ELGAR COMPANION TO HAYEKIAN ECONOMICS

In Memory of
Norman Barry
1944–2008

Elgar Companion to Hayekian Economics

Edited by

Roger W. Garrison

Emeritus Professor of Economics, Auburn University, USA

Norman Barry

Professor of Social and Political Theory, University of Buckingham, UK

Edward Elgar
PUBLISHING

Cheltenham, UK • Northampton, MA, USA

© Roger W. Garrison and Norman Barry 2014

All rights reserved. No part of this publication may be reproduced, stored in a retrieval system or transmitted in any form or by any means, electronic, mechanical or photocopying, recording, or otherwise without the prior permission of the publisher.

Published by
Edward Elgar Publishing Limited
The Lypiatts
15 Lansdown Road
Cheltenham
Glos GL50 2JA
UK

Edward Elgar Publishing, Inc.
William Pratt House
9 Dewey Court
Northampton
Massachusetts 01060
USA

Paperback edition 2016

A catalogue record for this book
is available from the British Library

Library of Congress Control Number: 2014941543

This book is available electronically in the Elgaronline
Economics subject collection
DOI 10.4337/9780857931115

ISBN 978 0 85793 110 8 (cased)
ISBN 978 0 85793 111 5 (eBook)
ISBN 978 1 78347 526 1 (paperback)

Typeset by Servis Filmsetting Ltd, Stockport, Cheshire
Printed and bound in Great Britain by TJ International Ltd, Padstow

Contents

List of contributors		vii
Acknowledgments		viii
A tribute to Norman Barry by Martin Ricketts		ix
1	Introduction Roger W. Garrison	1
2	Hayek in the history of economic thought Denis O'Brien	11
3	Hayek and economic theory in the 1930s Martin Ricketts	47
4	Hayek's *Pure Theory of Capital* Gerald R. Steele	71
5	Hayek and Keynes Roger E. Backhouse	94
6	Hayek and Friedman Roger W. Garrison	116
7	Hayek and Mises Richard M. Ebeling	138
8	Hayek and Lachmann Peter Lewin	165
9	Hayek: from economics as equilibrium analysis to economics as social theory Paul Lewis	195
10	Hayek and spontaneous order Craig Smith	224
11	Hayek on socialism Mark Pennington	246
12	Hayek versus the neoclassicists: lessons from the socialist calculation debate Peter J. Boettke, Christopher J. Coyne and Peter T. Leeson	278

13	Spontaneous order, free trade and globalization *Steven G. Horwitz*	294
14	Hayek on labor unions *Charles W. Baird*	314
15	Hayek and economic policy (the Austrian road to the third way) *Enrico Colombatto*	343
16	What remains of Hayek's critique of 'social justice'? Twenty propositions *Robert Nef*	364

Index 381

Contributors

Roger E. Backhouse, University of Birmingham, UK

Charles W. Baird, California State University – East Bay, USA

Peter J. Boettke, George Mason University, USA

Enrico Colombatto, University of Turin, Italy

Christopher J. Coyne, George Mason University, USA

Richard M. Ebeling, The Citadel, USA

Roger W. Garrison, Auburn University, USA

Steven G. Horwitz, St. Lawrence University, USA

Peter T. Leeson, George Mason University, USA

Peter Lewin, University of Texas at Dallas, USA

Paul Lewis, King's College, University of London, UK

Robert Nef, Liberales Institut, Switzerland

Denis O'Brien, University of Durham, UK

Mark Pennington, King's College, University of London, UK

Martin Ricketts, University of Buckingham, UK

Craig Smith, University of Glasgow, UK

Gerald R. Steele, University of Lancaster, UK

Acknowledgments

The editors of this volume – Norman Barry until his untimely death in 2008, and myself afterward – are grateful for the efforts of all those who have written chapters on the various aspects of Friedrich A. Hayek's contribution to economics: Roger E. Backhouse, Charles W. Baird, Peter J. Boettke, Enrico Colombatto, Christopher J. Coyne, Richard M. Ebeling, Steven G. Horwitz, Peter T. Leeson, Peter Lewin, Paul Lewis, Robert Nef, Denis O'Brien, Mark Pennington, Martin Ricketts, Craig Smith and Gerald R. Steele. Each with his own special expertise, these economists have offered critical assessments of Hayek's contributions in the various fields of the discipline and, collectively, have produced an enlightening mosaic of Hayekian economics.

We are also grateful to the personnel at Edward Elgar Publishing, especially to Megan Ballantyne, Jo Betteridge, Laura Mann and Francine O'Sullivan, all of whom have been exceedingly patient in seeing this publication effort through to completion. The mid-project change in editorial responsibility entailed a time-consuming recovery effort which required the patience of both the publisher and the contributors. Martin Ricketts, a close colleague of Norman Barry's, is to be thanked for timely help in making the transition.

We gratefully acknowledge the permission granted by the University of Chicago Press (Grant No. 107705) in coordination with Taylor & Francis Books UK (Routledge) to use the excerpts in Charles W. Baird's Chapter 14 taken from Friedrich A. Hayek's *Constitution of Liberty* (1960). We also acknowledge the permission granted by the Institute for Economic Affairs to use excerpts from Friedrich A. Hayek's *1980s Unemployment and the Unions*, 2nd edition (1984). Finally, it should be noted that Baird's Chapter 14, 'Hayek on labor unions', though originally drafted for inclusion in the present volume, was subsequently withdrawn and published as two separate articles in the *Journal of Private Enterprise*, 2007, 23 (1) and 2008, 23 (2). We gratefully acknowledge *JPE*'s permission to publish the now recombined articles as Chapter 14.

A tribute to Norman Barry (25 June 1944 – 21 October 2008)
Martin Ricketts

Delivered on 6 November 2008

It is my sad task today to address the congregation at the funeral of a great scholar, a close colleague and a staunch personal friend. I first met Norman when he took up his post at Buckingham in 1982 and for the next 25 years we shared the ups and downs of life here as well as many overlapping interests. It turned out that we had much in common and had a similar intellectual outlook, even though Norman's background was in politics and mine was in economics. Having read and studied Hayek, Norman had a grasp of economics that was very rare among political theorists, while as a student of Stanley Dennison, John Jewkes, Jack Wiseman and Alan Peacock, I had been schooled in political economy and public finance, and had been introduced to the history of economic thought. I would not like to calculate how many hours we must have sat in pubs, offices and seminar rooms discussing questions of common interest. To be able to spar with Norman over such an extended period with the utmost good humor was one of the most formative experiences of my life. It helped that we came from differing disciplines because it reduced our perception of personal rivalry to very manageable proportions. We questioned and tutored one another out of mutual interest. The education that he provided in political theory, constitutional law and social philosophy did not threaten him. My attempts to help with Austrian economics, public choice and the economics of social policy did not threaten me. It was a pure form of intellectual barter that strengthened us both. It must say something about us, however, that we did not write a single joint paper.

Norman graduated from the University of Exeter and arrived at Buckingham after stints at Queens Belfast (where he met the economist George Shackle) and Birmingham Polytechnic. He was immensely proud to be a member of the University of Buckingham. Of course, like all things that are important to us, it could occasionally be the object of criticism. Indeed we are more inclined to voice our disappointments over things we care about than over things that we can take or leave. But, for Norman, the University of Buckingham became a central feature in his life and career. It was not just a place where he happened to have a job. The University gave him a freedom that he could not feel elsewhere. And he gave the University intellectual firepower in defense of its independence and even of its existence. In 1994 he wrote *The Case for Independent Universities*, a pamphlet that was used by the University during the National Committee of Enquiry into Higher Education in 1997 under the chairmanship of Sir Ron Dearing.

One has to remember that, in the 1970s, Norman's views were deeply unfashionable. Not only did he defend classical liberal social science, he was a political theorist who was interested in economics and who introduced economic analysis into his politics. He was one of the first political theorists in the UK to master 'public choice' theory – the so-called economics of politics. He admired the work of James Buchanan and Gordon Tullock in *The Calculus of Consent* and Anthony Downs's *Economic Theory of Democracy*. He was one of the first to consider the implications for political theory of the economic analysis of public goods. He had read Charles Tiebout's 1956 article 'A pure theory of local expenditures' [*Journal of Political Economy*, 64 (5), 416–24] and deduced the implications for the economic analysis of competitive federalism long before his professional colleagues, and this marked him as an unreliable outsider if not a defector to the enemy.

Escaping from an uncongenial consensus was important. But equally important was a psychological benefit from being at the University of Buckingham. As a critic of state power and more specifically of state finance of higher education, he could avoid all charges of hypocrisy by coming to Buckingham. Here he was paid by his students, just as Adam Smith would have approved. He could be at one with himself. Buckingham was his natural home.

On his arrival in Buckingham, Norman had already published *Hayek's Social and Economic Philosophy*, a work admired by Sir Alan Peacock who was then Vice-Chancellor. He had also produced a textbook – *An Introduction to Modern Political Theory* – that went to four editions. Norman particularly enjoyed meeting alumni of Oxford or Cambridge who admitted to him that his textbook was widely used and greatly appreciated for its clarity and coverage – even if (as Norman liked to believe) it had to be circulated in brown paper envelopes. In the following two decades, a stream of high-quality work came from his pen (and later his keyboard). His books on classical liberalism and libertarianism, welfare policy and business ethics were translated into Japanese, Chinese, Turkish, Italian and Swedish. He published papers in internationally respected journals including the *British Journal of Political Science*, the *Cornell Law Review* and the top-ranking journal in the United States, *Political Theory*. Here he engaged seriously with the top minds of the time. In his 1984 article 'Unanimity, agreement and liberalism' [*Political Theory*, 12 (4), 579–96], he offered a powerful critique of the philosophical foundations used by the future Nobel Laureate James Buchanan in his approach to constitutional choice. His inaugural lecture at Buckingham contrasted the philosophical problems encountered by end-state theories of justice compared with theories of justice derived from rules of just conduct.

Norman produced over 150 publications on a wide-ranging set of issues. The pensions problem; marriage and divorce; Austrian economics; German neo-liberalism (he was an ardent admirer of Ludwig Erhard and the German Ordoliberals); essays on the history of political thought including the work of Edmund Burke, Hume, Smith, Rousseau and Bastiat; varieties of capitalism and issues of corporate governance; insider dealing; citizenship and rights; and constitutional law. He was happy to stoop to journalism – defending the financial innovator Michael Milken, the takeover raider T. Boone Pickens and Gordon Gekko from their detractors during the 1980s era of 'greed is good'. Essentially he saw these figures as protectors of shareholders against the depredations of arrogant and unaccountable managers. As he put it when reviewing the more recent Enron, WorldCom and Tyco scandals in the *Financial Times*, 'All the players of the 1990s were very hot on business ethics but they were much cooler on right and wrong'.

Although Norman was at home at Buckingham, his world was actually much wider and far-flung. From his lair he could foray out to wage a continual guerrilla campaign of disruption against the advance of collectivist thinking. His network ran through the Institute of Economic Affairs in London, where he was a member of the Advisory Council, through to contacts in think tanks and associations across the world. He was a regular visitor to the Philosophy Centre at Bowling Green, Ohio where he once stayed at the Buck-Eye Budget Motor Inn – a residence, he delighted in telling me, as impersonal as it was possible to imagine and therefore the nearest to his ideal of abstract market coordination. Yet this vaunted disdain for all communal ties was pure affectation, and the irony was transparent. I can attest to the affection in which he was held at the Philosophy Centre by the flow of emails that I have received enquiring after him. He regularly attended and occasionally arranged conferences organized by the Liberty Fund. I remember attending one in Bruges arranged with the expert administrative help of our own Anne Miller [i.e. of Buckingham]. He lectured in New Zealand, Australia, Japan, Italy and many other countries. And, of course, he was a regular visitor to the Association for Liberal Thinking in Turkey, a connection that has brought us recently a stream of welcome visitors to the Beloff Centre for the Study of Liberty. As he himself would have put it – again heavy with irony – he was indeed 'big' in Turkey.

One of the great delights of Norman's company was his ability to use humor for the serious purposes of communicating ideas. If he was joking, he was probably also trying to draw attention to a serious point. Indeed, to some degree, the more serious the point, the more likely he would be to joke about it. In this he was in a great English tradition. On the other hand he enjoyed pure flippancy. He liked the idea of persiflage – the lightest of banter – although, even here, he took his banter seriously. This derived from his libertarianism. As a clever man he relished pure wordplay and sharp wit. But I think he also actually enjoyed annoying his socialist opponents whom he rightly or wrongly took to be almost completely humorless. Why should all these pompous fools insist that we have to be serious all the time? He once recounted with great pleasure, for example, the story of Noel Coward's riposte to the newspaper reporter who asked how, during the depression years of the 1930s he could enjoy his champagne breakfast – 'Doesn't everyone'?

But, as well as the short flippant observation or witty wordplay, Norman was capable of gradually constructing the most elaborate and whimsical flights of fancy. In the early days he managed to establish a surreal link between the competition within a group of us to produce the most academic papers in each calendar year and the Tour de France. A whole vocabulary developed of which the most important element concerned the metaphorical 'yellow jersey' supposedly worn by the race leader. This inevitably led to the invention of jerseys of more and more colors to represent more and more ridiculous (and provisional) achievements by his imaginary rivals. Like a game of Mornington Crescent, I might lay claim to being the wearer of the lime green jersey without necessarily having any idea what bizarre substage of the race this was supposed to signify – although Norman might always be expected to think of something. He was delighted when, in an early annual report, it was revealed that a member of the maintenance department had published an article in *Caravanning Weekly* (or some similarly titled magazine) and thereby had come higher in the publications race than many academic members of staff. Topsy-turvy figured, I think, significantly in Norman's humor – a Gilbert and Sullivan element.

In terms of musical theatre, however, his taste was less Gilbert and Sullivan and more Rodgers and Hart. The sophistication of the lyric seemed to be the key to his taste. He was genuinely knowledgeable about the history of the American musical – perhaps part of his overall love affair with the United States. He disliked sentimentality and preferred the words of Larry Hart, Cole Porter and Stephen Sondheim to

Oscar Hammerstein. He could be somewhat pedantic – criticizing the use of the line 'stamp me and mail me' in the song 'Get me to the church on time' sung by Eliza Doolittle's father in Lerner and Loewe's *My Fair Lady* – on the grounds that a cockney would never have used the American 'to mail' as a verb but the English 'to post'. Somehow 'stamp me and post me' did not work at all and required extensive re-writing of the rest of the song. I'm not sure whether he ever solved the problem to his satisfaction.

The plays of Tom Stoppard were another interest of Norman's and he acted as the organizer of a Liberty Fund conference to discuss them. He naturally liked the fact that Stoppard was seen as a right-wing playwright in an age of 'angry young men', 'kitchen sink' drama, and social protest. The characters in Stoppard's plays are often academics or other intellectuals facing ethical dilemmas. My *Oxford Companion to English Literature* says of the play *Jumpers*, for example, that 'the physical acrobatics of the jumpers of the title parallel the verbal gymnastics of (the central character's) lengthy speeches, which are brilliantly witty parodies of academic philosophy'. One can see immediately that this would appeal to Norman.

He reviewed theatrical performances and films and revealed in this journalistic output much about himself and his approach to politics. 'When I first read the Diaries,' he says in his review of *Bridget Jones*, 'I thought – at last a female reactionary . . . who smokes Silk Cut and drinks too much Chardonnay. She must be a conservative . . . I had not felt so confident about the future since I read that the Spice Girls were Thatcherites'. Actually he goes on to conclude that Bridget is actually not interested in politics at all, but he is nevertheless determined to claim her and does so with the observation that it is precisely because she has no interest in politics that she is a real conservative.

Norman himself often claimed that he disliked politics – a seemingly paradoxical observation for a Professor of Politics. But there is no doubt that he hated practical politics. For Norman, nothing could disguise the basic truth that politics is the business of making collective choices and that, in practice, it mostly involves one lot of people bossing around another lot of people. Politics must in the end confer power to coerce and this was always repellent to him. He preferred agreement and the gains that accrue to non-coerced trade. Hence his emotional preference for the study of economics and his devotion to Hayek. He studied politics, he said, in the way that a biologist studies a lethal bacterium. If people like Bridget Jones who are indifferent to politics are conservative, it is difficult to see Norman in the same camp. In the end, Norman was a classical liberal, hating politics but deeply interested in social and political theory and continuing the search for ways of gaining the collective benefits from a strong state whilst somehow imposing constitutional limits on its hydra-like tendency to grow.

It was in 1997 at a conference not far from Hamburg that I first became aware that Norman was finding it difficult to walk. I remember we made it to a suitable hostelry, ordered some beer, our talk turning to academic and other matters and, making light of the episode, he recovered fairly rapidly. Norman always made light of his condition. After he was diagnosed with multiple sclerosis, and even as his condition worsened so that relatively simple tasks became increasingly difficult, I never heard a single word of self-pity. He would occasionally admit to a bad day but in the tones of scientific detachment – a simple observation of the facts. His determination to continue was formidable. Even in the last months, as he concentrated intently on the task of holding a cigarette between his fingers, and I nervously anticipated the hot ash dropping onto a newspaper, we talked of academic papers still to be written. As Norman's physical and mental faculties were eroded, an unquenchable will remained untouched – an absolute determination, like Ulysses in a once much-admired poem by Tennyson, to go on to the bitter end:

> Come my friends,
> 'Tis not too late to seek a newer world.
> Push off, and sitting well in order smite
> The sounding furrows; for my purpose holds
> To sail beyond the sunset, and the baths
> Of all the western stars, until I die.

Those of us who remain should draw what courage we can muster from Norman's example. For, as the eponymous hero of Tennyson's poem says as he encourages his oarsmen to set out once more:

> Tho' much is taken, much abides; and tho'
> We are not now that strength which in old days
> Moved earth and heaven; that which we are, we are;
> One equal temper of heroic hearts,
> Made weak by time and fate, but strong in will
> To strive, to seek, to find, and not to yield.

1. Introduction
Roger W. Garrison

A BRIEF BIOGRAPHICAL SKETCH OF FRIEDRICH A. HAYEK[1]

Friedrich August von Hayek (1899–1992) was a notable contributor to twentieth-century economics and a central figure of the Austrian school. He is credited for advances not only in the field of economics but also in the fields of psychology, epistemology and political philosophy. His scholarly output spans seven decades.

Hayek was born in Vienna (then the capital of Austria-Hungary) on 8 May 1899. He served in the military as an artillery officer in World War I before entering the University of Vienna, where he obtained doctorates in law and political science. After spending a year at New York University (1923–24), Hayek returned to Vienna where he joined the celebrated Privatseminar conducted by Ludwig von Mises. In 1927 Hayek became the first director of the Austrian Institute for Business Cycle Research. His writing during the late 1920s reflected his experience in New York, during which time the US was experiencing the early phases of a dramatic economic boom, and his participation in Mises' seminar, during which his appreciation for the Austrian theories of money and business cycles were strengthened.

On an invitation from Lionel Robbins, chair of the economics department at the London School of Economics (LSE), Hayek delivered a series of lectures at the LSE in 1931 and subsequently accepted the Tooke Chair. With his lectures published as *Prices and Production* ([1931] 1935), Hayek emerged as the principal rival of John Maynard Keynes on the issues of business cycles and stabilization policy.

During the late 1930s and early 1940s Hayek's research centered on the role of knowledge and discovery in market processes and on the methodological underpinnings of the Austrian school. In particular, Hayek emphasized the subjectivism and methodological individualism that underlay the Austrians' thinking. His contributions in these areas were an outgrowth of his participation in the debate over the possibility of economic calculation under socialism. A key article during this period was his 'Economics and knowledge' (Hayek, 1937).

Though written for popular consumption, Hayek's *Road to Serfdom*

([1944] 1967) can be seen as an application of his theorizing about socialism in all its forms. He was able to foretell the sequential consequences of encroaching socialism in England with an acuity that derived from his having witnessed the same sequence in his native Austria 20 or 25 years earlier (Hayek, [1944] 1967, p. 2). Unfortunately, Hayek's reaching out to the intelligent layman was accompanied by – and, in all likelihood, helped bring about – his estrangement from the economics profession.

In 1950 Hayek left the LSE and joined the Committee on Social Thought at the University of Chicago. His research there encompassed the broader concerns of social, political and legal philosophy. It was during his Chicago years that he wrote *The Constitution of Liberty* (1960). He returned to Europe in 1962 with appointments at the University of Freiburg, West Germany and then (in 1969) at the University of Salzburg, Austria. His Freiburg–Salzburg years were devoted to producing the three-volume *Law, Legislation and Liberty* (1973, 1976 and 1979). Hayek returned to Freiburg in 1977, residing there until his death in 1992.

HAYEK'S EVOLVING PERSPECTIVES[2]

Beyond the present volume's Chapter 2, in which Denis O'Brien sets out the place of Hayek in the history of economic thought, the sequencing of the chapters reflects the twists and turns of Hayek's academic career. I have resisted dividing the book into parts out of concern that that would overemphasize the shifts in Hayek's focus, as outlined above, and eclipse the underlying continuity of Hayekian thought. I am aware of the special attention that has come to be given to Hayek's 'Economics and knowledge' (1937), an article which, according to Terence Hutchison (1981), marks Hayek's rejection of Mises' *a prioristic* thinking and his turn towards Karl Popper's falsificationism. Hutchinson took this perceived change of mind as implying a first-order distinction between 'Hayek I' and 'Hayek II'. In my judgment Bruce Caldwell has effectively countered Hutchison in part by quoting from a 1981 letter from Hayek to Hutchison indicating that 'I was *never* an *a priorist*' (emphasis in the original), and that '[t]he main intention of my [1937 article] was to explain gently to Mises why I could not accept his *a priorism*' (Caldwell, 2004, pp. 420–21).

Although Roy McCloughry, editor of a compilation of Hayek's early essays, swears off the task of interpreting Hayek, he identifies the 1937 article as a 'watershed in Hayek's thought' (McCloughry, 1984, p. viii) – almost as if this characterization involved no interpretation. The supposed watershed is taken to be the point when Hayek turned from the characteristics of an achieved equilibrium to the analysis of the equilibrating process. That is, before the watershed, he was concerned with the end-state relationships that can be set out in a general equilibrium framework; after the watershed, he was concerned with the dispersion of information and with the price system as a network for communicating that information. I question whether this bifurcation can survive a broader understanding of Hayekian economics.

At best McCloughry's distinction is overdrawn. In Hayek's early writings, he was always careful to square his own theorizing with the general equilibrium theory of the Lausanne school of economics rooted in the works of Léon Walras. But the emphasis was on 'general' rather than on 'equilibrium'. It would be more accurate to say that Hayek always paid explicit attention to the general interdependencies among all markets – whether or not the market forces associated with those interdependencies are conceived as having actually achieved a state of equilibrium.

Having absorbed the insights of Walras and other Continental economists, Hayek had a keen awareness of both the virtues and the limitations of Alfred Marshall's partial equilibrium analysis. When theorizing about money, capital accumulation or capital consumption, or about fluctuations in business activity and widespread employment, it is impermissible to focus the analysis on one or two broadly defined markets while impounding others by way of a *ceteris paribus* assumption. Hayek was aware of the fallacious doctrines and disastrous policies that could be – and were – derived from the unfounded use of *ceteris paribus*. The undue extension of partial equilibrium analysis was evident both in the unschooled thinking of politicians and businessmen and in the theorizing of Keynes and other British economists who were schooled in Marshallian economics. It can fairly be said of Keynes that he had ventured far away from Marshall in terms of the questions asked (about the macroeconomy) but had leaned heavily on Marshall (relying, in effect, on partial equilibrium analysis) for the answers given. Keynes's assumption of a fixed structure of industry in the context of changing rates of interest and dramatic movements in employment and income is an especially relevant case in point.

Hayek had witnessed the results of this mode of theorizing and was neither surprised nor impressed. And because he was schooled in Vienna, it is not surprising that Hayek himself did not adopt the same strategy. Nor is it surprising that, having studied under the Walras-inspired Friedrich von Wieser, he grounded his own thinking in the Lausanne school. It is misleading, though, to identify the early Hayek as a general equilibrium theorist, given what that term has come to mean. But it is to Hayek's credit that he focused his attention on the interdependencies identified by Walras. Hayek's response to Keynes's *Treatise on Money* demonstrated the edge that Walrasian thinking had over Marshallian thinking when macroeconomic relationships are at issue. And that edge was to become sharper with the subsequent writings of both Keynes and Hayek.

It is certainly possible to detect a change in the focus of Hayek's writings during his years of continuous interaction with British economists. In earlier years he was concerned predominantly with the questions of how the market process would have to operate if the preferences of consumers were to get transformed into the production plans of business firms and how government policy, particularly central-bank policy, could interfere with this process. With his post-Continental writings he became more concerned with the issue of how this same market process could in fact operate even though the information on which the process is based is incomplete and dispersed throughout the economy.

But Hayek was well aware of this second question in the early 1920s. In fact, as indicated by his own introductory remarks in the McCloughry edited volume (1984, p.1), he was already working with and under the influence of Mises when Mises' *Socialism* appeared in 1922. That book dealt at length with the critical issue of economic calculation. Hayek may well have believed as the 1920s wore on that the economics profession had understood – or soon would understand – the full significance of Mises' contribution. His own efforts, then, could be directed towards developing the Misesian vision by focusing on the intertemporal coordination made possible by unhampered credit markets and the intertemporal discoordination caused by misguided central-bank policy. If anything, the so-called watershed referred to by McCloughry marks the period during which Hayek became aware that the profession, at least in Britain, had in fact not absorbed Mises' insights at all. Hayek himself says as much when reflecting in the late 1970s on his putting together a volume on collectivist planning in the early 1930s. 'I found that certain new insights which were known on the Continent had not reached the English-speaking world yet' (Hayek, 1994, p.79). Hayek goes on to say that it was this revisiting of Mises' (and others') early ideas about socialism that led him to write the 1937 article 'Economics and knowledge' (ibid., p.80).

Also, Hayek's Copenhagen lecture, delivered in 1933 (halfway between the publication dates of the two editions of his *Prices and Production*), casts doubts on the notion of a watershed. Even a casual reading of the English translation, published six years later as 'Price expectations, monetary disturbances and malinvestments' (Hayek, [1939] 1975), reveals that his focus in that lecture is closer to his 1937 article than to his graph-laden exposition in *Prices and Production*. Hayek expresses concern about the gulf between the conventional statics and dynamics and about the inadequate treatment of time and hence of expectations, especially in theorizing about trade cycles. The ongoing change in his thinking, however, can be seen as an evolutionary one:

> Not very long ago [1928? 1931? – RG] I myself still believed that the best way to [deal with the gulf between statics and dynamics] was to say that the theory of the trade cycle at which we were aiming ought to be organically superimposed on the existing theory of equilibrium. I am now [1933, and later in 1937] more inclined to say that the general theory itself ought to be developed so as to enable us to use it directly in the explanation of particular industrial fluctuations. (Hayek, [1939] 1975, pp. 137–8)

In sum, it had gradually dawned on Hayek that his British colleagues could not appreciate *Prices and Production* and related writings because they lacked a fundamental understanding of the significance of decentralized decision-making in a market economy. In an attempt to overcome this obstacle, Hayek began to deal in a more explicit way with the coordination of individual plans on the basis of dispersed and incomplete information. But both the early Hayek and the later Hayek were Walrasian in the looser sense of attention to interdependencies, and both were concerned with the market process as a coordinating mechanism. Even Hayek's early (1928) essay, 'Intertemporal price equilibrium and movements in the value of money' (in McClaughry, 1984) provides much direct and indirect evidence of the continuity of Hayek's thinking.

ECONOMICS *CUM* POLITICAL PHILOSOPHY

Hayek's move in 1950 from the LSE to the University of Chicago was accompanied by another change in his focus – though, again, without any implied discontinuity in his thinking. Had he been accepted into the university's department of economics, he may well have resumed work on his technical economics. However, he was found unsuitable by his would-be colleagues – not because of his political views but because of his technical economics and, more specifically, his capital theory and business cycle theory. Beyond citing an internal issue concerning the procedure in hiring faculty, Milton Friedman mentioned only this one issue during an interview conducted by biographer Alan Ebenstein. The economics faculty 'didn't agree with [Hayek's] economics. *Prices and Production*, his capital theory – if they [Chicago's economics faculty] had been looking around the world for an economist to add to their staff, their prescription would not have been the author of *Prices and Production*' (Ebenstein, 2001, p. 174). Hayek himself sized up the situation a little differently: '[t]he econometricians didn't want me' (ibid., p. 175).

Fortunately, the University of Chicago's Committee on Social Thought did want him. And, all things considered, the snubbing by the economics department was not much of a bruising for Hayek. Interviewed in the late 1970s, Hayek indicated that by 1950 he had 'become somewhat stale as an economist' and would have 'found it difficult to return to systematic teaching of economic theory' (Hayek, 1994, p. 126). The Committee on Social Thought was conducive to his thinking and writing outside the field of economics narrowly conceived, a circumstance that meshed with his aspirations. As Ebenstein puts the matter, Hayek's focus on 'political economy and societal philosophy over technical academic economic theory during the last fifty years of his life reflected . . . his mature belief that the former is more important than and incorporates the latter' (Ebenstein, 2001, p. 176).

Hence, Hayek's writings post-1950 do not require that we extend Hutchison's bifurcation and declare a 'Hayek III'. Throughout his long career, the common concern was coordination in a free society. His understanding of equilibrium states, the equilibrating process and the requisite social institutions combine into a remarkably coherent perspective on both the narrow and the broad issues of a market economy. In the early years of the revival of Austrian economics in the United States, Gerald P. O'Driscoll, Jr wrote a book titled *Economics as a Coordination Problem: The Contribution of Friedrich A. Hayek* (1977). Hayek himself penned the 'Foreword'. In it he wrote:

> It is a curious fact that a student of complex phenomena may long himself remain unaware of how his views of different problems hang together and perhaps never fully succeed in clearly stating the guiding ideas which led him in the treatment of particulars. I must confess that I was occasionally myself surprised when I found in Professor O'Driscoll's account side by side statements I made at the interval of many years and on quite different problems, which still implied the same general approach. That it seemed in principle possible to recast a great part of economic theory in terms of the approach which I had found useful in dealing with such different problems as those of industrial fluctuations and the running of a socialist economy was [most] gratifying to me. (O'Driscoll, 1977, p. ix)

And had O'Driscoll's book been extended to include social philosophy, Hayek may well have been even more gratified.

Not all of the contributors to this volume would ascribe a lifetime of cohesiveness to Hayekian thought, especially in connection with aspects of Hayek's capital theory and business cycle theory of the 1930s and of the legal framework recommended by Hayek in his post-1950 writings. And as even I would concede, in Hayek's treatment of these and other topics, the devil is in the details. But the chapters in this volume suggest a preponderance of cohesiveness – in part by virtue of the unavoidable overlap among the contributions, where similar arguments are made in dealing with very different issues.

Some of the overlap, much of it helpful in revealing the interconnections among different aspects of Hayekian thought, derives from the different ways of narrowing the focus of the separate contributors. One focuses on a particular time period, the 1930s; another on a particular book, *The Pure Theory of Capital*. Four of the contributions focus on the relationship between Hayek's ideas and those of another economist: Keynes, Friedman, Mises and Lachmann. The rest focus on particular topics, broad and narrow, almost all of which tend to be interrelated: socialism, the socialist calculation debate, social justice, spontaneous order, globalization, free trade and trade unions.

A NOTE ABOUT THE ORIGIN AND DEVELOPMENT OF THIS VOLUME

The selection of contributors to this volume reflects, in large part, the good judgment and entrepreneurship of Norman Barry. More than a dozen invitees answered his call for contributions. Collectively, they produced a scholarly, even-handed and fairly comprehensive treatment of Hayekian thought. It was to be a long road, though, from the initial acceptances of invitations in 2003 to the eventual appearance in print of the final product. Understandably, these chapters, all of substantial length and worthy of inclusion in Norman's project, could not be written in haste. This aspect of the production time was to be expected.

However, Norman's health had begun to decline in the late 1990s and his condition became increasingly debilitating. Still, Norman pressed on with his academic career, but in his final years progress on his publication project was dramatically slowed.

I never had the privilege of knowing Norman Barry personally, but I knew him through his writings and through our correspondence about my own submission to the volume. These connections gave me some idea about his character. When I discovered from others sometime in 2008 that his health had become an issue, I contacted him through Linda Waterman, the University of Buckingham's Departmental Administrator, and offered to become co-editor of the volume. Somehow I wasn't surprised to learn that his resolve to finish the job himself despite his failing health had already ruled out any thought of a co-editor.

In October of 2008, I was contacted by Mrs Waterman with the sad news of Norman's passing and with encouraging remarks about the possibility of my taking over the editorial responsibility of his publication project. Subsequent overtures from Edward Elgar resulted in my becoming co-editor.

Norman's and my editing, then, has been strictly *seriatim*. And the transition was a rocky one despite the help and understanding of Edward Elgar and of Norman's close friend and colleague Martin Ricketts. Only a few of the contributions to the volume were found in Norman's files. Exhaustive searches over a period of many months failed to unearth any hard copies or electronic copies of any of the other papers. Not even a complete and up-to-date listing of submitted papers was found. And though there was reason to believe that edited copies of the papers and even a nearly completed introduction by Norman did exist, hope of finding any of them faded. Then, after getting a few leads from known contributors, I began to track down other contributors and to get still other leads. Eventually, there were enough chapters, all of good quality, to more than justify pushing forward with the project. I issued several new invitations, which in the end netted two additional contributions (by Richard Ebeling and Peter Lewin). And the pre-copy-editing finalization of the chapters allowed authors of some of the earliest submissions to include updated material and to cite recent literature.

On a personal note, let me say that I first became aware of Norman Barry shortly after my arrival at Auburn University in late summer of 1978. I had just completed a 15-month residency at the Institute for Humane Studies in Menlo Park, California, during which I worked toward completing my dissertation on the relationship between neoclassical and Austrian monetary theories. Happily, my stay overlapped Friedrich Hayek's residency at the Institute for Humane Studies – his during the summer of 1977. To say the least, opportunities to interact with Hayek did wonders for my enthusiasm for my dissertation topic.

While settling in at Auburn and beginning my teaching career, I paid a visit to the university bookstore and just happened to notice in the new-arrivals section *Hayek's Social and Economic Philosophy* by Norman Barry (1979). I didn't realize at the time how surprised I should have been to find such an academic publication at a state school bookstore that specialized mainly in textbooks and T-shirts. And now, on rereading large portions of Norman's book at the end of my teaching career, I am gratified to realize that my introduction to the *Elgar Companion to Hayekian Economics* is wholly compatible with his own view of Hayek's economic and philosophical writings. In the preface Norman wrote:

Professor Hayek has found academic recognition and very great world-wide respect for his contributions in a wide variety of disciplines and it is the aim of this book to present his social and economic philosophy as an integrated system of ideas in which seemingly very different subject areas can be seen as elements in a comprehensive framework. Thus, while Hayek is probably known publicly as a leading advocate of free market economics this standpoint finds its true significance only in a wider philosophical context. (Barry, 1979, p. ix)

Though critical of many specifics of Hayekian theory, the contributions to the present volume will stand in testament to the many ways in which Norman's summary assessment captures the essence of Friedrich A. Hayek.

NOTES

1. The first four paragraphs draw largely from Garrison and Kirzner (1987).
2. This section draws from and elaborates upon Garrison (1985).

BIBLIOGRAPHY

Barry, Norman P. (1979), *Hayek's Social and Economic Philosophy*, London: Macmillan Press.
Caldwell, Bruce, J. (2004), *Hayek's Challenge: An Intellectual Biography of F.A. Hayek*, Chicago, IL: University of Chicago Press.
Ebenstein, Alan (2001), *Friedrich Hayek: A Biography*, New York: Palgrave.
Garrison, Roger W. (1985), 'Review of *Money, Capital, and Fluctuations*: Early Essays by Friedrich A. Hayek, ed. by Roy McCloughry', *Market Process*, 3 (2), 7–9.
Garrison, Roger W. and Israel M. Kirzner (1987), 'Friedrich August von Hayek', in John Eatwell, Murray Milgate and Peter Newman (eds), *The New Palgrave: A Dictionary of Economics*, vol. II, London: Macmillan Press Ltd, pp. 609–14.
Hayek, Friedrich A. (1928), 'Intertemporal price equilibrium and movements in the value of money', translated and reprinted in Roy McCloughry (ed.) (1984), *Money, Capital and Fluctuations. Early Essays*, London: Routledge and Kegan Paul.
Hayek, Friedrich A. (1931), *Prices and Production*, 2nd edn, 1935, London: Routledge and Kegan Paul.
Hayek, Friedrich A. (1937), 'Economics and knowledge', *Economica*, n.s. 4 (Feb.), 33–54.
Hayek, Friedrich A. (1939), 'Price expectations, monetary distrubances and malinvestments', translated from the original German and printed in Hayek (1975), *Profits, Interest and Investment*, Clifton, NJ: Augustus M. Kelley, pp. 135–56.
Hayek, Friedrich A. ([1944] 1967), *The Road to Serfdom*, Chicago, IL: University of Chicago Press.
Hayek, Friedrich A. (1960), *The Constitution of Liberty*, Chicago, IL: University of Chicago Press.
Hayek, Friedrich A. (1973, 1976, 1979), *Law Legislation and Liberty*, 3 vols, Chicago, IL: University of Chicago Press.
Hayek, Friedrich A. (1994), *Hayek on Hayek*, Stephen Kresge and Leif Wenar (eds), London: Routledge.

Hutchison, Terence W. (1981), *The Politics and Philosophy of Economics: Marxians, Keynesians, and Austrians*, Oxford: Basil Blackwell.
McCloughry, Roy (ed.) (1984), *Money, Capital and Fluctuations. Early Essays by F.A. Hayek*, London: Routledge & Kegan Paul.
Mises, Ludwig von (1922), *Socialism: An Economic and Sociological Analysis*, New Haven, CT: Yale University Press.
O'Driscoll, Gerald P., Jr (1977), *Economics as a Coordination Problem: The Contributions of F.A. Hayek*, Kansas City, MO: Sheed Andrews & McMeel.

2. Hayek in the history of economic thought[1]
Denis O'Brien

[I]t is hardly remembered that there was a time when the new theories of Hayek were the principal rival of the new theories of Keynes. Which was right, Keynes or Hayek? There are many still living teachers of economics, and practical economists, who have passed through a time when they had to make up their minds on that question; and there are many of them (including the present writer) who took quite a time to make up their minds. (Hicks, 1967, p. 203)

INTRODUCTION: HAYEK'S BACKGROUND

In order to form a view on Hayek's place in the history of economic thought, it is necessary to look at his career, the impact of his ideas, their internal coherence, his relationships with his contemporaries and critics, and finally to consider the perspective two decades after his death. Each of these aspects of Hayek's life and work will be considered in sections of this chapter. However it is first necessary to look at his intellectual background.

Hayek was an Austrian economist, a product of the style of economics which developed under the leadership of Carl Menger in the four decades before 1914.[2] The Mengerian school developed a corpus of economic theory and an approach to economic problems which were quite distinct from other forms of marginalism.[3] Yet within its ranks there are diverse elements.

As Hayek himself made clear when writing about Schumpeter (1967, pp. 339–41; 1992, pp. 160–65), members of the Austrian school themselves followed different paths in their development. Hayek made it possible to attempt some evaluation of the importance of different members of the Austrian school, as seen from his own standpoint, through the series of essays he wrote on them (O'Brien, 1994b, pp. 366–7), and in this way he shed some light on their importance for him.

But the main sources for him are clear from the contents of, and acknowledgements in, his own economic writings. First comes Menger, whose emphasis on subjectivism proved a starting point, though Hayek later laid much more stress on the evolutionary elements in Menger's 1883 book. Second, from Böhm-Bawerk, Hayek took – with highly adverse intellectual and professional consequences – a non-subjective theory of capital, one which he ultimately (but belatedly) abandoned. Third, the greatest influence on Hayek was neither of these. It was Ludwig von Mises (Hayek, 1992, pp. 25–30).

Before Hayek came under the influence of Mises, his education in economics was narrow, although he was familiar with the work of Wieser and of the later Austrians such as Hans Mayer and Richard Strigl. Under Mises's influence, he embarked upon a wide self-education in economics through scholarship (Rosner and Winckler, 1989; O'Brien, 1994a). Hayek read enormously widely, and was scrupulous in his acknowledgment of predecessors.[4] Indeed the first of the four lectures which make up his *Prices and Production* is essentially a lecture on the history of economic thought. For Hayek, scholarly study of the history of economics was inseparable from the development of the subject of economics itself (O'Brien, 1994b).

In addition it was Mises who brought home to Hayek the full implications of a subjectivist approach to general equilibrium; and it was Mises's *Gemeinwirtschaft* which led directly to Hayek's abandonment of socialism (Hayek, 1992, pp. 133, 136). It was Mises who found employment for Hayek, in the study of the trade cycle, and it was under the influence of Mises that Hayek was working in the 1920s.

THE 1930s: AN OUTSIDER

As Hayek's Austrian colleague Ludwig Lachman has testified, Hayek 'made a triumphant entry into the University of London in 1931'; he 'had become a rather lonely figure by 1939' (Lachman, 1986, p. 225; see also Blaug, 1992, p. 31). In the intervening decade Hayek had been, as Hicks later remembered, a central figure in the intellectual dramas of the 1930s.

The story started with an invitation to Hayek from Lionel Robbins, newly established as Professor of Economics at the London School of Economics (LSE), to deliver a series of lectures, Prices and Production, which created a sensation (Schumpeter, 1954, p. 1120; Benassi, 1987, p. 263). Robbins read economic literature in German; something of an outsider himself, he sought to establish at LSE an alternative tradition to the Marshallian tradition embodied in the dominant Cambridge school of economics (Robbins, 1933, pp. xiv–xvi; 1930; 1934b, pp. xvii–xix). Menger's works were reprinted at LSE, with an introduction by Hayek; Mises's seminal book on money ([1924] 1934) (earlier reviewed by Keynes despite subsequently claiming that he could not read German – O'Brien, 1998a, p. 43) and his *Gemeinwirtschaft* (*Socialism*) (Mises, [1932] 1936) were translated under Robbins's auspices. Hayek, an outsider to the British system, and trained in a very different kind of economics, thus joined with Robbins in an attempt to alter fundamentally the centre of gravity of economics in Britain.

As if this were not enough, Hayek, like Robbins, was opposed to many of the fashionable academic nostrums of the day. His opposition to Marxism set him apart from a number of academics, notably at LSE itself, and his continuation of the criticisms of the idea of a planned socialist economy, following the work of Mises, ran entirely counter to the prevailing climate. His position was ultimately to be justified, but not before an academic myth had arisen (and been sedulously propagated) that Hayek had somehow been defeated on this issue by Lange who advocated such a system; but the justification came long after the decade now being considered. Hayek was to continue this critique into the 1940s, and to live long enough to see the breakdown of the East European Marxist regimes and the discoveries that followed; the Trabant plant in East Germany, supposedly the most efficient part of the old Soviet Empire, was described by one motoring journal as a 'toxic slag heap'. But such events were far in the future; in the 1930s Hayek's critical attitude won him few friends. The perception, which Hayek derived from Mises, that there was a core problem stemming from factor valuation, and a fundamental failure to understand all that markets achieved, was not welcome (Vaughn, 1980).

But it was the success of Keynes's *General Theory*, and of the quite extraordinarily swift Keynesian Revolution, which did the most fundamental damage to Hayek's standing. It was not just a question of operating on aggregate demand, but a fundamental methodological opposition to the kind of aggregation embodied in the IS–LM (investment saving–liquidity preference money supply) revolution which left Hayek such a lonely figure. In the view of Keynes's biographer, the impact of the *General Theory* was such that the Austrian outpost at LSE crumbled – Hayek and Robbins failed to reply, and Lerner, Kaldor and Hicks deserted to the Keynesian camp (Skidelsky, 1992, p. 573). The failure by Hayek to reply was probably a crucial blow to his reputation, and the reason that he later gave – that he thought that Keynes would change his mind yet again, as he had done between the *Treatise* and the *General Theory* – is unconvincing (O'Brien, 1994a, p. 362). It seems more likely that he had been worn down by the abuse directed at him by Cambridge writers early in the 1930s, a strategy on their part which thus proved successful.[5] At all events, as Leijonhufvud has observed, the Austrian approach to macroeconomics became of interest only to 'antiquarians' after 1936; it was abandoned by monetary economists (Leijonhufvud, 1981, p. 133) and indeed Hayek acknowledged defeat in some comments delivered at the Royal Statistical

Society in 1938. Critically he admitted that there might not be a regular periodicity of macroeconomic fluctuation and also rejected the idea of monocausal trade cycles (Hayek, 1938; Rühl, 1994, p. 190).

HAYEK AND CAMBRIDGE

The relationship between Hayek and Keynes got off to a bad start, with a 'strong disagreement' in 1928 (Hayek, 1978, p. 283). But it was Hayek's review of Keynes's *Treatise on Money* (1930) in 1931 that proved the starting point for what was effectively a feud which lasted for the decade and was only stilled by a reconciliation during the war (Caldwell, 1995).

There was much in Keynes's *Treatise* that was irritating to someone familiar with the work of Wicksell and of Mises. It even made the outrageous claim, as Laidler has noted, that there was at the time of its publication no pre-existing body of monetary theory (Keynes, 1930, vol. 1, p. xviii; Laidler, 1999, p. 130). Moreover, Hayek's review made a number of good points. Keynes's curious treatment of profit as something distinct from other income, which could be explained by an inequality between savings and investment, the unsatisfactory treatment of investment and of the capital stock, the subjective originality of the book, the laborious equations, the tortured terminology – it was hardly surprising that Hayek found much that was unsatisfactory. Even later enthusiasts for Keynes's work, such as Patinkin (1976), have had strong reservations about the *Treatise*. Moreover, as Hayek continued his critique into a second part, he was able to quote a passage from the *Treatise* which could well have been written by Wicksell, only to find that the Wicksellian mechanism had been obscured by peculiar definitions of savings and investment so that 'the rate of interest which will equilibrate "savings" and "investment" in Mr Keynes's sense is quite different from the rate which would keep them in equilibrium in the ordinary sense' (Hayek, 1932a, p. 66).

Nor was Hayek alone in his dismay at the *Treatise*. Robertson (1931) and Hawtrey were only two of those who were fundamentally unhappy about it. But Keynes's response to Hayek was abusive. He dragged into his response an attack upon Hayek's *Prices and Production*, which he described as 'one of the most frightful muddles I have ever read, with scarcely a sound proposition in it' (Keynes, 1931, pp. 55–6) and then, using his position as editor of the *Economic Journal*, he commissioned a review of Hayek's book by Sraffa. This managed to be both pompous and abusive. It was impossible from the content of Sraffa's review to see what Hayek's book actually said. The review began with the observation that:

all this in four lectures must have been a feat of endurance on the part of the audience as much as of the lecturer. For however peculiar, and probably unprecedented, the conclusions may be, there is one respect in which the lectures collected in this volume fully uphold the tradition which modern writers on money are rapidly establishing, that of unintelligibility. (Sraffa, 1932a, p. 86)

In the closed community of British academia, this abuse, delivered with the sanction of the editor of one of the leading journals in the world, did Hayek much harm, as Lachmann subsequently testified. Elsewhere it was recognized that Hayek had been wronged; the American economist Howard Ellis referred to the 'astonishing misrepresentations' of Sraffa's attack (Ellis, 1934, p. 365n). But the biggest problem with the Sraffa review – and it reflects ill on the academic community that it should have done Hayek harm – was its own unintelligibility. Sraffa was clearly unwilling to reveal the theoretical standpoint from which he was arguing, as with his 1926 attack on Marshallian price theory, though it subsequently became clear in that case that the starting point was Marx and Ricardo (O'Brien, 1984, pp. 251–2). It was Ludwig Lachmann who decoded Sraffa's review in the light of the latter's subsequent writings and pointed out that it marked the start of the neo-Ricardian counter-revolution, being, like Sraffa's 1926 article (though Lachmann does not mention this) both anti-subjectivist and anti-neoclassical. (Lachmann, 1986, pp. 226–7). But nobody appeared able or willing to sort this out at the time. Hayek challenged Sraffa to make explicit his theoretical starting point (Hayek, 1932b, p. 103), but Sraffa ducked the challenge (Sraffa, 1932b, p. 114).

It was thus impossible to have a dialogue with either Keynes or Sraffa. With Hayek's other critics it was possible. Thus Arthur Marget's (1932) review of *Prices and Production*, and that of Hansen and Tout (1933), both come like a breath of fresh air. The authors of these articles were outside Britain; Hayek did indeed have a debate with Hansen and Tout, responding to their review in an article in *Econometrica* (Hayek, 1934). Later critics within the UK such as Tom Wilson (1939–40) and Nicholas Kaldor (1939, 1942), as well as Hawtrey (1932, 1933, 1940, 1941), may have disagreed strongly (in the case of Hawtrey in particular, very strongly indeed) with Hayek's analysis; and their criticisms were very far from groundless. But at least it was possible for Hayek to read the criticisms and to respond to them. With Cambridge, however, there seemed no possibility of dialogue.

SUBJECTIVISM

One of the bases of Sraffa's attack upon Hayek had been his aversion to subjectivism. Indeed a thorough-going subjectivism of the kind to be found in Austrian economics did not play well with a British audience. Yet employed as a critical tool – as in Hayek's later critique of 'scientism' – the idea drew attention to fundamental issues. Subjectivism was to play a central role in Hayek's sustained and brilliant critique of a set of ideas which many of his academic contemporaries found seductive: historicism, socialism and scientism. We could only understand the development of society resulting from countless individual decisions, he argued, on the basis of introspection as a key to subjectivism, not by misguidedly attempting to posit the existence of metaphysical entities such as 'society'. It was a fallacy that the methods of natural science could be transferred to the much more complicated social and economic world, because in the latter, actions were based upon beliefs rather than upon objective facts, and there could not be an objective body of data on which a planner could operate (Hayek, 1941b, 1942–44).

To Anglo-Saxon tastes, Hayek was prone to overstate the claims for subjectivism, to claim indeed that it was the most important development in economics in the last hundred years (1942–44, I, p. 281), and even trying to find a subjective basis for the theory of rent (ibid., pp. 282–3). But the questions which subjectivism raised for such metaphysical entities as 'society', 'the economy', 'capitalism' and 'the class struggle' were real enough. If journalists and other political commentators seem unable to function without reference to such concepts in our own time, as well as the more recent, and even more nebulous, 'international community', Hayek's position has the merit of forcing recognition that such concepts are metaphysical and that statements such as 'society insists that . . .' literally have no meaning, and are merely rhetorical flourishes. Moreover, the reliance of scientism on such metaphysical concepts reveals the hollowness of its claims to be applying the methods of natural science to social phenomena.

Hayek's development of his critique of scientism was, for the most part, published in the early 1940s, by which time he had already become a lonely figure. But things did not improve much after the Second World War.

HAYEK IN THE POST-WAR WORLD

Hayek was to blame the 1944 publication of *The Road to Serfdom* – tremendous popular success though it was (Blundell, 2005, pp. 25–6) – for his becoming an outcast (Hayek, 1994, p. 103). Yet it is not clear that, at least as far as his fellow economists went, the reactions were extravagantly hostile. The review by Pigou expressed the opinion that '[f]ew who read through this earnest and admirably written plea will fail to be interested and stimulated by his treatment of it, and fewer still to close the book without a feeling of respect for and sympathy with the writer' (Pigou, 1944, p. 219). There were respectful reviews by Schumpeter (1946), Aaron Director (1945) and J.J. Spengler (1945). Even socialist writers such as Evan Durbin (1945) and Erich Roll (1945), however strongly they disagreed with Hayek, were prepared to debate the issues. The really vitriolic abuse came instead from those outside the ranks of economists.

But in 1950 on abruptly leaving LSE, Hayek was turned down by the Chicago economics department. This is unlikely to have been due, at least decisively, to *The Road to Serfdom*, though Hayek's book had been received with outrage by the American left, and academics have an instinct to conform. It is also true that Hayek's opponent Oscar Lange had recently enjoyed a successful spell in a chair in the Chicago department, before becoming an ambassador (Backhouse, 2002b). But it would be hard to argue that the majority of the Chicago department, or the Chicago tradition, were instinctively opposed to the message of Hayek's book.[6] Rather the problem seems to have lain with Hayek's economics. Milton Friedman has testified that the problem was partly internal – the department's right to choose staff rather than accord with the wishes of the administrators – but particularly that the department did not like Hayek's capital theory and the analysis of *Prices and Production*. According to Friedman, 'if they had been looking around the world for an economist to add to their staff, their prescription would not have been the author of *Prices and Production*' (Ebenstein, 2001, p. 174). Moreover Friedman has expressed himself strongly about the monetary theory espoused by Hayek and Robbins at LSE in the 1930s, which he considered a disastrous version of the quantity theory. Hayek, through the intercession of John Neff, was given a position on the Committee on Social Thought, and he occupied this chair for about 15 years. But he was there in the role of a social philosopher rather than that of an economist more narrowly defined.

As Hayek's career as a social philosopher developed, those who might have been expected to provide some intellectual support could be seen distancing themselves from him. In particular Robbins, having already distanced himself from *The Road to Serfdom* (O'Brien, 1988, p. 66), was unenthusiastic about Hayek's 1960 book, *The Constitution of Liberty* (Robbins, 1961). The same was true of Viner's (1961) review of the book, this despite testifying that Hayek was an economist 'of the first rank'. There were, one suspects, particular causes for this. Hayek's hostility to Bentham, whom he regarded with some justification (Rothbard, 1995, pp. 49–68) as a constructivist, would not have pleased Robbins (Hayek, 1960, pp. 55, 174, 435; cf. 1973–79, I, pp. 22, 128–9; 1973–79, II, pp. 17–23, 44–8). Hayek had indeed pointed to a fundamental fallacy of pain–pleasure evaluation: the assumption that all effects could be known at the outset, when in truth there were always unintended consequences.

More troublingly, there is a suspicion raised by the reviews that the strongly anti-religious Robbins, Viner and (especially) Frank Knight (1967), who could all otherwise be expected to be sympathetic to Hayek, seemed to have found the agnostic Hayek insufficiently hostile to religion.

Hayek thus became successively more isolated, even from those who might have been expected to have much in common with him. His influence and standing clearly faded during the 1960s. Indeed one commentator has pointed to the fact that an acknowledgment by Malinvaud of Hayek's work on prices in intertemporal equilibrium was later dropped and replaced by a reference to Hicks (Milgate, 1979). Most startlingly of all, George Shackle, who had been a graduate student of Hayek in the 1930s, and who was later to write appreciatively about him (Shackle, 1981), omitted almost all mention of Hayek's economics from his 1967 book *The Years of High Theory*, which was supposed to be about economic theory in the 1930s (Böhm, 1992, pp. 8–10).

In the Mont Pelerin Society and through the foundation of the Institute of Economic Affairs, Hayek managed to maintain some sort of contact with his contemporaries and some circulation for his ideas. But much of the 1960s was a bleak time for his reputation. It was with works by John Hicks from the mid-1960s that Hayek's reputation began to revive. First there was Hicks's pathbreaking *Capital and Growth* (1965), which undoubtedly helped to revive interest in the Austrian theory of capital. Secondly there was the discussion in Hicks's *Critical Essays in Monetary Theory* (1967). This provided a serious re-evaluation of Hayek's macroeconomics. Then, with the growing awareness in the early 1970s that inflation throughout the Western world was getting out of control, there was a reawakened interest in Hayek's approach to inflation (Spencer, 1975; Maling, 1975; Backhouse, 2002a). Moreover, as inflation was seen to distort economic signals in markets, there was renewed interest in Hayek's treatment of economics and knowledge.

The macroeconomic model together with Hayek's work on the framework for economic activity, much of which dated from the 1960s, were identified by the Nobel Memorial Prize committee as his key contributions when the prize was awarded to Hayek (Royal Academy of Sciences, 1974). With the resurgence of interest, Fritz Machlup, in paying tribute to Hayek's contribution, was able to claim that '[t]he victory of Keynes's theory on the political scene and in the halls of the universities did not mean that all scholars turned their back to Hayek's hypotheses' (Machlup, 1974, p. 202; 1976).

The resurgence of interest in Hayek's work was to last well into the next decade. Since it was Hayek's trade cycle theory and his approach to inflation which reawakened interest, it seems best to examine this in more detail.

TRADE CYCLE THEORY

Although Hayek had an extensive knowledge of the monetary literature in English, German, French and Italian, and had been working on monetary questions since the 1920s, the underlying mechanism for his analysis of the trade cycle was taken from Mises's reinterpretation of Wicksell's cumulative process. The idea was that, with a bank lending rate less than the marginal rate of profit, there would be a distortion of the relative prices of consumption and investment goods, compared with the relationship which would have existed in response solely to consumer preferences for present and future goods. Monetary expansion, which lay behind the lower bank lending rate, did not primarily affect the general price level but this relative price relationship, as both Mises and Hayek repeatedly emphasized. Then the expansion of the investment good market, resulting from the cheap credit, enabled producers of investment goods to capture resources from producers of consumption goods. This shifted leftwards the supply schedules for consumption goods. The resulting rises in their prices imposed forced savings on consumers. This was stage 1.

But an important – and often neglected – stage 2 followed. The enhanced factor incomes, resulting from factors being bid away from the production of consumption goods, shifted upwards the demand curves for consumption goods, restoring the pre-disturbance relative price ratio of consumption and investment goods, and the output of the former to their original levels. The increase in output involved the reattraction of resources back into the consumption goods industries. This led the producers of investment goods to seek yet further loans from the banking system, in order once more to bid up the prices of factors, and to try to complete the investment projects upon which they had embarked as a result of the initial credit expansion. Thus monetary expansion disturbed a general equilibrium in which, prior to the disturbance, the relative outputs of consumption goods and investment goods reflected consumer preferences for consumption goods and savings, and the social rate of time preference.

As Kaldor (1942) was to argue persuasively (though Hayek, 1942, denied this), Hayek departed significantly from this model in his later writings on the trade cycle. The version put forward by Hayek in *Profits, Interest and Investment* (1939) and in *The Pure Theory of Capital* (1941a) is different from the Mises-derived version described above, and which is to be found in *Prices and Production* (1931a) and *Monetary Theory and the Trade Cycle* ([1929] 1933). The later version is built around the (misnamed) Ricardo Effect. In this version, an increase in the demand for consumption goods, possibly because of a reduction in the rate of interest, raises profits in the consumption goods industries because real wages fall during a boom. Nominal wages are sticky, but the prices of consumption goods rise. The increased profitability leads to a demand for investment in capacity; but this is capital-widening, rather than the capital-deepening (more roundabout production processes), which was involved in the earlier model. However the fall in real wages reduces the equilibrium ratio of capital to labour; this is what Hayek called the Ricardo Effect. Hayek believed that this latter effect would be more powerful than the stimulating effect of demand for machinery for capital widening, so that there would be a slump in the capital goods industries as entrepreneurs substituted labour for capital. So, as Kaldor pointed out, the idea that production methods would become unduly roundabout was replaced in this later version by the idea that they might become unduly direct.

This later version was clearly not very satisfactory. As Wilson (1939–40) pointed out, the arithmetical examples in which Hayek showed a direct and dramatic effect of changes in real wages on profitability were highly sensitive to the unrealistically short turnover rates for capital which he posited.

By the time Hayek centred his trade cycle model around the so-called Ricardo Effect, he was engaged in what can be seen in retrospect to have been a defensive exercise; in Lakatosian terms, the scientific research programme of his trade cycle model was in a degenerating phase. But the earlier, Mises-derived, model is a much more impressive structure. It is true that the argument was developed within the context of a closed economy, a key assumption of which Hayek seems to have been scarcely conscious though it was pointed out by Haberler (1937, pp. 32, 66) and by subsequent critics (Hummel, 1979, p. 134), and it was subject to sustained and accurate criticism. Dennis Robertson, who like Hayek attached importance to the phenomenon of forced saving (or 'induced lacking' as he called it) (Presley, 1978, p. 115), found the Austrian model oversimplified (Robertson, 1940, pp. 184–8). He made the fundamental empirical criticism of the basic model that Hayek exaggerated the difficulty which a change in the interest rate, as the boom came to an end and banks moved to protect their reserves, would cause to those engaged in investment where this had been financed from retained profits or from long loans at lower rates of interest than those now prevailing (ibid., p. 100n). Robertson believed that Hayek exaggerated the sensitivity of investment to small changes in the interest rate.

More damagingly still, Hawtrey, the largely unsung hero of interwar British macroeconomics, made two fundamental criticisms of the Mises model. First – and this criticism was primarily directed at Keynes's *Treatise* – Hawtrey argued that changes in the bank lending rate did not have a significant effect upon the long-run rate of interest (Hawtrey, 1938, pp. 184–95). Secondly, Hawtrey (1941) argued that Hayek had fundamentally misunderstood how investment worked. Capital could not be viewed apart from the enterprise, and within the enterprise the costs and returns associated with investment were only part of a much wider picture involving marginal costs and returns. The aim of the enterprise was to maximize the net return, not to maximize the return per unit of capital, a point made also by Kaldor (1942). Moreover, increased investment could take the form of widening rather than deepening capital. Which of the two was more important was essentially an empirical question, but capital deepening was forced upon Hayek by the assumption that the cycle started from a position of general equilibrium with full employment.

But the assumption by Hayek was not arbitrary. All the factor-price effects of the model would not work if there were unemployed resources on which the capital goods industries could draw without bidding factors away from the consumption goods industries.

There were other difficulties. Hayek (1931a, p. 139) believed that the end of a boom involved uncompleted investment projects. Like much else in the theory this was an empirical question, though the belief seems to have been grounded on Central European experience around 1930. But in the logic of the theory investment projects must be incomplete, as Neisser pointed out (Haberler, 1937, pp. 49–50). Otherwise the whole resource-recapture cycle would not be necessary because the extra investment, as it came on stream, should be able to provide the required consumer goods (as consumers ceased to suffer forced saving) without competition for resources.

The original version of Hayek's trade cycle theory was thus distinctly shaky, and this was apparent to his contemporary critics. But the Ricardo Effect was even less convincing. First, it relies upon a stylized fact (which, like other stylized facts, turns out not to be a fact) that real wages fall during a boom. (It was however implied by the forced saving argument of the earlier trade cycle theory.) Put forward by Hayek on a number of occasions, the Ricardo Effect was criticized by Kaldor (1942) and by Tom Wilson (1939–40). It seems to be quite clear, despite attempts to defend it (O'Driscoll, 1975), that it is not even in Ricardo; and certainly not in the passages cited by Hayek in support of this origin (Kaldor, 1942; Ferguson, 1973; O'Brien, 1994b, p. 368). But, most damagingly of all, as Kaldor showed in a series of articles, the Ricardo effect did not provide a satisfactory theory of a trade cycle; in particular, as Wilson pointed out (1939–40, p. 234), the change in real wages would not necessarily influence the choice of method – it would raise profits on both capital-widening *and* capital deepening.

THE QUANTITY THEORY OF MONEY QUESTION

Hayek's theory of the trade cycle, at least in the version in *Monetary Theory and the Trade Cycle*, was a monetary theory (Colonna, 1994). This was clear enough to Hayek's contemporaries. Ellis (1934, pp. 162–5) saw the Mises theory as part of the cash balance approach. Haberler (1937, pp. 31ff.), surveying trade cycle theories, classified Hayek as offering a monetary overinvestment theory. Friedman (1974, p. 158) identified the LSE theory in the 1930s as a distorted version of the quantity theory.

There are dissenters from this last view. Hicks (1977, p. 63) has denied the quantity theory classification on the surprising ground that a direct link between the money supply and the price level is broken by the possibility of holding balances, where credit supply is unconstrained by bank liquidity. O'Driscoll and Rizzo have argued that the theory differs from the quantity theory because of the microeconomic focus of the argument (O'Driscoll, 1977, pp. 135–42; O'Driscoll and Rizzo, 1985, pp. 188–228). But there is no genuine microeconomics in Hayek's trade cycle theory, because the myriad of prices somehow become aggregated into representative consumer and producer goods prices and factor rewards.

As has been pointed out by Hageman (1994), Hayek was actually trying in 1929 to reintroduce money into the dominant German trade cycle theory. His treatment of historical figures such as Thornton, and above all Cantillon, show causality as running from money supply changes to prices (O'Brien, 1994b, p. 360). Fundamentally, all that is different from the quantity theory is that one price level is replaced by two, representing the prices of consumer and investment goods respectively. Hayek says explicitly that a change in the money supply is central to the argument ([1929] 1933, pp. 101–2, 107). Indeed several writers (Humphrey, 1984; Bellante and Garrison, 1988; Seccareccia, 1994) have noted parallels with Fisher's treatment of the quantity theory. Undoubtedly Hayek ([1929] 1933, pp. 106–7) confused the issue because, following Mises's own emphasis, and in common with Haberler (1937), and later Robbins, he dismissed the concept of a general price level as without significance.

Hayek, like Mises, maintained that changes in the general price level could not cause a trade cycle ([1929] 1933, p. 13), but the way in which he presented this has caused confusion. It has been suggested that he did not believe that changes in the money supply caused cyclical fluctuations at all (Rühl, 1994, p. 195) and he has even been hailed as an opponent of the quantity theory (Aréna, 2002). But the inescapable fact is that the price level must rise in Hayek's model: first the price of investment goods rises, and then that of consumption goods rises, restoring the original relative price ratio. Furthermore, since (as we shall see) Hayek envisaged the acceleration of inflation, he must indeed have had some concept of the general price level.

Hayek's exposition caused further confusion because some believed – even so perceptive a critic as Hicks (1967, p. 208) – that the secondary recovery in the consumption goods industries had been left out of *Prices and Production*. Even an acute critic like Marget (1932) believed that Hayek's theory was compatible with a stable overall price level. This was something that Hayek asserted, but overall price stability could only be explained by productivity rising so fast that, without the trade cycle-induced changes, the general price level would have fallen. But were productivity rising that fast, it is by no means obvious that a restoration of expenditure on consumer goods would have caused their prices to rise.

In summary, Friedman's perception of the fundamental similarity of Hayek's approach with the quantity theory was not misplaced. Rather it was Hayek's exposition which has misled later commentators. Indeed it has been plausibly argued by Bellante and Garrison (1988; Garrison, 1989; Bellante, 1994) that Hayek's and Friedman's two versions of monetary disequilibrium can be regarded as complementary: Friedman focuses upon labour market disequilibrium, Hayek upon capital market disequilibrium.

CAPITAL THEORY

Perhaps the major problem raised by Hayek's treatment of macroeconomic fluctuations is to be found in capital theory. Hayek started from the position that the period of production – Böhm-Bawerk's concept – was related to the preferences of individuals for present and future goods, and its length determined marginal investment and profitability. Hayek refers to Böhm-Bawek in an essay on factor rewards dating from 1926, a 1927 essay on interest theory, and in the essay on intertemporal equilibrium of 1928 (McCloughry, 1984, pp. 33–54, 55–70, 71–117); and the period of production features in *Prices and Production* (*P&P*) (Hayek, 1931a, Ch. 2).

It was an unfortunate theoretical path to follow. Hawtrey took the trouble to understand as fully as was possible the model underlying *P&P*, unlike those in Cambridge who simply abused Hayek. He also reviewed the English version of Hayek's *Monetary Theory and the Trade Cycle* (*MTTC*) (Hawtrey, 1933) and was scathing about the capital theory. Of that in *P&P* he wrote:

> I feel bound to say that Dr Hayek has spoiled an original piece of work which might have been an important contribution to monetary theory, by entangling his argument with the intolerably cumbersome theory of capital derived from Jevons and Böhm-Bawerk. This theory, when it was enunciated, was a noteworthy new departure in the metaphysics of political economy. But it is singularly ill-adapted for use in monetary theory, or indeed in any practical treatment of the capital market.
>
> The result has been to make Dr Hayek's work so difficult and obscure that it is impossible to understand his little book of 112 pages except at the cost of many hours of hard work. And at the end we are left with the impression, not only that this is not a necessary consequence of the difficulty of the subject, but that he himself has been led by so ill-chosen a method of analysis to conclusions which he would hardly have accepted if given a more straightforward form of expression. (Hawtrey, 1932, p. 125)

Indeed it was apparently the capital theory which had led Hayek to the belief that an extension of credit would necessarily be spent in lengthening the period of production. But, as Hawtrey pointed out, not only was extra credit used to hold increased stocks, but Hayek's view did not of itself produce a trade cycle. It was apparently necessary, Hawtrey (1933, pp. 185–7) argued in his review of *MTTC*, to introduce non-monetary causes to do this. As we shall see, in the discussion of a falling price level, this was not necessarily the case; but even Hawtrey missed that.

It was clear to Hayek's colleagues that the period of production was an encumbrance. Lionel Robbins (1934a) omitted it from his Hayekian *The Great Depression* (O'Brien, 1988, pp. 106–7), and Kaldor, one of the two translators of *MTTC*, attacked the concept (Kaldor, 1939).

It is easy to show that it is impossible to arrive at a scalar measure of capital stock (Laidler, 1999, pp. 33–4). But in truth nothing hinges on a scalar measure of this kind. Though Hayek talked about shortening or lengthening of the production process, he frequently avoided reference to a 'period of production' (e.g. Hayek, 1934; O'Brien, 1994b, p. 359). The period of production was essentially an irrelevance, a fifth wheel to which Occam's Razor must necessarily apply. It has no empirical counterpart, and nothing in the theory stands by its presence, as Hayek admitted in controversy with Frank Knight (Hayek, 1936, pp. 206–7). If removed, we are simply left with the proposition that investment may become greater than voluntary saving. This can be clearly seen if we look at John Presley's (1978) illuminating discussion of Dennis Robertson. The crucial indication for both Hayek and Robertson that something was wrong was not a lengthening of the immeasurable – the period of production – but the occurrence of forced saving (Robertson's induced lacking). The policy implication is clear enough: an increase in the rate of interest. But it only differs in detail from Wicksell, whose policy prescription, as Tom Humphrey (1992) has shown, requires both an inflation and a price level target for stability. What Hayek required for his model was a relative price target. There is no role for the metaphysical idea of a period of production.

Hayek could have seen clearly enough from Robbins's 1934 book that it was possible to give a clear exposition of his theory without the period of production. Perhaps the book did help to turn Hayek away from the concept. It had already received little emphasis in *MTTC*, dating originally from 1929, though it was prominent in *P&P* of 1931. But that book was designed to impress a London audience with the difficult novelty of an alternative tradition. Later Hayek rejected the period of production concept outright, as in his *The Pure Theory of Capital* (1941a). The last link with Böhm-Bawerk had gone (Blaug, 1992, p. 32).

In some ways it is puzzling that Hayek stuck with the concept for as long as he did. In so doing he left himself open to Cambridge critics who, even now, focus upon the concept (e.g. de Vivo, 1994). Yet Mises himself was to reject the period of production as an 'empty concept' (1949, p. 489; Moss, 1976, p. 54).

There were, I think, three reasons why Hayek persevered with this unfortunate concept. Firstly, it was part of the programme to establish the legitimacy of an Austrian alternative to Anglo-Saxon economics. For this, a lineage was necessary, and Böhm-Bawerk was a founding father of the line. Never mind that the period of production in the latter's work is crude. This can be put down to inferior technique. Secondly, the period of production was part of Hayek's ill-judged product differentiation, distinguishing his trade cycle theory from that of Fisher. This was a mistake. It had the unfortunate effect of alienating a potential source of support in the Chicago department, and it later enabled those who wished to dismiss Hayek's work to point to his ill-advised use of the period-of-production concept. Thirdly, the sad truth is that, in his review of Keynes's *Treatise*, Hayek had painted himself into a corner. He made great play of the absence of capital theory from the *Treatise*, and with Keynes's failure to acquaint himself with Böhm-Bawerk's work (Hayek, 1931b, pp. 7–8; 1931c, p. 63; 1932a, pp. 81–3; Butos, 1994, p. 473). He thus placed himself in the position of having to show why capital theory is of central importance.

The triangles through which Hayek sought to explain his theory of capital, and which involve a scalar quantity, one which is thus vulnerable to the standard criticism that its value will change with a change in relative prices, really make no sense, and there is ample testimony that they confused contemporaries (e.g. Robinson, 1972). Jevons, whose priority Hayek scrupulously acknowledged (1931a, p. 38), had a clear understanding of such triangles, with time on the horizontal axis and investment on the vertical one. But Hayek attempted to use the vertical axis both for inputs – 'intermediate products', the Austrian 'higher-order' goods – and outputs of consumer goods. Howard Ellis, in his book on German monetary theory saw clearly enough that the triangles were meaningless (Ellis, 1934, pp. 353–4); but others persevered in an attempt to make sense of them. One of the particular difficulties which they encountered was the problem of fixed capital (Hicks and Weber, 1973, p. 192; Steedman, 1994, p. 14). There was no correspondence between inputs and outputs where capital lasted a long time. Even Lutz (1943, p. 304), who tried to solve the dimensionality problem of the triangles by arguing that they could only be interpreted by measuring inputs in terms of the output to which they gave rise, had to accept that with fixed capital there was an insoluble problem.

Modern Austrians – with some exceptions (Steele, 1993) – have understandably distanced themselves from this part of Hayek's work. He has been criticized for the abandonment of subjectivism in *P&P* (O'Driscoll and Rizzo, 1985); and most recent Austrian writers, from Lachmann (1956) onwards, employ a thoroughgoing subjective treatment of capital as a structure of plans (e.g. Horwitz, 1996, 2000), without any idea of a scalar.

THE INFLATION ACCELERATION ISSUE

Hayek undoubtedly expected that, if inflationary bank lending were allowed to occur, inflation itself would accelerate unless the banks were constrained by reserve considerations (Hayek, 1934, pp. 155–7; 1960, pp. 330–33, 336–9; 1972). For this he has been criticized. Yet it would be surprising if Hayek had not given some thought to the matter, given that he had witnessed the hyperinflation in Continental countries after the First World War (Rosner and Winckler, 1989), and given that he was to maintain this theme in his later work, though without reliance upon his trade cycle model, relying subsequently on the erosion of money illusion (Hayek, 1967, pp. 282, 295–9).

The acceleration mechanism in the trade cycle model is however perfectly comprehensible in terms of the model. Starting from full employment, resources have to be bid away from the production of consumer goods, and they are then recaptured by the consumer goods industries once factors with enhanced incomes spend those incomes. We thus have a sequence involving a rise in the price of producer goods, a rise in the price of labour, a rise in the price of consumer goods, another rise in the price of labour, and so on. Assuming for simplicity that all the price rises are at an equal percentage rate r, we have a series of the form $(1 + r)^n$. If the money supply increases to finance these price increases is proportionate to the price increases, and if we assume that the proportion is unity for simplicity, the money supply increases will be of the form (with the first term set to unity) $1 + (1 + r) + (1 + r)^2 + \ldots + (1 + r)^n$. Over any finite period of time the series will produce a finite sum, and that sum will provide the starting value for the next run of the series. Thus the money supply is growing at an increasing rate.

This was recognized by contemporaries, even Haberler (1937, pp. 44, 46, 51) despite his resistance (1927) to the idea of a general price level. For the mechanism to work it is necessary that the initial monetary expansion should occur in an economy at full-employment general equilibrium. While this was understood, it was not fully appreciated that the resource recapture played a central role. As already noted, Hicks mistakenly believed it to be absent from *P&P*, even though it is present both in that book (Hayek, 1931a, pp. 57, 89) and in *MTTC* ([1929] 1933, p. 217). It was clearly recognized by Haberler, who cited it in his *Prosperity and Depression* (1937, pp. 45–6).

The fear of an acceleration of inflation undoubtedly underlay the opposition of Hayek to monetary and fiscal expansion in the 1930s. Hayek consistently maintained this position (Skidelsky, 1992, p. 469; O'Brien, 1994a, p. 360), arguing in his 1934 reply to Hansen and Tout (1933) that boosting demand was mistaken, thus ensuring that the 'LSE Austrians' repelled their potential allies in Chicago as Friedman (1974, pp. 162–3) has subsequently testified. Hayek later softened his opposition to government macroeconomic policy (1960, pp. 223, 324–39); but not very much.

THE FALLING PRICE LEVEL ISSUE

In controversy with Wicksell, the Swedish economist Davidson had pointed out that equality of the bank lending rate with the marginal rate of profit would not produce a stable price level (Hayek, [1929] 1933, pp. 113–15; Hayek, 1932c, pp. 122–4, 129; Uhr, 1960, pp. 279–92; Uhr, 1975, pp. 21–2). With a trend growth in productivity, the price level would fall unless the money supply were steadily increased, for which it would be necessary to have the bank lending rate below the 'natural rate'. Mises and Hayek, as Wicksell's successors, were then faced with the realization that in this dilemma lay the key to a periodic cycle. For if the bank lending rate were kept below the 'natural rate', the whole process of expansion which they envisaged would be set in motion; and it would only be checked, after successive rounds of price increases, when banks became concerned about their liquidity positions. Thus aiming for a stable price level entailed a commitment to a trade cycle (Hayek, [1929] 1933, p. 119).

Faced with this difficulty, Hayek, Haberler and Robbins were prepared instead to envisage a price level falling in line with the secular increase in productivity. But such a policy raised a host of difficulties: not merely the distributive implication of increasing rentier income, which was hardly likely to be popular in the 1930s, but, as Hummel (1979) has pointed out, a falling price level would have the effect of raising the value of the deflated rate of interest (where inflation was now negative), which could thus rise above the marginal rate of profit and produce a depression without a preceding boom. As subsequent controversy has shown (Dowd, 1995; Selgin, 1995a, 1995b) there exist many difficulties with the falling price level policy prescription.[7] But it was a logical outcome of the Mises–Hayek model, as is indeed clear from Hayek's paper on intertemporal equilibrium, where it is argued that if future prices are not expected to fall (in line with productivity) then more investment than is warranted will take place (1928, pp. 92–3).

THE ROLE OF GENERAL EQUILIBRIUM

Perhaps the difficulties concerning the future price level may explain why Hayek showed some signs of moving away from equilibrium theorizing from 1937, as Bruce Caldwell (1988) has argued. Others believe that his commitment to at least Lausanne general equilibrium was rather superficial in the first place. Aréna (1994, p. 211) has pointed out that the passage frequently cited as evidence of Hayek's commitment to general equilibrium ([1929] 1933, pp. 42–3) is normally curtailed before the point at which it goes on to refer not merely to Lausanne but also to James Mill and to Say. There is also a discernible change in Hayek's work from about 1937, in a much increased emphasis on evolutionary forms, linking this with the same element in Menger's work (O'Brien, 1994a, pp. 351–2, 357). Moreover, as Lachmann (1940) pointed out, general equilibrium involves reversibility, whereas Hayek's apparatus does not.

But, all that conceded, it is still true, as Smithies (1941) pointed out in his perceptive review of Hayek's *Pure Theory of Capital*, that the later book is still about equilibrium, albeit a moving equilibrium in which all plans are fully realized. This is a matter of some importance in relation to modern developments in economics which cite Hayek as a forerunner, as we shall see.

METHODOLOGY

There is considerable controversy about Hayek's methodological position. By many commentators, including the present writer (O'Brien, 1994a, p. 364), he has been seen as an *a priorist* in the Misean mould. Bruce Caldwell (1994) has maintained that Hayek never was an *a priorist*. Terence Hutchison, as a middle way, has argued that Hayek, having read the original German version of Popper's *Logik des Forschungs*, changed his approach in 1937 (Hutchison, 1981, p. 125; 1994, p. 217; Hamouda and Rowley, 1994, p. 186).

But the weight of the evidence from Hayek's writings seems clear enough. He was, and he remained, an *a priorist*, and somebody who was led seriously astray by this methodological stance. In this methodological position, which dates at least back to J.E. Cairnes, and which was espoused also by Robbins (O'Brien, 1988, Ch. 3; Hutchison, 1978, pp. 210, 224), reasoning to a necessary conclusion proceeds on the basis of assumptions. Any contact with reality takes the form of 'verification': checking the validity of the assumptions in order to be satisfied that the theoretical approach used was appropriate for the particular conditions to which it was applied. This still seems a reasonable reading of Hayek's 1937 paper which is sometimes taken of evidence of his change of view. Of course if introspection is regarded as a source of assumptions – and it certainly was by Hayek (O'Brien, 1994a, pp. 351–3) – verification becomes very tricky. There can be no assurance of uniformity of psychological response, as Robbins himself emphasized strongly when attacking attempts to justify progressive taxation by reference to diminishing marginal utility (O'Brien, 1988, pp. 23–5, 39).

But it is even doubtful whether Hayek took very seriously the idea of verification. After all it was assumed in his writing, and in that of his allies, that the US money supply had increased, and that this had produced a boom followed by a depression (e.g. Hayek, 1934, p. 161). But this was an assumption which was eminently subject to verification, and it was simply wrong (O'Brien, 1998a, pp. 33–5). Hayek's position here led him seriously astray and damaged his standing forever; indeed the Austrians have been charged, however unfairly, with facilitating the rise of Hitler by opposing reflationary measures (Hutchison, 1992, pp. 110–12).

Latterly Austrian writers have accepted that the US money supply had actually fallen; Haberler (1986) is an example. But the whole of Hayek's trade cycle theory suffered from a fundamental empirical weakness. For Hayek, like Keynes in the *Treatise*, believed that the bank rate influenced short-term rates of interest, that these in turn affected long-term rates, which influenced investment in fixed capital. In fairness to Keynes, he did attempt to justify this on the basis of what was, it later emerged, an unsatisfactory run of data. Ralph Hawtrey, who was very much better at this kind of work than Keynes, denied all these connections, and showed in *A Century of Bank Rate* (1938, pp. 184–95) that Keynes was mistaken. Reviewing the evidence, Hicks (1940) in turn accepted the argument. Hawtrey established that the short-term rate had very little influence on capital outlay. This result was fundamentally damaging to Hayek; far more damaging than to Keynes, who had moved on from the apparatus of the *Treatise*. Yet Hayek appears to have been unmoved, and to have regarded the empirical results as irrelevant.

After shifting the balance of his argument concerning the trade cycle towards the Ricardo Effect, he supervized the doctoral research of Tsiang (1947). The latter, though phrasing his findings very cautiously, did not find empirical support either for the Ricardo Effect or for the idea that real wages fell in the upswing of the cycle, which underpinned the effect. (Tsiang's result here confirmed earlier work concerning the behaviour of real wages in the cycle – 1947, pp. 2–3.) Yet there is no sign that Hayek responded to these findings. In his comments at the Royal Statistical Society in 1938, Hayek had remained sceptical about empirical work, despite his putative change of heart in 1937, and he does not seem to have altered his view, leaving a legacy of suspicion of empirical work in the later Austrian literature (Dolan, 1976, pp. 6–7; Spadaro, 1978, p. 212).

HAYEK AND NEW CLASSICISM

In 1977 Robert Lucas, the leading figure in new classicism, explicitly linked his work to Hayek's *MTTC* ([1929] 1933). In particular he argued that the book accepted the need, recognized until Keynes's *General Theory*, to incorporate trade cycle theory into Lausanne general equilibrium. He made the point that Keynes had redirected professional effort towards 'the apparently simpler question of the determination of output at a point in time, taking history as given' (Lucas, 1977, p. 7). He went on to argue that the trade cycle literature 'had been directed at identifying institutional sources of instability, with the hope that, once understood, these sources could be removed or their influence mitigated by appropriate institutional change' (ibid., p. 8). By contrast Keynes offered a way of rectifying the economy however the position in which it found itself had come about.

It is true that Lucas rejected Hayek's reliance upon the interest mechanism, as requiring interest-elasticities of investment which were far too high to be plausible. But there was clearly a link in Lucas's mind between what he was trying to do, as signalled in particular by his 1975 paper, and what Hayek had done.

Subsequently a number of writers have argued that any similarity between Hayek's work and new classicism is superficial. Thus some (Butos, 1985; Cochran and Glahe, 1999) have argued that the new classical models require markets to clear continuously, which was not true of Hayek, and that the new models are equilibrium models, whereas in Hayek the economy is out of equilibrium. Rühl (1994) has concluded that Hayek's analysis has little in common with the new classical one, even though the question of a trade cycle within an equilibrium model remains a concern because the problem has not been solved. Aréna (1994) has argued that the new classical approach is very much closer to Walras than Hayek was, and Hamouda and Rowley (1994) have rejected the new classical parallel on the grounds that such an approach involves a closed probability distribution, as distinct from something like Shackle's 'possibility' (1972, pp. 364–404).

The most fundamental criticisms have come from Kevin Hoover (1988, 1994). He argues, firstly, that the new classicals ask how a Walrasian economy adapts, with given tastes, endowments and production possibilities, to exogenous or policy-generated fluctuations; the Austrians ask much broader questions with the evolution of tastes, expectations and technology involved. Secondly, the new classicals want a predictive model, and they use mathematics and econometrics. The Austrians do not use these tools, and want understanding rather than prediction. Thirdly, the latter take the dispersal of information as fundamental; for the former it is limited to the degree necessary to produce fluctuations. Fourthly, Lucas et al. duck out of real disaggregation of macroeconomics by the use of representative-agent models. Finally, equilibrium of new classicals is market clearing, while for Austrians it is plans becoming compatible – a distinction short-circuited by new classicals using *tâtonnement* to achieve market clearing. (Hoover, 1994, p. 579).

Hoover has also pointed out that the use of rational expectations, which puts the economy close to, if not at, equilibrium, poses a real problem for Austrians and that the new classicals have incorporated a cycle into general equilibrium via stochastic elements. However such stochastic differential equations are still deterministic. The new classical model assumes that plans are already in existence, whereas for the Austrians they are part of a continual learning process operating through the market mechanisms (1988, pp. 235–6, 247).

Rational expectations blur the distinction between risk and uncertainty (Hoover, 1988, p. 239), and Hayek's work provides a good basis for criticizing rational expectations in whichever of the competing definitions one accepts (O'Driscoll and Rizzo, 1985, pp. 214–26). Furthermore Hayek's doctrine of unintended consequences sits very ill with the rational expectations concept. The idea of some physics-type model, as constructed by the new classicals, being in any way acceptable to Hayek is clearly strained (Hoover, 1988, p. 240).

While there is substantial weight in all these points, there is more to be said. It is true that the attempt to use representative agents as a micro-reduction of macroeconomics is regarded as at best a failure and at worst as bogus (Hoover, 1988, pp. 243–4; Hausman, 2003). But it has been persuasively argued that an individualist reduction of macroeconomics is probably impossible (Levy, 1985); and in any case, Austrian trade cycle theory itself involves aggregation. We have production goods lumped together as one category, and consumption goods in another category. The trade cycle hinges on a change in the relative prices of these two aggregated sectors.

In summary, new classical economics has encountered some of the same problems which Hayek and his successors encountered. The new classicists have, with technical apparatus, attempted to deal with what Hayek regarded as an important question – a trade cycle in the context of general equilibrium. While, viewing Hayek's work as a whole, it is possible to argue that he was concerned with the broad range of issues which critics of the new classical parallel have cited, there are important parts of Hayek's later theoretical work, including *The Pure Theory of Capital* (1941a), which did indeed involve an equilibrium trade cycle. The links between Hayek's trade cycle writings and those of the new classicists are perhaps rather greater than the assembled critics have allowed.[8]

OVERVIEW

Hayek's career fits into a recognizable pattern. First there were the late 1920s and the 1930s, when Hayek rose to considerable prominence as a theorist and was, up to 1936, the main intellectual opponent of Keynes. But the victory of Keynes's *General Theory* (1936) undoubtedly led to a significant reduction in Hayek's personal standing, and it did not recover as a result of his later theoretical work which culminated in *The Pure Theory of Capital*.

What brought Hayek to a new peak (Table 2.1) was his critique of scientism and of the roots of totalitarianism. This encompassed both his

Table 2.1 Hayek citations (1926–2003)

Time span	No. of yrs	Cites	Citations/year
1926–30	5	7	1.4
1931–36	5	32	6.4
1937–43	7	26	3.7
1944–45	2	751	375.5
1946–59	14	116	8.3
1960–70	11	228	20.7
1971–80	10	291	29.1
1981–90	10	104	10.4
1991–2003	13	17	0.8

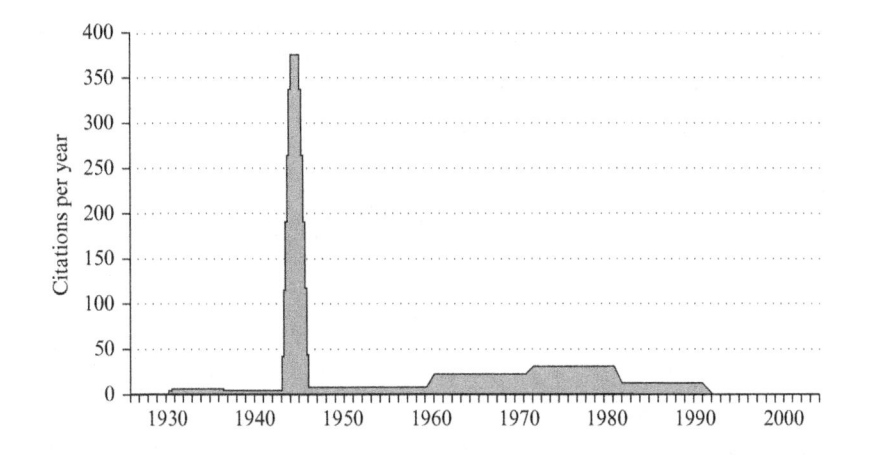

continuation of Mises's exposition of the impossibility of central planning, his withering examination of the work of Saint Simon and Comte (1941b, 1942–44), and his brave (and possibly personally disastrous) attack upon the direction in which he saw Western society going after the Second World War, which found expression most notably in *The Road to Serfdom* (1944) (O'Brien, 1994b, pp. 351–9). The third and most sustained peak was that in which he worked out, with great care and scholarship, a vision of economic activity based upon a legal framework, which was essentially developing Smith's vision of the constraint of economic activity by law, religion and custom (O'Brien, 1998c). This effort found its expression in two great works, *The Constitution of Liberty* of 1960, and *Law, Legislation and Liberty*, the three volumes of which appeared over the years 1973–79. It was in the 1970s also that he received the Nobel Prize, when his earlier

Table 2.2   Hayek citations (2003–2011)

Year	Citations
2003	68
2004	70
2005	95
2006	122
2007	119
2008	154
2009	173
2010	159
2011	149

work on the trade cycle and his most recent on a free society were cited as particular achievements.

The most recent citation data show, not surprisingly, that as the world financial system suffered a series of shocks of a kind not included in the conventional probability distributions, there has been an upsurge of interest in Hayek's work. This upsurge is evident in Table 2.2 and the accompanying chart.

The pattern of citations shown in Table 2.1 corresponds to this outline of his career. Only in the 1990s did the citations almost cease. Furthermore, from analysis of relative citations by Deutscher (1990, pp. 189–202), it is evident that Hayek was amongst the most cited authors in the great theoretical controversies of the 1930s.[9]

Yet a large part of Hayek's work has experienced years of neglect. As Dostaler (1994, p. 148) has emphasized, it is important to read what Hayek actually wrote. Like Adam Smith, he is cited but unread (Hamouda and Rowley, 1994, p. 178), which leads to inaccuracy and distortion. Yet even in his Teutonic professor style, his work has much greater immediacy than the secondary literature. Return to this work is both necessary and profitable. Hayek quite clearly anticipated Rawls's principle by suggesting maximizing the income potential of the least well-off (1967, p. 173)[10] – yet it is possible for the secondary literature to contest this because few readers will be familiar with the original.

There is also a quite extraordinary mainstream hostility to Austrian economics in general and to Hayek in particular (Rizzo, 1992). Some of the latter seems visceral.[11] Despite this hostility, there are still those who attempt to carry the Austrian flag. There are different kinds of Austrians, but the gaps between them are much smaller than the gulf between all of them and mainstream economics; and the heritage which the Austrians share, as Backhouse (1985, p. 378) has pointed out, is not Böhm-Bawerk or Schumpeter, it is Menger, Mises and Hayek. The main Austrian centre, formerly New York University, seems now to have moved to George Mason University in Fairfax, Virginia. Austrian views have been kept alive by the Foundation of Economic Education (Irvington, NY) dating from the 1940s, and in more recent years the Ludwig von Mises Institute (Auburn, AL) has greatly increased the visibility of the Austrian school. However, the list of contributors to volumes on Hayek (and their academic affiliations) reveals a much wider constituency. Particular Hayekian themes are also being developed, such as the sustained work by Roger Garrison (1985, 1989, 2001) on Hayek's trade cycle model.

Moreover an Austrian approach to economics provides a good basis for criticizing the mainstream literature. Although Spadaro (1978, pp. 206–7) has suggested that such an approach, at least if primarily defensive, is a misallocation of resources, it is apparent from the Austrian literature that criticism can be a good method of developing an alternative research programme.[12] The intellectual descendants of Hayek have been good at asking awkward questions (e.g. Lachmann, 1978). The vulnerable areas of mainstream economics are many, and Hicks himself has testified to the inadequacy of so central a part as the Paretian system (1967, p. 138). Hayek and other Austrians asked the awkward questions that mainstream theory sidesteps. Such questions include economic actors taking decisions on the basis of a constantly changing supply of knowledge which causes, in turn, constant revision of plans. This difficulty extends to the problem of intertemporal coordination and the revision of plans across time (Garrison, 1985). More generally, what meaning has the concept of rational behaviour with time-dependent knowledge? (Boland, 1978; Langlois, 1985). Again, the Hayekian treatment of expectations is much less constrained than the mechanistic treatment of rational expectations, and far more suggestive than the arbitrary changes in expectations which Keynes employed in the *General Theory*. The questions raised by Hayek's treatment of knowledge[13] are fundamental to an understanding of how a real economy works, as Leijonhufvud has argued (1968, p. 401). Yet the mainstream is averse to even acknowledging the existence of such questions.[14] Indeed, the Keynesian mainstream for long largely ignored the time dimension of investment (Tsiang, 1949).[15]

But Hayek bequeathed more than awkward questions. There are possibilities of developing his understanding of markets through experimental economics (Smith, 1982) and game theory (Schmidt, 2002), though the closed probability distributions would not have appealed to Hayek (cf. Shackle, 1972, pp. 24, 161, 422). Even the capital theory may not be a dead end: following the pioneering work of Hicks, writers such as Desai and Redfern (1994) and Zamagni (1984, 1987) have produced highly mathematical interpretations of 'traverses' between equilibria.

Less promising is Hayek's work on the denationalization of money. While the free banking literature has taken its inspiration from Hayek (Dowd, 1994), there has been serious criticism of the idea of competition in currencies (King, 1983; Summers, 1983). The transaction costs of multiple issues (Edwards, 1980), and the possibility of moral hazard, are so serious that it is unlikely that any unitary state would follow this path although, as Hayek himself pointed out, in border areas, especially in Europe, competing currencies have in the past operated in parallel. But they are currencies originating with national issuers, not commercial organizations. Of course, as Hayek stressed, states have abused their powers of issue; but currency competition has to be considered as a remedy for this not in isolation but in comparison with other possible remedies such as inflation targeting (Howard, 1977).

On the other hand his treatment of competition in the markets for goods and services has proved important. Hayek insisted on analysing the way in which competition works, as distinct from the sterile definitional approach of Lausanne general equilibrium. The fixation of economists with perfect competition led them grossly to underestimate the achievements of the competitive system (Hayek, 1949, pp. 102–6; 1967, p. 174; 1973–79 III, pp. 65–8). As Backhouse (2002a, pp. 278–9) has emphasized, Hayek focused on rivalry, new products and new processes; to put it another way, Hayek addressed not maximization subject to constraints but the much more fundamental issue of moving the constraints. Competition should be viewed as a continuous discovery process, as Smith understood, not a set of conditions like perfect competition. Such a view has lasting validity.[16] Moreover it has had an important policy impact, for competition policy illustrates perfectly why Austrian, and specifically Hayekian, economics lacks fashionable appeal. It undermines the idea of an active competition policy (in which many economists have found highly remunerative employment) and thus accords with the devastatingly successful Chicago anti-antitrust school.[17] (O'Brien, 1998a, p. 29). Indeed a key member of that school cites Hayek (Demsetz, 1988; 1989, pp. 219, 223; Demsetz, 1995, p. 171; DiLorenzo, 1994).

CONCLUSION

Hayek came into the English-speaking world as an economist, not as a philosopher. But his work broadened out to embrace philosophical considerations relating to the framework of economic activity, which linked with his overriding concern with freedom and responsibility. He thus found a key role in the development of British liberalism, as Cockett (1995) has shown at length. The influence of Mises led Hayek on to Smith, Burke, Ferguson and Hume, and to the concept of spontaneous order, and ultimately to some of the most important writing that economists have produced about the framework of economic activity (O'Brien, 1998c). The Austrian understanding of the operation of markets, with which this is associated, has been of great importance, notably at those times when fashionable opinion has favoured planning, whether indicative (as in the 1960s) or directive (Lavoie, 1986; O'Brien, 1998b, p. 115).

The line of development goes from Menger to Mises to Hayek. The combined direct influence of the last two continues, and historians of economic thought cannot neglect the importance of Hayek in the story of the development of the subject. Hayek has been called Böhm-Bawerk's greatest pupil (Blaug, 1985, p. 541). The link is unfortunate; it has been argued above that Hayek would have done well to steer clear of Böhm-Bawerk's capital theory. He was Mises's greatest pupil far more, and he managed, starting from that base, to counter the vanity of academics who wished to plan society, to explain the fundamental nature of markets, and also – and this is worth emphasizing in an academic climate in which scholarship is at a discount – he was one of the last of the great scholar economists. The questions which he asked were not trivial, and they do not permit of easy answers. They are thus not attractive to the economist-as-technician. To be blunt, Austrian economics is not good for outside career opportunities and, because of the ruling mainstream, it is not good for academic career opportunities either.[18] But of its importance as one of the strands in the development of our subject there can be no doubt.

NOTES

1. Though edited for the present volume, this chapter, which serves as a foundation for many of the subsequent chapters, originally appeared as Chapter 10 in Denis P. O'Brien (2007), *History of Economic Thought as an Intellectual Discipline*, Cheltenham, UK and Northampton, MA, USA: Edward Elgar.
2. For a fascinating account of the Austrian background see Caldwell (2004).
3. It is now clear that Schumpeter's claim (1954, pp. 837, 918), that there was no fundamental difference between Menger, Walras and Jevons, was wrong (Jaffé, 1976).
4. I am quite unable to understand the implication in Streissler (1994, p. 48) that Hayek was grudging with acknowledgments.
5. It is true that Pigou, himself the victim of such abuse, did courageously take up the challenge and review the *General Theory*, in the LSE journal *Economica* (Collard, 1981, pp. 125–6); but he did at least enjoy the status of an insider, unlike Hayek.
6. It is however surprising to learn that the 'left' was predominant among social scientists in Chicago in the 1930s (Caldwell, 2004, p. 233).
7. As Howard (1977) has pointed out, Hayek later settled for a stable price level. Haberler (1986) also came to recognize problems with a falling price level.
8. It seems that Lucas himself has accepted Hoover's view (Snowdon and Vane, 1998, p. 121).
9. In the period 1931–35, Hayek was third in the list of most cited macroeconomists (behind Keynes and Robertson), and for 1936–39 he was seventh (Deutscher, 1990, pp. 190–93). I owe this data on citations to John Creedy.
10. Rawls, it is true, focuses on the distributive outcome. But experience shows that, precisely because of unintended consequences, we have limited control over that. Hayek instead looked to the creation of conditions for the attainment of such equality.
11. Thus Fischer (1986, p. 433), in a very hostile article, accuses Hayek (1976) of ignorance of Klein (1975) – yet Hayek explicitly cites Klein's article (1976, p. 37). See also the comments by Ackley quoted by Bellante and Garrison (1988, pp. 335–6) and Solow's description of Hayek's trade cycle model as 'completely incomprehensible' cited by Garrison (2001, p. 4).
12. O'Driscoll and Rizzo (1985) provide a good example of this.
13. Or Hayek's and Morgenstern's; see Caldwell (1994) and Foss (1995).
14. Hutt, whose work on search was belatedly acknowledged by Leijonhufvud (1969, p. 31), with chagrin, was simply pushed out of mainstream consciousness.
15. In Leijonhufvud's view (1981, p. 173), Keynes gave little thought to capital or economic growth.
16. It is thus capable of further development. It has been argued that Kirzner's theory of entrepreneurship derives from Hayek (Kirzner, 1997; Palermo, 1999, pp. 104–5). The suggestion (Hamouda and Rowley, 1994, pp. 191–2) that the Japanese *keiretsu* system might render Hayek's vision of competition irrelevant now seems, two decades later, rather quaint.
17. In destroying anti-trust policy, the Chicago economists destroyed industrial economics, creating a desert in which game theory took root.
18. For exploration of possible links with another 'outside' branch of economics – institutionalism – see Boettke (1989), Caldwell (1989), Samuels (1989) and Rutherford (1989, 1994).

REFERENCES

Aréna, Richard A. (1994), 'Hayek and modern business cycle theory', in M. Colonna and H. Hagemann (eds) *Money and Business Cycles; The Economics of F.A. Hayek*, Vol. I, Aldershot, UK and Brookfield, US: Edward Elgar, pp. 203–17.
Aréna, Richard A. (2002), 'Monetary policy and business cycles: Hayek as an opponent of the quantity theory tradition', in Jack Birner, Pierre Garrouste and Thierry Aimar (eds), *F.A. Hayek as a Political Economist*, London: Routledge, pp. 64–78.
Backhouse, Roger E. (1985), *A History of Modern Economic Analysis*, Oxford: Blackwell.
Backhouse, Roger E. (2002a), *The Penguin History of Economics*, London: Penguin.
Backhouse, Roger E. (2002b), 'Don Patinkin: interpreter of the Keynesian revolution', *European Journal of the History of Economic Thought*, 9 (2), 186–204.
Bellante, Don (1994), 'The Phillips curve', in Peter J. Boettke (ed.), *The Elgar Companion to Austrian Economics*, Aldershot, UK and Brookfield, VT, USA: Edward Elgar, pp. 372–7.
Bellante, Don and Roger W. Garrison (1988), 'Phillips curves and Hayekian triangles: two perspectives on monetary dynamics', *History of Political Economy*, 20 (2), 207–34.
Benassi, Corrado (1987), 'An input–output formulation of the "coefficient of money transactions": a note on Hayek's trade cycle theory', *Economica Internazionale*, 40 (1), 1–19, reprinted in John C. Wood and Ronald N. Woods (eds) (1991), *Friedrich A. Hayek. Critical Assessments*, vol. 4, London: Routledge, pp. 263–79.
Blaug, Mark (1985), *Economic Theory in Retrospect*, 4th edn, Cambridge: Cambridge University Press.
Blaug, Mark (1992), 'Commentary', in Bruce Caldwell and Stephan Böhm (eds), *Austrian Economics: Tensions and New Directions*, Boston, MA: Kluwer, pp. 31–4.
Blundell, J. (2005) Hayek, Fisher and the Road to Serfdom. London: Institute of Economic Affairs.
Boettke, Peter J. (1989), 'Evolution and economics: Austrians as institutionalists', *Review of the History of Economic Thought and Methodology*, 6, 73–89.
Böhm, Stephan (1992), 'Austrian economics between the wars: some historiographical problems', in Bruce J. Caldwell and Stephan Böhm (eds), *Austrian Economics: Tensions and New Directions*, Norwell, MA: Kluwer, pp. 1–30.
Boland, Lawrence A. (1978), 'Time in economics vs. economics in time: the "Hayek problem"', *Canadian Journal of Economics*, 11 (2), 240–62.
Butos, William N. (1985), 'Hayek and general equilibrium analysis', *Southern Economic Journal*, 52 (2), 332–43.
Butos, William N. (1994), 'The Hayek–Keynes macro debate', in Peter J. Boettke (ed.), *Edward Elgar Companion to Austrian Economics*, Aldershot, UK and Brookfield, VT, USA, pp. 471–7.
Caldwell, Bruce J. (1988), 'Hayek's transformation', *History of Political Economy*, 20 (4), 513–41.
Caldwell, Bruce J. (1989), 'Austrians and institutionalists: the historical origins of their shared characteristics', *Review of the History of Economic Thought and Methodology*, 6, 91–100.
Caldwell, Bruce J. (1994), 'Four theses on Hayek', in M. Colonna, H. Hagemann and O. Hamouda (eds), *Capitalism, Socialism, and Knowledge; The Economics of F.A. Hayek*, vol. II, Aldershot, UK and Brookfield, VT, USA: Edward Elgar, pp. 117–30.
Caldwell, Bruce J. (ed.) (1995), *Contra Keynes and Cambridge. The Collected Works of F.A. Hayek*, vol. 9, London, UK: Routledge and Chicago, IL, USA: University of Chicago Press.
Caldwell, Bruce J. (2004), *Hayek's Challenge. An Intellectual Biography of F.A. Hayek*, Chicago, IL: University of Chicago Press.
Cochran, John and Fred Glahe (1999), *The Hayek–Keynes Debate – Lessons for Current Business Cycle Research*, Lampeter: Edwin Mellen.
Cockett, Richard (1995), *Thinking the Unthinkable: Think-Tanks and the Economic Counter-revolution 1931–1983*, London: Harper Collins.

Collard, David (1981), 'A.C. Pigou, 1877–1959', in Denis P. O'Brien and John R. Presley (eds), *Pioneers of Modern Economics in Britain*, London: Macmillan, pp. 105–39.
Colonna, Marina (1994), 'Hayek's trade cycle theory and its contemporary critics', in M. Colonna and H. Hagemann (eds), *Money and Business Cycles; The Economics of F.A. Hayek*, vol. 1, Aldershot, UK and Brookfield, VT, USA: Edward Elgar, pp. 27–52.
Demsetz, Harold (1988), *Ownership, Control, and the Firm*, Oxford: Blackwell.
Demsetz, Harold (1989), *Efficiency, Competition and Policy*, Oxford: Blackwell.
Demsetz, Harold (1995), *The Economics of the Business Firm*, Cambridge: Cambridge University Press.
Desai, Meghnad and Paul Redfern (1994), 'Trade cycle as a frustrated traverse: an analytical reconstruction of Hayek's model', in M. Colonna and H. Hagemann (eds), *Money and Business Cycles; The Economics of F.A. Hayek*, vol. 1, Aldershot, UK and Brookfield, VT, USA: Edward Elgar, pp. 121–43.
Deutscher, Patrick (1990), *R.G. Hawtrey and the Development of Macroeconomics*, London: Macmillan.
de Vivo, Giancarlo (1994), 'Comment', in M. Colonna and H. Hagemann (eds), *Money and Business Cycles; The Economics of F.A. Hayek*, vol. 1, Aldershot, UK and Brookfield, VT, USA: Edward Elgar, pp. 94–7.
DiLorenzo, Thomas J. (1994), 'Industrial organization and the Austrian school', in Boettke, Peter J. (ed.), *The Elgar Companion to Austrian Economics*, Aldershot, UK and Brookfield, VT, USA: Edward Elgar, pp. 382–8.
Director, Aaron (1945), 'Review of F.A. Hayek, *The Road to Serfdom*', *American Economic Review*, 35 (2), 173–5.
Dolan, Edwin. G. (ed.) (1976), *The Foundations of Modern Austrian Economics*, Kansas City, MO: Sheed & Ward.
Dostaler, Gilles (1994), 'The formation and evolution of Hayek's trade cycle theory', in M. Colonna and H. Hagemann (eds), *Money and Business Cycles; The Economics of F.A. Hayek*, vol. 1, Aldershot, UK and Brookfield, VT, USA: Edward Elgar, pp. 147–67.
Dowd, Kevin (1994), 'Free banking', in Peter J. Boettke (ed.) *The Elgar Companion to Austrian Economics*, Aldershot, UK and Brookfield, VT, USA: Edward Elgar, pp. 408–13.
Dowd, Kevin (1995), 'Deflating the productivity norm', *Journal of Macroeconomics*, 17 (4), 717–32.
Durbin, E.F.M. (1945), 'Professor Hayek on economic planning and political liberty', *Economic Journal*, 55 (220), 357–70.
Edwards, J.R. (1980), 'Monopoly and competition in money', *Journal of Libertarian Studies*, 4 (1), 107–17, reprinted in John C. Wood and Ronald N. Woods (eds) (1991), *Friedrich A. Hayek. Critical Assessments*, vol. 3, London: Routledge, pp. 145–55.
Ebenstein, Alan (2001), *Friedrich Hayek: A Biography*, Basingstoke, UK and New York, USA: Palgrave.
Ellis, Howard S. (1934), *German Monetary Theory, 1905–1933*, Cambridge, MA: Harvard University Press.
Ferguson, C.E. (1973), 'The specialization gap: Barton, Ricardo, and Hollander', *History of Political Economy*, 5 (1), 1–13.
Fischer, Stanley (1986), 'Friedman versus Hayek on private money', *Journal of Monetary Economics*, 17 (3), 433–9.
Foss, Nicolai J. (1995), 'More on Hayek's transformation', *History of Political Economy*, 27 (2), 345–64.
Friedman, Milton (1974), 'Comments on the critics', in Robert J. Gordon (ed.), *Milton Friedman's Monetary Framework. A Debate with his Critics*, Chicago, IL: University of Chicago Press, pp. 132–77.
Garrison, Roger W. (1985), 'Intertemporal coordination and the invisible hand: an Austrian perspective on the Keynesian vision', *History of Political Economy*, 17 (2), 309–21.
Garrison, Roger W. (1989), 'The Austrian theory of the business cycle in the light of modern macroeconomics', *Review of Austrian Economics*, 3, 3–29.

Garrison, Roger W. (2001), *Time and Money. The Macroeconomics of Capital Structure*, London: Routledge.
Haberler, Gottfried (1937), *Prosperity and Depression*, Geneva: League of Nations.
Haberler, Gottfried (1986), 'Reflections on Hayek's business cycle theory', *Cato Journal*, 6 (2), 421–35, reprinted in John C. Wood and Ronald N. Woods (eds) (1991), *Friedrich A. Hayek. Critical Assessments*, vol. 4, London: Routledge, pp. 249–62.
Hageman, Harold (1994), 'Hayek and the Kiel school: some reflections on the German debate on business cycles in the late 1920s and early 1930s', in M. Colonna and H. Hagemann (eds) (1994), *Capitalism, Socialism, and Knowledge; The Economics of F.A. Hayek*, vol. 1, Aldershot, UK and Brookfield, VT, USA: Edward Elgar pp. 101–20.
Hamouda, Omar F. and Robin Rowley (1994), 'Rational processes: markets, knowledge and uncertainty', in M. Colonna, H. Hagemann and O. Hamouda (eds) (1994), *Capitalism, Socialism, and Knowledge; The Economics of F.A. Hayek*, vol. 2, Aldershot, UK and Brookfield, VT, USA: Edward Elgar, pp. 178–94.
Hansen, Alvin H. and Herbert Tout (1933), 'Investment and saving in business cycle theory', *Econometrica*, 1 (2), 119–47.
Hausman, Daniel M. (2003), 'Taking causal questions seriously', *Journal of Economic Methodology*, 10, 259–69.
Hawtrey, Ralph G. (1932), 'Review of F.A. Hayek's *Prices and Production*', *Economica*, 12, 119–25.
Hawtrey, Ralph G. (1933), 'Review of F.A. Hayek's *Monetary Theory and the Trade Cycle*', *Economic Journal*, 43, 669–72.
Hawtrey, Ralph G. (1938), *A Century of Bank Rate*, reprinted (1962), London: Frank Cass.
Hawtrey, Ralph G. (1940), 'The trade cycle and capital intensity', *Economica*, n.s. 7, 1–15.
Hawtrey, Ralph G. (1941), 'Professor Hayek's pure theory of capital', *Economic Journal*, 51 (201–203), 281–90.
Hayek, Friedrich A. (1928), 'Intertemporal price equilibrium and movements in the value of money', translated and reprinted in Roy McCloughry (ed.) (1984), *Money, Capital and Fluctuations. Early Essays*, London: Routledge & Kegan Paul.
Hayek, Friedrich A. ([1929] 1933), *Monetary Theory and the Trade Cycle*, transl. Nicholas Kaldor and H. Croome, London: Cape.
Hayek, Friedrich A. (1931a), *Prices and Production*, 2nd edn, London: Routledge & Kegan Paul, 1935.
Hayek, Friedrich A. (1931b), 'Reflections on the pure theory of money of Mr. J.M. Keynes (I)', *Economica*, 11 (33), 270–95, reprinted in John C. Wood and Ronald N. Woods (eds) (1991), *Friedrich A. Hayek. Critical Assessments*, vol. 1, London: Routledge, pp. 1–23.
Hayek, Friedrich A. (1931c), 'A rejoinder to Mr. Keynes', *Economica*, 11 (34), 398–403, reprinted in John C. Wood and Ronald N. Woods (eds) (1991), *Friedrich A. Hayek. Critical Assessments*, vol. 1, London: Routledge, pp. 60–64.
Hayek, Friedrich A. (1932a), 'Reflections on the pure theory of money of Mr. J.M. Keynes (continued) (II)', *Economica*, 12 (35), 22–44, reprinted in John C. Wood and Ronald N. Woods (eds) (1991), *Friedrich A. Hayek. Critical Assessments*, vol. 1, London: Routledge, pp. 65–85.
Hayek, Friedrich A. (1932b), 'Money and capital: a reply', *Economic Journal*, 42 (June), 237–49, reprinted in John C. Wood and Ronald N. Woods (eds) (1991), *Friedrich A. Hayek. Critical Assessments*, vol. 1, London: Routledge, pp. 102–12.
Hayek, Friedrich A. (1932c), 'The fate of the gold standard', translated in Roy McCloughry (ed.) (1984), *Money, Capital and Fluctuations. Early Essays by F.A. Hayek*, London: Routledge & Kegan Paul, pp. 118–35.
Hayek, Friedrich A. (1934), 'Capital and industrial fluctuations', *Econometrica*, 2 (April), 152–67, reprinted in John C. Wood and Ronald N. Woods (eds) (1991), *Friedrich A. Hayek. Critical Assessments*, vol. 1, London: Routledge, pp. 148–63.
Hayek, Friedrich A. (1936), 'The mythology of capital', *Quarterly Journal of Economics*, 50 (2), 199–228.

Hayek, Friedrich A. (1937), 'Economics and knowledge', *Economica*, n.s. 4 (Feb.), 33–54.
Hayek, Friedrich A. (1938), 'Discussion on the trade cycle', *Journal of the Royal Statistical Society*, 101, Part III, 578–80.
Hayek, Friedrich A. (1939), *Profits, Interest and Investment*, London: Routledge.
Hayek, Friedrich A. (1941a), *The Pure Theory of Capital*, London: Routledge.
Hayek, Friedrich A. (1941b), 'The counter-revolution of science', *Economica*, n.s. 8, Part I, 9–36, Part II, 119–50. Part III, 281–320.
Hayek, Friedrich A. (1942), 'A comment', *Economica*, n.s. 9, 383–5.
Hayek, Friedrich A. (1942–44), 'Scientism and the study of society', Part I, *Economica*, n.s. 9, 267–91; Part II *Economica* n.s. 10, 34–63; Part III *Economica*, n.s. 11, 27–39.
Hayek, F.A. (1844), *The Road to Serfdom*, Chicago, IL: University of Chicago Press.
Hayek, Friedrich A. (1949), *Individualism and Economic Order*, London: Routledge.
Hayek, Friedrich A. (1960), *The Constitution of Liberty*, London: Routledge & Kegan Paul.
Hayek, Friedrich A. (1967), *Studies in Philosophy, Politics, and Economics*, London: Routledge.
Hayek, Friedrich A. (1972), *A Tiger by the Tail*, ed. Sudha R. Shenoy, London: Institute of Economic Affairs.
Hayek, Friedrich A. (1973–79), *Law, Legislation and Liberty*, London: Routledge & Kegan Paul.
Hayek, Friedrich A. (1976), *Denationalisation of Money*, 2nd edn (1978), London: Institute of Economic Affairs.
Hayek, Friedrich A. (1978), *New Studies in Philosophy, Politics, Economics and the History of Ideas*, London: Routledge.
Hayek, Friedrich A. (1992), *The Fortunes of Liberalism*, The Collected Works of F.A. Hayek, vol. 4, Peter Klein (ed.), London: Routledge.
Hayek, Friedrich A. (1994), *Hayek on Hayek*, Stephen Kresge and Leif Wenar (eds), London: Routledge.
Hicks, John R. (1940), 'Mr. Hawtrey on Bank Rate and the long term rate of interest', *Manchester School*, 10, 21–37.
Hicks, John R. (1965), *Capital and Growth*, Oxford: Clarendon.
Hicks, John R. (1967), 'The Hayek story', *Critical Essays on Monetary Theory*, Oxford: Clarendon, pp. 203–15.
Hicks, John R. (1977), *Economic Perspectives*, Oxford: Clarendon.
Hicks, John R. and Wilhelm Weber (eds) (1973), *Carl Menger and the Austrian School of Economics*, Oxford: Clarendon.
Hoover, Kevin D. (1988), *The New Classical Macroeconomics. A Sceptical Enquiry*, Oxford: Blackwell.
Hoover, Kevin D. (1994), 'The new classical economics', in Peter J. Boettke (ed.) *The Elgar Companion to Austrian Economics*, Aldershot, UK and Brookfield, VT, USA: Edward Elgar, pp. 576–81.
Horwitz, Steven G. (1996), 'Capital theory, inflation and deflation: the Austrian and monetary disequilibrium theory compared', *Journal of the History of Economic Thought*, 18, 287–308.
Horwitz, Steven G. (2000), *Microfoundations and Macroeconomics*, London: Routledge.
Howard, David H. (1977), 'Review of F.A. Hayek's *Denationalisation of Money*', *Journal of Monetary Economics*, 3 (4), 483–5.
Hummel, Jeffrey R. (1979), 'Problems with the Austrian business cycle theory', *Reason Papers*, no. 5, 41–53, reprinted in John C. Wood and Ronald N. Woods (eds) (1991), *Friedrich A. Hayek. Critical Assessments*, London: Routledge, pp. 124–36.
Humphrey, Thomas M. (1984), 'On nonneutral relative price effects in monetarist thought: some Austrian misconceptions', reprinted in T.M. Humphrey (1993), *Money, Banking and Inflation*, Aldershot, UK and Brookfield, VT, USA: Edward Elgar, pp. 280–86.
Humphrey, Thomas M. (1992), 'Price-level stabilization rules in a Wicksellian model of the cumulative process', *Scandinavian Journal of Economics*, 94 (30), 509–18.
Hutchison, Terence W. (1978), *On Revolutions and Progress in Economic Knowledge*, Cambridge: Cambridge University Press.

Hutchison, Terence W. (1981), *The Politics and Philosophy of Economics*, Oxford: Blackwell.
Hutchison, Terence W. (1992), *Changing Aims in Economics*, Oxford: Blackwell.
Hutchison, Terence W. (1994), *The Uses and Abuses of Economics*, London: Routledge.
Jaffé, William (1976), 'Menger, Jevons and Walras de-homogenized', *Economic Inquiry*, 14 (4), 511–24.
Kaldor, Nicholas (1939), 'Capital intensity and the trade cycle', *Economica*, n.s. 6 (21), 40–66.
Kaldor, Nicholas (1942), 'Professor Hayek and the concertina-effect', *Economica*, n.s. 9 (36), 359–82.
Keynes, John Maynard (1930), *A Treatise on Money*, vol. I *The Pure Theory of Money*, vol. II *The Applied Theory of Money* reprinted (1971) as vols V and VI of *The Collected Writings of John Maynard Keynes*, London: Macmillan for the Royal Economic Society.
Keynes, John Maynard (1931), 'The pure theory of money. A reply to Dr. Hayek', *Economica*, 2, 387–97, reprinted in John C. Wood and Ronald N. Woods (eds) (1991), *Friedrich A. Hayek. Critical Assessments*, vol. 1, London: Routledge, pp. 50–59.
Keynes, John Maynard (1936), *The General Theory of Employment, Interest and Money* reprinted as vol. VII of *The Collected Writings of John Maynard Keynes*, London: Macmillan for the Royal Economic Society.
King, Robert G. (1983), 'On the economics of private money', *Journal of Monetary Economics*, 12 (1), 127–58.
Kirzner, Israel M. (1997), 'Entrepreneurial discovery and the competitive market process: an Austrian approach', *Journal of Economic Literature*, 35 (1), 60–85.
Klein, Benjamin (1975), 'The competitive supply of money', *Journal of Money, Credit and Banking*, 6 (4), 423–54.
Knight, Frank H. (1967), 'Laissez faire: pro and con', *Journal of Political Economy*, 75 (Dec.), 782–95.
Lachmann, Ludwig M. (1940), 'A reconsideration of the Austrian theory of industrial fluctuations', *Economica*, n.s. 7 (26), 179–96.
Lachmann, Ludwig M. (1956), *Capital and Its Structure*, reprinted (1978), Kansas City, KS: Sheed Andrews & McMeel, 1978.
Lachmann, Ludwig M. (1978), 'The Austrian stocktaking: unsettled questions and tentative answers', in Spadaro, Louis M. (ed.), *New Directions in Austrian Economics*, Kansas City, KS: Sheed Andrews & McMeel, pp. 1–18.
Lachmann, Ludwig M. (1986), 'Austrian economics under fire: the Hayek–Sraffra duel in retrospect', in Wolfgang Grassl and Barry Smith (eds), *Austrian Economics: Historical and Philosophical Background*, New York: New York University Press, pp. 225–42.
Laidler, David (1999), *Fabricating the Keynesian Revolution*, Cambridge: Cambridge University Press.
Langlois, Richard N. (1985), 'Knowledge and rationality in the Austrian school: an analytical survey', *Eastern Economic Journal*, 9 (4), 309–30, reprinted in John C. Wood and Ronald N. Woods (eds) (1991), *Friedrich A. Hayek. Critical Assessments*, vol. 4, London: Routledge, pp. 118–40.
Lavoie, Donald C. (1986), 'The market as a procedure for discovery and conveyance of inarticulate knowledge', *Comparative Economic Studies* 28 (1), 1–19, in John C. Wood and Ronald N. Woods (eds) (1991), *Friedrich A. Hayek. Critical Assessments*, vol. 4, London: Routledge, pp. 213–33.
Leijohnhufvud, Axel (1968), *On Keynesian Economics and the Economics of Keynes*, Oxford: Oxford University Press.
Leijohnhufvud, Axel (1969), *Keynes and the Classics*. London: Institute of Economic Affairs.
Leijohnhufvud, Axel (1981), *Information and Coordination*, Oxford: Oxford University Press.
Levy, David M. (1985), 'The impossibility of a complete methodological individualist reduction when knowledge is imperfect', *Economics and Philosophy*, 1 (1), 101–8.
Lucas, Robert E. (1975), 'An equilibrium model of the business cycle', *Journal of Political Economy*, 83 (6), 1113–44.
Lucas, Robert E. (1977), 'Understanding business cycles', in Karl Brunner and Allan

H. Meltzer (eds), *Stability of the Domestic and International Economy*, Amsterdam: North Holland, pp. 7–30.

Lutz, Friedrich A. (1943), 'Professor Hayek's theory of interest', *Economica*, n.s. 10 (Nov.), 302–10.

McCloughry, Roy (ed.) (1984), *Money, Capital and Fluctuations. Early Essays by F.A. Hayek*, London: Routledge & Kegan Paul.

Machlup, Fritz (1974), 'Friedrich von Hayek's contribution to economics', *Swedish Journal of Economics*, 76 (4), 498–531, reprinted in John C. Wood and Ronald N. Woods (eds) (1991), *Friedrich A. Hayek. Critical Assessments*, vol. 2, London: Routledge, pp. 193–229.

Machlup, Fritz (ed.) (1976), *Essays on Hayek*, New York: New York University Press.

Maling, Charles E. (1975), '*The Austrian business cycle theory and its implications for economic stability under laissez faire*', *Reason Papers*, no. 2, 65–90, reprinted in John C. Wood and Ronald N. Woods (eds) (1991), *Friedrich A. Hayek. Critical Assessments*, vol. 2, London: Routledge, pp. 248–68.

Marget, Arthur W. (1932), Review of F.A. Hayek *Prices and Production*, *Journal of Political Economy*, 40 (2), 261–6.

Menger, Carl (1883), *Untersuchungen über die Methoden der Socialwissenschaften und der Politischen Oekonomie insbesondere*, trans. F.J. Nock, reprinted as Louis Schneider (ed.) (1963), *Problems of Economics and Sociology*, Urbana, IL: University of Illinois Press.

Milgate, Murray (1979), 'On the origin of the notion of intertemporal equilibrium', *Economica*, n.s. 46 (181), 1–10.

Mises, Ludwig von ([1924] 1934) *The Theory of Money and Credit*, 2nd edn (1924), transl. H.E. Batson (1934), London: Cape.

Mises, Ludwig von ([1932] 1936) *Gemeinwirtschaft*, transl. as *Socialism* by J. Kahane (1936), London: Cape.

Mises, Ludwig von (1949) *Human Action*, 3rd edn (1966), Chicago, IL: Regnery.

Moss, Laurence S. (ed.) (1976), *The Economics of Ludwig von Mises*, Kansas City, KS: Sheed & Ward.

O'Brien, Denis P. (1984), 'The evolution of the theory of the firm', reprinted in D.P. O'Brien (1994), *Methodology, Money and the Firm*, Aldershot, UK and Brookfield, VT, USA: Edward Elgar, vol. 1, pp. 247–76.

O'Brien, Denis P. (1988), *Lionel Robbins*, London: Macmillan.

O'Brien, Denis P. (1994a), 'Friedrich August von Hayek', *Proceedings of the British Academy*, 84, pp. 347–66.

O'Brien, Denis P. (1994b), 'Hayek as an intellectual historian', in Jack Birner and Rudy van Zijp (eds), *Hayek, Co-ordination and Evolution*, London: Routledge, pp. 343–74.

O'Brien, Denis P. (1998a), 'Four Detours', *The Journal of Economic Methodology*, 5 (1), 23–41.

O'Brien, Denis P. (1998b), 'Information and investment in a wider context', in Nicholai J. Foss and Brian J. Loasby (eds), *Economic Organisation, Capabilities and Co-ordination*, London: Routledge, pp. 104–20.

O'Brien, Denis P. (1998c), 'Hayek, Friedrich August von', in Peter Newman (ed.), *The Palgrave Dictionary of Economics and the Law*, vol. 2, London: Macmillan, pp. 217–28.

O'Driscoll, Gerald P., Jr (1975), 'The Specialization gap and the Ricardo effect: comment on Ferguson', *History of Political Economy*, 7 (2), 261–9.

O'Driscoll, Gerald P., Jr (1977), *Economics as a Coordination Problem. The Contributions of Friedrich A. Hayek*, Kansas City, KS: Sheed, Andrews & McMeel.

O'Driscoll, Gerald P., Jr and Mario J. Rizzo (1985), *The Economics of Time and Ignorance*, Oxford: Blackwell.

Palermo, Sandye (1999), *The Evolution of Austrian Economics*, London: Routledge.

Patinkin, Don (1976), 'Keynes' monetary thought: a study of its development', *History of Political Economy*, 8 (1), 1–150.

Pigou, Arthur C. (1944), 'Review of F.A. Hayek, *The Road to Serfdom*', *Economic Journal*, 54 (214), 217–19.

Presley, John R. (1978), *Robertsonian Economics*, London: Macmillan.
Rizzo, Mario J. (1992), 'Afterword: Austrian economics for the twenty-first century', in Bruce J. Caldwell and Stephan Böhm (eds), *Austrian Economics: Tensions and New Directions*, Boston, MA: Kluwer, pp. 245–55.
Robbins, Lionel (1930), 'The economic works of Philip Wicksteed', *Economica*, 10, 245–58.
Robbins, Lionel (1933), 'Introduction', in Philip H. Wicksteed (1910), *The Commonsense of Political Economy*, London: Routledge.
Robbins, Lionel (1934a), *The Great Depression*, London: Macmillan.
Robbins, Lionel (1934b), 'Introduction', in Knut Wicksell, *Lectures in Political Economy*, trans. E. Classen, London: Routledge.
Robbins, Lionel (1961), 'Hayek on liberty', *Economica*, n.s. 28 (109), 66–81.
Robertson, Dennis H. (1931), 'Mr. Keynes' theory of money', *Economic Journal*, 41 (163), 395–411.
Robertson, Dennis H. (1940), *Essays in Monetary Theory*, reprinted (1956), London: Staples.
Robinson, Joan V. (1972), 'The second crisis of economic theory', *American Economic Review*, 62 (2), 1–10.
Roll, Eric (1945), 'Review of F.A. Hayek *The Road to Serfdom*', *American Economic Review*, 35 (2), 176–80.
Rosner, Peter and Georg Winckler (1989), 'Aspects of Austrian economics in the 1920s and 1930s', *Research in the History of Economic Thought and Methodology*, 6, 19–30.
Rothbard, Murray N. (1995), *Classical Economics*, Aldershot, UK and Brookfield, VT, USA: Edward Elgar.
Royal Academy of Sciences (1974), 'The Nobel Memorial Prize in Economics 1974', *Swedish Journal of Economics*, 76, 46–71.
Rühl, Christof (1994), 'The transformation of business cycle theory: Hayek, Lucas and a change in the notion of equilibrium', in M. Colonna and H. Hagemann (eds), *Money and Business Cycles; The Economics of F.A. Hayek*, vol. 1, Aldershot, UK and Brookfield, VT, USA: Edward Elgar, pp. 168–202.
Rutherford, Malcolm (1989), 'Some issues in the comparison of Austrian and institutional economics', *Research in the History of Economic Thought and Methodology*, 6, 159–72.
Rutherford, Malcolm (1994), 'Austrian economics and American (old) institutionalisation', in Peter Boettke (ed.) *The Elgar Companion to Austrian Economics*, Aldershot, UK and Brookfield, VT, USA: Edward Elgar, pp. 529–34.
Samuels, Warren J. (1989), 'Austrian and institutional economics: some common elements', *Research in the History of Economic Thought and Methodology*, 6, 53–71.
Schmidt, Christian (2002), 'Hayek, Morgenstern and game theory', in Jack P. Birner, Pierre Garrouste and Thierry Aimar (eds), *F.A. Hayek as a Political Economist*, London: Routledge, pp. 53–63.
Schumpeter, Joseph A. (1946), 'Review of F.A. Hayek *The Road to Serfdom*', *Journal of Political Economy*, 54 (3), 269–70.
Schumpeter, Joseph A. (1954), *History of Economic Analysis*, London: Allen & Unwin.
Seccareccia, Mario (1994), 'Credit money and cyclical crises: the views of Hayek and Fisher compared', in M. Colonna and H. Hagemann (eds), *Money and Business Cycles; The Economics of F.A. Hayek*, vol. 1, Aldershot, UK and Brookfield, VT, USA: Edward Elgar, pp. 53–73.
Selgin, George A. (1995a), 'The "productivity norm" versus zero inflation in the history of economic thought', *History of Political Economy*, 27 (4), 705–35.
Selgin, George A. (1995b), 'The case for a "productivity norm": comment on Dowd', *Journal of Macroeconomics*, 17 (4), 733–40.
Shackle, G.L.S. (1967), *The Years of High Theory*, Cambridge: Cambridge University press.
Shackle, G.L.S. (1972), *Epistemics and Economics*, Cambridge: Cambridge University Press.
Shackle, G.L.S. (1981), 'F.A. Hayek, 1899–', in Denis P. O'Brien and John R. Presley (eds), *Pioneers of Modern Economics in Britain*, London: Macmillan, pp. 234–61.
Skidelsky, Robert (1992), *John Maynard Keynes. Vol.2. The Economist as Saviour 1920–37*, London: Macmillan.

Smith, Vernon L. (1982), 'Markets as economizers of information: experimental examination of the "Hayek Hypothesis"', *Economic Inquiry*, 20 (2), 165–79.
Smithies, Arthur (1941), 'Professor Hayek on *The Pure Theory of Capital*', *American Economic Review*, 31 (4), 767–79.
Snowdon, Brian and Howard R. Vane (1998), 'Transforming macroeconomics: an interview with Robert E. Lucas Jr.', *Journal of Economic Methodology*, 5, 115–46.
Spadaro, Louis M. (ed.) (1978), *New Directions in Austrian Economics*, Kansas City, KS: Sheed Andrews & McMeel.
Spencer, Roger W. (1975), 'Inflation, unemployment, and Hayek', *Federal Reserve Bank of St Louis – Review*, reprinted in John C. Woods and Ronald N. Woods (eds) (1991), *Friedrich A. Hayek. Critical Assessments*, vol. 2, London: Routledge, pp. 230–38.
Spengler, Joseph J. (1945), 'Review of F.A. Hayek, *The Road to Serfdom*', *Southern Economic Journal*, 12 (1), 48–55.
Sraffa, Piero (1932a), 'Dr. Hayek on money and capital', *Economic Journal*, 42 (165), 42–53, reprinted in John C. Wood and Ronald N. Woods (eds.) (1991), vol. 1, pp. 86–96.
Sraffa, Piero (1932b), 'A rejoinder', *Economic Journal*, 42 (166), 249–51, reprinted in John C. Wood and Ronald N. Woods (eds) (1991), *Friedrich A. Hayek. Critical Assessments*, vol. 1, London: Routledge, pp. 113–15.
Steedman, Ian (1994), 'On *The Pure Theory of Capital* by F.A. Hayek', in M. Colonna, H. Hagemann and O. Hamouda (eds), *Capitalism, Socialism, and Knowledge; The Economics of F.A. Hayek*, vol. 2, Aldershot, UK and Brookfield, VT, USA: Edward Elgar, pp. 3–25.
Steele, Gerald R. (1993), *The Economics of Friedrich Hayek*, London: Macmillan.
Streissler, Erich W. (1994), 'Hayek on information and socialism', in M. Colonna, H. Hagemann and O. Hamouda (eds), *Capitalism, Socialism, and Knowledge; The Economics of F.A. Hayek*, vol. 2, Aldershot, UK and Brookfield, VT, USA: Edward Elgar, pp. 47–75.
Summers, Lawrence H. (1983), 'Comment', *Journal of Monetary Economics*, 12 (1), 159–62.
Tsiang, Sho-Chieh (1947), *The Variations of Real Wages and Profit Margins in Relation to the Trade Cycle*, London: Pitman.
Tsiang, S.C. (1949), 'Rehabilitation of time dimension of investment in macrodynamic analysis', *Economica*, n.s. 16 (63), 204–17.
Uhr, Carl G. (1960), *Economic Doctrines of Knut Wicksell*, Berkeley, CA: University of California Press.
Uhr, Carl G. (1975), *Economic Doctrines of David Davidson*, Uppsala: Almqvist & Wiksell.
Vaughn, Karen I. (1980), 'Economic calculations under socialism: the Austrian contribution', *Economic Inquiry*, 18 (4), 535–54.
Viner, Jacob (1961), 'Hayek on freedom and coercion', *Southern Economic Journal*, 27 (4), 230–36.
Wilson, Tom (1939–40), 'Capital theory and the trade cycle', *Review of Economic Studies*, 7 (3), 169–79.
Zamagni, Stefano (1984), 'Ricardo and Hayek effects in a fixwage model of traverse', *Oxford Economic Papers*, 36 (suppt), 135–51.
Zamagni, Stefano (1987), 'Ricardo–Hayek effect', in John Eatwell, Murray Milgate and Peter Newman (eds), *The New Palgrave Dictionary of Economics*, vol. 4, London: Macmillan, pp. 198–9.

3. Hayek and economic theory in the 1930s
Martin Ricketts

THE YEARS OF HIGH THEORY

It was Shackle (1967) who coined the term 'the years of high theory' to describe the period between 1926 and 1939. These were years of upheaval in economic ideas accompanying momentous economic events. The First World War seemed to have swept away an entire self-regulating economic as well as social order. By comparison with the relative stability of the Victorian and Edwardian world and its accompanying economic theory (associated in England with Alfred Marshall, and on the Continent with economists such as Carl Menger and Leon Walras) the new world was harsh and seemingly highly unstable. A price system, until 1914 widely perceived as acting like a barely noticed thermostat successfully adjusting a heating system to take account of changing weather conditions, began instead to plunge people into bouts of stifling heat and icy cold. By the late 1920s large-scale resource unemployment and the study of the business cycle were at the centre of economic attention. Dynamics rather than equilibrium statics became the focus of theoretical effort.

Hayek played a leading part in the theoretical debates of this era although the period ended with his efforts mainly rejected, and Shackle does not think it necessary to discuss his contribution. Hicks (1967) reflects that Hayek was 'a leading character in the drama' of the 1930s though his economic writings were not widely studied after the Second World War. 'It is hardly remembered that there was a time when the new theories of Hayek were the principal rival of the new theories of Keynes' (p. 203). In this chapter an attempt is made to set out the basic features of Hayek's economics up to 1945 and to discuss why he failed in his aim of 'bridging the gulf between "statics" and "dynamics"' (Hayek, [1935a] 1939, p. 137).

'AUSTRIAN' CAPITAL THEORY AND THE STRUCTURE OF PRODUCTION

Hayek was director of the Austrian Institute for Trade Cycle Research (1927–31). His thinking on industrial fluctuations was heavily influenced by Ludwig von Mises (who played a major role in establishing the Institute) and the Austrian tradition of capital theory going back to Böhm-Bawerk. Much of Hayek's effort in the 1930s was taken up with an attempt to show that the disruptive crises to which the market system was from time to time subject could be traced to the influence of monetary disturbances upon entrepreneurs' decisions about capital structure. During 1930–31 Hayek delivered a series of lectures at the University of London setting out his provisional ideas and these were published as *Prices and Production* (1931).

Lecture 2 of *Prices and Production* sets out the basic conceptual apparatus of Austrian capital theory. Essentially, Hayek envisages a world in which final consumers' goods are produced in a series of stages. The 'original means of production' (labour and natural resources) are applied over time and produce a sequence of 'intermediate goods' of rising value. Eventually the goods are complete and are available for consumption. In this early formulation Hayek imagines that each stage of production requires a constant application of the original means of production and that each stage is of the same length of time. The system can be thought of as a version of Adam Smith's treatment of division of labour by which production is broken into specialized activities undertaken one after the other. If each activity takes the same length of time and each involves the same additional application of labour and materials, the result is a particular example of Hayek's 'structure of production'. Because resources are assumed to be applied at a constant rate over time, attention is focused on the only other structural feature – the number of stages into which production is divided or the 'length' or 'roundaboutness' of the production process.

Hayek used triangular diagrams originally devised by Stanley Jevons and Knut Wicksell to illustrate the value added over time to intermediate products by the process of investment and the relationship of consumption to the stock of intermediate products (circulating capital). He preferred to deal in discrete periods and arithmetic examples although the elementary results are probably easier to illustrate using continuous time. If payments to 'original means of production' in the manufacture of consumers' goods deliverable after a process of length t^* are made at a constant rate θ, the value V of intermediate goods at any specified point in the process of production t will simply be given by $V(t) = \theta t$. For the given 'length' (t^*) of the production process and the given rate of gross investment θ, the value of final consumers' goods produced will be θt^*. If this output of consumption goods is to be maintained at a continuous rate over time, total payments to the original means of production will have to occur at a rate θt^* (that is, there must exist at all stages $0 \leq t \leq t^*$ of the production process a stock of intermediate goods valued at θt and accumulating at the rate θ). The value of the total stock of intermediate goods (and hence the stock of circulating capital) in such an 'evenly rotating economy' will then be given by $_0\int^{t^*}\theta t dt = 0.5\theta t^{*2}$. Notice that there is no net saving or investment in this economy. The flow of payments to the means of production (θt^*) is just enough to pay for the flow of consumers' goods, and the capital stock remains constant over time. Value added per period equals consumption per period.

Setting $\theta = 1$ for convenience, it is easy to see that a longer absolute length of the production process will increase the capital intensity of production. With $t^* = 4$, the rate of output of consumption goods per unit time is 4 while the capital stock is 8. The capital output ratio is thus $8/4 = 2$. With $t^* = 6$ and $\theta = 1$ the capital stock will be 18 and the capital output ratio will have risen from 2 to $18/6 = 3$. Indeed the ratio of capital to output is simply $0.5t^*$, a concept known to Austrian capital theory as 'the average period of production'. Clearly the entire capital stock is not invested for the full period t^*. Because investment is undertaken at a constant rate, some capital is tied up for almost the entire period of production while some will be invested at a late stage in the process. The average period for which a unit of capital is invested is $0.5t^*$.

Objections to this conceptual apparatus are not difficult to formulate and a vigorous discussion of Austrian capital theory took place in the 1930s.[1] Would an increase in the number of stages of production necessarily imply a longer overall duration of the production process? Perhaps different stages could last for different lengths of calendar time? Roundaboutness in terms of 'number of stages' and roundaboutness in terms of elapsed time might be quite different. Would the production of some goods require a greater application of the 'original means of production' at some stages than at others? Other questions also suggest themselves. As presented by Hayek in lecture 2 of *Prices and Production* all capital is 'circulating capital', the accumulation of 'work in progress'. How might the theory be adapted to cope with the existence of durable items of capital equipment? Would technical advance and the use of specialized machinery necessarily 'lengthen' the production process as Böhm-Bawerk supposed? These and other issues were at the heart of controversies over capital theory in the 1930s. Such was the central importance of capital theory to Hayek's thinking on business cycles that his work on *The Pure Theory of Capital* (1941) was to be a major intellectual commitment during the late 1930s. It was a commitment that apparently left him intellectually exhausted,[2] and the resulting theoretical structure is discussed in detail elsewhere in this volume.

INDUSTRIAL FLUCTUATIONS

For the purposes of this chapter, however, Hayek's commitment to the Austrian theory of capital is important because he regarded it as an integral part of his explanation of business fluctuations. A change from one capital structure to another required such intricate adjustments to prices and resource flows that it was here that Hayek looked for potential coordination failures. A rise of t^* from 4 to 6, as we have seen, increases the proportion of capital to output from 2 to 3. Such a process is likely to be disruptive as it involves a period of reduced consumption while the capital stock is augmented and additional stages are inserted into the structure of production, followed by a return to a new steady state. Presumably this lengthening of the production process will only occur if entrepreneurs at the relevant stages find it profitable to adjust their activities in an appropriate way. The crucial signal inducing this adjustment is provided by the interest rate.

As goods move through the stages of production their value is increased not only by the application of additional labour and raw materials but also by the interest payments that are necessary to compensate for 'waiting'. Positive time preference implied that holders of assets had to be compensated for agreeing to delay consumption. The prices of all existing assets at every production stage thus had to rise by this rate of time preference if they were to be held, and the 'price margins' established when capital goods passed between stages of production would reflect this time preference rate. Hayek gave great attention to these 'price margins', seeing them as providing the signals for changes in the structure of production. If people became more 'patient' and this was reflected in a willingness to support more roundabout production processes, net saving would occur at the existing market interest rate which would then tend to fall. Existing price margins between stages of production would now be more than sufficient to compensate for waiting and the incentive to lengthen the structure of production by holding assets for longer and laying them down sooner (and thus adding to circulating capital) would be in place.[3] New savings would thus, according to Hayek, be taken up and used as part of the stock of circulating capital. Equilibrium would be restored when the rate of interest in the market had fallen and the price margins between stages had narrowed sufficiently to reflect the lower prevailing rate of time preference. The market interest rate and the resulting capital structure would then once more be fully compatible with the willingness of the population to support a greater total stock of capital.

It was therefore characteristic of Hayek's treatment of capital structure in *Prices and Production* that he did not see saving as a danger that might lead to a depression. Indeed new saving was the only reliable means to permanently greater consumption: 'Every increase in consumption, if it is not to disturb production, requires previous new saving ... If the increase of production is to be maintained continuously, it is necessary that the amounts of intermediate products in all stages is proportionately increased' (p. 95). A falling rate of interest associated with more patient consumers will be correctly interpreted by producers as a sign that more roundabout processes are now economically sustainable. For Hayek the factor that gave rise to crises and industrial fluctuations was a falling market rate of interest not associated with more patient consumers but artificially contrived by the banking system.

THE INFLUENCE OF MONEY

Money was at the root of industrial fluctuations, which is why Hayek is usually described as supporting a monetary or overinvestment theory of the trade cycle. Expansions of credit leading to falls in the market rate of interest unrelated to the real time-preference of consumers were for Hayek a recipe for disaster. Here he followed the monetary theory of Wicksell. Wicksell distinguished between the 'natural rate of interest', which reflected the real time-preference of economic agents, and the 'market rate of interest', which reflected the terms upon which loans could be had from the banking system. In static equilibrium these two rates would be the same and, indeed, individual utility-maximizing equilibrium required that economic agents adjusted their intertemporal consumption patterns through borrowing and lending so as to bring their rates of time preference into line with the market rate of interest.

The activities of the banks, however, could induce a disequilibrium situation. If the market rate of interest fell below the natural rate, bank loans and bank deposits increased as entrepreneurs undertook additional investments. This monetary expansion permitted producers to bid resources away from consumers who had no plans to reduce their demands for final goods. For so long as the market rate of interest was held below the natural rate, the money supply would increase and more investment would be undertaken than warranted by the real time-preference of the population. However, consumers would eventually find that their real levels of consumption were reduced by unanticipated increases in the prices of consumers' goods. The introduction of longer production processes would, for a period, reduce the flow of 'mature' consumers' goods. 'For some time society as a whole will have to put up with an involuntary reduction of consumption' (p. 88). Inflation caused by monetary expansion thus would lead to 'forced saving', and 'an unforeseen retrenchment of ... real income' – the ultimate source of the additional resources used for investment.[4]

Hayek regarded the 'lengthening' of the production process induced by monetary expansion and 'forced saving' as unsustainable. 'These elongations ... are likely to be partly or wholly reversed as soon as the cause of the forced saving disappears' (p. 135). In 1931 he did not stumble across the ideas of adaptive or rational expectations that came to play such an important role after the 1960s in explaining the unsustainability of continuous monetary expansion. He was clear, however, that 'for obvious reasons the banks cannot continue indefinitely to extend credits; and even if they could, the other effects of a rapid and continuous rise of prices would, after a while, make it necessary to stop this process of inflation' (p. 90). Once monetary expansion is ended, however, the return to a shorter structure of production is what constitutes a crisis or depression. The structure of production is too roundabout or, as we would now say, capital-intensive, and only a return to a more appropriate capital structure will end the crisis.

In a model based upon circulating capital the severity of the disruption entailed by a return to a shorter structure of production seems difficult to understand. Where capital takes the form of semi-finished goods, transferring attention to completing final goods in order to satisfy consumers' demands rather than investing in the earlier stages of production would not appear such a difficult adjustment problem. Hayek, therefore, explains large-scale resource unemployment during a shortening of the production process by introducing the concept of capital 'specific' to particular stages of production in the form of specialized equipment. If entrepreneurs have invested in specific machinery and equipment suited to a longer production process than is eventually warranted, it may stand idle because of lack of the additional resources required to 'complete' it. 'This phenomenon of a scarcity of capital making it impossible to use the existing capital equipment appears to me the central point of the true explanation of crises' (Hayek, 1939, p. 149). In other words resources have to be moved from investment to consumption, which means that some specific types of partly finished capital designed mistakenly for a highly capital-intensive structure of production cannot be sustained in the long run and will remain uncompleted.

The movement to less capital-intensive methods accompanying the crisis is associated by Hayek (1939, p. 8) with what he calls 'the Ricardo effect'. Ricardo argued that a change in the wages of labour:

would not equally affect commodities produced with machinery quickly consumed, and commodities produced with machinery slowly consumed. Every rise of wages ... would lower the relative value of those commodities which were produced with a capital of a durable nature. A fall of wages would have precisely the contrary effect'.[5]

As already discussed, Hayek expected the prices of consumers' goods to increase during the boom phase of a cycle as entrepreneurs bid resources away from consumption. This rise in prices would imply a fall in the real wage and this would lead entrepreneurs to substitute labour for machinery and begin the process of shortening the structure of production.

Hayek's interpretation of business fluctuations as successive 'lengthening' (in the upswing) and 'shortening' (in the downswing) of the structure of production led him to the view that government policy should not try to suppress the adjustment process. Once the monetary damage had been done and entrepreneurs had taken decisions in response to false price signals the scope for government policy to help the situation appeared limited. One way or another, the structure of production would return to a configuration that was compatible with underlying 'real' factors. Attempts at further credit expansion could not avert an eventual crisis, while higher levels of government spending on final output would make the imbalance between demand for consumers' and producers' goods even worse and produce further 'shortening' in the structure of production. Hayek did not therefore recommend an active monetary or fiscal policy. The important thing was to prevent further confusion of price signals and the mistaken decisions that accompanied them. No doubt the more flexible were prices and the fewer the 'frictions' within the system, the more rapid would be the recovery. But the process could not be expedited by government action.

MONETARY POLICY AND FLUCTUATIONS

The main policy question that concerned Hayek was how to avoid getting into a crisis in the first place. This led immediately to a consideration of the role of monetary policy in preventing the type of credit expansion that Hayek saw as ultimately responsible for industrial fluctuations. What was required was 'neutral money', a term that referred to a situation in which 'relative prices would be formed, as if they were influenced only by the "real" factors which are taken into account in equilibrium economics' (p. 130). In the static Walrasian world of general equilibrium theory, money appeared merely as a 'numeraire'. It did not itself influence the relative exchange ratios of goods and factors but was simply a common 'good' in terms of which it was convenient to express equilibrium prices.

Hayek realized that there was a paradox here. As a student in the tradition of Carl Menger he viewed money as an institution that had evolved to cope with the uncertain future. It was a means by which people avoided commitment and kept their options open. It permitted a far more extensive division of labour, but it implied a reduction in the scope of barter. Goods supplied no longer carried with them an immediate demand for something else and the fixing of a 'real' exchange ratio. The existence of money inevitably raised the possibility that hoarding (the accumulation of money balances and thus supply unmatched by demand) or dishoarding (spending out of money balances and thus demand unmatched by new supply) might occur. The behaviour of transactors would now depend upon factors such as 'confidence' or the state of 'expectations', while if people tried to tie things down by contracting for the future delivery of goods using money prices, these could only be guesses as to what the 'real' equilibrium prices would turn out to be.

There was thus a paradox in defining money as 'neutral' with reference to a static equilibrium world in which the peculiar function of a medium of exchange was not required. Conversely, in a world of 'indirect exchange' and an uncertain future it was not easy to see how money could ever be neutral in quite the sense implied by the injunction that it should not disguise or distort 'real' factors. These 'real factors' could only finally be known in an equilibrium that would effectively deprive money of its principal purpose. These considerations led Hayek to remark that identifying the necessary conditions required for the neutrality of money is 'practically impossible' and that perhaps 'the ideal could not be realized by any kind of monetary policy' (p. 131).

Nevertheless, Hayek in lecture 4 of *Prices and Production* does offer some thoughts on how monetary policy might be conducted so as to avoid the periodic crises that so preoccupied all economic thinking in the 1930s. His basic proposition is that so far as possible the authorities should try to keep constant over time the flow of money payments. The title of the lecture is 'The case for and against an "elastic" currency'. Contemporary opinion, according to Hayek, favoured an 'elastic' currency, one that expanded and contracted with the demands of trade so as to keep constant an index of prices. For Hayek this was a dangerous doctrine. Index numbers of consumer goods prices could not reveal what was happening to the 'price margins' between stages of production which, as we have seen, influenced entrepreneurial decisions about the structure of production. A rule that some average of consumer goods prices should be kept constant would not, in principle, prevent monetary disturbance to the structure of production. Hayek preferred to keep money payments constant so that any increase in productivity and hence real output brought about through a 'natural' lengthening of the production process would lead to gradually falling prices. Such falling prices would not be harmful and indeed would represent 'the only means of avoiding misdirections of production' (p. 105).

Constancy in the flow of money payments did not, however, constitute an easily implemented policy. In the first place Hayek took what we would now call a 'broad' view of money: 'When I speak of changes in the quantity of money, this is always meant to include that *total* of all kinds of media of exchange (including all so-called "substitutes" for money)' (p. 109). He was therefore confronted with the problem of establishing a clear way of measuring the total money supply and a means of controlling it. Here he relied on the ability of the central bank to expand or contract its own credits with consequential knock-on effects up the 'inverted pyramid' of the credit system. Knowing what these effects would be was a serious problem, particularly as reserve ratios were themselves not entirely fixed but could vary with business conditions.

A second important problem was that keeping the flow of money payments constant would require the authorities to counteract any spontaneous changes in the 'velocity of circulation' caused by technical changes in the methods of payment or by other factors leading to a greater or lesser demand for money. A third (related) matter that concerned the structure of production directly was what Hayek termed the 'co-efficient of money transactions'.[6] Here the point at issue was the degree to which the various stages of production were carried out within vertically integrated firms rather than by the transfer of intermediate products from one firm to another through a relatively disintegrated supply chain. Hayek argued that the relationship between the 'structure of production' (in terms of its capital intensity or 'roundaboutness') and what we might call the 'structure of business organization' (in terms of the number of stages undertaken within a single administrative unit) was a significant matter.[7] A lengthening structure of production organized within vertically integrated concerns would not require the use of additional monetary transactions. If, however, more 'stages' required more market transactions as the intermediate products advanced through the production process there would, in the absence of other countervailing changes in the velocity of circulation or in the quantity of money, be a depressing effect on prices. In effect, a process of vertical integration reduces the demand for money balances and disintegration increases it. Both were seen by Hayek as inconsistent with the objective of trying to maintain the 'neutrality' of money.

Monetary policy for Hayek was therefore far from straightforward and his work is littered with statements emphasizing that practical implementation of the theoretical ideal would be difficult if not impossible and that monetary analysis was in its infancy. Monetary disturbance was at the root of industrial fluctuations but avoiding these disturbances seemed to require monetary authorities with extraordinary technical and informational capabilities to adjust the money stock in response to changing conditions and thus to maintain a constant flow of money payments. 'Even under the best practicable monetary system, the self-equilibrating mechanism of prices might be seriously disturbed by monetary causes' (p. 161).

A summary of Hayek's thinking on money in 1931 might therefore run as follows. Decision-making in an economy which uses highly capital-intensive processes of production and with a highly advanced division of labour puts an enormous strain on the co-coordinating power of the price system. Price movements must convey real information if they are to serve their purpose. A fall in interest rates and price margins, for example, that reflects greater saving and lower time preference, will lead entrepreneurs to take decisions that are less likely to be proved mistaken by future events than a fall in interest rates that is induced by monetary expansion.

EXPECTATIONS AND EQUILIBRIUM

The formation of expectations is crucial here. It is expectations of profits that will determine the willingness of entrepreneurs to invest in more roundabout methods. 'If these entrepreneurs entertain correct views about the price changes that are to be expected as a result of the changes in the method of production, the new rate of interest should correspond to the system of price margins which will ultimately be established' (p. 84). In other words Hayek might be interpreted as saying that entrepreneurs, although not always correct in their expectations, will not make systematic errors in the absence of monetary disturbances. If they have some broadly correct view of the underlying 'real' forces at work, they can form a more accurate conception of future developments than if they are viewing the world through a distorting monetary lens. Given that the option of dispensing with the monetary glasses entirely would greatly reduce potential gains to trade, the aim of monetary policy must be to correct for any inherent defects in sight that might develop over time and to equip entrepreneurs with as near perfect vision as imperfect nature makes possible.

A 1933 lecture on price expectations sets out clearly the importance that Hayek began to attribute to the formation of expectations. Equilibrium in traditional analysis abstracts from time and 'could not be of great value'. If the problems accompanying the passage of time were to be addressed:

we must make very definite assumptions about the attitude of persons to the future. The assumptions of this kind which are implied in the concept of equilibrium are essentially that everybody foresees the future correctly and that this foresight includes not only the changes in the objective data but also the behavior of all the other people with whom he expects to perform economic transactions. (Hayek, 1939, pp. 139-40)

Equilibrium required that decision-makers were not disappointed by events and that the expectations held by transactors were mutually compatible. Thus it was important, given that existing prices would inevitably play a large role in the formation of expectations, that actual prices should not encourage false ideas and contain 'the germ of such disappointments'.

Perhaps it is possible to discern in these ideas the influence of Gunnar Myrdal whose great contribution to monetary theory was to distinguish clearly between *ex ante* plans embodying intentions based upon expectations, and *ex post* outcomes. Monetary equilibrium required the equality of *ex ante* plans to invest with *ex ante* plans to save. Only then would the *ex post* bookkeeping equality of saving with investment not turn out to disappoint expectations. It was in a paper published by Hayek in 1933 that Myrdal first 'works out in detail the vitally important distinction between "looking forward" and "looking backward"'.[8] Hayek did not, however, incorporate these developments systematically into his thinking or advance the analysis of expectations. He confined himself to the argument that monetary changes could play no role in re-establishing equilibrium once it had been disturbed, and that a constant money supply would be least likely to cause trouble by inducing incompatible expectations. Such a contention made more intuitive sense in the context of trying to maintain a pre-existing equilibrium than in a situation of disequilibrium and depression. It was this that lay behind the criticism that Hayek was too inclined to start his analysis assuming a well-functioning system satisfying the requirements of a static equilibrium, and that this betrayed a mind-set unlikely to advance understanding of disequilibrium processes.

THE ECLIPSE OF AUSTRIAN CAPITAL THEORY

This somewhat harsh judgement on Hayek's work on the economics of business cycles in the early 1930s is supported by the fact that it did not play a prominent role in the future development of the discipline. A major problem for Hayek was that the economics profession ultimately rejected his conviction that fluctuations could not be properly understood without the support of the Austrian theory of capital. Not only was the theory of capital itself subject to objections, but its use in the analysis of fluctuations was swept away by the Keynesian revolution. A 'timeless' capital–output ratio took the place of the Austrian average period of production in models of long-run growth, and the tradition of Böhm-Bawerk disappeared from mainstream textbooks. In the 1960s the 'Cambridge capital controversies' concerned problems in the measurement of aggregate capital, the coherence of the notion of its 'marginal productivity' and the theoretical reliability of any systematic association between the rate of interest and the 'capital intensity' or 'roundaboutness' of production techniques.[9] Although these difficulties were at the heart of the 'Austrian' theory of capital, the debate in the 1950s and 1960s did not particularly emphasize this historical association. The battle was viewed mainly as a struggle between 'neoclassical' rather than 'Austrian' economists and their Cambridge (England) critics. Harcourt's (1972) summary of these controversies does not contain a reference to Hayek's work, while Böhm-Bawerk appears in a single scholarly footnote.

In the late 1930s, Hawtrey (1939) still made the period of production and the structure of production central pillars in his approach to capital and devoted a whole chapter to a consideration of Hayek's *Prices and Production*. Hicks (1939, p. 192) commented that 'nearly everyone who comes to the study of capital falls a victim to Böhm-Bawerk's theory at some stage or other'. But although Hicks admired the achievement of Böhm-Bawerk and accepted that the theory was basically correct with respect to the simplest special cases that it analysed (such as tree harvesting or wine production), he, along with most of the post-war generation of economists, abandoned it. It was perhaps a misfortune for Hayek that he was so immersed in the tradition of Böhm-Bawerk that he was 'unable to let the matter go' (O'Brien, 2004, p. 503).

THE ROLE OF THE STATIONARY STATE IN DYNAMIC ANALYSIS

In a revealing paragraph in *Value and Capital*, Hicks (1939) throws the problem with which Hayek was wrestling in *Prices and Production* into sharp focus. The dependence of current quantities supplied and demanded not simply on current prices but on the history of past expectations and on current expectations of future prices was 'the first main crux of dynamic theory; and it marks the first parting of the ways' (p. 117). We could either face the issue or 'evade the issue by concentrating on the case where these difficulties are at a minimum. The first is the method of Marshall; the second (broadly speaking) is the method of the Austrians. Its hallmark is concentration on the case of a Stationary State'.

Difficulties are at a minimum in stationary states because, as we have seen, there is no net saving or investment and conditions replicate themselves period by period. Entrepreneurs (if we can call decision-makers in stationary conditions by this name) will correctly expect existing prices to continue so that current and expected future prices for each class of good will be the same. This is, of course, precisely the method of Hayek in *Prices and Production*. Preoccupation with stationary conditions, argued Hicks, had a 'baneful influence'. It was not that Austrian economists like Hayek were not interested in disequilibrium. Hayek's whole aim was to explain fluctuations. But 'stationary-state theorists naturally regarded reality as "tending" towards stationariness' although the theory itself supplied no grounds for confidence that any such tendency actually existed. The result was a preoccupation with an ideal capital structure that required certain price ratios and static expectations for its perpetuation but that 'told us nothing about anything actual at all' (p. 119).

Actual conditions were not stationary. The important question was how the economic system would behave outside a stationary state in an uncertain and monetized world. What were the forces, if any, that might lead towards the stationary state and that underlay the assumed 'tendency' towards equilibrium? As we have seen, Hayek in *Prices and Production* presented no real theory of expectations. This does not mean, of course, that his insight that instability in the supply of money might lead to mistaken investment decisions was wrong, or that stability in monetary conditions is not a sensible policy objective. But neither of these propositions is necessarily dependent upon the validity of the Austrian theory of capital which was his main focus of attention.

From the perspective of the early twenty-first century, however, some of Hicks's observations about 'Austrian' thinking in the 1930s appear curious. We are used to thinking of the Austrian School as being particularly associated with an analysis of disequilibrium situations, with recognition of pervasive uncertainty, with an emphasis on the role of entrepreneurship, and so forth. It seems strange to think of 'Austrian' thinking as directing attention away from disequilibrium adjustment because of an obsessive interest in stationary states. Yet this was the way it seemed to many economists at the time. It was, however, another strand in Hayek's economic writing in the 1930s that played a central part in establishing our modern conception of the Austrian School.

This issue was the markets-versus-planning debate or the possibility of socialist economic calculation. Information and economic change were central concerns in this dispute. Here, the boot was on the other foot and it was Hayek who was able to accuse his opponents of an obsession with static equilibrium constructs in unreal worlds. As Blaug (1992) remarks, however, static general equilibrium analysis was by the late 1930s already 'becoming the standard for theoretical sophistication in microeconomics, in terms of which Austrian price theory stood condemned as antediluvian'. For contemporary critics Hayek's approach to fluctuations was too much influenced by underlying concepts of stationary states. His approach to the traditional theory of prices was, in contrast, too lacking in general equilibrium rigour. Hayek had managed to fall foul of prevailing fashions in both areas for apparently diametrically opposing reasons. There is a strong case, however, that this is explained not by any lack of consistency on his part but by the reverse. He had a highly consistent view of the nature of the economic system at a time of huge theoretical innovation. It is to Hayek's approach to the price system that I turn in the next section.

THE CALCULATION DEBATE

The debate concerning the possibility of rational economic calculation in a socialist state originated with a paper by Mises (1920, reprinted in Hayek, 1935b, pp. 87–130). In this paper Mises asserted that the absence of private ownership of the means of production made any kind of rational approach to resource allocation impossible. It was impossible because collective ownership suppressed market transactions and this in turn prevented the emergence of market prices to indicate the value of resources in different potential employments. 'Where there is no free market, there is no pricing mechanism; without a pricing mechanism, there is no economic calculation' (Hayek, 1935b, p. 111). The top officials in a socialist state might have some set of objectives that they wish to fulfil, but in the absence of prices for the resources at their disposal they cannot know how best to go about achieving them. Prices of factors of production in a market economy provide decision-makers with imperfect information about the value of alternatives forgone and thus implicitly carry the message: 'to make sure that you do not waste my services you should make sure that the value of my marginal product exceeds this price'. Socialist officials would have no such assistance with their decision-making and would 'be without any means of testing their bearings' (p. 106). 'Socialism', argued Mises, 'is the abolition of rational economy' (p. 110).

This paper had a massive impact and Hayek's economics was clearly heavily influenced by it. Hayek summarized his own view of market processes in a famous paper on 'The use of knowledge in society' (1945). It represented an extension and elaboration of Mises' argument. Knowledge is not universally available. It is dispersed across the entire population and the great economic question is how to make the greatest social use of it. One method might be to construct a system that tried to transfer this knowledge to a central organizer who could then use it rationally in pursuit of some specified set of objectives. Hayek made the point that the volume of possibly relevant information was virtually limitless; including as it did not simply technical or scientific knowledge but also idiosyncratic 'knowledge of time and place'. He added that a large part of this potential stock of knowledge was of a type ('tacit knowledge') that was by its nature incapable of being communicated by means of blueprints or statistics or even words. For good measure he emphasized that knowledge was in an endless state of flux so that any attempt at documentation would always be out of date.

Hayek's main point was that the 'market' was a decentralized solution to this fundamental problem of making use of widely dispersed knowledge. Decentralized decision-making meant that the people with local knowledge could use it. In order to use it to good effect, however, they needed to combine it with knowledge of things concerning which they had no direct experience. The prices of resource inputs conveyed in a highly economical form just enough information to make sure that the inputs were appropriately allocated. Detailed information about why certain price changes were occurring – political upheaval, technological change, the development of new products that made use of or dispensed with various inputs, freak weather conditions and so forth – were not necessary. Price changes would induce decentralized responses that reflected the new social valuation of the resource at the margin. Handling change was the central problem. 'It is, perhaps, worth stressing that economic problems arise always and only in consequence of change' (Townsend, 1971, p. 21). Mises also had emphasized this point when he conceded that a socialist system might theoretically continue to replicate unchanged a status quo established by the market. This, however, would be 'impossible in real life'. A static situation was only a theoretical construct 'necessary ... for our thinking' about economics but 'corresponding to no real state of affairs' (Hayek, 1935b, p. 109).

The socialist answer to Mises and Hayek was provided by Lange (1938). This is not the place to review the entire calculation debate in detail but a few of the main lines of argument are important because they help to isolate what was distinctive about Hayek's economic thought in his years at the London School of Economics. Lange's aim was to show that the price system and socialism were not incompatible. He did this by confronting the challenge head on. He contended that valuations for goods and services could be generated in a socialist system. He interprets Hayek (1935b) as saying that the function of the market is 'to provide a method of allocating resources by trial and error' (Townsend, 1971, p. 37).

Such a 'trial and error' procedure was possible under socialism. Some of the details depended upon what kind of socialist system was envisaged – whether, for example, the rate of saving was determined by individual decisions or centrally imposed – but the main components were a straightforward application of a Walrasian '*tâtonnement*' process.

Provisional prices of goods and labour would be established centrally. Local decision-makers (whether consumers or producers) would face these 'parametric' prices rather like transactors in a 'perfectly competitive market'. Producers would be asked to adjust their outputs so that the marginal cost of production (evaluated using the provisional prices of labour, intermediate goods and materials) of each good and service was equal to its price. Of course there would be excess supplies and demands at these provisional prices and the Walrasian price adjustment process would be implemented. The central administrators would increase the prices of goods and labour for which there was excess demand and lower the prices of those for which there was excess supply. This would be an 'ongoing' process mimicking the behaviour of a 'competitive' market. As for new capital, the (politically determined) quantity would be allocated 'competitively' and a shadow price attached for use by local officials in their investment appraisal. Lange goes so far as to conjecture that a planning board, because of 'its wider knowledge of what is going on in the whole economic system than any private entrepreneur can ever have' might be able to approach an equilibrium price structure 'by a *much shorter* series of successive trials than a competitive market actually does' (p. 55).

For 25 years after the end of the Second World War it was generally accepted that Lange's reply to Hayek and Robbins was decisive. Perhaps it was Lange's use of Walrasian general equilibrium ideas that made his opponents seem unsophisticated, if not, as Blaug puts it, 'antediluvian'. Townsend (1971) summarized the view of the time when he commented that socialist countries were mostly centralized dictatorships but that Lange had shown 'there is no reason in economic theory why they should be this way' (p. 15). This seems quite correct. It was possible in theory to think of a scheme that would make socialist calculation, *pace* Mises, at least possible and, *pace* Hayek and Robbins, compatible with a trial and error process. Given that the origins of the dispute concerned the very possibility of any kind of rational economic calculation under socialism it is perhaps understandable that Lange's article was widely seen as a knockout punch. The more subtle question, however, was whether the trial and error process that Lange had identified for his socialist state did indeed mimic the market well enough to fool everyone as he claimed, or whether it was a distorted and lifeless caricature.

CHARACTERISTICS OF HAYEK'S VIEW OF THE PRICE SYSTEM

For Hayek, the calculation debate was not about the possibility of any kind of rational approach to resource allocation under socialism. He had already accepted, as noted by Lange, that this was 'not an impossibility in the sense that it is logically contradictory' (Hayek, 1935b, p. 207). The point for Hayek was that a socialist state would have to jettison the competitive market, and this was so irrespective of the name attached to whatever ersatz scheme it was necessary or expedient to introduce as a substitute. Lange's market process simply did not pass muster and would not do the job as effectively as the real thing.

The central difference between Lange and Hayek concerned the formation of prices and the means by which they changed. For Lange, the competitive market functions by confronting consumers and producers with given prices to which each person has to adjust their behaviour. These prices then mysteriously change, period by period, in response to excess supplies and demands. 'As a result we get a *new* set of prices, which serves as a new basis for the individuals' striving to satisfy their subjective equilibrium condition' (p. 42). This is Lange's attempt to specify in theoretical terms how markets actually work and, having conceived markets as working in this way, he found it possible to replicate the process under socialism.

Hayek could not accept that this was a reasonable theoretical abstraction capable of encapsulating and explaining the social potential of markets. Prices convey information, but changes are not communicated to all participants at once. He considers some new opportunity for the use of tin. Only some people will know of this. Their actions will create market gaps that will 'in turn' be filled from other sources and 'the effect will rapidly spread throughout the whole economic system'. 'The whole acts as one market ... because [its members'] limited individual fields of vision sufficiently overlap so that through many intermediaries the relevant information is communicated to all' (p. 25). Lange is substituting a planning board as a single all-encompassing intermediary which signals to all market participants at the same time to replace a mass of traders continually adapting their prices to changing conditions. For Hayek, by means of the price system, information is spread, in turn, through many intermediaries.

This difference in perception of market processes was of the greatest importance even if it was only dimly understood in the debates of the time. Lange's trial and error process was centralized in the sense that any changes required in the structure of prices were centrally determined.

Hayek's trial and error process was decentralized in the sense that all market participants adjusted the terms of their agreements as circumstances changed. The result would be that trade would not take place at a single price for each good or service across the entire market. It is true that Hayek talks of the existence of 'one price for any commodity' but it is clear from the context (immediately following the description of a continuing process) that this is the situation arrived at once the ramifications of any change have been worked through and 'might have been arrived at by one single mind possessing all the information'. In Lange's system administrators always make their decisions on the basis of a common understanding of prices. It is one of the fundamental requirements of his planning process that prices are parametric and identical for all administrators. For Hayek, if all traders are in agreement about the relative prices of goods and factors across the entire economy it shows that economic change has subsided and price adjustments have come to an end as people have fully adjusted to a certain unchanging set of conditions and no further arbitrage possibilities exist.

There is no doubt that differing ideas about how to model market processes were capable of generating great confusion. Looking at Hayek's work during this period as a whole, however, it is difficult not to credit him with a consistent position. The first lecture of *Prices and Production*, 'The influence of money on prices', discusses the history of ideas on how changes in the money supply come to affect prices not all in one go but in a continuing adjustment process. Immediate and full adjustment of all prices to monetary change would imply that monetary change would have no 'real' impact. In fact, as we have seen, Hayek believed that money was far from 'neutral' and that the path to a new price structure following a monetary disturbance could be painful. This, of course, was the essence of his approach to the structure of production. Changes in the market rate of interest would not immediately be reflected in the prices of all intermediate goods. The world could not be seen in terms of 'simultaneous determination' and solutions to systems of simultaneous equations. His was a classical world of 'cause and effect'.

The consequences of taking a Hayekian view of the market process rather than the view espoused by Lange were wide-ranging. Lange asserted, for example, that the criticism that a socialist system would require the solution of millions of equations was misplaced. The same 'equations' would require to be solved in his system as would be required in the market system, 'and the persons who do the "solving" are the same also' (p. 54). Further, socialist administrators would have 'exactly the same knowledge, or lack of knowledge, of the production functions as the Capitalist entrepreneurs have' (p. 34). Lange was fully justified in replying to the 'millions of equations' objection in the context of his proposed system. But once more, each protagonist was curiously missing or misinterpreting the points raised by the other.

When Hayek complained about the complexity of the problems involved in planning an economic system he was drawing attention to the fact that the number and variety of goods and services (including intermediate goods) that exist in the market was so enormous that it was effectively beyond the capacity of a planning system to handle – even one based upon Lange's model. If a central authority was to set 'parametric' prices it would inevitably have to specify the 'goods' to which the prices applied and it would have to know at each point in time the extent of 'excess supply or demand' in order to approve a price adjustment. In practice, of course, index numbers might be employed, but index numbers were anathema to Hayek. They inevitably concealed variations in relative prices between items in the 'basket' of goods considered. Further, the characteristics of goods and services in a market were changing endlessly. New goods and services were being introduced and old ones improved. Solving equations was not therefore the only issue. Simple administration was quite sufficient to present massive difficulties. Under Hayek's system, this administrative apparatus was not required because there was no necessity for a central register of every description of input and output. Transactors knew the subtleties of their different trades and could assess whether an available price was attractive or not. They did not need to describe all the detailed features of goods and factors to a planning board nor wait for instructions about what 'parametric' prices were to be used at any particular time.

The other misunderstanding concerned the nature of individual decisions in a market. In Lange's system all decisions are 'calculations' in the following sense. Administrators are assumed to know the (centrally given) accounting prices and the technical production opportunities that they face. They then calculate and implement the input combinations that minimize costs of production and the output at which marginal cost is equal to price. For Lange this is precisely equivalent to the activity of 'capitalist entrepreneurs'. We have seen, however, that for Hayek this could not be the case. It would only be the case if prices were parametric for capitalist entrepreneurs. No doubt there might be instances where the richness of a particular market was so great and conditions so stable that the market approached this 'equilibrium' situation. In general, however, change was the rule and with change came economic problems and non-parametric prices rather than routine administration and equilibrium prices. The economic problems associated with change were not amenable to solution through mere 'calculation'. They required adjustments based upon judgements about the future. In a Hayekian competitive market, prices had to be negotiated and marginal cost was a matter of subjective assessment. There was an inevitable speculative and information-discovery dimension to the activities of the participants in Hayek's market process that has been completely purged from Lange's system. Socialist administrators and capitalist entrepreneurs do not perform the same function in spite of Lange's ingenious attempt to prove the contrary.

THE COMPETITIVE ORDER

Many of these points are precursors of more fully worked-out ideas that Hayek developed later in the 1950s and 1960s. Hayek (1948, 1968) explicitly discusses the idea that competition is a 'discovery procedure' and that this conception is quite different from, and indeed incompatible with, the textbook notion of perfect competition. Perfect competition requires that transactors cannot influence prices and it is precisely this feature that Lange used to simulate the results of 'competition' in his 'trial and error' process. Competition properly understood is more akin to scientific research by which competing hypotheses are tested and either survive or are refuted by emerging events. This element in Hayek's economics greatly influenced later work by writers such as Kirzner (1973) on the role of the entrepreneur. This stressed the importance of alertness to hitherto unnoticed opportunities in the competitive process and the nature of 'entrepreneurial profit', a category that finds no place in perfectly competitive analysis.

This distinctive Hayekian view of the competitive market process was refined after he had moved away from pure economics and further into social philosophy in the years following the Second World War. He took particular care to distinguish between an order created by design and a 'spontaneous order' which emerges from a continuous process of individual adaptations to changing conditions. The market order he termed a 'catallaxy' to distinguish it from an economy proper which implies conscious organization in pursuit of known ends. The competitive market cannot be seen as pursuing or achieving specified collective ends. It simply proceeds.[10] Although Hayek's ideas on spontaneous order came to prominence later in his career, his work in economics in the 1930s does reveal their influence from the beginning. His (1933) inaugural lecture at the London school of Economics (LSE) indicates that *Prices and Production* and all his economic writing in the 1930s should be read as discussions concerning the conditions that are necessary to the maintenance of a spontaneous order. 'We discover again and again that necessary functions are discharged by spontaneous institutions', institutions that 'at first we did not even understand when we saw them'. He writes of 'the spontaneous interplay of the actions of individuals' and suggests, citing Mises, that we still mistakenly 'refuse to recognize that society is an organism and not an organization' (Hayek, 1933a, in Bartley and Kresge, 1991, vol. 3, pp. 26–7).

It is this last sentence that perhaps best explains the gulf in interpretation and understanding between Hayek and his critics during his time at LSE. In the case of his account of business fluctuations Hayek was attempting something very ambitious and ultimately not persuasive to contemporary opinion. The structure of production was itself the product of a spontaneous order. It involved the interplay of vast numbers of economic agents trading and processing intermediate products in every stage of development. The process was aided by the institution of money, itself originally the outcome in Hayek's Austrian conception (following Carl Menger) of spontaneous evolutionary forces. Like a modern-day ecologist fretting about the consequences of man's interventions in nature, Hayek feared the destructive potential of ill-conceived policies on a possibly delicate, organic and complex evolved order. This order was constantly and incrementally changing but Hayek had only the tools of Austrian capital theory to bring to bear on the problem and his account therefore seemed dominated by the idea of the stationary state, a concept not unrelated to a static equilibrium. In the depths of a depression this seemed an unpromising starting point.

In the calculation debate Hayek's economics was informed by the same philosophical understanding. The order arising out of a market catalaxy was one thing and the order arising out of Lange's organizational substitute was another. One process was evolutionary and organic; the other was consciously designed. Whether the 'natural' or the 'artificial' version was better depended on what objectives were being pursued, and was difficult to resolve by appeal to pure reason. The question would have to be settled by experience. To contemporary opinion, however, as indeed probably to modern opinion, the idea that it was better to trust in an evolved system that had no intrinsic purpose, rather than in a system cleverly designed with the eventual achievement of an efficient equilibrium in mind, was difficult to grasp. It therefore either eluded the grasp of most people or, where the idea was understood, was rejected. What Hayek later termed the 'fatal conceit' of constructivist rationalism was simply too powerful to be resisted and Lange's use of general equilibrium theory proved more palatable to prevailing tastes than did Hayek's account of market process.

CONCLUDING COMMENTS

The years between the wars saw economists struggling to understand the processes of economic change. Static and comparative static theories were widely seen as inappropriate tools for the task of explaining industrial fluctuations or long-run growth. Hayek, Kaldor and Knight might all have found room to agree with such a statement. If these methods still made their appearance it was because alternative theoretical constructs were so difficult to devise. Explanations of economic change still required some lags, frictions, rigidities or other imperfections somehow to impede a move from one equilibrium state of affairs to another as a result of an exogenous disturbance. Given the possible number of exogenous influences that might be suggested, the number of possible imperfections that might arise, and the technical difficulty of then predicting a time path of results for a complex and interdependent system of autonomous agents, it is hardly surprising that the field was so controversial.

Hayek played, as has been seen, a distinctive part in these discussions about dynamic analysis. Perhaps he was all along too much of a social philosopher ever to be fully understood by pure economists. His thinking always had an evolutionary and biological element that did not mesh with the 'mechanical' and deterministic models with which economists were familiar and which he still employed in his work during the 1930s. Both in his theory of fluctuations and in his approach to the 'calculation debate' Hayek took a position that was rejected by contemporary opinion. Keynesian analysis swept away concern with the Austrian structure of production, while the nationalization of industry and rational planning characterized the post-war agenda. Nevertheless, economic debates are rarely finally settled. Economists continue to argue about the distinction between competition as a state and competition as a process, while experience with planning mechanisms was disappointing enough for Hayek's views to gain a more respectful hearing from the mid-1970s onwards. Hayek may not have triumphed in the 1930s but many of the problems of dynamic analysis that preoccupied him remain unresolved to this day.

NOTES

1. Blaug (1968, Chapter 12) provides a detailed review of the main protagonists of this debate in the 1930s. Kaldor (1937) summarizes the controversy and contrasts his views with those of Knight (another of the main critics of the Austrian theory).
2. See D.P. O'Brien's entry on Hayek in Rutherford (2004, p. 503).
3. The simplicity of this basic 'Austrian' theory of capital is very seductive. Unfortunately the inverse relation between the market rate of interest and the 'capital intensity' of

production processes does not generalize from cases involving even rates of flow of circulating capital to cases involving heterogeneous capital goods and differing structures of 'waiting'. The intertemporal flow 10, 0, 16, for example, has a higher present value than the flow 5, 15, 5 when evaluated at a rate of interest below 28 per cent and above 72 per cent. It has a lower present value evaluated at rates of interest in between.
4. A succinct account of Hayek's model that is true to the original conception is not easy to formulate. As Hicks (1967) points out, the 'Hayek story' was always perplexing. In particular his assumption that the prices of producers' goods initially rose relative to consumers' goods only for this relationship to be reversed later seems inconsistent with 'forced saving'. Why the lag between higher payments to labour and the demand for consumers' goods? Does this not imply 'voluntary saving'? Why would consumers' goods prices not respond almost immediately, thus short-circuiting any prolonged 'real effects' from monetary expansion and avoiding the 'lengthening' of the production process'?
5. Ricardo ([1817] 1891, Gonner Edition, Chapter 1, section 5, p. 33). Ricardo's statement might make more intuitive sense to a modern reader if the word 'cost' is substituted for the word 'value'. Ricardo refers to 'time which must elapse before (a good) can be brought to the market' (p. 31) and sees durable equipment as releasing its stored up labour slowly over a long period. The context of the labour theory of value is, of course, alien to the Austrian tradition but the connection between capital intensity and 'time to market' is very compatible with the analysis of Böhm-Bawerk.
6. Hayek (1931) defines this as 'the proportion between the total flow of goods to that part of it which is effected by money' (p. 121).
7. Hayek does not attempt to explain the degree of vertical integration in production. For this he would have required some concept of 'transaction cost' which was to be formulated by Coase (1937). He nevertheless realized that economic organization changed over time and that it had monetary implications.
8. The quote is from an account by Bertil Ohlin of the development of the interwar Stockholm School reported in Shackle (1967), p. 229. Myrdal's paper was published in Hayek (1933b).
9. For a retrospective on these debates see Cohen and Harcourt (2003).
10. These ideas are fully explored in Hayek (1976, vol. 2).

REFERENCES

Bartley, William W., III and Stephen Kresge (eds) (1991), *The Trend of Economic Thinking, The Collected Works of F.A. Hayek*, vol. III, London: Routledge.
Blaug, Mark (1968), *Economic Theory in Retrospect*, 2nd edn, London: Heinemann.
Blaug, Mark (1992), 'Commentary', in B.J. Caldwell and S. Boehm (eds), *Austrian Economics: Tensions and New Directions*, Boston, MA: Kluwer Academic Publishers, pp. 31–4.
Coase, Ronald H. (1937), 'The nature of the firm', *Economica*, 4 (16), 386–405.
Cohen, Avi J. and Geoffrey C. Harcourt (2003), 'Whatever happened to the Cambridge capital theory controversies?' *Journal of Economic Perspectives*, 17 (1), 199–214.
Harcourt, Geoffrey C. (1972), *Some Cambridge Controversies in the Theory of Capital*, Cambridge: Cambridge University Press.
Hawtrey, Ralph G. (1937), *Capital and Employment*, Longmans, London: Green & Co.
Hayek, Friedrich A. (1931), *Prices and Production*, 2nd edn (1935), London: Routledge.
Hayek, Friedrich A. (1933a), 'The trend of economic thinking', in William W. Bartley III and Stephen Kresge (eds) (1991), *The Trend of Economic Thinking, The Collected Works of F.A. Hayek*, vol. III, London: Routledge, pp. 17–34.
Hayek, Friedrich A. (ed.) (1933b), *Beiträge zur Geldtheorie*, Vienna: Springer.
Hayek, Friedrich A. (1935a), 'Price expectations, monetary disturbances and malinvestments',

reprinted in F.A. Hayek (1939), *Profits, Interest and Investment and Other Essays on the Theory of Industrial Fluctuations*, London: Routledge, pp. 135–56.
Hayek, Friedrich A. (ed.) (1935b), *Collectivist Economic Planning*, London: Routledge & Kegan Paul.
Hayek, Friedrich A. (1939), *Profits, Interest and Investment and Other Essays on the Theory of Industrial Fluctuations*, London: Routledge.
Hayek, Friedrich A. (1941), *The Pure Theory of Capital*, London: Routledge.
Hayek, Friedrich A. (1945), 'The use of knowledge in society', *American Economic Review*, 35 (4), 519–30, reprinted in Townsend (ed.) (1971), *Price Theory*, Harmondsworth: Penguin, pp. 17–31.
Hayek, Friedrich A. (1948), 'The meaning of competition', *Individualism and Economic Order*, Chicago, IL: University of Chicago Press, pp. 92–118.
Hayek, Friedrich A. (1968), 'Competition as a discovery procedure', in F.A. Hayek (1978), *New Studies in Philosophy, Politics, Economics and the History of Ideas*, London: Routledge & Kegan Paul, pp. 179–90.
Hayek, Friedrich A. (1976), *Law Legislation and Liberty*, vol. 2, London: Routledge & Kegan Paul.
Hicks, John R. (1939), *Value and Capital: An Inquiry into Some Fundamental Principles of Economic Theory*, 2nd edn (1946), Oxford: Clarendon Press.
Hicks, John R. (1967), 'The Hayek story', *Critical Essays in Monetary Theory*, Oxford: Clarendon Press, pp. 203–15.
Kaldor, Nicholas (1937), 'The controversy on the theory of capital', reprinted in Nicholas Kaldor (1960), *Essays on Value and Distribution*, London: Duckworth, pp. 153–205.
Kirzner, Israel (1973), *Competition and Entrepreneurship*, Chicago, IL: University of Chicago Press.
Lange, Oscar (1938), 'On the economic theory of socialism', reprinted in Townsend (ed.) (1971), *Price Theory*, Harmondsworth: Penguin, pp. 32–56.
Mises, Ludwig von (1920), 'Economic calculation in the socialist commonwealth', reprinted in F.A. Hayek (ed.) (1935b), *Collectivist Economic Planning*, London: Routledge & Kegan Paul, pp. 87–130.
O'Brien, Denis P. (2004), 'Hayek', in Donald Rutherford (ed.), *The Biographical Dictionary of British Economists*, vol. 1, Bristol: Thoemmes Continuum, pp. 499–504.
Ricardo, David (1817), *Principles of Political Economy and Taxation*, E.C.K Gonner (ed.) (1891), London: George Bell.
Rutherford, Donald (ed.) (2004), *The Biographical Dictionary of British Economists*, Bristol: Thoemmes Continuum.
Shackle, G.L.S. (1967), *The Years of High Theory: Invention and Tradition in Economic Thought 1926–1939*, Cambridge: Cambridge University Press.
Townsend, Harry (ed.) (1971), *Price Theory*, Harmondsworth: Penguin.

4. Hayek's *Pure Theory of Capital*
Gerald R. Steele

INTRODUCTION

In 1941, *The Pure Theory of Capital* was too late – and too obscure – to catch the attention of an economics profession that was fixated upon John Maynard Keynes. Although capital is central to issues of market coordination, capital theory held no broad interest, even prior to the developing era of Keynesian economics:

> In the Cambridge tradition that governed Keynes's brief study of economics, the Mill-Jevons theory of capital, later developed by Böhm-Bawerk and Wicksell was not seriously considered. By about 1930, these ideas had been largely forgotten in the English-speaking world. (Hayek, 1983, p.48)

By Hayek's own description, *The Pure Theory of Capital* is a 'highly abstract study of a problem of pure economic theory' that attempts to establish the 'fundamentals' that must serve 'more concrete work on the processes which we observe in the real world' (Hayek, 1941, p.v). In particular, Hayek wished to remedy earlier expositions of a monetary theory of business cycles (Hayek, 1933, 1935, 1939) and to respond to criticisms that arose primarily from 'the inadequacy of its presentation of the theory of capital which it presupposed' (Shackle, 1981, p.242).

The protracted and interwoven development of Hayek's capital theory and business cycle theory was set against the background of an intense rivalry between Hayek and Keynes in the 1930s. Hayek had seen that 'an elaboration of the still inadequately developed theory of capital was a prerequisite for a thorough disposal of Keynes's argument' (Hayek, 1983, p.46); and, in retrospect, he considered it an error of judgement that he had given no time to an immediate and studious critique of Keynes's *General Theory*. So, in addition to serving Hayek's own exposition of a monetary theory of business cycles, *The Pure Theory of Capital* serves to expose the fallacy of the central tenet of Keynes's *General Theory* – one that sits firmly in the mainstream of modern economics – for a 'direct dependence of investment on final demand' (Hayek, 1983, p.48). Yet, Hayek's exposé remains generally ignored, with the effect that Keynesian demand management (macroeconomics) together with marginal analysis (microeconomics) remain the dominant instruments of economic analysis. The issues could scarcely be more important. To understand *The Pure Theory of Capital* is to question the relevance of mainstream economics.

ANGLO-AMERICAN AND AUSTRIAN ECONOMICS

Referenced by Hayek as the 'Anglo-American approach', the marginal analysis of modern microeconomics presents a theory of production such that, with given technology (a 'production function' that relates output to the input of capital and labour), factor productivities, hiring costs and the level of activity, there exists an optimal combination of capital and labour. Whenever the relative cost of hiring capital and labour changes, a simple substitution takes place until the new optimal combination for production is reached; that is, where the ratio of the marginal product of capital to its hiring cost is equal to the ratio of the marginal product of labour to its hiring cost. These are the familiar textbook details of neoclassical optimality, that derive from the implausible assumptions that inputs of capital and labour are unambiguously quantifiable, independently priced and readily substitutable. Although neoclassical theory sees capital as machinery, the time required to build machines is not discussed. Instead, there is either short-run analysis (where capital is immutably fixed) or long-run analysis, where the combination of capital and labour and the level of output are already optimally adjusted to the relative hiring costs and to the technical parameters of the production function.

The crucial oversight is that capital plant (durable capital) is a produced means of production; that is, machines are themselves produced by labour, usually working with other machines. The implication is that when the cost of hiring labour increases, so too does the cost of producing machines; and the neoclassical notion of a simple economically efficient substitution between capital and labour is no longer obvious. The oversight is a corollary of abstracting from the requirement 'for time to elapse between effort and result in production' (Shackle, 1981, p. 253), from the practical issue that some production methods require more time than others, and from the idea that capital is destroyed in the process of producing goods and services.

The use of labour to produce items of capital that are then employed, together with labour, to produce consumption goods is described (in the Austrian approach to economics) as an indirect, or 'roundabout', method of production. Working capital is also required. To illustrate: in the manufacture of bread, wheat and yeast are separately cultured (using chemical nutrients and water) to reproduce themselves; the wheat is milled to produce flour; yeast and water are added, the mix is kneaded, allowed to prove and then baked to produce bread. This process involves durable capital (tractor, plough, grindstone and oven) and working capital (the 'intermediate products' of seed, yeast, nutrients, and a 'wage fund' from which to remunerate workers in the period before their contribution to the production of bread can be sold at market). Such considerations are lost to neoclassical economics, where labour is set alongside durable capital to the exclusion of working capital and the consideration of time.

The more revealing Austrian approach to production has its origins in the work of David Ricardo. In the early nineteenth century, Ricardo had shown that the labour theory of value – according to which relative product prices are determined by the amounts of labour required to produce each product – could not be true when capital is used. The nub of his explanation is that, if machine-X were capable of producing the same output as that produced by (say) 100 labour-years, machine-X must embody (that is, can be produced by) fewer than 100 labour-years of work. Otherwise, there would have been no point in building that machine. It follows that a rise in the cost of hiring labour must increase the cost of 100 labour-years by more than it increases the cost of machine-X. So, a rise in the cost of labour would trigger the substitution of machines for labour, but not in the simplistic manner of the neoclassical approach. In the development of this idea, William Stanley Jevons is credited with the first explicit introduction of time into the theory of production (see Hayek, 1941, p. 113), following upon which Austrian capital theory emerged in the work of Eugen von Böhm-Bawerk, Knut Wicksell ('honorary Austrian'), Ludwig von Mises and Friedrich Hayek.

Roundaboutness comes both in the time taken to produce capital, and in the productive life of capital. Although Jevons focused upon continuous inputs, other possibilities present themselves given that resources may be committed as investments over varying periods of time. Similarly, corresponding returns may also be obtained over varying periods of times. At one extreme, a product may require inputs over an extended time-scale to give virtually instantaneous consumption (continuous input/point output); for example, a firework display. At the other extreme, a product that is produced virtually instantaneously may give service over many years (point input/continuous output); for example, a walking stick that is cut from a tree. Most cases are hybrids in varying degree (continuous input/continuous output). Whatever the profile, the expenditures necessary to purchase inputs are most commonly incurred in advance of the revenues received from the sale of outputs. This is the perspective of the Austrian theory of capital.

In the Austrian approach, capital is presented as 'equivalent to a "fund" out of which incomes, and particularly wages' (Hayek, 1941, p. 325) are paid. For example, Robinson Crusoe might set aside fish (thereby saving from current production to accumulate a wage fund) to sustain himself during the period necessary to build a boat (durable capital). A successful investment would see all of his circulating capital – the fund of fish and, via Crusoe's effort, their transformation into felled trees and vine and, still further, into a boat – finally 'turned over' as fish are finally caught by this roundabout method. In combining his direct with his indirect labour efforts, Crusoe's investment increases his capacity to catch fish.

Now, even by the simple illustrations of baking bread and catching fish, relationships are shown to be sufficiently 'complex' to render it 'seriously misleading' to 'treat one part of capital as being permanent, and the other part as involving no waiting whatever' (Hayek, 1941, p. 330). Indeed, while capital stock (tractor, plough and Crusoe's boat) may have the appearance of permanence, even the most durable item of capital will depreciate in use, through natural deterioration and with obsolescence. In stressing this impermanence, Hayek places the greater emphasis upon circulating (rather than durable) capital. Circulating capital:

> possesses the characteristics of capital in a higher degree than fixed capital, and ... those theories which tend to stress the importance of goods in process rather than of durable goods have contributed more to the understanding of the important problems in this field. (Hayek, 1941, p. 330)

The reasons are: that inputs are necessary to produce outputs; that inputs are used up (however slowly) in their contribution to production; and that time is required both to apply inputs and to obtain outputs. At some stage, all elements of capital (tractor, plough, Crusoe's boat, wheat grindstone, yeast, water, oven and the wage fund) become transformed into final consumption goods (bread and fish). At the end of its period of circulation – as final consumption goods are eventually sold at market – capital is 'turned over' and released in 'free form' (as income) and becomes available either for reinvestment or for commitment elsewhere. Changes in the deployment of capital stock are achieved through this release of capital in free form as income together with the application of new saving from income.

Changes in the deployment of capital over time 'mainly depend on the foresight of the entrepreneur capitalist' whose main function is 'to attempt to maintain his capital so that it will yield the greatest possible return' (Hayek, 1941, p. 332). Entrepreneurs with the greatest perception gain at the expense of others but, in the uncertain world, new capital may be financed as much from unanticipated windfall capital gains as from income generated by normal business success. With poor entrepreneurship and business losses, investments are unlikely to be repeated in those areas where yields were low. Contrariwise, the gains to successful entrepreneurship release funds for further investments in areas of high yield, 'which means not only that new capital is formed in place of that lost elsewhere, but that it is formed exactly where it is most needed, and placed in the hands of those most qualified to use it' (Hayek, 1941, p. 333).

Capital is heterogeneous, existing in many different forms and the incentives to invest are equally diverse; but, since every investment has some impact upon the market valuation of output across all stages of production, investments are necessarily interdependent.

Investment delivers consumption goods across a wide range of near and distant future periods. For example, current investments might be directed to provide a new ferry for next year and a bridge five years hence, when the ferry may (or may not) be rendered obsolete. Against a limitless range of possibilities, the most important consideration concerns the compatibility of components within a capitalistic structure of production as it is developed continuously in the face of changing incentives and new opportunities. Hayek points to the narrower confines for a coherent configuration of capital goods than for consumption goods. Whereas price adjustments make it relatively easy to sell any consumption good that is brought to market, in regard to capital goods, 'there are definite proportionalities between the different parts of the capitalistic structure of production, which must be preserved if those parts are not to become completely useless' (Hayek, 1941, p. 25).

For example, however much the price of a railway locomotive is reduced, an absence of rail track leaves that investment with a very low yield. Only in a static world might it be possible to link a given stock of capital uniquely to a given constant stream of income. If a unit of input were relocated from a shorter to a longer period of investment, this would raise the stream of output forthcoming at a later date and reduce the stream of output at an earlier date. The value of those two output streams would be correspondingly affected; and so, too, would the respective yields on the shorter (less roundabout) and the longer (more roundabout) investments. This is a general feature and the context for two related and important issues. How is the productivity of capital explained; and how might the aggregate stock of capital be quantified?

HOW CAPITAL IS PRODUCTIVE

Capital is used because roundabout methods raise production above the capacity of direct labour methods. So, where lies the source by which machine-X has a greater productive capacity than the 100 labour-years that it takes to build; 'why should the more time-consuming methods of production yield a greater return? Ever since the time when it was first put forward, this proposition as been the source of endless confusion' (Hayek, 1941, p. 60).

(It still is.) The advantages that might be gained from a roundabout method of production are often confused with those that can arise from the division of labour or from technical progress. Technical progress is separate and distinct from the application of a roundabout method. The yield from a roundabout method per se is not derived from superior technology. Indeed, the choice of a method of production might be taken in the context of a given state of knowledge.

The introduction of capital lengthens the period of production. While greater efficiency might derive from the division of labour – the performance of a given set of operations by a larger number of men – this would shorten the period of production. Even so (and this may explain the confusion), the division of labour might accompany the introduction of a more roundabout production process, since 'it becomes possible to use certain capacities, materials and tools which could not have been used if all the labour had to be applied in the way that would give the final result by the shortest possible route' (Hayek, 1941, p. 71). Here a distinction is drawn between the vertical division of labour (through a series of successive processes) and the horizontal division of labour (which involves the simultaneous application of different skills). Only the former would necessitate an extension to the period of production and, thereby, contribute to the yield attributable to capital per se.

In principle, a new technique or a more effective division of labour should be discounted as explanations of a positive yield from the use of a roundabout method; each of these would as readily apply to a direct labour method. In practical terms, however, capital might be essential to facilitate those gains (in which case the contribution of capital would be inseparable from that of technology or skill specialization).

Beyond the role of capital as a vehicle for new techniques or in allowing a greater division of labour and skill specialization, Hayek points to 'one general fact' to explain the productivity gain from roundabout methods; namely, that:

> there will almost always exist potential but unused resources which could be made to yield a useful return, but only after some time; and that the exploitation of such resources will usually require that other resources, which could yield a return immediately or in the near future, have to be used in order to make these other resources yield any return at all. This simple fact fully suffices to explain why there will always be possibilities of increasing the output

obtained from the available resources by investing some of them for longer periods. (Hayek, 1941, p. 60)

So, for Hayek, the greater productive capacity of machine-X derives from the latent resources (whose use would otherwise be non-viable) that are drawn into the production process. Capital investment creates economic resources out of non-economic 'resources'; and, from the released potential of the latter, further opportunities to enhance productive capacity may arise:

> There are always an infinite number of natural forces which are capable of being turned to some human use, and which are in this sense potential or latent resources ... the reason why resources which are capable of being turned to some useful purpose are not actually ... so used is that they would have to be combined with other resources which are more urgently needed elsewhere. (Hayek, 1941, pp. 60–61)

The absence of illustrative examples in *The Pure Theory* might have been expected. Waterpower is introduced here to serve that purpose. Even as a farming community chooses to set aside foodstuffs (as a wage fund) to support the construction of its first waterwheel and mill house, time must elapse before development raises riverbank sites to the status of economic resources. Once they are fully occupied, any further increase in demand would allow riverbank sites to command an economic rent.

In the earliest stage, the illustration shows how 'investments' constitute 'only the services of those resources which might also have given an immediate return' (Hayek, 1941, p. 63); that is, final consumption goods in the form of foodstuffs. Then, during the period of construction of the waterwheel and mill house, the output of final consumption goods must fall as direct labour is diverted to work elsewhere; but eventually waterpower not only delivers an enhanced capacity to produce final consumption goods, it may also present further opportunities to draw other previously uneconomic resources into the productive process; and so, 'as investment proceeds more and more of those natural resources which were only potential resources are utilised and gradually drawn into the circle of scarce goods, and have in their turn to be counted as investments' (Hayek, 1941, p. 64).

More generally, the use of roundabout processes might also release the potential of latent techniques, latent specialization of labour and latent raw materials.

THE STOCK OF CAPITAL

In physical terms, the overall capitalistic structure of production undergoes continuous change as entrepreneurs set their investments according to their expectations and anticipations of yield from different choices regarding future production and income. Since those decisions constantly redefine the values of the components that comprise the aggregate stock of capital, this brings into question the (neoclassical) notion of a measurable quantum of capital.

A roundabout method is defined by the requirement for time to produce plant and machinery, together with the time of its productive life. A simple average period of production (suggested by Böhm-Bawerk) is possible when inputs and outputs flow at a constant rate. The application of compound interest (suggested by Wicksell) brings some refinement to the concept. However, the measurement difficulties are intractable, and it remained for Hayek to show that the quest for an unambiguous quantum was futile:

> there is no way in which the variety of technical periods during which we wait, either for the products of different kinds of input or for particular units of the product, can be combined into an aggregate or average which can be regarded as a technical datum. No matter what procedure we were to adopt, the same technical combination of different inputs would, under different conditions, appear to correspond to different aggregate or average periods, and from among the different combinations sometimes another would appear to be the 'longer'. (Hayek, 1941, p. 145)

Hayek's elucidations show that the 'supply of capital' can be described only in 'terms of the totality of all the alternative income streams between which the existence of a certain stock of non-permanent resources (together with the expected flow of input) enables us to choose' (Hayek, 1941, p. 147). Together with various combinations of other resources, each constituent part of the stock of capital may be used in many different ways; but the sacrifice made in order to achieve any particular income stream can be stated only in terms of the potential income streams that might otherwise have been achieved.

As the output stream at an earlier date falls when resources are reallocated to a longer-term project, 'the value of the marginal products of units of input invested for that earlier date increases, with the result that it becomes profitable to invest more for that date' (Hayek, 1941, pp. 190–91). However, this is as far as it is possible to take the notion of a marginal productivity of capital, because capital is only periodically available in a free form, to be applied readily in an endless variety of different uses. Entrepreneurs optimize their aggregate yield by equating yields at the margin; but the valuation of their capital (and, hence, the quantum of capital; or, in Hayek's original terminology, the 'aggregate figure of the amount of waiting') is an outcome of their deliberation, rather than a datum against which to make their decision:

> In order to arrive at an aggregate figure of the amount of waiting involved in each process we have to assign different weights to the different units of input, and these weights must necessarily be expressed in terms of value. But the relative values of the different kinds of input will inevitably depend on the rate of interest, so that such an aggregate cannot be regarded as something that is independent of, or as a datum determining, the rate of interest. (Hayek, 1941, p. 143)

However, those comments were unheeded by the participants in a long needless dispute that extended beyond a decade into the early 1970s.

THE CAPITAL THEORY CONTROVERSY

Capital was central from the earliest stages in the development of 'classical economics' to the analysis of the distribution, accumulation and growth processes of a capitalist economy. The respective shares of wages and profits were regarded as the outcome of historical social class relationships. This contrasts sharply with neoclassical economics, where the application of marginal analysis to factor markets drives the conclusion that, as more of a factor is hired, its marginal productivity falls as its marginal hire cost rises. If the former exceeds the latter, factors are hired; and if the latter exceeds the former, factors are fired. Hence the neoclassical conclusion: the real value of the hire cost of a factor tends to reflect the marginal productive contribution of the last factor hired or fired.

In pointing to the result that the aggregate amount of heterogeneous capital is quantifiable only by the discounted present value of its prospective future product, Joan Robinson (1953) initiated the capital theory controversy. Equilibrium within the neoclassical paradigm requires the marginal product of capital to be known; which requires the quantum of capital to be known; which requires the remuneration of capital to be known; which requires the marginal product of capital to be known. In short: the quantum of capital employed is decided by its marginal productivity; but its marginal productivity is decided by the quantum of capital employed. This was not new. Frank Knight had indicated the problem in 1936:

> Difficulty and complexity arise because the relation between capital and interest take different forms and especially because of the danger of circular reasoning. On the one hand, capital is usually and properly defined as 'income' capitalized at some 'rate of return'. But the interest rate is usually thought of as the ratio between the net annual yield and a quantity of capital. On the face of it, this is a vicious circle; interest cannot be a rate of return; i.e. a ratio to a principal, unless the terms of the ratio are definable independently of the rate return itself, yet in the same units of both numerator and denominator. (Knight, 1936, p. 433)

And, thereafter, the feature was incorporated (as indicated by the citation above) into Hayek's subsequent work. Yet, Knight and Hayek feature neither in the debates nor in the definitive summary (see Harcourt, 1972) of the futile and protracted Cambridge controversies in the theory of capital.

The attack (from Cambridge, England) upon the 'profound truths' of the neoclassical 'parables' (see Harcourt, 1972: p. 122) was an attack upon an easy but inappropriate opponent, whose own defence (from Cambridge, Massachusetts) was predicated upon the simplistic timeless notion of constrained optimization. The respective paradigms have little common ground. Indeed, the neoclassical concept of a factor's marginal product is irretrievably lost, once production is acknowledged to be a series of outputs following upon a series of inputs. Within the Austrian framework, many of the issues raised in the controversies have little relevance; these include the distribution of income between homogeneous factors of production and the quantification of capital. Many other issues, relating to the admission of capital as a factor of production, to the ideological stances taken in respect of capitalism, to the incentives for capital accumulation, to the array of choice requiring investment decisions, and to the causes and consequences of economic growth, were already adequately addressed within the Austrian framework.

HAYEK'S RIVER ANALOGY

Whereas *The Pure Theory of Capital* is short on illustration, Hayek later employed a river analogy to deliver a revealing insight into the complex time-lapse relationships that may exist between investments and the output of final consumption goods (Hayek, 1983). Tributaries flowing into the upper reaches of a river deliver ever-changing volumes of water. These are analogous to flows of new and replacement investment that are determined by relative factor prices, technological change and the interest rate. Analogous to a constant rainfall (but changing dispersion) within the catchment of the river and its tributaries are variations in the allocation of investment funds to diverse projects of different life duration. In the broadest perspective, the river represents the structure of capitalistic production that (given the dispersion of rainfall) delivers varying volumes of water (supply of final goods) quite independently of the level of the tide (demand for final goods) in the estuary. Of course, though independently determined, spontaneous adjustments to prices and supply volumes are expected where supply and demand are not in equilibrium.

Hayek's most important claim is his denial of a direct causal relationship between sales of consumption goods and changes in the upper reaches of the stream of capitalistic production; and between sales of consumption goods and the level of employment. So, Hayek rejects the Keynesian argument that the path to full employment might begin with general measures to boost consumers' expenditure; that a modest increase in consumption goods' prices would encourage new investments and employment. Both theoretically and empirically, there is no single correspondence between sales of final goods and changes in the upper reaches. Indeed, Hayek believed it to be more generally the case that a revival of final demand in a slump was 'an effect rather than a cause of a revival in the upper reaches of the stream of production' (Hayek, 1983, p. 46). That initial impetus is most likely to emerge through spontaneous entrepreneurship – alertness to opportunities and anticipation of change – in the widest sense:

> if entrepreneurs . . . never altered their plans until after a change in final demand (or any other change) had actually occurred . . . the adaptation of production to change would be so expensive as to make it in many cases impossible . . . because the capital available for investment in new forms would be so scarce. (Hayek, 1941, p. 330)

CAPITAL INVESTMENT, MONETARY DISEQUILIBRIUM AND THE BUSINESS CYCLE

Intertemporal preferences determine the pace of capital investment and the extent of capital accumulation. Only by sacrificing the production of final consumption goods are resources diverted (as saving) to investment projects. The vital need for any community to maintain minimum levels of sustenance determines: (1) the maximum rate of input into a wage fund (that is, saving in order to provide the resources to undertake investment); and, by implication; (2) the lowest value to which positive time preference (that is, the discount rate) might fall; and (3) the maximum rate of economic growth (that is, the increase in productive capacity through capital accumulation). All are inextricably tied. Where consumers' choices set the discount rate above the minimum vital level, saving is below the maximum attainable level and capital accumulates at less than the maximum rate. Choice determines the rate of capital accumulation: if more jam is consumed today, less jam can be produced tomorrow. Yet, capital's inherent productivity can influence that choice: the more enticing is the jam promised for tomorrow, the greater the amount of today's consumption that is likely to be postponed.

The decision to lengthen the process of roundabout methods of production makes it possible to obtain a greater volume of final goods from a given outlay; but these goods reach the market at a later date than the lesser volume of goods from a shorter process. Whether it is more profitable to maintain or to alter the structure of production depends upon the balance between the prices received for final output at different dates and the cost of providing capital. In a setting of diverse capital stock of different life duration, the situation is complex in that a redirection of investments may lead to different outcomes at different dates in terms of the stock of capital and the level of output.

The ultimate yield of any particular investment is determined by many factors including a multitude of unrelated decisions taken by many individuals. In general, the success of any particular investment depends upon how well each production plan fits within a structure to which every plan contributes. Machines are potentially commercially viable when their productive capacity is greater than that of the labour needed to build them. In using capital, time is required both to build and to realize the potential of machines; so, their commercial viability rests upon the time discount factor. When roundabout methods are used, resources are committed (in early stages of production) some time before final consumption goods (from late stages of production) are ready for market. This implies that 'backing' (someone's saving) is needed for the enterprise. The alternative source of finance – bank credit – gives the linkage to Hayek's monetary theory of the business cycle.

Financial markets allow potential creditors (that is, savers who supply 'loanable funds') and debtors (that is, investors, who demand 'loanable funds') to trade to mutual advantage. The natural rate of interest is the price that equalizes the demand for loans with the supply of credit. Whereas saving (that is, the non-consumption of current production) allows the transfer of purchasing power from income recipients to potential investors, the provision of bank credit involves no tangible resource transfer. Rather, bank credit creates purchasing power with no resource backing.

Although the natural rate of interest rises with any increased demand for loanable funds, an expansion of bank credit would hold the market rate below the level of the natural rate. As the amount of bank credit varies (both rising and falling), the market rate of interest diverges (both negatively and positively) from the natural rate of interest. So, if bankers apply set commercial criteria for extending credit, any bunching of investment opportunities (arising, say, from advances in technology or product development) could lead to a bunching of bank credit. In that circumstance, it would be likely for the market rate of interest to be forced below the natural rate. When the process of bank credit creation is terminated – as commercial banks hit the constraint of their finite reserve assets, or as the central bank restricts the supply of reserve assets in order to maintain the value and (hence) acceptability of high-powered money – the market rate of interest would be forced above the natural rate.

Variations in the process of bank credit creation disturb the natural state of equilibrium in the market for loanable funds. The application of capital theory in a context of monetary disequilibria is the key element in Hayek's business cycle theory, which views production as an intertemporal sequence of stages: investment goods are produced at stages that are early in relation to the eventual emergence of consumption goods. Whenever there is an increased willingness to save, the natural rate of interest falls, so raising the incentive to invest in early stages of production. New saving provides resources to create capitalistic (roundabout) methods of production and to deliver sustainable economic growth (that is, permanently higher levels of output of consumption goods, when roundabout methods eventually come on line).

The origins of intertemporal economic instability (the business cycle of boom and slump) derive from the monetary instability that is associated with variations in bank credit creation. When new bank credit holds the market rate of interest below the natural rate, the monetary theory of business cycles shows there to be too much investment (overinvestment) and the wrong type of investment (malinvestment). Overinvestment occurs because 'the case most frequently to be encountered' (Hayek, 1967, p. 54) is where new bank credit primarily delivers additional purchasing power to investor-debtors. That increased demand for investment goods diverts resources from the production of consumption goods. Too few consumption goods are produced and there is too much investment. Malinvestment occurs because unnaturally low interest rates give an extra incentive to invest in the very earliest stages of production: too much investment is directed to early stages of production, and too little is directed to late stages of production. The forces setting the incentive to overinvest and to malinvest are examined in the next section.

When new bank credit holds the market rate of interest below the natural rate, more resources are in demand for investment purposes, but the incentive to save is diminished. The corollary of that reduced saving is an increased demand for consumption goods. Initially, this is likely to be met from stock, from the existing structure of production and from other practical considerations:

> capital and labor can be employed more intensely than is possible on a sustainable basis. Routine maintenance of machinery can be postponed and the machinery can be kept running more hours per day or more days per week than usual. Additional workers can be drawn into the labor force, some workers can work overtime, and others can postpone retirement. These considerations allow for the production of both investment goods and consumption goods to increase simultaneously but, of course, not on a sustainable basis. (Garrison, 2004, pp. 335–6)

It is because Hayek's business cycle theory is built upon the assumption that factors of production are fully employed that simultaneous increases in demand for investment goods and consumption goods are incompatible, so that something must give. Ultimately the attempts to save less and to consume more are thwarted (as 'forced saving') by the diversion of resources from the (late-stage) production of consumption goods to the (early-stage) production of investment goods. 'Forced saving' delivers the necessary real resources for the capital investments that are encouraged by new bank credit and, thereby, create shortages in the supply of consumption goods.

The overall effect is intertemporal disequilibria; that is, inconsistent patterns between the implied schedules of supply and demand for consumption goods, with excessive demands in the present and excessive supplies in the future. In this scenario, the general tendency is for current prices of consumption goods to rise, with subsequent consequences for incentives to invest such that, even with the diversion of real resources to the production of investment goods, the growth that is stimulated is unsustainable.

AN ILLUSTRATION

A numerical illustration shows the twin forces that are at work. There is the interest rate effect that is caused by bank credit creation; and there is the relative prices effect that is caused by shortages in the supply of consumption goods. Consider two roundabout production methods: one (single late stage) delivers net revenue of £110.00 after one year; and the other (single early stage) delivers £259.37 after ten years. (In a primitive Crusoe context, these might be the alternatives of collecting saplings for immediate use as fuel and planting saplings to deliver mature trees for use as fuel.) At a 10 per cent discount rate, the capitalized values (£100) of the net revenue from each project are identical:

$$£100.00 = £110.00 \times (1.1000)^{-1}$$
$$£100.00 = £259.37 \times (1.1000)^{-10}$$

Now, with an expansion of bank credit that causes the discount rate to fall to 8 per cent, the capitalized values would rise to £101.85 for the late-stage project and to £120.14 for the early-stage project:

$$£101.85 = £110.00 \times (1.0800)^{-1}$$
$$£120.14 = £259.37 \times (1.0800)^{-10}$$

This illustrates how a reduction in the discount rate gives an extra incentive to invest in the earlier stage of production.

The consequential incentive to divert resources (from the late to the early stage) would have the subsequent effect of creating a shortfall in the supply of consumption goods and a general tendency for their prices to rise. Now, if those higher prices were to increase net revenues from the sale of consumption goods by (say) 3 per cent (so as to raise net revenues from £110.00 to £113.30 and from £259.37 to £267.16, respectively), the capitalized values (at a 10 per cent discount rate) would also rise by 3 per cent from £100.00 to £103.00. However (assuming that the capital outlay required for each project remains unchanged at £100.00) the internal rate of return from the late-stage project would rise to 13.30 per cent, as compared with a rise to only 10.33 per cent for the early-stage project:

$$£100.00 = £113.30 \times (1.1330)^{-1}$$
$$£100.00 = £276.16 \times (1.1033)^{-10}$$

This illustrates how an increase in the prices of consumption goods (relative to the prices of associated investment goods) gives a greater incentive to invest in the late-stage project; that greater incentive derives from the possibility of repeated investments earning 13.30 per cent, with the potential to net £348.58 over ten years:

$$£348.58 = £100.00 \times (1.1330)^{10}$$

a sum whose capitalized value of £134.39,

$$£134.39 = £348.58 \times (1.1000)^{-10}$$

is directly comparable with that of only £103.00 for the early stage project.

To summarize: a fall in the discount rate gives an incentive to invest in the more roundabout method (early stage) of production; and a rise in the prices of consumption goods (in relation to the capital outlay necessary to produce them) gives an incentive to invest in the less roundabout method (late stage) of production. Now, if the initial reduction in the discount rate were caused by bank credit creation, these results (generalized) allow a business cycle theory to be built upon capital theory and the impact of two price distortions: the interest rate effect and the relative prices effect.

BUSINESS CYCLES: THEORY AND PRACTICE

Hayek's business cycle theory shows how intertemporal distortions to the price mechanism can adversely affect a market economy. So long as bank credit creation holds the market rate of interest below the natural rate, incentives exist (the interest rate effect) to divert investment from late stages of production (that is, from the more imminent production of consumption goods) to early stages of production (that is, to the less imminent production of consumption goods). Even once that diversion of resources is under way, intermediate goods previously and irrevocably committed might sustain the flow of consumption goods for some time; but, sooner or later, this must end. As resources continue to be diverted to early stages, a scarcity of consumption goods is inevitable, so creating a tendency for consumption goods prices to rise in relation to the prices of investment goods (the relative prices effect). Ultimately, with the eventual cessation of bank credit creation, a period of readjustment begins as (with the market rate now rising) investment incentives become redirected to favour late stages of production.

PRICE EXPECTATIONS

With the development of business cycle theory in the 1930s, the relevance of a constant proportional rate, as against an accelerating rate, of monetary expansion was debated; but the role of price expectations was neglected. At one extreme, in the absence of price expectations, it is a logical proposition that, '[i]f capital is to become progressively deeper, inflation must accelerate, but . . . a constant proportional rate of monetary expansion would suffice to sustain and render viable a once and for all step change in the time structure of production' (Laidler, 1994, pp. 12–13). At the other extreme, if agents fully adjust their behaviour according to rationally formed price expectations so that prices move instantaneously to new equilibrium levels, the key issue of whether 'further injections of bank credit' might 'enable the economy finally to achieve and then to sustain indefinitely a more roundabout structure of production', invites the 'standard Austrian argument that attempts to stave off trouble by further credit creation would lead to rising inflation and the ultimate collapse of the currency' (Laidler, 1994, p. 11).

Keynes's *General Theory* had encouraged central bankers to pursue 'the policy of an autonomous rate of interest, unimpeded by international preoccupations' (Keynes, 1936, p. 349). In that macroeconomic context, monetary disturbances to real economic activity were less likely to be the unwitting and unintended consequence of established commercial banking practice. They were intended to achieve real macroeconomic objectives; but while fully fledged Keynesian economics subsequently invoked the full paraphernalia of monetary and fiscal demand management policies, the goal of full employment without inflation proved elusive. Even as aspirations became progressively diminished through the last quarter of the century, the one instrument left in play – the interest rate – was, and continues to be, routinely tailored as if it were relevant to the amelioration of every perceived macroeconomic underperformance.

Now, in regard to the issue of whether economic growth fostered by bank credit creation is necessarily unsustainable, the outcome turns on whether forced saving delivers sufficient real resources to meet capital investment commitments in full. The issue is whether investment projects, encouraged at relatively early stages of production by monetary expansion, might be completed, either before a monetary expansion is curtailed, or before rises in the prices of consumption goods switch incentives to favour late stages of investment. In the primitive context of Robinson Crusoe having set aside (as saving) some fish, in order to provide time to build a boat (committing resources to an early stage of production), an inadequate amount of saving would soon be apparent and cause Crusoe to revert to fishing (recommitting resources to a late stage of production). In a less primitive context, the principle remains: real resources are necessary to undertake real capital investments. Given the direction of bank credit creation that is presumed by Hayek's business cycle theory (placing new buying power in the hands of investor-debtors), real resources are diverted from late to early stages of production, and an investment boom is initiated. Given the presumption that bank credit creation cannot extend indefinitely, simple practicalities suggest that some investment projects would be completed (before a monetary expansion is curtailed, or before rises in the prices of consumption goods switch incentives to favour later stages of investment) and that some would be left unfinished (like Crusoe's boat).

Projects, whose capital completely turns over, before the market rate of interest reverts to the higher natural rate, would be retrospectively viewed as sound investments. Those that come on-line, but are still time-discounting future earnings as the market rate of interest begins its rise towards the natural rate, less so. At the furthest extreme, some projects would be abandoned on the basis that sunk costs are no justification for further commitments. Yet, in retrospect, such a boom would have proven no less sustainable than one drawing from simultaneous reductions in the market and natural rates of interest; that is, a boom initiated by an increase in voluntary saving. The explanation lies with three practicalities: that the (macroeconomic) saving function is not robust; that saving is intertemporally unpredictable; and that every historical increase in real voluntary saving (in proportion to income) has always been reversed. It might even be argued that bank credit creation gives a more reliable basis (in terms of duration) for investment decisions; but that case would be a misleading diversion. Even with the most favourable outcome to a bank credit-led investment boom, the overall situation would be one where too few consumption goods are produced sooner rather than later, and too many consumption goods are produced (or were planned to be produced) later rather than sooner. This, rather than whether a bank credit-led investment boom is or is not sustainable, is the more telling point.

Investment per se is not necessarily a good thing; not even if, by the sacrifice of jam today, a greater abundance of jam is gained tomorrow. That outcome would be desirable only if it were desired. So, although a credit-led investment boom might be capable of sustaining a higher economic growth rate, the net benefits accruing to consumers would be negative: the benefit from an increased future volume of consumption goods would be more than countered by the negative impact of forced saving. It is because new bank credit is never distributed uniformly across all sections of the community that relative prices are affected and the efficiency of a market economy compromised. However, with a bank credit-led consumption boom, the interest rate effect and the relative prices effect would be active simultaneously and with offsetting tendencies. So, the particular distortions that were emphasized in the 1930s would have less emphasis today.

DISPENSING WITH KEYNES: INVESTMENT INCENTIVES AND THE MULTIPLIER

Hayek represents Keynes's idea – that new investment is profitable only when there is an increase in consumers' demand – as 'part of the same widespread fallacy to which the businessman is especially prone' (Hayek, 1978, p. 213). The error lies in applying what holds for a single industry, to industry as a whole:

> While, of course, the relative magnitude of the demand for equipment of a particular industry will depend upon the demand for the product of that industry, it is certainly not true to say that the demand for capital goods in general is directly determined by the magnitude of the demand for consumers' goods. (Hayek, 1935, p. 143)

Any dependency of investment upon consumption applies only to existing techniques; it cannot be relevant to 'investment which can increase productivity per head of worker by equipping a given labour force with more capital equipment' (Hayek, 1978, p. 213). That first possibility might relate, for example, to investing in an additional shop (with an assistant) to meet an increased demand for sweets; and the second possibility might relate to investment in automatic sweet dispensers. The latter would be 'encouraged by low product (consumer good) prices (which make it necessary to save on labour costs) and discouraged by high ones' (Hayek, 1978, p. 213). Indeed, by Hayek's formal analysis, a general rise in consumption goods' prices enhances the relative profitability of less roundabout processes, and vice versa.

Hayek's economic theory is predicated upon the assumption of full employment, which he defends as relevant even to an economy in recession:

> An analysis on the assumption of full employment, even if the assumption is only partially valid, at least helps us to understand the functioning of the price mechanism, the significance of the relations between different prices and of the factors which lead to changes in these relations. But the assumption that all goods and factors are available in excess makes the whole price system redundant, undetermined and unintelligible. (Hayek, 1972, p. 103)

Where resources are fully employed, there is an obvious trade-off between the provision of goods for current consumption and the provision of goods for future consumption. Advance through economic growth can be achieved only by present sacrifice. Any attempt to force growth by monetary expansion has immediate inflationary implications that cannot be ignored. Yet, according to Keynes's *General Theory*, this difficulty is absent in the presence of widespread unemployment among productive factors.

Keynes argues that, with high unemployment, a bond-financed credit-led investment boom could achieve quantity adjustments (that is, higher levels of output) without the consequences that derive from forced saving. This is not to say that consumption goods prices would not be affected. Indeed, more highly priced consumption goods were expected to reflect diminishing returns to labour and higher unit costs. Involuntarily unemployed labour would acquiesce in the real wage reductions that this implies, and so there would be no inflationary impetus. However, the case was made by default, because Keynes failed to show the processes of adjustment. Investment instantaneously raises aggregate real income and the instantaneous multiplier provides the exact amount of new saving to finance the original investment. However, in admitting the practical limitations of this instantaneous multiplier, Keynes discusses the extreme case, where new investment expenditure is a total surprise so that, in the first instance, no additional consumption goods are available to meet the increase in demand. Then, 'the efforts of those newly employed in the capital-goods industries to consume a proportion of their increased incomes will raise the prices of consumption-goods ... causing a postponement of consumption' (Keynes, 1936, p. 123).

Keynes saw the postponement of consumption ('forced saving') as temporary, lasting for the time necessary to allow consumption goods industries to increase their production. Consumption would then rise above its normal level – to compensate for the temporary postponement – before reverting back to that normal level. While recognizing that these adjustments were relevant to the analysis of business cycles, Keynes maintains that they do not 'in any way affect the significance of the theory of the multiplier ... nor render it inapplicable as an indicator of the total benefit to employment to be expected from an expansion in the capital-goods industries' (Keynes, 1936, p. 124).

And, as if haunted by this problem, he states that 'Price-instability arising in this way does not lead to the kind of profit stimulus which is liable to bring into existence excess capacity' (Keynes, 1936, p. 288). Why not? For some unexplained reason, the unexpected abnormal profits would be universally recognized to be windfall gains accruing to those just fortunate enough to have products 'at a relatively advanced stage of production'.

Keynes describes no route that avoids the consequences of forced saving. Furthermore, his 'aggregations conceal the most fundamental mechanisms of change' (Hayek, 1931, p. 277) and implicitly deny the importance of the composition of any idle resources that are readily available. Appropriate resources must be immediately at hand in the form of factors of production, in the form of work in progress at every stage of completion and in the form of consumption goods. Only then might there be no bottlenecks or shortfalls in levels of production to meet new demands from formerly unemployed workers. Yet, the message of Keynes's *General Theory* is that higher levels of investment might be financed by monetary expansion; that is, without inflation and without any significant shortfall in the provision of consumption goods.

Such events are only made possible by the unrealistic assumption of elastic and appropriate supplies of factor inputs and intermediate products. That such propositions were countenanced reflects upon the limited objectives of Keynes's *General Theory*. Investment appraisal, periods of gestation, cash flow, pay-back periods, and problems of finance are not pertinent to the problem of raising aggregate expenditure to a level that generates full employment. That narrow focus has led, and continues to lead, economic policy to be targeted upon full employment, with little consideration of the consequences for the composition of production or the implications for cyclical activity or economic growth.

HAYEK'S ACHIEVEMENT

Hayek's intention was for *The Pure Theory of Capital* to provide a basis from which to elucidate the function of capital in a money economy. That second stage was never achieved. In retrospect, Hayek believed that Austrian capital theory had stalled and he regretted that others had not been drawn to the task (Hayek, 1994, p. 96). Yet, while Hayek's contribution in advancing Austrian capital theory is acknowledged to contain 'some of the most penetrating thoughts on the subject that have ever been published' (Machlup, 1976, p. 29), a general view is that it provides 'little in the way of specific constructive results' (Steedman, 1994, p. 23), being an exercise in pure logic and of 'doubtful practical value' (Fletcher, 1989, p. 246). So, although *The Pure Theory of Capital* is described as 'a remarkable contribution to knowledge', that assessment is qualified by the fact that it is 'inconceivable that any statistical or practical use can be made of the Austrian theory of capital' (Shackle, 1981, p. 250).

There is no argument in relation to statistics. *The Pure Theory of Capital* does not lend itself to applied statistical work and that is enough to condemn it to modern eyes:

> To an economist today . . . only that is true which can be proved statistically, and everything that cannot be demonstrated by statistics can be neglected . . . the modern fashion demands that a theoretical assertion which cannot be statistically tested must not be taken seriously and has to be disregarded. (Hayek, 1975, pp. 6–7)

And yet:

> Nobody would probably seriously contend that statistics can elucidate even the comparatively not very complex structures of organic molecules, and few would argue that it can help us to explain the functioning of organisms. Yet, when it comes to accounting for the functioning of social structures, that belief is widely held. (Hayek, 1967, p. 31)

In advancing Austrian capital theory beyond the early fraught attempts to achieve meaningful quantification, Hayek's work achieved much deeper insights into the structures of capitalistic production. The quality that distinguishes Austrian capital theory from the more widely appreciated neoclassical theory of production is its close proximity to entrepreneurial experience. Business practice recognizes that time is essential to the gestation of capital; and, thereafter, that production and earnings extend into a finite and uncertain future. These features are fundamental to entrepreneurial activity. Rational entrepreneurial decisions – to incorporate (present and future levels of) costs, the (present and future levels of) availability of labour, plant and machinery, the (present and future levels of) interest rates, periods of gestation and the duration of earnings – are captured by Austrian theory. By contrast, the out-of-time constrained optimization of neoclassical theory offers no basis to analyse entrepreneurial activity. With that appreciation of *The Pure Theory of Capital*, a paradox is resolved: that an exercise in pure logic should be deemed too realistic to serve as a tool for analysis: 'Degrees of realism range from K (for capital) to an aerial photograph of the Rust Belt. K is too simple; everything from the Pure Theory to the aerial photograph is too realistic' (Garrison, 2001, p. 11).

If simplification is to be judged by the versatility of theory in practical application, *The Pure Theory of Capital* is certainly too complicated (or realistic) either to deliver tractable microeconomic conclusions or to serve macroeconomic forecasting. However, in revealing the deficiencies of earlier presentations and in pointing to its own omissions, *The Pure Theory of Capital* propagates the important message that dynamic complexity is rarely overstated and – for the same reason – that economic coordination is mostly likely to be achieved in the highest practical degree as a spontaneous order within a liberal market system of production and exchange.

REFERENCES

Fletcher, Gordon A. (1989), *The Keynesian Revolution and Its Critics*, 2nd edn, London: Macmillan.
Garrison, Roger W. (2001), *Time and Money: The Macroeconomics of Capital Structure*, London, UK and New York, USA: Routledge.
Garrison, Roger W. (2004), 'Overconsumption and forced saving in the Mises–Hayek theory of the business cycle', *History of Political Economy*, 36 (2), 323–49.
Harcourt, Geoffrey C. (1972), *Some Cambridge Controversies in the Theory of Capital*, London: Cambridge University Press.
Hayek, Friedrich A. (1931), 'Reflections on the pure theory of money of Mr J.M. Keynes, part 1, *Economica*, 11 (33), 270–95.

Hayek, Friedrich A. (1933), *Monetary Theory and the Trade Cycle*, London: Jonathan Cape.
Hayek, Friedrich A. (1935), *Prices and Production*, 2nd edn, revised and enlarged, London: Routledge & Kegan Paul.
Hayek, Friedrich A. (1939), 'Profits, interest and investment', *Profits, Interest and Investment and other Essays on the Theory of Industrial Fluctuations*, London: Routledge, pp. 3–72
Hayek, Friedrich A. (1941), *The Pure Theory of Capital*, Chicago, IL: University of Chicago Press.
Hayek, Friedrich A. (1967), *Studies in Philosophy, Politics, and Economics*, London and Henley: Routledge & Kegan Paul.
Hayek, Friedrich A. (1972), *A Tiger by the Tail*, London: Institute of Economic Affairs.
Hayek, Friedrich A. (1975), *A Discussion with Friedrich von Hayek*, Washington, DC: American Enterprise Institute for Public Policy Research.
Hayek, Friedrich A. (1978), *New Studies in Philosophy, Politics, Economics and the History of Ideas*, London and Henley: Routledge & Kegan Paul.
Hayek, Friedrich A. (1983), 'The Austrian critique', *The Economist*, 11 June, pp. 45–8; reprinted in F.A. Hayek (1995), *Contra Keynes and Cambridge: Essays, Correspondence*, vol. IX, ed. Bruce J. Caldwell, London: Routledge, pp. 247–54.
Hayek, Friedrich A. (1994), *Hayek on Hayek: An Autobiographical Dialogue*, ed. Stephen Kresge and Leif Wenar, Chicago, IL: University of Chicago Press.
Keynes, John Maynard (1936), *The General Theory of Employment, Interest and Money*, New York: Harcourt, Brace & Company.
Knight, Frank H. (1936), 'The quantity of capital and the rate of interest', *Journal of Political Economy*, 44 (5), pp. 434–5.
Laidler, David (1994), 'Hayek on neutral money and the cycle', in M. Colonna and H. Hagemann (eds), *Capitalism, Socialism and Knowledge, The Economics of F.A. Hayek*, vol. I, Aldershot, UK and Brookfield, VT, USA: Edward Elgar, pp. 3–26.
Machlup, Fritz (1976), *Essays on Hayek*, Hillsdale, MI: Hillsdale College Press.
Robinson, Joan (1953), 'The production function and the theory of capital', *Review of Economic Studies*, 21 (2), 81–106.
Shackle, G.L.S. (1981), 'F.A. Hayek, 1899 –', in D.P. O'Brien and J.R. Presley (1984), *Pioneers of Modern Economics in Britain*, London: Macmillan Press, pp. 234–61.
Steedman, Ian (1994), 'On The Pure Theory of Capital by F.A. Hayek', in M. Colonna, H. Hagemann and O. Hamouda (eds), *Capitalism, Socialism and Knowledge, The Economics of F.A. Hayek*, vol. II, Aldershot, UK and Brookfield, VT, USA: Edward Elgar, pp. 3–25.

5. Hayek and Keynes
Roger E. Backhouse

POLITICAL PHILOSOPHY AND ECONOMIC THEORY

Friedrich Hayek and John Maynard Keynes have come to represent two sharply opposed political philosophies, thereby creating the danger that their economic theories will be interpreted against the background of the ideas currently associated with their names. The claim made in this chapter is that to read their work this way is mistaken, for their economic ideas changed significantly, even if (at least once Hayek had abandoned his youthful socialism) there was considerable continuity in their political positions. Keynes's economic theory changed, as is well known, with the *General Theory* ([1936] 1973), though the extent of his break with the past should not be exaggerated. Hayek's ideas changed significantly with his article 'Economics and knowledge' (1937), though in his case too, earlier ideas were not abandoned completely. However, although the two facets of their thinking need to be separated, their political philosophies provide important background to their economic theories.

Keynes never had great faith in the self-regulatory powers of capitalism (see Backhouse and Bateman, 2009, 2011 for more extensive discussions of his view of capitalism). The pre-1914 prosperity had been inherently fragile, as he had argued in *The Economic Consequences of the Peace* ([1919] 1971), a view confirmed by the interwar experience of economic dislocation and, eventually, mass unemployment. Throughout his career, he was concerned to find a way to manage a capitalist economy so as to mitigate its worst features. Policy could be placed in the hands of an intellectual elite, driven by a sense of duty to pursue policies that were in the public interest: the 'presuppositions of Harvey Road' (Harrod, 1972, pp. 214, 226). He also had a strong belief in the power of social science to solve the world's problems. Moreover, the government's position in the economy was such that it was an illusion to think that it could abdicate from taking responsibility for the economic situation by leaving things to market forces, even if it wished to do so. He expressed this view that government had no choice but to act most forcefully in the *Tract on Monetary Reform* ([1923] 1971) where he argued that behind all the technical arguments about monetary policy, inflation and the exchange rate, lay the reality that the government could not avoid taking a decision. He lambasted those who thought that the gold standard absolved policymakers from this task:

> In truth, the gold standard is already a barbarous relic ... Advocates of the ancient standard do not observe how remote it now is from the spirit and the requirements of the age. A regulated non-metallic standard has slipped in unnoticed. *It exists.* Whilst the economists dozed, the academic dream of a hundred years, doffing its cap and gown, clad in paper rags, has crept into the real world by means of the bad fairies – always so much more potent than the good – the wicked ministers of finance. (Keynes, [1923] 1971, p. 138)

In thinking that the gold standard absolved them from responsibility for taking a decision over the value of the currency, policymakers were deluding themselves. The only issue was whether policymakers would recognize this or would persist in the illusion that they had no responsibility to take a decision. Keynes took this idea further in 'The end of laissez faire' (1926) in which he argued that the role of the state was not to do things better than private enterprise would do them, but to do things that otherwise would not be done at all. As the 1920s went on, with high unemployment in Britain, and even more following the disaster of the Great Depression, it was clear to Keynes that the economic system was not working and the need was for an economic theory that would provide that guidance. By the *General Theory* (Ch. 24) he was arguing that the state now had to take a decision about the level of investment (though, interestingly, he wanted decisions about the allocation of investment to remain as much as possible in private hands): if government could achieve full employment, the private sector could be left to deal with the allocation of resources – the 'classical' theory would come into its own. Policymaking was always his primary concern, all his other major works being directly addressed to policy issues and so it is not accidental that, though the *General Theory* was presented as a work of economic theory, it was taken as of direct relevance to policy.

Hayek, in contrast, was converted from his youthful socialist, or social democratic, leanings by his encounter with Ludwig von Mises in the 1920s. He turned to the problem of the business cycle, offering a new theory that he developed through the 1930s, culminating in *The Pure Theory of Capital* (1941). Throughout this period he persisted in the belief that theory was fundamental, and that statistical analysis could prove little. There was, however, an important change in his theory. In the late 1920s and early 1930s his theory of the cycle was based on the theory of economic equilibrium, developed by Leon Walras and integrated with Böhm-Bawerk's capital theory by Knut Wicksell. This view was first stated clearly in two articles in 1927–28 on the theory of interest and intertemporal price movements, in which he developed the notion of an intertemporal equilibrium (Hayek, 1984, Chs 3–4). His work prior to this (Hayek, 1925, in Hayek, 1984, Ch. 1) could be seen as in the tradition of the English currency school, emphasizing the dangers of an elastic currency: though present, capital theory was marginal. The notion of intertemporal equilibrium provided the framework within which his major theory of the cycle was developed, in his *Monetary Theory and the Trade Cycle* (1933, first published in German 1929) and *Prices and Production* ([1931] 1935a). In this work the idea of intertemporal equilibrium, and beneath that the more general notion of a general equilibrium of the price system, was central in his arguments about how monetary policy could disrupt the economic system. In Hayek's debates with Keynes during the early 1930s, he was working within this framework, but prompted by his work on collectivist economic planning (Hayek, 1935b) he moved towards a radically different conception of markets as information-storing and processing mechanisms.

The changes in the theories of both Keynes and Hayek should establish clearly the dangers attached to viewing their economic theories through the lens of their political philosophies. Clearly, both believed that their economic theories supported and helped to justify, their political positions, but it is arguable that both should be seen as using economic arguments to support policies that they found attractive for philosophical, political or ethical reasons. Keynes's doubts about the stability of capitalism and the efficiency of unimpeded free enterprise could find expression in the Cambridge quantity theory framework, the Wicksellian framework of the *Treatise on Money* ([1930] 1971) or the approach of the *General Theory*, in which he attempted to break free of all 'classical' theories. In the same way, Hayek used both equilibrium theory and information theory to justify his scepticism about whether stimulating demand could do anything to improve the operation of the economic system. Thus although Keynes and Hayek were reaching opposed policy prescriptions, and at times were focusing on very different theoretical arguments, they were nevertheless thinking about the issues in ways that had much in common (see Steele, 2001). Moreover, their technical economic theories were capable of being used to support a range of policy prescriptions. To illustrate this, note that Hayek's focus on knowledge and intertemporal equilibrium could be used, as in Axel Leijonhufvud's widely read reappraisal of Keynesian economics (1968), to argue that Keynes's theory was, about an intertemporal coordination failure. Leijonhufvud argued that even though Keynes had a much better 'Gestalt-conception of what happens during business cycles' (that is, that competitive markets fail to sustain an adequate level of aggregate demand and that forces to restore full employment may be very weak) it was Hayek who had a better view of the fundamental theory (Leijonhufvud, 1968, p. 401; see Backhouse and Boianovsky, 2013)

HAYEK'S ENCOUNTERS WITH KEYNES AND KEYNESIANISM

Hayek seems to have first met Keynes in 1928 at a meeting of representatives of European business-cycle institutes (Hayek, 1994, p. 89), after which their paths crossed repeatedly till Keynes's death in 1946. Hayek was then in charge of the Vienna Institut für Konjunkturforschung, having previously worked in New York, where he had learned the latest methods of statistical cycle analysis from Wesley Clair Mitchell at Columbia. Before that, he had come from studies in law and political science. However, despite working in this environment he was skeptical about the scope for what could be achieved purely through statistical analysis and was already developing his economic theories.

By 1928, Keynes had become established as an expert on monetary economics, having leapt to prominence as a public figure in 1919 with *The Economic Consequences of the Peace*. Before that, he had obtained a Fellowship at King's College Cambridge on the basis of a philosophical thesis on the theory of probability and had made a career in the Civil Service, rising to be leader of the Treasury delegation at Versailles. Despite achieving a reputation as the economist who best understood financial relations between Britain and India (*Indian Currency and Finance*, [1913] 1971), he was hardly prominent as a major economist. In 1919, however, he became the most prominent economist of the day and during the 1920s he acquired a reputation as one of the world's leading monetary theorists.

The first public exchange between Keynes and Hayek came in 1931, after which they came to be seen as rivals. From 1931 to 1936 they and their associates were arguing over the causes of the business cycle and the appropriate remedies. During the Second World War, Keynes and Hayek came closer together, personally and intellectually, through their common concern with non-inflationary finance of the war. By the time of Keynes's death, Hayek felt able to claim Keynes as an ally against younger Keynesians. His battles were then with Keynesianism, not with Keynes personally.

One of the remarkable features of Keynesian economics was the rapidity with which Keynesian ideas spread; what one commentator (McCormick, 1992) has called 'the Keynesian avalanche'. (Some of these ideas are explored in the essays by Backhouse, Bateman, Laidler and Peden in Backhouse and Bateman, 2006.) Keynes's victory was total (cf. Dostaler,

1991). Hayek soon came to believe that, rather than depriving Keynesian economics of its main supporter, the effect of his death was to raise Keynes to a position analogous to sainthood. In Keynes's absence, the fate of Keynesianism passed entirely to his followers and in the ensuing decades 'Keynesianism' became a label that was applied to a wide range of ideas. It was the term used to denote the political philosophy of a mixed economy that Hayek and many libertarians considered a greater threat than outright socialism, fostering the illusion (so they believed) that extensive state intervention could take place without undermining the foundations of a free society. It also represented both an approach to policymaking and a type of technical economics. Keynesian economics was about managing the level of aggregate demand, mainly through variations in taxation and government expenditure, so as to lower the average level of unemployment and to smooth out the business cycle. In economic theory, it was also the label for a certain type of economic modelling, centred on the determinants of aggregate demand, found in both elementary textbook theory and in large-scale empirical models run by forecasting agencies and bodies such as the Brookings Institution and the UK Treasury. Keynesianism also became the name for an approach to economic policy that centred on the management of aggregate demand to control unemployment and the business cycle. It is very uncertain how far these quite different incarnations of Keynesianism would have received Keynes's approval. (Left-wing Keynesians, such as Joan Robinson, have referred to the bastardization of his ideas, and there has been an extensive literature on what Keynes really meant to say in his *General Theory*.) The point is that from the 1950s onwards, it was Keynesianism rather than Keynes's economics that was the principal target of Hayek's arguments about policy. On occasion, Hayek even used Keynes as an authority against Keynesian policies, as when he argued that Keynes, just before his death, was as worried about the inflationary implications of so-called Keynesian policies as he (Hayek) was (Hayek, 1994, p. 92; 1995, p. 232).

The context of Hayek's writing in relation to Keynesian economics was also changed by his move to the United States and his changing relationship to the economics profession. In the 1930s, Hayekian theories were part of the mainstream of business cycle theory. He published in the main journals, his ideas were debated by leading theorists and he helped to set the agenda. After 1950 Hayek's position in relation to the economics of the economics profession changed dramatically. His main work lay elsewhere, in political philosophy and psychology among other areas. Not only were his ideas on the cycle almost totally eclipsed, but he was no longer taken seriously as an economist: even where economists knew about him, he was someone who may once have done serious (though now outdated) work on macroeconomics, but who had abandoned not just business cycle theory but economics. His work on psychology and political philosophy was not seen as relevant to economics and he disappeared from syllabuses and textbooks. When he started writing on policy, though he may have influenced politicians, few economists took him seriously: he was an ideologue (or even a crank) who had not kept up with recent developments in economics. (Leijonhufvud is hardly a counter-example, because his interest in Hayek was unusual, and even he was focusing on just one aspect of his ideas.)

The situation changed to a certain extent after his award of the Nobel Prize in 1974, but even then recognition of his work as something that needed to be taken seriously was arguably confined to a small minority. The profession might be moving towards more conservative views about economic policy and towards a view of Keynesian economics that was much closer to Hayek's, but with the advent of the new classical macroeconomics, it moved to a more mathematical style of theorizing that made Hayekian ideas seem even further from the frontiers of macroeconomic research than they had been in the Keynesian era. The fall of communism in the 1980s and 1990s raised Hayek's star still further but made little difference to economists' views of his macroeconomic thinking. If there was a change, it was that Keynes increasingly joined Hayek in the pantheon of historical figures whose work, though it might provide ideas and inspiration, did not fall into the category of 'serious' macroeconomic theory.

Discussion of Hayek's economics in relation to Keynes's therefore falls into three clearly separated phases. The first is their debates on the business cycle and other matters in the period from Hayek's arrival in London till just before the *General Theory* (approximately 1929–35). The second is the period from the *General Theory* to Keynes's death in 1946. During both these phases Hayek was engaging with Keynes personally as well as with the various versions of Keynesian theory that were appearing. The two phases are distinguished in several ways: Keynes's ideas changed dramatically; Hayek's concerns and economic thinking changed substantially; the policy context changed from that of the Depression to that of the Second World War. The third phase is Hayek's debates with Keynesianism from the 1950s onwards, which reflected not only the changing nature of Keynesianism, but also the new macroeconomic currents associated primarily with Milton Friedman and Robert Lucas.

DEBATING SAVING AND INVESTMENT, 1929–36

Keynes's theoretical framework was the Cambridge quantity theory of money developed by his teacher Alfred Marshall, and his colleague A.C. Pigou. Keynes used it creatively, focusing on the short run, emphasizing even more than did his colleagues the role of expectations, and integrating it with the theory of purchasing power parity. He drew the conclusion that governments had a choice over whether to stabilize the price level (the internal value of money) or the exchange rate (the external value of money): they could not do both. However, his modifications to the theory were hardly substantial. His *Tract on Monetary Reform* was, as its title indicates, an application of standard theory to an urgent policy issue, not a systematic treatise on monetary economics.

Through the 1920s, though Keynes lectured on monetary economics at Cambridge, and was heavily involved in discussions of theory with Dennis Robertson and others, his publications were short and oriented towards policy: Britain's return to the gold standard, German reparations payments and unemployment policy were the main concerns of this period. Hirai (2004) has argued that there was a clear gap between Keynes the policy analyst and Keynes the theorist, with the latter failing to keep up with the former (much as Clarke has argued for the years after 1930). Then, in 1930, Keynes published his *Treatise on Money*, the book that, had all gone well, would have provided the solid academic foundation for the reputation he had already acquired. This marked a break with the Marshallian tradition in that the central theoretical analysis, his so-called 'fundamental equations', drew on Wicksell. Keynes moved away from the quantity theory tradition towards an income–expenditure analysis in which price level changes depended on the balance between saving and investment, and through them on monetary policy; exactly the theoretical framework towards which Hayek had rapidly moved in the late 1920s, although in his case he reached it via Mises. The similarity between their theoretical frameworks is crucial to understanding the exchange between them in 1930–31.

Central to Keynes's theory was a definition of income that included wages, interest on capital, 'regular monopoly gains' and 'normal remuneration of entrepreneurs' (Keynes, [1930] 1971, vol. 1, p. 111). It excluded windfall profits – the difference between entrepreneurs' actual earnings and their normal earnings. He then defined saving as the difference between income and consumption. Because of the way Keynes defined income, windfall profits were not included in saving. Investment was defined as the value of the net increase in the capital stock during the relevant period. The result was a set of accounts in which investment equalled saving plus windfall profits.

Windfall profits were important for Keynes because their level would determine whether firms wished to change output. In equilibrium they would be zero, indicating that entrepreneurs were receiving their normal remuneration. This provided a mechanism through which investment would be linked to windfall profits and hence to output and the price level. Investment would depend on the difference between the anticipated return on investment and the rate of interest (Bank Rate, the rate of interest set by the Bank of England). A reduction in the rate of interest would lower saving and raise investment, opening up a gap between saving and investment, creating windfall profits, and an increase would have the opposite effect. Keynes ([1930] 1971, vol. 1, p. 139) followed Wicksell in defining the natural rate as the rate of interest at which windfall profits were zero (and savings would equal investment), and the market rate as the actual rate of interest determined by the banking system.

Policy implications followed directly. The banking system determined the terms on which credit was available to entrepreneurs, this determining the level of windfall profits and hence whether output and the price level were rising or falling. If credit conditions were such as to cause windfall profits to be zero, then output and the price level would be stable. Though Keynes recognized that other factors could also affect the situation, he concluded that '[b]ooms and slumps are simply the expression of the results of an oscillation of the terms of credit about their equilibrium position' ([1930] 1971, vol. 1, p. 165).

This conclusion and much of the argument parallels Hayek's argument in *Prices and Production*. In his first lecture he distinguished two strands in the development of monetary theory since the eighteenth century. One was the link between the rate of interest, the money supply and the price level; the other was 'forced saving', the doctrine that monetary expansion can raise the level of investment through transferring purchasing power from consumers to investors. He acknowledged ([1931] 1935b, p. 25) that this part of his theory was similar to ideas developed by Dennis Robertson in *Banking Policy and the Price Level* (1926), a book that had played an important part in the development of Keynes's thoughts on the subject. Keynes was thus working squarely in the monetary tradition that Hayek was attempting to develop.

When Hayek reviewed Keynes's *Treatise*, he relieved himself of the task of explaining Keynes's theory by choosing to address his review to 'expert readers who [had] read the book in its entirety' and referring English readers, unfamiliar with the capital theory on which much of his argument rested, to *Prices and Production* (Hayek, 1995, p. 122). The reason he gave for his failure to provide a more conventional review was, essentially, that he could not understand it:

It is here [Books III and IV of the *Treatise*] that all the force and all the weaknesses of the argument are concentrated, and it is here that the really original work is set forth. And here, unfortunately, the exposition is so difficult, unsystematic, and obscure, that it is extremely difficult for the fellow economist who disagrees with the conclusions to demonstrate [the] exact point of disagreement and to state his objections. There are passages in which the inconsistent use of terms produces a degree of obscurity which, to anyone acquainted with Mr. Keynes's earlier work, is almost unbelievable. It is only with extreme caution and the greatest reserve that one can attempt to criticize, because one can never be sure whether one has understood Mr. Keynes aright. (Hayek, 1995, p. 122)

This incomprehension was mutual, and Keynes, when responding to Hayek, replied in kind:

The book [*Prices and Production*], as it stands, seems to me to be one of the most frightful muddles I have ever read, with scarcely a sound proposition in it beginning with page 45, and yet it remains a book of some interest, which is likely to leave its mark on the mind of a reader. It is an extraordinary example of how, starting with a mistake, a remorseless logician can end up in Bedlam.

Yet Dr. Hayek has seen a vision, and though when he woke up he has made nonsense of his story by giving the wrong names to the objects which occur in it, his Khubla Khan is not without inspiration and must set the reader thinking with the germs of an idea in his head. (ibid., p. 154)

This mutual incomprehension and the way in which their exchange developed are explained by the fact that they were working in the same Wicksellian theoretical framework, but they interpreted it in very different ways. They each had their own view of how the Wicksellian concepts of saving, investment and monetary equilibrium should be interpreted, and each criticized the other by presenting his own interpretation of the theory that they shared: they argued over details in a way that would not have happened had there not been significant overlap between their theories. Hayek found objections with Keynes's definition of profits and his assumption that changes in aggregate profits could be seen as the cause of price changes using his own theory to explain why production might change even when profits as defined by Keynes were zero. He used capital theory taken from *Prices and Production* to offer a critique of Keynes's concept of investment and its relation to the capital stock. Keynes responded by claiming the crucial issue was whether all changes in the amount of money in circulation were due to investment differing from saving. Keynes denied that this was true, and claimed that Hayek's misunderstanding arose from attributing this belief to him. There was some discussion of capital, but it did not lead to any examination of the broader issues on which they differed.

Keynes, following Wicksell, considered a neutral monetary policy to be one in which the price level was constant and windfall profits were zero. Hayek, in the thesis that became *Monetary Theory and the Trade Cycle*, had argued that neutrality should be defined, instead, in terms of a constant money supply. His starting point was full equilibrium in a barter economy, on the grounds that it was essential to start with a theory that was fully understood and this was the only candidate. In such a barter economy, saving and investment had to be equal and there would be an equilibrium set of relative prices. Because it would lead to forced saving, raising investment above voluntary saving, any increase in the money supply, Hayek argued, would raise the price of investment goods relative to consumption goods, causing production to be distorted even if the overall price level did not change.

He developed this idea that monetary policy could alter production, even without any change in the overall price level, in *Prices and Production*. His theory was based on the idea, taken from Böhm-Bawerk, that production needed to be seen as taking place over time, with capital being measured by the 'length' of the production process. If the production took place over three periods, it would be as represented in Figure 5.1 (patterned after Hayek, 1931, pp. 44, 52, 56, 59). The broken set of boxes denotes the labour and capital applied to production in each of three periods: 40 per period. In period 1 of the process, intermediate goods worth 40

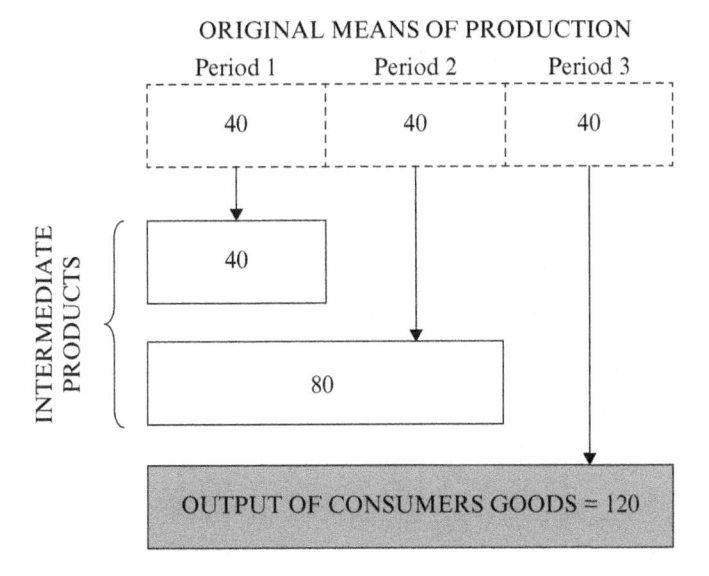

Figure 5.1 Hayekian triangle (three-period process)

are produced. In period 2, these are combined with a further 40 units of capital and labour to produce intermediate goods worth 80 units. In the final period the application of a further 40 of capital and labour leads to the production of consumer goods worth 120. In a stationary economy, there will always be three processes operating (or a multiple of three), one at each stage of the productive process. In each period, therefore, 120 of consumer goods will be produced, along with 120 of intermediate goods. The ratio of consumer goods to intermediate goods is (80 + 40)/120 = 1.

Now suppose that the rate of interest falls, causing entrepreneurs to adopt more capital-intensive methods. This will take the form of a longer period of production. If the total resources in the economy are the same and the length of the production process increases to 4 periods, the result will be as in Figure 5.2. Total resources are still valued at 120, and in equilibrium there are four processes operating, each employing 30 of capital and labour. The significant point about this example is that, due to the lengthening of the production process, the ratio of consumption goods to intermediate goods has declined to 2:3.

Because he started from the assumption of an equilibrium in which all resources were employed, for Hayek the only way an increase in investment could raise production was through changes in the structure of production,

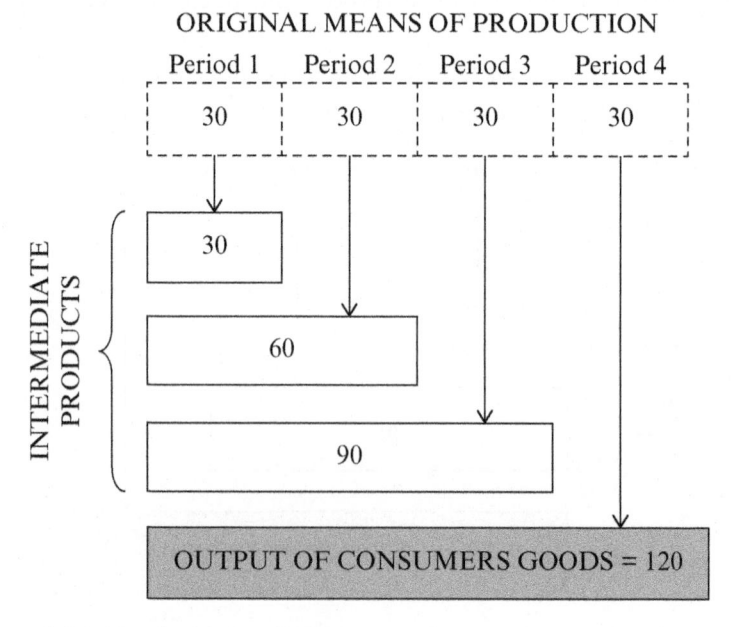

Figure 5.2 Hayekian triangle (four-period process)

such as that illustrated in these diagrams. Investment had to be understood in these terms, which led him find Keynes's alternative conception of investment, which involved adding new capital goods to an already-existing stock, inadequate, something to which he devoted much of his review.

This concept of capital is central to Hayek's explanation of unemployment. If the money supply were expanded, the interest rate would be too low and the economy would move to a longer period of production, such as shown in Figure 5.2. At some point, he argued, the expansion would have to cease and the economy would have to move back to a shorter period, such as shown in Figure 5.1. If intermediate goods were all the same, this would not cause any problem. However, the intermediate goods involved in each process are physically different, with the result that when shorter processes of production are started up, some of the intermediate goods used in the longer processes will simply stop being used: part of the capital stock becomes obsolete and is effectively lost. The result will be that there will be insufficient capital to employ the entire labour force and the result will be unemployment until the economy has worked its way through to a new equilibrium where the right stock of intermediate goods is available for the whole labour force to be employed using the new, less capital-intensive methods of production.

Some scholars have criticized Keynes for turning his response to Hayek's review of the *Treatise* into a review of *Prices and Production*, suggesting that his motive for doing so must have been to distract attention from his own book. However, given the nature of Hayek's critique, it was hard for Keynes to do otherwise. Arguments about the time-structure of production lay behind his criticisms of Keynes's concept of profits and his understanding of saving and investment (Hayek, 1995, pp. 127, 130). He went so far as to say that Keynes would have made his task easier had he familiarized himself not only with the descendants of Wicksell's theory, but also with Wicksell's theory itself (ibid., p. 131). Hayek effectively invited Keynes to consider his own theory.

There followed an exchange of letters between Keynes and Hayek, in which they explored some of the definitional problems that divided them. Hayek responded in print to Keynes's reply, and in February 1932 published the second half of his review. At the time of this exchange, Keynes's book was also being debated by a group of his younger Cambridge colleagues (the 'Circus', coordinated by Richard Kahn) and it is thought that they persuaded him that its theoretical structure did not properly allow for changes in output; though not expressed in the same way, this was a question that had also concerned Hayek. In March 1932, Keynes wrote to Hayek that he was unlikely to respond to the main points in his review: 'I am trying to reshape and improve my central position, and that is probably a better way to spend one's time than in controversy' (ibid., p. 173). Hayek (1994, p. 90) has said that he found this very discouraging, though others might have interpreted Keynes's retreat as a vindication of some of his arguments. A few months later, Piero Sraffa, one of Keynes's Cambridge colleagues, challenged Hayek's use of the concepts of forced saving and the natural rate of interest, and Hayek responded, but debates with Keynes were over.

Over the next few years, Keynes and Hayek both developed their ideas significantly. Keynes's passage to the *General Theory* is well documented (see, e.g., Patinkin, 1982; Dimand, 1988; Clarke, 1998, Ch. 4). He abandoned the definition of saving that he had used in the *Treatise* which Hayek had criticized, and moved to a theory where the level of investment determined the output and employment directly, through aggregate demand. The *General Theory* was carefully formulated to avoid many of the theoretical pitfalls into which the *Treatise* had fallen. For example, Keynes tried to avoid the aggregation problems to which Hayek had pointed by the device of measuring output in 'wage units' (sums of money divided by the wage rate). In perhaps the most radical departure from his previous theory, he argued that investment was not the result of rational calculation but the result of a spontaneous urge to take action: the long-term expectations on which investment decisions were based were effectively exogenous, based on conventions and animal spirits.

Hayek continued to believe that capital theory was fundamental to any explanation of the business cycle, but he nonetheless modified his theory very substantially. His early work was based on the notion of static equilibrium:

> It is my conviction that if we want to explain economic phenomena at all, we have no means available but to build on the foundations given by the concept of a tendency towards an equilibrium. For it is this concept alone which permits us to explain fundamental phenomena like the determination of prices or incomes, an understanding of which is essential to any explanation of fluctuation of production. (Hayek, [1931] 1935, p. 34)

He went so far as to say that the existence of unemployed resources was 'not explained by static analysis, and accordingly we are not entitled to take it for granted' (ibid.), presumably implying that if it were explained by static analysis, it could be taken for granted, a remarkably strong claim for static equilibrium theory.

During the 1930s, Hayek moved away from this extreme faith in equilibrium theory, in the process redefining the notion of equilibrium. In 'Economics and knowledge' (1937), he questioned whether the concept of equilibrium had meaning when applied to the actions of a group of individuals, and moved to a broader concept of equilibrium that took account of the subjective character of knowledge. Equilibrium involved consistency of beliefs with outcomes, and hence with the beliefs of other individuals. He therefore focused much more on expectations, arguing that the static equilibrium framework of *Prices and Production* was inadequate for analysing the cycle, moving instead to a concept of equilibrium based on fulfillment of expectations. Faced with these verity of the depression, he paid greater attention to how downturns in the economy might get amplified, developing theories in which prices and wages and technical coefficients were rigid, and in which perverse expectations might become self-fulfilling; for example, faced with expectations of falling prices, consumption might fall, causing those expectations to be fulfilled (1939, p. 177).

SUPPORTING KEYNES OVER INFLATION, 1936–46

Keynes's *General Theory* swept away all before it. Even Hayek's colleagues and students at the London School of Economics (LSE), such as Nicholas Kaldor, Abba Lerner and George Shackle, became Keynesians. Eventually, even Robbins, Hayek's patron at LSE, accepted that his opposition to Keynes in the early 1930s, the result of his adherence to Hayek's theory of the business cycle, was the greatest mistake of his professional career, disowning his book, *The Great Depression* (1934) (Robbins 1971, p. 154; see Howson, 2011 for a more extensive discussion of the relationship between Robbins and Hayek). Within a decade, economists were speaking of the 'Keynesian revolution' as marking a radical break with what went before. Not only did the *General Theory* provide economists with a welter of theoretical puzzles that needed solving (the debate over what Keynes really meant remained central to macroeconomics as late as the 1960s) but it also coalesced with the parallel revolutions in national income accounting and econometrics. Economics became more technical, focused around constructing and analysing the properties of economic models, and by around the late 1950s, almost the entire business cycle literature looked profoundly out of date. By the new standards it was simply not rigorous. Many of the lessons that economists had learned in the interwar period were lost (see Backhouse and Laidler, 2004). This affected not only Hayek's work but also that of his many contemporaries.

In Hayek's case, there was the further factor that economists came round to the view that Keynes had been right to attribute the Great Depression to a lack of effective demand and to argue that it would be cured only by expansionary monetary or fiscal policy. Keynes seemed vindicated as rearmament and then the Second World War restored full employment. *The Pure Theory of Capital* (1941) provided a restatement of his capital theory that was much more systematic than he had been able to do in *Prices and Production*, or in any of his articles. However, it did nothing to turn the tide of Keynesian economics.

Hayek chose not to review the *General Theory*. He offered a number of reasons for this. Though he later discounted this explanation, Hayek claimed that he did not want to risk discouragement a second time: having changed his mind soon after publishing the *Treatise*, Keynes might do the same after the *General Theory*; he had become tired of controversy with an opponent who was hard to pin down (Hayek, 1995, p. 60, cf. pp. 40–43; cf. Hayek, 1994, p. 90). There was also the problem that *Economica* had published Pigou's very critical review, and it was thought that another one would be inappropriate (Howson, 2001; cf. Caldwell, 1998 and introduction to Hayek, 1995). Later, he claimed that, given the success of Keynesian ideas, to proclaim his dissent from views that were held almost universally would have made it harder for him to be heard on other matters that he considered important (Hayek, 1999b, p. 116). He also suggested a deeper reason: a realization that the difference between them 'did no longer concern particular points of analysis but rather the whole method of approach':

> there had been a gradual change in Keynes's whole view of the proper scope and method of theoretical analysis which went far beyond the particular issues with which he was concerned. As I saw it, an examination of the validity of the *General Theory* would have made it necessary to take issue with the whole macrodynamic approach, the treatment of the economic process in terms of aggregates and statistical totals, a theory which was concerned only with price levels and total income streams and in effect took the whole structure of relative prices for granted and provided no tools to explain changes in relative prices or their effects. (Hayek, 1995, p. 60)

In short, he would have to tackle not just economics but methodology. He came to realize that, though Keynes played a part in the transition that was taking place, it was much broader than Keynes. It was a theme to which he turned in 'Scientism and the study of society' (1952, Part 1).

Further reasons for Hayek's changed attitude towards controversy with Keynes may be found in external circumstances. In the late 1930s and during the Second World War, the main threat to liberalism came not from socialism or communism but from fascism. He and Keynes were on the same side. Keynes also shared with Hayek a concern with inflation, which manifested itself as early as 1937. During the war, Hayek supported Keynes's attempts to design policies that would enable war to be waged without creating inflation; he may not have shared Keynes's theoretical framework, but he supported his aims and many of his policies, such as schemes for compulsory savings and deferred pay (Hayek, 1997, pp. 164–72). Hayek and Keynes became close when LSE moved out to Peterhouse College in Cambridge for the duration of the war, and Hayek was given dining rights in Kings College. They found common interests ranging from book collecting to the history of ideas, and Keynes helped with matters such as finding a suitable school for Hayek's son.

A good illustration of the changed relationship between Keynes and Hayek is provided by an exchange in the *Economic Journal* in 1943. The problem with which they were both concerned, and over which Keynes became locked in negotiations with the United States (Skidelsky, 2000, Part 2), was the monetary standard that should operate in the post-war period to replace the chaos that followed the breakdown of the gold standard in the early 1930s. Hayek's (1943, in Hayek, 1999b, Ch. 2) solution was a commodity reserve currency. There were great advantages, he argued, in having a currency based on a commodity whose value was regulated by its cost of production rather than by the decisions of a monetary authority. For centuries there was a widely held 'superstitious prejudice' in favour of gold as the commodity on which the value of the currency should be based (Hayek, 1999b, p. 107), but with confidence in gold shaken it was considered whether there might be a better alternative. Hayek proposed that currency be based on warehouse receipts for bundles of storable commodities: a unit of currency would be defined not in terms of gold, but, for example, as a quantity of wheat plus a quantity of sugar, a quantity of copper and a quantity of rubber.

The advantage of such a currency over credit money was that its value would be determined solely by the production costs of the commodities included in the bundle, not by a monetary authority. Compared with gold, it had the advantage that if there was an increase in demand for currency (perhaps because of a general increase in uncertainty) the price of currency would rise, providing an incentive for producers to supply more of the commodities on which it was based, leading to an increase in the supply of money. Similarly, if demand for currency fell, commodities could be withdrawn from warehouses and consumed.

Keynes's (1943) response (which incidentally did not even mention Hayek) showed the extent to which his views remained close to those he had expressed 20 years earlier in his *Tract on Monetary Reform*. He favored an International Clearing Union, with the power to grant credit, on the grounds that it would not only provide currency when this was required, but would also allow countries freedom to deal with their internal price levels in ways that they considered appropriate. As in the *Tract*, he was not prepared to insist that countries sacrifice internal stability (of the price level) for external stability (of the exchange rate).

During this period Hayek increasingly began to differentiate between

Keynes's own ideas and those of his younger disciples (though he sometimes refrained from mentioning them, he had in mind Richard Kahn, James Meade and Joan Robinson). Reviewing William Beveridge's *Full Employment in a Free Society* (1944) he was careful to compare its theoretical framework with 'that of Lord Keynes as seen by his younger disciples and familiar to American readers mainly through the writings of Professor A.H. Hansen' (Hayek, 1945, in Hayek, 1995, p. 234). Hayek liked to recount a conversation he had with Keynes, in Kings College, shortly before his death:

> Later, a turn in the conversation made me ask him whether he was not concerned about what some of his disciples were making of his theories. After a not very complimentary remark about the persons concerned, he proceeded to reassure me by explaining that those ideas had been badly needed at the time he had launched them. He continued by indicating that I need not be alarmed; if they should ever become dangerous I could rely upon him again quickly to swing round public opinion – and he indicated by a quick movement of his hand how rapidly that would be done. But three months later he was dead. (Hayek, 1995, p. 232)

At least when it came to economic policy, the line Hayek drew between Keynes and 'Keynesian' economics was becoming sharp, Keynes being a potential ally against his disciples.

HAYEK AGAINST KEYNESIAN ECONOMICS, 1946–92

After his *Pure Theory of Capital*, Hayek moved away from business cycle theory. The economics profession had moved on and Hayek no longer fitted in. Even in Chicago, he did not fit into the Economics Department and when he was offered a position it was in the interdisciplinary Committee for Social Thought. There were, however, more positive reasons for moving on from his early work on business cycles: as has been explained already, he was moving away from his early confidence in the method of equilibrium analysis and he was becoming aware that the fundamental differences between himself and Keynesian economics were methodological as much as substantive. His methodological inquiries resulted in 'The counter revolution of science' (1941–42) and 'Scientisim and society' (1942–44) (combined in Hayek, 1952). He also became convinced that it was necessary to work more actively to defend a free society, hence *The Road to Serfdom* (1944) and his work towards organizing the Mont Pelerin Society. Both of these projects, which were his main focus in the 1950s, took him away from technical economics and into the social sciences more generally, from which it was a smaller step to the work on psychology.

After his essay on commodity money in 1943, there was a gap of over three decades before Hayek published anything else on money. The context was the breakdown of the Keynesian consensus following the sharp rise in both inflation and unemployment following the 1973–74 oil shocks. Exchange rates had been allowed to float and governments were searching for new frameworks for monetary policy. Hayek's interventions were published, not in academic journals, but by the Institute of Economic Affairs, a London-based think tank that he had been instrumental in setting up in the 1950s. In two pamphlets he argued for 'Choice in currency' and the 'Denationalization of money' (Hayek, 1999b, Chs 3–4). The first of these argued that in countries within the European Union, the best way to achieve monetary union would be for all governments to commit themselves to allowing their citizens to hold whichever country's money they chose. Thus people in Britain might choose to hold French francs if that currency offered the prospect of falling in value less than other European Union (EU) currencies.

In 'Denationalization of money', Hayek took the argument a stage further, arguing that governments should allow people to hold not only monies issued by other countries' central banks, but also money issued by any private firm that decided to issue it. Explaining the steps by which a private bank could set about issuing a new currency (denominated in its own, unique, unit of account, not in terms of any national currency) he argued that competition would ensure that issuers would be more concerned to maintain the value of their currency than would government-owned and run central banks.

Though, in the 1940s, Hayek had emphasized Keynes's opposition to inflation, 30 years later, perhaps encouraged by the movement within economics against Keynesian economic theory, he painted a rather different picture of Keynes:

> The chief root of our present monetary troubles is, of course, the sanction of scientific authority which Lord Keynes and his disciples have given to the age-old superstition that by increasing the aggregate of money expenditure we can lastingly ensure prosperity and full employment ... It was John Maynard Keynes, a man of great intellect but limited knowledge of economic theory, who ultimately succeeded in rehabilitating a view long the preserve of cranks with whom he openly sympathized. He had attempted by a succession of new theories to justify the same, superficially persuasive, intuitive belief that had been held by many practical men before, but that will not withstand rigorous analysis of the price mechanism. (Hayek, 1999b, pp 115–16)

He did not claim that this was Keynes's intention, but he clearly blamed Keynes for the post-war inflation and he reverted to his earlier charge, made in his review of the *Treatise*, that Keynes did not understand economic theory. His main evidence for Keynes's error was that the two centuries of the gold standard (1714–1914 in Britain and 1749–1949 in the United States) were the only period in human history when prices stayed roughly constant; these were precisely the centuries during which these economies had industrialized and grown rapidly.

CONCLUSIONS

This chapter has told the story of the interactions between Keynes and Hayek, perhaps the two most influential economists of the twentieth century. Keynes was 16 years Hayek's senior, but as a result of rather different career paths, their theories of the business cycle emerged into the public arena almost simultaneously, in 1929–30. The age difference was important, because as a 30-year old who was challenging the leading representative of the establishment, Hayek exhibited the brashness and perhaps even the arrogance that is typical of young economists challenging their elders. Keynes, renowned for his power with the English language, responded in kind. Given that their disagreements concerned the most important economic question of the day, that Keynes was a major public figure, and that Hayek found a powerful supporter in Robbins, it was inevitable that they captured the attention of the economics profession. It is hardly going too far to say that the major question confronting economists in those years of depression was whether Keynes or Hayek was right.

Doubts about who would win that contest were ended with Keynes's *General Theory*. This decisively changed the terms of macroeconomic debate and by the 1950s there had emerged a dominant Keynesian orthodoxy. At the same time, Keynesian ideas spread, gradually, into policy-making. Keynes's triumph was so decisive because it involved economic theory, applied economics, economic policy and political philosophy or ideology. The period that ended in the 1970s was undoubtedly the Age of Keynes.

In the closing decades of the century Hayek's star rose and Keynes's fell; though far from completely, however much critics tried to argue this, for there remained many Keynesian economists and after the 2008 financial crisis, there was an enormous, though lopsided, upsurge of interest in Keynes (see Backhouse and Bateman, 2011). However, even in the 1990s, after the fall of Communism, Hayek never had the pervasive influence exerted by Keynes in the 1950s and 1960s. Hayek's main influence was on the prevailing ideology: it was Thatcher, Reagan and people in the ex-Soviet economies who were most attracted by Hayek. On the other hand, only a few economists accepted Hayek's theories or even regarded his work as worth taking seriously. It was Milton Friedman, not Hayek, who had persuaded economists to question Keynesian theory; though ideologically close to Hayek, his economics was, with its highly empirical tone, methodologically very different from Hayek's. Robert Lucas, one of the architects of the new classical macroeconomics that became fashionable in the 1970s, at first thought of himself as an Austrian (like Hayek, his economics was based on the assumptions of individual rationality and intertemporal equilibrium) but was soon persuaded that this was a mistake (Hoover, 1988).

Macroeconomic theory, though it moved away from supporting Keynesian policy prescriptions, and though it took on board many ideas from the interwar literature of which Hayek's was a part, had been profoundly influenced by Keynes and never lost those scars. Hayek's belief in theory and his disdain for statistical work never had any appeal to the mainstream of the economics profession, however much it might emphasize the importance of grounding models on rational choice foundations. It was Friedman's expectations-augmented Phillips curve (together with evidence from the 1970s), not Hayek's arguments about the structure of production, that convinced economists that expansionary monetary policies might have adverse long-term consequences, just as his *Monetary History of the United States* (Friedman and Schwartz, 1963) had persuaded them to take the money supply seriously. Furthermore, despite efforts to create a macroeconomics based on market clearing and intertemporal optimization by consumers, macroeconomists realized, after the initial enthusiasm for the new classical macroeconomics (in the 1970s) and real business cycle theory (in the 1980s), that it was impossible to explain observed behaviour without taking account of the lags and rigidities that had come to be associated with Keynesian economics.

Hayek wrote that Keynes had tried, with a succession of theories, to justify the belief that raising the aggregate of money spending would raise employment. Similar remarks could be made about Hayek, except that in his case he sought to demonstrate that monetary expansion would, eventually, lead to higher unemployment than if adjustments had been allowed to take their course: that inflation caused unemployment. Keynes had a strong belief in the power of social science to provide solutions to the world's problems, and in the ability of the ruling elite to implement those solutions. Hayek shared neither of these beliefs, with the possible exception of the wartime emergency. In both cases, critics might argue that political philosophy came first, and economic theory second, leaving both of them exposed to the charge that theory provided but a cover for ideology. An alternative, less critical perspective might be that each had a strong intuitive view of how the economic world worked, and that they tried to capture this view in their formal theory.

REFERENCES

Backhouse, Roger E. and Bradley W. Bateman (eds) (2006), *The Cambridge Companion to Keynes*, Cambridge: Cambridge University Press.
Backhouse, Roger E. and Bradley W. Bateman (2009), 'Keynes and capitalism', *History of Political Economy*, 41 (4), 645–71.
Backhouse, Roger E. and Bradley W. Bateman (2011), *Capitalist Revolutionary: John Maynard Keynes*, Cambridge, MA: Harvard University Press.
Backhouse, Roger E. and Mauro Boianovsky (2013), *Transforming Modern Macroeconomics: Exploring Disequilibrium Microfoundations, 1956–2003*. Cambridge: Cambridge University Press.
Backhouse, Roger E. and David Laidler (2004), 'What was lost with IS-LM', *History of Political Economy*, 30 (Supplement: The IS-LM model: its rise, fall and strange persistence), 25–56.
Beveridge, William (1944), *Full Employment in a Free Society*. London: George Allen & Unwin.
Caldwell, Bruce J. (1998), 'Why didn't Hayek review Keynes's *General Theory*?' *History of Political Economy*, 30 (4), 545–70.
Clarke, Peter F. (1998), *The Keynesian Revolution and its Economic Consequences*, Cheltenham, UK and Lyme, NH, USA: Edward Elgar.
Dimand, Robert W. (1988), *The Origins of the Keynesian Revolution*, Aldershot, UK and Brookfield, US: Edward Elgar.
Dostaler, Gilles (1991), 'The debate between Hayek and Keynes', in William J. Barber (ed.), *Perspectives on the History of Economic Thought, Volume VI: Themes in Keynesian Criticism and Supplementary Modern Topics*, Aldershot, UK and Brookfield, VT, US: Edward Elgar, pp. 77–101.
Friedman, Milton and Anna J. Schwartz (1963), *A Monetary History of the United States, 1867–1960*, Princeton, NJ: Princeton University Press.
Harrod, Roy F. (1972), *The Life of John Maynard Keynes*, Harmondsworth: Penguin Books.
Hayek, Friedrich A. (1933), *Monetary Theory and the Trade Cycle*, transl. N. Kaldor and H.M. Croome, London: Jonathan Cape.
Hayek, Friedrich A. (1935), *Collectivist Economic Planning*, London: George Routledge, 1st German edn 1929.
Hayek, Friedrich A. (1935), *Prices and Production*, 2nd edn, London: George Routledge, 1st edn 1931.
Hayek, Friedrich A. (1937), 'Economics and knowledge,' *Economica*, n.s. 4 (13), 33–54.
Hayek, Friedrich A. (1939), *Profits, Interest and Investment*, London: George Routledge.
Hayek, Friedrich A. (1941), *The Pure Theory of Capital*, London: Routledge & Kegan Paul.
Hayek, Friedrich A. (1944), *The Road to Serfdom*, London: Routledge.
Hayek, Friedrich A. (1952), *The Counter Revolution of Science*, Glencoe, IL: Free Press.
Hayek, Friedrich A. (1984), *Money, Capital and Fluctuations: Early Essays*, ed. Roy McCloughry, London: Routledge & Kegan Paul.
Hayek, Friedrich A. (1994), *Hayek on Hayek: An Autobiographical Dialogue*, ed. Stephen Kresge and Lief Wenar, London: Routledge.

Hayek, Friedrich A. (1995), *Contra Keynes and Cambridge, The Collected Works of F.A. Hayek*, vol. 9, ed. Bruce Caldwell, series ed. Stephen Kresge, London: Routledge.
Hayek, Friedrich A. (1997), *Socialism and War: Essays, Documents, Reviews. The Collected Works of F.A. Hayek*, vol. 10, ed. Stephenn Kresge, London: Routledge.
Hayek, Friedrich A. (1999a), *Good Money, Part I: The New World. The Collected Works of F.A. Hayek*, vol. 5, ed. Stephen Kresge, London: Routledge.
Hayek, Friedrich A. (1999b), *Good Money, Part II: The Standard. The Collected Works of F.A. Hayek*, vol. 6, ed. Stephen Kresge, London: Routledge.
Hirai, Toshiaki (2004), 'Keynes as a theorist and as a commentator during 1923–1930', unpublished paper, Sophia University, Tokyo.
Hoover, Kevin D. (1988), *The New Classical Macroeconomics*, Oxford: Basil Blackwell.
Howson, Susan (2001), 'Why didn't Hayek review Keynes's *General Theory*? A partial answer', *History of Political Economy*, 33 (2), 369–74.
Howson, Susan (2011), *Lionel Robbins*, Cambridge: Cambridge University Press.
Keynes, John Maynard (1913), *Indian Currency and Finance. The Collected Writings of John Maynard Keynes*, vol. I (1971), London: Macmillan.
Keynes, John Maynard (1919), *The Economic Consequences of the Peace. The Collected Writings of John Maynard Keynes*, vol. II (1971), London: Macmillan.
Keynes, John Maynard (1923), *A Tract on Monetary Reform, The Collected Works of John Maynard Keynes*, vol. IV (1971), London: Macmillan.
Keynes, John Maynard (1926), 'The end of laissez faire', in *Essays in Persuasion. The Collected Writings of John Maynard Keynes*, vol. IX (1972), London: Macmillan, pp. 272–94.
Keynes, John Maynard (1930), *A Treatise on Money*, 2 vols, in *The Collected Works of John Maynard Keynes*, vols V–VI (1971), London: Macmillan.
Keynes, John Maynard (1936), *The General Theory of Employment, Interest and Money. The Collected Writings of John Maynard Keynes*, vol. VII (1973), London: Macmillan.
Keynes, John Maynard (1943), 'The objective of international price stability', *Economic Journal*, 53, 185–7.
Leijonhufvud, Axel (1968), *On Keynesian Economics and the Economics of Keynes*, Oxford: Oxford University Press.
McCormick, Brian J. (1992), *Hayek and the Keynesian Avalanche*, Brighton: Harvester Wheatsheaf.
Patinkin, Don (1982), *Anticipations of the General Theory*, Chicago, IL: Chicago University Press.
Robbins, Lionel C. (1934), *The Great Depression*, London: Macmillan.
Robbins, Lionel C. (1971), *Autobiography of an Economist*, London: Macmillan.
Robertson, Dennis H. (1926), *Banking Policy and the Price Level*, London: Macmillan.
Skidelsky, Robert (2000), *John Maynard Keynes*, vol. 3: *Fighting for Britain, 1937–1946*, London: Macmillan.
Steele, Gerald R. (2001), *Keynes and Hayek: The Money Economy*, London: Routledge.

6. Hayek and Friedman
Roger W. Garrison

In the grand battle of ideas, Friedrich A. Hayek and Milton Friedman were, at the same time, soul mates and adversaries. Hayek's *Constitution of Liberty* (1960) and Friedman's *Capitalism and Freedom* (1962) are rightly seen as companion volumes. By contrast, Hayek's *Monetary Theory and the Trade Cycle* ([1928] 1975) and Friedman's *Optimum Quantity of Money and Other Essays* (1969) are worlds apart. The tenets of classical liberalism unite these two thinkers; the methods and substance of their economics, particularly the economics of money and business cycles, divide them. A thorough understanding of both the common ground and the battleground requires attention to several different fields of study, including philosophy of science, methodology, political economy and economics. The comparison is facilitated by a wealth of literature produced by Hayek and Friedman as well as a voluminous and still-growing secondary literature aimed at reconciling the differences or at sharpening them.[1] But sorting it all out requires careful attention to the changing views of these two leaders of their respective schools of thought and to the various contexts in which particular arguments were made.

Hayek's own characterizations of the relationship between his views and those of Friedman are sometimes less than helpful. In a mid-1980s interview conducted by W.W. Bartley III, for instance, Hayek (1994, p. 144) claimed that 'Milton and I agree on almost everything except monetary policy'. A full accounting of their actual differences could well take the form of identifying all the ways in which this claim is wrong or misleading. Differing views about monetary policy follow directly from the more fundamentally differing judgments about the macroeconomic significance of money in a market economy.

Hayek theorized in terms of the market process that governs relative prices. His macroeconomic theorizing focused especially on the rate of interest, which, broadly conceived, reflects the pattern of various categories of capital goods in relation to the anticipated prices of the corresponding consumer goods. Monetary expansion can distort relative prices, causing resources to be misallocated.

Friedman focused on the strong relationship between changes in the monetary aggregates and subsequent movements in the overall level of prices, as demonstrated statistically during the heyday of monetarism for many economies and for many time periods. With possible effects on resource allocation considered to be at most a secondary issue, the focus is on the price level and total real output, and the empirical findings bolster the claim that the long-run effect of monetary expansion is overall price and wage inflation.

The differing orientations – theoretical for Hayek and empirical for Friedman – reflect a fundamental difference in methodological precepts. While actually allied on many policy issues (including even monetary policy when their policy recommendations are constrained by considerations of practicality and political viability), Hayek and Friedman are radically at odds with one another about the very nature of the requisite analytical framework.

The difficulties of comparing Hayek and Friedman can be illustrated by one of Hayek's prescriptions for monetary policy. A decade before he suggested that monetary policy was the primary basis for their disagreement, his own policy recommendations were almost indistinguishable from Friedman's. In a lecture delivered in Rome in 1975, Hayek (1978, p. 208) agreed that 'we will have to try to get back to some more or less automatic system for regulating the quantity of money'. He suggested that the rate of monetary growth should be reduced to match 'the rate of real growth of production' (p. 206). His only reservations about adopting such a monetary rule were based on: (1) doubts that the money supply was sufficiently well defined to make the rule practicable; and (2) belief that the monetary authority should have some discretion in order to deal with liquidity crises.[2] The first reservation is one that came to haunt monetarism starting in the early 1980s when monetary reforms in the US (including the phasing out of Regulation Q) blurred the distinction between money and savings. The second reservation, which reflects concerns about significant variations in money demand, suggests a deviation from monetarism in the direction of Keynesianism.

But largely because of his attention to the market process and relative prices, Hayek was critical of Keynesian theory from the beginning. Keynes's macroeconomic aggregates, such as investment, consumption, income and employment, tend to mask more than they reveal. A regret that Hayek often expressed is that he failed to review Keynes's *General Theory* (1936).[3] Undoubtedly, Keynes's methods and especially his neglect of relative-price considerations would have been Hayek's focus. But there was also regret for not having reviewed Friedman's *Essays in Positive Economics* (1953), 'which in a way', according to Hayek, 'was quite as dangerous a book' (Hayek, 1994, p. 145).

It is curious that Hayek's 'dangerous book' remark was part of the same response in which he expressed nearly complete agreement with Friedman (except for monetary policy). In another interview (by Leo Rosten in Hayek, 1983, p. 95), Hayek criticized Friedman for concentrating too much on statistical relationships (between the quantity of money and the price level), claiming that matters are not quite that simple. Nonetheless, he indicated that for all practical purposes, he and Friedman were 'wholly on the same side'. Here Hayek qualified this claim only with the parenthetical remark, 'our differences are fine points of abstruse theory'.

Friedman's account of his differences with Hayek puts the 'fine points of abstruse theory' into perspective: 'I am an enormous admirer of Hayek, but not for his economics. I think *Prices and Production* [([1935] 1967)) is a flawed book. I think his capital theory book [*The Pure Theory of Capital* (1941)] is unreadable. On the other hand, *The Road to Serfdom* (1944) is one of the great books of our time' (Ebenstein, 2001, p. 81). In Friedman's view, the alliance is based on their adherence to the principles of classical liberalism; their economics – and especially their macroeconomics – is quite another matter.

OPPOSING VIEWS ABOUT 'THE RIGHT KIND OF MACROECONOMICS'

Hayek's early work on capital theory was, in the first instance, an exercise in price theory with special attention to the market economy's temporal dimension. The Hayekian triangle, as it came to be called, was introduced in his 1931 London School of Economics (LSE) lectures (which became *Prices and Production*) as a highly stylized depiction of the economy's time structure of production. Hayek demonstrated just how the allocation of resources among the temporally sequenced stages of production can be guided by the price system. Changes in people's preferred pattern of consumption over time, as registered by their saving behavior, get translated through the price system – and in particular through interest rate movements – into an altered pattern of investment among temporally sequenced stages of production. In a well-functioning economy, investment decisions in the current period will not be systematically at odds with people's current saving propensities or with their future demands for consumption goods. His account of how markets work to coordinate production decisions with consumer preferences is an exercise in price theory; that is, in microeconomics. But it is foundational, in Hayek's view, to any subsequent theorizing about macroeconomic issues of boom and bust.

Long before the search for microeconomic foundations was added to the agenda of modern macroeconomics, Hayek ([1935] 1967, p. 127) insisted that price theory is a strict prerequisite to monetary theory, business cycle theory and, it might be added, to macroeconomics in general: the 'task [of monetary theory] is to cover a second time the whole field which is treated by pure theory under the assumption of barter, and to investigate what changes in the conclusions of pure theory are made necessary by the introduction of indirect exchange'. The mere statement of this agenda for monetary theory (and for macroeconomics) seems to command assent, with only one point of clarification. The broader context in which this mission statement appears suggests that his reference to 'barter' as an assumption that underlies 'pure theory' is unnecessarily strong, even to the point of being misleading. His 'pure theory' is simply value theory, or price theory, which assumes away not money itself but rather all problems that might originate from the sphere of money.[4] Monetary theory, then, beyond the accounting of money's evolution and of its essential role in facilitating exchange, is concerned with the problems that stem from breaking the direct links between supplying and demanding. Money, that is, puts some slack in the price system, allowing for the possibility of economy-wide disequilibrium conditions that can persist for some time.

In Hayek's *Pure Theory of Capital* (1941, p. 408), the potential for problems arising in the monetary sphere are attributed to money's status as a 'loose joint': 'money by its very nature constitutes a kind of loose joint in a self-equilibrating apparatus of the price mechanism which is bound to impede its working – the more so the greater play in the loose joint'. By implication, pure theory assumes a tight joint. The introduction of this tight/loose distinction in the closing pages of Hayek's otherwise 'pure theory' facilitated a summary assessment of Keynes's loose-joint theorizing: 'the existence of such a loose joint is no justification for concentrating attention on that loose joint and disregarding the rest of the mechanism, and still less for making the greatest possible use of the short-lived freedom from economic necessity which the existence of this loose joint permits' (p. 408).

In the context of Hayek's theorizing as it compares to Friedman's, the tight/loose distinction is significant in a different way. It helps identify the 'right kind of macroeconomics'. The origins of a conspicuous macroeconomic problem, such as a cyclical downturn, possibly followed by a spiraling of the economy into deep depression, are to be found in the loose-jointedness of the allocation mechanism that can allow for a systemic disequilibrium in the period preceding the downturn. Unlike the macroeconomic *consequence* of the systemic disequilibrium (a sometimes dramatic collapse), the *cause* of the problem is not so conspicuous. The inherent looseness, especially if that looseness is being exploited by policymakers for political gain, can allow for a more vigorous economic expansion than can be sustained. But the disequilibrium that characterizes the investment boom – that is, its unsustainability – does not reveal itself until the boom is eventually brought to an end by the cumulative mismatching of production plans and consumer preferences.

The role of the economist, Hayek points out (1941, p. 409), is precisely to identify such aspects of the situation that are 'hidden from the untrained eye'. For Hayek, the cause-and-effect relationship between the short-run exploitation of the price system's loose-jointedness and the subsequent economic downturn has a first-order claim on our attention despite the more salient co-movements in macroeconomic magnitudes that characterize the post-downturn spiraling of the economy into deep depression.

On the question of the 'right kind of macroeconomics', Friedman's judgment stands in stark contrast to Hayek's. In his general approach to theorizing, Friedman (1986, p. 48) is a soul mate to Keynes: 'I believe that Keynes's theory is the right kind of theory in its simplicity, its concentration of a few key magnitudes, its potential fruitfulness'. As described by Allan Meltzer (1988, p. 18), 'Keynes was the type of theorist who developed his theory after he had developed a sense of relative magnitudes and of the size and frequency of changes in these magnitudes. He concentrated on those magnitudes that changed most, often assuming that others remained fixed for the relevant period'. Friedman's own professed agreement with Keynes in this regard is confirmed by his adoption of a 'simple common model', to set out the key differences between monetarism and Keynesianism (Friedman, 1970a). This simple common model is the algebraic rendition of the once-standard Keynesian analytical framework (IS–LM: Investment Saving–Liquidity preference Money supply).[5] Here and elsewhere Friedman sees his differences with Keynes as empirical and not theoretical.

Friedman's 'right kind of macroeconomics' restricts the theorizing to measurable magnitudes whose variations are of a 'substantial size and frequency'. Ruled out of consideration from the outset, then, are any subtle but cumulative deviations in the pattern of investments from the pattern that would be consistent with sustainable growth. With an empirical orientation and a focus on a few key magnitudes, Friedman's research agenda was limited in its scope by an untenable methodological maxim: big effects must have big causes. (Strict adherence to this maxim would require us to reject the possibility that a forest fire was caused by a discarded cigarette butt.) It is true, of course, that some causes and corresponding effects are both big. (Mount Vesuvius and Pompeii come to mind.) And these, of course, are the ones for which there can be strong empirical support. But some causes – and sometimes the more fundamental causes – can be 'hidden from the untrained eye'.

A big change in the quantity of money in circulation has a big effect on the general level of spending. This empirical finding, which is bedrock for Friedman's monetarism, has as its theoretical expression the equation of exchange: $MV = PQ$, where M is the money supply, V is its velocity of circulation, and PQ (the price level times the economy's total output) is total nominal expenditures E. Largely because of considerations of data availability, the monetarists' actual empirical testing made use of total nominal income (Y) rather than nominal expenditures. In the long run, the economy's circular flow of earning and spending keeps any difference between these two magnitudes (Y and E) empirically trivial and justifies the substitution of Y for E in the equation of exchange.

Though a profoundly limited methodology, Friedman's empiricism was enormously successful during the quarter-century following his seminal restatement of the quantity theory of money (Friedman, [1956] 1969). The validity of the proposition that changes in PQ are associated with proportional or near-proportional changes in M rests on the constancy or near-constancy of V. And, in fact, the bulk of the empirical work done during the ascendency of monetarism was aimed at showing that in many different countries and in many different time periods, the demand for money – as gauged summarily by the reciprocal of the money's income velocity – is a stable demand. The empirical finding in the 1950s and 1960s of a well-behaved demand for money (a near-constant V with only a slight upward trend) was of great significance. It effectively countered the Keynesian vision in which money hoarders can play a major causal role in determining the economy's level of income and expenditures. Driven by psychological factors, or so Keynes would have us believe, people's hoarding propensities – that is, their liquidity preferences – can change in unpredictable ways. In the absence of rapidly adjusting prices, the fetishistic behavior of money holders can keep the economy from functioning at its full employment level.

Friedman's idea of 'the right kind of macroeconomics' together with his empirical finding of stable money demand puts into clear perspective his own claim that 'We're all Keynesians now'. Insisting that he was quoted out of context, Friedman offered an in-context statement that established more accurately his relationship to Keynes: 'in one sense, we are all Keynesians now; in another, no one is a Keynesian any longer'. He went on to identify the two senses: 'We all use the Keynesian language and apparatus; none of us any longer accepts the initial Keynesian conclusions' (Friedman, 1968, p. 15) – which is to say: we all set out our macroeconomics in terms of the same few highly aggregated magnitudes, but we reject, among other specifics, the conclusion that variations in those magnitudes are caused by a fetish-driven and unstable money demand.

We should note here that Friedman's 'all', whatever the intended context, is too inclusive. It should include Keynesians and monetarists but not Austrians. The contrast between Keynes's (and Friedman's) 'variations of substantial size and frequency' and Hayek's 'aspects hidden from the untrained eye' was specifically at issue when Hayek (1978, p. 25) remarked in his Nobel address – which he aptly titled 'The pretense of knowledge': 'there may ... well exist better "scientific" evidence [empirically demonstrated regularities among "key" magnitudes] for a false theory, which will be accepted because it is more "scientific", than for a valid explanation, which is rejected because there is no sufficient quantitative evidence for it'. The target of his remark was Keynesianism, which features the empirically demonstrable short-run co-movements of spending and employment, but the remark also has implications for monetarism, which features, almost exclusively, the empirically demonstrable co-movements of the money supply and nominal income, the movements in the latter ultimately taking the form of movements in the overall price level.

The contrast between the two methodologies is also directly at issue when Friedman claims, in reference to interwar expansion and subsequent contraction, that 'Everything going on in the 1920s was fine', and that 'what happened in the thirties explains the thirties, not what happened in the twenties' (Skousen, 2005, pp. 166, 181 fn 9). Friedman's 'everything going on the 1920s' must be understood to mean everything that can be described with the Keynesian language and apparatus.

Although Friedman's monetarism was methodologically incapable of exposing those hidden aspects of the boom that were key to Hayek's theory, its empirical demonstrations of the stability of money demand did have its intended effect of focusing attention on the money supply. That is, if the variations of the Keynesian macroeconomic magnitudes were not attributable to fetish-driven money demanders, then they must be attributed to the bungle-prone money supplier. Much more often than not, it is a change in M and not a change in V that leads to a change in PQ. In the long run, money-induced changes in PQ resolve themselves into changes in P – with the economy's real output (Q) ultimately being determined solely by real inputs (and hence not at all by the quantity of money in circulation). However, it follows almost as a corollary that until the price level fully adjusts itself to a changed quantity of money, quantity adjustments, possibly severe ones, will characterize the adjustment process.

The combination of the classical proposition about the long-run neutrality of money together with the empirically demonstrated stability of money demand underlies Friedman's claim that the Great Depression, or more specifically, the severe economic contraction that began after the 1929 stock market crash and lasted well into 1933, was almost wholly attributable to the collapse of the money supply. Similarly, his classically inspired empirical studies underlie his claim that 'inflation is always and everywhere a monetary phenomenon' (Friedman, 1968, p. 39). In the long run, increases in M in excess of increases in real output are followed by proportionate increases in P.

When qualified with due allowances for allocation effects and wealth effects, which can last well beyond Friedman's short run, this long-run proposition about the relationship between the money supply and the general level of prices was disputed neither by Hayek nor by any of the other Austrian economists. In fact, Ludwig von Mises incorporated the quantity theory of money into his own thinking in *The Theory of Money and Credit* ([1912] 1953, pp. 146–51). He defended this theory, which he simply took to be the supply-and-demand approach to explaining money's value, against the then prevalent theory that money is imbued with value by the state. But, for Hayek (as well as for Mises), establishing P's long-run near-proportionality to M is only a minor part of the task of monetary theory. More demanding – and more relevant to the issues of the business cycle, monetary policy and monetary reform – is the task of identifying the shorter-run non-neutral aspects of money. What can be said about the movements of real output during a monetary expansion, and about money-induced changes in relative prices and hence in the pattern of output? More specifically, how is the relationship between the valuation of outputs and the corresponding valuation on inputs affected by changes in the money supply? The answers to these and related questions, by virtue of the nature of the questions themselves, must be firmly anchored in what Hayek calls 'pure theory', by which he simply means the underlying microeconomic relationships, which may be distorted in a protracted and systematic way by changes in the money supply.

MACROECONOMIC AGGREGATES AND MACROECONOMIC PATTERNS

It has long been perceived that Keynes is the father of macroeconomics. There is an important sense in which this perception is correct. Keynes's *General Theory* certainly represents a break with ongoing developments in economics and even a break with his own earlier work. Reflecting years later on Keynes's influence and expressing regret for not having reviewed Keynes's book, Hayek identified the 'decisive reason' for failing to write a review (one reason among several; again, see Caldwell, 1998): Hayek had an aversion to macroeconomics per se. His exact remarks require close scrutiny. Although ripe for misinterpretation, they can be revealing about the key difference between Hayek and Keynes, and *a fortiori* between Hayek and Friedman.

> There was [one] reason which I then only dimly felt but which in retrospect appears to me the decisive one: My disagreement with that book did not refer so much to any detail of the analysis as to the general approach followed in the whole work. The real issue was the validity of what we now call macro-analysis, and I feel now that in a long-run perspective the chief significance of the *General Theory* will appear that more than any other single work it decisively furthered the ascendancy of macroeconomics and the temporary decline of microeconomic theory. (Hayek, 1978, p. 284)

Was it Hayek's intent to declare all of macroeconomics invalid? That could hardly be so. Students at the London School of Economics in the 1930s were immersed in Hayekian thought and at the same time were well aware of the Keynesian alternative. The oft-quoted reckoning by John Hicks (1969, p. 203) features Keynes and Hayek as the major contenders for the field. And the field, of course, was macroeconomics, though the term itself was not yet in common use. Both Keynes and Hayek theorized about business cycles and particularly about the unemployment associated with downturns and depressions. They both wrote about the relationship between saving and investment, and about money, interest rates and wage rates. In short, they were both macroeconomists.

At most, what Hayek 'only dimly felt' was the categorical difference between his kind of macroeconomics and Keynes's kind of macroeconomics. Some two decades after the publication of the *General Theory*, the difference that emerged between Friedman and Keynes was relatively minor compared to the difference between Hayek's macroeconomics and Keynes and Friedman's macroeconomics. Still, Hayek's claim of a dim feeling even in this sense is puzzling. The major theme in his *Monetary Theory and the Trade Cycle* ([1928] 1975) which was published years before Keynes's *General Theory*, is that the quantity theory of money has relevance beyond the simple across-the-board relationship between the quantity of money and the overall level of prices. Perceiving an undue emphasis on the price level that characterized then prevalent monetary theory, Hayek showed that the quantity theory can serve as the starting point for an analysis of relative price changes that are induced by the extension of bank credit. How, then, could his general dissatisfaction with the sort of macroeconomics as set out in the *General Theory* be 'only dimly felt'?

Hayek's criticism of the crude 'Quantity Theory school', as he called it, was extended years later to apply to Keynesian crudities. In a 1979 interview, Hayek explicitly categorized 'Keynes's economics as just another branch of the centuries-old Quantity Theory school, the school now associated with Milton Friedman' (Minard, 1979, p. 49). Keynes, according to

Hayek, 'is a quantity theorist, but modified in an even more aggregative or collectivist or macroeconomic tendency' (ibid.). Modern mainstream macroeconomists may be puzzled that Hayek – or anyone – would associate Keynes of the *General Theory* with Friedman of the 'optimum quantity of money'. But Keynes and Friedman are similar in Hayek's perception in terms of their macroeconomic methodologies; a perception that is confirmed by Friedman himself when he praised Keynes for pursuing the 'right kind of macroeconomics'.

The contrast between monetarism and Keynesianism stems from Friedman's considerably narrowed conception of the quantity theory. He began his 1956 restatement with the claim that, 'The quantity theory is in the first instance a theory of the *demand* for money' (Friedman, 1969, p. 52). In Friedman's hands, it is a theory that, contra Keynes, the demand for money is stable. And with V not changing much, PQ moves with M. The centuries-old Quantity Theory that united Keynes and Friedman in Hayek's mind was characterized by its high level of aggregation which allows the role of money to be analyzed exclusively in terms of the price level and without regard to the pattern of prices or the corresponding mix of outputs. With this definition, Keynes's conception of macroeconomic equilibrium as an equality between total income and total expenditures ($Y = E$), where the Y and E change in real terms when economic activity is below its full employment potential, and change only in nominal terms when the economy is pressured to move beyond its full employment potential, falls comfortably into the quantity theory tradition.

For Hayek, what mattered was the patterns of spending on consumable output and on the various factors of production. To focus on total expenditure and total income is to overlook the foundational microeconomic relationships that give meaning to the notion of a macroeconomic equilibrium. This is the point of Hayek's early charge that 'Mr. Keynes's aggregates conceal the most fundamental mechanisms of change' (Hayek, 1931, p. 227). On this count, Friedman's quantity theory reckoning was less attractive – that is, more aggregative – than Keynes's circular flow. Keynes, after all, did disaggregate the total expenditures of the private sector into consumption expenditures and investment expenditures: $E = C + I$. Friedman combined the two categories of output into a single aggregate output: $Q_C + Q_I = Q$. Hence, the output magnitude in Friedman's quantity theory does not differentiate in any substantial way between consumption and investment.

In Hayek's macroeconomics, the wrong mix of consumption and investment and the wrong temporal pattern of investment activities can constitute a macroeconomic disequilibrium; even though total spending in the current period might equal current income, and even if the overall price level is constant. In Hayek's view, something important is missing from any macroeconomic theory that does not give emphasis to this aspect of macroeconomic disequilibrium.

THE MISSING TRADE-OFF: BETWEEN CONSUMPTION AND INVESTMENT

As in other respects, the contrast between Hayek's and Friedman's macroeconomics is best put into perspective by first reviewing Hayek's dissatisfaction with Keynesian theory. As already indicated, Hayek considered Keynes's theorizing to be in the quantity theory tradition; this despite Keynes's dividing total private spending into two constituent components. Keynes's distinction between consumption spending and investment spending was not made in order to allow for a trade-off between these two magnitudes but rather in recognition that one of the components, namely investment spending, was subject to unpredictable changes in both magnitude and direction.

Keynes's 'animal spirits', which motivate investors and which wax and wane with the winds of business psychology, cause investment spending to rise and fall and cause total spending to change in the same direction and with an amplified magnitude. When investors are moved by the animal spirits, the high investment spending and higher total spending generates correspondingly higher incomes, out of which people engage in more consumption spending and more saving. Similarly, if consumption spending were to decrease, say as a result of an increase in saving propensities, then total spending ($C + I$) would decrease, too. Further, the resulting slack economy would likely dampen the animal spirits that had been motivating the investment community. Here, the principle of derived demand is in play. In Keynes's construction, then, the two spending magnitudes (C and I) move together (though at different rates). Neither ever moves at the expense of the other. There is no allowance for a trade-off between consumption and investment.

Reflecting on the Keynesian Revolution three decades after the publication of the *General Theory*, Hayek ([1966] 1978, p. 285) focused on the 'relation between the demand for consumers' goods and the volume of investment' in order to establish this critical difference between Keynes's theorizing and his own. 'There are undoubtedly certain conditions in which an increase of the demand for consumers' goods *will* lead to an increase in investment. But Keynes assumes that this will always be the case'. The 'certain conditions', of course, are conditions of economy-wide unemployment of labor and other factors of production. But at least sometimes, scarcity is a binding constraint. Under these conditions, consumption (in the current period) and investment (which will allow for increased consumption in some future period) must present themselves as trade-offs.

Abba Lerner and others who were learning from both Keynes and Hayek in the 1930s were alive to this defining distinction (Colander and Landreth, 1996). For Keynes, consumption and investment move up and down together, their path of possible movements only occasionally (and quite by accident) bumping up against the constraint imposed by scarcity; for Hayek, these two magnitudes must be traded off against one another at full employment. And understanding the market process that can facilitate the desired trade-off, Hayek insisted, is a strict prerequisite to understanding how that process might malfunction (or be derailed) in such a way as to result in the widespread unemployment of labor and other factors of production.

While Keynes's theoretical construction effectively denied even the possibility of a trade-off, his highly aggregative treatment of investment concealed the market mechanisms that make such a trade-off possible. Hayek's alternative construction entailed a multi-stage structure of production whose separate stages are affected differentially by a change in consumption spending. For instance, an increase in saving, which means a reduction of consumption spending, impinges in a twofold way on the stages of production. Late-stage production activities are curtailed by the derived-demand effect. But early-stage production activities are bolstered by the decreased interest rates, which are the direct consequence of increased saving. Resources are allocated away from the production of current and near-future consumables and toward the production of more-remote-future consumables. This reallocation, which is consistent with the change in the hypothesized spending and saving propensities, is achieved by the interplay of the derived-demand effect and the interest rate effect. It was Keynes's failure to recognize this interplay and its significance that led him to articulate his infamous paradox of thrift, according to which an increase in savings (implying a decrease in consumption spending), leads to a general decrease in spending and hence in income, which in turn counters the initial increase in saving.

The ruling out of any consumption–investment trade-off and the neglect of the market mechanisms that might facilitate it was rightly seen as the Achilles' heel of the Keynesian construction. Unfortunately, these critical issues were put into total eclipse by the monetarist counter-revolution. The equation of exchange makes no first-order distinction between consumption and investment. These two components of the economy's output make only a summary appearance, as the Q in the equation of exchange,

$MV = PQ$, where Q represents the sum of the economy's consumable output and the additions to its capital stock. And further removing the critical trade-off from view, the monetarists do not write the equation of exchange explicitly in terms of output (Q) but rather in terms of the empirically equivalent real income (y) paid to labor and other inputs in the process of producing it. (Using lower case to indicate a real magnitude, that is, $y = Y/P$, is standard in monetarist literature.) The issues that are central to Hayek's macroeconomics and key to exposing the oversights and fallacies in Keynes's, are buried deep in Friedman's $MV = Py$.

THE MONETARISTS' TRADE-OFF AND THE 'MISSING EQUATION'

While the Austrians' macroeconomic construction features the relative movements of consumption and investment, the monetarists' construction features the distinction between nominal and real changes in the economy's total output (of both consumption goods and investment goods). That is, in the short run, a change in nominal output (as measured by nominal income, Py) entails some combination of a change in the general level of prices (P) and a change in real output, or real income (y). Of particular interest to the monetarists, of course, are the consequences for P and y of an increase (or decrease) in the money supply. The general issue here resolves itself into the question of the $P - Q$ split or, equivalently, the $P - y$ split.

The hard core of monetarism is its demonstration of the nature of the $P - y$ split in the context of the long run. The proposition for which Milton Friedman is best known is that, in the long run, money-induced changes in Py consist wholly of proportionate changes in P and hence not at all in changes in y. The long run is understood to be a period sufficiently long (typically 18–30 months) for market mechanisms, whatever their particulars, to adjust the level of prices to the higher money supply.

In the simple case of a constant velocity of money and no economic growth, the long-run relationship between the money supply and the price level is one of strict proportionality. For an economy that experiences a growth rate in the low single digits, a money supply that is made to grow at that same rate results in an unchanging price level. This is the basis for Friedman's monetary rule: year in and year out, the growth rate of the money supply should be made to match the long-run trend of economic growth.

The short run is a different story – and a variously told story. The issue of the $P - y$ split during the economy's adjustment to a change in the money supply constitutes the soft underbelly – a 'major unsettled issue' Friedman (1992, p. 49) – of monetarism. Recognizing that the monetarist framework was not a closed system of equations except in its long-run application, Friedman discussed the short-run $P - y$ split in terms of a 'missing equation'. In a 1974 exposition (in Gordon, 1974, pp. 31ff) he combines the main Keynesian variables (consumption, investment, income and the interest rate) with the essential monetarist variables (the money supply, money demand and the price level) into what he calls a 'simple common model'. Tellingly, the common model has six equations and seven unknowns; hence a missing equation. Friedman points out that the two simplest ways to close the system of equations are: (1) to take the price level as given, which gives the system of equations a short-run Keynesian orientation; or (2) to take real income as given, which gives them a long-run monetarist orientation. Friedman then provides a lengthy account of a 'third approach' (Gordon, 1974, pp. 34–40) in which the system of equations is closed by dealing only with nominal income, Py, and not addressing the issues of the $P - y$ split. Offering as monetarism's hardest-core proposition the near proportionality between the money supply and nominal income, while remaining agnostic about the nature of the $P - y$ split, has since become monetarism in its most defensive mode. The near-proportionality is a direct implication of the empirically demonstrated near-constancy of the velocity of money. This mode of thinking is consistent with the statement of Friedman and Schwartz in which they adopt an agnostic attitude about the 'transmission mechanism' through which changes in the money supply affects the economy's real variables:

> We have little confidence in our knowledge of the transmission mechanism, except in such broad and vague terms as to constitute little more than an impressionistic representation rather than an engineering blueprint. Indeed, this is the challenge our evidence poses: to pin down the transmission mechanism in specific enough detail that we can hope to make reasonably accurate predictions of the course of a wide variety of economic variables [i.e., the seven unknowns] on the basis of information about monetary disturbances. (Friedman and Schwartz, [1963] 1969, p. 222)

At this point, we have three approaches to dealing with the missing equation: a short-run constant Keynesian P, a long-run constant monetarist y, and a short-run agnostic monetarist Py.[6] In his preliminary remarks, Friedman rightly and revealingly recognizes that these three approaches are nowhere near exhaustive. He points out that to close the seven-variable, six-equation system, '[s]ome one of these variables must be determined by relationships outside the system' (p. 31). And in a footnote, he immediately expands the possibilities: 'It is not necessary that a single variable be so determined. What is required is an independent relation connecting some subset of the seven endogenous variables with exogenous variables, and that subset could in principle consist of all seven variables' (p. 31 fn 18).

Here, Friedman may be seen as recognizing the open-endedness of ways to close the system. But his open-ended possibilities are constrained by Keynes and Friedman's 'right kind of macroeconomics'. There is a pre-emptive ruling out of transmission mechanisms that may be operating within one or more of the seven variables. As dictated by his methodology, attention is limited to measurable magnitudes whose variations are of a substantial size and frequency.

Ironically, Friedman's earliest attempt to deal head-on with the lag that separates a change in the money supply and the eventual change in the price level focused on market mechanisms that work within one of the seven variables. Why should this time lag between the injection of new money into the economy and the full adjustment of the price level be so long? To answer this question, Friedman focuses largely on market mechanisms within the investment aggregate – mechanisms that are triggered by the initial holders of the injected money:

> Holders of cash will . . . bid up the price of assets. If the extra demand is initially directed at a particular class of assets, say, government securities, or commercial paper, or the like, the result will be to pull the prices of such assets out of line with other assets and thus widen the area into which the extra cash spills. The increased demand will spread sooner or later affecting equities, houses, durable producer goods, durable consumer goods, and so on, though not necessarily in that order . . . These effects can be described as operating on 'interest rates', if a more cosmopolitan [i.e., Hayekian] interpretation of 'interest rates' is adopted than the usual one which refers to a small range of marketable securities. (Friedman, [1961] 1969, p. 255)

Assuming that his consumer durables qualify as investment, Friedman is dealing with different sub-aggregates that make up the investment magnitude. The distinction between durables and non-durables is a rough proxy for Hayek's distinction between various stages of production: 'durable' translates into 'earlier stage'. What Friedman has in mind, of course, is the distinction between 'sources' and 'services' or, equivalently, stocks and flows. This is the distinction that underlies Frank Knight's capital theory. Nonetheless, Friedman's characterization of the market process that occurs between the increase in the money supply and the eventual rise in the price level has a distinct Austrian flavor, including the temporarily low rate of interest and the inherently self-reversing character of the adjustment process. In the continuation of his account Friedman's 'reactions' that 'undo the initial effects' are Hayek's self-reversing process:

> The key feature of this process [during which interest rates are low] is that it tends to raise the prices of sources of both producer and consumer services relative to the prices of the services themselves ... It therefore encourages the production of such sources and, at the same time, the direct acquisition of the services rather than of the source. But these reactions in their turn tend to raise the prices of services relative to the prices of sources, that is, to undo the initial effects on interest rates. The final result may be a rise in expenditures in all directions without any change in interest rates at all; interest rates and asset prices may simply be the conduit through which the effect of the monetary change is transmitted to expenditures without being altered at all (pp. 255–6)

The idea that artificially low interest rates govern resource allocation during the boom and that this market process is inherently self-reversing are, of course, central to the Austrian account of boom and bust. All that is lacking in Friedman's stock-flow (or source-service) accounting of the process is the recognition of a more thoroughgoing intertemporal capital structure. But even this aspect of the process is brought into view when Friedman breaks loose from the Knightian stock-flow straitjacket and breathes some life into the issue of capital allocation:

> It may be ... that monetary expansion induces someone within two or three months to contemplate building a factory; within four or five, to draw up plans; within six or seven, to get construction started. The actual construction may take another six months and much of the effect on the income stream may come still later, insofar as initial goods used in construction are withdrawn from inventories and only subsequently lead to increased expenditure by suppliers. (p. 256)

Friedman's objective in this 1961 article is to make plausible the empirical finding of an otherwise implausibly long lag between the increase of the money supply and the eventual near-proportional increase in the price level. But while he makes the long lag plausible, he inadvertently created doubts that: (1) the overall price level (rather than relative-price changes and hence resource misallocations) should be central to his theory; and (2) the full adjustment to the monetary injection is complete once the price level has risen. Essentially, Friedman's long lag is a reflection of Hayek's loose joint. From his earliest writings, Hayek had insisted that the misallocation of resources into long-term but unsustainable capital should be the central focus.

The 1961 article is particularly revealing in the context of the subsequent search for the missing equation. Friedman's monetary framework, set out on the basis of Keynesian variables, is in fact one equation short. But adding a seventh equation in terms of those seven variables fails to close the system in a satisfying way. And on the basis of Friedman's 1961 discussion of the lag, we see that what is actually missing is Hayek.

No candidate seventh equation, whether $P = P_0$, $y = y_0$, $Y = Py$ (or any other equation restricted to the seven Keynesian variables), will do the job. Rather, the short-run variations are to be accounted for in terms of money-induced movements of resources that are eclipsed by the Keynesian – and monetarist – aggregates. Hayek's early criticism of Keynes applies equally to Friedman: '[Mr Friedman's] aggregates conceal the most fundamental mechanisms of change'.

Why, we must ask, couldn't – or didn't – Friedman put his earlier treatment of the lag into play when setting out his own analytical framework? The answer to this question is readily at hand: because doing so would be contrary to his fundamental methodological precepts. Teasing the cause of the downturn out of the pattern of resource allocation during the boom is not the right kind of macroeconomics, especially as applied to the interwar experience of boom and bust. During the 1920s, there were no macroeconomic magnitudes undergoing such dramatic change as to capture Friedman's attention. And undramatic changes, such as those that may well have been going on within the output aggregate, were *ipso facto* seen as incapable of having dramatic consequences. Besides, any attempt to track capital movements at a low level of aggregation would be fraught with measurement problems and, in any case, would be irrelevant in view of the Knightian stock-flow conception of capital and income. Finally, actual movements in interest rates during the 1920s appeared minor at best and hence hardly warranted any concern about money-induced effects on resource allocation.

HAYEK AND THE HIDDEN FORCES DURING THE 1920s BOOM

The task of the economist, according to Hayek, is precisely to look for aspects of market forces that are apt to be hidden from the untrained eye. There is probably no better example of such hidden forces than those that occurred during the boom of the 1920s. The combination of technological advance and accommodating monetary policy leaves interest rates largely unaffected but skews the pattern of investment, putting it in conflict with intertemporal preferences and hence with the pattern of consumer spending.

As conventionally told, the story of the business cycle entails an actual lowering of the interest rate by the central bank. The artificially cheap credit results in excessive investment in long-term (and hence interest rate sensitive) projects. At the same time, the low return on saving results in an increase in current and near-term consumption. In short, an artificially low interest rate drives a wedge between saving and investment and sets the economy off on an unsustainable growth path.

A conceptually separate story, the story of technological advance, entails a temporarily high market rate of interest. Improvements in technology, such as occurred during the 1920s (electrification, home appliances, processed foods, industrial chemicals, cosmetics and the mass production of automobiles) meant increased returns to investment spending. Had there been no central bank accommodation, the correspondingly increased demand for investment funds would put upward pressure on interest rates while the increased investment activity, would in time would result in more and/or better consumer goods being available. The higher interest rates would call forth an additional amount of saving, whose magnitude would set the pace at which the new technological possibilities could be exploited.

Consumers, however, would be eager to take at least some of those gains in the form of current consumption. Expanded employment opportunities resulting from the technological advance would provide increased incomes, which would translate into increased saving *and* increased spending on currently available consumables. Put differently, the increased saving out of the rising incomes would not allow for a full-throttle implementation of the new technology. Inventories of consumer goods would be drawn down, and hence some resources would be drawn in this direction to accommodate the increased consumer demands. In short, the competition for investment funds – to accommodate increased current consumer demand and to implement the new technology – would cause the interest rate to rise.

In his earliest writings on monetary theory, Hayek ([1928] 1975) identified the temporary increase in interest rates during the implementation period as the interest rate brake. That is, while increased earnings and increased saving allow for the implementation of new technologies, the actual spending patterns of consumers sets a limit on the rate of implementation so as to allow for some increased consumption to be enjoyed during the implementation period.

When the basic story of the business cycle (entailing a reduced interest rate) is superimposed onto the story of technological advance (entailing an increased interest rate), it is not surprising that the interest rate seems not to play a major role. It undergoes little or no change because the downward pressure of credit expansion offsets the upward pressure of the interest rate brake. The fact that there is no clearly discernible net movement in the interest rate during the 1920s is not a matter of coincidence. The Federal Reserve's policy of 'accommodating the needs of trade', a policy based on the real bills doctrine, meant that any increased demand for investment funds would be met by an increased supply of credit rather than by an increased interest rate. That is, as a matter of policy, the Federal Reserve overrode the interest rate brake, allowing the pattern of investment to get cumulatively out of line with the pattern of spending. Hayek's own summary assessment is to the point, although in his early work on business cycles he attributed the cycles to any system of elastically supplied credit rather than to ill-fated policies of a central bank:

> The immediate consequence of an adjustment of the volume of money to the 'requirements' of industry is the failure of the 'interest brake' to operate as promptly as it would in an economy operating without credit. This means, however, that new adjustments are undertaken on a larger scale than can be completed; a boom is thus made possible, with the inevitably recurring 'crisis'. (Hayek, [1928] 1975, p. 179)

The 'crisis' in this passage refers to the inevitable downturn that eventually comes about as a result of the cumulative mismatch of the pattern of investment and the pattern of spending. This was his theory – more broadly, the Austrian theory – of boom and bust. And his judgment that the 1920s boom was not sustainable was made well before the bust. In 1923, while studying at New York University and watching the Federal Reserve, Hayek began work on a PhD thesis to answer the question, 'Is the function of money consistent with an artificial stabilization of purchasing power?' (Hayek, 1984, p. 7). In retrospect, we might rephrase the question: 'Is Friedman's monetary rule consistent with sustainable growth?' No doubt, had Hayek completed that thesis, the interest rate brake and the perversities of the real-bills doctrine would have been central to his argument.

In Hayek's view, the particulars of the market process that characterize the boom have a first-order claim on the economist's attention, despite any subsequent spiraling downwards of income and spending and despite subsequent ill-conceived fiscal and monetary policies that, along with tax policies, trade policies, price supports and relief programs made the ensuing depression much deeper and much longer than it otherwise would have been. The fact that movements in the macroeconomic aggregates can be large ones and the correlations among the aggregates can be strong ones does not detract from the significance of the policy-driven market process that preceded the bust.

A SUMMARY JUDGMENT: METHODOLOGY AS TRUMPS

A careful reading of Hayek's and Friedman's monetary theory reveals some common ground. Neither Hayek nor Austrian economists generally have denied the kernel of truth in the quantity theory of money. No doubt, the long-run relationship linking the price level to the money supply (as well as its implications for monetary reform) accounts for the occasions in which Hayek minimized the differences between Friedman and himself. The merits of a Hayek–Friedman alliance were especially obvious in the 1970s, when monetary restraint in almost any form had to be considered preferable to a continuation of the money-driven, double-digit price and wage inflation. This aspect of the common ground is, no doubt, fairly widely understood.

Hardly recognized at all, however, is that Friedman, who has issued emphatic and wholesale dismissals of Hayek's *Prices and Production*, actually wrote his own *Prices and Production* in the form of 'The lag in effect of monetary policy'. The key excerpts from that article (presented above) have an undeniable Hayekian flavor. A Friedman–Hayek alliance would seem to be in order especially in the context of the 1920s, when the story to be told could not be convincingly told in terms of the Keynesian aggregates. Friedman's own story of the $M - P$ lag and hence the $P - y$ split fills in the blanks and aligns his own understanding of the boom with Hayek's.[7]

It can only be that Friedman's pre-commitment to Keynes's kind of macroeconomics stood in the way of such an alliance. For Friedman, methodology was trumps. But with the methodological issues fully in view, modern readers can appreciate both Friedman's post-boom empirical findings and Hayek's pre-bust economic insights.

NOTES

1. Enduring or renewed interest in this comparison of ideas is evidenced by Mark Skousen's *Vienna and Chicago: Friends or Foes?* (2005) and Lanny Ebenstein's separate biographies of *Friedrich Hayek* (2001) and *Milton Friedman* (2007).
2. In his early writings, Hayek ([1928] 1984) had suggested that, as a policy ideal, the product of money and its velocity of circulation, that is, MV, should be kept constant. The constant product implies that M should be varied to offset any variation in V. This aspect of the policy is aimed at dealing with liquidity crises. But the rule also implies that increased economic output should be accommodated by a declining price level. That is, a constant PQ that matches the constant MV requires that P and Q must move in opposing directions. The apparent difference here between the early and late Hayek, that is, between a recommended constancy of MV and a recommended increase in M to match the increase in Q, does not constitute a change of mind but rather is a difference between Hayek's notions of ideal policy and practical policy. See Garrison (1985).

3. See Caldwell (1998) for an assessment of the various reasons that Hayek offered for his not reviewing Keynes's book.
4. '[I]t is clear that [in Hayek's writings] the monetary economy is not to be compared with an actual barter economy, but with the abstract type of an economy where money is not needed because there are no frictions or imperfections' (Klausinger, 1989, p. 172).
5. Nearly three decades after introducing the 'common model', Friedman identified this particular tactic (of setting out his own ideas in the language of Keynesianism) as his 'biggest academic blunder' (Weinstein, 1999). However, any alternative tactic he might have adopted would not likely have lessened the difference between his kind of macroeconomics and Hayek's.
6. Left out of account here is the common textbook exposition of short-run/long-run Phillips curve analysis. True, the market process that moves the economy along a short-run Phillips curve and then causes the curve itself to shift was set out by Friedman himself. But his analysis was intended, as I argue elsewhere (Garrison, 2001, pp. 199–203), primarily as an immanent criticism of the 1960s-style Keynesian policy menu and not as the monetarist account of the $P - y$ split. The very notion that it is rising prices, as differentially perceived by employers and employees, that lead to an increase in output is directly at odds with one of the fundamental propositions of monetarism: according to Friedman (1970b, p. 23), 'the change in the growth rate of nominal income [following an increase in the money supply] typically shows up *first* in output and hardly at all in prices'; that is, Q rises first and hence cannot have been caused by an initial rise in P. Also, the supposed labor-market dynamics that are central to the Phillips curve story imply that the real wage rate falls in the early phase of a money-driven boom – an implication that, to my knowledge, has no empirical support.
7. Importantly, the story of the so-called 'Great Moderation' (beginning in the mid-1980s), during which Friedmanian magnitudes were relatively well behaved, can in retrospect be better understood by focusing attention on interest rates and Hayekian sub-aggregates. And the more recent period (circa 2003–05) during which low interest rates gave an artificial boost to housing and other interest rate-sensitive investments, cannot be understood without an appreciation for the Hayekian insights.

REFERENCES

Caldwell, Bruce J. (1998), 'Why didn't Hayek review Keynes's *General Theory*?' *History of Political Economy*, 30 (4), 545–69.
Colander, David and Harry Landreth (1996), *The Coming of Keynesianism to America: Conversations with the Founders of Keynesian Economics*, Cheltenham, UK and Brookfield, VT, USA: Edward Elgar.
Ebenstein, Alan (2001), *Friedrich Hayek: A Biography*, New York: St Martin's Press.
Ebenstein, Alan (2007), *Milton Friedman: A Biography*, New York: Palgrave Macmillan.
Friedman, Milton ([1956] 1969), 'The quantity theory of money: a restatement', in Milton Friedman (1969), *The Optimum Quantity of Money and Other Essays*, Chicago, IL: Aldine, pp. 51–67.
Friedman, Milton ([1961] 1969), 'The lag in effect of monetary policy', in Milton Friedman (1969), *The Optimum Quantity of Money and Other Essays*, Chicago, IL: Aldine, pp. 237–60.
Friedman, Milton (1962), *Capitalism and Freedom*, Chicago, IL: University of Chicago Press.
Friedman, Milton (1968), *Dollars and Deficits*, Englewood Cliffs, NJ: Prentice Hall.
Friedman, Milton (1969), *The Optimum Quantity of Money and Other Essays*, Chicago, IL: Aldine.
Friedman, Milton (1970a), 'A theoretical framework for monetary analysis', in Robert Gordon (ed.), *Milton Friedman's Monetary Framework: A Debate with His Critics*, Chicago, IL: University of Chicago Press, pp. 1–62.

Friedman, Milton (1970b), *The Counter-Revolution in Monetary Theory*, London: Institute of Economic Affairs.
Friedman, Milton (1984), *Money, Capital and Fluctuations*, Roy McCloughry (ed.), Chicago, IL: University of Chicago Press.
Friedman, Milton (1986), 'Keynes's political legacy', in John Burton (ed.), *Keynes's General Theory: Fifty Years On*, London: Institute for Economic Affairs, pp. 47–55.
Friedman, Milton (1992), *Money Mischief: Episodes in Monetary History*, New York: Harcourt Brace Jovanovich.
Garrison, Roger W. (1985), 'Review of Friedrich A. Hayek's *Money, Capital and Fluctuations*', *Market Process*, 3 (2), 7–9.
Garrison, Roger W. (2001), *Time and Money: The Macroeconomics of Capital Structure*, London, UK and New York, USA: Routledge.
Gordon, Robert J. (ed.) (1974), *Milton Friedman's Monetary Framework: A Debate with His Critics*, Chicago, IL: University of Chicago Press, pp. 1–62.
Hayek, Friedrich A. ([1928] 1984), 'Intertemporal price equilibrium and movements in the value of money', in Friedrich A. Hayek, *Money, Capital, and Fluctuations: Early Essays*, ed. Roy McCloughry, Chicago, IL: University of Chicago Press, pp. 71–117.
Hayek, F.A. (1931), 'Reflections on the pure theory of money of Mr J.M. Keynes', *Economica*, 11 (31), 270–95.
Hayek, F.A. (1941), *The Pure Theory of Capital*, Chicago, IL: University of Chicago Press.
Hayek, F.A. ([1935] 1967), *Prices and Production*, 2nd edn, New York: Augustus M. Kelley.
Hayek, F.A. ([1928] 1975), *Monetary Theory and the Trade Cycle*, New York: Augustus M. Kelley.
Hayek, F.A. (1944), *The Road to Serfdom*, Chicago, IL: Chicago University Press.
Hayek, F.A. (1960), *The Constitution of Liberty*, Chicago, IL: Chicago University Press.
Hayek, Friedrich A. [1966] 1978, 'Personal reflections of Keynes and the "Keynesian Revolution"', in Friedrich A. Hayek, *New Studies in Politics, Economics and the History of Ideas*, Chicago, IL: University of Chicago Press, pp. 283–9.
Hayek, F.A. (1978), *New Studies in Philosophy, Politics, Economics and the History of Ideas*, Chicago, IL: Chicago University Press.
Hayek, F.A. (1984), *Money, Capital and Fluctuations*, Roy McCloughry (ed.), Chicago, IL: University of Chicago Press.
Hayek, F.A. (1994), *Hayek on Hayek: An Autobiographical Dialogue*, Stephen Kresge and Leif Wenar (eds), Chicago, IL: University of Chicago Press.
Hicks, John R. (1967), 'The Hayek story', *Critical Essays in Monetary Theory*, Oxford: Oxford University Press, pp. 203–15.
Keynes, John Maynard (1936), *The General Theory of Employment, Interest, and Money*, New York: Harcourt, Brace, & Company.
Klausinger, Hansjoerg (1989), 'On the history of neutral money', in Donald A. Walker (ed.), *Perspectives on the History of Economic Thought*, vol. 2, Aldershot, UK and Brookfield, VT, USA: Edward Elgar, pp. 171–86.
Meltzer, Allan H. (1988), *Keynes's Monetary Theory: A Different Interpretation*, Cambridge: Cambridge University Press.
Minard, Lawrence (1979), 'Wave of the past? Or wave of the future?' *Forbes*, 24 (1, Oct. 1), pp. 45–52.
Mises, Ludwig von ([1912] 1953), *The Theory of Money and Credit*, New Haven, CT: Yale University Press.
Skousen, Mark (2005), *Vienna & Chicago: Friends or Foes?*, Washington, DC: Capitol Press.
Weinstein, Michael M. (1999), 'Milton Friedman: my biggest mistake', *New York Times*, 4 July, sec. 3, p. 2.

7. Hayek and Mises
Richard M. Ebeling

There is no single man to whom I owe more intellectually, even though he [Ludwig von Mises] was never my teacher in the institutional sense of the word ... Although I do owe him a decisive stimulus at a crucial point in my intellectual development, and continuous inspiration through a decade, I have perhaps most profited from his teaching because I was not initially his student at the university, an innocent young man who took his word for gospel, but came to him as a trained economist ... Though I learned that he was usually right in his conclusions, I was not always satisfied with his arguments, and retained to the end a certain critical attitude which sometimes forced me to build different constructions, which however, to my great pleasure, usually led to the same conclusions. (F.A. Hayek, 'Coping with ignorance', 1978, pp. 17–18)

LUDWIG VON MISES AND FRIEDRICH A. HAYEK IN VIENNA

In the twentieth century, the two economists most closely identified as representing the Austrian School of economics were Ludwig von Mises and Friedrich A. Hayek. Indeed, more than any other members of the Austrian School, Mises and Hayek epitomize the academic and public perception of the 'Austrian' approach to economic theory and method, as well as a free-market-oriented view of social and economic policy. Their names have been inseparable from the conception of the 'Austrian' theory of the business cycle; or the 'Austrian' critique of socialist central planning and government intervention; or the 'Austrian' view of competition and the market process; or the 'Austrian' emphasis on the unique characteristics that separate the social sciences from the natural sciences.[1]

Yet, as Hayek emphasizes in the quotation with which the chapter begins, he never directly studied with Mises as a student at the University of Vienna; and while considering him the thinker who had the most influence on him in his own intellectually formative years of the 1920s and early 1930s, he approached Mises' ideas with a critical eye. Not always satisfied with the particular chain of reasoning by which Mises may have reached a conclusion on questions of economic theory or policy, Hayek said, he nonetheless often ended up with the same (or similar) results, although through a somewhat different logical process.

That Hayek appreciated his intellectual debt to Mises' own writings was not simply a reflective afterthought in later years following the winning of the Nobel Prize in Economics in 1974. He was appreciative of Mises' intellectual stature from the time he came into Mises' orbit in Vienna in the years shortly after the end of the First World War.

Ludwig von Mises was Hayek's senior by 18 years, having been born in September of 1881 in Lemberg, the capital of the Hapsburg Crownland of Galicia, a far eastern corner of the Austro-Hungarian Empire bordering on the Russian Empire. Among Mises' family were prominent members of the orthodox Jewish community in Galicia, who were strongly liberal in their views on social reform; a few months before Ludwig was born, his great-grandfather had been ennobled by Emperor Franz Joseph with the hereditary 'Edler von' in recognition of his service as a leader of the Jewish community in that part of the Hapsburg domains.

Ludwig's father moved his branch of the family to Vienna in the early 1890s. After attending the Acedemisches Gymnasium (a high school geared toward those destined for higher education), Mises entered the University of Vienna in 1900 planning to specialize in history. But in 1903 he discovered Carl Menger's *Principles of Economics* (1871), the founding work of the Austrian School, and it had such a profound impact on the 22-year-old Ludwig that he decided to become an economist. He graduated in 1906 with a doctorate in jurisprudence, since economics was studied through the law faculty at the University of Vienna.[2]

Mises had already started making a controversial figure of himself even before the First World War. He had caused a minor stir in some official circles when he challenged, in a series of articles published in scholarly journals between 1907 and 1910, the reluctance of the Austro-Hungarian Bank to complete the monetary reforms that had begun in 1892 to formally put the Hapsburg Empire on the gold standard with legally required redemption of Austrian notes and deposits for specie currency (Mises, 1907, pp. 3–20; 1909, pp. 31–82; 1910a, pp. 95–103).[3] And he was already a strong liberal critic of the growing fiscal and regulatory burdens of the Austrian government on the country's economic and industrial development (Mises, 1910b, pp. 117–30).

Mises published his first major work in June 1912, *The Theory of Money and Credit* (Mises, 1912), and on its basis was awarded in February 1913 the status of *Privatdozent* (an unsalaried lecturer) at the University of Vienna, permitting him to offer a seminar each term; he was promoted to 'professor extraordinary' in 1918, an honorific title of 'tenure' as an unsalaried lecturer.[4]

The Theory of Money and Credit attempted to advance monetary theory in several directions. First, following the lead of Carl Menger's 1892 monograph on 'Money' (Menger, 1892, pp. 25–107), Mises developed a 'subjectivist' and 'marginalist' formulation of the cash balance approach for explaining the general value or purchasing power of the monetary unit, based on the individual's demand for money. Second, he developed a thoroughly micro-based theory of the non-neutrality of money through an analysis of the time-sequential process resulting from changes in the quantity of money in terms of its impact on the structure of relative prices and wages, relative income shares, and the allocation of resources among competing uses in the economy, the longer-run outcome of which would be an overall change in the general scale of prices in the economy.

And, third, Mises attempted to integrate Eugen von Böhm-Bawerk's theory of capital and interest with the more recent work of Knut Wicksell which showed how changes in the supply of money and credit could bring about a discrepancy between the 'natural rate' and the 'money rates' of interest. The result was a theory of the business cycle emphasizing the unsustainable boom that set the stage for an economic downturn: a misdirection of resources and mal-investment of capital caused by a credit expansion that pushed the money rates of interest below the 'natural rate', thus bringing about a time-structure of investments inconsistent with the available amount of real savings.[5]

While his early scholarly reputation was based upon his writings as a monetary theorist, Mises made his living for almost of a quarter of a century, from 1909 to 1934, as a senior economic analyst at the Vienna Chamber of Commerce, Crafts and Industry. He was responsible for policy evaluation and recommendations on behalf of the Vienna business community relating to a wide variety of monetary, fiscal and regulatory legislative matters that came before the Austrian parliament.[6]

His first, full-time academic position came in 1934 – at the age of 53 – when he was invited by the Graduate Institute of International Studies in Geneva, Switzerland to take up a visiting chair in International Economic Relations. Mises held this position until the summer of 1940 when he escaped to the United States from the uncertainties of an increasingly war-ravaged Europe as the Lowlands countries and France were falling under Hitler's control in May and June of that year.

Friedrich Hayek was born in 1899, the year before Mises entered the University of Vienna. By late 1918 Hayek had returned from fighting in the Austrian army on the Italian front during the First World War; he enrolled at the University of Vienna shortly after returning home. As a war veteran he was able to enter an accelerated program that allowed him to earn his doctorate in jurisprudence in 1921. He had been undecided about whether to focus on psychology or on economics, and ended up choosing the latter because it offered a more likely career track, given the employment situation in post-war Vienna. He earned a second doctoral degree in political science in 1923 (Caldwell, 2004, pp. 133–49).

But it was after earning his first degree in 1921 that he began his decade-long close relationship with Mises. At the university, Hayek had studied with one of the leading figures of the 'older' Austrian School, Friedrich von Wieser. Carl Menger, the founder of the Austrian School, had retired from his teaching position at the university in 1903 and was replaced by Wieser, who had been a professor at the German University of Prague.

Eugen von Böhm-Bawerk, Wieser's brother-in-law and the other major figure who had helped establish the international reputation of the Austrian School in the last decades of the nineteenth and the early years of the twentieth centuries, had died in 1914. Böhm-Bawerk had offered a renowned graduate seminar at the University of Vienna for nearly a decade during which both Mises and Joseph A. Schumpeter had been among the attendees.

Hayek tells us that he was greatly taken by Wieser as a scholar and a personality, and even suffered from a degree of student hero-worship.[7] When he graduated in 1921 and was in need of employment, Wieser wrote a letter of introduction for him addressed to Mises, who at that time, besides his duties at the Chamber of Commerce, was in charge of a special Office of Accounts established by the League of Nations to sort out Austrian government prewar debts among the 'successor states' that had replaced the Hapsburg Empire. More than once, Hayek recounted that first meeting with Mises:

> I remember vividly how, after presenting to Mises my letter of introduction by Wieser, in which I was described as a promising young economist, Mises said, 'Well, I've never seen you in my lectures.' That was almost completely true. I had looked in at one of his lectures and found that a man so conspicuously antipathetic to the kind of Fabian [socialist] views that I then held was not the sort of person to whom I wanted to go. But of course things changed. That meeting was the beginning. After a short conversation, Mises asked, 'When can you start work?' This led to a long, close collaboration . . . During [the] next ten year he certainly had more influence on my outlook of economics than any other man. (Hayek, 1978, pp. 17–18)

Hayek found Mises to be an extraordinarily productive economist and efficient administrator. He was, Hayek said:

> the kind of man who, as was said about John Stuart Mill, because he does a normal day's work in two hours, has always a clear desk and time to talk about anything. I came to know him as one of the best-educated and best-informed men I had ever known, and what was most important at the time of great inflation [as Austria and Germany were experiencing in the early 1920s], as the only man who really understood what was happening. (Hayek, 1992, p. 132)

For Hayek, Mises was not simply an economist. In Hayek's eyes, Mises' 'acute knowledge' and 'profound wisdom' was more 'in the tradition of the great moral philosophers' such as Montesquieu, Voltaire, Adam Smith or Alexis de Tocqueville.

When Hayek was in the United States in the mid-1920s and 'tried to explain Mises' position in pretty much the same words to Wesley Clair Mitchell in New York, [he] only encountered – perhaps understandably – a politely ironic skepticism' (Hayek, 1992, p. 153).

What began that influence on Hayek's views on economics and social philosophy in general was the impression made by Mises' *Socialism: An Economic and Sociological Analysis* (Mises, 1922). The book had grown out of a journal article that Mises had published two years earlier on 'Socialist calculation in the socialist commonwealth' (Mises, 1920). As the First World War ended, there was the rise to power of the Bolsheviks in Russia in 1917, then short-lived Marxist regimes in Hungary and Bavaria in 1919, and large socialist movements in Germany and Austria calling for the abolition of private property and the implementation of centrally planned economies.

Mises raised a fundamental question about the instituting of a socialist planned society: how would the newly established central planners know how to rationally and efficiently plan an economy once private property in the means of production was abolished, market competition had been done away with, and market-generated money prices no longer existed?

Mises' essential argument was that the only realistic and meaningful way to determine the value that people placed upon alternative consumer goods and services they could buy, and the only way to effectively determine the opportunity costs of employing the scarce means of production in their potential competing uses, was through a market-based pricing system. The heterogeneous physical 'things' of the world that were potentially suitable for men's uses could be reduced to a valuational common denominator through which entrepreneurs could rationally calculate the most profitable ways to direct production for the purpose of satisfying the most urgently expressed wants of the buying public. Socialism, by doing away with the crucial institutions without which this would be 'impossible', meant not a greater and more productive 'horn of plenty' for humanity, but instead meant economic 'planned chaos'.

This critique of the economic viability of a socialist economy was placed in a far wider setting in Mises' treatise on *Socialism*. Here Mises broadened the analysis to include the social, political, historical, ethical and cultural dimensions of a fully and comprehensively implemented collectivist order. And from virtually every angle, Mises found that the socialist dream was in reality a doorway to social stagnation, political tyranny and economic irrationality. Indeed, as Hayek suggested, it went outside the far more narrow range of the mere economist's frame of reference.

Years later, Hayek stated that:

> When *Socialism* first appeared in 1922, its impact was profound. It gradually altered the outlook of many of the young idealists returning to their university studies after the World War. I know, for I was one of them ... Socialism promised to fulfill our hopes for a more rational, more just world. And then came this book. Our hopes were dashed. *Socialism* told us that we had been looking for improvement in the wrong direction ... [T]o those of us who experienced its first impact, *Socialism* will always be his [Mises'] decisive contribution. It challenged the outlook of a generation and altered, if only slowly, the thinking of many ... To none of us young men who read the book when it appeared the world was ever the same again. If [Wilhelm] Röpke, stood here, or [Lionel] Robbins, or [Bertil] Ohlin (to only mention those of exactly the same age as myself) they would tell you the same story ... Although there were few unquestioning followers at first, he attained interest and admiration among a younger generation and attracted those who were concerned with the borderline of social theory and philosophy ... [F]or our generation it must remain the most memorable and decisive production of Professor Mises' career. (Hayek, 1992, p. 133–40)

After spending over a year in the United States, Hayek returned to Vienna and went back to work for Mises at the League of Nations Office of Accounts on prewar Austrian debt obligations. Hayek also began to regularly attend Mises' already famous *Privatseminar*, which brought together economists, political scientists, sociologists, philosophers, and historians for wide-ranging discussions on virtually all facets of the human sciences, many of whom became internationally renowned in their particular scholarly fields. Many of those who participated in the seminar recalled in later years that they considered it to be one of the most rewarding and challenging intellectual experiences of their lives because of the consistent quality of the papers delivered and the discussions that followed (Mises, 1940b, pp. 81–3; Mises, Margit von, 1984, pp. 202–11).[8] The partial lists of the themes and topics discussed in the papers presented at the private seminar that are among Mises' 'lost papers' show that during the years when Hayek was participating he delivered presentations on the theory of imputation, credit and banking policy, price level stabilization, and a variety of related subjects.

After Mises stepped down from his administrative role at the Office of Accounts in February 1925 and returned to his full-time duties with Vienna Chamber of Commerce, Hayek searched for a better-paying position, since he had recently married. Unable to get Hayek a job with the Chamber of Commerce, Mises proceeded with an alternative plan to assist his young friend. While in the United States, Hayek had spent a good deal of time studying various statistical methods developed by American economists for investigating the phases of the business cycle. While many of these statistical methods are certainly out of date now, in the Vienna of the mid- and late 1920s, Hayek had cutting-edge knowledge of empirical techniques that few others possessed in the German-speaking world, and most certainly not in the Austria of that time.[9]

Mises, who through his position at the Chamber of Commerce was well known and highly respected in Austrian business circles, arranged for the financing and legal approval for the establishment of the Austrian Institute for Business Cycle Research, with Hayek proposed as its director.[10] In November 1926, Mises explained the purpose for such an institute at a conference of the executive directors of the various Austrian Chambers of Commerce. Central to the case for such an institute, Mises argued, would be its unbiased independence in its analytical and statistical studies of the economic conditions in Austria; its autonomy would place it above and separate from politics, something that would not be the case if such studies were done within the Chamber of Commerce, since it was understood to speak for the interests of business. As Mises stated matters:

> The Institute for Business Cycle Research will never compete with such agencies of economic policy as the Chambers of Commerce. Rather, it will use, in the analysis of statistical data, its entire spectrum of scholarly knowledge in the field of economics, so as to distill truths from mere numbers, irrefutable evidence from the plethora of subjective and corruptible data. Only thus will statistical material have reached a level of qualification and maturity to be considered and employed by economic policy makers. Statistics in themselves are merely instruments for the understanding and exploitation of economic data. Only after a thorough, an objective, and a scientific treatment will such statistical data attain the status of objective truth and serve the common good, and only then will the full value of the efforts of those who collected such data be appreciated . . . The Institute's findings will offer to all political parties and all politico-economic interests, a solid foundation for reliable decision-making. (Mises, 1926)

The Austrian Institute for Business Cycle Research opened its doors in January 1927 in the same building housing the Vienna Chamber of Commerce, with Hayek as its founding director at the age of 28. Until his departure for Geneva in the summer of 1934, Mises served as an acting vice-president for the Institute. In 1930 Mises had also helped arrange financial support for Hayek and the Institute from the Rockefeller Foundation, a support that continued until 1938 (Leonard, 2011, pp. 92–3). Especially with the start of the Great Depression, the Rockefeller subsidy became crucial. Already in December of 1930, Hayek reported to the Institute's Board of Trustees that the Austrian dues-paying membership to the organization had stagnated, and recommended that a public relations (advertising) campaign be initiated. Mises, according to the minutes of the discussion that followed, strongly argued, however, that the format of any advertisements should avoid being 'too American' in style.

Within a short time, the Institute was publishing a monthly bulletin on economic conditions and trends in Austria and in Central Europe in general (with the issues virtually all written by Hayek in the first years). It was in one of these bulletins in the spring of 1929 that Hayek has sometimes been credited with predicting the coming of the Great Depression in the United States. He suggested that the economic depression that was already affecting parts of Europe was not likely to end until interest rates declined, and this depended upon an end to the economic boom in the US, which he thought likely to happen within the next few months (Hayek, 1975, p. 2).

The archives of the Austrian Institute for Business Cycle Research and the League of Nations in Geneva show that the Institute was periodically working with and preparing reports for the League's economic intelligence service. For instance, only a little over a year after the Institute had starting functioning, in March 1928 it hosted a two-day meeting of Central European business cycle institutes in Vienna at which Hayek recommended a partnership for standardizing of the methodology used by the organizations in their collection of statistical data, especially in terms of price-level indices, interest rates, production levels, stock market prices, railway traffic, and unemployment and foreign trade; and that these institutes should synchronize the publication of their respective monthly findings.

In 1930, Hayek prepared graphical and statistical data exhibitions for two business cycle institute conferences held in London and Berlin that were well received at both events. In March of 1931, Hayek traveled to Geneva for a League-sponsored conference of economic research institutes on the economic crisis, for which he summarized the origins and impact of the Great Depression up to that point in Austria. And he, again, attended a League-organized meeting in Geneva in July 1931 as part of an effort to coordinate the research activities of the various economic and business cycle institutes.

The Institute also began a book series, under the general title of 'Contributions to Business Cycle Research', the first volumes of which were Hayek's *Monetary Theory and the Trade Cycle* (Hayek, 1929), Fritz Machlup's *The Stock Market, Credit, and Capital Formation* (Machlup, 1931) and Hayek's *Prices and Production* (Hayek, 1931).

Hayek delivered the four lectures that became *Prices and Production* at the London School of Economics (LSE) in late January 1931. Shortly afterward he was offered the Tooke Chair in Economic Science and Statistics at LSE, and moved to England in the summer of 1931 to take up his teaching duties in the fall term.[11] [12]

Around the time Hayek arrived in London, *Prices and Production* was beginning to make an impact on the economics profession and debates over business cycle theory and policy. He was also invited to deliver guest lectures at many other universities across Great Britain, and he was soon hailed as an original and creative thinker offering unique insights on monetary theory and policy, the business cycle, and the economic crisis through which the world was passing.[13]

But the international recognition only made Hayek even more aware of how much he owed to Ludwig von Mises in terms of the many ideas for which he was being so widely praised. In a letter to Mises written in November 1931, Hayek expressed the debt he owed to his mentor:

> [Lionel] Robbins presented me as an eminent authority, so that people always want to hear my opinion on all matters. I am aware for the first time, that I owe you virtually everything that gives me an advantage as compared to my colleagues here and to most economists even outside my narrow field of research (here my indebtedness to you goes without saying). In Vienna one is less aware of [this intellectual debt to you] because it is the unquestioned common basis of our circle. If I do not deceive too many expectations of the people here at LSE, it is not to my credit but to yours. However [my] advantage [over the others] will disappear with your books being translated and coming generally known. (quoted in Hulsmann, 2007, p. 635)[14]

With Hayek's move to Great Britain, his frequent, if not daily, association and interaction with Mises came to an end. Their correspondence clearly shows that rarely did much time pass that they were not communicating with each other, sharing their experiences, ideas and frustrations over the political and economic trends over the years and decades before Mises' death in 1973. But they never again lived so directly in one another's company as in those years in Vienna in interwar Austria, nor influenced each other's lives in so immediate a way.

THE MASTER AND THE PUZZLER

In 1975, Hayek published an article titled 'Two types of minds' (Hayek, 1975, pp. 50–56). He contrasted two types of thinkers. First, the 'master of his subject', the one who has read virtually everything in his field and has the ability to recall, explain and critically analyze all the literature, controversies, and competing views within his discipline. The second kind of thinker Hayek labeled the 'puzzler', or he even suggested the 'muddler'.

He is the person who constantly finds it necessary to rethink arguments that he has heard or read before, who never finds it easy to systematically formulate the ideas of others, and is more likely to take bits of ideas from others and incorporate them in various ways into his own thoughts that often seem not to have fully coherent and logical themes from some clear first principles. The puzzler muddles through, groping his way, rather than reasoning from any carefully thought-out starting premises or 'first principles'.

Hayek suggested that examples of these two types of minds among the Austrian economists had been Eugen von Böhm-Bawark, a true 'master' of his subject who could restate all of his own and his opponents' arguments in economics with great logical clarity; and Friedrich von Wieser, who was clearly more of the 'puzzler' in the way he thought and wrote through a maze of ideas that often seemed to lack any reasoned coherence or relationship to the ideas of others (other than from Menger, Hayek suggested, from whom Wieser had drawn his early inspiration).[15]

I would like to suggest that one way to approach the relationship between Mises' and Hayek's ideas on various themes in economics is in the contrast between the 'master' and the 'puzzler'. Ludwig von Mises, in this comparison, was surely the 'master'. When Hayek at the age of 22 first met Mises, who was already 40, Mises was in the process of formulating an entire logical system of economic thought from a set of core principles. Hayek, on the other hand, was groping toward his general conception of the monetary and market processes.

Unlike Athena who emerged full-grown and ready for combat in warrior dress from Zeus's forehead, Mises' theory of human action, or 'praxeology' as he later came to call it, did not take shape in his mind all at once. It took form over 20 years, from before the time *The Theory of Money and Credit* originally appeared in 1912, to the early 1930s when he published a collection of methodological essays (Mises, 1933). By this time Mises had formulated an 'axiomatic-deductive' conception of human action and choice; constructed a theory of conceivable social and economic orders in the form of a contrast of the alternatives of capitalism, socialism and interventionism; and developed a theory of money, the monetary order and the business cycle. It is true that Mises' 'system' was not presented as an integrated whole until 1940 when he published *Nationalökonomie: Theorie des Handelns und Wirtschaftens* (Mises, 1940a) in Geneva in the midst of the Second World War, and then reformulated it almost a decade later in its English-language version, *Human Action: A Treatise on Economics* (Mises, 1949). But nonetheless, together, Mises' writings from this earlier 20-year period offer a systematic view of man, society, and the economic and social order.[16]

Hayek never wrote a systematic treatise on economics in which he integrated and formulated his overall conception of human choice, the social order and the economic system. The two treatises that he wrote later in life, *The Constitution of Liberty* (Hayek, 1960) and his three-volume *Law, Legislation, and Liberty* (Hayek, 1973, 1976, 1979), are primarily concerned with the social, legal and political orders of a free society. All of his ideas on the nature and workings of the economic system and market order are clearly embedded in and centrally inform the content and orientation in these works. Indeed, his economic writings during the 1920s, 1930s and 1940s are the essential foundations for his later profound work on social and political philosophy. But Hayek the economist never offered his version of Mises' *Human Action*.

Instead, what one finds in Hayek's economic writings from the interwar period and after is the work of a scholar often being 'inspired' by some theme earlier developed by Mises, and then, as he expressed it, proceeding to reformulate the problem and its analytical construction in his own 'puzzler's' way in response to the economic theory and policy controversies of his own time.

THE NATURE OF THE ECONOMIC ORDER AND MARKET COORDINATION

In early February 1933, Hayek sent Mises a draft of his paper, 'The trend of economic thinking', which Hayek delivered as an inaugural lecture at the London School of Economics in early March. A week after receiving the draft of the lecture, Mises sent Hayek his comments, in which he said:

> There is a substantial divergence in our views in that you discuss the issue of laissez-faire in the tradition manner rather than from the standpoint of the various organizational possibilities of societal collaboration (i.e., individual property, communal property, etc.), a distinction that I make in my own work. From my standpoint it is essential that the issue is not whether to choose laissez-faire or an omnipotent state, but rather which of a limited number of conceivable types of organization is best suited or the only appropriate organization for allowing human cooperation in the economy. (Mises, 1933)

What Mises seemed to object to in Hayek's lecture was the absence of a particular ordering principle in the context of which Mises believed questions concerning economic systems needed to be investigated. In this LSE inaugural lecture, Hayek emphasized the misdirection the German Historical School has given to economic reasoning by rejecting 'theory' in place of a narrow study of 'the facts' of history; he also focused on the failure of later economists who were influenced by these German Historicists from any longer having a full appreciation of the 'spontaneous institutions' that generate an order to economic and social processes, the recognition of which demarcates economic science's distinct subject matter.

Hayek suggested that socialists had slowly come to realize that many of the features that they most objected to in the market economy – such as interest in the savings–investment relationship – would have to be incorporated in a planned economy if a rational use of resources were to occur. 'The best a dictator could do in such a case would be to imitate as closely as possible what would happen under free competition', Hayek said. The leading hurdle preventing the 'wise planner' from doing so, in Hayek's view, was the pressure of special-interest groups who lobbied for the maintenance of the status quo upon which their present income positions were dependent.

He also argued that appreciation of the spontaneous order of the market did not imply a 'purely negative attitude' toward the role of the state in economic affairs. Indeed, Hayek hoped that the generally critical stance against government intervention by economists, due to the often naïve and uninformed policy prescriptions of the 'lay mind', would 'not prevent economists from devoting more attention to the positive task of delimiting the field of useful State activity ... To remedy this deficiency must be one of the main tasks of the future' (Hayek, 1933, pp. 26, 29–31).

For Mises the most important contribution to economic theory in his time had been the discovery of the logical impossibility of rational economic calculation under a system of comprehensive socialist central planning.[17] The nature and requirements for economic calculation were the cornerstones for evaluating and judging the political practicability of alternative economic systems.

In both his 1920 essay on economic calculation and his 1922 book on *Socialism*, Mises had emphasized that there would be no difficulty in solving resource allocational problems under socialist planning if, on the day before the socialist revolution, markets were in equilibrium, and if nothing changed in the society after central planning was introduced. But neither of these conditions could be presumed to be true. Change was inescapable and inevitable in the real world, and decisions would have to be made anew all the time concerning how best to arrange the productive activities in the socialist society of tomorrow (Mises, 1922, p. 105). Thus, the central planner could not simply inherit the capitalist economy of the day before, and then continue things as under capitalism.

Seeds of Hayek's later emphasis on the division of knowledge in society and the informational role of prices in the economy were already in Mises' analysis. As Mises saw it, 'In societies based on division of labor, the distribution of property rights affect a kind of mental division of labor, without which neither economy nor systematic production would be possible' (Mises, 1922, p. 101). And:

> This is the decisive objection that economics raises against the possibility of a socialist society. It must forgo the intellectual division of labor that consists in the cooperation of all entrepreneurs, landowners, and workers as producers and consumers in the formation of market prices. But without it, rationality, i.e., the possibility of economic calculation, is unthinkable. (Mises, 1927, p. 50)

Thus, issues concerning the role and extent of government control, planning or regulation of economic activities were inseparable from whether or not a functioning and competition-based price system was in operation and allowed to determine the best and most efficient uses of the means of production to serve consumer ends, as guided by those using their own capital and resources in the division of labor as they considered most profitable. Without such a price system, participants in that 'intellectual division of labor' could not, as consumers, inform producers of what goods they desired and the relative value they placed upon them, and could not, as entrepreneurs and factor owners, decide what lines of production were the ones most consist with those consumer preferences, given the opportunity costs of resource uses in other ways as they saw them.

This idea binds together most of Mises' arguments about the nature of the market order. If the absence of a functioning price system under comprehensive central planning does away with all economic rationality (in terms of efficient and effective uses of means in the achieving of ends in the social system of division of labor), then government interventions through either price controls or production regulations represent 'sand in the machine' that prevents prices from conveying the information without which market coordination through economic calculation is diminished or made impossible, and prevents entrepreneurs from using their best judgments as to how to arrange resource uses that satisfy consumer demands on the basis of what prices are interpreted as telling them.

Thus, the idea that one could pick and choose what one desired to be the functions of government in terms of government ownership, or regulation, control or redistribution, was inconsistent with an appreciation that the fundamental issue concerning the role of government in society concerned the extent to which government intervention or planning interfered with the existence and effective operation of those institutions – private property, competitive exchange and market-based prices – without which a cooperative system of division of labor could not properly solve the 'economic problem'.

When Hayek edited the collection of essays on *Collectivist Economic Planning* (Hayek, 1935) just two years after his inaugural lecture at LSE, his views on the central role of the price system and its crucial role for ordering the productive activities of the society were expressed in ways much closer to Mises' view of things. But as a number of commentators have suggested, the real turn in Hayek's conception of the workings of the market order emerged out of the challenge of the 'market socialists' and the proposed 'mathematical solutions' to the economic problem. Already in his own contributions to *Collectivist Economic Planning*, Hayek had pointed out the implied (and unrealistic) assumption that all the detailed and dispersed technical and related 'data' was somehow known or could be made available to the planners, without which they could not effectively know how to best use the 'society's' collective means to serve its collective ends (Hayek, 1992, pp. 93–7).

It was grappling with these issues that clearly led Hayek to questions and answers that he tried to deal with in 'Economics and knowledge' (1937), 'Socialist calculation: the competitive "solution"' (1940), 'The use of knowledge in society' (1945) and 'The meaning of competition' (1946). Reading them in succession, one sees the evolution of Hayek's thinking about what he came to regard as the fundamental weaknesses of the emerging neoclassical microeconomic framework that, building on the perfect competition model, assumed away all the problems of economic coordination in the real world of constant change and imperfect and decentralized knowledge.

This also, it seems, made him reflect on how his own emergent ideas on these themes related to those of Ludwig von Mises, whose writings were a central starting point for his own intellectual discovery process. More specifically, Hayek began to wonder if Mises' methodological starting point was a sufficient one to fully explain the competitive procedure through which coordination of multitudes of interdependent individual plans could be successfully and fully accomplished.

Hayek accepted Mises' (and Wieser's) argument that the social sciences construct their understanding of the human world from a different type of knowledge than the natural sciences. To understand 'human action' it was necessary to draw upon a particular source of knowledge: the introspective reflection about the logical workings of the human mind. 'Action', after all, can be seen as nothing more than 'reason' applied to purpose. And if this is so, then to comprehend the 'logic' in men's actions, it is necessary to look into that mind of which any one of us has the closest knowledge: the workings of our own.[18]

Understanding the logical relationships that can be 'discovered' from thinking about our own actions concerning the meanings and relationships between ends and means, or costs and benefits, or trade-offs and 'marginal' decision-making enable us to fully grasp how the formal economic logic of individual minds generate coordination between the various actions being undertaken by those individuals, respectively. But what does this tell us about how, or through what mechanism, the planned actions of multitudes of individuals become coordinated with one another?

An individual can certainly attempt to bring his own actions into a consistent 'equilibrium', given the circumstances he finds himself in and the 'data' of those circumstances as he knows and understands them. But if we take for granted that the actors do not have a 'perfect knowledge' or 'perfect foresight' of all circumstances that might affect the outcomes of their own actions – including the planned actions of others with whom they are interdependent in various direct and indirect ways in the division of labor – then by itself our understanding of the formal logic guiding each individual's own actions does not tell us how their potentially inconsistent interactions might be or are brought into coordinated equilibrium with each other (Hayek, 1937, p. 36).

In later years Hayek stated that this way of expressing the 'economic problem' as a knowledge 'coordination problem' in his article on 'Economics and knowledge' was meant as an 'gentle' criticism of Ludwig von Mises, who, Hayek believed, had claimed that the entire logic of how market processes brought about economy-wide coordination could be deduced 'a priori' from introspective knowledge of the individual's formal 'logic of choice' (Caldwell, 2004, pp. 220–23).

Hayek was persuaded that an 'empirical' element had to be introduced into the economic analysis concerning how individuals learned that their plans may be inconsistent with those of others and discovered in what directions they had to adapt their actions so as to move them into a more coordinated pattern with the planned actions of those others.

One would imagine that this would have led Hayek to propose a particular theory of expectations formation to explain how individuals came to hold views about the relationship of their own actions to that of others, and how experienced disappointments brought about 'revisions' in those interdependent expectations in a more coordinated direction. In other words, one would expect Hayek to have suggested an empirically based theory of 'learning' in a complex market setting.

Instead, he pursued a different path, and that was to show how individuals did not have to have any detailed knowledge of the actions and plans of others in the complex market order. The 'problem' has its solution, in realizing that the prices that Mises had emphasized as so crucial for purposes of economic calculation are also the means for economizing on the vast and specific knowledge about the intentions of others on both the demand and the supply sides of the market.

Each market participant in their own corner of society needed merely to follow and appropriately respond to the registered price changes that they observed and that were relevant to their own decision-making. At the same time, each individual could then adapt to what those relevant prices told him about the possible actions of others by using the particular knowledge that he or she possessed about their own circumstances and possibilities which those others could not know or appreciate in the same way. This was how 'society' could take advantage of all the types and bits of dispersed knowledge that only exist in the minds of multitudes of individuals without any centralized direction or control (Hayek, 1945).

Thus, by a slightly different chain of reasoning and emphasis, Hayek reached a conclusion parallel and complementary to Mises' earlier argument. Prices are the essential institutional mechanism by which rational use may be made of the means of production relative to the demands for various and competing goods and services in society. But for Hayek the 'calculating' acts which those prices made possible were due to the fact that all the minimum relevant information about the actions of others that individuals needed to know are encapsulated into those market-generated terms of trade.

Mises considered Hayek's development of how knowledge is used in society through the price system to be 'Hayek's valuable contribution to knowledge'. Mises went on to say that:

> The fact that knowledge exists dispersed, incomplete, and inconsistent, in many individual minds has been pointed out by Hayek and this is very important. Hayek says that if we are talking about the knowledge of our age, we are making a mistake if we think that this knowledge exists in all minds, or even that all of it exists in the mind of one man. He pointed out, for instance, in the case of the socialistic society that the progress possible is limited by the mind of one man. It is important for the capitalist economy that everybody, who has a better knowledge about some particular problem, can try to profit from this superiority and his attempts contribute to the improvement of the general conditions. In the socialistic economy, knowledge has value only insofar as it is available to the central authority, to the dictators who are making the central plan. Under capitalism, the coordination of the various bits of knowledge is brought about through the market. In a socialistic society it must be effected either in the mind of the dictator or in the minds of the members of the dictator's committee. (Greaves, 1958)

INTROSPECTION, UNDERSTANDING AND METHODOLOGICAL SUBJECTIVISM

One of the hallmarks of the 'Austrian' approach to economic and social analysis has been methodological subjectivism, the idea that if we are to understand and interpret the actions of individuals in the world the starting point must be the meanings that actors give to their own actions, the actions of others, and to the objects in the world.

While this 'subjectivist' approach was clearly present in the works of the 'older' Austrian School, the form that it has taken in the writings of the later Austrians, including Mises and Hayek, is surely derived from Max Weber in his *Economy and Society* (1922). Weber defines 'action' as behavior to which the actor assigns a personal or 'subjective' meaning, with the 'meaning' defining the purpose or goal of the action. 'Social action' is that human conduct in which an individual is conscious of and orients some aspects of his activities to the presence of another human agent. Such social action can be either one-sided or mutual (Weber, 1922, p. 88).[19]

The same applies to objects. Regardless of their specific physical characteristics, what makes one sharp object a warrior's weapon and another a surgeon's scalpel is the purpose for which the object may have been designed and the goal for which it is applied. Neither archeologist, nor sociologist, nor historian, nor economist would know how to understand the actions of human beings or the things men use for various purposes if the attempt was not made to appreciate these 'subjective' meanings that give the intelligibility that may be found in human 'movements' and social 'objects'.

Hayek devoted a part of his scholarly time in the 1940s to analyzing and explaining the significance and importance of 'subjectivism' in response to the rise and influence of positivism and behaviorism, and why he considered the misplaced use of the methods of the natural sciences in the social sciences to be not only faulty science – what he referred to as 'scientism' – but potentially harmful when applied to questions of social policy (Hayek, 2010, pp. 77–168).[20]

In *The Counter-Revolution of Science*, Hayek emphasized Mises' unique place in the consistent application of a subjectivist approach in economics:

> it is probably no exaggeration to say that every important advance in economic theory during the last one hundred years was a further step in the consistent application of subjectivism . . . This is a development which has probably been carried out most consistently by Ludwig von Mises, and I believe that most of the peculiarities of his views which at first strike many readers as strange and unacceptable trace to the fact that in the consistent development of the subjectivist approach he has for a long time moved ahead of his contemporaries.

> Probably all the characteristic features of his theories – from his theory of money (so far ahead of its time in 1912) to what he calls his *a priorism* ... all follow directly (although, perhaps, not all with the same necessity) from this central position. (Hayek, 2010, p. 94)

Yet, to speak of such a subjectivist approach for analyzing and understanding social and economic phenomena already implies an empirical element in the analysis. It is strange, then, that Hayek failed to see this in Mises' own writings. Mises in his writings in the late 1920s and early 1930s on the methods of the social sciences had already delineated between the 'formal' and abstract character of the universal and 'a priori' theorems of economics, and those elements that could only be known from 'experience' or 'empirical' information.

What it means for men to pursue ends and apply means, to weigh costs and benefits, to make trade-offs, and evaluate alternatives either categorically or at 'the margin', can all be derived from and can only be known through introspective reflection on the logical workings of our own mind. But what it is that men desire, which things or activities they view as means to attain those desired ends, what they consider the 'cost' or the 'benefit', from a choice, what they may view as a 'consumer good' or a 'producer good', and what and how much they may be willing to trade away of one thing to get another – these things can only be known through the 'empirical' facts of the specific circumstances and situations in which men may find themselves. The economist and the social analyst cannot know these things 'a priori'. Rather, it is the logic of human action and choice that provides the analytical schema in the context of which the 'empirical' data may be arranged and ordered to give that interpretive intelligibility to any and all of conscious human conduct (Mises, 1933, 25–31).

But what is the 'empirical' method for understanding how men coordinate their actions toward each other for mutual compatibility in pursuit of their plans in the market place? It must be said that when Hayek wrote 'Economics and knowledge', it is true that Mises had not articulated this in the detail that might have made unnecessary Hayek's 'gentle' criticism of what he considered to be the limits of Mises' 'a priori' logic of choice.

Perhaps it was in response to Hayek's criticism that Mises was stimulated to more explicitly formulate his theory of 'expectations' or 'learning' in his 1940 treatise, *Nationalokonomie* (1940a), which he restated in *Human Action* (1949) and refined in *Theory and History* (1957) and *The Ultimate Foundations of Economic Science* (1962).[21] Here, too, Mises' starting point was Max Weber. Weber had argued that a central tool of the historian was the method of the 'ideal type', a theoretical construction of essential features or characteristics discerned for interpretive purposes in the study of the actions of individuals, groups or institutions in which men act and interact. What does it mean to say someone had a 'Napoleon complex', or that the individual's actions were 'typical' of a 'South American military dictator', or that a group of individuals were acting in ways 'typical' of 'religious fanatics'? Or that the actions of people and the activities undertaken were 'typical' of a 'developing industrial city' or that the procedures for electing people to political office were 'typical' of the 'democratic spirit'? Thus, Weber once wrote a monograph on 'The city' meant to historically explain the characteristics that could be gleaned from the actual evolution of towns into cities, to highlight those qualities that could be conceptualized as 'typical' in the development and nature of cities in Europe.

In Mises' refined analysis, Weber's tool of interpretive 'understanding' – the 'ideal type' – is argued to be not only a mental schema to analyze aspects of the past, but also the mental process through which people anticipate and coordinate their actions with those of others looking to the future.

In interacting with other human beings we accumulate knowledge of others, and 'out of what we know about man's past behavior, we construct a scheme about what we call his character', Mises said (1962, p. 50). The source for constructing such composite 'images', or 'pictures' of the qualities and characteristics of others, obviously cannot be known 'a priori'. They can only be derived from 'experience'. This knowledge, Mises stated, is 'acquired either directly from observing our fellow men and transacting business with them or indirectly from reading or hearsay, as well as out of our special experience acquired in previous contacts with the individuals concerned'. And with this knowledge, 'we try to form an opinion about their future conduct' (1957, p. 313).

Actors in the market, using such 'empirical experience', form 'ideal types' that serve as the anticipatory framework in the context of which people form expectations about the likely actions of others with whom they may interact, and whose actions need to be anticipated precisely because what those others may do can influence the outcomes of one's own actions.

If one could say that Hayek's emphasis on the role of prices in economizing and disseminating information, in the context of which individuals might better utilize that special and particular knowledge they possess that others do not, refined and extended Mises' analysis of prices for purposes of economic calculation, the same could be said about Mises' conception of 'ideal types', in that it completed a missing element in Hayek's theory of prices as a communication mechanism.

That is, what are the prices conveyed to the respective actors in the market telling them? In other words, prices need to be interpreted in order to know what they may be telling someone about the actions of others, to which he must respond in some way. Every seller accumulates in their mind 'images' or typifications of those with whom they regularly interact on the demand or supply side. They use these 'ideal types' to decide whether a price change is permanent or temporary; whether it means that consumers are interested in some new features in the product they market; or whether it reflects some new competitive activity by a rival to which they need to respond.[22]

When, in 'The use of knowledge in society', Hayek referred to the special knowledge of particular time and place that only belongs to each individual in his own specific corner in the extended system of division of labor, one of the aspects of that knowledge is the complex of ideal typifications that, say, an entrepreneur has formed in his mind from interacting with the specific buyers he normally deals with and the specific sellers against whom he regularly competes. These anticipatory images derived from market experience enable the formation of expectations to try to coordinate one's own actions with those of others. Disappointments, errors and failures generate shifts (at the margin) in the ideal typifications each is using in directions that, it is hoped, reduce similar discoordinating actions or responses in the future.

Thus, the 'subjectivist' agenda is extended from understanding the logic of action and choice to the formation of expectations, for understanding how actors may better coordinate their activities on the basis of the communications provided by the prices formed on the competitive market.

CONCLUSIONS

No two thinkers ever think exactly alike. This is no less true even among those who may share common philosophical, methodological and theoretical ideas. Mises and Hayek were not carbon copies of each other.[23] Yet, their contributions may be thought of as complements rather than substitutes. Indeed, it is difficult to imagine how Hayek the economist and social philosopher would have been possible without Mises, the grand 'subjectivist' system-builder, the elements of which often became the starting point and the intellectual challenge for Hayek to 'puzzle' through to conclusions not much different from and often refined elaborations of those of his mentor.[24]

For Mises, Hayek was certainly his most valued 'student', if not, as Hayek pointed out, in the literal sense. Together, their contributions in fact are the basis and framework for the entire edifice of modern Austrian economics. It does not detract from the significance of Hayek's body of work to say that in many of its facets, it was the ideas of Ludwig von Mises that were being carried on.

NOTES

1. On the ideas of the Austrian economists from the founding of this school of thought in the 1870s to around the time of the First World War, see Ebeling (2010b).
2. On Mises' family background, education and the general Viennese cultural milieu when he was a young man in Austria, see Ebeling (2010a, pp. 36–56) and my introduction to Ebeling (2012).
3. According to Mises' *Memoirs* (1940b, pp. 35–9), it seems that while the central bank had been *de facto* redeeming notes and deposits for gold since the end of the nineteenth century, the central bank authorities and members of the Austrian parliament were reluctant to make redemption *de jure* because some of the revenues from foreign exchange transactions were used for various corrupt purposes by bank and government officials, and they were afraid of the greater transparency that legal convertibility would shine on the central bank's accounting methods. On Mises' monetary writings before the First World War, see Ebeling (2010a, pp. 57–87).
4. In Mises' inaugural lecture at the University of Vienna, 'On rising prices and purchasing power policies' (Mises, 1913a, pp. 156–67), he was already showing his strong views against monetary 'activism' by governments and central banks. See also 'The general rise in prices in the light of economic theory' (Mises, 1913b, pp. 131–55), in which he also, in his opening remarks, demonstrates his criticisms of misplaced inductive methods in the construction of economic theory.
5. '[F]or many years', Hayek considered Mises' *The Theory of Money and Credit* to be 'the most profound and satisfying work on the subject available' (Hayek, 1992, p. 127).
6. On Mises' work and writings for the Vienna Chamber of Commerce during the interwar period, see Ebeling (2010a, pp. 88–140) and my introduction to Ebeling (2003).
7. But, like Mises, Hayek also remarked that a 'decisive influence' on his thinking about economics was Menger's *Principles* (Hayek, 1994, p. 57).
8. For some reminiscences by participants in Mises' private seminar, which met twice a month in his Chamber of Commerce office between October and June of each year from 1920 to 1934, including those by Gottfried Haberler and Fritz Machlup, see Margit von Mises' *My Years with Ludwig von Mises* (Mises, Margit von, 1984, pp. 202–11). For Mises' own brief description and clearly fond recollection of the private seminar, see Mises (1940b, pp. 81–3).
9. The uses and limits of statistical methods in economics was, in fact, a significant theme among several of the younger Austrian economists during this time. For example, Gottfried Haberler's first book was on *Der Sinn der Indexhahlen* [The meaning of index numbers] (Haberler, 1927), an analysis of the microeconomic problems and difficulties with aggregated price indexes for estimating changes in real incomes and the real value of deferred payments over time. He also emphasized the limits of macroeconomic price aggregates for any successful analysis of the nature and phases of the business cycle (Haberler, 1928, pp. 107–17). See, also, his 1931 monograph on, 'The different meanings attached to the term, "fluctuations in the purchasing power of gold", and the best instrument or instruments for measuring such fluctuations' (Haberler, 1931). In 1928, Oskar Morgenstern published a book, his first, on *Wirtschaftsprognose, eien Untersuchung ihrer Verasussetzungen und Moglichkeiten* [Economic forecasting: an analysis of its assumptions and possibilities] (Morgenstern, 1928), in which he concluded that the application of statistical techniques for successful prediction of future economic events was virtually impossible. One finds here, in the questions raised about human knowledge and how people form interpersonal expectations, ideas that were

later clarified and formalized in his contribution to the theory of games (Von Neumann and Morgenstern, 1944). For a summary and critical evaluation of Morgenstern's arguments on the limits and impossibilities for economic forecasting, see Marget (1929).

10. See Hayek (1994, pp. 68–9): 'Once I was employed in that office [the Office of Accounts], our contacts rapidly became close, and for the following eight years Mises was unquestionably the personal contact from whom I profited the most, not only by way of intellectual stimulation, but also for his direct assistance in my career ... It was also Mises to whom I owe the creation of the Austrian Institute for Business Cycle Research, conceived by him, I believe, largely for the purpose of providing for me after he had failed to get me as a sort of scientific assistant into the chamber of commerce where he held his main job (for the purpose of building up there under his direction an economic research division).'

11. The minutes of the Austrian Institute's board meeting in the summer of 1931, at which Oskar Morgenstern was appointed as Hayek's successor as director, makes clear that Hayek's position at LSE was viewed as a temporary position for one year, after which he would return to Vienna and again take up his duties as Institute director. In fact, Hayek remained at the London School of Economics until 1948. And Morgenstern served as director of the Austrian Institute for Business Cycle Research until March 1938, when he found himself exiled in the United States during a lecture tour at the time of the annexation of Austria by Nazi Germany. The Institute's documents also show that Hayek ran the organization from 1927 to 1931 in a rather chaotic form of 'spontaneous order', with little system or care with paperwork or records. Organizational *Ordnung* only arrived with Morgenstern's appointment as director, after Hayek had moved to London. From that point on, discipline reigned, with a careful keeping of all Institute correspondence, research and financial statements.

12. I might mention a story Oskar Morgenstern related to me in the mid-1970s, a story that I have never seen recounted anywhere. Morgenstern said that one morning in the spring of 1931, after Hayek had returned from having delivered the London lectures that became *Prices and Production*, he ran into Hayek at the elevator in the Vienna Chamber of Commerce building where the Institute then had its offices (and where Morgenstern was employed as Hayek's assistant). Morgenstern told me that while riding up on the elevator together he turned to Hayek and said, 'We are going to enter the office, you are going to look through your mail, and you will find a letter inviting you to be a professor at the London School.' And they both laughed. In the office, Hayek sat down at his desk and went through his mail. He came to a letter from the London School of Economics, opened it, and found the invitation for the position as the Tooke Professor of Economic Science and Statistics. Not saying a word, Hayek handed the letter to Morgenstern, and they looked at each other in a chilled silence. I must have looked incredulous after being told this story, because Morgenstern said to me with dead seriousness, 'It happened just that way.'

13. See the excellent discussion of this period of Hayek's intellectual life by Hansjoerg Klausinger, in his introduction to volume 7 of Hayek's *Collected Works* (Hayek, 2012).

14. Mises' influence on Lionel Robbins, who had invited and brought Hayek to LSE, was no less of note at this time. In the preface to his *An Essay on the Nature and Significance of Economic Science*, Robbins had acknowledged his 'especial indebtedness to the works of Ludwig von Mises' (Robbins, 1932, pp. viii–ix). But this was made even clearer in the letter that Robbins enclosed with the copy of the book that he sent to Mises on 20 May 1932, just after it was published: 'I send you herewith a copy of my modest attempt to popularize for English readers the methodological implications of modern economic science. I hope you will not mind my especial mention of your name in the preface. I have no wish to make you in any way responsible for my crudités of exposition, but if there is anything of value in what I have said it would be most unjust that your name should not be associated with it. It is not easy for me to put into suitable words the magnitude of my intellectual debt to your work.' Mises replied on 18 June 1932, expressing his thanks and complete agreement with Robbins's contribution: 'Only today, I have

the time to thank you for the pleasure that I found in having received your book. I have read it with great interest. It is needless to say that I fully agree with your arguments. I only regret that you did not expand your book to include the treatment of a number of other important problems. I am, however, convinced that your latest work will prove to be very successful.' And as Hayek later pointed out, 'Robbins' own most influential work, *The Nature and Significance of Economic Science*, made what had been the methodological approach to microeconomic theory established by the Austrian school the generally recognized standard [within the wider economics profession]' (Hayek, 1992, p. 53).

15. In conversation in 1977, Hayek said to me that when he wrote this article, the real comparison that he had in mind was between Lionel Robbins and himself. Robbins, Hayek stated, was the epitome of the 'master' of his subject, who seemingly had read everything in economics, who could restate and explain every theory, and could easily express the ideas of others in their own words almost verbatim. Hayek saw himself as the 'puzzler' who had to recast his ideas every time a problem arose, and never was sure how it all might hang together until long after, when a mental glance backwards made him see connections and relationships among his own ideas that he had not seen when first thinking them through. This 'puzzler' aspect to Hayek's own thinking process was implied in the forward to Gerald O'Driscoll's, *Economics as a Coordination Problem: The Contributions of Friedrich A. Hayek*, in which Hayek said, 'It is a curious fact that a student of complex phenomena may long himself remain unaware of how his views of different problems hang together and perhaps never fully succeed in clearly stating the guiding ideas which led him to the treatment of particulars. I must confess that I was occasionally myself surprised when I found in Professor O'Driscoll's account side by side statements I made at the interval of many years and on quite different problems, which still implied the same general approach' (O'Driscoll, 1977, p. ix).

16. See Hayek (1992, p. 128): 'During these years, the 1920s and early 1930s, Mises was extraordinarily fertile, and in a long series of monographs on economic, sociological, and philosophical problems built up the comprehensive philosophy of society that he first expounded in a German work [*Nationalökonomie*] and then summed up in his *magnum opus* by which he is mainly known to his American readers, *Human Action*.'

17. See Mises (1933, p. 157): 'Insomuch as money prices of the means of production can be determined only in a social order in which they are privately owned, the proof of the impracticability of socialism necessarily follows. From the standpoint of both politics and history, this proof is certainly the most important discovery made by economic theory ... It alone will enable future historians to understand how it came about that the victory of the socialist movement did not lead to the creation of the socialist order of society.'

18. See Mises (1933, pp. 12–35) and Wieser (1914, pp. 8–9).

19. In his review of Mises' *Human Action*, Ludwig Lachmann made a point of emphasizing that, 'In reading this book we must never forget that it is the work of Max Weber that is being carried on here' (Lachmann, 1977, p. 95).

20. A peculiar missing element in Hayek's discussions of the subjectivist approach in social and economic analysis is the seemingly total absence of any explicit references to the fact that one of the leading influences in the development of methodological subjectivism was Max Weber. This is peculiar since Mises, especially, emphasized Weber's significance in this area for the social sciences, and even published in 1929 a lengthy essay on Weber in the form of a 'eminent criticism' of Weber's ideas for economic theory (Mises, 1933, 68–129). Weber's theory of 'subjective meaning' and 'ideal types' was also a frequent discussion topic in Mises' private seminar, where Hayek was, of course, a regular participant.

21. Another impetus for Mises to articulate more clearly his theory of how men use interpretive 'understanding' of the 'facts' of the market settings in which they find themselves to form expectations and adapt to unexpected outcomes and events very likely was the appearance of Alfred Schutz's, *The Phenomenology of the Social World* (1932).

Schutz applied Max Weber's 'ideal type' concept to develop a theory of how men interpret and anticipate the actions of others when looking to the future. Schutz, like Hayek, was an active member in Mises' *Privatseminar* in Vienna, and remained one of Mises' closest friends after they both had moved to the United States. On Schutz's relationship to the Austrian economists, see Ebeling (2010a, pp. 332–47).
22. For a more detailed explanation and analysis of the uses of the 'ideal type' for constructing an 'Austrian' theory of expectations and expectations formation, see Ebeling (1986, 1987, 1994, 1999).
23. Differences that may be found in Mises' and Hayek's approaches to economics in general and Austrian economics in particular have been emphasized by Salerno (1993). However, I think a stronger case can be made that the similarities are greater than the differences, if one keeps in mind the common 'Mengerian' starting point for both: methodological individualism and subjectivism; the market as a dynamic process through time, rather than a focus on end-state market equilibrium; attention to capital complementarity and the time structure of production; and many social and market institutions as the cumulative result of unintended societal evolution. For an interpretation that focuses more on the 'complementarities' of their contributions within the Austrian tradition, see Kirzner (1992, pp. 119–36).
24. See Hayek (1992, p. 158): 'I must admit that often I myself did not initially think his arguments were completely convincing and only slowly learned that he was mostly right and that, after some reflection, a justification could be found that he had not made explicit.'

REFERENCES

Caldwell, Bruce J. (2004), *Hayek's Challenge: An Intellectual Biography of F.A. Hayek*, Chicago, IL: University of Chicago Press.
Ebeling, Richard ([1986] 1995), 'Toward a hermeneutical economics: expectations, prices, and the role of interpretation in a theory of the market process', reprinted in David L. Prychitko (ed.), *Individuals, Institutions, Interpretations: Hermeneutics Applied to Economics*, Brookfield, VT: Avebury, pp. 138–53.
Ebeling, Richard ([1987] 1995), 'Cooperation in anonymity', reprinted in David L. Prychitko (ed.), *Individuals, Institutions, Interpretations: Hermeneutics Applied to Economics*, Brookfield, VT: Avebury, pp. 81–92.
Ebeling, Richard (1994), 'Expectations and expectations-formation in Mises' theory of the market process', in Peter J. Boettke and David L. Prychitko (eds), *The Market Process: Essays in Contemporary Austrian Economics*, Aldershot, UK and Brookfield, VT, USA: Edward Elgar, pp. 83–95.
Ebeling, Richard ([1999] 2010), 'Human action, ideal types, and the market process: Alfred Schutz and the Austrian economists', reprinted in *Political Economy, Public Policy, and Monetary Economics: Ludwig von Mises and the Austrian Tradition*, London, UK and New York, USA: Routledge, pp. 332–47.
Ebeling, Richard (2003), *Austrian Economics and the Political Economy of Freedom*, Cheltenham, UK and Northampton, MA, USA: Edward Elgar.
Ebeling, Richard (2010a), *Political Economy, Public Policy, and Monetary Economics: Ludwig von Mises and the Austrian Tradition*, London, UK and New York, USA: Routledge.
Ebeling, Richard (2010b), 'An "Austrian" interpretation of the meaning of Austrian economics: history, methodology, and theory', in Roger Koppl, Steven Horwitz and Pierre Desrochers (eds), *Advances in Austrian Economics*, 14, Bingley: Emerald Group, pp. 43–68.
Ebeling, Richard (ed.) (2012), *Selected Writings of Ludwig von Mises*, Vol. 1, *Monetary and Economic Policy Problems Before, During and After the Great War*, Indianapolis, IN: Liberty Fund.

Greaves, Bettina Bien (1958), Stenographic notes of Ludwig von Mises' New York University Seminar, 20 March (unpublished).
Haberler, Gottfried (1927), *Der Sinn der Indexzahlen*, Munich: J.C.B. Mohr.
Haberler, Gottfried ([1928] 1993), 'A new index number and its meaning', reprinted in Anthony Y.C. Koo (ed.), *The Liberal Economic Order*, vol. II, *Money, Cycles and Related Themes*, Aldershot, UK and Brookfield, VT, USA: Edward Elgar, pp. 107-17.
Haberler, Gottfried (1931), 'The different meanings attached to the term "fluctuations in the purchasing power of gold" and the best instrument or instruments for measuring such fluctuations', Geneva: League of Nations, F/Gold/74, March.
Hayek, F.A. ([1929] 2012), *Monetary Theory and the Trade Cycle*, reprinted in Hansjoerg Klausinger (ed.), *The Collected Writings of F.A. Hayek*, vol. 7, *Business Cycles, Part I*, Chicago, IL: University of Chicago Press, pp. 49-165.
Hayek, F.A. ([1931] 2012), *Prices and Production*, reprinted in Hansjoerg Klausinger (ed.), *The Collected Works of F.A. Hayek*, vol. 7, *Business Cycles, Part I*, Chicago, IL: University of Chicago Press, pp. 167-283.
Hayek, F.A. ([1933] 1991), W.W. Bartley and Stephen Kresge (eds), *The Collected Works of F.A. Hayek*, vol. 3, *The Trend of Economic Thinking: Essays on Political Economists and Economic History*, Chicago, IL: University of Chicago Press.
Hayek, F.A. (ed.) (1935), *Collectivist Economic Planning: Critical Studies on the Possibilities of Socialism*, London: George Routledge
Hayek, F.A. ([1937] 1948), 'Economics and knowledge', reprinted in F.A. Hayek, *Individualism and Economic Order*. Chicago, IL: University of Chicago Press, pp. 33-56.
Hayek, F.A. ([1940] 1948), 'Socialist calculation: the competitive "solution"', reprinted in F.A. Hayek, *Individualism and Economic Order*, Chicago, IL: University of Chicago Press, pp. 181-208.
Hayek, F.A. ([1945] 1948), 'The use of knowledge in society', reprinted in F.A. Hayek, *Individualism and Economic Order*, Chicago, IL: University of Chicago Press, pp. 77-91.
Hayek, F.A. ([1946] 1948), 'The meaning of competition', in F.A. Hayek, *Individualism and Economic Order*, Chicago, IL: University of Chicago Press, pp. 92-106.
Hayek, F.A. ([1960] 2011), *The Constitution of Liberty: The Definitive Edition*, Ronald Hamowy (ed.), *The Collected Works of F.A. Hayek*, vol. 17, Chicago, IL: University of Chicago Press.
Hayek (1973, 1976, 1979), *Law, Legislation, and Liberty*, 3 vols, Chicago, IL: University of Chicago Press.
Hayek, F.A. (1975), 'Interview with Dr. Friedrich A. von Hayek', *Gold and Silver Newsletter*, Monex International Limited, June.
Hayek, F.A. ([1978] 1983), 'Coping with ignorance', reprinted in *Knowledge, Evolution and Society*. London: Adam Smith Institute, pp. 17-27.
Hayek, F.A. (1992), *The Collected Writings of F.A. Hayek*, vol. 4, *The Fortunes of Liberalism, Essays on Austrian Economics and the Ideal of Freedom*, ed. Peter G. Klein, Chicago, IL: University of Chicago Press.
Hayek, F.A. (1994), *Hayek on Hayek*, ed. Stephen Kresge and Leif Wenar, Chicago, IL: University of Chicago Press.
Hayek, F.A. (2010), *Studies in the Abuse and Decline of Reason*, Bruce Caldwell (ed.), *The Collected Works of F.A. Hayek*, vol. 13, Chicago, IL: Chicago University Press.
Hayek, F.A. (2012), *The Collected Writings of F.A. Hayek*, vol. 7, *Business Cycles, Part I*, ed. Hansjoerg Klausinger, Chicago, IL: University of Chicago Press.
Hulsmann, Jorg Guido (2007), *Mises: The Last Knight of Liberalism*, Auburn, AL: Ludwig von Mises Institute.
Kirzner, Israel M. (1992), *The Meaning of Market Process: Essays in the Development of Modern Austrian Economics*, New York: Routledge.
Lachmann, Ludwig M. (1977), *Capital, Expectations, and the Market Process: Essays on the Theory of the Market Process*, Kansas City, KS: Sheed, Andrews & McMeel.
Leonard, Robert (2011), 'The collapse of interwar Vienna: Oskar Morgenstern's community, 1925-1950', *History of Political Economy*, 43 (1), pp. 83-130.

Machlup, Fritz ([1931] 1940), *The Stock Market, Credit, and Capital Formation*, London: William Hodge.
Marget, Arthur W. (1929), 'Morgenstern on the methodology of economic forecasting', *Journal of Political Economy*, 37 (June), pp. 312–39.
Menger, Carl ([1871] 1981), *Principles of Economics*, New York: New York University Press.
Menger, Carl ([1892] 2002), 'Money', in Michael Latzer and Stefan W. Schmitz (eds), *Carl Menger and the Evolution of Payments Systems: From Barter to Electronic Money*, Cheltenham, UK and Northampton, MA, USA: Edward Elgar, pp. 25–107.
Mises, Ludwig von ([1907] 2012), 'The political-economic motives of the Austrian currency reform', in Richard M. Ebeling (ed.), *Selected Writings of Ludwig von Mises*, Indianapolis, IN: Liberty Fund, pp. 3–20.
Mises, Ludwig von ([1909] 2012), 'The problem of legal resumption of specie payments in Austria-Hungary', in Richard M. Ebeling (ed.), *Selected Writings of Ludwig von Mises*, Indianapolis, IN: Liberty Fund, pp. 31–82.
Mises, Ludwig von ([1910a] 2012), 'On the problem of legal resumption of specie payments in Austria-Hungary', in Richard M. Ebeling (ed.), *Selected Writings of Ludwig von Mises*, Indianapolis, IN: Liberty Fund, pp. 95–103.
Mises, Ludwig von ([1910b] 2012), 'Financial reform in Austria', in Richard M. Ebeling (ed.), *Selected Writings of Ludwig von Mises*, Indianapolis, IN: Liberty Fund, pp. 117–30.
Mises, Ludwig von ([1912] 1980), *The Theory of Money and Credit*, Indianapolis, IN: Liberty Fund.
Mises, Ludwig von ([1913a] 2012), 'On rising prices and purchasing power policies', in Richard M. Ebeling, (ed.), *Selected Writings of Ludwig von Mises*, Indianapolis, IN: Liberty Fund, pp. 131–55.
Mises, Ludwig von ([1913b] 2012), 'The general rise in prices in the light of economic theory', in Richard M. Ebeling (ed.), *Selected Writings of Ludwig von Mises*, Indianapolis, IN: Liberty Fund, pp. 156–67.
Mises, Ludwig von ([1920] 1935), 'Economic calculation in the socialist commonwealth', in F.A. Hayek, (ed.), *Collectivist Economic Planning: Critical Studies on the Possibilities of Socialism*, London: George Routledge & Sons, pp. 87–130.
Mises, Ludwig von ([1922] 1981), *Socialism: An Economic and Sociological Analysis*, Indianapolis, IN: Liberty Fund.
Mises, Ludwig von (1926), 'On the necessity of objective and scholarly treatment of statistical data by "The Austrian Institute for Business Cycle Research"', remarks delivered before the Executive Directors' Conference of all [Austrian] Chambers of Commerce, Crafts, and Industry, 15 November.
Mises, Ludwig von ([1927] 2005), *Liberalism: The Classical Tradition*, Indianapolis, IN: Liberty Fund.
Mises, Ludwig von ([1933] 1981), *Epistemological Problems of Economics*, New York: New York University Press.
Mises, Ludwig von (1940a), *Nationalökonomie: Theorie des Handelns und Wirtschaftens*, Geneva: Editions Union.
Mises, Ludwig von ([1940b] 2009), *Memoirs*, Auburn, AL: Ludwig von Mises Institute.
Mises, Ludwig von ([1949] 1966), *Human Action: A Treatise on Economics*, Chicago, IL: Henry Regrary.
Mises, Ludwig von (1957), *Theory and History: An Interpretation of Social and Economic Evolution*, New Haven, CT: Yale University Press.
Mises, Ludwig von (1962), *The Ultimate Foundations of Economic Science: An Essay on Method*, Princeton: D. Van Nostrand.
Mises, Margit von (1984), *My Years with Ludwig von Mises*, 2nd enlarged edn, Cedar Falls, IA: Center for Futures Education.
Morgenstern, Oskar (1928), *Wirtschaftsprognoses, eine Untersuchung ihrer Voraussetzungen und Morglichkeiten*, Vienna: Julius Springer Verlag.
O'Driscoll, Gerald P. (1977), *Economics as a Coordination Problem: The Contributions of Friedrich A. Hayek*, Kansas City, KS: Sheed Andrews & McMeel.

Robbins, Lionel (1932), *An Essay on the Nature and Significance of Economic Science*, London: Macmillan.
Salerno, Joseph T. (1993), 'Mises and Hayek dehomogenized', *Review of Austrian Economics*, 6 (2), 113–46.
Schutz, Alfred ([1932] 1967), *The Phenomenology of the Social World*, Evanston, IL: Northwestern University Press.
Von Neumann, John and Osker Morgenstern (1944), *The Theory of Games and Economic Behavior*, Princeton, NJ: Princeton University Press.
Weber, Max ([1922] 1978), *Economy and Society: An Outline of Interpretive Sociology*, Berkeley, CA: University of California Press.
Wieser, Friedrich von ([1914] 1927), *Social Economics*, New York: Adelphi.

8. Hayek and Lachmann
Peter Lewin

INTRODUCTION

Friedrich Hayek was a scholar of uncommon breadth and depth whose work will be the subject of study and discovery for a long time to come. The span of his career makes it difficult, probably impossible, to account for all of the influences that the many scholars who crossed his path might have had on his work, or the influences that he might have had on theirs. No doubt this will motivate diverse contributions. Some of the usual suspects appear in other chapters of this volume. In this chapter I investigate the intellectual relationship between Hayek and his student and younger colleague Ludwig M. Lachmann. I begin at the beginning, the London School of Economics (LSE) years, during which Hayek and Lachmann both worked on the related topics of the trade cycle and capital theory. I follow with an examination of their diverging but related subsequent work. The capital theory experience is pivotal.

THE LSE YEARS: IN CLOSE PROXIMITY

Though he could with justification be described as a fellow 'Austrian economist', Ludwig Lachmann was born and educated in Germany, not in Austria. He became acquainted with and enamored of Austrian economics as a young student in his twenties, discovering the work of Joseph Schumpeter and Ludwig von Mises. (He met Mises for the first time in 1932.) He spent the rest of his long professional life working within and fighting for the causes of the 'Austrian School' as he saw them (Mittermaier, 1992; also Grinder, 1977b).

In 1933 he left Germany (with his future wife Margot) for England. He was unable to find an academic appointment and decided to go to the London School of Economics as a student, even though he already had a doctorate from Berlin (Mittermaier, 1992, p.9). This placed him at the very center of the vibrant new 'Hayekian' school of economics, together with such scholars as Lionel Robbins, John Hicks, Nicolas Kaldor, Abba Lerner, George Shackle and others, and at the very center of the fast-developing battle between the Hayekians and the emerging Keynesians.

He was already a Hayekian when he arrived (Mittermaier, 1992, p. 9). As Mittermaier points out, being a 'Hayekian' at that time referred to an appreciative interest in the Austrian theory of capital and the business (trade) cycle.[1]

Thus, the first and strongest connection between Hayek and Lachmann grew out of these topical preoccupations with the Austrian version of the business cycle, deriving from Mises and from the Austrian theory of capital, which was a crucial building block for that theory. The Austrian theory of capital (ATC), originating with Carl Menger (1871), was the most well-known contribution of the Austrian School at that time, owing mainly to the extensive work of Eugen von Böhm-Bawerk on the subject. Böhm-Bawerk's work had achieved worldwide recognition (1959, three volumes originally published during the period 1884–1912). In his influential work on the trade cycle (1933a, 1935a), Hayek had referred to, and made use of, a highly stylized version of the ATC. And much of his work in the 1930s was dedicated to the attempt to elaborate and make this theory more widely accessible, especially to English speakers. In the process, he was led to a thorough re-examination of the ATC, writing a number of important articles (some of which are collected in Hayek 1939a)[2] and culminating in *The Pure Theory of Capital* (1941). This body of work constitutes the greatest Hayekian influence on Lachmann. It was crucial to his own subsequent work on capital theory and also his enduring preoccupation with the topic of expectations.

Lachmann had for a while been troubled by the influence of people's expectations on their actions, and felt that in *Price and Production* (1935a) and *Monetary Theory and the Trade Cycle* (1933a)[3] and in his debate with Keynes subsequent to the publication of Keynes's *Treatise* (1930), Hayek had neglected to adequately address expectations in the trade cycle story offered as a counter-argument to Keynes. Reading Keynes's *General Theory* (1936) upon its publication, he was surprised to find Keynes's extensive treatment of the subject.

Lachmann always maintained that the quarrel (the Hayek–Keynes debate) was unnecessary and that no important economic principles were at stake. It concerned empirical questions about how markets work in the modern industrial world (that is, which markets were fix-price and which were flex-price, in Hicks's terminology) although there were also some political undertones. Keynes had won, he thought, partly because he had introduced expectations most effectively into his theory, at least where it suited his purposes, whereas neither Mises nor Hayek responded in like manner. In 1934 Paul Rosenstein-Rodan had said to Lachmann that the question of expectations was 'the major flaw in Hayek'. Keynes had not made the same mistake. As Lachmann wrote once (unpublished):

I bought a copy of the *General Theory* the week it came out (February 1936).
At first I understood very little. But when I came to the definition of 'marginal
efficiency of capital', I realized: Keynes too was bothered about expectations.
Investment depended on expectations! As I had reached the same conclusion
before, that was a great help. (Mittermaier 1992, p. 10)

Mittermaier's claim that Lachmann believed that the Austrians had inappropriately neglected expectations in the context of this debate is no doubt true. Indeed, the implications of subjectivism for expectations became a theme that motivated his work for the rest of his life.[4] Nevertheless, it is clear that in his work in the 1930s (subsequent to *Prices and Production*) Hayek too was much exercised about the question of expectations, and by the time the *General Theory* came out, Hayek had published a number of articles carefully examining their influence.[5] His seminal article 'Economics and knowledge' (1937a), which many see as a dividing line presaging Hayek's work on the meaning and consequences of disequilibrium, was preceded by much in-depth investigation of similar issues in connection with the ATC and expectations. It is reasonable to assume that Lachmann was strongly influenced by this work. The nature of that influence is, however, somewhat ambiguous. Lachmann considered his view of expectations to be more fundamental than Hayek's. As he later wrote:

For in the general equilibrium perspective Hayek adopted in the 1930s it is
convergence, and the nature of the economic processes promoting or impeding
it, that must be of primary interest. The divergence of expectations appears in
this perspective mainly as an obstacle to equilibrium, if not as a reflection of a
temporary distorted view of the world. (Lachmann, 1979, p. 314n)

To investigate this further we should look at Lachmann's work on capital theory and expectations.

HAYEK AND LACHMANN ON CAPITAL THEORY AND EXPECTATIONS

Lachmann's work on capital theory began in the late 1930s, continued into the 1940s and developed together with his work on expectations (Lachmann, 1937, 1938, 1939, 1941, 1943, 1944, 1945, 1947, 1948).[6] This work begins in the context of the Hayek–Keynes debate and the onset of the Great Depression, with Lachmann exploring the nature of 'secondary depressions', but it soon develops beyond this. It culminates ultimately in his book *Capital and its Structure* published much later in 1956 (Lachmann, 1978 [1956]), by which time he was far away, and most other economists' interest in capital theory had disappeared with the triumph of the Keynesian revolution.

BACKGROUND

Lachmann's capital theory is clearly Hayekian in spirit, and he acknowledges Hayek's important influence. 'My greatest debt of gratitude is to Professor F.A. Hayek whose ideas on capital have helped me to shape my own thought more than any other thinker' (Lachmann, 1978, p.xvi). It is, however, also closely connected to the work of Böhm-Bawerk, whose insights Lachmann sought to carefully and critically rehabilitate in a form applicable to modern real world production contexts.[7] As such, it bears an interesting relationship to Hayek's last and most extensive work on capital, *The Pure Theory of Capital*, of which more later.

Lachmann's approach reflects what he saw to be the inextricable connection between capital, knowledge and expectations, the implications of which he clearly thought needed to be spelled out in order to provide a satisfactory answer to the Keynesian challenge. According to Lachmann:

> The generic concept of capital without which economists cannot do their work has no measurable counterpart among material objects; it reflects the entrepreneurial appraisal of such objects. Beer barrels and blast furnaces, harbor installations and hotel room furniture are capital not by virtue of their physical properties but by virtue of their economic functions. Something is capital because the market, the consensus of entrepreneurial minds, regards it as capable of yielding an income . . . [But] the stock of capital used by society does not present a picture of chaos. Its arrangement is not arbitrary. There is some order to it. (Lachmann, 1978, p.xv)

The value of the capital stock, being dependent on individual expectations and evaluations (time preferences included), is not an objectively observable phenomenon. Only in equilibrium, where all individuals' expectations were consistent one with another, would such a value have any meaning. He thus offers a theory of the capital structure rather than the capital stock and emphasizes the heterogeneity of capital. The fact that capital goods are physically very dissimilar is significant precisely because of the existence of disequilibrium. Physical heterogeneity could be reduced to value homogeneity if the values of the various capital goods could be simply added together. Where disequilibrium means that individuals have different and frequently inconsistent expectations, one cannot simply add together individual valuations.

EXPECTATIONS

On the matter of both expectations and heterogeneity, Hayek and Lachmann are clearly on the same page. Those familiar with Lachmann's work on expectations and his emphasis on their disparate, incompatible nature will find the following similarity with Hayek's early pronouncement striking:

> It is evident that the various expectations on which different individuals base their decisions at a particular moment either will or will not be mutually compatible; and if these expectations are not compatible those of some people at least must be disappointed. (Hayek, 1933b, p. 140)

Compare this with a typical statement of Lachmann's on expectations:

> Different people may hold different expectations at the same time; the same person may hold different expectations at different times. These are quite insoluble problems as long as we regard expectations as independent of each other. Why should they be consistent with each other? (Lachmann, 1978, p. 21)

Hayek's preoccupation with expectations (influenced by his involvement in both the Hayek–Keynes debate and the socialist-calculation debate, which occurred also in the 1930s), led him to develop some of his most important early insights as evident in his seminal 1937 and 1945 articles (Hayek, 1937a, 1945). Lachmann seems to have picked up mostly from the work that preceded this.

INVESTMENT AND THE HETEROGENEITY OF CAPITAL

According to Lachmann, though the capital-stock is heterogeneous, it is not amorphous. The various components of the capital stock stand in sensible relationship to one another because they perform specific functions together. That is to say, they are used in various capital combinations. If we understand the logic of capital combinations, we give meaning to the capital structure and, in this way, we are able to design appropriate economic policies or, even more importantly, avoid inappropriate ones (e.g., Lachmann, 1947; 1978, p. 123).

Understanding capital combinations entails an understanding of the concepts of complementarity and substitutability. These concepts pertain to a world in which perceived prices are actual (disequilibrium) prices, in the sense that they reflect inconsistent expectations, and in which changes that occur cause protracted visible adjustments. Capital goods are complements if they contribute together to a given production plan. A production plan is defined by the pursuit of a given set of ends to which the production goods are the means. As long as the plan is being successfully fulfilled, all of the production goods stand in complementary relationship to one another. They are part of the same plan. The complementarity relationships within the plan that may be quite intricate and no doubt involve different stages of production and distribution.

Substitution occurs when a production plan fails (in whole or in part). When some element of the plan fails, a contingency adjustment must be sought. Thus some resources must be substituted for others. This is the role, for example, of spare parts or excess inventory. Thus, complementarity and substitutability are properties of different states of the world. The same good can be a complement in one situation and a substitute in another.[8] Substitutability can only be gauged to the extent that a certain set of contingency events can be visualized. There may be some events, such as those caused by significant technological changes, that, not having been predictable, render some production plans valueless. The resources associated with them will have to be incorporated into some other production plan or else scrapped; they will have been rendered unemployable. This is a natural result of economic progress which is driven primarily by the trial-and-error discovery of new and superior outputs and techniques of production. What determines the fate of any capital good in the face of change is the extent to which it can be fitted into any other capital combination without loss in value. Capital goods are regrouped. Those that lose their value completely are scrapped. That is, capital goods, though heterogeneous and diverse, are often capable of performing a number of different economic functions.

Though Lachmann develops the theme of capital heterogeneity, complementarity, specificity and order in a way that Hayek never did (of which more below) it is clear that Hayek was very much aware of the importance of the heterogeneity of capital (and, surprisingly, of labor)[9] in the work he did between *Prices and Production* and *The Pure Theory of Capital*:

> There is every reason to believe that there are as great differences between the position of the different kinds of capital good industries as there are great differences between them and the consumer goods industries ... [and these differences underlie] the importance of the specificity of existing equipment to a particular method of production. (Hayek, 1939b, p. 21)

Hayek's scattered remarks along these lines provided the impetus for Lachmann's development of his theory of the capital structure. In his 1948 article Lachmann refers to Hayek (1937b) and says, 'The ideas set forth by Professor Hayek have been the main inspiration of this paper' (Lachmann, 1948, p. 308n). This 1948 article titled 'Investment repercussions' is a fascinating extension of the ideas found in his first articulation of the capital, structure, complementarity, specificity and substitutability story in 1947, inspired by Hayek's (1937b) article which is tantalizingly titled 'Investment that raises the demand for capital'. In the light of Lachmann's later work, this last-mentioned article might be expected to be about capital complementarity (as investment, by adding to existing heterogeneous and complementary capital items, increases the expected rate of return of the capital combination and, thus, the demand for capital), but it is not, at least not directly. It is mostly about how past investment funds in diverse capital goods constitute a sunk cost and thus raise the prospective rate of return of any investment going forward. This is relevant to the question of investment and Keynes's marginal efficiency of capital (investment) and the trade cycle (never far from consideration during those times). Lachmann might have been expected to combine this with his capital structure ideas to address investment policy questions, including the question of the trade cycle.

A simple example illustrates Hayek's point. Consider an n-period investment in which the revenue earned in the first two periods is (and is expected to be) zero while expenses are positive, so that:

$$FV_1, FV_2 < 0$$

where FV_i refers to the expected net revenue (future value) for period i. The rate of return expected for the n periods (from the perspective of period 1) can be computed as r in:

$$\frac{FV_1}{(1+r)} + \frac{FV_2}{(1+r)^2} + \frac{FV_3}{(1+r)^3} + \ldots + \frac{FV_n}{(1+r)^n} = 0$$

Assume that r marginally exceeds the variable interest rate at which the project is being financed. The project is financed with a series of loans. If after two periods the interest rate unexpectedly rises, it might be expected that the project would be abandoned, since the n-period investment is now earning a rate of return less than the cost of financing it. However, this is no longer an n-period investment. Instead it is an $n-2$-period investment. The expenditures incurred in the first two periods are sunk costs and are irrelevant to the computation of the rate of return going forward (from the perspective of period 3). This can be computed using:

$$\frac{FV_3}{(1+r)^3} + \ldots + \frac{FV_n}{(1+r)^n} = 0$$

and r will clearly be higher and may well be substantially higher than when it was first computed. These considerations suggest that, with the passage of time, the rise in the rate of interest that is sufficient to deter the completion of any multi-period investment project may be significantly higher than the current rate at any period:[10]

> Anything which will lead people to expect a lower rate of interest, or a larger supply of investible funds, than will actually exist when the time comes for their utilization, will in the way we have suggested force interest rates to rise much higher than would have been the case if people had not expected such a low rate. But, while it is true that an unexpected decrease in the rate of saving, or an unforeseen appearance of a new demand for capital – a new invention for instance – may bring about such a situation, the most important cause practically of such false expectations probably is a temporary increase in the supply of such funds through credit expansion at a rate which cannot be maintained.[11] In this case, the increased quantity of current investment will induce people to expect investment to continue at a similar rate for some time and in consequence to invest now in a form which requires for its successful completion further investment at a similar rate. It is not so much the quantity of current investment but the direction it takes – the type of capital goods being produced – which determines the amount of future investment required if the current investments are to be successfully incorporated in the structure of production. [Thus] an increase in the rate of investment, or the quantity of capital goods, may have the effect of raising rather than lowering the rate of interest if this increase has given rise to the expectation of a greater future supply of investable funds than is actually forthcoming. (Hayek, 1937b, pp. 80f, footnote removed)

That these telling points were not more persuasive at the time in explaining the origins of the cycle – and in exposing the superficial nature of Keynes's analysis of investment behavior – must be attributed to the nature of the times and its preoccupation with the deep secondary depression in which the world economy found itself. But it is clear that here, and in similar contemporaneous work, Hayek can hardly be accused of neglecting the importance of expectations. So by this point in time at least, Lachmann's criticism on that score had been forcefully answered. Indeed, we see here the building blocks for Lachmann's exploration of the implications of the heterogeneity of capital in a changing world in which disappointed expectations feature so prominently:

> The modern theory of investment, set forth by Lord Keynes in *The General Theory*, has had its many triumphs these last twelve years, but it still has a number of gaps. Conceiving of investment as simple growth of a stock of homo-

geneous capital, it is ill-equipped to cope with situations in which the immobility of heterogeneous capital resources imposes a strain of the economic system. In particular, it can tell us little about the 'inducement to invest' in a world where scarcity of some capital resources co-exists with abundance of others. (Lachmann, 1948, p. 131)

In this article (1948) Lachmann then proceeds to lay out a detailed analysis of the implications of capital heterogeneity, perhaps even more fully and clearly than in his earlier 1947 article on complementarity and substitutability. He links these concepts to the theory of investment (which he points out must contain an implicit theory of capital), and specifically to Keynes's marginal efficiency concept (which lacks any recognition of such a theory).[12] The effect of an increase in investment on the demand for capital depends, in his account, on the shape of the already existing capital structure and the degree of its complementarity with the new investment. So he is, like Hayek, examining the implications of time and changes in expectations in response to experience (including the experience of the results of economic policy), but he does so from a much broader point of view, and the importance of Hayek's narrower point concerning sunk costs and the change in the expected rate of return of any project, as outlined above, does not feature prominently; though it is, of course, implied.

HAYEK'S WORK ON CAPITAL AND THE *PURE THEORY*

With the completion of *The Pure Theory of Capital*, Hayek's concentrated work on capital theory comes to an end. By his own admission he felt somewhat disillusioned with the project. Looked at retrospectively, this may have been an auspicious development. Hayek's experience in grappling with the intricacies of capital seems to have provided both motivation and insight for his later projects, in particular for his 'shift of methodological perspective from one that emphasized the dualism of the social and natural sciences to one that explored the distinction between "simple phenomena and complex phenomena"' (Horwitz, 2008, p. 144).

Caldwell (2004) points to the period of the 1940s as the time when Hayek began to undergo this shift. Hayek's decision to revisit theoretical psychology and publish *The Sensory Order* (1952) brings together both this emphasis on complex phenomena and Hayek's attempts to provide a scientific underpinning for traditional Austrian subjectivism (Horwitz, 2008, p. 144).

More specifically, Horwitz suggests, 'a new framework for conceptualizing the relationship between the natural and social world' was the outcome, at least in part, of:

> his work on capital theory in the late 1930s that culminated in 1941's *The Pure Theory of Capital*, along with similar contributions and extensions by Ludwig Lachmann. It is striking how similar the Austrian theory of capital is to Hayek's work on cognition. Many of the same underlying ideas of function, complementarity, and structure are present in both. (Horwitz, 2008, 144–5)

We can explore this a bit further. Hayek's extensive work on capital, while involving many insights pertinent to a theory of capital in a dynamic world, was never consummated in a fully fledged 'dynamic' theory of capital (indeed, one may wonder if such a theory is even possible in the way in which 'theory' is usually understood). But it was his intention to produce one that was the original motivation for *The Pure Theory of Capital*, an intention he never fulfilled. His objectives are clearly stated:

> The problems that are raised by any attempt to analyze the dynamics of production are mainly problems connected with the interrelationships between the different parts of the elaborate structure of productive equipment which man has built to serve his needs. But all the essential differences between these parts were obscured by the general endeavor to subsume them under one comprehensive definition of the stock of capital. The fact that this stock of capital is not an amorphous mass but possesses a definite structure, that it is organized in a definite way, and that its composition of essentially different items is much more important than its aggregate 'quantity', was systematically disregarded. (Hayek, 1941, p. 6)

Much of the book is, however, taken up with a discussion of how an economy directed by a central dictator might make decisions regarding the formation and use of capital goods in an environment devoid of change. This, of course, abstracts from any dynamic issues. There is, by assumption, no disequilibrium problem; heterogeneity is seen not to matter. Hayek does this as a foil, a relief against which to illuminate the real-world problems of heterogeneity and change. His method is first to get the abstract problem right. But, though the final section of the book does contain a valuable discussion of some dynamic issues, it is not the fulfillment of the project Hayek had originally envisaged.

There is some evidence to suggest that both Hayek and Lachmann saw Lachmann's work as a continuation of Hayek's project. From Lachmann's side we know this to be true from his many references to Hayek's work, some of which, as already indicated, are specific on this:

> The notion of intertemporal equilibrium ..., occupies a central place in Hayekian capital theory. All analysis in the *Pure Theory* is such equilibrium analysis. But Hayek also regards it as a means to an end, *viz.* causal analysis, and we shall have to question whether it is an adequate means to this end. (Lachmann, 1975, pp. 200–201)

The means are not adequate, something which he worked to remedy.

From Hayek's side the situation is less clear. When asked about the *Pure Theory*, Hayek once remarked, 'I think the most useful conclusions drawn from what I did are really in Lachmann's book on capital', and he suggests that what Lachmann said is perhaps as much as could be said. Hayek continues:

> Like so many things, I am afraid, which I have attempted in economics, this capital-theory work more shows a barrier to how these things I've stressed – the complexity of the phenomena in general, the unknown character of the data, and so on – really much more point out limits to our possible knowledge than [are] contributions that make specific predictions possible. (quoted in Kresge and Wenar, 1994, p. 142)

So it seems that Hayek's often frustrating and exhausting experience of working on capital theory provided an unintentional proving ground for his later fundamental philosophical investigations that led him away from a preoccupation with theories that could make 'specific predictions' to those that, because of the essentially complex nature of the world, were suited to making only 'predictions in principle' or 'pattern predictions'.

Capital theory is an area of inquiry that contains seemingly endless potential for further insight. Both Hayek and Lachmann were provoked to consider more general social issues; in Lachmann's case most particularly it was action in disequilibrium. This has implications for both how we do economics (or any social science) and how the people we study are able to gain sufficient knowledge in order to act in a coherent manner; that is, for methodology and epistemology. For both Hayek and Lachmann, doing capital theory implied considering the nature and limitations of social science, what can and cannot be said or predicted, and the role that social institutions play in orienting people's behavior. Both are led away from classical formal modeling to the consideration of 'complex phenomena': Hayek very extensively and explicitly, Lachmann more by implication. Consider the following remarks that Lachmann made later in considering Hayek's capital theory:

> There are two possible types of social process. (There may be more.) We may describe the first as 'mechanical', the second (for want of a better term) as 'orientative'. In the first, whatever men do within a period depends on the position they have reached. A 'feedback' mechanism in which each subsequent step

depends on 'distance from equilibrium' is a special instance of it. Actors, when in disequilibrium, plan to take their next steps in the direction of equilibrium. This is what Hayek must have had in mind:

> The direction in which an entrepreneur will have to revise his plans will depend on the direction in which events prove to differ from his expectations. The statement of conditions under which individual plans will be compatible is therefore implicitly a statement of what will happen if they are not compatible. (Hayek, 1941, p. 23)

> But in a footnote to this passage we are warned: 'This is strictly true only if we are thinking of a single deviation of a particular in a situation which is otherwise in equilibrium, that is, on the assumption that all other expectations are confirmed. If more than one element turns out to be different from what was expected, the relation is no longer so simple'. (Lachmann, 1975, p. 204)

For Lachmann this is his cue to explore the world of incompatible expectations writ large in which feedback mechanisms guiding action cannot be taken for granted. For Hayek one might wonder if it was one of those things that pushed him to the consideration of a world in which things are 'no longer so simple', a world of complex phenomena.

FROM CAPITAL COMPLEMENTARITY TO COMPLEXITY

By the time Lachmann took up his post at the University of the Witwatersrand in 1950, both Hayek and the wider economics world had moved on from capital theory and the trade cycle, and although he remained interested in capital theory, Lachmann gradually expanded his scope of inquiry to more abstract big-picture methodological issues (and, to a lesser extent, economic policy).[13] He and Hayek were never again to be working in close proximity.

WHAT IS COMPLEXITY?

Capital theory forces us to focus on the elemental fact that all human action in society is embedded in networks of shared, but (by definition) subjective meanings that propel and arise from the interaction between individuals – in a nutshell, that all human action in society is human interaction. The 'data' that inform human decisions are not given 'objectively' in the sense that data on the physical world are, but, rather, include prominently the expected actions of others upon whom the success of our actions depend (Hayek, 1937a; see also Lewin, 1997). Planned actions need to be coordinated in order to succeed.

Both Hayek and Lachmann devote considerable effort to examining the consequences of this. For Hayek this leads him from an initial attempt to define, examine, refine, and if possible save, the concept of equilibrium (understood as the achievement of plan coordination), to his abandoning the notion of equilibrium in favor of the broader concept of order (see Lewis, Chapter 9 of this volume). His later work on methodology, cognition, law and social institutions anticipates and develops his ideas on the methods associated with the study of complex adaptive (classifying) systems (Hayek, 1952, 1967, 1978; McQuade and Butos, 2009).

Complex systems are systems (networks, structures) with many elements that relate to one another in limited, but complicated and often numerous, multilevel (to be explained below), ways that lead to outcomes that are essentially unpredictable (in their details, though the possible 'patterns' may be known). Complex adaptive systems are complex systems whose multiple interactions lead to outcomes that are in some significant sense 'ordered' or 'functional' or 'organized' (Hayek, 1974, p. 26; also 1955, 1964). In these systems, complex interaction leads adaptively to outcomes that are coherent and useful according to some scheme of action and evaluation. For example, evolution in nature is a complex adaptive system that works through some selection-replication process (constrained by the physical environment) to produce outcomes that are better adapted to the environment (Hayek, 1964). The evolution framework is very generalizable and has been applied in multiple contexts, including of course to human societies (in which connection it was first conceived). As Hayek discerned very early on, the brain itself is a complex adaptive system (Hayek, 1952, based on work done in the 1920s).

Though it is the subject of an increasing body of research effort, and though it has a clearly commonsense-type meaning, there is no readily agreed-upon definition of the concept of 'complexity' (Page, 2011, pp. 24–32; Mitchell, 2009, pp. 94–111). For Hayek, complexity is in essence a matter of 'too many variables':

> what we regard as the field of physics may well be the totality of phenomena where the number of significantly connected variables of different kinds is sufficiently small to enable us to study them as if they formed a closed system for which we can observe and control all the determining factors; we may have been led to treat certain phenomena as lying outside physics precisely because this is not the case (Hayek, 1955, p. 4, footnote removed)

> The situation is different, however, where the number of significantly interdependent variables is very large and only some of them can in practice

be individually observed. The position will here frequently be that if *we already know* the relevant laws, we could predict that if several hundred specified factors had the values $x_1, x_2, x_3, \ldots, x_n$, then there would always occur $y_1, y_2, y_3, \ldots, y_n$. But in fact all that our observation suggests may be that if $x_1, x_2, x_3, \ldots, x_n$, then there will occur [some recognizable subset of $y_1, y_2, y_3, \ldots, y_n$ and there may be a large unknown number of subsets; or that perhaps some relation P *or* Q could result from a $x_1, x_2, x_3, \ldots, x_n$, or similar input]. There may be no possibility of getting beyond this by means of observation, because it may in practice be impossible to test all the possible combinations of the factors $x_1, x_2, x_3, \ldots, x_{n_s}$. If in the face of the variety and complexity of such a situation our imagination cannot suggest more precise rules than those indicated, no systematic testing will help us over this difficulty. (Hayek, 1955, p. 8)[14]

It is not a question of *merely* too many variables. The difference in conceptual structures to which Hayek is referring is of a huge magnitude.[15] It is in the first instance a practical matter, but it is most likely also more fundamental and elusive, in that in order to successfully model essentially complex structures we would have to engage in a degree of complex classification that is intrinsically beyond the capacity of the human brain to accomplish, being that the brain itself is a classifying mechanism of lower complexity than the observed structures (a point that emerges from his 1952 work on cognitive psychology). In addition there are some systems that are intrinsically non-computable/decidable (see Koppl, 2010); the imputation problem in capital theory comes to mind.

The implications of complexity in a system (structure, network) are typically that, though intelligible, the outcomes that result from their operation do not provide us with precise value (quantitative) predictions. Instead, they are intelligible in that we are able to understand (comprehend the meaning of) the types of outcomes that are possible and are observed. Thus patterns rather than values are what can be predicted. As Hayek is anxious to point out, and as has perhaps been insufficiently emphasized, this does not preclude the possibility of an important type of (Popperian) falsification or refutation (a criterion taken by many scientists as the hallmark of acceptable 'scientific' investigation). Certain resulting patterns are ruled out by this type of investigation. The observation of a pattern of results not within the range predicted by a model of complex phenomena would refute the model (Hayek, 1964, pp. 32–41; 1974, pp. 30–32). Confirmed observations of inherited traits acquired in a Lamarckian manner would refute the Darwinian version of evolution. Observations of 'stagflation' lent credence to Monetarist and Austrian accounts of macroeconomic structure as opposed to the Keynesian story. The fact that such 'refutations' are hard to come by, or indeed to sustain, counts no more against the scientific nature of these methods (that lack quantitative predictive capacity) than do the same limitations in more traditional refutations based on deviant quantitative outcomes. The latter are also notoriously hard to come by.

I spoke earlier of multilevel interaction. Hayek's description of complex phenomena implies the phenomenon of emergence (see Lewis, 2012). Complex adaptive systems are (most) often hierarchical in nature, exhibiting 'lower' and 'higher' levels. Elements existing at the lower level interact in ways that result in the 'emergence' of qualitatively different (to be explained below) elements at a higher level. But interaction is not limited to any level. Elements at a lower level may be affected (in a 'downward' direction) by the emergent elements at a higher level B, as when individual action is influenced by social structures (like institutions and standards) that are themselves the result of prior individual actions; hence multilevel interaction. The observation that the changes are 'qualitative' in nature is basically a recognition that they cannot be fully accounted for by changes in the elements at the lower level. The new characteristics appear to emerge in a not fully explicable way from the interactions that occur at a lower level. This is a discernible aspect of the 'too many variables' problem, one that is commonly found with complex phenomena. Indeed it, and the other typical aspects of complex systems, are clearly apparent in capital structures as portrayed by both Hayek and Lachmann.

HETEROGENEITY AND COMPLEXITY; QUALITY AND QUANTITY

As we have seen, drawing on the work of Hayek, Lachmann made much of the fact that capital goods are heterogeneous and built his theory of the capital structure, based on complementary capital-good combinations, around this. Both Hayek and Lachmann emphasized that the heterogeneous nature of capital goods precluded adding them up to obtain an overall aggregate capital stock. Capital goods cannot be measured by adding them up. There is no simple dimension along which this could be accomplished (for example Lachmann, 1941; 1978, Ch. 4; see also Hayek, 1941, pp. 36–9; 1935b, pp. 86–8). For reasons already explained, aggregation in terms of the money values of the capital goods ignores the diverse subjective estimations of their 'worth' in terms of the prospective earnings they are expected to provide. The heterogeneity of capital goods is a derivative of the heterogeneity of expectations surrounding them.

Until recently this point was mostly ignored by scholars and policymakers. Lately, however, many aspects of heterogeneity have come to be considered very relevant: in the social and biological sciences and, notably, in management studies, where 'firm heterogeneity' strikes at the core of the neoclassical microeconomic theory of production. It is frequently invoked also in 'complexity studies' (as 'variety') (see also Harper and Endres, 2010, 2012). This growing literature, provoking more in-depth examination of the concept of heterogeneity, reveals hitherto insufficiently appreciated connections between the early and later work of both Lachmann and Hayek. Most fundamentally, considering the concept of heterogeneity throws light on the relationship between quantity and quality.

All observation and explanation proceed on the basis of classification (categorization). Phenomena are grouped into categories according to our perception of their essential similarity (homogeneity). The elements of any category (class) might be different in some respects, but in all respects that matter to us they are identical. Items within a particular category can be counted, quantified. The ability to quantify is crucially dependent on being able to count items in this manner. The number and type of categories (variables) is known and fixed. Thus, the arrival of a new category cannot be accommodated within a scheme of simple quantitative variation and must be considered to be a change in quality. Qualitative differences are categorical differences.

All quantitative modeling proceeds on the basis of the assumption that the individual elements of any given quantifiable variable are identical (homogeneous) and are different in some important respect from those of another variable. Variables are essentially distinguishable categories. In addition the elements of a quantifiable category do not interact with each other – else they could not be simply counted. Each element is an independent, identical instance of the class. (Most obvious is the case of 'identical randomly distributed variables'.) This does not preclude the elements themselves being complex – being the result of lower-level interactions, like identical molecules or biological cells, which are incredibly complex phenomena.

We may think of this in terms of structure. Structure implies connections and interactions. As indicated earlier, a structure is composed of heterogeneous items that are more than simply a list of those items. There is a sense of how the heterogeneous items work together to 'produce' something. (We see here how a capital structure is both a metaphor for and a particular case of the phenomenon of complex structures in the world.) A structure is an 'order' in Hayek's sense, in which it is possible to know something about the whole by observing the types and the ways in which they are related, without having to observe a totality of the elements. Structures are relational. Elements are defined not only by their individual characteristics but also by the manner in which they relate to other elements. These interactions are, in effect, additional variables.

Thus, though the elements of a quantifiable category may be

unstructured, these elements may be composed of structured sub-elements. This is the basis of the phenomenon of modularity. Self-contained (possibly complex) modules may be quantified. This dramatically simplifies the organization of complex phenomena, as has been noted in a fast-growing literature on the subject. Modularity is a ubiquitous phenomenon both in nature and in social organizations. It is an indispensable principle of hierarchically structured complex systems. The benefits of modularity in social settings include the facilitation of adjustment to change, and of product design, and the reaping of large economies in the use and management of knowledge (see e.g. Baldwin and Clark, 2000; Langlois, 2002, 2013) and it is clearly an aspect, perhaps the key aspect, of Lachmannian capital structures. Capital goods themselves are modules, which are creatively grouped into capital combinations which constitute the modules of the (non-quantifiable) capital structure.

Returning to the theme of the relationship between quantity and quality, quantitative modeling works when both the independent and dependent variables are meaningful, identifiable quantifiable categories that can be causally related. The model 'works' then in the sense of providing quantitative predictions. The inputs and outputs can be described in quantitative terms. But when the outcome of the process described by the model is a new (novel) category of things, no such quantitative prediction is possible. Ambiguity in the type and number of categories in any system destroys the ability to meaningfully describe that system exclusively in terms of quantities. We have a sense then of the effects of heterogeneity. Variation applies to quantitative range. Heterogeneity (variety) applies to qualitative (categorical) range. Diversity incorporates both, but they are significantly different. Heterogeneity may not be necessary for complexity, but heterogeneity does militate in its favor. For example, compound interaction between quantitative variables (categories) can be an important characteristic of complex systems, but complex systems are likely to result from substantial heterogeneity, especially where heterogeneity is open-ended, in the sense that the set of all possible categories of things is unknown and unknowable. These considerations strongly suggest that the capital structure of a market economy is a complex phenomenon (in the technical sense discussed above).

Heterogeneity rules out aggregation, which in turn rules out quantitative prediction and control, but certainly does not rule out the type of 'pattern prediction' of which Hayek spoke. In fact, as we have seen, erroneously treating heterogeneous capital as though it were a quantifiable magnitude has led to misunderstandings and policy errors, such as those associated with the connection between investment and interest rates; errors that could have been avoided with a better understanding of capital heterogeneity and its effects. The capital structure is complex, but it is intelligible. We can understand and describe in qualitative (abstract) terms how it works and render judgment on economic policies that affect it. And, as a result of Hayek's insights into complex phenomena, we have an enhanced appreciation of what is involved. Lachmann's work on capital is thus enriched by this broader perspective, in a way that perhaps he had not yet come fully to appreciate.

FURTHER OBSERVATIONS ON CAPITAL COMPLEXITY: THE IMPORTANCE OF CHANGE

Lachmann reaches for the increasing number of productive stages as an indication of the growing complexity of the capital structure. Though not spelled out, considering the importance of complementarity (a form of interaction between elements) at multiple levels (capital combinations, plans), complexity in this context seems to imply an increasingly complicated network of production linkages: a progressively expanding network of complicated, multilevel mutual dependencies between increasingly specialized elements. And the more complex the system, the more complex the disparate expectations of the agents that operate within it. Disparate expectations imply error and uncertainty. Thus, capital complexity is related to the ubiquity of (unexpectable) change. This is an important part of Lachmann's theory. It is in the connection between capital accumulation and technological progress that this is most evident.

Lachmann proposed a reinterpretation of a controversial aspect of Böhm-Bawerk's theory, his famous proposition concerning the superior productivity of roundabout production (that is, of production processes that are more indirect, that take more 'production time') (Lachmann, 1978, Ch. 5). Like his contemporary Austrian school colleagues, Lachmann regarded Böhm-Bawerk's use of time as a unit of measurement for the capital stock as untenable and seriously misleading, an indefensible attempt at quantification. He felt strongly, however, that Böhm-Bawerk's intuition about the sources of economic progress was correct: 'the intuitive genius of Böhm-Bawerk gave an answer [that], to be sure we cannot fully accept and which, moreover, is marred by an excessive degree of simplification, yet an answer we cannot afford to disregard' (1978, p. 73). Therefore he suggested dispensing with the notion of 'period of production' and replacing it with the notion of 'degree of complexity'. Whereas Böhm-Bawerk argued that the period of production increased with capital accumulation, Lachmann argued that capital accumulation results in the increasing complexity of the production process. In this way he hoped to have given a new and more appropriate meaning to the notion of increased roundaboutness.

Lachmann argued that Böhm-Bawerk's ideas were closely related to those of Adam Smith (1978, p. 79). Both were concerned about the sources of economic progress. Both lived in a world that was 'neither a stationary nor a fully dynamic world' (1978, p. 79). Our world is, however, a dynamic world, one in which technical progress is an outstanding feature. 'For Adam Smith the division of labor was the most important source of progress. The same principle can be applied to capital. As capital accumulates there takes place a "division of capital", a specialization of individual capital items, which enables us to resist the law of diminishing returns' (1978, p. 79). Böhm-Bawerk's thesis about the higher productivity of roundabout production is an empirical generalization. It can be applied, reinterpreted, to our own world. We have achieved, and will continue to achieve, greater productivity – that is, the production of more and (qualitatively) better consumption goods and services – by the continuing introduction of new indivisible production goods (which embody new production techniques); in other words, essentially qualitative changes. This can be cast in terms of Böhm-Bawerk's idea of 'stages of maturity'. Böhm-Bawerk argued that capital accumulation will take the form of an increase in the number of stages of production. 'The richer a society the smaller will be the proportion of capital resources used in the later stages of production, the stages nearest to the consumption end, and *vice versa*' (Lachmann, 1978, p. 82). The increased number of stages is indicative of increased complexity which, in turn, is indicative of increased productivity. Increased complexity implies 'an ever more complex pattern of capital complementarity' (Lachmann, 1978, p. 85).[16]

Capital accumulation (the progressive creation of capital value over time) necessarily implies an evolving capital structure, that is, a capital structure that is becoming more 'complex'. Lachmann's theory is a theory of progress reflected in and achieved by a continuing specialization of economic activities, a growing division of function. Heterogeneity matters because heterogeneous capital goods perform qualitatively different functions in combination with other human and physical resources. New goods, new methods of production, new modes of organization, new resources (capital goods) (Schumpeter, 1947, pp. 84–5) – all of these are part of the market process, all this change is part of the 'information age' (understood more broadly to encompass modern industrial and post-industrial economies).

It is not the fact of changes in technology that is revolutionary; it is the speed with which it is occurring that is new. The pace of change is not only quicker, it is accelerating. Lachmann's considerations suggest, however, that our ability to absorb and adjust to change has dramatically increased; it must have, or else we would not be able to observe these changes, occurring as they do within a well-ordered social framework, a framework that remains intact in spite of the ubiquity of change. So, during this period of his professional life, Lachmann turns his attention to the investigation of the institutional setting within which economic activity exists (1971, 1979), to be examined below.

The increasing complexity of the capital structure can now be understood in broader terms, especially if we include human capital (as we should). In some respects this is only the latest in a line of similar revolutions like the original emergence of language and the development of writing, accounting and printing. The latest, and to date most profound, in this line of developments is electronic communication, of which the telephone, the computer, the video and audio recorder, and of course the internet, are all part. Electronic communication in all of these aspects is responsible for the developments of global markets, of desktop publishing, of fuel injectors for automobiles, of computer-aided design of everything from microchips to airplanes, and so on.

Thus to understand the phenomenon of accelerating structural change occurring together with our enhanced abilities to adapt to change, we must realize that the scope and pace of technological change itself is governed by our ability to generate and process relevant information. This means that the current pace of technical change is dependent on the results of past technical advances, particularly the ability to generate and process information. This is a complex process involving multilevel interactions over time.

If technological change is seen as the result of many trial-and-error selections (of production processes, of product types, of modes of distribution, and so on) then the ability to generate and perceive more possibilities will result in a greater number of successes. It will, of course, also result in a greater number of failures. Lachmann's proposition that capital accumulation, proceeding as it does hand in hand with technological change, necessarily brings with it capital regrouping as a result of failed production plans, appears in this perspective to be particularly pertinent. '[E]conomic progress ... is a process which involves trial and error. In its course new knowledge is acquired gradually, often painfully, and always at some cost to somebody' (Lachmann, 1978, p. 18). Today, new knowledge acquisition is not so gradual.

COMPLEXITY AND INSTITUTIONS

Many of the issues that arise in capital theory generalize readily to all social situations, such as the interaction of individual expectations. The most important bridging concept is the concept of the 'plan', the basis of all human action.

Lachmann sees the market process as tending to integrate the capital structure, in other words, rendering individual production plans more consistent, although he is careful to add that the forces of equilibrium may be overwhelmed by the forces of change. At the individual level, disparate elements of the production plan are brought into consistency by the planner. These elements are all present in a single human mind. There is no such mechanism guaranteeing consistency between different production plans. The market process does, however, tend to eliminate inconsistencies between plans insofar as not all of them can succeed. In this way plans that are consistent with (complementary to) one another tend to prevail over those that are not. So whereas the individual planner ensures the complementarity of all of the resources within a production plan, the market process tends towards a situation of overall plan complementarity. But there is absolutely no guarantee that in the face of continuing changes in the 'data', that such a tendency will be the dominant one. Lachmann was clearly more skeptical than Hayek (or Mises or Kirzner) about the question of the predominance of equilibrating over disequilibrating forces. For him it was an empirical issue.

> Professor Hayek and Mises both espouse the market process, but do not ignore equilibrium as its final stage. The former, whose early work was clearly under the influence of the general equilibrium model, at one time appeared to regard a strong tendency towards general equilibrium as a rare phenomenon of the market economy. Mises, calling the Austrians 'logical' and the neoclassicals 'mathematical' economists, wrote: 'Both the logical and the mathematical economists assert that human action ultimately aims at the establishment of such a state of equilibrium and would reach it if all further changes in date were to cease' (Mises, 1949, p. 352). It is this view of the market process as at least potentially terminating in a state of long-run general equilibrium that now appears to require revision.
>
> What emerges from our reflections is an image of the market as a particular kind of process, a continuous process without beginning or end, propelled by the interaction between the forces of equilibrium and the forces of change. General equilibrium theory only knows interaction between the former. (Lachmann, 1976b, p. 239)

Lachmann thus rejects the notion of the predominance of equilibrating tendencies even in 'theory'. He did not see it as legitimate to omit from the theory the undeniably disequilibrating effects of the inevitable change in knowledge that must occur with the passage of time. But this disagreement is not about whether or not equilibrium is ever reached. There is no disagreement that it is not. What emerges as an issue for all these economists then is the question of how people can act in a world which is always subject to changes in the 'data' so that it is always *de facto* in disequilibrium. And the answer they all give in one form or another is the existence of social institutions: the existence of rules, habits, customs, mores, and so on that serve to anchor people's expectations about the actions of others in such a way as to permit them to act coherently in anticipation of predictable consequences.

The problem is particularly acute for Lachmann the 'radical subjectivist'. For him expectations are autonomous. Although they may be influenced by events, they are not wholly determined by them. All experience must be interpreted, and may be interpreted differently by different individuals. This creates unavoidable uncertainty and error. It is the world in which there is work for the entrepreneur who pits his vision of the future against those of his rivals. It is a kaleidic world. This implies what Roger Koppl has called the 'Lachmann problem' (Koppl, 1998, p. 61). Action is by definition goal-oriented, informed by knowledge of a causal mechanism that presupposes a tight connection between action and outcome. But if outcomes are radically uncertain, why are people not debilitated? How is action possible in a radically uncertain world? Stated differently, on the one hand there are the undeniable facts of novelty and disequilibrium and the inability to foresee all consequences. On the other hand, there is the undeniable fact of order in society in which people seem able to act by relying on successfully predicting the actions of others. How is one to reconcile these apparently irreconcilable perspectives?

This issue has been the subject of some recent research (e.g. McMullen, 2010, pp. 114, 131; Foss and Garzarelli, 2007; Lewis and Runde, 2007) which turns to Lachmann's work on social institutions (mainly Lachmann, 1971; see also Lachmann, 1979) for a resolution. Compared to Hayek, Lachmann's work on institutions is tiny. Hayek's work is extensive and well-known, forming the basis for comprehensive analysis and defense of decentralized market economies. Yet, the inspiration for Lachmann on this is not Hayek, his former mentor, but rather Max Weber.[17] In his analysis Lachmann does not even cite or refer to Hayek. Clearly he either was not sufficiently familiar with the later Hayek or else he was not enamored of this work but, given their history, was reluctant to engage on it – most likely the latter (see Mittermaier, 1992, p. 10).[18]

It is not even that their approaches are that different, though clearly Hayek's concerns range much wider and deeper. Both stress the role that institutions play in orienting individual action, in providing the 'rules of the game' that provide individuals with sufficient knowledge, about the possible range of actions of others, to be able to form reliable expectations. Both speculate about the origin and change of these institutions. Hayek has a full-blown theory of cultural evolution. Lachmann has a few pages on innovations in institutions and on how individual imitation of behavior may lead to the emergence of institutions (Lachmann, 1971). Both agree that institutional change must be orderly and slow if it is not to disturb the institutional framework.

CONCLUDING REMARKS

I will conclude this chapter by offering a few, perhaps presumptuous, remarks on where I think Lachmann's – and maybe Hayek's – analysis might be augmented to provide further insight into how action is possible in a kaleidic world (Lewin, 1997; [1999] 2011, Ch. 3).

The Lachmann problem revolves around the autonomy of expectations. Because they are autonomous they are likely to be disparate; hence the unavoidability of substantial numbers of errors. Of the disparate expectations of any given future only one (at most) can be correct. If, indeed, this were all there was to it, action would be impossible. It is no answer to say that institutions provide points of orientation that enable action unless we can somehow explain how institutions act to reduce the spread of expectations or render the consequences of that spread harmless. Both solutions emerge from a different way of looking at it.

We need to unpack the concept of 'expectations' and ask the question, 'Expectations of what?' Obviously individuals have expectations about many different things. Only some of these are likely to differ much across individuals. Those that form the basis of institutions, expectations about the 'rules of the game', are likely to be very uniform across individuals. We may say that these expectations are informed by knowledge of the 'social laws' concerning how others will (almost) invariably behave in given situations,[19] analogous to their knowledge of natural laws (like the law of gravity). Those expectations that are informed by these two kinds of knowledge are likely to be very congruent. By contrast those expectations relating to the outcomes of introducing a new product, a new advertising approach, a new technology, a new competitive strategy, are not informed by such 'hard' knowledge. These are likely to be all over the place. Yet, such actions will not be deterred on account of the spread of expectations. The entrepreneur acts precisely because he believes he is different and he knows better than the rest, absent which there would be no profit in it. Thus, somewhat paradoxically, predictability in one sphere is the necessary ingredient for coping with its absence (novelty) in another sphere (Loasby, 1991, 1994). To invoke once again the analogy of a sports game, the fact that the outcome (the score, and the details of the action) cannot be predicted with any degree of certainty does not prevent the game from being played. On the contrary, it is the very unpredictability that adds to its attraction. What are predictable are the consequences of any infringement of the rules of the game, the fact that the losers will probably accept the result peacefully, and so on. And it is the latter that allows the game to be played.

Finally there is the question of the origin of these institutional frameworks within which action can take place. Lachmann tries to invoke the idea of a process like a market process to explain how functional institutions win out. He was, like Hayek, looking to some kind of evolutionary selection process. He also appeals to individual imitation of successful action (Lachmann, 1971). No doubt both forces are at work. But, it seems to me he misses a key element. An individual walks across the mall full of snow and leaves a trail of footprints. Someone following him finds it helpful to walk in his footprints (pun intended). Those who follow do the same and eventually they make a path through the snow that is of benefit to all who walk it (Kirzner, 1992, Introduction). The original trailblazer is an unintentional institutional entrepreneur. The general principle is the operation of network effects: the more people use the network, the greater the benefits for each (Liebowitz and Margolis, 1994). Social institutions are complex phenomena and they are networks. A network of this kind is one in which the individuals who participate benefit from a shared (frequently tacit) understanding of how to proceed, a common standard (like a telephone technology, a language group, a religious group, a commonly accepted means of payment, a system of commercial laws, and so on). These 'external benefits' are the network effects that imply that there is feedback from individual action to other individuals, in the direction of producing uniform expectations regarding each other's behavior (choices). We can provide plausible choice-theoretic arguments showing how individuals perceive the benefits of choosing common modes of behavior. In other words, social institutions are likely to emerge spontaneously from individual action and to grow spontaneously to an optimum size. They have exactly the properties whose absence Lachmann emphasized in dynamic market processes. They produce a convergence of individual expectations. There are many examples of convergent social processes, perhaps the most familiar being the emergence of money (Menger, 1871).

Convergence and permanence are no doubt relative. Nevertheless they are necessary in some degree for the existence of, and for the understanding of, dynamic economic processes. The hectic procession of new products and productive processes – the result of the activities of a multitude of individuals organized as firms, operating within the constraints of contract and property law, some of whom succeed in their endeavors, many of whom do not – is dependent on underlying social institutions. Experience suggests that while we cannot predict who will succeed and who will not, while we cannot predict which products will emerge and be popular, while we cannot foresee the nature of future technologies, we strongly believe that the process will be peaceful and will be orderly; we confidently expect those who are unsuccessful to accept their losses peacefully and perhaps try something else, those who lose their jobs to move on in the hope of greener pastures, and those who do succeed to continue to try to do so. The fruits of this dynamic process depend crucially on our (predictable) willingness to accept the consequences of its unpredictability. That willingness is the vital predictable part. Indeed, as with other complex adaptive orders, we have the emergence of 'order' and we are able to explain the process in a readily accessible and intuitive way as deriving from human action.

ACKNOWLEDGEMENTS

Thanks to Roger Garrison, Roger Koppl, Paul Lewis and Richard Ebeling for very helpful comments and editorial assistance, with the usual disclaimer.

NOTES

1. Hayek's contributions to philosophy, politics and methodology were yet to come, and though Mittermaier claims correctly that Lachmann was never a Hayekian in this later and broader sense, I shall have some things to say about the relationships between Lachmann and the later Hayek.
2. About the articles collected in the 1939 volume, Hayek says: they 'are a selection from the various attempts made in the course of the last ten years to improve and develop the outline of a theory of fluctuations contained in two small books on *Monetary Theory and the Trade Cycle* and *Prices and Production*' (Hayek, 1939a, vii).
3. Written originally in German in the late 1920s.
4. 'Austrian economics reflects a subjectivist view of the world. The subjective nature of human preferences is its root. But in a world of change the subjectivism of expectations is perhaps even more important than the subjectivism of preferences. The assumption of "static expectations", however, means not merely that expectations as autonomous forces causing economic change are ignored so that a mechanism of other forces may be exhibited in its "pure form" but also that the diversity of expectations, the pattern of inconsistent expectations held by different individuals at the same time, which we find in the real world, cannot even come into sight' (Lachmann, 1976a, 22).

5. The work at both LSE and Cambridge was influenced by the writings of the 'Stockholm School' of economics, starting with Wicksell and including Lindahl and especially Myrdal on the effects of expectations.
6. During this time he was still in England (holding a variety of short-term positions), though he spent five months in the United States where he met Alfred Shutz and Frank Knight, both of whom had a lasting impression on him (Mittermaier, 1992, pp.11f).
7. In an important sense, Lachmann's capital theory is also Mengerian (see Lewin, [1999] 2011, Ch. 8).
8. Lachmann uses the example of a delivery company (Lachmann, 1947, p.199; 1978, p.56). The company possesses a number of delivery vans. Each one is a complement to the others in that they cooperate to fulfill an overall production plan. That plan encompasses the routine completion of a number of different delivery routes. As long as the plan is being fulfilled, this relationship prevails, but if one of the vans should break down, one or more of the others may be diverted in order to compensate for the unexpected loss of the use of one of the productive resources. To that extent and in that situation they are substitutes.
9. '[E]ven if aggregate demand for labor at the existing wage level ... continues to increase, it will be an increase in the demand for kinds of labor of which no more is available, while at the same time the demand for other kinds of labor will fall and total employment will consequently decrease' (Hayek, 1939b, p.26).
10. I am referring here to the (internal) rate of return because this affords easy comparison with the rate of interest and is equivalent to Keynes's marginal efficiency of capital (investment). Strictly speaking one should judge the efficacy and attractiveness of a project (in financial terms) using the net present value criterion.
11. As current experience with the dot-com boom–bust shows, both of these causes may exist. The arrival of a new technology, which leads to an unexpected increase in the demand for capital, may be underwritten by a very expansive monetary policy; and this would plausibly have the effects described by Hayek in this paragraph (see also Garrison, 2011, p.447; also Chapter 7 in this volume).
12. Anticipating his future preoccupations he also explores the role of changing and inconsistent expectations and points out that this implies the enduring existence of disequilibrium. We find here also perhaps his earliest articulation of the nature and importance of the 'plan' in analyzing investment behavior. Perhaps the most important general implication of a disequilibrium approach to capital is the proposition that all capital accumulation entails technological change. Most technical change is embodied in new (improved) capital goods and/or involves the production of new consumption goods. It is very likely that government expenditure 'crowds out' not only private sector investment but also private sector investment-induced technical progress. The shape of the capital structure will be different and, because capital assets are heterogeneous, specific and durable, will remain different from what it would otherwise have been.
13. For example, both he and Hayek developed similar but different variations of the Austrian business cycle theory to apply to the world of their time. Both emphasized the role of labor unions. Lachmann considered the power of unions to be such as to have created a situation in which prices could no longer fall and in which unions were seen to be the main culprits for the occurrence of inflation. Referencing John Hicks, he suggested that the world had abandoned the gold standard for a 'labor-standard' (Lachmann, 1967; see also Hayek, 1959 and Baird, Chapter 14 of this volume).
14. '[S]ocial sciences, like much of biology, but unlike most fields of the physical sciences, have to deal with structures of *essential* complexity, i.e. with structures whose characteristic properties can be exhibited only by models made up of relatively large numbers of variables' (Hayek, 1974, p.26). It is illuminating to view this problem in the context of statistical modeling and the well-known difficulty of inferring from the estimated reduced-form parameters the fundamental structural parameters of the model. The model is supposedly an 'accurate' depiction of reality. This is the 'Lucas critique' leveled at econometric practice. The response has been to try to find better (more easily

identifiable) models. But, in the context of the discussion in the text, it may be seriously doubted that such a strategy is ever likely to be viable. The structural parameters of real-world complex processes are the result of multilevel interaction an order of magnitude far beyond the capacity of any statistical modeler to specify. For a 'critical realist' analysis of the 'Lucas critique' see Lawson (1995), which contains many (independently perceived) 'Hayekian-type' insights, but without reference to Hayek.

15. Hayek (1964, p.25n, references removed) quotes von Neumann (1951): 'we are dealing here with parts of logic with which we have practically no experience. The order of complexity is out of all proportion to anything we have ever known'. Hayek continues: 'It may be useful to give here a few illustrations of the orders of magnitude with which biology and neurology have to deal. While the total number of electrons in the Universe has been estimated at 10^{79} and the number of electrons and protons at 10^{100}, there are chromosomes with 1,000 locations [genes] with 10 allelomorphs 10^{1000} possible combinations; and the number of possible proteins is estimated at 10^{2700}. C. Judson Herrick suggests that during a few minutes of intense cortical activity the number of interneuronic connections actually made (counting also those that are actuated more than once in different associational patterns) may well be as great as the total number of atoms in the solar system (i.e. 10^{56}); and Ralph W. Gerard has estimated that in the course of seventy years a man may accumulate 15×10^{12} units of information ("bits"), which is more than 1,000 times larger than the number of nerve cells. The further complications which social relations superimpose upon this are, of course, relatively insignificant. But the point is that if we wanted to "reduce" social phenomena to physical events, they would constitute an additional complication, superimposed upon that of the physiological processes determining mental events.' See also Fiori (2009).

16. Mises points this out in a particularly graphic way. An increase in the number of stages of production – that is, an increase in specialization – necessarily implies an increase in complexity in that those stages closer to the final product are more complex than those stages further from it. Complexity is related to specificity: the construction of artifacts for specialized purposes implies more internal structure, and more linkages between the stages. 'Iron is less specific in character than iron tubes, and iron tubes less so than iron machine parts. The conversion of a process of production [to another purpose, in response to unexpected change] becomes as a rule more difficult, the farther it has been pursued and the nearer it has come to its termination, the turning out of consumers' goods' (Mises, 1949, p.500).

17. Though, as Roger Koppl suggests, Weber was no doubt an inspiration for Hayek (as for Mises) as well.

18. This is a genuine puzzle, since Lachmann showed no reluctance to part company on the issue of equilibration.

19. They will drive on the right-hand side, they will mark time in the same way, they will not resort to violence if their business fails, and so on.

REFERENCES

Baldwin, Carliss Y. and Kim B. Clark (2000), *Design Rules*, Cambridge, MA: MIT Press.
Böhm-Bawerk, Eugen von (1959), *Capital and Interest*, South Holland, IL: Libertarian Press.
Caldwell, Bruce J. (2004), *Hayek's Challenge*, Chicago, IL: University of Chicago Press.
Fiori, Stefano (2009), 'Hayek's theory on complexity and knowledge: dichotomies, levels of analysis, and bounded rationality', *Journal of Economic Methodology*, 16 (3), 265–85.
Foss, Nicolai J. and Gaimpaolo Garazarelli (2007), 'Institutions as knowledge capital: Ludwig M. Lachmann's interpretive institutionalism', *Cambridge Journal of Economics*, 31, 789–804.
Garrison, Roger W. (2011), 'Alchemy leveraged: the Federal Reserve and modern finance', *Independent Review*, 16 (3), 435–51.

Grinder, Walter E. (ed.) (1977a), *Capital, Expectations and the Market Process, Essays on the Theory of the Market Economy*, Kansas City, KS: Sheed, Andrews & McMeel.

Grinder, Walter E. (1977b), 'In pursuit of the subjective paradigm', in Grinder (ed.) (1977a), pp. 3–24.

Harper, David A. and Anthony M. Endres (2010), 'Capital as a layer cake: a systems approach to capital and its multi-level structure', *Journal of Economic Behavior and Organization*, 74, 30–41.

Harper, David A. and Anthony M. Endres (2012), 'The anatomy of emergence, with a focus upon capital formation', *Journal of Economic Behavior and Organization*, 82 (2–3), 352–67.

Hayek, Friedrich A. (1933a), *Monetary Theory and the Trade Cycle*, London: Jonathan Cape.

Hayek, Friedrich A. (1933b), 'Price expectations, monetary disturbances and malinvestment', lecture delivered in Copenhagen, December; reprinted in Hayek (1939a), pp. 135–56.

Hayek, Friedrich A. (1935a), *Prices and Production*, London: Routledge & Kegan Paul.

Hayek, Friedrich A. (1935b), 'The maintenance of capital', *Economica*, n.s. 2 (Aug.); reprinted in Hayek (1939a), pp. 83–134.

Hayek, Friedrich A. (1937a), 'Economics and knowledge', *Economica*, n.s. 4 (Feb.); reprinted in Hayek (1948), pp. 33–6.

Hayek, Friedrich A. (1937b), 'Investment that raises the demand for capital', *Review of Economic Statistics*, 19 (4), 174–7; reprinted in Hayek (1939a), pp. 73–82.

Hayek, Friedrich A. (1939a), *Profits, Interest and Investment*, London: Routledge.

Hayek, Friedrich A. (1939b), 'Profits, interest and investment', in Hayek (1939a), pp. 3–72.

Hayek, Friedrich A. (1941), *The Pure Theory of Capital*, Chicago, IL: University of Chicago Press.

Hayek, Friedrich A. (1945), 'The use of knowledge in society', *American Economic Review*, 35 (4), 519–30; reprinted in Hayek (1948), pp. 77–91.

Hayek, Friedrich A. (1948), *Individualism and Economic Order*, Chicago, IL: University of Chicago Press.

Hayek, Friedrich A. (1952), *The Sensory Order: An Inquiry into the Foundations of Theoretical Psychology*, London and Henley: Routledge & Kegan Paul.

Hayek, Friedrich A. (1955), 'Degrees of Explanation', *British Journal for the Philosophy of Science*, 6 (23), 209–25; reprinted (with small additions) in Hayek (1967), pp. 3–21.

Hayek, Friedrich A. (1959), 'Unions, inflations and profits', in Philip D. Bradley (ed.), *The Public Stake in Union Power*, Charlottesville, VA: University of Virginia Press; reprinted in Hayek (1967), pp. 280–94.

Hayek, Friedrich A. (1964), 'The Theory of Complex Phenomena', in Mario A. Bunge (ed.), *The Critical Approach to Science and Philosophy: Essays in Honor of K.R. Popper*, New York: Free Press; reprinted in Hayek (1967), pp. 22–42.

Hayek, Friedrich A. (1967), *Studies in Philosophy, Politics and Economics*, London: Routledge & Kegan Paul.

Hayek, Friedrich A. (1974), 'The Pretense of Knowledge', *Les Prix Nobel en 1974*; reprinted in Hayek (1978), pp. 23–34.

Hayek, Friedrich A. (1978), *New Studies in Philosophy, Politics, Economics and the History of Ideas*, London and Henley: Routledge & Kegan Paul.

Horwitz, Steven G. (2008), 'Analogous models of complexity: the Austrian theory of capital and Hayek's theory of cognition as adaptive classifying systems', *Advances in Austrian Economics*, 11, 143–66.

Keynes, John Maynard (1930), *A Treatise on Money*, 2 vols, London: Macmillan.

Keynes, John Maynard (1936), *The General Theory of Employment, Interest and Money*, London: Macmillan.

Kirzner, Israel M. (1992), *The Meaning of Market Process: Essays in the Development of Modern Austrian Economics*, London, UK and New York, USA: Routledge.

Koppl, Roger G. (1998), 'Lachmann on the subjectivism of active minds', in Roger G. Koppl and Gary Mongiovi (eds), *Subjectivism and Economic Analysis: Essays in Memory of Ludwig Lachmann*, New York: Routledge, pp. 61–79.

Koppl, Roger G. (2010), 'Some epistemological implications of economic complexity', *Journal of Economic Behavior and Organization*, 76, 859–72.
Kresge, Steven and Leif Wenar (eds) (1994), *Hayek on Hayek: An Autobiographical Dialogue*, Chicago, IL: University of Chicago Press.
Lachmann, Ludwig M. (1937), 'Uncertainty and liquidity preference', *Economica*, n.s. 4 (15), 295–308; reprinted in Don Lavoie (ed.) (1994), pp. 29–41.
Lachmann, Ludwig M. (1938), 'Investment and costs of production', *American Economic Review*, 28 (3), 469B81; reprinted in Don Lavoie (ed.) (1994), pp. 42–56.
Lachmann, Ludwig M. (1939), 'On crisis and adjustment', *Review of Economics and Statistics*, 21, 2–68; reprinted in Don Lavoie (ed.) (1994), pp. 76–90.
Lachmann, Ludwig M. (1941), 'On the measurement of capital', *Economica*, n.s. 8 (32), 367–77; reprinted in Don Lavoie (ed.) (1994), pp. 91–106.
Lachmann, Ludwig M. (1943), 'The role of expectations in economics as a social science', *Economica*, n.s., 10 (37), 12–23; reprinted in Walter E. Grinder (ed.) (1977a), pp. 65–80.
Lachmann, Ludwig M. (1944), 'Finance capitalism', *Economica*, n.s. 11 (42), 64–73; reprinted in Don Lavoie (ed.) (1994), pp. 107–23.
Lachmann, Ludwig M. (1945), 'A note on the elasticity of expectations', *Economica*, n.s. 12 (48), 248–53; reprinted in Don Lavoie (ed.) (1994), pp. 124–30.
Lachmann, Ludwig M. (1947), 'Complementarity and substitution in the theory of capital', *Economica*, n.s. 14 (54), 108–19.
Lachmann, Ludwig M. (1948), 'Investment repercussions', *Quarterly Journal of Economics*, 62 (5), 698–713; reprinted in Don Lavoie (ed.) (1994), pp. 131–46.
Lachmann, Ludwig M. (1967), 'Causes and consequences of the inflation of our time', *South African Journal of Economics*, 35, 281–91; reprinted in Walter E. Grinder (ed.) (1977a), pp. 289–307.
Lachmann, Ludwig M. (1971), *The Legacy of Max Weber*, Berkeley, CA: Glendessary Press.
Lachmann, Ludwig M. (1975), 'Reflections on Hayekian capital theory', presentation at the Allied Social Science Associate Meeting in Dallas, TX; reprinted in Lavoie (ed.) (1994), pp. 198–212.
Lachmann, Ludwig M. (1976a), 'Austrian economics in the present crisis of economic thought', in Walter E. Grinder (ed.) (1977a), pp. 25–44.
Lachmann, Ludwig M. (1976b), 'From Mises to Shackle: an essay on Austrian economics and the kaleidic society', *Journal of Economic Literature*, 14 (1), 54–62; reprinted in Lavoie (ed.) (1994), pp. 229–40.
Lachmann, Ludwig M. (1978 [1956]), *Capital and its Structure*, Kansas City, KS: Sheed, Andrews & McMeel.
Lachmann, Ludwig M. (1979), 'The flow of legislation and the permanence of the legal order', *ORDO*, 30 (1), 69–70.
Langlois, Richard N. (2002), 'Modularity in technology and organization', in Nicolai J. Foss and Peter G. Klein (eds), *Entrepreneurship and the Firm: Austrian Perspectives on Economic Organization*, Cheltenham, UK and Northampton, MA, US: Edward Elgar, pp. 24–47.
Langlois, Richard N. (2013), 'The Austrian theory of the firm: retrospect and prospect', *Review of Austrian Economics*, 26 (3), 247–58.
Lavoie, Don (ed.) (1994), *Expectations and the Meaning of Institutions: Essays in Economics by Ludwig Lachmann*, New York: New York University Press.
Lawson, Tony (1995), 'The Lucas critique: a generalization', *Cambridge Journal of Economics*, 19 (2), 257–76.
Lewin, Peter (1997), 'Hayekian equilibrium and change', *Journal of Economic Methodology*, 4 (2), 245–66.
Lewin, Peter ([1999] 2011), *Capital in Disequilibrium*, Auburn, AL: Ludwig von Mises Institute.
Lewis, Paul (2012), 'Emergent properties in the work of Friedrich Hayek', *Journal of Economic Behavior and Organization*, 82 (2–3), 368–78.
Lewis, Paul and Jochen Runde (2007), 'Subjectivism, social structure and the possibility of

socio-economic order: the case of Ludwig Lachmann', *Journal of Economic Behaviour and Organization*, 62 (2), 167–86.
Liebowitz, Stanley J. and Stephen E. Margolis (1994), 'Network externality: an uncommon tragedy', *Journal of Economic Perspectives*, 8 (2), 133–50.
Loasby, Brian (1991), *Equilibrium and Evolution: An Exploration of Connecting Principles in Economics*, Manchester: Manchester University Press.
Loasby, Brian (1994), 'Evolution within equilibrium', *Advances in Austrian Economics*, 1, 69–11.
McMullen, Jeffery S. (2010), 'Perspective taking and the heterogeneity of the entrepreneurial imagination', *Advances in Austrian Economics*, 13, 113–44.
McQuade, Thomas J. and William N. Butos (2009), 'The adaptive systems theory of social orders', *Studies in Emergent Order*, 2, 76–108.
Menger, Carl (1871), *Principles of Economics*, transl. James Dingwall and Bert F. Hoselitz (1976), New York: New York University Press.
Mises, Ludwig von (1949), *Human Action*, Chicago, IL: Henry Regnery; 1998 edn, Auburn, AL: Ludwig von Mises Institute.
Mitchell, Melanie (2009), *Complexity*, Oxford: Oxford University Press.
Mittermaier, K.H.M. (1992), 'Ludwig Lachmann (1906–1990). A biographical sketch', *South African Journal of Economics*, 60 (1), 7–25.
Neumann, John von (1951), 'The general and logical theory of automata', *Cerebral Mechanism in Behavior*, Hixon Symposium, New York.
Page, Scott E. (2011), *Diversity and Complexity*, Princeton, NJ: Princeton University Press.
Schumpeter, Joseph A. (1947), *Capitalism, Socialism and Democracy*, New York: Harper.

9. Hayek: from economics as equilibrium analysis to economics as social theory
Paul Lewis

INTRODUCTION

Friedrich Hayek, a scholar of enormous range and scope, made major contributions both to pure economic theory and also to a wide variety of fields in social theory and philosophy. Historians of thought usually attempt to impose some order on Hayek's work by distinguishing between the early (pre-1937) Hayek, whose attention was largely confined to matters of pure economic theory, and the later (post-1937) Hayek, whose interests extended well beyond the conventional boundaries of economics to embrace fields as diverse as political philosophy, jurisprudence, theoretical psychology, the philosophy of science and the history of ideas.

The impetus for Hayek's transformation from narrow economic theorist to wide-ranging social theorist and philosopher, a transformation whose origins are usually traced to Hayek's 1937 paper on 'Economics and knowledge' (Hayek, [1937] 1948), derived from his increasing dissatisfaction with the principal methodological tool to which he had been committed in his pre-1937 writings on price theory, capital theory and business cycles, namely equilibrium analysis. By 1937 Hayek's participation in the socialist calculation debate had led him to realize that the epistemological presuppositions of equilibrium theory – that is, the assumptions it makes about people's knowledge – preclude a satisfactory answer to what Hayek had come to see as the central question of economics: namely how (if at all) people learn enough about each other's actions to be able to form mutually compatible plans.

Although Hayek's concerns in this regard ultimately led him to abandon the very methodological tool he had previously regarded as indispensable for economic theory, namely equilibrium analysis, he did not completely forsake studying the problem of plan coordination. On the contrary, he remained concerned with it throughout his post-1937 career. What did change, however, was the methodology which Hayek employed in addressing the problem, with his pre-1937 commitment to equilibrium analysis gradually giving way to a broader, social-theoretic approach which placed considerable emphasis on the causal and explanatory significance of the social-structural context in which people conduct their economic affairs, and whose central organizing concept was not that of general equilibrium but rather that of socio-economic order (Fleetwood, 1995; Vaughn, 1999).

Underpinning Hayek's shift from economics as equilibrium analysis to economics as social theory was an increasing preoccupation on his part with issues of socio-economic ontology, that is, with issues concerning the nature of (the constituents of) the socio-economic world. Hayek's dissatisfaction with equilibrium analysis, although initially expressed in epistemic terms, led him to elaborate in considerable detail on various issues of socio-economic ontology. In time, Hayek arrived at an ontology which portrayed people both as having distinctly limited cognitive powers – so that there are insurmountable limits to their ability to know, to predict and therefore to control the socio-economic world – but also as being situated within a nexus of social structures (rules and institutions) which, by limiting the range of people's actions and therefore making them more predictable, facilitates purposeful human conduct. In this way, the insight first articulated in Hayek's 1937 paper, namely that the key to explaining the working of decentralized market economies lies in developing an account of the causal processes through which people acquire knowledge of one another's (current and future) actions, also informed his later writings on political philosophy and social theory, where he examined how the social rules and institutions of a liberal polity provide the information required for private citizens to coordinate their plans and so achieve their individual goals in peace and harmony. And it was in his later social-theoretic work on the role of social institutions and rules in shaping people's expectations and guiding their actions that Hayek was finally able to provide a convincing answer to the question, first posed in his narrow technical work on economics, of how socio-economic order is possible in decentralized market economies.

HAYEK'S TRANSFORMATION: 'ECONOMICS AND KNOWLEDGE'

While in his early work Hayek was never completely sanguine about the use of equilibrium constructs, being careful to distinguish those problems for which intertemporal rather than static notions of equilibrium were appropriate, and while he was always careful to emphasize the importance of disequilibrium adjustment processes, he consistently maintained that a genuinely economic explanation of some phenomenon must be couched in the language of equilibrium analysis. In his 1928 paper on monetary economics, for instance, Hayek writes that the static equilibrium construct is a 'methodologically valuable fiction [whose] field of application is identical with that of economic theory' ([1928] 1984, pp. 72, 75). Similarly, in *Monetary Theory and the Trade Cycle,* Hayek contends that any economic explanation of the cycle must build on the foundations provided by the theory of equilibrium ([1933] 1966, pp. 28–30). Prior to 1937, then, Hayek virtually defined economics as equilibrium analysis, maintaining that any legitimate economic explanation must employ some notion of equilibrium (Caldwell, 2004, pp. 155–62).

However, a number of factors, most notably his participation in the socialist calculation debate of the 1930s, prompted Hayek to question both the merits of the equilibrium concept and also his views on the relationship of Austrian to neoclassical economics. Prior to the calculation debate, the majority of Austrians thought of themselves as part of the neoclassical or marginalist tradition, along with Marshallian and Walrasian economists, not as representatives of, and advocates for, a distinctive Austrian school of thought.[1] However, the use of general equilibrium theory to justify market socialism led Hayek to revise his understanding of his own approach to economics and to begin to distance himself, and the Austrian approach more generally, from the emerging neoclassical orthodoxy. For in responding to the arguments of the market socialists – arguments that were couched in terms of the neoclassical framework by which he himself had set such store in the past – Hayek came to realize that his developing understanding of the market as a dynamic process of adjustment was one to which equilibrium analysis singularly failed to do justice. More specifically, as Hayek argued in a paper that is widely held to be a landmark in his transformation from a neoclassical economist preoccupied with equilibrium analysis to a wide-ranging social theorist articulating a distinctively Austrian view of economic issues, namely, 'Economics and knowledge' ([1937] 1948), the problem with equilibrium analysis is that by confining itself to situations in which people's plans are already coordinated, it ignores the most important question that must be answered both in explaining how market economies work, and also in evaluating the feasibility of central planning: namely that of how (if at all) people acquire the information they need to coordinate their plans and thereby achieve an orderly allocation of resources.[2] And it was because general equilibrium analysis fails to address this key issue, upon which (as we shall see) Hayek believes the superiority of free markets over socialism to depend, that it could be used to justify social planning (Kirzner, 1988; Caldwell, 2004, pp. 209–20).[3]

Hayek's aim in 'Economics and knowledge' was to question the epistemological presuppositions of economic theory, that is, to subject to critical scrutiny 'the role which assumptions and propositions about the knowledge possessed by the different members of society play in economic analysis'. In doing so Hayek hoped to illuminate the extent to which formal equilibrium analysis conveys knowledge about the real world ([1937] 1948, p. 33). Hayek identifies two epistemological issues which economic theory must take into account if it is to yield an adequate analysis of the working of modern industrial economies. First, people's actions are informed not by a direct (theoretically unmediated) knowledge of their objective circumstances but rather by their subjective perceptions of those circumstances. Economic analysis must therefore begin not with the 'objective facts' of people's circumstances (as they are known, say, to an observing economist), but rather with people's perceptions of and beliefs about their situation, for it is such 'subjective data' which are the key influence on how people choose to act: 'It is important to remember that the so-called data from which we set out in this sort of analysis are all facts given to the person in question, the things as they are known to (or believed by) him to exist, and not, strictly speaking, objective facts' (Hayek, [1937] 1948, p. 36).[4]

Furthermore, knowledge of the 'objective data' which, however indirectly and shakily, inform people's subjective beliefs is dispersed among the members of society in such a way that any one person is aware of no more than a few of the relevant facts. '[T]here is here', Hayek ([1937] 1948, p. 50) contends, 'a *division of knowledge* which is quite analogous to, and at least as important as, the problem of the division of labor'. Hayek elaborates on this point in his 1945 essay on 'The use of knowledge in society', arguing that the division of knowledge reflects the importance of what he terms 'the knowledge of the particular circumstances of time and place ... knowledge of people, of local conditions and of special circumstances':

> To know of and put to use a machine not fully employed, or somebody's skill which could be better utilised, or to be aware of a surplus stock which can be drawn upon during an interruption of supplies, is socially quite as useful as the knowledge of better alternative techniques. The shipper who earns his living from using otherwise empty or half-filled journeys of tramp-steamers, or the estate agent whose whole knowledge is almost exclusively one of temporary opportunities, or the *arbitrageur* who gains from local differences of commodity prices – are all performing eminently useful functions based on special knowledge of circumstances of the fleeting moment not known to others. (Hayek, [1945a] 1948, p. 80)

The existence of such dispersed and fragmented knowledge implies that no one person can possess any more than a tiny fraction of the total knowledge available in society. This 'constitutional limitation' on man's knowledge is the second epistemological issue emphasized by Hayek in his assessment of the presuppositions of equilibrium analysis (Hayek, [1945b] 1948, p. 14).

Hayek reformulates the notion of equilibrium, as it applies both to the behavior of isolated individuals and also to the interdependent actions of a group, and evaluates its usefulness for understanding real-world economic phenomena, in the light of the aforementioned epistemological issues. Hayek is sanguine about the applicability of the notion of equilibrium to the conduct of individual people, considered in isolation. An individual's (proposed) actions are in equilibrium, Hayek avers, if in the light of that individual's beliefs about his circumstances they form part of a single plan (that is, if they constitute a consistent and integrated set of intended actions through time). While it may subsequently transpire that the beliefs upon which the individual's plan was based were mistaken, leading to the disruption of the equilibrium between his actions and thereby to a revised plan and a new equilibrium, it remains the case that his actions were in equilibrium when his initial plan was first formulated, given his beliefs at that time. For Hayek, then, given that an individual's plan is based not on the objective facts of his situation per se, but rather on the individual's subjective perceptions of his objective circumstances, it follows from the 'pure logic of choice' that at any given moment in time a rational individual will always be in equilibrium (Hayek, [1937] 1948, pp. 35–7).

Having outlined what the notion of equilibrium entails when applied to a single person, Hayek turns to the task of reworking the concept so that it can be used to analyse the interaction of a number of different people. 'Equilibrium exists in this connection', Hayek ([1937] 1948, p. 37) maintains, 'if the actions of all members of the society over a period are all [successful] executions of their respective individual plans on which each decided at the beginning of the period'. The requirements for a general equilibrium of this type extend well beyond those necessary for the equilibrium of an isolated individual, a fact that had hitherto gone unappreciated by the vast majority of economists:

> I have long felt that the concept of equilibrium itself and the methods which we employ in pure analysis have a clear meaning only when confined to the analysis of a single person and that we are really passing into a different sphere and silently introducing a new element of altogether different character when we apply it to the explanation of the interactions of a number of different individuals. (Hayek, [1937] 1948, p. 35)

More specifically, in addition to the need for each individual to have a coherent plan of action informed by their own subjective understanding of their circumstances, as demanded by the notion of individual equilibrium, a general equilibrium calls for two additional conditions to be met

(Hayek, [1937] 1948, pp. 37–9). In the first place, people will be able to bring their plans to fruition only if those plans are based on the expectation of the same set of objective facts. For if people formulated their plans on the basis of conflicting expectations about their external environment, it would be impossible for any set of objective facts to make the execution of all of those plans feasible. The existence of a general equilibrium demands, therefore, that people hold common expectations concerning external events. This requirement is rendered more exacting by the fact that, in a society based on exchange, the external events which influence the outcome of one person's action, and which that person must therefore take into account in deciding what to do, include not only natural events but also the conduct of other people, so that one person's intended actions become part of the set of objective facts that others must take into account in devising their own plans. The second requirement for the existence of a general equilibrium is, therefore, that people's plans are compatible in the sense that one individual's proposed actions do not disrupt the plans of the others. This in turn demands that people are able to form accurate expectations of the actions of their fellow men: 'since some of the data on which any one person will base his plans will be the expectation that other people will act in a particular way, it is essential for the compatibility of the different plans that the plans of one contain exactly those actions which form the data for the plans of the other' (Hayek, [1937] 1948, p. 38).

Hayek summarizes the results of his investigations into the epistemological presuppositions of general equilibrium theory by noting that the existence of a general economic equilibrium entails that 'the foresight of the different members of the society is in a special sense correct':

> It must be correct in the sense that every person's plan is based on the expectation of just those actions of other people which those people intend to perform and that all these plans are based on the expectation of the same set of external facts, so that under certain conditions nobody will have any reason to change his plans. Correct foresight is then not, as it has sometimes been understood, a precondition which must exist in order that equilibrium may be arrived at. It is rather the defining characteristic of a state of equilibrium. (Hayek, [1937] 1948, p. 42)

Will people in the real world acquire the knowledge required for them to be able to form such expectations? The fact that decentralized market economies typically do generate an orderly allocation of resources, in which people are for the most part able successfully to execute their plans, suggests that this question – the question of the existence of a 'tendency toward equilibrium', as Hayek ([1937] 1948, p. 44) terms it – ought to be answered in the affirmative ([1937] 1948, pp. 51, 55).[5]

However, while the empirical evidence suggests that the inhabitants of decentralized market economies have tended to be remarkably successful in formulating mutually compatible plans even in the face of the existence of subjectively held, dispersed knowledge, economic theory is rather less successful in explaining how such plan coordination is actually brought about in practice. Standard economic analysis simply assumes that the same objectively correct data – the same knowledge of people's tastes, of what constitutes an economic good, and of the lowest-cost technologies for producing those goods – is given to all people, thereby ignoring the subjectivity and dispersal of knowledge which are the defining characteristics of the epistemic problem which must be solved if plan coordination is to be achieved. Hence, while 'the question why the data in the subjective sense of the term should ever come to correspond to the objective data is one of the main problems we have to answer', Hayek is forced to conclude that 'pure equilibrium analysis is not concerned with the way in which this correspondence is brought about. In the description of an existing state of equilibrium which it provides, it is simply assumed that the subjective data coincide with the objective facts' ([1937] 1948, pp. 39, 44). And because of this, general equilibrium analysis fails to solve 'the really central problem of economics as a social science', namely the problem of how socio-economic order is generated in decentralized market economies:

> The problem which we pretend to solve is how the spontaneous interaction of a number of people, each possessing only bits of knowledge, brings about a state of affairs in which prices correspond to costs, etc., and which could be brought about by deliberate direction only by somebody who possessed the combined knowledge of all those individuals. Experience shows us that something of this sort does happen, since the empirical observation that prices do tend to correspond to costs was the beginning of our science. But in our analysis, instead of showing what bits of information the different persons must possess in order to bring about that result, we fall in effect back on the assumption that everybody knows everything and so evade any real solution of the problem. (Hayek [1937] 1948, pp. 50–51)[6]

What Hayek is arguing in his 1937 paper, then, is that the epistemological presuppositions of general equilibrium theory are so radically at variance with the epistemic problem that is actually solved in decentralized market economies that equilibrium analysis cannot provide a satisfactory account of how people in practice solve the economic problem that confronts them.

The upshot of all this, according to Hayek, is that general equilibrium analysis will necessarily be confined to the realm of pure logic, inapplicable to the real world, unless and until a satisfactory account is provided of the causal processes through which people acquire the knowledge required to form mutually compatible plans:

> [T]he tautologies, of which formal equilibrium analysis in economics essentially consists, can be turned into propositions which tell us anything about causation in the real world only in so far as we are able to fill those formal propositions with definite statements about how knowledge is acquired and communicated. The significant point here is that it is these apparently subsidiary hypotheses or assumptions that people do learn from experience, and about how they acquire knowledge, which constitute the empirical content of our propositions about what happens in the real world. (Hayek, [1937] 1948, pp. 33, 46)

Far from being 'given' to people, as equilibrium analysis supposes, knowledge of the objective facts of relevance to economic affairs – knowledge of the lowest-cost technologies, and of the associated costs; knowledge of consumers' preferences, including the type of goods they desire and the prices they are willing to pay for them; and knowledge of who is a reliable supplier of such goods – is discovered only through the process of market competition. As Hayek puts it in his essay on 'Competition as a discovery procedure':

> economic theory sometimes appears at the outset to bar its way to a true appreciation of the character of the process of competition, because it starts from the assumption of a 'given' supply of scarce goods. But which goods are scarce, or which things are goods, and how scarce or valuable they are – these are precisely the things which competition has to discover. (Hayek, [1968] 1978, p. 181)[7]

What is needed, therefore, is an (empirical) account of the causal processes through which knowledge is discovered and transmitted in actual market economies.

HAYEK'S ONTOLOGICAL TURN, PART 1: PEOPLE AS CONSTITUTIONALLY IGNORANT BEINGS

Before examining Hayek's efforts to fill this lacuna in economic theory, it is important to note that a rationale for Hayek's epistemology can be found in his account of human nature and, in particular, in his conception of the human mind, as expounded in his 1952 book, *The Sensory Order*. Although Hayek did not explicitly connect the theory of mind advanced in that book to his economics, the two are (as we shall see) eminently compatible, so that (with the benefit of hindsight) *The Sensory Order* can be thought of as providing an (ontological) account of the psychological underpinnings of Hayek's (epistemological) claim that knowledge is inevitably dispersed and belief subjectively held. While *The Sensory Order* was published only in 1952, it was conceived, and a first draft was written, in 1920, during Hayek's time as an undergraduate in Vienna. However, with Hayek's interest in psychological issues having been rekindled by his participation in the socialist calculation debate – and, more specifically, by his efforts to understand, to explain and ultimately to undermine (what he saw as) the scientific view of human reason which underpinned the arguments advanced by advocates of government intervention and by their (behaviorist) supporters in the social sciences – he decided to return to his undergraduate manuscript, to update it and to develop it into a book-length treatment of human physiological psychology.[8] Thus, while Gray (1998, p. 134) is correct in claiming that Hayek's 1937 paper on 'Economics and knowledge' marks an epistemological turn in his work, it was closely followed by an ontological turn as Hayek revisited his earlier work on the nature of the human mind in order to provide what can, in retrospect, be viewed as an ontological grounding for his account of the character of knowledge in modern, decentralized market economies (Caldwell, 2004, p. 256–79).[9]

In the first place, Hayek denies that man possesses the capacity to know things as they are in themselves. He contends that there is no Archimedean viewpoint from which people can view the entirety of the world as it is in itself, untainted by theoretical presuppositions. Even our most basic sensory impressions are the product of a process of classification whereby we attend to only a few of the infinite aspects of the physical world in order to parse it into different categories of object. Indeed, according to Hayek, the mind 'just is' a classificatory system, a complex neural process whereby stimuli from the physical world are transformed into the phenomenal world of our perceptions. On this view, perception is always interpretation, so that the phenomenal, or sensory, order which characterizes our experiences is the product of the creative activity of our minds rather than something given to us by the world itself (Hayek, 1952, pp. 42, 48–53, 142). Moreover, while Hayek maintains that the capacity to classify is a general human characteristic, and that there are sufficient commonalities in the structures of different people's minds to ensure that they categorize and so experience the world in similar ways, he also contends that rather than being fixed, the structure of the central nervous system evolves over time, with connections among neurons gradually forming in response to stimuli. Different people encounter different environments, and therefore receive different stimuli, so that their minds evolve in different ways over the course of their lives. Consequently, while the classificatory apparatus possessed by any two individuals will share many common features, so that their sensory experiences will be ordered in similar ways, they will not be identical. Different people will experience the world in different ways (Hayek, 1952, p. 110). Thus, Hayek's claim that knowledge is subjective and dispersed reflects his beliefs about human nature and, more specifically, about the human mind: people only perceive the world through conceptual spectacles (so that their knowledge consists in an interpretation of the objective facts rather than a direct acquaintance with the latter) (Hayek, [1962] 1967, p. 54); and different people interpret the world in different ways, attending to and learning about different aspects of the world (so that the totality of knowledge about the world is dispersed throughout the population rather than being concentrated in a single mind).

Hayek's first major attempt to provide an account of the causal processes through which knowledge is discovered and transmitted in actual market economies, and thereby to explain how order is generated in such a setting, is to be found in his famous essay on 'The use of knowledge in society', in which he highlights the coordinating role of freely adjusting market prices ([1945a] 1948). Hayek argues that when individuals act on the basis of their local knowledge, they generate changes in relative prices which indicate the consequences of their actions for the scarcity of various goods and thus convey to others hints about the (local, at times tacit and always dispersed) knowledge which informs their plans, thereby enabling people successfully to coordinate their plans with one another. To take Hayek's classic example of the market for tin, suppose that some entrepreneurs perceive that new and lucrative opportunities for the use of tin have arisen. Anticipating the profits to be had from exploiting those opportunities, entrepreneurs purchase more tin, driving up demand. The ensuing rise in the relative price of tin will inform other people of its increased scarcity, inducing them to economize on their own use of the resource and thereby to free some of it to be employed in the new business ventures. The higher value of tin will also induce other entrepreneurs both to seek out new sources of supply and also to search more assiduously for substitutes for tin. In this way, people are induced to adapt their behaviour to changes in their circumstances without most of them 'knowing anything at all about the original cause of these changes':

> The most significant thing about this system is the economy of knowledge with which it operates, or how little the individual participants need to know in order to be able to take the right action. In abbreviated form, by a kind of symbol, only the most essential information is passed on and passed on only to those concerned. It is more than a metaphor to describe the price system as a kind of machine for registering change, or a system of telecommunication which enables individual producers to watch merely the movement of a few pointers in order to adjust their activities to changes of which they may never know more than is reflected in the price movement. (Hayek, [1945a] 1948, pp. 86–7)

For Hayek, then, prices act as 'knowledge-surrogates', enabling people to adjust their behavior to circumstances about which they have little or no direct awareness. More specifically, two main ways in which prices convey knowledge may be distinguished: first, prices guide people's decisions *ex ante* by informing them of the relative scarcities of goods and thereby alerting them to the existence of opportunities for profit of which they were ignorant hitherto; second, calculations of profit and loss facilitated by prices indicate *ex post* the success or otherwise of those decisions (Hayek, ([1945a] 1948, pp. 83–90; [1968] 1978, pp. 181–2, 187).[10]

HAYEK'S ONTOLOGICAL TURN, PART 2: SOCIAL STRUCTURES

Important though relative prices are, Hayek is quick to admit that they are not the only source of the information required for people to formulate mutually compatible plans. As early as his 1937 paper on 'Economics and knowledge', Hayek situates the price mechanism within the broader context provided by social rules and institutions:

> It has become customary among economists to stress only the need of knowledge of prices . . . But . . . price expectations and even the knowledge of current prices are only a very small fraction of the problem of knowledge as I see it. The wider aspect of the problem of knowledge with which I am concerned is the knowledge of the basic fact of how the different commodities can be obtained and used (Hayek, [1937] 1948, p. 51)

For Hayek, there is a whole gamut of institutions, such as the press, within which the price mechanism is embedded and which communicate knowledge and thereby help to coordinate the activities of market participants. Hayek returns to this point in '*Individualism*: true and false', where he writes of the importance for plan coordination of 'the traditions and conventions which evolve in a free society and which, without ever being enforceable, establish flexible but normally observed rules that make the behavior of other people predictable in a high degree' ([1945b] 1948, p. 23). Even in his 1945 paean to the price mechanism, where he might be forgiven for exaggerating the significance of the role of freely adjusting relative prices, Hayek acknowledges that '[t]he price system is *just one* of those formations which man has learned to use' in dealing with the problem of forming feasible plans in a decentralized market economy:

> We make constant use of formulas, symbols and rules whose meaning we do not understand and through the use of which we avail ourselves of the assistance of knowledge which individually we do not possess. We have developed

these practices and institutions by building on habits and institutions which have proved successful in their own sphere and which have in turn become the foundation of the civilisation we have built up. (Hayek, [1945a] 1948, p. 88)

Even in the late 1930s and 1940s, then, Hayek recognized that the price mechanism is insufficient to explain the degree of plan coordination observed in practice in decentralized market economies. Rather than being the product solely of the price system, plan coordination is the product of 'the whole organisation of the market' (Hayek [1946] 1948, p. 96).

Before considering in detail how Hayek's thought developed in the 1960s, it is worth noting that there are good reasons for attending to the role played by institutions, as well as to that of relative prices, in the generation of plan coordination. In particular, although Hayek does not justify the significance accorded to institutions in his work from the early 1960s onwards in quite this way, a truly thoroughgoing commitment to subjectivism implies that the information provided by price signals simply cannot be sufficient to enable people to dovetail their plans with one another. The reason, as later generations of Austrian economists, most notably Ludwig Lachmann, have argued, is that a thoroughgoing commitment to the principle of subjectivism will see the latter applied not only to people's perceptions of their circumstances but also to the expectations which they form on the basis of those perceptions (Lachmann, [1976] 1994; 1986, pp. 22–58). Perhaps most notably, the subjectivism of interpretation implies that there cannot be a mechanical link between people's circumstances and their expectations. On the contrary, at any given point in time people have to exercise their subjective judgement in interpreting what their circumstances, including the relative prices prevailing on the market at that moment, signify about the conditions that will obtain in the future, when the plans which people are currently formulating will be being implemented. The problem, of course, is that as soon as it is acknowledged that people have to exercise their judgement in interpreting and forming expectations on the basis of a given array of relative prices, then the possibility arises that different people may interpret those prices in a variety of different ways, yielding a diverse spectrum of (subjective) expectations of the future, which in turn underwrite a host of mutually incompatible plans. In a nutshell, then, according to a radical subjectivist like Lachmann, invoking the informational role of prices does not by itself dispose of the problem of explaining how market economies generate orderly outcomes, because while market prices do indeed convey information about the relative scarcities of goods and the intentions of other people, they do not do so unambiguously. However, as Lachmann himself suggests, and as I discuss in greater detail below, shared rules of interpretation play a crucial role in ensuring that the difficulties which the subjectivism of interpretation creates for the formation of mutually incompatible plans are usually overcome (Lachmann, 1970, pp. 49–50, 61).[11]

Returning to Hayek's work on rules, one may begin by noting that it was only in his post-1960 work on social theory and political philosophy that Hayek developed his earlier insights into the role of institutions in facilitating plan coordination into a full-fledged, and convincing, account of the possibility of socio-economic order in decentralized market economies. In those writings, Hayek argues that the dissemination of knowledge required for plan coordination is facilitated not only by price signals but also by a network of formal and informal social rules (such as the laws of property, tort and contract; and norms of honesty and promise-keeping, respectively). The significance of social rules and, in particular, their role in the generation of mutually compatible plans, is a theme that rises to prominence in Hayek's work in the 1960s. Before elaborating on the latter theme, however, it is worth discussing a little more detail Hayek's views on social rules and, in particular, about the implications of Hayek's account of rule-following for his account of the ontological and epistemological issues which must be addressed by a satisfactory theory of the coordination of economic activities in decentralized market economies.

Developing ideas first aired in *The Sensory Order*, Hayek in the 1960s argues that the human mind is a classificatory system whose operation is governed by an (evolving) system of rules. Perception, along with all of the other activities of our minds and much of human action, is a rule-guided activity (Hayek, [1962] 1967, pp. 43–6; [1969] 1978, pp. 38–42). Significantly, according to Hayek, people are usually unable to state explicitly many of the rules which govern their perceptions and actions. People's knowledge of the rules in question is 'tacit' or 'practical' in the sense that, while they know how to act in accordance with the rules, they lack the propositional knowledge required to articulate them discursively (Hayek, [1962] 1967, pp. 43–5, 53; [1969] 1978, pp. 38–9). For instance, according to Hayek, much of the knowledge which is important in everyday business life consists in things like an entrepreneur's hunches and intuitions about the sort of product which is likely to prove attractive to consumers, or in a production engineer's knowledge of how to solve various technical problems, or in a businessman's capacity to glean information about new sources of finance, rather than in a grasp of particular facts which people could list and state explicitly if required to do so (Hayek, 1960, p. 25; [1968] 1978, p. 182; 1979, p. 190 n. 7; 1988, p. 78).

Hayek argues that one of the most important implications of his thesis that the mind is a rule-governed classificatory system is that there is an absolute limitation on human knowledge. Hayek's argument here is premised on the claim that any classificatory apparatus must possess a structure of a higher order of complexity than is possessed by the objects it classifies. It follows that the human mind can never fully understand itself – it is incapable of explaining fully its own operations – because, like any classificatory device, the mind will only be able fully to comprehend objects of a lesser degree of complexity than itself. If the mind is the indispensable means by which people interpret and understand the world, then there is no scope for people to step outside of their minds to obtain a God's-eye view of the latter, untainted by theoretical presuppositions. To borrow an analogy from Michael Polanyi, one simply cannot examine one's spectacles while simultaneously wearing them (Hayek, 1952, pp. 184–90; [1962] 1967, pp. 60–63). According to Hayek, therefore, people are intrinsically incapable of stating discursively all the rules which govern the working of their minds:

> [W]e always know not only more than we can deliberately state but also more than we can be aware of ... [M]uch that we successfully do depends on presuppositions which are outside the range of what we can either state or reflect upon ... [T]hought must, if we are not to be led into an infinite regress, be assumed to be directed by rules which in turn cannot be conscious – by a supra-conscious mechanism which operates upon the contents of consciousness but which cannot itself be conscious. (Hayek, [1962] 1967, p. 61)

And the fact that our perceptions, thoughts and deeds are directed by a hierarchy of rules, some of which are necessarily beyond our powers of conscious identification and articulation, implies that there is 'an inherent limitation of our possible explicit knowledge' (Hayek, [1962] 1967, p. 60). The fact that much of the knowledge which informs our actions is tacit in nature, and that there are insuperable limits to man's capacity to articulate this knowledge, is a third epistemological issue which economic theory must take into account if it is to yield an adequate analysis of the working of modern industrial economies. The epistemological task which faces society is not simply that of utilizing knowledge which is fragmented and dispersed throughout the population; it is the even more fundamental problem of utilizing knowledge which is practical in the sense that it is embodied in skills, habits and rules, rather than being explicitly known to people.

However, while the tacit nature of our knowledge of social rules marks a qualitative increase in the severity of the epistemological problem which must be solved by society, Hayek argues that man's reliance on social rules also provides the key to understanding how orderly social outcomes remain possible in decentralized market economies. The reason lies in the fact that, according to Hayek, social rules are storehouses or repositories of practical social knowledge, embodying wisdom accumulated down the ages about how people should (in general terms) both interpret and also (if they wish to achieve particular goals) respond to various situations. And it is the fact that different people act in accordance with the same abstract social rules, following the same general guidelines about how to interpret and act in various kinds of situation, that makes it possible for them to form reliable expectations of each other's future conduct, enabling them to foresee with some confidence the outcome of their own actions and thereby facilitating (without, of course, guaranteeing) the formation of mutually compatible plans:

> What reconciles the individuals and knits them into a common and enduring pattern of a society is that they respond in accordance with the same abstract rules. What enables them to live and work together in peace is that in the pursuit of their individual ends the particular monetary impulses which impel their efforts are guided and restrained by the same abstract rules. If emotion or impulse tells them what they want, the conventional rules tell them how they will be able and be allowed to achieve it. The action, or act of will, is always a particular, concrete, and individual event, while the common rules which guide it are social, general, and abstract. (Hayek, 1976, p.12; also see [1967b] 1978, p.85)

The social rules to which Hayek refers are 'abstract' in the sense that they provide general guidelines about how people should act in various types of situation, often merely forbidding particular kinds of action. They are, to borrow Michael Oakeshott's (1983) felicitous phrase, 'adverbial rules', specifying certain requirements that a person's behaviour must satisfy in various types of situation, without dictating that the person must take a specific action or pursue a particular goal. Hence, people whose conduct is guided by such rules still enjoy considerable freedom to act in accordance with their local knowledge. It follows that, for Hayek, people's actions are not a unique, deterministic response to their circumstances and are therefore not predictable in every last detail. Nonetheless, the fact that people act in accordance with a common, and relatively stable, set of intellectual, legal and moral rules ensures that there are reasonable bounds as to how they are likely to act, ensuring that the general form, if not the precise details, of their future conduct is predictable enough to facilitate the effective coordination of people's activities even without the direction of an overarching, commanding intelligence (Hayek, 1960, pp.148–61; 1976, pp.123–8).

In highlighting the importance of social rules for the coordination of economic activity, Hayek portrays people not only, as we have seen, as 'constitutionally ignorant', but also as intrinsically social beings whose very capacity to reason, and therefore whose beliefs, goals and conduct, are all profoundly shaped (but not entirely determined) by the inherited traditions, customs and rules of their society.[12] This brings us the second aspect of Hayek's post-1937 ontology, namely his view of society as being composed not only of individual people but also of shared social structures. For Hayek, people can be 'individuals' – in what Hayek terms the 'true' sense of that oft-misused term – only within the context provided by the institutions, rules and relations of which their society is composed:

> What, then, are the essential characteristics of true individualism? The first thing that should be said is that it is primarily a *theory* of society, an attempt to understand the forces which determine the social life of man, and only in the second instance a set of political maxims derived from this view of society. This fact should by itself be sufficient to refute the silliest of the common misunderstandings: the belief that individualism postulates (or bases its arguments on the assumption of) the existence of isolated or self-contained individuals, instead of starting from men whose whole nature and character is determined by their existence in society. (Hayek ([1945b] 1948, p. 6)

The fact that people are social beings who draw on shared traditions, customs and rules in order to act helps us to understand how the dangers of the solipsism raised by the subjectivity of interpretation can be avoided. When it comes to judging the significance of disequilibrium prices, say, people are able to transcend the confines of their own subjective point of view by drawing on shared interpretive frameworks. The use of the latter helps to ensure that people reach similar interpretations of the meaning and significance of price signals, making it easier for them to predict one another's actions and thereby increasing the likelihood of their developing mutually compatible plans (Ebeling, 1986; Fleetwood, 1995, p. 125–5; Lewis 2012: 373–4).[13]

For Hayek, therefore, society is composed not only of individual people but also of social rules, traditions and customs (Fleetwood, 1995, pp. 82–6, 107; Runde, 2001). People's reliance on the latter enables them to devise mutually compatible plans, even in the face of their irremediable ignorance of most of the facts which will determine the consequences of their actions. For Hayek, this picture of the socio-economic world as constituted not only by individual people but also by inherited social structures, which shape people's attributes and goals and facilitate purposeful human conduct, 'provides a true theory of human nature. It is a view of mind and society which provides an appropriate place for the role which tradition and custom play in their development' ([1964a] 1967, p. 95). More specifically, as I shall discuss in more detail below, Hayek's ontology is one which leads him to advocate an approach to the analysis of socio-economic affairs which is 'anti-rationalistic' in the sense that it is 'a view which in general rates rather low the place which reason plays in human affairs, which contends that man has achieved what he has in spite of the fact that he is only partly guided by reason, and that his individual reason is very limited and imperfect':

> One might even say that [the anti-rationalistic approach] is a product of an acute consciousness of the limitations of the individual mind which induces an attitude of humility toward the impersonal and anonymous social processes by which individuals help to create things greater than they know ... [It] regards man not as a highly rational and intelligent but as a very irrational and fallible being, whose individual errors are corrected only in the course of a social process, and which aims to make the best of a very imperfect material (Hayek, [1945b] 1948, pp. 8–9)

And it is to a more detailed account of Hayek's conception of the orderly socio-economic process generated by people's rule-governed activity to which I now turn my attention.

FROM MARKET EQUILIBRIUM TO SOCIO-ECONOMIC ORDER

How is the meshing of plans generated by people's rule-governed behaviour to be conceptualized? Hayek rejects the idea that such plan coordination is best understood as an equilibrium, arguing that this idea 'presupposes that the facts have already all been discovered and competition therefore has ceased' ([1968] 1978, p. 184; also see Caldwell 2004, pp. 226–7). For Hayek, the equilibrium concept applies only to 'economies', defined more narrowly than in everyday discourse as organizations, such as households or firms, in which a single intelligence deliberately allocates resources in the service of a 'given' objective. Such situations are not representative of the free market as a whole, for the latter is populated by a whole host of individual economies with a multiplicity of separate, often conflicting and incommensurable goals, each of which is informed by its author's local knowledge of their circumstances, and which therefore cannot be known by any one person in their totality. Hayek terms the dovetailing of plans brought about by the mutual, rule-governed adjustment of the individual economies within the market, a 'catallaxy'. A catallaxy is thus a coordinated network which, though lacking a common purpose of its own, facilitates the achievement of a great variety of different individual purposes and thereby makes possible the use of knowledge which nobody possesses in its entirety (Hayek, [1967b] 1978, pp. 90–92; 1976, pp. 107–9).

As both Fleetwood (1995) and Vaughn (1999) have perceptively emphasized, in conceptualizing the coordination of economic activity in a catallaxy, Hayek proposes to replace of the notion of equilibrium with that of 'order':

> By 'order' we shall describe *a state of affairs in which a multiplicity of elements of various kinds are so related to each other that we may learn from our acquaintance with some spatial or temporal part of the whole to form correct expectations concerning the rest, or at least expectations which have a good chance of proving correct*. (Hayek, 1976, p. 36; also see [1967b] 1978, p. 72–4)

The orderliness of social activity therefore manifests itself in the fact that individuals can, for the most part, implement plans of action in the confident expectation that the contributions from their fellow men which are required to bring those plans to fruition will in actual fact be forthcoming.

More specifically, according to Hayek, the market order or catallaxy is an example of a spontaneous order, that is, a set of social arrangements that appear to have been planned by some single intelligence but which, in actual fact, arise as the mutually beneficial, but unintended, consequence of human actions aimed at individual purposes:

> Such an order involving an adjustment to circumstances, knowledge of which is dispersed among a great many people, cannot be established by central direction. It can arise only from the mutual adjustment of the elements and their response to the events that act immediately upon them. It is what Michael Polanyi has called the spontaneous formation of a 'polycentric order': 'When order is achieved among human beings by allowing them to interact with each other on their own initiative – subject only to the laws which uniformly apply to all of them – we have a system of spontaneous order in society' [Polanyi, 1951, p. 159]. (Hayek, 1960, p. 294)

For Hayek, then, a catallaxy is a particular kind of spontaneous order, produced by the market through people acting in accordance with various social rules, the 'result of human action, but not the execution of any human design' (Adam Ferguson, quoted in Hayek, 1967a, p. 96; 1978, p. 109).

Moreover, if it is indeed the case that the market order arises as the unintended consequence of rule-governed human action – with purposeful human conduct being possible only because people act in accordance with social rules – so it is equally true that continued existence of the rules which underpin and facilitate social order depends on human action. For while the rules, customs and traditions which provide the context for current economic activity were inherited ready-made by the current generation of people, having been shaped in the past by the actions of earlier generations, both Hayek's strictures against collectivism, and also his work on cultural evolution, make clear that the continued existence of those rules depends upon current human agency (Hayek, [1942–44] 1979,

p. 152; 1967a, pp. 72–80; see also Fleetwood, 1995, pp. 145–6; Lange von-Kulessa, 1997, pp. 276–82). In drawing upon the stock of inherited rules, traditions and customs in order to act, people reproduce (or, if individuals break away from traditional rules and engage in new forms of conduct which others subsequently imitate, transform) those structures, thereby ensuring their continued existence into the future (perhaps in a modified form). Hayek can thus be seen to subscribe to a transformational conception of socio-economic order, according to which the social structures which facilitate the formation of mutually compatible expectations, and which therefore underpin the possibility of socio-economic order, are the ever-present condition for, and also the continually (and often unintentionally) (re)produced outcome of, people's actions:

> [W]e often observe in spontaneous social formations that the parts move as if their purpose were the preservation of the wholes. We find again and again that *if* it were somebody's deliberate aim to preserve the structure of these wholes and *if* he had the knowledge and the power to do so, he would have to do it by causing precisely those movements which in fact are taking place without any such conscious direction. In the social sphere these spontaneous movements which preserve a certain structural connection between the parts are, moreover, connected in a special way with our individual purposes: the social wholes which are thus maintained are the condition for the achievement of many of the things at which we as individuals aim, the environment which makes it possible even to conceive of our individual desires and which gives us the power to achieve them. (Hayek, [1942–44] 1979, pp. 145–6)

On this view, social order just is the (never-ending) process whereby people draw on (pre-existing, historically given) social structures (such as the legal system) in order to act and, in doing so, subsequently either reproduce or transform those structures, a conception which 'has the advantage that we can meaningfully speak about an order being approached to various degrees, and that order can be preserved throughout a process of change' (Hayek, [1968] 1978, p. 184; see also Fleetwood, 1995, pp. 135–55).[14]

ECONOMICS AS SOCIAL THEORY: HAYEK'S COMPARATIVE INSTITUTIONAL ANALYSIS

Hayek's research in economics and his later investigations in social theory and political philosophy can thus be seen to form a more coherent body of work than might at first glance appear to be the case. Hayek's insight that the problem of economic order is primarily one of knowledge informed his post-1960 writings on political philosophy and social theory, where he examined how the rules and institutions of a liberal polity enable even 'constitutionally ignorant' people to anticipate one another's actions accurately enough to form mutually compatible plans (Hayek, 1960, p. 29). Indeed, as we have seen, it was only in this later work that Hayek was finally able to provide a convincing answer to the question, first posed in his narrow technical work on economics a quarter of a century earlier, of how socio-economic order is possible in decentralized market economies. As Hayek himself put it when reflecting upon the development of his research:

> [T]hough at one time a very pure and narrow economic theorist, I was led from technical economics into all kinds of questions usually regarded as philosophical. When I look back, it seems all to have begun, nearly thirty years ago, with an essay on 'Economics and knowledge' in which I examined what seemed to me some of the central difficulties of pure economic theory. Its main conclusion was that the task of economic theory was to explain how an overall order of economic activity was achieved which utilized a large amount of knowledge which was not concentrated in any one mind but existed only as the separate knowledge of thousands or millions of different individuals. But it was still a long way from this to an adequate insight into the relations between the abstract rules which the individual follows in his actions, and the abstract overall order which is formed as a result of his responding, within the limits imposed upon him by those abstract rules, to the concrete particular circumstances which he encounters. It was only through a re-examination of the age-old concept of freedom under the law, the basic conception of traditional liberalism, and of the problems of the philosophy of the law which this raises, that I have reached what now seems to me a tolerably clear picture of the nature of the spontaneous order of which liberal economists have so long been talking. (Hayek, [1964a] 1967, pp. 91–2; also see 1960, p. 3)

In moving away from the concept of equilibrium utilized in his narrow technical economics towards the notion of socio-economic order, Hayek can in his later work be thought of as attempting to devise an interdisciplinary, social-theoretic approach to the study of economic issues (Hayek, 1973, p. 4; see also Boettke, 1999; Vaughn, 1999). More specifically, Hayek's later work is social-theoretic in the sense that, rather than attempting to account for market order solely in terms of the (inter)actions of purposeful economic agents, as neoclassical economics would demand, it places significant explanatory weight on the properties of the social-structural context in which that interaction takes place. Hayek downplays the significance of (behavioral postulates about) the rationality and morality of human conduct, emphasizing instead people's irremediable ignorance, and arguing that what matters for the coordination of economic activity is less people's precise motivations and more whether the institutional framework within which they are embedded enables them to learn what they need to know to coordinate their plans. Hayek's key insight, therefore, is that, however principled they may be, people will be able to generate an orderly allocation of resources only if the prevailing institutions enable them to learn enough about each other's intentions to coordinate their plans. While some institutional arrangements, in particular those comprising a liberal polity, facilitate the requisite learning, others, most notably those found in socialist economies, hamper or even preclude it. Irrespective of their morality, people's constitutional ignorance will prevent them from developing plans which dovetail unless they act against a backdrop provided by the institutions of private property, money and money prices, and contract and tort law (Hayek, 1960, pp, 156–7). On this view, Hayek can be thought of as developing a comparative institutional approach to social theory, the central tenet of which is that social systems should principally be analysed and assessed not in terms of their moral content, but rather by reference to their (epistemic) capacity to facilitate (or hamper) the effective use of the (often dispersed and tacit) knowledge existing in society (Gray, 1998, pp. 40–41, 134–5; Boettke, 1999; Vaughn, 1999).

In examining how different institutional arrangements affect the scope for people to learn and use various kinds of knowledge, and thus to coordinate their activities and bring their plans to fruition, Hayek is investigating the social-structural causes of knowledge acquisition and, therefore, of socio-economic order in decentralized market economies. Thus conceived, Hayek's work lends itself to elaboration in terms of the notion of contrastive causal explanation. The latter approach to explanation has been developed by realist social theorists and philosophers and suggests that to explain some phenomenon of interest is to provide an account of its causal history.[15] Of course, the provision of a complete causal history of something as complex as the market economy is an undertaking whose demands far exceed the capabilities of even the most talented and learned social theorist or historian. However, the task of providing a causal explanation can be reduced to manageable proportions by focusing on a subset of the relevant causal factors, in particular those whose influence is indicated by the existence of differences or contrasts between the history of the phenomenon under investigation (termed, the 'focus') and the history of another, similar (but not identical) phenomenon (the 'foil'). The result will be an explanation which (it is hoped) identifies the causes, not of the focus per se, but rather of the difference or contrast between the focus and the foil. For instance, rather than attempting to do justice to all of the influences which have shaped the history and performance of market economies, Hayek concentrates on those causal factors which (he believes) account for the key differences between the history and performance of market economies and that of centrally planned economies. More specifically, according to Hayek, while the existence of purposeful human conduct is common to both types of economy, the cause of the superior performance of market economies is a social-structural one, namely the capacity of the institutions of the market economy to facilitate a more effective use of knowledge than is possible under central planning (Hayek, [1937] 1948, pp. 46–55; Boettke, 1999, p. xxiv; also see Hayek, [1964b] 1967, p. 26).

That Hayek advances a causal explanation of the performance of the market relative to that of a planned economy reflects his belief, expressed in *The Sensory Order* and elsewhere, that the human mind is a classificatory device which can fully comprehend only those phenomena of a lower order of complexity than itself. When investigating something as complex as the market order, therefore, the nature of the human mind implies that all that is possible is an explanation of certain general and highly abstract features of, or patterns in, the phenomenon under investigation, not the explanation (still less the prediction) of its detailed properties. Hence, while Hayek's account explains some of the key qualitative features of the market order, in particular its capacity to facilitate the implementation of more individual plans than can be achieved in central planned economies, it does not yield precise explanations or predictions of the detailed outcomes generated by the market. It does not, for instance, predict or guarantee that the plans of any specific person will succeed (Hayek, 1976, pp. 126–8). Hayek can thus be thought of as advancing an explanation of the general principles governing the working of market economies, focusing in particular on the role played in the generation of market order by a few social structural (institutional) causes, not as attempting to illuminate every last one of the relevant casual factors or to provide detailed, quantitative predictions of the outcomes yielded by the market. Once again, the picture of human nature to which Hayek subscribes provides an (ontological) grounding for (aspects of) his methodology – in this case his commitment to explanations of the principle and to pattern prediction (Hayek, 1952, pp. 179–90; [1964b] 1967, pp. 26–36; 1967a, pp. 71–6).

The fact that, in his later work, Hayek focuses on the social-structural causes of socio-economic order should not be taken to indicate that he denies the causal impact of purposeful human conduct. People are the driving force of socio-economic life in the sense that nothing would happen in the socio-economic world were it not for intentional human agency. For instance, social rules and institutions persist over time only because they are (re)produced through human action. However, as we have seen, purposeful human conduct is possible only because of the existence of the institutions of private property, the law and other social rules, and money and money prices. This can be thought of as a specific case of the point, made earlier, that Hayek views people as social beings whose powers of reasoning – in this case their ability to engage in rational economic calculation – and therefore whose actions, are profoundly shaped by the particular configuration of social rules and institutions in which they are embedded (Hayek, 1960, pp. 60–65; 1979, pp. 75–7). For Hayek, therefore, social structures and intentional human agency are recursively related, that is, each is both a cause and a consequence of the other (Hayek, [1964a] 1967, p. 84). It is simply the case that the focus of Hayek's later work is on the role of social rules and institutions in facilitating human action, so that the role of intentional human agency per se fades into the background, without of course being denied or entirely neglected (Fleetwood, 1995, pp. 146–7; Runde, 2001, pp. 13–15).

Hayek's emphasis on the contrastive or comparative performance of the free market economy manifests itself in the fact that, rather than basing his normative case for the market on the (optimal) properties of perfectly competitive equilibria, he instead makes a comparative institutional claim, namely that a market economy will yield a greater degree of coordination than any other social system. While Hayek extols the virtue of the market, he is careful not to claim that the outcomes it produces are efficient in any absolute sense. He does not, for example, claim that the allocation of resources produced by free markets will satisfy the criteria for Pareto optimality. Indeed, according to Hayek, the fact that equilibrium analysis ignores the very (informational) problems which real-world markets have to solve implies that the normative criteria to which it gives rise, such as Pareto efficiency, provide an inappropriate benchmark for evaluating the merits of real-world market economies. The relevant comparison is not between a real-world system of competitive markets and some fictitious state of equilibrium, but rather between the former and other, non-market methods of resource allocation:

> The peculiarity of competition – which it has in common with scientific method – is that its performance cannot be tested in particular instances where it is significant, but is shown only by the fact that the market will prevail in comparison with alternative arrangements... [W]e do injustice to the achievement of the market if we judge it, as it were, from above, by comparing it to an ideal standard which we have no known way of achieving... [W]e judge it, as we ought to, from below, that is against what would be produced if competition were prevented. (Hayek, [1968] 1978, pp. 180, 185)[16]

Thus, Hayek shifts our attention from the more or less absolute notion of efficiency associated with the concept of a competitive equilibrium towards a more relativistic notion (Rizzo, 1990, pp. 24–6). The fact that people must decide how to act in a world which is shaped by other people's (constantly evolving) plans implies that there will inevitably be mistaken expectations and failed plans, so that the allocation of resources yielded by the market will not be optimal in the sense of exhausting all possible gains from trade. The great virtue of the market, however, is that it constitutes the most effective means known to man of ensuring that people have both the information, and the incentives, required to correct erroneous expectations, so that a closer (albeit still imperfect) degree of coordination of people's plans is achieved than is possible under any other social system (Hayek, [1945a] 1948, pp. 82–3; 1976, pp. 124–5).

METHODOLOGICAL IMPLICATIONS

Viewed in this light, Hayek's approach is not well described by the term 'methodological individualism'. While at times, especially in his discussion of the so-called compositive method in his *Scientism* essay (Hayek, [1942–44] 1955), Hayek's rhetoric makes it seem as if he is endorsing a form of methodological individualism,[17] in actual fact the substance of Hayek's post-1937 work has little in common with methodological individualism, at least as the latter is commonly understood. Methodological individualism is usually taken to demand that social phenomena be explained solely in terms of the actions of isolated, atomistic individuals. Hayek's explanation of socio-economic order departs from this approach in a number of ways. He deals not with self-contained individuals whose properties are fixed independent of their social environment, but rather with thoroughly social beings whose essential characteristics and capacities – whose ability to reason, to calculate, to act, indeed to be human – are all profoundly shaped by inherited social structures (rules, traditions and institutions). Moreover, Hayek accords significant causal and explanatory weight to the social-structural context in which people act, arguing that the key determinant of the possibility of socio-economic order is social-structural in nature, namely the capacity of the institutional framework within which people are embedded to provide them with sufficient knowledge to coordinate their plans. In arguing that social systems should be analysed in terms of their (emergent epistemic) capacity to promote (or impede) the effective use of all the various kinds of knowledge in society, Hayek is invoking an emergent, social-structural cause of knowledge acquisition and, therefore, of socio-economic order (Lewis 2012, 2014). This is quite at odds with the methodological individualism's (reductionist) desideratum that explanations should be couched solely in terms of the properties (the goals, the beliefs and the actions) of individual people.

This suggests that to continue to describe the work of the later Hayek's as an example of methodological individualism is legitimate only if that term is defined so broadly that it is stripped of almost all its usual connotations. Such an approach would be more likely to cause confusion, hampering the accurate interpretation of Hayek's work and also making it more difficult for advocates of Hayek's approach to economics to engage in a fruitful dialogue of supporters of other schools of thought. A more accurate approach would be either to describe Hayek's work as an example of institutional or holistic individualism, or to say that he subscribed to a transformational model of social activity.[18]

ACKNOWLEDGEMENTS

I am very grateful to the late Norman Barry, Roger Garrison, Jochen Runde and, in particular, Bruce Caldwell for perceptive comments on an earlier draft of this chapter. Any remaining deficiencies are solely my responsibility.

NOTES

1. An important precursor to Hayek's (1937) paper was provided in 1932 by the Viennese economist Hans Mayer, who anticipated some of the points later made by Hayek by drawing attention to differences between the Austrians and the other supporters of marginalist economics. In particular, Mayer contrasted the former's emphasis on the (causal) processes through which prices are formed with the latter's (functionalist) emphasis on the properties of (static) equilibrium states (Mayer, [1932] 1994).
2. The contention that the essence of Hayek's post-1937 transformation lies in his dissatisfaction with equilibrium analysis is defended by Caldwell (1988; 1992; 2004, pp. 409–22). For an alternative view, see Hutchison (1981, pp. 210–19; 1992).
3. '[I]t is difficult to suppress the suspicion that this particular proposal [market socialism] has been born out of an excessive preoccupation with problems of the pure theory of stationary equilibrium' (Hayek, [1940] 1948, p. 188).
4. Hayek's most famous statement of this subjectivist position is perhaps to be found in *The Counter-Revolution of Science*, where he writes that, 'In fact, most of the objects of social or human action are not "objective facts" in the special narrow sense in which this term is used by the Sciences and contrasted to "opinions", and they cannot at all be defined in physical terms. So far as human actions are concerned the things are what the acting people think they are' ([1942–44] 1979, p. 44).
5. As Hayek later put it, 'The orderliness of social activity shows itself in the fact that the individual can carry out a consistent plan of action that, at almost every stage, rests on the expectation of certain contributions from his fellows. That there is some kind of order, consistency and constancy in social life is obvious. If there were not, none of us would be able to go about his affairs or satisfy his most elementary wants' (1960, p. 160).
6. Also see Hayek ([1937] 1948, pp. 52, 54; [1945a] 1948, pp. 77–8, 82–3, 90–91; [1946] 1948, pp. 92–5; [1968] 1978, pp. 181, 184).
7. For more on this topic, see Hayek's essay on 'The meaning of competition' ([1946] 1948, pp. 95–7, 100–101, 106).
8. 'In the end it was concern with the logical character of social theory which forced me to re-examine systematically my ideas on theoretical psychology' (Hayek, 1952, p. v).

9. The ontology presuppositions of Hayek's theoretical psychology and, in particular, the role of emergent properties in his account of the working of the mind are discussed in more detail in Lewis (2012, pp. 370–73).
10. Contemporary Austrian economists argue, contrary to neoclassical interpretations of Hayek's work on the informational role of prices, that it is disequilibrium (as distinct from equilibrium) prices which are the key to the coordination of economic activity in decentralized market economies. For it is disequilibrium prices, and more specifically the opportunities for profit to which they give rise, which both alert entrepreneurs to the existence of poorly coordinated decisions and also provide them with the incentive to exploit those newly discovered opportunities and thereby to bring people's activities more closely into conformity with each another (Hayek, 1979, pp. 71–2, 80–88; also see Kirzner, 1984; Thomsen, 1992).
11. For more on Lachmann's account of order, see Lewis and Runde (2007) and Lewis (2011). The relations between Lachmann's and Hayek's work is discussed in Lewin (Chapter 8 of this volume).
12. '[W]e should regard human reason as the product of a civilization which was not deliberately made by man but which had rather grown by a process of evolution . . . [E]ven man's capacity to think is not a natural endowment of the individual but a cultural heritage' (Hayek, [1964a] 1967, p. 86; also see Hayek, 1960, 1973, pp. 17–19; 1988, pp. 22–3). Also see Lewis (2012, pp. 374–6).
13. Hence, according to Hayek, such rules 'could almost be described as a kind of instrument of production, helping people to predict the behavior of those with whom they must collaborate' ([1944] 2001, p. 77).
14. Hayek develops an evolutionary account of the social institutions and rules which underpin the catallaxy, arguing that they emerge as the unintended outcome of people's actions via a process of cultural selection. For Hayek, those institutions and rules which have survived the test of time have done so because they enable people to deal effectively with the problems posed by the intrinsic limitations of their knowledge (Hayek, 1960, 1967a, 1978, 1979, 1988). Hayek's theory of cultural evolution has proven to be one of the most controversial aspects of his work, stimulating considerable debate. See, for instance, Vanberg (1986), Boettke (1990), Vaughn (1999), Caldwell (2000, 2002), Gaus (2006), and Lewis (2014).
15. See, for instance, Lipton (1991) and Lawson (1997, pp. 199–226). For more on the relevant notion of (social-structural) causation, see Lewis (2000, 2012, 2013).
16. Also see Hayek ([1935] 1948, pp. 156–7; [1945a] 1948, p. 87; [1946] 1948, p. 104–6; [1967b] 1978, p. 91).
17. See, for example, Hayek ([1942–44] 1979, p. 67).
18. For similar points, see Sciabarra (1995, pp. 15–19), Koppl (2002, p. 35), Caldwell (2004, pp. 279–87, 411–18), Lewis (2005, pp. 309–11) and Hodgson (2007).

REFERENCES

Boettke, Peter J. (1990), 'The theory of spontaneous order and cultural evolution in the social theory of F.A. Hayek', *Cultural Dynamics*, 3 (1), 61–83.
Boettke, Peter J. (1999), 'Introduction: which enlightenment, whose liberalism? Hayek's research program for understanding the liberal society', in Peter J. Boettke (ed.), *The Legacy of Friedrich von Hayek. Volume I: Politics*, Cheltenham, UK and Northampton, MA: Edward Elgar, pp. xi–lv.
Caldwell, Bruce J. (1988), 'Hayek's transformation', *History of Political Economy*, 20 (4), 513–41.
Caldwell, Bruce J. (1992), 'Hayek the falsificationist? A refutation', *Research in the History of Economic Thought and Methodology*, 10, 1–15.

Caldwell, Bruce J. (2000), 'The emergence of Hayek's ideas on cultural evolution', *Review of Austrian Economics*, 13 (1), 5–22.
Caldwell, Bruce J. (2002), 'Hayek on cultural evolution', in Uskali Mäki (ed.), *Fact and Fiction in Economics: Models, Realism and Social Construction*, Cambridge: Cambridge University Press.
Caldwell, Bruce J. (2004), *Hayek's Challenge: An Intellectual Biography of F.A. Hayek*, Chicago, IL, USA and London, UK: University of Chicago Press.
Ebeling, Richard M. (1986), 'Towards a hermeneutical economics: expectations, prices, and the role of interpretation in a theory of the market process', in Israel M. Kirzner (ed.), *Subjectivism, Intelligibility and Economic Understanding: Essays in Honour of Ludwig M. Lachmann on his Eightieth Birthday*, New York: New York University Press.
Fleetwood, Steve (1995), *Hayek's Political Economy: The Socio-Economics of Order*, London, UK and New York, USA: Routledge.
Gaus, Gerald F. (2006), 'Hayek on the evolution of society and mind', in Edward Feser (ed.), *The Cambridge Companion to Hayek*, Cambridge: Cambridge University Press.
Gray, John (1998), *Hayek on Liberty*, 3rd edn, London, UK and New York, USA: Routledge.
Hayek, Friedrich A. (1928), 'Intertemporal price equilibrium and movements in the value of money', in Roy McLoughry (ed.) (1984), *Money, Capital and Fluctuations: Early Essays of F.A. Hayek*, London: Routledge & Kegan Paul.
Hayek, Friedrich A. ([1933] 1966), *Monetary Theory and the Trade Cycle*, trans. Nicholas Kaldor and Honor M. Croome, New York: Kelley.
Hayek, Friedrich A. (1935), 'Socialist calculation II: the state of the debate', in Hayek (1948).
Hayek, Friedrich A. (1937), 'Economics and knowledge', in Hayek (1948).
Hayek, Friedrich A. (1940), 'Socialist calculation III: the competitive "solution"', in Hayek (1948).
Hayek, Friedrich A. (1942–44), *The Counter-Revolution of Science: Studies on the Abuse of Reason*, 2nd edn 1979, Indianapolis, IN: Liberty Fund.
Hayek, Friedrich A. ([1942–44] 1955) Part 1: 'Scientism and the Study of Society', *The Counter-Revolution of Science: Studies in the Abuse of Reason*, Glencoe, IL: Free Press of Glencoe; and London: Collier-Macmillan, pp. 11–102.
Hayek, Friedrich A. ([1944] 2001), *The Road to Serfdom*, London, UK and New York, USA: Routledge.
Hayek, Friedrich A. (1945a), 'The use of knowledge in society', in Hayek (1948).
Hayek, Friedrich A. (1945b), '*Individualism*: true and false', in Hayek (1948).
Hayek, Friedrich A. (1946), 'The meaning of competition', in Hayek (1948).
Hayek, Friedrich A. (1948), *Individualism and Economic Order*, Chicago, IL: University of Chicago Press.
Hayek, Friedrich A. (1952), *The Sensory Order: An Inquiry into the Foundations of Theoretical Psychology*, London and Henley: Routledge & Kegan Paul.
Hayek, Friedrich A. (1960), *The Constitution of Liberty*, London, UK and New York, USA: Routledge.
Hayek, Friedrich A. (1962), 'Rules, perception and intelligibility', in Hayek (1967).
Hayek, Friedrich A. (1964a), 'Kinds of rationalism', in Hayek (1967).
Hayek, Friedrich A. (1964b), 'The theory of complex phenomena', in Hayek (1967).
Hayek, Friedrich A. (1967a), 'Notes on the evolution of systems of rules of conduct', *Studies in Philosophy, Politics and Economics*, London: Routledge & Kegan Paul.
Hayek, Friedrich A. (1967b), 'The confusion of language in political thought', in Hayek (1978).
Hayek, Friedrich A. (1968), 'Competition as a discovery procedure', in Hayek (1978).
Hayek, Friedrich A. (1969), 'The primacy of the abstract', in Hayek (1978).
Hayek, Friedrich A. (1973), *Law, Legislation and Liberty: A New Statement of the Liberal Principles of Justice and Political Economy, Volume I: Rules and Order*, London, UK and New York, USA: Routledge.

Hayek, Friedrich A. (1976), *Law, Legislation and Liberty: A New Statement of the Liberal Principles of Justice and Political Economy, Volume II: The Mirage of Social Justice*, London, UK and New York, USA: Routledge.

Hayek, Friedrich A. (1978), *New Studies in Philosophy, Politics, Economics and the History of Ideas*, London and Henley: Routledge & Kegan Paul.

Hayek, Friedrich A. (1979), *Law, Legislation and Liberty: A New Statement of the Liberal Principles of Justice and Political Economy, Volume III: The Political Order of a Free People*, London and New York: Routledge.

Hayek, Friedrich A. (1988), *The Fatal Conceit: The Errors of Socialism*, ed. W.W. Bartley III, London: Routledge.

Hodgson, Geoffrey M. (2007), 'Meanings of methodological individualism', *Journal of Economic Methodology*, 14, 211–226.

Hutchison, Terence W. (1981), *The Politics and Philosophy of Economics: Marxians, Keynesians and Austrians*, Oxford: Blackwell.

Kirzner, Israel M. (1984), 'Prices, the communication of knowledge and the discovery process', in Kurt R. Leube and Albert H. Zlabinger (eds), *The Political Economy of Freedom: Essays in Honour of F.A. Hayek*, Munich: Philosophia Verlag; reprinted in I.M. Kirzner (1992), *The Meaning of Market Process: Essays in the Development of Modern Austrian Economics*, London, UK and New York, USA: Routledge.

Kirzner, Israel M. (1988), 'The economic calculation debate: lessons for Austrians', reprinted in I.M. Kirzner (1992), *The Meaning of Market Process: Essays in the Development of Modern Austrian Economics*, London, UK and New York, USA: Routledge.

Koppl, Roger G. (2002), *Big Players and the Economic Theory of Expectations*, Basingstoke: Palgrave.

Lachmann, Ludwig M. (1970), *The Legacy of Max Weber*, London: Heinemann.

Lachmann, Ludwig M. (1976), 'From Mises to Shackle: an essay on Austrian economics and the kaleidic society', reprinted in Don Lavoie (ed.), *Expectations and the Meaning of Institutions: Essays in Economics by Ludwig Lachmann* (1994), London, UK and New York, USA: Routledge.

Lachmann, Ludwig M. (1986), *The Market as an Economic Process*, Oxford: Basil Blackwell.

Lange-von Kulessa, Juergen (1997), 'Searching for a methodological synthesis: Hayek's individualism in the light of recent holistic criticism', *Journal of Economic Methodology*, 4 (2), 267–87.

Lawson, Tony (1997), *Economics and Reality*, London, UK and New York, USA: Routledge.

Lewis, Paul A. (2000), 'Realism, causation and the problem of social structure', *Journal for the Theory of Social Behaviour*, 30 (3), 249–68.

Lewis, Paul A. (2005), 'Agency, structure and causality in Austrian economics: tensions and resolutions', *Review of Political Economy*, 17 (2), 291–316.

Lewis, Paul A. (2011), 'Far from a Nihilistic Crowd: Lavoie and Lachmann's theoretical contribution', *Review of Austrian Economics*, 24, 185–98.

Lewis, Paul A. (2012), 'Emergent properties in the work of Friedrich Hayek', *Journal of Economic Behavior and Organization*, 82 (2–3), 368–78.

Lewis, Paul A. (2013), 'On Hayek, social theory and the contrastive explanation of social order', *Critical Review*, 25 (3–4), 1–23.

Lewis, Paul A. (2014). 'Notions of order and process in Hayek: The significance of emergence', Forthcoming in the *Cambridge Journal of Economics*.

Lewis, Paul A. and Jochen Runde (2007), 'Subjectivism, social structures and the possibility of socio-economic order', *Journal of Economic Behavior and Organization*, 62, 167–86.

Lipton, Peter (1991), *Inference to the Best Explanation*, London: Routledge.

Mayer, Hans (1932) 'The cognitive value of functional theories of price', reprinted in Israel M. Kirzner (ed.) (1994), *Classics in Austrian Economics: A Sampling in the History of a Tradition, Volume II: The Interwar Period*, London: William Pickering.

Oakeshott, Michael J. (1983), 'The rule of law', *On History*, Oxford: Basil Blackwell.

Polanyi, Michael (1951), *The Logic of Liberty*, Chicago, IL: University of Chicago Press.

Rizzo, Mario J. (1990), 'Hayek's four tendencies toward equilibrium', *Cultural Dynamics*, 3 (1), 12–31.
Runde, Jochen H. (2001), 'Bringing social structure back into economics: on critical realism and Hayek's *scientism* essay', *Review of Austrian Economics*, 14 (1), 5–24.
Sciabarra, Chris M. (1995), *Marx, Hayek, and Utopia*, Albany: State University of New York Press.
Thomsen, Esteban F. (1992), *Prices and Knowledge: A Market Process Perspective*, London, UK and New York, USA: Routledge.
Vanberg, Victor (1986), 'Spontaneous market order and social rules: a critical examination of F.A. Hayek's theory of cultural evolution', *Economics and Philosophy*, 2 (1), 75–100.
Vaughn, Karen I. (1999), 'Hayek's implicit economics: rules and the problem of order', *Review of Austrian Economics*, 11 (1–2), 128–44.

10. Hayek and spontaneous order
Craig Smith

When one discusses political philosophy with an informed, but non-expert, layperson, it is usual to find that they associate particular thinkers with a key term or concept that they have picked up from their general reading. Mention Rawls and the 'veil of ignorance' may be referenced; cite Nozick and something about 'Wilt Chamberlain' will likely be mumbled back; mention Hayek and there is a good chance that the phrase 'spontaneous order' will pop up. Hayek's association with the idea of spontaneous order is well deserved as he is the most significant theoretical exponent of the idea in modern times. The aim of this chapter is to examine the central role that the idea of spontaneous order plays in shaping Hayek's theoretical approach to social science and social theory in general. Hayek once stated that, during his career, he had made one discovery ('the approach of the utilization of dispersed knowledge') and two inventions (the 'denationalization of money' and his 'system of democracy') (Caldwell, 2004, p. 206). However, on examining the body of his work, it becomes clear that the guiding concepts behind his various research projects and his inventions and discovery are the 'twin ideas of evolution and the spontaneous formation of order' (Hayek, [1978] 1984a, p. 177). So pervasive is the idea of spontaneous order in Hayek's work, and so profitably did he explore its implications, that it is no exaggeration to say that it forms the spine of his life's work. The aim of the present chapter is to examine Hayek's treatment of spontaneous order as it develops through the body of his work. In order to begin my examination I should start by saying something about the pedigree of the idea.

HISTORICAL ORIGINS

There appear to be two distinct strains of development of the idea of spontaneous order that run, respectively, through Austrian economics and Scottish moral philosophy.[1] The first strain of spontaneous order thought emerges in the moral philosophy of the Scottish Enlightenment. For the sake of clarity it is perhaps best, as Hayek does, to trace the notion to the work of Bernard Mandeville. Mandeville's exposition of the concept of unintended consequences in *The Fable of the Bees* famously examined the notion that 'private vices' can produce 'publick benefits' (Mandeville, [1732] 1988, p. 1). The idea that beneficial social outcomes can be produced as a result of the interaction of individuals pursuing their own ends proved to be highly controversial. This was chiefly because of the language of 'vice' in which Mandeville framed his argument. His critics, such as Francis Hutcheson, attacked the idea that vice can produce beneficial outcomes; however they took on board the idea that the outcome of social interaction may be something that no one actor intended. From Mandeville and Hutcheson the notion of the unintended generation of social order can be traced in the work of all of the major theorists of the Scottish Enlightenment. Hume's theory of property and justice is conducted against the backdrop of an appreciation that social-level phenomena are the result of individual-level adjustments that become codified through habit and custom. While Adam Ferguson famously noted, in a passage often cited by Hayek, that: 'Every step and every movement of the multitude, even in what are termed enlightened ages, are made with equal blindness to the future; and nations stumble upon establishments, which are indeed the result of human action, but not the execution of any human design' (Ferguson, [1767] 1995, p. 119). Most famously though, the theory found expression in the work of Adam Smith ([1776] 1981) through his theory of the evolution of common moral rules from 'sympathy' and his examination of the operation of a commercial society. From Smith onwards the idea of spontaneous order became associated with the 'invisible hand'. For Smith the invisible hand provides a metaphor for the non-deliberative generation of order in society. In other words, on the macro-level social orders arise that are the product, or unintended consequence, of the micro-level actions of individuals.

This Scottish take on spontaneous order was continued and developed through three distinct paths in the nineteenth century. The classical economists, notably Jean-Baptiste Say, developed Smith's economic approach and explored the internal operation of a commercial society and the concept of entrepreneurship in an attempt to elucidate the operation of the invisible hand. The notion of evolved social institutions was continued through the influence of Burke's writings, and the idea of evolution was picked up by Darwin and applied to natural science before being re-imported to the social sciences by Herbert Spencer. Hayek was keen to note though that he felt Spencer's development of the tradition of thought was misplaced. Hayek rejected 'social Darwinism' because he believed that it implied an individual-level survival-of-the-fittest principle in economic competition. Partly as a result of this unfortunate eugenic diversion, and partly as a result of its misplaced association with 'naïve' progressive theories, the idea of unintended order passed out of favor in moral philosophy, living on only in the economic thought of the Austrian school. The Scottish tradition of moral philosophy provides a social theory that accounts for social order and institutions in terms of a gradual evolution conducted through the medium of the interaction of individuals pursuing their own ends in the circumstances in which they find themselves.

The second strain of spontaneous order argument is developed in the field of Austrian economics. The Austrians' contribution to the development of spontaneous order thought lies chiefly in their introduction of a subjective theory of value in economics. While Smith and the Scots appeared to accept that 'objective' social institutions were the result of a process of inter-subjective development, they did not go so far as to apply this systematically to the notion of value. Where Smith continued to propagate the idea of some objective measure of value (in labor) he proved an influence on Marx's economic theories. The Austrians, on the other hand, developed a more fully subjectivist approach that viewed the only accurate measure of value to be market prices that reflected the inter-subjective valuation of goods.[2]

The theory of order presented in the economic writings of the Austrians obviously influenced Hayek's technical economic theory through the idea that social orders, such as prices, can be generated in an unintended manner. The most developed Austrian statement on the methodological significance of the spontaneous generation of order is to be found in Carl Menger's writings.[3] Here Menger advances a theory that seeks to account for the origins of social institutions through understanding them as the unintended consequences of human action. He set himself the question: 'How can it be that institutions which serve the common welfare and are extremely significant for its development come into being without a common will directed towards establishing them?' (Menger, [1963] 1996, p. 124).

Outside of Austrian circles the idea of spontaneous order remained in something of a malaise throughout the early twentieth century. However, it was at this time that Hayek was absorbing the ideas of Menger and Mises and familiarizing himself with the tradition of moral philosophy that had developed from the Scottish Enlightenment. It was only in the second half of the twentieth century, with the writings of Hayek and his contemporary Michael Polanyi, that the tradition of spontaneous order thought was revived in mainstream social theory. Hayek's accomplishment was to devote serious attention to the development of both the Scottish and the Austrian strains of spontaneous order thought, bringing them together in a comprehensive approach to the study of social institutions.[4] Before going further though, it is necessary to pause and consider precisely what we understand by the term 'spontaneous order'.

WHAT'S IN A NAME?

The term 'spontaneous order' applies to a body of social theory that has developed concerning the unintended generation of order in society. The first use of the term appears to be in Michael Polanyi's 1951 essay 'Manageability of social tasks' (Jacobs, 1998, p. 19), though Polanyi had used similar terms in his earlier, 1941, essay 'The growth of thought in society'. Spontaneity is used here to identify a particular way in which order may emerge. Indeed it is interesting to note that Hayek's technical definition of order in *Law, Legislation and Liberty* is deliberately couched in neutral language to stress that there are a number of ways in which order may arise. He defines an order as: 'a state of affairs in which a multiplicity of elements of various kinds are so related to each other that we may learn from our acquaintance with some spatial or temporal part of the whole to form correct expectations concerning the rest, or at least expectations which have a good chance of proving correct' (Hayek, [1982] 1993, vol. 1, p. 36).[5] Hayek wants to avoid the intellectual error of identifying order as something that must be imposed from without.

Hayek and Polanyi adopted the term 'spontaneous order' because it distinguished exogenously imposed orders from endogenously generated orders. That is, spontaneous, or endogenous, order is that type of order which was not deliberately, externally imposed, but rather which developed from the mutual adjustment of individual particles reacting to common circumstances. Spontaneous order is order that has not been deliberately designed but rather which has emerged from a process of mutual adjustment. A crude example of the distinction noted here would be between a machine designed by an engineer and a biological organism produced as a result of a process of evolution.[6] Hayek would later admit that the term 'spontaneous' is not without ambiguity and instead would offer the terms 'self-generating order' and 'self-organizing structures' (Hayek, [1982] 1993, vol. 1, p. 37) as more precise alternatives. Despite this, 'spontaneous' is the term that has stuck in the critical discourse and Hayek himself continued to use it out of 'conveniency' (Hayek, [1982] 1993, vol. 1, p. 37).

One of Hayek's favorite examples of spontaneous order is the formation of crystals, and this is instructive because it offers a glimpse at the key elements of spontaneously generated order. Crystals are formed by the mutual adjustment of individual particles during a particular chemical reaction. The particles follow a series of identifiable general rules in a specific set of circumstances (the chemical reaction); however the precise form of the individual crystal is determined not by the rules, but rather by the reaction of the particles to these rules and to each other. As Hayek observes: 'the important point is that the regularity of the conduct of the elements will determine the general character of the resulting order but not all the detail of its particular manifestation' (Hayek, [1982] 1993, vol. 1, p. 40). While it is possible for us to predict the formation of a crystal with certain characteristics in a particular set of circumstances, and even for us to arrange the occurrence of those circumstances, it is impossible for us to foresee the precise form of that crystal down to the position of each individual particle. Spontaneous orders are not externally imposed plans, but rather represent patterns that develop from internal adjustment. We see in this example the key elements of a spontaneous order explanation. An order is formed by the mutual adjustment of individual particles following general rules in specific circumstances. The order cannot be predicted in a precise manner, because it is the result of mutual adjustment by individual particles in reaction to each other, but we are able to identify the rules that are followed and are thus able to predict that a particular pattern (a crystal) will form. Why this should be significant will become obvious when we consider that Hayek believed that human social order is largely a product of spontaneous ordering, and that this had profound methodological consequences for the social sciences.

The care with which Hayek sets down his understanding of spontaneous order reveals that he views it as the basis of a particular 'approach' to understanding the development of order. His work is characterized by a series of attempts to apply the approach to social phenomena and through these applications to develop a clearer understanding of the concept itself. As has been widely noted by critics, Hayek regards spontaneous order as 'a methodological tool rather than an ethical postulate' (Gissurarson, 1987, p. 42), or as a 'value-free explanatory system' (Gray, 1986, pp. 119–20). This fits with the view that Hayek's social theory approaches political philosophy in a particular manner. Kley has argued that Hayek develops a 'distinct body of descriptive and explanatory theory' (Kley, 1994, p. 3); and this explanatory theory is characterized throughout by its reliance on the idea of spontaneous order. In other words Hayek's interest in spontaneously generated orders shapes both his research agenda and his mode of argumentation.

SPONTANEOUS ORDER AND CRITICISM

Hayek's interest in the idea of spontaneous order began to develop in his early work on technical economics. Inspired by the writings of the Austrian school, Hayek's early work is characterized by an interest in monetary theory and the business cycle. Though the idea of spontaneous order does not appear in an explicit form in this technical economic work, its influence is nonetheless apparent in some of the concerns that Hayek expressed with regards to the concept of static equilibrium. From the late 1920s through to the early 1940s Hayek produced a series of books and articles on technical economics that display a growing ambivalence about the practical and theoretical value of the concept of static equilibrium for the understanding of complex market economies.

While accepting that the notion of equilibrium was a useful conceptual tool, Hayek was concerned that it failed accurately to account for economic models that included money and, moreover, that a static equilibrium model failed as an explanatory device when time became a factor in the process of production. These doubts about the explanatory potential of static equilibrium models were further developed when he began to consider the central role of knowledge in economic processes. When Hayek developed his 'discovery' of the division of knowledge he became increasingly skeptical about the explanatory use of static models that assumed perfect knowledge on the part of the actors involved. Indeed he moved towards the position that the accurate analysis of market economies demanded recognition of the role of trade and prices in the coordination of dispersed knowledge through mutual adjustment. This central economic phenomenon was excluded from models based on static equilibrium, rendering them misleading when applied to real economies precisely because they ignored the process of spontaneous ordering that lies at the heart of market economies. The notion of static equilibrium becomes an abstract model of explanation that is useful for the study of idealized situations – in effect it provides what Hayek would later come to refer to as an explanation of the 'principle' – but when applied to complex monetary economies carried out over time and under conditions of imperfect knowledge, it loses much of its explanatory force.

What we see in this technical economic work are the beginnings of Hayek's concerns with the position of the abstract explanation of complex phenomena in the social sciences. As he moves towards his 'discovery' of the significance of dispersed knowledge he increasingly moves away from technical economics and towards social and political theory. This is not to say that Hayek rejected the study of technical economics, for he maintained an interest in it throughout his career, but rather that as he became more aware of the significance of the concept of spontaneous order his attention was drawn to explaining the development of the social institutions that make the coordination of economic behavior possible.

Hayek first begins to develop the spontaneous order approach in his critical examination of what he regards as an erroneous approach to the study of social phenomena.[7] Hayek deploys the term 'constructivist rationalism' to describe the common errors that have plagued many of the social sciences since their development. The main error ascribed to this school of thought is precisely that it neglects the role played by spontaneous orders in social interaction. He refers to constructivist rationalism as 'the innocent sounding formula that, since man has himself created the institutions of society and civilization, he must also be able to alter them at will so as to satisfy his desires or wishes' (Hayek, [1982] 1993, vol. 1, p. 59). Hayek's response to this is not to argue against the moral imperatives that drive the projected reforms of the constructivist rationalists; rather he wishes to stress that the attitude embodies a factual error about the nature of society and social institutions.

The factual error takes the form of an anthropomorphic fallacy and is traced by Hayek to a confusion in thought that has persisted since ancient Greece. The dichotomy drawn between *physei* (by nature) on the one hand, and *nomo* (by convention) or *thesei* (by deliberate design) on the other, has misled many of those operating in the social sciences (Hayek, [1982] 1993, vol. 1, p. 20). Constructivist rationalism is responsible for perpetuating a crude dichotomy that conflates *nomo* and *thesei* in such a way as to regard what is not 'natural' as being necessarily the product of deliberate human design. This conflation is an intellectual error that ignores the category of spontaneous order and leads to an excessive focus on deliberative human design as a mode of explanation in social science. This attitude is compounded by a related tendency to view the products of deliberate design as being superior, or more rational, and therefore more desirable than the products of convention. This leads to the 'hubris of reason' (Hayek, [1982] 1993, vol. 1, p. 33): the belief that society is a deliberate rational construction that can and should be deliberately and rationally reconstructed. For Hayek this is an intellectual error of staggering proportions and one that finds its practical manifestation in the politics of socialism.

Hayek draws on the tradition of spontaneous order thought and credits the Scottish Enlightenment with being the first group of thinkers to take seriously the distinction between *nomo* and *thesei* (Hayek, 1967, p. 97). By this understanding the social is a product of human action, but not necessarily a product of human design. With this view in place Hayek's criticism of constructivist rationalism and socialism are set in a wider dispute about the methodology of social science. Hayek's development of his 'discovery' of the role of knowledge in a market society is combined with an understanding of social order that is grounded in the spontaneous order approach. His 'discovery' that human knowledge is dispersed among individuals in a manner that precludes its centralization is combined with the insight that the institutions that have been developed to deal with dispersed knowledge rely on mutual adjustment and spontaneous ordering for their success. Thus the 'synoptic delusion' – 'the fiction that all the relevant facts are known to some one mind, and that it is possible to construct from this knowledge of the particulars a desirable social order' (Hayek, [1982] 1993, vol. 1, p. 14) – is the characteristic error of socialism. The root of this factual error is as much a failure to appreciate the spontaneous development of order in society as it is a failure to comprehend the role of market prices. As a result the socialist calculation debate, in which Hayek participated on the 'Austrian' side, is not a debate over moral value systems; it is a debate about the practical ability of constructivist rationalism and socialism to attain their stated goals. If the spontaneous order, subjectivist approach to social science is a more accurate model for understanding social formations, and if Hayek and the Austrians are right about the knowledge transferral role of the price system, then socialism will fail to deliver on its promises.

In his later work Hayek extends this methodological critique into political philosophy when he comes to consider the idea of social justice. If the extended order of society is the product of unintended consequences and is correctly to be understood as a macro-level spontaneous order, then it becomes 'meaningless' (Hayek, [1982] 1993, vol. 2, p. 103) to attribute to society the human value of justice. This is simply an extension of the anthropomorphic error of constructivist rationalism. If a social order is not the product of the deliberate actions of human minds, but is rather a spontaneous order created by the mutual interaction and adjustment of a vast number of individuals, then the term 'justice' cannot apply to the end result. Without an actor to whom we may attribute responsibility, the term 'justice' is rendered little more than a confusing political slogan. Hayek notes the irony that it is possible to refer to justice in the end results of a planned economy. Here responsibility can be attributed to the planner who issues commands, and as a result the end state can be considered in terms of justice. Social justice is a concept that can only meaningfully be understood in a planned economy; but this is not because planned economies are superior to market economies in attaining it, rather it is because planned and market economies are conceptually distinct from each other just as designed orders and spontaneous orders are distinct from each other. This insight leads to the view that justice can only be meaningfully understood as a procedural principle in societies that operate through mutual interaction under general rules. The actions of individuals may be adjudged to be just or unjust in reference to general rules, but the macro-level final outcomes are the product of no one individual will and, as a result, cannot be considered in terms of justice.

SPONTANEOUS ORDER IN PSYCHOLOGY AND SCIENCE

Having developed the basis of the spontaneous order approach in his critical engagement with socialist planning and constructivist rationalism, what was then required was to add some positive flesh to the critically developed bones of the approach. If constructivist rationalism is mistaken, then clearly what is required is a new understanding of the nature of science and social science. Hayek's attempt to provide such a theory is permeated by the idea of spontaneous order. The fleshing out of the spontaneous order approach begins in Hayek's psychological work published as *The Sensory Order*. Without delving into too much detail, it is possible to discern the theme of spontaneous order in the basis of the theory that Hayek developed from his early student essays on psychology. For Hayek the human mind is an order of regularity derived from the classification and comparison of sensory perceptions. Human understanding is characterized by the development of mental 'maps' and 'models' (Hayek, [1952] 1976, p. 115, 179) that develop into a neural order. The mind classifies experience through comparison and the mental 'maps' that are created as a result of this process produce a complex, self-ordering system that constitutes human consciousness. The neural impulses that operate in the human mind provide a series of interdependent connections and comparisons that constitute a form of spontaneous order.

Hayek extends this model of human mental order into his theory of the nature of science. Scientific enquiry is a formalization of the process that is carried on in the subconscious operations of the human mind. It is the conscious pursuit of the process of classification, the refinement of the 'maps' of the mind, aimed at clarifying human understanding. As Hayek puts it:

> Science consists in a constant search for new classes, for 'constructs' which are so defined that general propositions about the behaviour of their elements are universally and necessarily true. For this purpose these classes cannot be defined in terms of sensory properties of the particular individual events perceived by the individual person; they must be defined in terms of their relations to other individual events. (Hayek, [1952] 1976, p. 174)

This approach to the psychology of science lends itself, in Hayek's view, to a Popperian, hypothetico-deductive or evolutionary approach to science.[8] The pursuit of science is about the refinement of knowledge that advances in such a way as to develop and discard theories concerning the mental models. The human mind, and by extension scientific enquiry, are orders of classification where a regularity of neural impulses is affected by regularities in external phenomena discerned from comparative observation. The mind and science are understood through the lens of spontaneous order.

Towards the end of his career Hayek extended this view when he argued that the human mind and reason were products of a process of cultural evolution. Socialized individuals developed human rationality at the same time as they developed other social institutions. For Hayek it is a mistake to regard social institutions as the product of human rationality, and it is far more accurate to say that the human mind and rationality develop in tandem with the evolution of other cultural factors. Hayek denied that this represented a rejection of the value of human rationality. He argued that 'reason properly used' (Hayek, 1988, p. 8) is 'not an abdication of reason but a rational examination of the field where reason is appropriately put in control' (Hayek, 1960, p. 69). By understanding the limits and nature of human reason we will be able to make more effective use of it. If the purpose of science is to clarify the mental maps of human understanding through the careful use of reason, then the purpose of social science is to achieve this clarity with regards to social phenomena.

SPONTANEOUS ORDER AND METHODOLOGY

Throughout his career Hayek attempted to refine his methodological views in the light of his appreciation of the idea of spontaneous order. One dimension of this is his attachment to a version of methodological individualism.[9] He develops this attachment from his 'discovery' about the role of the division or dispersal of knowledge through society. As Hayek notes:

> the concrete knowledge which guides the action of any group of people never exists as a consistent and coherent body. It only exists in the dispersed, incomplete, and inconsistent form in which it appears in many individual minds, and the dispersion and imperfection of all knowledge are two of the basic facts from which the social sciences have to start. (Hayek, [1952] 1979, p. 50)

For Hayek the social sciences are concerned with individuals and the ideas and opinions which they possess and which shape their actions (Hayek, [1952] 1979, p. 64). This point of view does not take the extreme view that individuals are detached atoms, nor does it deny that individuals associate in social groupings. What it does do is note that social groupings are not objective 'facts' in any real sense. The subject matter of many of the social sciences is subjective rather than objective. The point of this assertion is to stress that the starting point of enquiry about social phenomena should be on the level of the behavior of the individual. Social phenomena are the product of an 'inter-individual' process (Hayek, [1952]

1979, p. 152). As a result of this the mental categories that we make use of to understand social phenomena are constructed from the actions and opinions of the individuals that compose them. They are not 'real' or objective entities, but rather they are theories about opinions held by individuals.[10]

The 'truly social' (Hayek, [1948] 1984, p. 134–5) institutions are those that are the product of a process of unintended consequences. As Hayek puts it:

> The problems which they [the social sciences] try to answer arise only insofar as the conscious action of many men produce undesigned results, insofar as regularities are observed which are not the result of anybody's design. If social phenomena showed no order except insofar as they were consciously designed, there would indeed be no room for theoretical sciences of society and there would be, as is often argued, only problems of psychology. It is only insofar as some sort of order arises as a result of individual action but without being designed by any individual that a problem is raised which demands a theoretical explanation. (Hayek, [1952] 1979, p. 68–9)

This observation, which Hayek draws from Menger, is actually startlingly obvious when considered coolly. If, as constructivist rationalists argue, an individual designs something in a deliberate, rational manner, then it is simple to explain. They made it. If, however, something is the product of human interaction but not of human design, if it is genuinely a 'social' formation, then constructivist rationalism must be a defective approach to its explanation. True social science, in the sense of the examination of complex macro-level social formations and beliefs, is the study of the unintended consequences of the actions of individual humans. For example, language cannot meaningfully be understood as a deliberate construction of a single human mind. As a social phenomenon it can only properly be appreciated as having resulted from the interaction of individuals striving to communicate. Thus an explanation of the linguistic features of a particular language only makes sense if they are viewed as the gradual accumulation of the unintended consequences of particular attempts at communication. As a result an explanation of linguistic usage must be based on a process of theorizing about the use of ideas made by individuals in a social context.

The significance of this facet of the spontaneous order approach becomes more succinct when Hayek moves to consider how social science ought properly to be undertaken. The social sciences should proceed according to a subjectivist method that acknowledges the centrality of the role of individuals and their opinions. When social scientists talk of social wholes or categories they must always qualify their assertions by noting that these wholes and categories are themselves theories about individuals interacting to produce unintended consequences. Social phenomena are composed from the actions of individuals. Indeed Hayek uses the term 'compositive social theory' (Hayek, [1952] 1979, p. 151) to describe this approach. Social scientists – and here Hayek delves back into the work of the Scottish Enlightenment on 'conjectural history' (Hayek, [1982] 1993, vol. 3, p. 156) and Menger on social investigation – operate by creating theoretical models that account for social phenomena. These models are not 'facts' (Hayek, [1952] 1979, p. 128) in an objective or physical sense, and we ought not to operate as though they were. As a result the study of truly social phenomena must be undertaken through the development of composite models that account for the regularities of behavior within social formations. However such an approach to the study of society is again limited by the scope of individual human knowledge. As Hayek notes:

> The inevitable imperfection of the human mind becomes here not only the basic datum about the object of explanation but, since it applies no less to the observer, also a limitation on what he can hope to accomplish in his attempt to explain the observed facts. The number of separate variables which in any particular social phenomenon will determine the result of a given change will as a rule be far too large for any human mind to master and manipulate them effectively. In consequence our knowledge of the principle by which these phenomena are produced will rarely if ever enable us to predict the precise result of any concrete situation. (Hayek, [1952] 1979, p. 73–4)

Hayek is keen to distinguish the methodology of compositive social theory from the erroneous approaches of constructivist rationalism. To this end he stresses what he refers to as the difference in 'degrees' of prediction that are associated with each approach. Constructivist rationalists, inspired by positivist science, believed that the scientific credentials of a social science lay in its ability to provide for the precise prediction of the form of social phenomena which could then be used to guide social policy. This manifests itself in a number of ways. For example the approach that Hayek terms 'historicism' is based on the assumption that social science is capable of the accurate prediction of the course of future historical events. This form of prediction claims too much in Hayek's view. Among his arguments against it is the assertion that the vast complexity of social phenomena, and the consequent existence of the unintended consequences of individual actions, precludes detailed predictions of future events because the human mind is incapable of centralizing all of the information necessary to make such a prediction or of foreseeing all of the unintended consequences. While he wishes to stress the significance of what he calls 'pattern' prediction, he is aware that this is prediction of a different degree than that claimed by historicists.

Pattern prediction is intimately related to the spontaneous order approach. It is concerned with identifying 'types' of phenomena that are produced by producing theories about the regularities that govern them. To return to the example of crystals mentioned above: a pattern prediction identifies the regularities that produce a particular type of order in a given set of circumstances. It provides an explanation of the 'principle' involved. Thus we are able to identify the chemical reaction that will produce a certain sort of crystal. However we are not able to predict the precise form that the crystal will take because we cannot anticipate the precise mutual adjustments of individual particles. Pattern predictions arise from theories about the behavior of individual particles that follow certain regularities of behavior. As a result a compositive social theory makes theoretical predictions about the likelihood of the occurrence of types of phenomena by producing explanatory theories that describe the 'principles' or regularities involved.[11] The form of compositive social theories is that they are conditional on a set of regularities. They make no claim as to the inevitability of these circumstances actually occurring (and thus avoid the error of historicism). If we understand the 'principle' that produces a complex 'pattern' we are able to make use of the abstract formulation in our understanding of social phenomena even if it does not allow us precise powers of prediction.

Accurate social science is to be understood as that which advances by the compositive approach. As a result social science should not be expected to be capable of absolute, detailed prediction. In his early writings Hayek believed that this marked a distinction between the methodology of the social sciences and that of the natural sciences. The mistake of the constructivist rationalists, which Hayek termed scientism, was to believe that the methodology of the natural sciences, with its claims of precise foresight and prediction, was applicable to the entirely more complex field of social science. Mesmerized by the success of the natural sciences, these thinkers undertook an erroneous attempt to achieve comparable degrees of prediction in the social sciences. Indeed some took it as a mark of the scientific validity of their work that they were able to provide such predictions. However in his later work, under the influence of Karl Popper, Hayek began to downplay this distinction between the natural and social sciences and to move closer to Popper's view that constructivist rationalism represents a mistaken understanding of the nature of science itself rather than a misapplication of the methodology of the natural to the social sciences. To this end Hayek began to distinguish between simple and complex phenomena as the demarcation line in terms of methodological approach.[12]

The advantage of this shift for Hayek was that he moved from the weaker criticism that constructivist rationalism misapplied scientific methodology to a stronger position that they misapprehended the nature of science itself. This view sits more comfortably with his criticisms of socialism and attempts at social planning. If accurate social prediction, down to the level of accuracy necessary for the efficient planning of a complex society, is an unscientific claim, then socialism's chief vindication is undercut from the start. This clearly connects with the argument about the impossibility of socialist calculation as a result of the impossibility of the centralization of all of the knowledge necessary to direct an entire economy.

APPLICATIONS OF THE SPONTANEOUS ORDER APPROACH

Having refined his spontaneous order approach through his critical and methodological writings, Hayek went on to deploy the approach to the understanding of a broad range of social phenomena. Hayek's social theory is characterized by a focus on the significance of rule-following behavior in the generation of the wider spontaneous social order. He regards the development of moral norms as a process of the non-deliberative pursuit of established regularities drawn from experience and socialization. Social groups develop regularities of behavior that facilitate social interaction and the survival of the species. These rules are formed from the conventional acceptance of mutually adjusted forms of behavior. That is to say, individuals adjust to each other's behavior and repeat these practices gradually forming a system of accepted moral behavior.[13] Morality is an adjustment to the circumstances in which social groups find themselves. As a result moral traditions are plastic to a high degree and evolve or change as the circumstances of the people change. This is not to say that all moral rules are subject to constant change: Hayek was no relativist. Some, such as the prohibition against murder, remain in essence the same, as a result of their importance in facilitating social order. Morality is an evolved spontaneous order that develops over time within a social group. Its rules embody a form of knowledge that allows individuals to interact with each other and to order their expectations and plan their lives in an efficient manner. When such moral rules begin to be codified by judges called upon in cases of dispute we experience the beginnings of law and government. Thus, just as science is the formalization of the way our minds operate, so law develops from formalization of the moral regularities that develop as conventions among individuals.

Social change is best understood as an evolutionary process that occurs when individual changes in belief, brought about by changed circumstances, filter up to the macro-level and change the traditional attitudes of the group. In his later work Hayek attempted to develop this spontaneous order approach to morality into a more ambitious theory of cultural evolution by group selection. In this theory, competition between groups and the efficiency of the order provided by their respective traditions and institutions leads to a process of evolution that favors groups with efficiently functioning orders. The key functional advantage that Hayek identifies here is the stability of expectations created by private property and the rule of law. Clearly delineated property and law, governed by what Hayek calls 'rules of just conduct' (Hayek, [1982] 1993, vol. 2, p. 31), facilitate the interaction of individuals in a smooth manner.[14] This order and stability in turn allows individuals to exploit their individualized knowledge and to maximize their opportunities to attain their individual goals. Thus cultures that develop stable government, law and property facilitate the interests of individuals and allow efficient economic and social interaction. Hayek's arguments about spontaneous order and the division of knowledge come together to provide an instrumental justification of liberal principles. The spontaneous order of society is free to develop because these key regularities of law and property are stable.

One policy implication of this spontaneous order approach to society refers to the role of government. If Hayek's model of social order as a spontaneous order is accurate then we are able to draw certain conclusions about the necessary role of government in the facilitation of the wider social order. The primary role of government must be to provide a stable legal framework that allows the efficient operation of mutual interaction between individuals. This implies that the first task of government is the maintenance of the rule of law, where law is understood as generalized formulations that provide the regularities necessary for the wider order to cohere. Hayek identifies two types of law: 'The use of enforceable generic rules in order to induce the formation of a self-maintaining order and the direction of an organization by command towards particular purposes' (Hayek, [1982] 1993, vol. 2, p. 55). It is clear that his spontaneous order approach, combined with his 'discovery' of the division of knowledge, led him to favor the former as the more efficient mode of macro-level social organization. The gradual refinement of the legal system in line with experience is the most pressing role for government.[15] Consequently, because this role is derived from the need for regularity and the subsequent provision of stable expectations, this implies that cultures that adopt institutions that restrict arbitrary interference with the actions of individuals (whether by government or by other individuals), will be more successful in maintaining an extended order and will have an advantage in the process of cultural evolution. The primary function of the government is to provide the generalized legal framework that allows individuals to pursue their lives and to develop the extended, spontaneous, social order. Hayek uses the metaphor of a gardener to describe the proper function of government. He notes that man will 'have to use what knowledge he can achieve, not to shape the results as the craftsman shapes his handiwork, but rather to cultivate a growth by providing the appropriate environment' (Hayek, [1978] 1984b, p. 276). In other words compositive social science identifies the explanations of principle that can then help guide the actions of government in providing the best general conditions to allow individuals to utilize their own abilities in order to live flourishing lives.

SPONTANEOUS ORDER AND FREEDOM

We have begun to see how Hayek develops the results of his spontaneous order approach to understanding society in such a way as to allow him to draw certain, factual, conclusions about the relative efficiency of social orders. He believed that his theory lent clear support to the institutions of liberalism, markets and freedom. If cultural evolution moves the process of social change in a spontaneous order then it stands to reason that a degree of freedom is necessary in order for individual actors to adapt to changing circumstances. Laws and regularities are required for the social order to cohere, but the development of the wider order in reaction to changing circumstances demands a degree of freedom for adaptation. This is an extension of Hayek's arguments concerning the utilization of human knowledge. Indeed his 'discovery' of the division of knowledge comes together with his spontaneous order approach to provide a strong case for individual freedom. Individual actors must be given scope to make the most efficient use of their own local stocks of knowledge within the spontaneous order of society. As Hayek puts it, each individual must be 'free to make full use of *his* knowledge and skill, that he must be guided by his concern for the particular things of which *he* knows and for which *he* cares, if he is to make as great a contribution to the common purposes of society as he is capable of making' (Hayek, [1948] 1984, p. 140).

The spontaneous order of society is a framework that facilitates the attainment of individual goals. It allows the efficient coordination and exploitation of knowledge dispersed among individuals. Hayek's defence of the market through the significance of knowledge in the economy is vitally connected to his adoption of a spontaneous order approach to social explanation. Freedom is instrumentally justified as an organizational principle that allows the development of spontaneous orders that facilitate social and material progress. As a result the conclusion of Hayek's spontaneous order approach to social analysis is that it can be construed as a defence of the liberal market order from factual arguments about the nature of society.[16]

TWIN CONCEPTS

Thus far we have seen how Hayek draws on the traditions of spontaneous order expounded by the Scottish Enlightenment and the Austrian economists to develop a spontaneous order approach to social theory. Throughout Hayek stresses the vital importance of the 'twin' concepts of spontaneous order and evolution. The close link that Hayek draws between these two concepts is underlined by his claim that:

> It makes no difference for our present purpose whether the process extends over a long period of time, as it does in such cases as the evolution of money or the formation of language, or whether it is a process which is constantly repeated anew, as in the case of the formation of prices or the direction of production under competition. (Hayek, [1952] 1979, pp. 71–2)

However a number of commentators have noted that Hayek might be making a conceptual error by running the 'twin' concepts together. Norman Barry summarizes the problem by noting that Hayek appears to conflate two meanings of spontaneous order. Namely 'a complex aggregate structure which is formed out of the uncoerced actions of individuals' as opposed to 'the *evolutionary growth* of laws and institutions through a kind of Darwinian "survival of the fittest" process' (Barry, 1982, p. 11,).[17] Another way of viewing this is that Hayek fails to make sufficient distinction between explanations of the emergence of an order and explanations of the endurance of that order.[18] The basic point is that there are important conceptual differences between the formation of a spontaneous order and its subsequent evolution through a form of natural selection. Hayek's failure to appreciate the significance of this distinction is more than likely a result of the 'sketchy and unfinished' (Witt, 1994, p. 187) nature of his later work on cultural evolution. However it need not pose too serious an issue so long as we note that Hayek's claim was that the concepts are 'twins', and we recall that, as with all twins, they need not be identical and one is always born before the other. Thus what emerges from an original mutual adjustment may change gradually over time in reaction to changing conditions through a process best described as evolutionary adaptation.

There are however several more significant problems with Hayek's attempts to extend the spontaneous order approach into a theory of cultural evolution. The first of these is the controversial position of theories of group selection in general. For example there is the very real problem of explaining how rules that encourage group survival come to be favored by individuals. In terms of social practices it is perfectly possible that rules which encourage group survival are not necessarily the same as those that bring benefits to specific individuals (the free-rider problem is perhaps the clearest example of this).[19] But more importantly there appear to be difficulties about reconciling group selection with Hayek's commitment to a version of methodological individualism.[20] Group selection explanations are clearly holistic in manner and in order to fit them comfortably within the tenor of the rest of Hayek's spontaneous order approach would require a significant amount of work on the theoretical link between the individual mutual adjustments and the group-level outcomes. Perhaps, as Jeremy Shearmur (1996) has suggested, this unfinished work of Hayek's should serve as the foundations of a future research project that seeks to refine the spontaneous order approach.

There remain two further significant problems with the 'twin' concepts in respect of their relationship to the liberal conclusions that Hayek seeks to draw from his spontaneous order approach. First, there is nothing in Hayek's theory of cultural evolution that necessarily leads to liberal outcomes.[21] As a description of a process of social change, the liberal conclusions that Hayek draws rely mainly on his 'discovery' of the division of knowledge for the strength of their instrumental justification of individual freedom. However the process of the natural selection of institutions is descriptive and cannot make claims about the environmental characteristics that will shape the course of adaptations. More dangerously for the 'twinning' of spontaneous order and evolution is the point that it is perfectly plausible that rationally designed rules may prove more efficient at facilitating the formation of spontaneous orders than those that have evolved through cultural evolution.[22] In order to respond to both of these criticisms Hayek would be forced to fall back on his arguments about the dispersed and imperfect nature of human knowledge and the dangers of social engineering. However, as I have noted, though Hayek often attaches his arguments about knowledge to his spontaneous order approach, it is the knowledge arguments that do most of the 'work' in the attachment of liberal conclusions to the spontaneous order approach. This aside, the spontaneous order approach that Hayek refined throughout his career stands as an innovative methodological approach to theoretical social science.

CONCLUSION

By now it will be sufficiently obvious that the spontaneous order approach characterizes the basis of Hayek's research in a broad variety of fields throughout his career. By bringing together the ideas of the Scottish Enlightenment with those of Austrian economics Hayek sets the scene for his lifetime's work of elucidating the significance of spontaneous order for the understanding of social phenomena. This development of a conceptual approach suited to the study of social phenomena characterized by divided and dispersed knowledge is perhaps Hayek's greatest legacy, and one that forms the basis of an ongoing project for new generations of social theorists.

NOTES

1. Aside from Hayek's own discussion in the essay 'Dr Bernard Mandeville' the clearest delineation of the development of the idea appears in Norman Barry's 1982 article 'The tradition of spontaneous order'. For a discussion of its development in Scottish moral philosophy see Hamoway (1987) and in Austrian economics see Caldwell (2004). For a discussion of the relationship between Scottish and Austrian approaches to spontaneous order see Smith (2006).
2. The idea of the unintentional generation of order can be seen in the work of the 'School of Salamanca' (Barry, 1982, p. 12; Grice Hutchinson, 1978). The 'Spanish Schoolmen', as Hayek called them (Hayek, [1982] 1993, vol. 1, p. 170 n. 8–9) developed a subjective approach to value that they applied to monetary theory. They appear to be the first group of thinkers to devote attention to the idea that markets operate through self-regulation based on the subjective valuation of goods through prices. This strain of thought displays obvious similarities to the later work of the Austrian school of economics of which Hayek was a part. However it is questionable whether the Schoolmen were a direct inspiration to the Austrians, and more likely that the Austrians developed the idea independently and only later noted the similarity of their ideas to those of their Spanish precursors.
3. Alan Ebenstein quotes Hayek as describing Menger's writings as the most 'beautifully' worked-out version of the spontaneous generation of institutions (Ebenstein, 2003, p. 20).
4. Hayek observed that 'what I told my students was essentially what I had learned from those writers and not what they chiefly thought, which may have been something quite different' and that what he read did not allow him to 'reproduce their thought but altered my own thought' (Hayek, 1978, pp. 52–3). The honesty of this statement largely renders redundant studies that seek to criticize Hayek's appropriation of the work of past thinkers. The model of spontaneous order that Hayek developed was his own and did not depend on the work of his predecessors for the strength of its formulation: the role of the Scots and the Austrians is that of inspirations rather than authorities.
5. It is no accident that Hayek's definition focuses on the informational or knowledge-providing role of orders as his 'discovery' of the division of knowledge is intimately linked to the idea of spontaneous order.
6. Hayek's contemporary at the London School of Economics (LSE), Michael Oakeshott, developed a similar analysis of types of order that he termed 'enterprise association' and 'civil association'. One of the key distinctions drawn by Oakeshott was that enterprise associations are consciously designed to pursue a purpose whereas civil associations have 'no extrinsic substantive purpose' (Oakeshott, [1975] 1990, p. 110). The significance of this observation is that in the case of enterprise association the order aims at some external goal pursued through hierarchical commands while in civil association the only 'purpose' is preservation of the order itself through mutual adherence to generalized rules of behavior.

7. Hayek traces the development of the error to the French Enlightenment and Continental rationalism. He spends considerable time discussing the divergence of this tradition of thought from the other, in his view more accurate, tradition of the Scottish Enlightenment (Hayek, 1960, pp. 54–62).
8. There has been considerable debate about the degree of compatibility between Hayek's and Popper's respective thought. While it seems clear that Hayek came to accept and endorse a great deal of Popper's conclusions on scientific methodology, there remain several points of tension between the two and it is doubtful whether Hayek was ever fully won over to Popper's position on the unity of method between the natural and social sciences. For a discussion of this see Gray (1986, p. 120) and Kley (1994, p. 44).
9. We should be clear here that Hayek did not subscribe to the classical version of methodological individualism. For a discussion of Hayek's formulation of methodological individualism see Caldwell (2004, pp. 283–6).
10. Some have interpreted these comments to indicate that Hayek's thought takes an interpretative or hermeneutic turn. However, as Bruce Caldwell (2004, p. 437) has demonstrated, it is more likely that Hayek retained a commitment to a form of realism that is, in places, obscured by the language he uses to attack the more forceful claims of positivists about the reality of social categories such as class.
11. Another example of pattern prediction that Hayek provides is the Darwinian theory of evolution (Hayek, [1967] 1994, pp. 60–61). According to Hayek, Darwin's theory describes a process that has occurred in natural history but provides us with no specific predictions as to the precise outcomes of future manifestations of the process. This is because the theory of evolution is based on adaptation to changing environmental and biological conditions that cannot be foreseen.
12. For an argument to this effect see Caldwell (2004, pp. 304–6).
13. Galeotti provides an excellent summary of this: 'Hayek's conjectural reconstruction of social spontaneity and rule formation is the following: From casual human interactions in the various spheres of social interchange, patterns emerge unintentionally. Given the human need for rules, there is a tendency to repeat those patterns as a guideline for action in future instances of similar behavior. Then, among the number of spontaneous patterns that emerge in a given community at a given time, the most successful one has a chance to be repeated until it rules out the others' (Galeotti, 1987, p. 171).
14. We should note here that this assertion about the rule of law takes the form of a pattern prediction or 'explanation of the principle' and results from Hayek's compositive social theory.
15. Hayek develops this idea in his 'invention' of a constitutional model that assigns legislation concerning the two different types of law to separate assemblies in order to avoid their conflation.
16. Lessnoff notes how Hayek attempts to draw support for liberal institutions from his theory of social evolution: 'by this stage it is clear that Hayek's social theory is no longer a neutral account of the evolution of human social structures, but is a defence of a particular kind of evolved social structure, one incorporating private property and a market economy' (Lessnoff, 1999, p. 155).
17. The same point is noted by Gissurarson, who refers to the 'co-ordinating consequences of certain traditions' and 'an evolutionary selection of traditions' (Gissurarson, 1987, p. 61), and Kley, who notes that Hayek 'fails to distinguish two fundamentally different types of spontaneous order, orderly patterns of co-operation forming within a given system of rules on the one side, and systems of rules developing in a process of cultural evolution by natural selection on the other' (Kley, 1994, pp. 38–9). Similar doubts are aired by Petsoulas (2001, p. 17), Shearmur (1996, p. 115) and Gray (1986, pp. 33–4).
18. This point is made by Ullmann-Margalit (1978, pp. 275–8), Nozick (1994, p. 314) and Heath (1989, p. 108).
19. This is a criticism of Hayek's group selection developed by Kley (1994, p. 162), Petsoulas (2001, p. 63), Shearmur (1996, pp. 84–5), Gray (1989, p. 247) and Paul (1988, p. 259).

20. See Hodgson (1991, p. 79), Kley (1994, p. 23), Birner (1994) and Gray (1986, pp. 52–4). Although Bruce Caldwell has sought to downplay this issue by noting that Hayek was not a doctrinaire methodological individualist (Caldwell, 2004, pp. 355–6).
21. For this point see Kley (1994, p. 191), Petsoulas (2001, p. 17), Barry (1982, p. 30) and Gray (1986, p. 142).
22. As has been noted by Barry (1982, p. 42), Buchanan (1977, pp. 33, 37) and Rothschild (2001, p. 145).

REFERENCES

Barry, Norman P. (1982), 'The tradition of spontaneous order', *Literature of Liberty* 5 (2), pp. 7–58.
Birner, Jack (1994), 'Hayek's grand research programme', in Jack Birner and Rudy van Zijp (eds), *Hayek, Co-ordination and Evolution: His Legacy in Philosophy, Politics, Economics and the History of Ideas*, London: Routledge, pp. 1–21.
Buchanan, James M. (1977), *Freedom in Constitutional Contract: Perspectives of a Political Economist*, College Station, TX: Texas A&M University Press.
Caldwell, Bruce J. (2004), *Hayek's Challenge: An Intellectual Biography of F.A. Hayek*, London, UK and Chicago, IL, USA: University of Chicago Press.
Ebenstein, Alan (2003), *Hayek's Journey: The Mind of Friedrich Hayek*, Basingstoke, UK and New York, USA: Palgrave Macmillan.
Ferguson, Adam ([1767] 1995), *An Essay on the History of Civil Society*, ed. Fania Oz-Salzberger, Cambridge: Cambridge University Press.
Galeotti, Anna Elisabetta (1987), 'Individualism, social rules, tradition: the case of Friedrich A. Hayek', *Political Theory*, 15 (2), 163–81.
Gissurarson, Hannes H. (1987), *Hayek's Conservative Liberalism*, London: Garland Press.
Gray, John (1986), *Hayek on Liberty*, 2nd edn, Oxford: Basil Blackwell.
Gray, John (1989), *Liberalisms: Essays in Political Philosophy*, London: Routledge.
Hamoway, Ronald (1987), *The Scottish Enlightenment and the Theory of Spontaneous Order*, Carbondale, IL: Southern Illinois University Press.
Hayek, Friedrich A. ([1948] 1980), *Individualism and Economic Order*, Chicago, IL: University of Chicago Press.
Hayek, Friedrich A. ([1948] 1984), 'Individualism: true and false', in Chiaki Nishiyama and Kurt R. Leube (eds), *The Essence of Hayek*, Stanford, CA: Hoover Institution Press, pp. 131–59.
Hayek, Friedrich A. ([1952] 1976), *The Sensory Order*, London: Routledge & Kegan Paul.
Hayek, Friedrich A. ([1952] 1979), *The Counter-Revolution of Science: Studies on the Abuse of Reason*, Indianapolis, IN: Liberty Fund.
Hayek, Friedrich A. (1960), *The Constitution of Liberty*, London: Routledge.
Hayek, Friedrich A. (1967), *Studies in Philosophy, Politics and Economics*, London: Routledge & Kegan Paul.
Hayek, Friedrich A. ([1967] 1994), 'The theory of complex phenomena', in Michael Martin and Lee C. McIntyre (eds), *Readings in the Philosophy of Social Science*, Cambridge, MA: MIT Press, pp. 55–70.
Hayek, Friedrich A. (1978), *New Studies in Philosophy, Politics, Economics and the History of Ideas*, London: Routledge & Kegan Paul.
Hayek, Friedrich A. ([1978] 1984a), 'Dr Bernard Mandeville', in Chiaki Nishiyama and Kurt R. Leube (eds), *The Essence of Hayek*, Stanford, CA: Hoover Institution Press, pp. 176–94.
Hayek, Friedrich A. ([1978] 1984b), 'The pretence of knowledge', in Chiaki Nishiyama and Kurt R. Leube (eds), *The Essence of Hayek*, Stanford, CA: Hoover Institution Press, pp. 266–77.
Hayek, Friedrich A. ([1982] 1993), *Law, Legislation and Liberty*, 3 vols, London: Routledge.

Hayek, Friedrich A. (1988), *The Fatal Conceit: The Errors of Socialism*, ed. William W. Bartley III, London: Routledge.
Heath, Eugene (1989), 'How to understand liberalism as gardening: Galeotti on Hayek', *Political Theory*, 17 (1), pp.107–13.
Hodgson, Geoffrey M. (1991), 'Hayek's theory of cultural evolution: an evaluation in the light of Vanberg's critique', *Economics and Philosophy*, 7 (1), 67–82.
Jacobs, Struan (1998), 'Michael Polanyi and spontaneous order 1941–1951', *Tradition and Discovery: The Polanyi Society Periodical*, 24 (2), 14–28.
Kley, Roland (1994), *Hayek's Social and Political Thought*, Oxford: Clarendon Press.
Lessnoff, Michael H. (1999), *Political Philosophers of the Twentieth Century*, Oxford: Blackwell.
Mandeville, Bernard ([1732] 1988), *The Fable of the Bees or Private Vices, Publick Benefits*, 2 vols, ed. F.B. Kaye, Indianapolis, IN: Liberty Fund.
Menger, Carl ([1963] 1996), *Investigations into the Method of the Social Sciences*, trans. Francis J. Nock, Grove City, PA: Libertarian Press.
Nozick, Robert (1994), 'Invisible-hand explanations', *American Economic Review*, 84 (2), 314–18.
Oakeshott, Michael ([1975] 1990), *On Human Conduct*, Oxford: Clarendon.
Paul, Ellen Frankel (1988), 'Liberalism, unintended orders and evolutionism', *Political Studies*, 36 (2), 251–72.
Petsoulas, Christina (2001), *Hayek's Liberalism and its Origins: His Idea of Spontaneous Order and the Scottish Enlightenment*, London: Routledge.
Polanyi, Michael (1941), 'The growth of thought in society', *Economica*, n.s. 8 (32), 428–46.
Polanyi, Michael (1951), 'The manageability of social tasks', *The Logic of Liberty*, London: Routledge, pp.154–200.
Rothschild, Emma (2001), *Economic Sentiments: Adam Smith, Condorcet, and the Enlightenment*, Cambridge, MA: Harvard University Press.
Shearmur, Jeremy (1996), *Hayek and After: Hayekian Liberalism as a Research Programme*, London: Routledge.
Smith, Adam ([1776] 1981), *An Inquiry into the Nature and Causes of the Wealth of Nations*, Roy Harold Campbell, Anthony S. Skinner and William B. Todd (eds), Indianapolis, IN: Liberty Fund.
Smith, Craig (2006), *Adam Smith's Political Philosophy: The Invisible Hand and Spontaneous Order*, London: Routledge.
Ullmann-Margalit, Edna (1978), 'Invisible-hand explanations', *Synthese*, 39, 263–91.
Witt, Ulrich (1994), 'The theory of societal evolution: Hayek's unfinished legacy', in Jack Birner and Rudy van Zijp (eds), *Hayek, Co-ordination and Evolution: His Legacy in Philosophy, Politics, Economics and the History of Ideas*, London: Routledge, pp.178–89.

11. Hayek on socialism
Mark Pennington

INTRODUCTION

In his *Friedrich Hayek: A Biography*, Alan Ebenstein (2001) describes the Austrian economist as the greatest 'anti-socialist' theorist of the twentieth century. This epitaph would doubtless have pleased a man who dedicated *The Road to Serfdom* (Hayek, 1944) to 'the Socialists of all Parties' and, in his final book, declared an intention to show that 'socialist aims and programmes are factually impossible to achieve or execute' (Hayek, 1988, p. 7). That such words should emanate from a man praised throughout his career for modesty when dealing with opponents, was testament to the scale of events then about to unfold in Eastern Europe and Hayek's sense of personal vindication after decades of scholarly isolation.

Notwithstanding the recognition that Hayek has achieved in recent years, the significance of his work to contemporary debates continues to be underappreciated and, worse still, misunderstood. In economic theory a raft of arguments justifying all manner of government interventions continue to be forthcoming under the guise of an equilibrium-centred view that Hayek rejected in the 1940s. In political theory and sociology meanwhile, there continues to be a ceaseless stream of assaults against the supposed 'atomism' of individualist philosophy, notwithstanding Hayek's view that the purpose of 'true' individualism was to understand the 'life of man as a social being'. Finally, the determination to put the pursuit of 'social justice' at the heart of public policy continues unabated in spite of Hayek's contention that the term was meaningless in the context of a 'Great' or 'Open' society.

This chapter explores the elements of Hayek's anti-socialism and demonstrates its continued relevance to contemporary debates. The analysis is structured in three sections. The first section examines Hayek's economics and in particular his confrontation with socialist economists in the 'calculation debates' of the 1930s and 1940s. The latter experience led Hayek to develop a far-reaching appreciation of the conditions necessary to generate social coordination and resulted in his sweeping account of societal evolution as an example of 'complex phenomena' or spontaneous order. The second section of the chapter explores the significance of spontaneous order theory in both the economic realm and in Hayek's application of this notion to political and cultural evolution. Finally, the third section turns to Hayek's critique of egalitarianism and the doctrine of social justice. The latter occupied a considerable proportion of Hayek's work towards the end of his life and in many ways constitutes one of the most radical elements of his anti-socialism. Each of the three sections summarizes the essentials of the Hayekian contribution at the time of their writing followed by an assessment of their ongoing relevance in light of contemporary responses from socialists in the fields of economic and political theory.

ANTI-SOCIALIST ECONOMICS: MARKETS, COMPETITION AND THE USE OF KNOWLEDGE IN SOCIETY

If Friedrich Hayek was the twentieth century's greatest anti-socialist theorist then nowhere was the prescience of his anti-socialism more evident than in the 'calculation debates' of the 1930s and 1940s. In the course of these debates Hayek, following his mentor Ludwig von Mises, enunciated a set of principles which demonstrated why a socialist economic system could not possibly hope to achieve an equivalent level of material well-being as a market order based on largely private ownership.

The Socialist Calculation Debate

Hayek's contribution to the socialist calculation debates is contained in the edited collection *Collectivist Economic Planning* (1935) and culminated with a series of articles subsequently printed under the title *Individualism and Economic Order* (1948). The latter contains the essays 'Economics and knowledge', 'The use of knowledge in society' and 'The meaning of competition', which Hayek himself described as his most significant contributions to economic theory (Ebenstein, 2001, p.97). These essays offer the most compelling theoretical explanation for the economic failure of state socialism and continue to throw light on difficulties caused by the milder forms of government interventionism that still prevail today. As will be shown in due course, the full significance of these essays and their radical implications are not properly appreciated, or even understood, by some of the most exalted names in contemporary economics.

Hayek's contribution to the socialist calculation debate is best seen as an enrichment of ideas that were implicit in Mises' famous assertion that it was impossible for a socialist economy to match the productive performance of the market owing to its inability to calculate (Mises, 1920). The

Misesian argument was that in the wake of the abolition of private property exchange, government planners would be unable to make calculations of economic value owing to the absence of relative resource prices. Seen in this light, the economic problem is not merely a 'technical' issue of discovering which goods can be produced under existing technology. Rather, the problem is primarily one of deciding which goods should be produced and how, in light of conflicting individual preferences and a multitude of alternatives for the use of the same production inputs. Without access to market prices for competing inputs and outputs, decision-makers lack the capacity to determine which of all the possible combinations of resource uses should be adopted. According to Mises, such information could be generated only through the exchange of property titles in the means of production, and since market exchange relationships and hence relative prices would be abolished under the classical socialist model, rational calculation of economic value would thus become impossible.

Hayek considered Mises' argument to constitute a decisive objection against socialist theory since it made no assumptions about the motivations of decision-makers. It did not, for example, assume that individuals were insufficiently altruistic and lacking the necessary incentives under socialism, but maintained that in the absence of market prices even the most public-spirited of planners would lack the information to allocate resources in the appropriate way. Nonetheless, Hayek sought to clarify and extend what has become known as the 'Austrian' critique of planning, owing to erroneous implications drawn from the socialist side of the argument.

Initial commentaries on the socialist calculation debate suggested that the proponents of 'market socialism' had refuted Mises' position. Oscar Lange, in particular, conceded Mises' point about the necessity for economic calculation in any social system, but maintained that if the conditions underlying the orthodox neoclassical model pertained, then planners would be able to allocate resources by arriving at an appropriate set of 'accounting prices' (Lange, 1936, 1937). Under conditions of perfect information and perfect competition, where knowledge of production possibilities, consumer preferences and hence relative resource scarcities is objectively given, the same information used by market participants would also be available to government planners. Planners, therefore, could perform the function of the 'Walrasian auctioneer', adjusting prices up or down until equilibrium was achieved. In this manner a socially optimal allocation of resources could be realized by instructing plant managers what to produce and by setting prices so that marginal revenues equalled marginal costs. Indeed, for Lange such procedures would be more efficient than a system based on private property, because 'real-world' markets do not meet the criterion of perfect competition and require the complex paraphernalia of contract which would not be necessary under a government-administered system.

Lange's response to Mises demonstrated the apparently counterintuitive conclusion that the neoclassical economic model, often used to justify market resource allocation, was equally, if not more compatible with support for a planned economy. As Caldwell (2003) has argued, it was this realization that prompted Hayek to recognize how little his own appreciation of the market economy had to do with underlying assumptions that neoclassical economics took for granted.

Hayek on 'Given' Knowledge

Central to Hayek's critique of the neoclassical framework is the assumption of 'given' knowledge underlying the notion of general equilibrium, originally enunciated by Walras and now formally articulated in the so-called Arrow–Debreu model. In making the assumption of objectively 'given' knowledge equilibrium theory fails to address how the relevant knowledge of relative resource scarcities is acquired, and indeed completely ignores the institutional conditions that are capable of bringing about the necessary process of social communication. Rather than explain how different institutional arrangements facilitate or inhibit the transmission of knowledge, according to Hayek neoclassical equilibrium models amount to little more than an 'exercise in pure logic' (Hayek, 1948, p. 45). Thus:

> In the usual presentations of equilibrium analysis it is generally made to appear as if these questions of how the equilibrium comes about were solved. But if we look closer, it soon becomes evident that these apparent demonstrations amount to no more than the apparent proof of what is already assumed. (Hayek, 1948, p. 45)

It was Hayek's contention that the knowledge needed to determine the content of relative resource prices could not be generated as effectively, if at all, by a socialist system of centrally derived accounting prices as it could by a system of private property exchange. There are several dimensions to his critique of the 'given' knowledge assumption in this regard.

First, knowledge of the various facts that contribute to the formation of prices in a free market is not 'given' to any one agency or group in its totality, but is divided among the various actors that make up the market concerned. Individuals and organizations make bids on the basis of knowledge of 'circumstances of time and place', including personal preferences, the availability of substitutes and entrepreneurial innovations, known only to themselves. As they do so, however, they contribute incrementally to the formation of prices, transmitting in coded form their personal 'bit' of information to actors with whom they exchange. The latter may then adapt their own behaviour in light of their own preferences and knowledge, which will inform subsequent market transactions with still other agents, and so on in a network of ever-increasing complexity. What matters is that in order to adjust their production or consumption patterns (substituting more for less expensive alternatives, for example) in response to changes in the relative scarcity of goods, market actors need not know very much about the complex network of events that contributes to a rise or fall in price; what they do need to know is that the price has changed. As Hayek (1948, p. 86) put it, 'The whole acts as one market, not because any of its members survey the whole field, but because their limited individual fields of vision sufficiently overlap so that through many intermediaries the relevant information is communicated to all'.

In Hayek's view, the advantage of market exchange is that it utilizes a complex 'division of knowledge', or what Mises had earlier described as a 'mental division of labor' in the coordination of economic affairs. For a socialist system to achieve an equivalent level of coordination would require that an organized group be aware of all the relevant conditions that affect the changing behaviour of dispersed social actors. The latter is, however, a cognitive impossibility. Government-determined prices will, therefore, fail to reflect the economic conditions facing individuals and organizations and will result in a massive misallocation of resources.

It must be emphasized that the adjustment process that Hayek has in mind is not, as some critics have implied, a mechanical or instantaneous one (e.g. O'Neill, 1998, Ch. 10). Market prices do not act as 'marching orders', telling people how to respond to changing conditions. Rather, they provide an invaluable prompt to 'economizing' behaviour. The information provided by shifting relative prices constitutes a necessary, though by no means sufficient, condition for economic coordination. The specific response of producers and consumers in rearranging their production and consumption bundles will be dependent on other factors, such as gossip with neighbouring actors about new techniques, prices and production processes and the ingenuity of the entrepreneurs concerned in creating alternative resource combinations.

The latter point leads to the second aspect of Hayek's challenge to the notion of 'given' knowledge: the assumption that the 'bits' of information possessed by market agents concerning the plans of those with whom they intend to exchange are necessarily accurate. This assumption is apparent in the notions of perfect information and the idea of a perfect market, which pervade neoclassical models and that frequently lead to demands to 'correct' so-called 'market failures' under conditions where information is deemed not to be perfect. From a Hayekian perspective, such models simply assume away the processes by which individuals and organizations are able to improve the accuracy of their expectations over time.

For Hayek, the primary economic problem is not the one examined by the general equilibrium model. On the contrary, the task of attaining economic coordination occurs under conditions of uncertainty, where information is highly imperfect and often contradictory (Hayek, 1948). It is the subjective and contradictory nature of the relevant 'data' dispersed amongst different market agents that precludes any central attempt (by computer simulation, for example) to replicate the results of private property exchange. Government planners (democratically elected or otherwise) could never set prices reflecting the subjective perceptions of economic opportunities dispersed amongst a myriad of actors who have the freedom to exchange property titles in the market. Only under private ownership can individuals and firms make bids for resources reflective of their own subjective interpretations, and only via the generation of profits and losses can these expectations be tested against the objective facts of other people's behaviour. It is the signals of profit and loss generated by the clash of competing ideas of dispersed market agents that enables trial-and-error learning, as participants imitate the behaviour of the successful and learn not to make the same errors as the unsuccessful.

The third and final element of the Hayekian challenge to neoclassical theory, which is the most radical in its implications, turns to the preferences of market participants. For Hayek, the notion of 'given' knowledge is inappropriate not only because of the possibility of entrepreneurial errors in interpreting the demand for different goods, but also because the content of people's preferences, whether for consumption or for capital goods, is itself subject to dynamic change. Consumers are alerted to and acquire previously unforeseen tastes and organizational practices by the process of market competition itself. The market process, therefore, facilitates learning under conditions of 'radical ignorance' where actors on both the demand and supply sides become aware of information which they previously did not know was in existence. The latter notion is captured in Hayek's claim that participation in markets is akin to a 'voyage of exploration into the unknown' (Hayek, 1948, p. 101). Static notions of equilibrium are, therefore, utterly inappropriate to understanding what is fundamentally an open-ended process of dynamic evolutionary change. For Hayek, what matters is that markets and private property exchange facilitate a more thorough-going process of innovation and evolutionary learning than a socialist system could ever hope to achieve. The decentralized decision-rights provided by private property allow a variety of ideas dispersed across individuals and firms to be tested against one another without the need for approval by any one authority or majority. The most that a hierarchical or majoritarian system can do, by contrast, is to conduct consecutive experiments where there is only one or a very few options being tried out at any time. The scope for evolutionary discovery will, therefore, necessarily be less than in a context of private property exchange.

Hayek's evolutionary view of the market economy also suggests a much wider understanding of what is meant by competition than is envisaged in neoclassical models. Competition in the Hayekian sense is a process that facilitates the ongoing discovery of solutions to unfolding social problems and may occur on multiple different levels. This may include competition between different organizational forms and between different sets of rules to cope with potential externalities and collective-goods problems. Most tellingly, the process of competition is itself the best mechanism for determining how much 'planning' in society there should actually be. As Coase (1937) pointed out, corporate firms are 'planning organizations' that arise when the transaction costs of relying purely on decentralized pricing systems are too high. There comes a point, however, where the cognitive limits of large organizations are breached and where more flexible competitors stand at an advantage. As Coase (1992, p. 716), writing in a distinctly Hayekian vein, subsequently put it, '[to] have an efficient economic system it is necessary not only to have markets, but also areas of planning within organizations of the appropriate size. What this mix should be we find as a result of competition'.

The Hayekian contribution to the socialist calculation debate provides perhaps the most convincing explanation for the relative failure of planned economies in the twentieth century and constitutes the decisive objection to the claim made by neoclassical economists that a socialist system could, even in principle, match the performance of private markets. By equating the case for markets with equilibrium conditions, Oscar Lange and subsequent supporters of 'neoclassical socialism' did not even begin to address the 'Austrian' argument against planning because Hayek rejected the underlying assumptions on which the neoclassical model is based.

Hayekian Economics versus 'New' Market Failure Socialism

The Hayekian critique of the 'given' knowledge postulate highlights the need for a fundamental recasting of the standard against which the success of market institutions should be judged. Specifically, it is mistaken to cite examples of 'market failure' owing to imperfect information or the absence of 'perfect competition', since a world of perfect foresight and equally distributed knowledge cannot exist under any institutional setting. The key question for political economy is to ascertain which institutions are best suited to operate in a world where the assumptions that underlie the neoclassical model simply cannot exist. It is here that the comparative strengths of a market system are revealed. This does not exclude the possibility of genuine 'market failures' that limit the possibility of private property solutions, but at the very least Hayek suggests that the burden of proof should be shifted decisively in the direction of those who favour government intervention.

Notwithstanding the belated credit that Hayek received for his contribution to the socialist calculation debate, the full implications of rejecting the 'given' knowledge assumption continue to be ignored or misunderstood. Some of the most exalted names in the economics profession persist in judging the success of market institutions against a variant of the general equilibrium framework in an attempt to justify new forms of state planning and control. One of the most significant attempts to resurrect the case for 'market socialism' is evident in the rise of the so-called 'new public economics' and the 'new economics of information', as pioneered by the Nobel laureate Joseph Stiglitz.

Whilst offering lip service to Hayek's work on the informational role of prices, Stiglitz and various collaborators contend that, left to their own devices, market processes are informationally 'inefficient' and can be improved upon by an economy-wide programme of government action. Grossman and Stiglitz (1980, 1986), for example, use 'information search models' to contend that private markets lead to the 'underproduction' of information in situations where information is costly to obtain. According to this view, if the market price system works as effectively at distributing information as Hayek maintains, then private actors will lack sufficient incentives to acquire information themselves. Hayekian market prices have collective-goods and prisoner's dilemma attributes, which allow individuals to 'free-ride' on the efforts of other participants by observing prices and obtaining for nothing what would otherwise be costly to acquire. From this Grossman and Stiglitz conclude that markets cannot attain an efficient equilibrium in the absence of supplementary government action.

Stiglitz's contributions to the economics of information earned him a Nobel Prize and yet they completely misconstrue the Hayekian position. According to Stiglitz, the Hayekian account of markets suggests that freely determined prices perform the function posited to them in the general equilibrium framework where price information is equally and instantly accessible to all other participants in the relevant market. At no point in his writings on the 'knowledge problem', however, does Hayek suggest that the price system conveys information in such a manner. Indeed, the core of the Hayekian critique is that by assuming all information is already known, equilibrium models fail to explain the process by which the dispersed 'bits' of information divided amongst market participants are actually brought together.

For Hayek, private markets do their job under conditions that are inevitably characterized by an element of disequilibrium owing to the cognitive limits of the human mind. Competition, therefore, can never be perfect. Knowledge of market discrepancies is dispersed between competitors in a lumpy or uneven manner and is not instantly accessible to all. It is by responding to private knowledge of market discoordination that creative entrepreneurial action prompts a learning process as knowledge of profit opportunities and changes in price data ripples out across the overlapping perspectives of neighbouring market actors. The very essence of the Hayekian argument is that such processes occur incrementally, as reaction takes time and as each entrepreneur or firm in the relevant chain of events differs in assessing and reacting to the new situation and changing data. Stiglitz's claim that all other market actors are able to 'free-ride' on acts of private entrepreneurship is, therefore, completely misplaced. Under conditions of dispersed knowledge and where learning must occur over time, there are always 'first-mover' advantages from acting on private information and hence obtaining larger gains (profits) before competitors are alerted to the newly revealed data. It is precisely this sort of learning procedure that accounts for the greater capacity of private markets to facilitate economic coordination than centrally planned alternatives.

Moreover, as Kirzner (1997) has argued, the notion of 'information search' deployed by Grossman and Stiglitz is not even relevant to the type of 'knowledge problem' that forms the core of the Hayekian argument (see also Boettke, 1997). For Grossman and Stiglitz, profit is conceived merely as a reward for searching out costly information, with problems of 'imperfect' information attributed to a lack of incentives to acquire additional knowledge which is nonetheless 'known' to be available; a problem of 'rational ignorance'. For Hayek, however, the primary function of profit and loss signals is to alert market participants to instances of previously 'unknown' ignorance and to ensure effective adjustment to unforeseen circumstances; a problem of 'radical ignorance', which cannot be analysed in terms of a model of rational search.

It should also be noted that Stiglitz's account of 'market failure', owing to the rational ignorance of market agents, fails even on its own terms to generate an effective argument for widespread government intervention. One of the central tenets of contemporary public choice theory is that whilst market participants rarely have incentives to become 'perfectly' informed, they have considerably more incentives to acquire accurate information than do actors in a social democratic setting (Somin, 1998). Voters, in particular, have precious few incentives to acquire accurate political information because the outputs of the political process necessarily have the character of a collective good. Remarkably, in works such as *Whither Socialism?* (1994), where Stiglitz claims to offer a comparative institutions analysis, he makes only one reference (in a footnote, p. 304) to the work of James Buchanan (himself a Nobel laureate), and none to Gordon Tullock, or to any other writers in the public choice tradition.

Setting aside these theoretical mistakes, the policy conclusions derived from the Stiglitz framework are even more difficult to sustain. The notion that governments can correct for 'market failures' owing to imperfect information by, for example, setting an optimal set of taxes and subsidies, completely avoids the question of how government agencies are to acquire the information necessary to adjust prices in the appropriate direction. Stiglitz and his followers assume that the relevant data are somehow 'given' to planners and are, therefore, guilty of precisely the charges levelled by Hayek against more orthodox versions of neoclassical theory. In short, the case for Stiglitz's version of 'market socialism' fares little better in the face of the Hayekian knowledge problem than the original contribution of Oscar Lange in the socialist calculation debates.

ANTI-SOCIALIST POLITICS: SPONTANEOUS ORDER AND THE LIMITS TO REASON

The failure of contemporary economists to recognize the limited applicability of the general equilibrium framework as an institutional benchmark mirrors the reluctance of economists in the 1940s to recognize the significance of the 'knowledge problem'. It was this very reluctance by the mainstream of economic theory that prompted Hayek to effectively abandon the discipline and to turn instead to the development of a much wider social theory which could account for the discovery and communication of knowledge. The result was his sweeping account of the role of 'spontaneous order', not only in the economic realm, but also as the driving force behind moral, cultural and political evolution.

The emphasis on the significance of spontaneous order was already apparent in the 1940s, most notably in the essay 'Individualism: true and false', where Hayek noted that, 'the spontaneous collaboration of free men often creates things greater than their individual minds can fully comprehend' (1948, p. 7). It was not, however, until *The Constitution of Liberty* in 1960 and a variety of essays written during the 1950s and 1960s that

Hayek began to refer explicitly to the term 'spontaneous order' per se. The three-volume treatise *Law, Legislation and Liberty* (1982) and Hayek's last work *The Fatal Conceit* (1988) see the implications of spontaneous order and the related notion of cultural evolution set out in their most comprehensive form. In developing these ideas Hayek sets out a systematic assault on the foundations not only of socialist economics, but also on the methodological and epistemological mindset that characterized socialist political economy in the twentieth century and which are still evident in contemporary mutations of leftist social theory.

True Individualism, Spontaneous Order and Social Evolution

Central to Hayek's concern with spontaneous order is the notion that social evolution is able to achieve a more complex and advanced form if it is not subject to the conscious control of a designing mind or group. 'True' individualism recognizes that human beings are inherently social creatures that acquire many of their values and practices via the cultural environment, and must be distinguished from the 'false', Cartesian individualism which conceives of society as the rational creation of individuals seeking to design optimal social institutions.

For Hayek, the defining feature that distinguishes the individual as a 'social being' is their incapacity to comprehend more than a tiny fragment of the society of which they are a part, owing to the constitutional limits of human intelligence (Hayek, 1948, p. 14). Recognition that people are a product of their social and cultural environment does not, therefore, imply that society is or should be the result of deliberate human creation. On the contrary, the defining feature of social life is that there are always unintended consequences that flow from purposeful human action. Thus, the primary goal of social theory is to account for those regularities or patterns of order that emerge as the unintended consequence of interacting individual plans. Individuals and organizations are situated within much larger 'spontaneous ordering' processes, the results of which are far greater than, and hence beyond the comprehension of, their constituent parts.

An epistemological concern with spontaneous order stems from the view that, given conditions of complexity and the cognitive limits of the human mind, individuals and organizations must to a large extent operate in a world of institutions that they have not sought consciously to create. Phenomena such as language, money, respect for possessions and other social traditions are not 'natural' processes but neither are they the result of deliberate 'invention' by a group. Such practices may subsequently be codified (as in a dictionary) or in cases such as property law enforced by an organization such as the state, but the rules and practices themselves are not the deliberate creation of any particular organization. In the case of language, for example, as new words and phrases spread via a process of imitation and adaptation, their initiators are not consciously aware of how such practices will be used and adapted by others. Similarly, the users of language are typically unaware of the multiple individual nodes that have initiated the words and phrases in common usage and the 'reasons' why such symbols have been adopted.

Spontaneous traditions and practices offer signposts to individual action and facilitate coordination under conditions of complexity. They are not however static phenomena, but are subject to experimental modification. Since people 'voluntarily' observe the rules of the spontaneous orders into which they are 'born' rather than have them imposed coercively by an external organization, they are better conceived as flexible rules, which can be 'broken' incrementally. The primary mechanism through which society is able to draw upon the dispersed knowledge necessary for continued evolution in light of changing circumstances is that of competition. Within a market economy it is the 'winnowing and sifting' of competition that encourages the emulation of profitable ventures, and discourages the spread of erroneous ideas in the supply of goods. The process of competitive emulation however also applies to many of the morals, informal manners and traditions that provide a degree of regularity in people's lives. Just as economic innovators are those willing to break from the conventional wisdom, so in the wider social sphere acts of moral entrepreneurship involve the breaking of traditional practices by minorities willing to face disapproval in order to experiment with new practices that may subsequently be adopted by the majority. For Hayek, incremental change via competitive testing of alternate practices is able to draw on a much wider division of knowledge than socialist attempts to 'reconstruct' cultural practices, whole cloth. Such competitive processes are not, it should be noted 'Darwinian' in character, but simulate Lamarckism. Whereas the former excludes the inheritance of acquired characteristics, cultural evolution is dependent on the spread of practices which are not innate, but learnt. Neither is such evolution confined to the transmission of habits and practices from ones parents, but from an indefinite number of other social actors. It is for this reason that socio-cultural evolution proceeds at a much faster rate than biological or 'natural' evolution and why the use of organized power should be minimized so as not to thwart the further evolution of spontaneous social rules.

In his later works, most notably *Law, Legislation and Liberty* and *The Fatal Conceit*, Hayek applies the notion of evolutionary competition not only to the internal operation of markets and liberal institutions but also to the spread of market institutions themselves. Money, private property and trade emerged historically via a process of competitive emulation, and developed largely out of historical accident in those areas where individuals were able to break away from the closed morals of traditional society and to learn to engage with strangers. It was, in turn, the practice of respecting private property and engaging in trade that allowed a highly complex division of labour to evolve, which spread gradually over the centuries, owing to the success of the groups that imitated such practices.

While Hayek's account of the evolution of market practices is based on a 'conjectural history', there is now considerable evidence from historical and anthropological sources which confirms that many market practices did indeed develop precisely where centralized political structures were at their weakest. North (1990), for example, argues that the conditions of political anarchy in medieval Europe allowed scope for the evolution of extensive commercial trading relationships as merchants were able effectively to escape administrative controls. In contrast, the process of cultural evolution in China and in the ancient Mediterranean was effectively choked by the existence of monopolistic political arrangements, which stifled the potential for further evolutionary growth. Such evidence challenges the claim made by many twentieth-century social democrats, such as Karl Polanyi, that the 'free market' economy did not emerge spontaneously but was the result of deliberate imposition in the nineteenth century by a state heady on the ideology of classical economics (Hayek, 1988, p. 44; see also Hejeebu and McCloskey, 2000, for a summary of this evidence). While market institutions can be imposed by administrative fiat, in many contexts this has simply not been the case. In the context of Britain, for example, Postan (1966) and MacFarlane (1976) document the development of sophisticated agricultural and labour markets under the fragmented legal structure of medieval England with 'free' rather than 'administered' prices. To the extent that the eighteenth- and nineteenth-century British state engaged in deliberate attempts to further the development of market institutions, these efforts did not take place in a cultural vacuum but were the product of hundreds of years of incremental change.

Socialism and the Limits to Reason

For Hayek, it is the recognition that social institutions are often 'the result of human action, but not of human design' that challenges the core of socialist theory at the methodological and at the normative level.

At the methodological level the fundamental error of socialism lies in its determination to treat social formations as if they are unitary wholes. The doctrine of methodological holism espoused most notably by Auguste

Comte, the founder of modern sociology, is that terms such as 'society' and 'the economy' correspond to real actors on the social stage. Such theories fail to provide any account of the underlying processes that link individual actions together and hence give the appearance of unity to social formations. Thus, 'The social sciences... do not deal with "given" wholes but their task is to *constitute* these wholes by constructing models from the familiar elements – models which reproduce the structure of relationships between some of the many phenomena which we always simultaneously observe in real life' (Hayek, 1952, p. 98).

The notion of spontaneous order is fundamental to the task of constituting social relationships and hence understanding what may appear to be holistic entities. In economics, for example, a market which appears to act as if it were a whole may only be understood with reference to the manner in which the price system links the activities of a myriad participants by transmitting information from one actor to another.

From a Hayekian perspective, so-called 'holistic' approaches to the study of social phenomena are not the only ones guilty of methodological errors. Socialism also finds support from approaches that purport to fall under the canon of methodological individualism but which are equally guilty of neglecting the interpersonal processes by which people acquire and communicate knowledge. The principal culprit here is the rationalistic notion of *Homo economicus*, or as Hayek described it, 'the bogey of the economic man' (1948, p. 11). The assumption of the perfectly informed agent with a consistent and fixed set of preferences, which underlies neoclassical economics, inevitably leads to the 'scientism' and 'constructivist rationalism' which views society as amenable to conscious control by an omniscient mind or group. As evidenced by Hayek's challenge to the 'given' knowledge postulate in the socialist calculation debate, such 'false' individualism neglects the processes of social learning which enable individual actors to acquire the level of rationality they in fact have.

For Hayek, recognizing the coordinating role of spontaneous ordering processes implies humility on behalf of social scientists and would-be planners. The most that can be understood about such orders are the general principles which connect the multitude of component parts: such as the capacity for new words to enter language via a process of imitation; and in markets, the tendency for prices to rise when demand exceeds supply. How specific acts of coordination come about, however, and the likely magnitude of changes in the underlying data, may never be known in sufficient detail. The penchant in quantitative economics for developing ever more sophisticated modelling techniques in the hope of generating more precise predictions to inform public policy is, therefore, little more than a 'pretence of knowledge' (Hayek, 1978).

That social science must confine itself to 'explanations of principle' rather than 'explanations of detail', requires that all theories purporting to predict the evolution of society according to so-called historical 'laws' should be abandoned. Such notions are replete in the socialist tradition and most famously in the Marxist doctrine of historical materialism. For Hayek, evolutionary processes are, outside of their general characteristics, essentially unpredictable and especially so in the sphere of human relationships where the character of future developments is dependent on the battle between competing ideas and where progress can all too easily be reversed owing to error. The latter point is sufficient to refute the charge that Hayek is guilty of an end-of-history mentality that posits evolutionary laws leading to the emergence of universal free-market practices (see Gray, 1997; Hodgson, 1998, for examples of this charge). Nowhere does Hayek suggest any inevitability about the triumph of the 'free market'. On the contrary, the idea that social advance is more likely to occur when space is left for spontaneous evolution will have its own fate determined by the battle with alternative social and political theories and the subsequent choices that people make. Hayek's own normative advocacy of spontaneous ordering processes was itself offered as what he perceived to be necessary corrective to the then dominant influence of the socialist paradigm.

Neither is Hayek's account of social evolution based on a functionalist account of institutions. Functionalist theories posit that particular institutions exist because they perform a particular function, such as maintaining social order or enabling economic growth, or in the case of Marxism, providing the conditions which will lead ultimately to the creation of a socialist society. Social institutions for Hayek do indeed perform 'functions', but they are not there because of these specific roles. Rather, on Hayek's view social rules and institutions that maintain the peace and allow for economic growth are those that have secured a competitive advantage in an environment of evolutionary selection. The existence of these institutions is not, however, explained in terms of their function, but in terms of their history and the competitive pressures that existed which may have selected for institutions with these specific traits.

It is at the normative level that the notion of spontaneous order challenges the claim of socialism to represent a truly progressive ideology. For many nineteenth- and twentieth-century socialists the extent of progress could be judged by how far societal development had been brought under 'conscious control' and that dependence on processes that were not the product of deliberate design, such as the market, was evidence of a lingering pre-Enlightenment irrationality (Hayek, 1948, p.11). For Hayek, however, far from representing a progressive social theory, it is the insistence that processes which are consciously directed are necessarily superior to a spontaneous order that is based on an 'unfounded superstition' (Hayek, 1952, p.153). The socialist refrain that 'society is greater than the sum of its individual parts' and must therefore be subject to 'conscious control' rests on a complete *non sequitur*. If social wholes are indeed greater than the sum of their parts, then it follows that the constituent elements, even when acting as an organized group via institutions such as the state, can never comprehend all of the factors that contribute to the advance of the whole. Thus:

> the inherent weakness of the collectivist theories is the extraordinary paradox that from the assertion that society is in some sense more than an aggregate of all individuals, their adherents regularly pass by a sort of intellectual somersault to the thesis that in order that the coherence of this larger entity be safeguarded it must be subjected to conscious control ... It thus comes about that in practice it is regularly the theoretical collectivist who extols individual reason and demands that all forces of society be made subject to direction by a single mastermind, while it is the individualist who recognizes the limitations of the powers of individual reason and consequently advocates freedom as a means for the fullest development of the powers of the inter-individual process. (Hayek, 1952, p.153)

Hayek versus Marxian Socialism

In the *Counter-Revolution of Science* (1952), Hayek singles out L.T. Hobhouse and Karl Mannheim as representative of the belief that progress be defined in terms of the extension of conscious planning. There is, however, a more inspirational figure in the socialist lexicon who is the major casualty of Hayek's critique: that of Karl Marx.

References to Marx's work in Hayek's writings are relatively minimal, but there is little doubt that the intellectual legacy of Marx's thinking forms the central target of his critique against the primitivism of socialist theory. It is to Marx that we owe the 'substitution of the term society for the state or compulsory organization about which he is really talking, a circumlocution that suggests that we can deliberately regulate the actions of individuals by some kinder and gentler method of direction than coercion' (Hayek, 1988, p.108).

Of all socialist thinkers it is Marx who identifies social progress with the conscious control that will come with the advent of socialism. The frequent attacks by Marx and Engels against the 'anarchy of production', and the demand for an *ex ante* coordination of economic life where competition and spontaneous order give way to conscious human design, underlies the view that market society 'alienates' humankind from its character as a 'species being'. According to Marx, 'true' freedom requires an end to the subjugation of the worker (and the capitalist) to the 'blind power' of the market and its replacement by system where, 'production by freely associated men . . . is consciously regulated by them in accordance with a settled plan' (Marx, 1906, Ch. 1, section 4, p. 92). For Marx, the conditions for such an order are imminent in the historical progression of capitalism itself, with the increasing concentration of industry in the hands of fewer enterprises under 'monopoly capitalism', paving the way for the ultimate overthrow of the market and its replacement with conscious planning.

Seen in this context, the body of Hayek's work on spontaneous order constitutes a comprehensive refutation of Marxian theory. The only circumstances in which conscious control would be possible on a society-wide basis would be those where the conditions of economic life are so few and simple that they could be surveyed by a single person or board (Hayek, 1944, p. 55). If humankind is to rely on conscious direction as the principal tool of social organization then it must confine itself to a primitive form of existence. In a progressive society characterized by a complex division of labour, there is simply no alternative to a widespread reliance on spontaneous ordering processes. Conscious social control in an advanced civilization is epistemologically unachievable and the 'liberating' potential of such processes is thus illusory.

Out with the doctrine of the superiority of conscious control must also go the Marxian prognosis for the future of capitalism. The doctrine of the 'increasing concentration of industry' is untenable because there comes a point where the cognitive limits of planned organizations are breached and where more flexible competitors exhibit a market edge. It is for this reason that, far from showing a constant tendency towards greater monopoly, the size and number of firms in different industrial sectors varies markedly over time (Steele, 1992, pp. 272–80). Ironically, it is the process of market competition itself that must be used to discover and rediscover, in an open-ended manner, how much conscious coordination in society there should actually be.

Hayek versus Communitarian Socialism

Given its record in Eastern Europe and elsewhere, Marxian socialism today finds few serious adherents. This has not, however, prevented key elements of the socialist position from being resurrected under the guise of communitarianism. The latter is readily apparent in the critique of market liberalism in contemporary social democratic writings and the advocacy of 'citizenship' and 'stakeholder' models of deliberative or participatory democracy which are frequently offered as a 'third way' palliative to the unhampered market.

Contemporary communitarian theory, inspired by the writings of

Jurgen Habermas and Charles Taylor and popularized by writers such as Benjamin Barber (see, e.g., Barber, 1984), has rescinded the outright hostility to markets evinced by traditional socialism, but has replaced this with the notion that market processes should be kept 'in their place' by the collective decisions of the community at large. There is, according to this milder form of socialism, a large sphere of goods and services that should not be allocated on the basis of contractual exchange. In an echo of Marx's theory of alienation, markets are said to 'atomize' or fragment individual decisions, disconnecting people from their communities and preventing them from relating their choices to a shared conception of the good. The individualism of market-driven consumerism should, therefore, be checked by a more community centred conception of 'citizenship', which encourages people to think collectively about how their behaviour affects the health of the community as a whole.

Market institutions are also said to take individual preferences as fixed and pre-given and thus neglect the possibility that people can be educated to an appreciation of alternative lifestyles, given a context that encourages debate and argument rather than the gratification of individual wants. On this view, institutions should not be evaluated on their capacity to respond to individual desires, but on their ability to transform and elevate people's preferences and values; a process that, it is claimed, is more likely to occur under mechanisms based on collective rather than individual choice.

Finally, the use of a common denominator such as money to aggregate individual preferences into an efficient social welfare function is deemed entirely inappropriate where there are incommensurable moral ends involved and where the aggregation of conflicting values is, therefore, impossible. Moral conflicts over resource use should not be considered according to the utilitarian criterion of willingness to pay, but should instead be dealt with via democratic debate and compromise.

The conception of the market economy implicit in these critiques is understandable when considered against the asocial view of the individual presented by contemporary neoclassical economics. From a Hayekian perspective, however, it is irrelevant to the fundamental issues at hand. Spontaneous order theory rejects the atomistic model in favour of an approach that recognizes the social nature of the individual. Communitarian arguments are, therefore, based on a series of *non-sequiturs*, which replicate the same intellectual errors characteristic of earlier variants of socialist thinking.

First, to suggest that because social and economic systems are holistically related entities, citizens must be encouraged to think and act 'holistically', completely misses the point that it is precisely because human relationships are complexly related wholes that conscious social planning is unachievable. For Hayek, the notion of a 'socially conscious' citizen is an epistemological impossibility. The central problem of social coordination is to enable people to adjust to circumstances and interests of which they are not and cannot be directly aware; which is precisely the role performed by market-generated spontaneous order.

A second *non sequitur* is evident in the claim that economic liberalism assumes that preferences and character are fixed and that to recognize otherwise is to grant the case for social democracy in the preference-forming process. As Hayek ([1961] 1967) points out in his critique of J.K Galbraith's *The Affluent Society*, the case for economic liberalism does not rest on the assumption of 'given' individual preferences and a fixed human nature. Far from undermining the case for the market economy, recognition that preferences are fluid strengthens the case for the economic liberalism because open markets are more likely to expose people to new tastes, values and cultural practices than social democratic alternatives. Employing the option of 'exit' enables those individuals who dissent from the majority to follow their own ideas without impinging on the ability of those who support the majority opinion to follow theirs.

The latter point assumes particular significance when it is recognized that much of the knowledge necessary for the transmission of values is of a tacit nature, which cannot be articulated verbally. Minority interests may not be able to articulate what is of value in their modes of living, but may still help to spread successful practices, to elevate tastes and to challenge prejudices if they have the capacity to lead by demonstration. This is, according to Hayek, one of the most important functions of the institution of private property, which affords multiple minorities the space to try out ideas, the merits or demerits of which may not be readily discerned by the majority, but from which the latter may then learn. The capacity for such imitative learning is hampered, if not removed entirely, under majoritarian social democracy where articulate persuasion, as eulogized by Habermas and his followers, is seen as the primary source of social communication (see, e.g., Habermas, 1990).

A third *non sequitur* is the claim that the use of money prices is inappropriate where there are incommensurable moral ends involved. Hayek's argument for market prices is not that they facilitate the aggregation of values into a yardstick of social welfare, but that they allow people with conflicting ends to engage in an impersonal process of mutual adjustment. To speak of maximization or efficiency is only appropriate in the context of an individual household, organization or firm operating according to a unitary scale of values and hence to what is judged more or less important. The virtue of the market economy is not its capacity to generate an 'efficient' set of decisions, but its ability to allow the discovery and pursuit of a range of different and perhaps conflicting values. The common good meanwhile is facilitated by the generation of prices which enables people pursuing a diversity of plans to adjust their actions in such a way which increases the chance that any one of these ends might successfully be achieved.

Within this context a case can surely be made that it is precisely with the ends that people value most highly that they should be required to make a personal sacrifice, including perhaps a material sacrifice. Thus:

> If the people who protest against having the higher values of life brought into the cash nexus really mean that we should not be allowed to sacrifice our lesser needs in order to preserve the higher values and that the choice should be made for us, this demand must be regarded as rather peculiar and scarcely testifies to great respect for the dignity of the individual. That life and health, beauty and virtue, honor and peace of mind, can often be preserved only at considerable material cost, and that somebody must take the choice, is as undeniable as that we are all sometimes not prepared to make the material sacrifices necessary to protect these values against all injury. (Hayek, 1944, pp. 106–7)

Each of the above errors is reflective of a wider misunderstanding by communitarian socialists of what should properly be meant by the term 'community'. For Hayek, community involves the shared identification, morals and commitments associated with the observance of spontaneously evolving cultural rules, including language and social mores such as respect for property. Nonetheless, while individuals identify themselves through the social practices in which they are embedded, communitarians are wrong to suggest that individual actors are – or should be – consciously involved in the pursuit of some 'communal end'. To speak of a communal end would require that society operates as an instrumental organization, a sort of super-person that defines the ends of its citizens. The latter conception of social order is, according to Hayek, only appropriate to a tribal society operating according to a narrowly defined set of goals. It is, however, wholly inappropriate to an 'open society' or catallaxy, where people have communal attachments to the cultural rules and practices which order their behaviour, whilst also having the liberty to experiment in pursuit of a wider variety of different ends.

ANTI-SOCIALIST ETHICS: THE MIRAGE OF SOCIAL JUSTICE

The political consequences that follow from the deficiencies in social democratic variants of socialism were to form the centrepiece of Hayek's work towards the end of his life. Foremost amongst these was the effect of the doctrine of social justice. For Hayek it is not simply that socialism derives faulty institutional conclusions from its view of the human condition, but that the ethical basis of socialism rests on foundations incompatible with life in the 'Great Society'.

The Atavism of Social Justice

The notion that the distribution of benefits and burdens should accord with social justice is a theme common to all variants of socialism, past and present, and is usually expressed in the demand that the distribution of income should accord with a particular conception of fairness. From Hayek's perspective, however, this criterion of justice represents little more than an atavistic throwback to a primitive form of society in which people work according to a narrow and shared set of ends and where the position of each individual in the whole is consciously determined by the group. To judge the distribution of income according to a notion of fairness or merit is only appropriate within a single organization operating according to a unitary set of ends, and in which people are allocated to particular posts or stations in life via the issue of commands or orders.

The results that individuals receive from a spontaneous order or catallaxy, by contrast, cannot be considered just or unjust since they are not based on obedience to specific commands, but follow from the observance of general or abstract rules of conduct, such as respect for property and contract. In this context it is meaningless to refer to the justice or injustice of a particular distribution of income because there is no one distributing agent who could be considered to have acted justly or unjustly and who could be held accountable for the actions concerned. The latter point is what defines life in the 'Great' or 'Open Society', where people are at liberty to follow their own ends and where the income that they receive is in large part the result of the decisions they take, or fail to take, in response to impersonal market signals.

In stark contrast to many conservative defenders of capitalism, Hayek is at pains to point out that the market economy does not distribute resources according to any particular conception of merit (how hard people try, for example), but with regard to the value of the services they provide to others. While the effort exercised by an individual will increase their chance of success in the market, such effort offers no guarantees of success and indeed many who do well in markets may not be considered particularly meritorious. Where innovation and constant changes in the structure of production are a prerequisite of social progress, the rewards that people receive may be determined by chance discoveries and other random events, such as a shift in the demand for a particular skill, that have little to do with individual effort. Seen in this light Hayek is at one with John Rawls in recognizing that many of the factors that contribute to a person's income are not things that are 'deserved'. The genetic inheritance of looks, talents or abilities, the cultural inheritance of being born into an educated family, and the caprice of the market, are all determinants of an individual's income and life chances, none of which can properly be said to have been merited by the people concerned.

Beyond those with whom we are intimately familiar, we are never in a position to make judgements about the 'just deserts' of others. The virtue of the market order for Hayek is that it rewards people according to how much we value their services, and not on our view of their personal merits – judgement we are seldom in a position to take. In a society where people may choose between a range of alternatives offering different remuneration, and where the factors that determine what an individual receives are multifaceted, merit is an inappropriate standard by which to judge resource distribution. To presume otherwise is to presume that:

> we are able to judge ... how well people use the different opportunities and talents given to them and how meritorious their achievements are in the light of all the circumstances which have made them possible ... It presumes then what the argument for liberty specifically rejects: that we can and do know all that guides a person's action. (Hayek, 1960, p. 97)

Evolution versus Egalitarianism

Hayek's challenge to social justice extends beyond the claim that in a free society based on spontaneous ordering processes there is no way of judging whether one state of affairs is more 'just' than another, to the substantive purpose that lies behind most demands for social justice: that of attaining a more equal distribution of wealth. From Hayek's perspective there would be no moral basis for saying that a more equal distribution constitutes evidence of greater social justice. In addition, however, he highlights other deleterious consequences that follow from egalitarian policies.

First, the pursuit of greater equality, beyond a certain point, is incompatible with a progressive and technologically advancing society. The basis of this claim lies not with the reduced incentives that might result from egalitarian measures but with the very nature of technological advance. Technologically advanced products cannot, in their initial stages of development, be made available to more than a small number of people at considerable expense. It is only the possibility that a small number may have initial access to such goods that allows for cheaper methods of mass production to subsequently be brought into existence. While this claim may be greeted by some socialists as a 'piece of far-fetched and cynical apologetics ... a little reflection will show that it is fully valid' (Hayek, 1960, p. 45). It would be necessary in a socialist society to select members of the population who would be charged with trying out new products and entire modes of living, long before it would be possible to make them available to the rest of the population. Unless it is to entirely abandon the goal of material progress, therefore, socialism cannot eliminate a substantial degree of inequality. The principal difference between a socialist order and a liberal society would be that in the former, favoured individuals would be selected by the political authorities; whereas in the latter, the accidents of birth and the market process determine the relevant distribution of goods.

A deeper variant of this argument goes beyond issues concerning the dissemination of technological innovations, to the very heart of how human beings learn. Inequality is fundamental to any process that allows trial-and-error learning, and the case for private property and individual liberty rests in large part on the scope they create for evolutionary discovery and learning via emulation. Thus, 'If the results of individual liberty did not demonstrate that some manners of living were more successful than others, much of the case for it would vanish' (Hayek, 1960, p. 85). In markets, the unequal results of competition are central to the transmission of knowledge. Whether through luck or skill, the discovery of profit opportunities, by some, sends out a signal to other less successful actors and facilitates a learning process where success breeds success, via emulation. Similarly, with regard to family life and cultural and educational practices, the process of transmitting knowledge is in large part dependent on the existence of unequal results which enable the less successful to learn from and to imitate the more successful. Seen in this light, even milder forms of socialism, which purport to establish 'equality of opportunity' in areas such as educational provision, are likely to stultify the process of evolutionary growth. It is precisely the differences in opportunities between people that drive up the general standard of opportunities that are available to all by allowing the space for the discovery of what is better; a process that necessarily requires that some have advanced ahead of others.

Whether in the realm of technological advance or in the transmission of social and cultural values, Hayek argues that inequality is central to a progressive society. The differential rewards and opportunities that people receive in such a process cannot be considered just or unjust, since evolutionary processes necessarily involve a significant degree of luck (Hayek, 1988, p. 74). If socialism tries to eliminate such inequalities then it will stifle the process of evolutionary growth. If, on the other hand, socialism accepts the inevitability of inequality then it will face the task of determining the relevant distribution according to some criterion of merit or fairness. It is in the latter context that socialism leads to political consequences that few of its adherents wish to see. Confronted with the absence of a complete ethical code and a common standard of fairness with which to allocate income and life chances, the pursuit of social justice will take one of two roads. Either it will degenerate into a sort of 'bargaining democracy' characteristic of contemporary welfare states, where competing interests press the government for the realization of their own particular variant of social justice; or, faced with the absence of agreement over the merits of different cases, it will lead to the arbitrary imposition of a standard of fairness by the political authorities. In the former case the outcome will be determined by the relative strength of the respective interest groups and can scarcely be considered to owe anything to a criterion of justice. In the latter instance, government officials assume the despotic power to determine the life chances of individuals depicted in Hayek's *Road to Serfdom*. By contrast, while the distribution of income under the market is partly the result of caprice, more than any other conceivable system it minimizes the arbitrary power of some to judge on the merits of others.

Hayek versus the Critics

Hayek's critique of social justice is one of the most radical elements of his political economy and yet has received relatively little attention from contemporary social and political theorists. Insofar as it has received attention, moreover, this has tended to be of a highly critical nature. While a significant number of analysts are now willing to grant the persuasiveness of his critique of the centrally planned economy and his positive case for the market, few are willing to concede Hayek's arguments against the pursuit of social justice.

One line of criticism advanced against Hayek's argument focuses on the claim that market outcomes cannot be judged against a criterion of justice because there is no agency responsible for the distribution of income and the results are not the deliberate intention of market participants. Lukes (1997), for example, argues that even though market actors are not responsible for the occurrence of the relevant distributive outcomes they are nonetheless responsible for how they react to them (see also, Plant, 1994). According to this view, failure to react in an appropriate way to instances of poverty and deprivation may rightly be condemned as unjust. Indeed, choosing to maintain a society which operates on spontaneous ordering principles in the first place is to commit oneself to correct for the inequalities that such a process will inevitably produce. When we choose to rely on a spontaneous order we are in effect choosing a distributive principle, and if we choose not to correct at least some of the inequalities that such a system produces then our conduct may rightly be considered as morally questionable. Seen through this lens, social democratic institutions such as the welfare state are an attempt to modify the results of a spontaneous order and do not require the kind of limits on human freedom found under centrally planned forms of egalitarianism.

A second line of critique attacks Hayek's view that the pursuit of social justice is only appropriate to a tribal society characterized by adherence to a common set of ends. Johnston (1997), for example, contends that the pursuit of a more equal distribution of wealth does not require agreement on a shared set of ends. It requires that wealth be more equally distributed, but need not make any attempt to specify the ends on which the relevant wealth should be applied. According to this view, the pursuit of social justice as a primary aim of public policy need make no more assumptions about the ultimate ends of the actors that make up society than the pursuit of other objectives such as an increase in aggregate wealth. Social justice is a general-purpose objective that increases the chance that any one of a number of possible ends may have a chance of being achieved. The latter is, of course, the very criterion that Hayek himself uses in support of the market economy.

Building on the above arguments it might be argued that for all his critique of the idea of social justice, Hayek's own advocacy of the market order is based on a particular distributional ideal, and one not dissimilar in formulation to that provided by the great architect of modern social justice theory, John Rawls. Given his critique of merit-based distributions Rawls maintains that criteria of social justice should not be applied to the results that specific individuals in a society receive or to the character of particular decisions or exchanges, but should apply instead to the overall character of political economic institutions: to the 'basic structure' of society (Rawls, [1971] 1999, p. 274). It is at this level of analysis that criteria of distributive justice should have force. The distributive principle that Rawls favours is what he calls the difference principle: that socioeconomic institutions should be organized such that any inequalities work to the greatest advantage of representative members from the least advantaged class (Rawls, [1971] 1999, p. 302). Rawls derives support for this principle from a contractarian thought experiment designed to simulate the conditions required for an impartial choice of social rules, where hypothetical parties behind a veil of ignorance – not knowing anything about their personal characteristics or social status – choose the basic ordering principles for their society.

Hayek himself has some favourable things to say about the Rawlsian approach and indeed appears to make moral claims for market institutions by attempting to judge basic social rules from a similarly impartial point of view. Thus, 'there unquestionably exists a genuine problem of justice in connection with the deliberate design of institutions, the problem to which Professor John Rawls has recently devoted an important book'. And, writing about such institutions in distinctly Rawlsian vein, he maintains that, 'we should regard as the most desirable order of society one which we would choose if we knew that our initial position in it would be determined purely by chance (such as the fact of our being born into a particular family' (Hayek, 1982, p. 132).

The only difference between Hayek and Rawls, it might be argued, is not over the need for social justice, but over the particular distributive principle that is chosen to evaluate the 'basic structure' of society. For Rawls it is the difference principle (maximizing the position of the worst off), whereas for Hayek, – it is something closer to improving the general standard of living such that all people in society benefit in some way from the operation of basic institutions such as markets and the laws of property. Since Rawls is not advocating a radical form of egalitarianism and indeed recognizes that inequalities are justified where these operate to raise the position of the least advantaged, it is not obvious why Hayek's arguments against full-blown egalitarian socialism should apply against the more moderate social democratic or welfare state policies that are typically advocated by those supporting the Rawlsian approach. Hayek's perspective does not seem to provide any basis for challenging the legitimacy of this approach and offers no reason to suppose that the pursuit of it will lead down some inexorable 'road to serfdom'.

The critiques sketched above appear to many commentators as decisive objections against Hayek's position, and to some as proof that his views on social justice are not even worth bothering to discuss (see, e.g., Haworth, 1994). Notwithstanding the prevalence of this viewpoint, however, it underestimates some of the basic issues which Hayek raises. Lukes's argument, for example, that the lack of a distributing agent in a market economy should not prevent people from being held responsible for how they react to the distribution concerned, avoids the fundamental question of what an appropriate response would be. It is only meaningful to say that people are failing in their responsibilities towards social justice if they are in a position to know what the relevant distribution should be and yet fail to act on this knowledge. For Hayek, the fact that no one is in control of market distributions is inextricably linked to the fact that no one can know what a 'socially just' distribution would be. The factors that determine what people receive in a free society are far too complex and varied for people to judge whether one particular distribution is more 'just' than another. This does not, of course, prevent people from responding to particular instances of hardship as and when they encounter them, but in no way can such actions be said to 'increase' the level of distributive justice across society as a whole.

Even if there is agreement on a particular distributive standard, such as Rawls's difference principle, people lack the cognitive capacity to know how they should act to bring about the desired principle. In order to be held responsible for their actions in this regard it would be necessary for people to anticipate the choices and thus effectively to 'read the minds' of countless other individuals and organizations in order to coordinate their actions in accordance with the principle. In the absence of this capacity then the decisions that people take to exchange goods and services or to give resources and time to others will continually transform the distribution of income in unanticipated ways.

It will not suffice to reply here that holding people responsible for their actions refers not to every specific exchange or act of giving, but to their willingness to uphold a 'basic structure' which provides the background opportunities and resources, commensurate with a particular distributive principle. The difficulty is precisely that knowledge of which opportunities and resource allocations constitute the relevant 'structure' can never be made available either individually or to a collective institution such as the state. In the case of rates of taxation, for example, a tax rate that secures a given level of inequality at a particular point in time may not be commensurate with such inequality at a subsequent point, because ongoing changes in technology, tastes, spending and employment patterns will continually alter the distribution that results from that level of taxation in countless unanticipated ways. In these circumstances it would be impossible for those charged with implementing the relevant tax to know in what direction to change it in response to the myriad factors affecting the distribution of income.

Where people retain freedom of action, therefore, it is of questionable value to speak of them acting justly or unjustly with respect to any particular macro-distributive pattern. There is, for example, no basis for any claim that the welfare state achieves the Rawlsian difference principle and is thus 'more just' in comparison to societies which lack such a state or where spending on redistributive programmes is lower. Quite simply, the knowledge required to perform the calculations necessary to judge the level of inequality required by the difference principle cannot be placed at the disposal of the agencies of the state, or any other actor or group within society.

In practice, of course, there may be no basis for agreement on a distributive standard against which to evaluate the performance of basic social institutions in the first place. Johnston's line of attack, therefore, fares little better than that of Lukes. To suggest that redistribution does not require agreement on the ends to which the wealth is finally applied ignores the point that the pursuit of an egalitarian distribution does require agreement on a shared moral end – an agreement which does not exist (Feser, 1997, p. 592). Moreover, Johnston ducks the fact that the pursuit of different ends has distributive consequences. This is well illustrated by the confusion apparent in the attitude towards cultural diversity and equality by contemporary theorists of what might best be described as 'multicultural socialism'. The latter support a commitment to cultural freedom while insisting that material inequalities between different groups are reduced as a condition of cultural empowerment (Young, 1990). Cultural toleration is, however, incompatible with the pursuit of egalitarian objectives for the simple reason that different cultural practices have different material consequences. A group that rejects the use of technological innovations, as do the Amish in the United States, is unlikely to generate the same number of opportunities for material advancement than a group that believes in technological progress. Attempts to secure 'equality of opportunity', therefore, may be at odds with cultural tolerance since they necessarily involve interference with the cultural practices of different groups. Either the state must intervene to redistribute away from the materially successful and hence inhibit the pursuit of their ends, or it must intervene to change the cultural ends of the poorer groups (see, e.g., Kukathas, 2003).

Though Hayek may himself appear to be advocating a principle of distributive justice when suggesting that institutions be judged in terms of their capacity to improve the chances of a representative agent achieving their ends, what he seems to have in mind here is a much 'thinner' conception of 'justice' than anything advanced in modern egalitarian social justice theory. The rules that Hayek emphasizes are the basic 'rules of just conduct' without which social progress of any kind would not be possible. These rules are essentially the classical liberal rights which include respect for person and property, contract and the prevention of force and fraud; and perhaps, though this is more questionable, support for a basic safety net to protect against destitution. Rules of this nature are what allow social cooperation to get off the ground and without which life is likely to disintegrate into permanent conflict (Gaus, 2011). As a consequence these are, on a Hayekian view, principles which may command widespread support from people who may differ about more substantive distributive ethics.

In addition, implementing such basic rules does not presuppose anything like the informational and calculational capacities that would be required in order to deliver a more substantive principle such as that favored by Rawls. Discerning whether people are abiding by the terms of private contracts and enforcing such agreements requires considerably less in the way of knowledge than the synoptic overview of resource allocations that would be required to implement the Rawlsian vision (Epstein, 1995). This argument may also apply in terms of the safety net provisions which Hayek allows for as a legitimate activity within a classical liberal framework of limited government. Ensuring that people are provided with basic food and shelter requires considerably less in the way of information than knowing which pattern of resource allocation maximizes the position of the worst-off.

In a sense, therefore, Hayek's 'basic structure' of rules are not rules of distributive justice per se but are better thought of as basic norms of interaction or Humean 'conventions' that enable people who may hold different conceptions of social or distributive justice to co-exist without permanent conflict (Barry, 2004). Though most of these rules have their origin in an evolutionary process – the groups that adhered to them are the ones that have survived and prospered – an understanding of the benefits such rules can bring may also be used to inform deliberate efforts towards institutional design. This may, for example, be required in the context of environmental protection where the creation of property rights to previously unowned or 'open access' resources may be needed in order to avoid resource depletion.

What the Hayekian approach rejects is the notion that widespread support can be generated for a more substantive set of distributive ethics such as those of Rawls which puts particular emphasis on maximizing the position of the worst-off; a principle which would require that billions of dollars be taken from the better-off even if the benefit to the worst-off from such transfers was nothing more than a few pennies per capita. In conditions of bounded rationality, of cultural diversity and where people have different evaluative standards, there may be no compelling way to generate agreement on such a specific moral standard. Rawls's own formulation of how to conceptualize the derivation of an impartial standard of justice assumes away the very conditions which require the need for social rules and institutions in the first place. Fully idealized rationality of the sort exhibited by actors behind the veil of ignorance implies that people can see costlessly and instantaneously all the consequences of their beliefs. The Rawlsian model assumes that everyone is equally rational, similarly situated and is convinced by the same arguments; the result being that the rules chosen are equivalent to what would be chosen by a single actor.

On a Hayekian view, the notion of full rationality when considering social morality is utterly inappropriate to passing judgement on real-world institutions which must operate in conditions where the limits of human reason are tightly bounded and standards of evaluation differ widely. Rawls's model has, for example, been criticized elsewhere for smuggling in an assumption of extreme risk aversion in order to justify the difference principle (e.g., Buchanan, 1977). If this assumption is dropped and those choosing social institutions are recognized to vary in their attitudes to risk, or do not know about these attitudes, then it is highly implausible to suggest that they would or should choose to bind themselves to a moral rule as specific as that favoured by Rawls. There is, therefore, no compelling moral reason why institutions that seek to maximize the position of the worst-off should be considered more (or less) just than those which emphasize improvements in the general standard of living.

There may, however, be reason to believe that attempts to make social justice the centrepiece of government activity when there is no basis for agreement over the relevant standards of distributive fairness run the constant risk of undermining the very basis of social order. The modern welfare state and the interest-group democracy that surrounds it has existed for little more than half a century, and whether these institutions prove capable of sustaining economic growth and social stability may only be revealed in a much longer time frame. At the very least, however, the social conflicts that have been precipitated by the debt crisis that has recently unfolded across many of the developed welfare states suggest that Hayek's analysis of the dangers associated with the pursuit of social justice is worthy of serious consideration.

CONCLUSION

This chapter has sought to explore the elements of F.A. Hayek's critique of socialism. While few would now deny that Hayek should be credited with highlighting the failures of East European-style economies, it has become a commonplace to argue that his insights are irrelevant to the milder forms of government intervention and their theoretical justification that prevail in contemporary social democracies. Hayek himself was aware of this charge, but was convinced that his theories were as pertinent in their application to milder forms of socialism as they were to its more radical manifestations. As this chapter has sought to demonstrate, whether it is 'new' market-failure interventionism, third-way communitarianism, or the continued advocacy of social justice as the primary justification for the welfare state, the Hayekian schema constitutes a systematic assault on the foundations of socialist theory in all its various guises and provides as many questions for socialists to answer today as it did throughout its author's lifetime.

REFERENCES

Barber, Benjamin R. (1984), *Strong Democracy*, Berkeley, CA: University of California Press.
Barry, Norman P. (2004) 'Political morality as convention', *Social Philosophy and Policy*, 21 (1), 266–92.
Boettke, Peter J. (1997), 'Where did economics go wrong? Equilibrium as a flight from reality', *Critical Review*, 11 (1), 11–64.
Buchanan, James M. (1977) *Freedom in Constitutional Contract*, College Station, TX: Texas A&M University Press.
Caldwell, Bruce J. (2003), *Hayek's Challenge: An Intellectual Biography of F.A. Hayek*, Chicago, IL: University of Chicago Press.
Coase, Ronald H. (1937), 'The nature of the firm', *Economica*, n.s. 4 (16), 386–405.
Coase, Ronald H. (1992), 'The institutional structure of production', *American Economic Review*, 82 (4), 713–19.
Ebenstein, Alan (2001), *Friedrich Hayek: A Biography*, London: Palgrave.
Epstein, Richard A. (1995) *Simple Rules for a Complex World*: Chicago, IL: Chicago University Press.
Feser, Edward (1997), 'Hayek on social justice', *Critical Review*, 11 (4), 581–606.
Gray, John (1997), *False Dawn: The Delusions of Global Capitalism*, London: Granta.
Grossman, Stanford J. and Joseph E. Stiglitz (1980), 'On the impossibility of informationally efficient markets', *American Economic Review*, 70 (3), 393–408.
Grossman, Stanford J. and Joseph E. Stiglitz (1986), 'Information and competitive price systems', *American Economic Review*, 66 (2), 246–53.
Gaus, Gerald (2011) *The Order of Public Reason*, Cambridge: Cambridge University Press.
Habermas, Jürgen (1990), *Moral Consciousness and Communicative Action*, Cambridge MA: MIT Press.
Hayek, Friedrich A. (1935), *Collectivist Economic Planning*, London: Routledge.
Hayek, Friedrich A. (1944), *The Road to Serfdom*, Chicago, IL: University of Chicago Press (1994, 50th Anniversary edition).
Hayek, Friedrich A. (1948), *Individualism and Economic Order*, Chicago, IL: University of Chicago Press.
Hayek, Friedrich A. (1952), *The Counter-Revolution of Science* (1979), Indianapolis, IN: Liberty Press.
Hayek, Friedrich A. (1960), *The Constitution of Liberty*, London: Routledge.
Hayek, Friedrich A. ([1961] 1967), 'The non sequitur of the "dependence effect"', *Studies in Philosophy, Politics and Economics*, Chicago, IL: University of Chicago Press, pp. 313–17.
Hayek, Friedrich A. (1978), 'The pretence of knowledge', in *New Studies in Philosophy, Politics, Economics and the History of Ideas*, London: Routledge, pp. 23–34.
Hayek, Friedrich A. (1982), *Law, Legislation and Liberty*, London: Routledge.
Hayek, Friedrich A. (1988), *The Fatal Conceit: The Errors of Socialism*, London: Routledge.
Haworth, Alan (1994), *Anti-Libertarianism*, London: Routledge.
Hejeebu, Santhi and Dierdre N. McCloskey (2000), 'The reproving of Karl Polanyi', *Critical Review*, 13 (4), 285–314.
Hodgson, Geoffrey M. (1998), *Economics and Utopia*, London: Routledge.
Johnston, David (1997), 'Hayek's attack on social justice', *Critical Review*, 11 (1), 81–100.
Kirzner, Israel M. (1997), 'Entrepreneurial discovery and the competitive market process: an Austrian approach', *Journal of Economic Literature*, 35 (1), 60–85.

Kukathas, Chandran (2003), *The Liberal Archipelago: A Theory of Diversity and Freedom*, Oxford: Oxford University Press.
Lange, Oskar R. (1936), 'On the economic theory of socialism I', *Review of Economic Studies*, 4 (1), 53–71.
Lange, Oskar R. (1937), 'On the economic theory of socialism II', *Review of Economic Studies*, 4 (2), 123–42.
Lukes, Steven M. (1997), 'Social justice: the Hayekian challenge', *Critical Review*, 11 (1), 65–80.
MacFarlane, Alan D.J. (1976) *The Origins of English Individualism*, Cambridge: Cambridge University Press.
Marx, Karl (1906), *Capital*, vol. 1, Chicago, IL: Charles H. Kerr & Co.
Mises, Ludwig von (1920), *Economic Calculation in the Socialist Commonwealth* (1990), Auburn, AL: Ludwig von Mises Institute.
North, Douglass C. (1990), *Institutions, Institutional Change and Economic Performance*, Cambridge: Cambridge University Press.
O'Neill, John (1998), *The Market*, London: Routledge.
Plant, Raymond (1994), 'Hayek on social justice: a critique', in Jack Birner and Rudy van Zjip (eds), *Hayek, Co-ordination and Evolution*, London: Routledge, pp. 164–77.
Postan, Michael M. (1966), 'Medieval agrarian society in its prime: England', in M.M. Postan (ed.), Cambridge History of England, vol. 1, 2nd edn, Cambridge: Cambridge University Press, pp. 548–632.
Rawls, John ([1971] 1999) *A Theory of Justice*, rev. edn, Cambridge, MA: Harvard University Press.
Somin, Ilya (1998), 'Voter ignorance and the democratic ideal', *Critical Review*, 12 (4), 413–58.
Steele, David Ramsay (1992), *From Marx to Mises*, La Salle, IL: Open Court.
Stiglitz, Joseph E. (1994), *Whither Socialism?* Cambridge, MA: MIT Press.
Taylor, Charles (1985), *Philosophy and the Human Sciences*, Cambridge: Cambridge University Press.
Young, Iris M. (1990), *Justice and the Politics of Difference*, Princeton, NJ: Princeton University Press.

12. Hayek versus the neoclassicists: lessons from the socialist calculation debate
Peter J. Boettke, Christopher J. Coyne and Peter T. Leeson

INTRODUCTION

An important question for any researcher who wishes to revisit the socialist calculation debate is: Why flog a dead horse? With the collapse of communism in 1991, there seems to be little value, other than for historical purposes, in rehashing the debate over socialism's feasibility. Nevertheless, we believe that there are at least two very good reasons to consider this debate once again.

The first reason has to do with the fact that socialism is an intellectually and emotionally powerful idea. This is particularly so as it is articulated by Karl Marx. Socialism is thus worthy of our most serious intellectual effort in analyzing its claims.[1] The classical political economy thought experiment that highlighted self-regulation and harmony of interests was called into direct challenge by Marx, who argued that the natural workings of the market economy led to a clash of interests among classes and to market failure in the cases of monopoly and crises.

In the wake of the collapse of real existing socialism, many intellectuals continue to find comfort in socialism's promise of a better world, even if the particulars of how to achieve that better world are a subject of dispute and puzzlement. It is often contended that the events of 1989–91 were the outcome of frail humanity that failed to live up to the demands of socialism. It is our contention that by revisiting the debate concerning socialism it becomes apparent that the opposite is actually true. Humanity did not fall short of the ideals of socialism; socialism fell short of the demands of humanity.

The second reason for reconsidering the socialist calculation debate is of a more parochial concern, but equally important nonetheless. This debate taught the Austrian economists how their understanding of the market system differed from the understanding of their neoclassical colleagues. In this regard, the debate was critical to the development of a unique Austrian paradigm represented in the work of thinkers like Ludwig von Mises and F.A. Hayek (Lavoie, 1985; Kirzner, 1988).

The Austrian theory of the market process is a direct descendant of the socialist calculation debate. Prior to the debate, the Austrian economists viewed themselves as a branch of the marginal revolution (Boettke and Leeson, 2003). The differences between the Walrasian, Marshallian and Mengerian branches of neoclassicism were perceived as stylistic, not substantive, in nature. The common enemy of neoclassicism was the atheoretical work of the historicists and institutionalists and the residue of classical economics that could be found in Marxism. Modern economics, defined as the marginal and subjective revolution in economics, was united in opposition to the intellectual forces of these schools. But as the debate over socialism moved to the English-speaking world, a peculiar twist occurred. The strongest arguments against the Austrian position in the debate came not from atheoretical institutionalists and historicists, nor from the Marxian scholars. On the contrary, the strongest arguments against the Austrian position came from neoclassical economists themselves.

This chapter is concerned with justifying the reasons for revisiting the socialist calculation debate, with particular emphasis on the contrast between neoclassical and Austrian views. In particular, in the course of reviewing the history of the debate regarding socialist calculation, we aim to draw attention to how the arguments made by F.A. Hayek launched specifically against socialism in fact constituted a much broader attack on the neoclassical paradigm.

BUILDING UP TO THE DEBATE: THE CLASSICAL ECONOMISTS AND MARX

The classical liberal political economy of David Hume and Adam Smith argued that the market system of private property, contract and consent could simultaneously achieve individual autonomy, peaceful domestic and international cooperation, and economic prosperity. Individuals pursuing their own interests within this setting would generate a pattern of outcomes that was socially beneficial. The argument of these thinkers was not that the pursuit of self-interest under any institutional regime would produce public benefits. Absent private property, for instance, unbridled self-interest would lead to the degradation of resources, not the creation of wealth.

Under the 'right' institutional conditions, however, individuals pursuing their own ends, Smith argued, would generate the same pattern of resource use that an omniscient and benevolent mind would have generated. Thus was born the contrast of designed and undersigned order. The proposition of self-regulation of the market economy was central to the 'invisible hand' story that Smith told. This proposition would be challenged on several fronts by subsequent generations of political economists.

The problem of monopoly, as understood at Smith's time, was not a problem inherent in the operation of the market system. Quite the opposite: it was understood as an outcome of government privilege. Nevertheless, those who came after Smith, like Marx, argued that the unregulated market economy necessarily led to the concentration of capital in the hands of a smaller and smaller group of individuals. The bigger the firm, the story goes, the better a position it is in to compete with smaller ones. Bigger firms possessed more market power and would use this power to dictate the terms of exchange in such a way that it led to their growth at the peril of small firms. Thus the logic of competition would favor the big and, with that, advantage their ability to thwart pressures of competition. In this fashion, the market economy was said to tend towards monopolization.

In addition to the problem of monopoly, the market economy was said to possess another inherent feature that undermined Smith's claim of self-regulation. This feature was the tendency towards overproduction. Contrary to J.B. Say and his 'law' which postulated a tendency for aggregate supply and demand to equate in the unhampered market economy, many political economists including Marx maintained that the market economy generated a general glut of goods. Met with general oversupply, the market was led to periodic business cycles, creating ups that were ultimately followed by economic crises in their wake.[2]

The upshot of these features of the market economy meant that rather than creating a 'harmony of interests' as they do in Smith's story, markets instead create conflicts of interests. Furthermore, due to the endemic waste brought on by crises, the unregulated market would generate less economic prosperity than might be obtained otherwise. Finally, given the abundance of idle resources including labor, workers would be disadvantaged in exchange relationships with firms and would be subjected to 'wage slavery', pushing wages to subsistence levels. In short, rather than simultaneously creating individual autonomy, social cooperation and economic prosperity, the market system would produce wage slavery, class conflict and irrational production.

By socializing the means of production, socialism would substitute production for use in the place of production for exchange. Whereas under capitalism the invisible hand operated to guide resource use, under socialism resource allocation would be 'rationalized'. Planned resource use would replace the anarchy of production in the market. In doing this, in addition to achieving the liberation of workers and the cooperation of mankind, socialism would generate greater prosperity than capitalism was ever capable of producing.

THE FIRST TWO STAGES OF THE DEBATE: 1920–37

In order to understand how the Austrian conception of the market, and in particular Hayek's, differed from that of their neoclassical cohorts, we must first understand the general stages that the debate concerning socialist calculation went through.[3] Only in doing this is it possible to realize – in the same way that the Austrians at the time did – what was unique and different in their approach.

In offering what they believed to be a refutation of capitalism, the socialists thought they had also established the fact that economic analysis (in addition to being incorrect) would be unnecessary in the socialist world. Against this claim, following the marginal revolution and in the years leading up to 1920, Friedrich von Wieser, Joseph Schumpeter, Leon Walras, Vilfredo Pareto, Enrico Barone, Fredrick Taylor and Frank Knight all pointed out that if socialism was to rationalize production, it would have to succeed in satisfying the same formal requirements that capitalism was said to achieve under conditions of equilibrium.[4] In other words, if rationalization implied the most efficient use of resources, which is the meaning it would have to have, then socialist rationalization would need to satisfy the optimality conditions which are described using marginalist principles. This point was little recognized by socialists until about 1920.

In 1920, Austrian economics' most prominent figure, Ludwig von Mises, published his article 'Economic calculation in the socialist commonwealth', in which he critiqued socialism on the grounds that economic calculation in a socialist system was impossible. We will discuss Mises' contribution in this regard below, and later when considering how Hayek formulated his argument against the socialists. For now it is sufficient to recognize that between the time this article appeared in 1920 and 1935, the debate concerning socialism was controlled by Mises' argument. Contributors believed that they had to respond to Mises' critique, and none had provided an argument that won the general consensus among theoretical economists.

With the coming of the Great Depression the underlying confidence many economists had in the self-regulating properties of the market was lost. In addition, theoretical developments by Joan Robinson and Edward Chamberlin, and casual empiricism by Berle and Means, had laid the groundwork for microeconomic criticisms of the efficiency of modern capitalism. Socialism now appeared as hope for a better arrangement of economic affairs.

Against the backdrop of this intellectual climate, the Polish economist Oskar Lange launched an attack on Mises' argument that met with long-lasting and overwhelming approval among technical economists.[5] Indeed, between 1937 and 1985, the basic consensus among professional economists was that the Austrian argument against socialism did not hold at a purely theoretical level and was empirically naïve.

Mises' 1920 article, which served as the core of this Austrian argument, proffered the following straightforward argument against socialism. Socialism, he pointed out, means the abolition of private property in the means of production. Furthermore, one of its fundamental goals is to achieve advanced material production in order to accomplish the transition from a condition of 'necessity' to a condition of 'freedom'. In order to achieve advanced material production, however, the socialist system of production must tend toward the optimal use of resources. Any suboptimal use of resources would need to be recognized and corrected or else advanced material production would not be possible.

In a system of private ownership, Mises argued, economists had come to understand how resource use was guided. Private property provided a strong incentive for people to use resources efficiently because they bore the costs and reaped the rewards of their activities. Prices established on the market provided signals to producers and consumers about the trade-offs they would have to make in purchasing inputs and outputs. And finally, profit-and-loss accounting would inform market participants about whether their business decisions accorded well with underlying tastes and technology.

In light of this, Mises posed the following question to the socialists: In the absence of the institution of private property and the business practices of a market economy, how would socialism motivate and inform its participants in order to achieve optimal production? Mises argued that socialism would be without any means to achieve its ends because the means chosen (abolition of private property) were fundamentally incoherent with regard to the ends sought (advanced material production).

Without private property in the means of production, Mises argued, there would be no market for the means of production. Without a market for the means of production, there would be no money prices for the means of production. Without money prices reflecting the relative scarcity of the means of production, there would be no way for economic planners to assess the opportunity cost of resource use. In short, economic planning would be groping in the dark. There would be no economic basis upon which to pursue project A rather than project B, decide what resources in what combination should be used to pursue one of these projects, establish whether or not the project was a success or a failure, or even if it should be undertaken at all. Rational allocation of resources under socialism was impossible. The notion of a 'socialist economy' was therefore oxymoronic. There could be no socialist economy, only planned chaos.

What was Lange able to say against this in 1936–37 that would so convince the profession of economists that Mises was wrong, and socialism was workable? In the belief that socialism, if it was to achieve its claimed outcomes of advanced material production, must satisfy the formal conditions of economic efficiency stipulated by marginalist principles, Frederick Taylor, Frank Knight, H.D. Dickinson and Abba Lerner began developing an argument that used modern neoclassical economics to assure the efficiency of socialist economic planning. Using the same line of neoclassical reasoning, Lange was able to formulate his critique of Mises.

In deploying the formal-similarity argument, Lange provided the following blueprint. First, allow a market for consumer goods and for labor allocation. Second, put the productive sector into state hands but provide strict guidelines for production to firms. Namely, inform managers that they must price their output equal to marginal costs, and produce that level of output that minimizes average costs. Adjustments can be made on a trial-and-error basis, using inventory as the signal. The production guidelines will ensure that the full opportunity cost of production will be taken into account and that all least-cost technologies will be employed. In short, these production guidelines will ensure productive efficiency is achieved even in a setting of state ownership of the means of production.

Lange went even further in his argument for socialism. Not only is socialism, by mimicking the efficiency conditions of capitalism, able theoretically to achieve the same level of efficient production as the market, but it would actually outperform capitalism by purging society of monopoly and business cycles that plague real-world capitalism. In the hands of Lange (and Lerner) neoclassical theory was to become a powerful tool of social control. Modern economic theory, which Mises had thought so convincingly established his argument, was now used to show that Mises was wrong. In the eyes of the economics profession, Mises had been decisively defeated with this argument.

HAYEK'S CHALLENGE

Lange's argument presented a formidable challenge for believers in the productive superiority of capitalism, a challenge that Mises' student, F.A. Hayek, would devote the better part of the 1940s attempting to meet.[6]

Hayek's response to Lange's model for market socialism came in the form of a multi-pronged argument. First, Hayek argued that the models of market socialism proposed by Lange and others reflected a preoccupation with equilibrium. The models possessed no ability to discuss the necessary adaptations to changing conditions required in real economic life. The imputation of value of capital goods from consumer goods represented a classic case in point. Schumpeter had argued that once consumer goods were valued in the market (as they would be in Lange's model), a market for producer goods was unnecessary because we could impute the value of corresponding capital goods *ipso facto*.

This 'solution' was of course accurate in the model of general equilibrium where there is a pre-reconciliation of plans (that is, no false trades). Hayek's concern, however (as was Mises'), was not with the model, but with how imputation actually takes place within the market process so that production plans come to be coordinated with consumer demands. This is not a trivial procedure and requires various market signals to guide entrepreneurs in their decision process on the use of capital good combinations in production projects. In a fundamental sense Hayek was arguing that Mises' calculation argument could not be addressed by assuming it away. Of course, if we focus our analytical attention on the properties of a world in which all plans have already been fully coordinated (general competitive equilibrium), then the process by which that coordination came about in the first place will not be highlighted.

This was Hayek's central point. Absent certain institutions and practices, the process that brings about the coordination of plans (including the imputation of value from consumer goods to producer goods) would not take place. Some alternative process would have to be relied upon for decision-making concerning resources, and that process would by necessity be one that could not rely on the guides of private property incentives, relative price signals, and profit-and-loss accounting since the socialist project had explicitly abolished them. In other words, the *ipso facto* proposition of competitive equilibrium was irrelevant for the world outside of that state of equilibrium. The fact that leading neoclassical economists (like Knight and Schumpeter) had not recognized this elementary point demonstrated the havoc that a preoccupation with the state of equilibrium, as opposed to the process which tends to bring about equilibrium, can have on economic science.

In Hayek's view, the problem with concentrating on a state of affairs as opposed to the process was not limited to assuming that which must be argued, but directed attention away from how changing circumstances require adaptations on the part of participants. Equilibrium, by definition, is a state of affairs in which no agent within the system has any incentive to change. If all the data were frozen, then indeed the logic of the situation would lead individuals to a state of rest where all plans were coordinated and resources were used in the most efficient manner currently known. The Lange–Lerner conditions would hold: prices would be set to marginal cost (and thus the full opportunity cost of production would be reflected in the price) and production would be at the minimum point on the firm's average cost curve (and thus the least-cost technologies would be employed). But what, Hayek asked, do these conditions tell us about a world where the data are not frozen? What happens when tastes and technologies change?

Marginal conditions, he noted, do not provide any guide to action; they are instead outcomes of a process of learning within a competitive situation. In a tautological sense, competition exists in all social settings and thus individuals find that in order to do the best that they can given the situation, they will stumble towards equating marginal costs and marginal benefits. This is true at the individual level no matter what system we are talking about. But this says nothing about the second optimality rule proposed in the Lange–Lerner model: that of producing at the level which minimizes average costs. Rather than being given to us from above, the least-cost methods of production and how best to satisfy consumer tastes must be discovered anew each day.

Effective allocation of resources requires that there is a correspondence between the underlying conditions of tastes, technology and resource endowments, and the induced variables of prices and profit-and-loss accounting. In perfect competition the underlying variables and the induced variables are in perfect alignment and thus there are no coordination problems. Traditions in economic scholarship that reject the self-regulation proposition tend to deny that there is any correspondence between the underlying conditions and the induced variables on the market.

Hayek, in contrast to both of these alternatives, sought to explain the lagged relationship between the underlying and the induced. Economics for him is a science of tendency and direction, not one of exact determination. Changes in the underlying conditions set in motion accommodating adjustments that are reflected in the induced variables on the market. The induced variables lag behind, but are continually pulled towards the underlying conditions. If the underlying conditions could be represented by a rabbit and the induced conditions by a dog, then perfect coordination (equilibrium) for the dog would be where the rabbit is; but as the dog moves, the rabbit moves. Thus we can tell a story about where the dog is heading even though the rabbit is constantly moving.

The detour on equilibration versus equilibrium in the core of economic theory was important because of the turn the debate took after Lange's paper and the transformation of basic language in economics. To Hayek and the Austrians, competition refers to a process of ongoing rivalry. To Lange, who was using a neoclassical conception, competition referred to a final state of affairs. Market efficiency is adaptive to Hayek, but to Lange and the neoclassicists it is a question of static efficiency. Similarly, to Hayek prices not only represent exchange ratios but also serve a crucial economizing and information role. For Lange and neoclassical economists they are merely the former.

Hayek's fundamental critique of Lange's contribution was that economists must not assume what must be demonstrated for their argument to hold. Informational assumptions were particularly problematic in this regard. As Hayek developed his argument, for the most part he steered clear of motivational issues by assuming that individuals (both privately and as planners) would have the best of intentions. However, while assuming moral perfection he refused to assume intellectual perfection. This was quite understandable. If one assumes both moral and intellectual perfection, then what possible objection could anyone raise to any social system of production? In fitting with our discussion above about equilibration versus equilibrium, Hayek argues that perfect knowledge is a defining characteristic of equilibrium but cannot be an assumption within the process of equilibration. The question instead is: How do individuals come to learn the information that is necessary for them to coordinate their plans with others?

In 'Economics and knowledge' (1937) and 'The use of knowledge in society' (1945), Hayek develops the argument that how economic agents come to learn represents the crucial empirical element of economics, and that price signals represent the key institutional guide post for learning within the market process. Traditional neoclassical theory taught that prices were incentive devices, which they indeed are. But Hayek pointed out that prices also serve an informational role, which is often unfortunately overlooked. Prices serve this role by economizing on the amount of information that market participants must process and by translating the subjective trade-offs that other participants make into 'objective' information that others can use in formulating and carrying out their plans.

As the debate progressed, Hayek emphasized different aspects of the argument developed in these two classic articles and came to place particular emphasis on the contextual nature of knowledge that is utilized within the market process. Knowledge, he pointed out, does not exist disembodied from the context of its discovery and use. Economic participants base their actions on concrete knowledge of particular time and place. This local knowledge that market participants utilize in orienting their actions is simply not abstract and objective and thus is incapable of being used by planners outside of that context to plan the large-scale organization of society.

Hayek's reasoning for why planning cannot work is not limited to the problem that the information required for the task of coordinating the plans of a multitude of individuals is too vast to organize effectively. The knowledge utilized within the market by entrepreneurs does not exist outside that local context and thus cannot even be organized in principle. It is not that planners would face a complex computational task; it is that they face an impossible task because the knowledge required is not accessible to them no matter what technological developments may come along to ease the computational task.

AUSTRIAN AND NEOCLASSICAL ECONOMICS DEHOMOGENIZED

Later, Mises buttressed Hayek's argument with his notion of the entrepreneur. The entrepreneur, Mises stated, is the driving force of the market process. Entrepreneurs both create and respond to the changes in market conditions, and through their profit-seeking push the market in the direction of clearing. Absent the institutional framework of private property that allows entrepreneurs to appraise the economic situation via the price system, socialist planning must fail. While Hayek's work in response to the market socialists focused on fleshing out the importance of the market as a process that generates a price system that enables us to make use of dispersed knowledge, Mises' subsequent work (1949) not only restated his argument on the impossibility of economic calculation under socialism, but also developed his notion of the entrepreneur as the driving force in the market economy.

It was only in the years following the third stage of the socialist calculation debate, in the late 1940s, that Hayek (and Mises) fully understood that their view of the nature of the economic process – the one we have described above – was fundamentally different from the view of the rest of the economics profession (see Kirzner, 1988). The increasing emphasis of Mises and Hayek on uncertainty, entrepreneurship, knowledge, equilibration (as opposed to equilibrium) and market processes all emerged in the course of the calculation debate. The calculation debate forced Mises and Hayek to carefully elucidate their understandings of the market process, and made them realize the implications of their own ideas. They were blind-sided by the fact that Lange (and Lerner) used neoclassical arguments to construct a defense of socialist economic organization. Although by the 1930s it seemed as though the mainstream had incorporated Austrian ideas rather fully, it became clear to those trained under them in the late 1940s and the 1950s that Mises and Hayek's understanding of the economic process was very different, and far from being accepted by the profession at large. The dividing line between Austrian and neoclassical ideas was drawn, and with it the Austrian school, as a distinct school of economic thought, was reborn.

At the same time as Mises and Hayek were realizing how their views differed from those of neoclassical economists, economic theory was increasingly moving towards greater formalization in style. This move, an outgrowth of economists' increasing desire to be scientific in the sense of the natural sciences, served not only to sideline Hayek's argument which had been rendered verbally, but also to drive a larger wedge between the Austrian approach to economics, described in terms of Hayek's arguments above, and mainstream neoclassical economics.

Although Lange's argument held sway over most of the profession for many years, by 1985 the socialist world was experiencing obvious shortcomings. Consumer frustrations were high, technological development was lagging behind the West, and even military superiority was questionable. In light of these developments many economists began to re-evaluate their previous thoughts regarding the status of socialism as an economic system.

Despite this, Hayek's ideas did not carry the day. In fact, after experiencing a brief spike in popularity, by 1990 consensus among economists held that although socialism suffered from serious problems in practice, Hayek's arguments, which as we saw above in many ways constituted an attack on central tenets of the neoclassical approach, could not be accepted. Although Hayek's arguments were seen as correct in conclusion, they had to be rejected in analysis because accepting them this way would demand a radical recasting of much of contemporary economic theory.

Thus economists such as Joseph Stiglitz (1994) are explicit in their judgment that modern information economics cuts equally against Lange and Hayek. Shleifer and Vishny (1994) are damagingly critical of socialist models, but they grant that Lange was correct in his critique of Mises on purely theoretical grounds, though they contend that he was completely ignorant of the real-world problems socialism would have to confront on public-choice grounds. The incentive problems that socialist planners would confront in organizing economic life are insurmountable and the scope for opportunistic behavior on the part of planning bureaucrats too great for an efficient economic organization to be realized. From the perspective of modern neoclassical economics, socialism cannot work; but not for the reasons emphasized by Hayek.

As was noted above, modern information economics was seen as cutting equally against the model of perfect competition and the model of market socialism. Asymmetric information and an imperfect-competition market structure assure that a market economy left to its own devices will not perform optimally, just as informational and incentive issues plague socialist models. The most ambitious attempt to reconstruct the case for socialism from the point of view of modern informational economics is the model of Pranab Bardhan and John Roemer (1992). This work builds on a series of papers in which Roemer attempts to recast Marxian theory on rational-choice foundations and also uses rational-choice logic to: (1) defeat the welfare claims of competitive equilibrium; and (2) challenge the government failure argument.

What is demonstrated in this literature – a conclusion that is reached by Stiglitz – is that the neoclassical defense of the market is a non-starter. If the neoclassical defense were valid, then the model of market socialism would work. If the model of market socialism fails to work for informational and incentive issues, then so does the neoclassical conception of the market. This conclusion is not only accurate, but perhaps one of the most important lessons we could learn from a century-long dispute over the nature of economic organization. None of the important characteristics that distinguish a market society from a non-market society can be adequately captured in the model that most believe is the foundation for studying a market society.

As Hayek pointed out, the neoclassical construct of perfect competition leaves no room for learning, bargaining and trading, entrepreneurship, innovation, variety and numerous other dimensions that constitute economic life in the real world. Each of these things, instead, is understood formally only as evidence of deviations from the ideal and thus as suboptimal from the standpoint of traditional welfare economics.

If the model of the market is suboptimal and the model of socialism is suboptimal, on what basis do we choose between them? Traditional neoclassical theory cannot adjudicate on grounds of efficiency; but Hayek's argument had nothing to do with the stylized neoclassical market. Thus we can turn to him to adjudicate between capitalism and socialism. The condition of uncertainty and imperfect information that is so problematic for the neoclassical model of the market is a virtue in Hayek's theory. As we discussed above, for Hayek, the market works precisely because it is not perfect. The great strength of the private-property market economy is not the optimality properties of a state of affairs where all the gains from exchange have been exhausted, but the fact that the market economy is in a constant state of flux where existing errors provide the incentive for future corrections and thus lead individuals to be less erroneous than before.

Markets prod and push; they are unsettling to all who wish to sit still. It is this constant activity that is the source of the adaptability to changing circumstances and the spur for innovation. Thus although neoclassical economics does not provide us with the means to establish the superiority of capitalism or socialism, the Austrian framework of both Hayek and Mises that places uncertainty, imperfect information, entrepreneurship and constant change at the center of our attention provides us with strong reason to believe that a private-property order will tend to push us in the direction of prosperity, while socialism cannot.

CONCLUSION

At the beginning of this century, economists debated whether economic law would even be necessary in the future socialist world. This is no longer part of the conversation. A century ago we also debated whether a market economy could be completely abolished. Today, except for extreme voices, the necessity of the market is widely recognized. However, there do remain several modern arguments for socialism. Besides that of Bardhan and Roemer, which we have already mentioned, there is the model proposed by Cottrell and Cockshot (1993), which uses developments in the theory of artificial intelligence to try and show that the problems faced by socialism according to Mises and Hayek are in fact surmountable. However, there are several problems with this model. Without going into depth, we should note that, as Horwitz (1996) points out, the argument of these authors fundamentally misunderstands the role of money and money prices in enabling economic calculation. Additionally, some have suggested a more decentralized workers' management model as means of rejuvenating socialism. Arguments against such arrangements have been leveled by those working in the property-rights tradition, as well as by modern Austrians, such as David Prychitko (1996, 1991), who has shown that such models do not escape the knowledge problem identified by Mises and Hayek.

While such attempts to resurrect socialism still exist, the debate has largely shifted and is now really about how to temper a market to serve egalitarianism. Joseph Stiglitz asks in his book *Whither Socialism?* whether modern economics can be used to serve the goals of nineteenth-century socialism (1994, pp. 269–77). Whatever the answer to this question, it is unclear that Stiglitz's offer has much argumentative weight beyond a very rarefied class of models where basically anything can be proven given certain assumptions.

The most important lesson we can take away from Hayek's arguments against the neoclassical framework in the socialist calculation debate is the necessity of moving away from idealizations of efficient systems and rarefied models that depend heavily on sensitive, specialized assumptions, to a conception of political economy that focuses on the robustness of systems.[7] We live in an imperfect world, populated by individuals caught between alluring hopes and haunting fears. Individuals who will make errors and individuals who will use whatever tools are available to them to take advantage of others exist side by side with individuals who willingly cooperate and those who want to be left alone. Neither moral nor intellectual perfection must be assumed.

A robust theory of political economy must instead challenge all models that assume either benevolence or omniscience. This is not because men are opportunistic as a description, but because in the event that we get an opportunistic ruler we want to constrain them to behave in a manner consistent with benevolence. Similarly, we do not build institutions with the idea that all men are largely ignorant because they are, but because by so doing we do not require that only the smart will be able to make the system work. Hayek's position in the debate against Lange, and implicitly the neoclassicists, underscores the importance of evaluating how alternative systems of economic organization perform under less than ideal conditions.

The arguments advanced by Mises and Hayek relaxed the assumption of planner self-interest in order to focus analytical attention on the informational issues socialist planners would confront. In doing this they created a 'best case' scenario for socialism and still were able to demonstrate the fragility of the system to deviations from ideal information conditions. Socialism, they showed, cannot perform adequately in light of the information problem planners face.

Drawing on the arguments of Adam Smith and David Hume, Mises and Hayek assumed the 'worst case' for capitalism. Not only were individuals assumed to be self-interested, but imperfect information was assumed as well. Hayek's arguments, building on Mises and Smith, demonstrate that the system of private property creates a strong tendency toward the efficient allocation of resources in the face of these 'worst-case' conditions. In other words, the market economy is robust.[8]

Regardless of whether one accepts these arguments advanced by Mises and Hayek, the lesson learned from their participation in the calculation debate remains valid. If we desire theories of political economy that correspond to the real world, which is characterized by highly imperfect conditions, our theories cannot begin by assuming perfection.

ACKNOWLEDGMENTS

The authors would like to thank the Mercatus Center, the Earhart Foundation, the Oloffson Weaver Fellowship and the Kaplan Fund for their generous support of this research. This chapter extends the arguments made in Boettke (2000b).

NOTES

1. Ludwig von Mises, in fact, argued that, 'Whatever our view of its utility or its practicality, it must be admitted that the idea of Socialism is at once grandiose and simple. Even its most determined opponents will not be able to deny it a detailed examination. We must say, in fact, that it is one of the most ambitious creations of the human spirit. The attempt to erect society on a new basis while breaking with all traditional forms of social organization, to conceive a new world plan and foresee the form which all human affairs must assume in the future – that is so magnificent, so daring, that it has rightly aroused the greatest admiration. If we wish to save the world from barbarism we have to conquer Socialism, but we cannot thrust it carelessly aside' ([1922] 1981, p.41).
2. An excellent discussion of Marx's theory of crisis under capitalism can be found in Paul Craig Roberts and Matthew Stephenson (1983).
3. For a documentary history of the socialist calculation debate see Boettke (2000a). This nine-volume reference collection reprints the main papers and excerpts from books dealing with the debate over socialism and the market economy and can be a convenient source for the original material discussed throughout our chapter.
4. The papers on this 'formal-similarity' argument and the subsequent attempts to develop a marginalist economics of socialism can be found in Boettke (2000a, vol. 4).
5. Lange's articles 'On the economic theory of socialism' were published in the *Review of Economic Studies* in 1936–37 and are reprinted in Boettke (2000a, vol. 4, pp.115–33, 139–60). Besides Lange, the other main contributor to the economic theory of socialism was Abba Lerner.
6. Hayek's essays are collected in his *Individualism and Economic Order* (1948). Also see Caldwell (1997) for a discussion of the development of Hayek's thought that was brought on by his debate over socialism.
7. This notion also played a prominent role in Mises' arguments regarding the practicability of socialism. For examples of recent work building in the Mises–Hayek tradition in this fashion see Boettke (2000b) and Boettke and Leeson (2004).
8. For a more detailed discussion of this issue see Boettke and Leeson (2004).

REFERENCES

Bardhan, Pranhab and John E. Roemer (1992), 'Market socialism: a case for rejuvenation', *Journal of Economic Perspectives*, 6 (3), 101–16.

Boettke, Peter J. (ed.) (2000a), *Socialism and the Market: The Socialist Calculation Debate Revisted*, 9 vols, New York: Routledge.

Boettke, Peter J. (2000b), 'Towards a history of the theory of socialist planning', in Peter J. Boettke (ed.), *Socialism and the Market: The Socialist Calculation Debate Revisited*, vol. 1, London: Routledge, pp.1–39.

Boettke, Peter J. and Peter Leeson (2003), 'The Austrian school of economics: 1950–2000', in Warren Samuels, Jeff Biddle and John Davis (eds), *A Companion to the History of Economic Thought*. Oxford: Blackwell, pp. 445–53.

Boettke, Peter J. and Peter Leeson (2004), 'Liberalism, socialism, and robust political economy', *Journal of Markets and Morality*, 7 (1), 99–111.

Caldwell, Bruce J. (1997), 'Hayek and socialism', *Journal of Economic Literature*, 35 (4), 1856–90.

Cottrell, Allin and W. Paul Cockshott (1993), 'Calculation, complexity, and planning: the socialist calculation debate once again', *Review of Political Economy*, 5 (1), 73–112.

Hayek, Friedrich A. (1937), 'Economics and knowledge', *Economica*, n.s. 4 (13), 33–54.

Hayek, Friedrich A. (1945), 'The use of knowledge in society', *American Economic Review*, 35 (4), 519–30.

Hayek, Friedrich A. (1948), *Individualism and Economic Order*, Chicago, IL: University of Chicago Press.

Horwitz, Seven G. (1996), 'Money, money prices, and the socialist calculation debate', *Advances in Austrian Economics*, 3, 59–77.

Kirzner, Israel M. (1988), 'The socialist calculation debate: lessons for Austrians', *Review of Austrian Economics*, 2, 1–18.

Lavoie, Don (1985), *Rivalry and Central Planning*, New York: Cambridge University Press.

Mises, Ludwig von ([1922] 1981), *Socialism: An Economic and Sociological Critique*, Indianapolis, IN: Liberty Fund.

Mises, Ludwig von (1949), *Human Action: A Treatise on Economics*, New Haven, CT: Yale University Press.

Prychitko, David L. (1991), *Marxism and Workers' Self-Management: The Essential Tension*, Westport, CT: Greenwood Press.

Prychitko, David L. (1996), 'The critique of workers' self-management: Austrian perspectives and economic theory', *Advances in Austrian Economics*, 3, 5–25.

Roberts, Paul Craig and Matthew Stephenson (1983), *Marx's Theory of Exchange, Alienation and Crisis*, Westport, CT: Praeger Publishers.

Shleifer, Andrei and Robert W. Vishny (1994), 'The politics of market socialism', *Journal of Economic Perspectives*, 8 (2), 165–76.

Stiglitz, Joseph (1994), *Whither Socialism?*, Cambridge, MA: MIT Press.

13. Spontaneous order, free trade and globalization
Steven G. Horwitz

INTRODUCTION

One of the interesting ironies of the resurgence of interest in the work of Friedrich Hayek in the last few decades is that he had very little to say about one of the most controversial economic issues of our time, namely the heightened importance and visibility of international trade. So-called 'globalization' remains a hotly contested issue and one that creates unusual coalitions on all sides. As Virginia Postrel (1998) argued, one way of viewing the debate over globalization is between 'dynamists' who do not fear uncontrolled and unplanned evolution and change, and 'stasists', who see only the costs of such change and attempt to limit it. The result is an unusual coalition in opposition to globalization that comes from the protectionist right and the 'progressive' left, with the former seeing only harm to the Western working class and the latter seeing globalization (or at least what they would call 'corporate-led' globalization) as impoverishing the developing world, both materially and culturally, by turning it into mini-Americas. What is striking about Postrel's framework is that it can be read in Hayekian terms even though Hayek himself had little to say on the issues at hand.

Hayek's relative silence on international trade is a curious phenomenon in and of itself. One suspects that there are two major explanations. First, with the debates over socialism and Keynesianism filling the journals, and the reality of the Great Depression and the rise of Stalinism and Nazism filling the newspapers, issues of international trade were hardly in the forefront of anyone's intellectual concerns during the most productive years of Hayek's life. In some ways, our contemporary worrying about international trade is a reflection of other major issues having been resolved, and resolved in ways sympathetic to Hayek. Second, and perhaps more interesting for the argument to follow, it was likely the case that Hayek believed that no educated person would doubt the argument for free trade; and certainly not those who imagined themselves talking publicly on economic issues. There was little need, in his mind, to rehash the arguments on free trade because they were long ago settled. An exploration of Hayek's views on international trade would therefore be little more than a repetition of textbook wisdom.

Instead, one can attempt what, for lack of a better term, we might call a 'Hayekian economic sociology' of globalization. From a Hayekian perspective, the argument for the free exchange of goods and services, and the free movement of people,[1] is an extension of Hayek's more general arguments about the role of competition as a knowledge-discovery process and the spontaneous ordering of human affairs under the rule of law. Put simply, peace and prosperity are most likely to emerge where the law treats everyone equally and leaves them to use their person and property in the ways that their localized knowledge deems best. Under a set of institutions that does so, there is no need for conscious direction of resources or 'trade policies', as the signals of the marketplace will guide actors to allocate resources in ways that contribute more to human wealth than any alternative. Unfortunately, the very uncontrolled nature of this process generates two reactions that undermine its benefits: protectionism and 'globophobia'. These two reactions are examples of two of the intellectual errors of modernity that Hayek warned about on numerous occasions: hubris and atavism, respectively. In what follows, I will explore Hayek's general themes about spontaneous order, the rule of law and competition, then turn to see how these can be applied to trade and examine in more detail the hubris of protectionism and the atavism of globophobia.

SPONTANEOUS ORDER, THE RULE OF LAW AND SOCIAL JUSTICE

The fundamental insight at the heart of Hayek's contributions to political economy and social theory is the concept of 'spontaneous order'. With the right set of social institutions, there is no need for human social interaction to be organized consciously and intentionally by other humans, rather the separate and dispersed actions of individuals will be coordinated by the feedback mechanisms of market signals and other analogous processes in other parts of the social world. For Hayek, this central idea was one rooted in the Scottish strand of the Enlightenment, which differed from the French and English strands in its more circumspect view of 'Reason'. For the more rationalist and narrowly utilitarian versions of the Enlightenment, Reason was the nearly infalliable guide to improving the human condition. In the wake of advances in the sciences just prior to and during the Enlightenment, this was an understandable position to take. However, the Scots rightly recognized that to make a god of Reason was to engage in the same sort of dogmatism that the Enlightenment attempted to overturn. In Hume's words, the idea was to 'use Reason to whittle down the claims of Reason'. The result was best captured by another Scot, Adam Ferguson, from whom Hayek (1967) took his definition of spontaneous order as 'the results of human action but not human design'.

The argument that the institutional order of modern society is the unintended outcome of human action runs in the face of our philosophical prejudices that lead us to think we can shape the social world to our wishes. The view that Hayek and others have called 'scientism' reflects this 'fatal conceit' that we can use the methods and procedures of science to organize human social activity. An understandable if mistaken outgrowth of the Enlightenment's belief in reason, scientism suggests that 'rationality' is something we can impose on the social world by better planning and organization. As Hayek (1952) has noted, this approach to the social world dates back over two centuries to the French and others. However, it found its most powerful voice in the Marxian critique of capitalism and that critique's implication for the socialist alternative. Understanding that backdrop is important for coming to grips with Hayek because so much of his system of thought emerged out of his own confrontation with these views in the socialist calculation debate of the interwar years.[2]

The core Marxian impulse is that the system of commodity production is inherently irrational and, in some sense, inefficient. Because capitalism relies on what one might call 'after the fact' coordination (that is, we only know what should have been produced after production takes place and profit and loss provide us with signals about how we did), it will be wasteful and irrational. The so-called 'anarchy of production' that characterizes capitalism, with no one overseeing the process as a whole, involves massive waste, not to mention the exploitation and alienation that Marx identified. The ways in which production and value creation under capitalism happen 'behind the backs' of workers is another instance of Marxian concerns with the uncontrolled nature of the system of commodity production. Because people are producing 'for exchange', it is only the outcomes of that exchange process that can provide feedback for the rationality of their choices.

The Marxian solution is to transcend commodity production by organizing the society as a whole to decide collectively what should be produced, how much should be produced, and what process should be used to produce it. Once agreement on the answers to those questions is obtained, then the work can be divided up among the members of the community and production can begin. When production is completed, the goods and services can then be allocated by some agreed-upon process. Note how this process substitutes an *ex ante* notion of coordination for the *ex post* coordination of capitalism. Marxists would argue that such comprehensive planning avoids the wastes of capitalism because we are in control of the production process from the outset and do not have to wait for profit or loss signals to tell us whether what we have done was right or not. This is what is meant by Marxists, and by later market socialists and economic planners well into the twentieth century, who speak of 'rationalizing' production.[3] Economic order must be imposed by intentional planning rather than emerging unplanned, out of the decentralized decisions of individual actors and organizations.[4]

The economic response to this argument has been covered in the scholarship surrounding Hayek's participation in the socialist calculation debate. The role that private property and a price system play in providing the knowledge necessary to answer the questions about production that Marxism just took for granted as being obvious is now much more clearly understood. The fundamental economic problem facing collective planning is really an epistemic one. Planners, no matter how democratically they were organized, could never access the information they would need to even come close to rationalizing production in the manner they imagined they could. The information discovered and made available via monetary exchanges of privately owned means of production that generate market prices enables *ex post* coordination to be as effective as it is. The dream of *ex ante* coordinating an economy of any significant degree of complexity is utopian in the strongest sense of the term. It is the height of hubris to imagine that one could take control of, and consciously plan, the productive activities of anything resembling a modern economy.

However, another line of argument in response to the Marxian critique is worth mentioning here. In *The Fatal Conceit* (1988) and a few other contributions later in his career, Hayek emphasized the sociological side of this Marxian impulse. In particular, he drew a distinction between the forms of social organization that might have been appropriate at a much earlier stage in human history, when societies were smaller and human relationships were 'face-to-face', and those forms that are appropriate for the anonymous world of what Hayek called the 'Great Society'. For Hayek, the attempt to decide collectively what to produce, how to produce it, and how to distribute it was an atavistic throwback to those earlier face-to-face societies. In a world where we all knew each other with that level of intimacy and where our groups were small and homogenous enough, then perhaps it would be possible to engage in that sort of collectivism. After all, we see that same sort of collectivism at work in smaller-scale organizations within the anonymous Great Society (for example, the family, firms, and other institutions of civil society).[5] From a social evolutionary perspective, Hayek argues that our moral instincts were honed in that early environment of face-to-face interaction where we really could take account of all the effects of our actions on others and make these collectivist decisions. Thus, our tendency to overlook the unintended consequences of our actions (whether good or bad) is deeply ingrained in our morality. We are morally disposed to count highly the direct help or harm we do closest to us and overlook the ripple effects of our choices, even if they dramatically outweigh the 'local' effects.

The problem with our moral instincts is that they are often inappropriate in the world we now inhabit. At the simplest level, our collectivist moral instincts may find it repugnant that some people earn annual incomes of millions of dollars while others live on the edge of poverty, often in the same city. The temptation is to engage in some sort of redistribution of wealth that will level out those differences, which is the sort of collectivist approach that characterized much of human history. However, we cannot afford to ignore the unintended consequences here, which might well result in reducing the incentive for the accumulation of wealth, which itself benefits the relatively worse-off through investment that creates jobs and raises the productivity of labor. Such redistribution might also change the incentives facing the relatively poor, creating dependency and perpetuating the very poverty we wish to eradicate. One can tell a similar story about the intended and unintended consequences of other policies (for example, minimum-wage laws), and in particular the subject at hand: international trade. The notion that human interaction can be a positive-sum game, as all forms of trade are, runs against the bulk of human history where conquest and predation were more likely to be the path to wealth accumulation, both of which are zero-sum at best. The clash between an evolved moral instinct that is disposed to think in terms of zero-sum interaction and the Great Society's success at encouraging positive-sum games plays out all around us. The assumption that one person's gain in wealth is brought about by the impoverishment of others characterizes a great deal of the critique of the globalization of trade.

This argument forms the basis of Hayek's critique of 'social justice'. In his view social justice requires that we take into account all of the possible effects, intended or unintended, that particular actions or policies might have and then determine how those effects match up against some metric or pattern of just outcomes. For example, whether a particular tax or wage policy forwarded social justice would depend upon the pattern of incomes it produced and, presumably, whether it promoted greater equality. In addition, one could render the judgment that, for example, the current pattern of incomes in the United States is 'socially unjust' because it fails to meet some predetermined notion of fairness or justice. Hayek's critique of this view is that most of the social outcomes in the Great Society cannot even have the concept of justice applied to them because we can only judge justice on the basis of individual, intended acts, not patterns of unintended consequences.

The desire to make patterns of social outcomes conform to predetermined notions of 'fairness' or justice, where these two terms are understood in terms of particular end-states, is seen by Hayek (1976) as a form of atavism in its longing for an earlier time when human social groups were small, simple and homogenous enough to make determinations of fairness in this way. The desire for social justice is the misguided attempt to apply the ethics of the tribe to the Great Society. The realities of the Great Society are such that we cannot obtain the knowledge necessary to determine whether any particular distribution of resources or income is in any sense of the word 'fair' or 'just'. Hayek (1976, pp. 31–3) argues that because those distributional patterns are the result of no one's intentions, we cannot even apply the concept of justice to them. Justice can only apply to the intended actions of human beings. Put another way, if one thinks the distribution of income generated by a market economy is unjust, who exactly has committed an injustice to generate that outcome? Individual incomes are the unintended results of all kinds of decentralized decisions by millions of people. If the outcome does not please us, who exactly has been unjust? Individual acts can be judged as just or unjust but not the unintended patterns of outcomes they produce. Any attempt to produce an intended pattern of outcomes will ultimately fail, as the underlying social and economic processes will upset any attempt at patterning, and will reduce the total amount of income or resources available in the process.[6]

The political problem, from a Hayekian perspective, is how to prevent our atavistic instincts from overriding what is necessary for the maintenance of the Great Society. We must, like Odysseus, lash ourselves to the mast to prevent ourselves from being tempted by the siren's song. For Hayek, the answer is the rule of law and constitutionalism. The law must treat people in similar circumstances similarly, and the goal is equality before the law, not equality in outcomes. For example, a law requiring the redistribution of income would not treat people equally in taxing them differently based on income. Justice, for Hayek, is procedural in that as long as individuals are not harming others, they are acting justly. This notion of the rule of law becomes enshrined one level higher in the form of constitutional limits on the power of the state. Rather than risk the temptation of either atavistic attempts at 'social justice' or hubristic attempts at various forms of social planning, constitutions can put reasonably firm limits on what the state can do, enabling it to avoid these ever-present temptations. Of course this often means that we have to live with results that we do not like and that appear as though they can be corrected. As Hayek (1988, p. 18) argued in *The Fatal Conceit*, we have to recognize that we live in 'two sorts of worlds at once' and that although our moral instincts may still be correct in the various organizations that we are part of (for example, families, firms, and so on), they cannot work in the broader social order. It requires an intellectually informed forbearance to accept constitutional limits as the public expression of the limits of our reason.

HAYEK ON INTERNATIONAL TRADE

As noted in the introduction, Hayek did not have much to say about international trade specifically. Whatever the reasons, the topic remains one of the least discussed in his dozens of books and essays. By way of example, there is no remotely extended discussion of the issue in *The Constitution of Liberty* (1960), nor in the three volumes of *Law, Legislation, and Liberty* (1973, 1976, 1979). In fact, the two places with any significant discussion of international trade issues are his *Monetary Nationalism and International Stability* ([1937] 1999) and the next-to-last chapter of *The Road to Serfdom* (1944). The discussion in *Monetary Nationalism* is fairly technical, as it focuses on the international monetary system more than trade generally. The chapter in *Serfdom* is more focused on trade, and with a particular emphasis on how international issues play into his more general thesis about the problems with planning. Neither is a full-blown discussion of the sorts of issues that today mark the debate on globalization, but both have relevance.

The central argument of *Monetary Nationalism* is that after the collapse of the international gold standard in the early 1930s, there was no longer any international monetary system worthy of the name. Individual countries now attempt to determine the share of their currencies in the world's money supply by conscious policy rather than the workings of an 'automatic' mechanism. That is, the proportionate shares are the result of a contest among national banks and policymakers, rather than the unintended result of the free flow of people, goods and services across national boundaries. Hayek sees the latter, which the pre-1931 gold standard approached, though imperfectly, as the more desirable situation as it does not pit country against country in a zero-sum (at best) struggle over shares in the international money supply. The ideal, Hayek argues, is a homogenous international currency that would result in the different shares in the total money supply accruing to individual countries no differently from the shares in national currencies that accrue to different states or regions. With a truly uniform currency over the effective trading area, the geographic distribution of that currency would be, in and of itself, irrelevant and would simply emerge as the unintended consequence of the various choices made by individuals. Such a currency would dramatically smooth international trade by reducing the transactions costs of such trade and by putting restraints on the ability of national governments to attempt to manipulate trade through changes in the supply of currency. An international currency system becomes an application of the constitutionalism and rule of law noted in the previous section.

Hayek argues specifically that a system of fixed exchange rates would be preferable to the floating and managed exchange rates that characterized the 'monetary nationalism' of which he was writing. He rightly recognized ([1937] 1999, p. 78) that the demand for floating exchange rates was really a way for each country to attempt to avoid the effects of an outflow of capital. The ability to change both domestic interest rates and foreign exchange rates is an attempt to 'postpone the necessity of more drastic credit contraction at home... and it may well be that it only passes on the necessity of credit contraction to another country' (p. 78). The end result of this 'beggar-thy-neighbor' process might be to bring 'about a violent contraction of credit at home' for each participant (p. 78). Hayek is also careful to note that this is not an inevitable result of any sort of international monetary system, rather it is the result of the 'mixed' systems then current that included central banks and the particular structure of reserves that they involved. He also recognized the larger implications of this sort of policy stance:

> But exchange control designed to prevent effectively the outflow of capital would really have to involve a complete control of foreign trade, since of course any variation in the terms of credit on exports or imports means an international capital movement... The truth of the whole matter is that for a country which is sharing in the advantages of the international division of labor it is not possible to escape from the effects of disturbances in these international trade relations by means short of severing all trade ties which connect it with the rest of the world. (pp. 82, 84)

He also notes that any such restrictions on capital movement would lead to dramatically different standards of living in different countries, which in turn would lead to increased international 'friction' (p. 85). The zero-sum nature of monetary nationalism is in sharp contrast to the positive-sum game of free international trade on a truly international monetary standard.

In the last substantive chapter of *The Road to Serfdom*, Hayek addresses the 'prospects of international order'. The context is the larger one of the book, namely the ways in which attempts to intentionally plan economies will gradually erode the other freedoms that we value. As most of the book examines the problems created for individual economies, this last chapter explores the effects on international order that might arise from national economic planning. Hayek (1944, p. 220) first notes a potential contradiction between concern about international trade and national economic planning by noting that: 'Many kinds of economic planning are indeed practicable only if the planning authority can effectively shut out all extraneous influences; the result of such planning is therefore inevitably the piling-up of restrictions on the movements of men and goods.'

Achieving national goals cannot take place without recognizing the effects of cross-national trade on those goals, and thus the likelihood of an attempt to harness international trade to national purposes. Hayek argues that there is a fundamental incompatibility between free international trade and national economic planning. The implication is that one of three things must happen: (1) the triumph of national interests over international ones will lead to a breakdown in international relations and threaten peace; (2) economic planning must become international in nature; or (3) faced with the impossibility of planning and the undesirability of perpetual conflict, we will see a return to free competition both nationally and internationally.

Leaving aside the third option for a moment, Hayek spends some time on both the first and second. Just after the earlier quote on the need for restrictions to maintain national goals, he notes the 'dangers to peace' created by the nationalism associated with economic planning. Specifically, he refers to the 'artificially fostered economic solidarity' of the citizens of the individual planning countries or of any coalitions that form among them (p. 220). The formation of these artificial solidarities create a number of faulty perceptions that Hayek sees as damaging to prosperity and international peace. For one, it leads people to believe that 'membership of a national group', rather than one's contribution to the creation of value, is what entitles one to a particular portion of world income. Given that 'it is neither necessary nor desirable that national boundaries should mark sharp differences in standards of living', the artificial solidarity fostered by national economic planning is likely to worsen conflict among nations by creating just the 'sharp differences' that Hayek rightly notes are unnecessary (p. 220). Rather than international trade being seen as a way for individual traders or firms to gain through mutually beneficial exchange, it increasingly becomes a struggle for portions of what is perceived to be a fixed pie. National economic planning turns a positive-sum game into a zero-sum one at best.

The result of moving the 'level of interest' from the individual to the national is that international frictions are increased. Hayek (1944, p. 220) is worth quoting at length here:

> If the resources of different nations are treated as exclusive properties of these nations as wholes, if international economic relations, instead of being relations between individuals, become increasingly relations between whole nations organized as trading bodies, they inevitably become the source of friction and envy between whole nations.

The irony here is that it is only when the effective unit of international trade is taken down to the smallest level possible (the household and the firm) that we truly get peaceful international interaction. Even the word 'international' is misleading because under a regime of free trade, the trade is not international but interhousehold or interfirm. It is precisely the interpolation of the 'nation' in the trading process that undermines the truly 'international' trade among firms and households.[7] Hayek furthermore sees the way in which national planning will move competition from the positive sum forum of the market to the zero sum forum of a contest of political force. Again, it is worth quoting Hayek (pp. 220–21) at some length:

> It is one of the most fatal illusions that, by substituting negotiations between states or organized groups for competition for market or for raw materials, international friction would be reduced. This would merely put a contest of force in the place of what can only metaphorically be called the 'struggle' of competition and would transfer to powerful and armed states, subject to no superior law, the rivalries which between individuals had to be decided without recourse to force. Economic transactions between national bodies ... must end in clashes of power.

Hayek concludes this discussion by claiming that the presumed Allied victory in the then-current war (World War II) could be put to no better use than to reverse the trend toward what was becoming 'a world of many national socialisms, differing in detail, but all equally totalitarian, nationalistic, and in recurrent conflict with each other' (Hayek, 1944, p. 221).

Hayek's treatment of the second option, the internationalization of economic planning, is fairly straightforward. Simply put:

> The problems raised by a conscious direction of economic affairs on a national scale inevitably assume even greater dimensions when the same is attempted internationally. The conflict between planning and freedom cannot but become more serious as the similarity of standards and values among those submitted to a unitary plan diminishes. (1944, p. 221)

Given that collective planning is only possible in situations of simplicity and homogeneity, the problems that plague even a small country with any degree of complexity and heterogeneity among its inhabitants will be magnified enormously if the scale is global. Aside from the insuperable problems of knowledge faced by any attempt to plan, getting agreement on any global ranking of ends will be impossible, forcing the international planning agency to determine whether, for example, the needs of Spanish farmers outweigh Scandinavian fishermen, or just how much Americans might have to be taxed to move resources to impoverished parts of Central or Southern Europe. These 'determinations' ultimately 'cannot be anything but a naked rule of force, an imposition by a small group on all the rest of that sort of standard and employment which the planners think suitable for the rest' (Hayek, 1944, p. 223).[8]

Hayek makes two other points that are worth mentioning, each involving attempts to plan across nations. First, one cannot assume that with a democratic planning process the interests of similar classes in similar nations will be in harmony. For example, members of the working class in richer countries can effectively exploit their counterparts in poorer countries by enforcing an international minimum wage law. As Hayek (1944, p. 225) puts it, such a law would deprive the worker in the poorer country 'of his only chance to better his conditions by overcoming natural disadvantage by working at wages lower than his fellows in other countries'. The other brief point he raises is that attempts to harmonize national planning across countries – and the restrictions in trade this would involve – would create 'objects of hatred and envy' out of the richer nations (p. 225). Once we move from a positive-sum regime of free trade to a zero-sum regime of contests of political force, those who come out worse might (legitimately perhaps) claim that their poverty is the result of the wealth of the rich. The example of the minimum-wage law fits this perception quite well. Hayek's point here is that it does not need to be this way, in that a regime of truly free trade among households and firms, regardless of nationality, would help to address the perception that one's fortune in the world economy is that of one's nation, rather than that of one's self. It would break the 'artificial' solidarity that Hayek referred to as one of the problems created by restrictions on trade promulgated in the name of national planning.

In the last section of this chapter, Hayek looks to solutions for the problems posed by national planning with respect to international trade. He argues for some sort of international body that would have the power not to direct resources in particular ways but to prevent national governments from undertaking nationalistic policies that would lead to a cascade of wealth-reducing and conflict-enhancing policies by other nations. In contemporary terms, he wants to find some form of communication and cooperation that will avoid the suboptimal outcome of a prisoner's dilemma game. Specifically, 'The need is for an international political authority which, without power to direct the different people what they must do, must be able to restrain them from action which will damage others' (1944, p. 232). He is careful to say that the powers given to such a body must be minimal, and not the power to plan or direct resources themselves. Moreover, 'it is essential that these powers of the international authority should be strictly circumscribed by the Rule of Law' (p. 232). And by 'Rule of Law' in this context, Hayek means a willingness to give up power and recognize that the law comes before the desires of men:

> We shall never prevent the abuse of power if we are not prepared to limit power in a way which occasionally may also prevent its use for desirable purposes. The great opportunity we shall have at the end of this war is that the great victorious powers, by themselves first submitting to a system of rules which they have the power to enforce, may at the same time acquire the moral right to impose the same rules upon others. (p. 236)

It is worth asking whether arrangements such as the GATT (General Agreement on Tariffs and Trade) and the WTO (World Trade Organization) fit this description. It is also worth asking the same question of regional trade agreements such as NAFTA (the North Atlantic Free Trade Agreement). The case for the latter is harder to make, given the various special interests embodied in the agreement. The GATT and the WTO, however, do seem to better fit the idea of an international body designed to adjudicate disputes with few powers of its own.

With these Hayekian thoughts on trade in mind, I turn to the two main issues of the present day, protectionism and globalization, and see what sense of them can be made from the perspective I have developed so far.

THE HUBRIS OF PROTECTIONISM

It is beyond the scope of an overview chapter such as this one to address every single argument for all the various forms of protectionism that continue to be raised in the popular media. Instead, the broad contours of these arguments can be explored from a Hayekian perspective to see what lines of response might be developed.

In general terms, most arguments for protectionism take one of two forms. Some are pure nationalism, in that they argue that domestic interests, especially labor interests, need to be protected at almost any cost. Other arguments are concerned with the effects of free trade on poor workers in other countries, and see the benefits of free trade as disproportionately accruing to larger, more developed countries. It is of note that these two forms of argument seem to run in contradiction to each other, as the first assumes that free trade harms large trading nations (or at least a substantial subset of citizens therein), while the second assumes free trade benefits them at the expense of poorer countries. It would seem that both cannot be true.

As has been argued for centuries, the benefits of free trade are positive and mutual. It is true that saying that nations on the whole benefit from trade is not the same thing as saying that each and every citizen benefits (on net) from it in every conceivable short run. In all forms of trade, shifts in demand or in the conditions of supply will cause changes in prices, which in turn will lead to resources, including labor, being shifted from sector to sector or place to place. International trade is no different. Whether through an increased openness of trade, or through changes or growth in the economies of trading partners, patterns of resource allocation will change as trade widens and deepens. Some domestic workers will find the value of their labor shrinking, or becoming prohibitively expensive. As a result, they will see their wages fall or their jobs disappear. As part of the same process, workers elsewhere in the world are seeing increased opportunities and rising wages as capital flows toward them. Moreover, domestic consumers see falling prices of the goods they consume, and consumers elsewhere in the world see greater opportunities to consume due to rising wages and a wider variety of goods at lower costs. Over time, those domestic workers made worse off by the changes in the terms of trade will find new opportunities either through adjustments in their human capital or through new jobs opened by new spending, resulting from domestic consumers spending less on new imports than they did on the same goods made domestically. In either case, free trade is not the cause of any longer-term unemployment or poverty.

In the face of these underlying processes, there is a desire to try to manage and control trade in ways that either prevent the localized short-term negative consequences, or try to offset those consequences with income transfers or other forms of economic intervention. In either case, the results are highly unlikely to be what the political process intends them to be. The belief that political actors can consciously regulate market processes to achieve their desired ends is an example of the hubris of the Hayekian 'fatal conceit'. In fact, political actors face three serious problems in their attempts to use protectionist measures to offset the effects of free trade. First, even if politicians could come up with a consistent coherent program to try to generate those consequences, such a plan is highly likely to be altered by the lobbying of various special interests, and not just those being 'protected'. Second, were politicians able to avoid doing what might be in their political self-interest to do, they would still face insuperable problems in marshaling the knowledge necessary to create a program that would have the results they in fact desire. Third, given the problems created by the first two concerns, the likely result of whatever is enacted is a set of unintended consequences that might worsen rather than improve the condition of those they wish to help, and that might create further problems that call forth another round of counterproductive intervention.[9]

For example, assume that increased international trade has led to the increased importation of clothing. Domestic garment industry workers might well complain about job losses and wage reductions in the face of cheaper imports. They might well lobby the legislature to impose a tariff or quota on imported clothing. What are the problems faced by the legislature? From a Hayekian perspective, they will first face a knowledge problem of what exactly it is that they should do to help. Would a tariff or a quota work better? How much of either? What would be the effects of such action on other related industries, whether higher or lower in the structure of production? Finding the 'right' answers to these questions is beyond the ability of anyone, including politicians. The Hayekian (1978) argument that competition is a process of discovery suggests that the only way to know precisely what markets 'should' do is to allow competition to unfold and discover that information. The knowledge about how best to allocate resources, or how various elements of the market are related, is not available outside the process of competition itself. Just as we learn who the best team is by actually playing the football game, so do we find out the best ways to allocate resources by watching what competition produces. Any protectionist policy that the political process generates will be of necessity arbitrary. The limits to the knowledge of political actors was central to Hayek's contributions to the socialist calculation debate, and protectionism is but a form of sectoral socialist planning.

Indeed, the very challenge of producing the 'right' policy will make the temptation to bend to the winds of political self-interest all the greater. Politicians tend to construct policies that will enhance their own electoral well-being rather than actually addressing the problem at hand (even if, as in this case, it is a pseudo-problem). More generally, the call for protectionist intervention itself often begins from those who are the specific groups made worse off by international trade. Trade is a classic case where the costs of an activity are concentrated and visible while the benefits are dispersed and subtle. Those upon whom the concentrated costs fall have the incentive to lobby to have those effects ameliorated, while the beneficiaries are often not even aware of the cause of their good situation, nor is the benefit to each sufficient to lead to political action to protect it. As Hayek recognized later in his career, this dynamic makes it increasingly difficult for constitutionally unconstrained legislatures to avoid special-interest legislation. Hayek's analysis of the political process in the third volume of *Law, Legislation, and Liberty* (1979) has direct application to the politics of protectionism. It will be very hard to resist the pleas of domestic garment workers whose livelihood is threatened by the world competition.

To complete the analysis, note that the results of the special-interest-driven legislation are likely to include some undesirable consequences not foreseen by the legislation's framers. Suppose that the garment workers are successful in getting the legislature to pass a tariff. As domestic consumers now are paying higher prices for clothing, they may well reduce their total expenditure on new clothes. The domestic retailers might react by lobbying for some sort of governmental assistance lest they too see job losses and firms closing down. And this would produce another cycle of knowledge and incentive problems for political actors, as well as a further set of unintended undesirable consequences. The interventionist process can quickly spiral out of control.

This analysis suggests that it is the very height of hubris to imagine that one can politically control the process of international trade. Even when protectionism is naked, in the sense that it aims only to help a specific few, there will be grave trouble in figuring out exactly what to do to help and how to avoid unintended effects on other actors in the process. Protectionists will also struggle to draw a line that makes some special-interest pleading legitimate and other pleading illegitimate. Well-intentioned protectionists who imagine that a country can be made better off through conscious direction of foreign trade suffer from the same hubris manifesting itself in a slightly different form. Here, imagining that they can produce greater social benefits than uncontrolled processes of international trade reflects an overvaluation of human intelligence at engaging in social design, and an undervaluation of the coordinative power of undesigned social institutions that further trade. For Hayek, the discipline of economics is centrally concerned with unmasking just this sort of hubris. As he argued in *The Fatal Conceit*, 'The curious task of economics is to demonstrate to men how little they really know about what they imagine they can design' (1988, p. 76). This applies no less to protectionism than to other forms of regulation and planning.

THE ATAVISM OF GLOBOPHOBIA

Traditional protectionist arguments have never really gone away, but in the last decade new versions of objections to free international trade have emerged. In particular, there is a line of thought that expresses a kind of generalized fear about the ongoing globalization of economic activity that is best captured by the term 'globophobia'. For the most part, this particular critique of free trade has come from the political left. This is somewhat surprising given the left's historical commitment to cosmopolitanism and objections to nationalism. In response, many of the left have qualified their criticisms of globalization to reflect a specific objection to 'corporate-led' globalization. The argument is that the ongoing globalization process is controlled by corporations and their collaborators within government and thus primarily benefits them, rather than the people in general. By contrast, the leftist critics of globalization argue that if globalization were 'directed from below' with workers and others controlling the processes by which global integration takes place, then these processes would be more fair and humane and provide greater benefits for more people.

This argument represents precisely the sort of atavistic view of economic and social interaction that Hayek criticized throughout his long career. Although there is no doubt that some 'free trade' agreements such as NAFTA include a variety of special-interest provisions that do indeed disproportionately and unfairly favor various producers, the belief that the wider processes of globalization are being 'directed' or 'managed' by the corporate sector, and that the benefits of these processes have mostly accrued to that same sector, reveals an inability both to see order without a designer and to understand how such an order can generate unintended, but beneficial, consequences. The critics of globalization appear to believe that economic processes can be and should be controlled for the benefit of particular identifiable groups.

From a Hayekian perspective the anti-globalization movement seems caught between two reactions: believing that globalization is being controlled by powerful interests and an inability to believe that globalization could happen, or at least could happen beneficially, without some group in control of it. In fact, much of what we call 'globalization' is the playing out of the unintended consequences of the falling costs of communication and transportation and the opening of the former Soviet bloc to domestic and international trade. It is certainly true that some owners of capital have benefitted greatly from these processes (and it is often overlooked that others have not, including a number of firms who have seen their market shares whittled away by more intense global competition), but the prime beneficiaries have been the citizenry of much of the world. The dramatic decline in the number of people living on less than $1 per day, as well as the major increases in per capita income in two of the world's most populous nations (China and India), suggest that whatever is happening is hardly benefitting the economically or politically powerful alone. Of course the financial crisis of 2008 and subsequent recession and slow recovery, as well as the fiscal problems of Western Europe, have caused a short-term slowdown, if not reversal, of the economic status of many people. Despite those troubles, the underlying long-run secular forces of progress continue and most measures of human well-being (for example, life expectancy, literacy rates, and the like) continue to improve even as economic indicators are more mixed.

Much of the globalization process is precisely the sort of mutually beneficial trade that characterizes markets. The patterns of unintended consequences that such trade causes are impossible to predict in their details and equally impossible therefore to control. Globalization is a dynamic process of uncontrolled change, but one that we have reason to believe will generate, on net, very beneficial results. The situation is a repeat at another level of complexity of the transition from traditional modes of economic production to modern market modes.[10] As individuals began to trade with strangers and allow pecuniary gain to determine their actions, they were often seen as threats to the traditional, collectivist ways of organizing economic activity. In the world of the face-to-face society, direct concern with the needs of the group was the primary ethical obligation and those who chose to do otherwise were potential threats to the group's survival. The typical story of the son who sets off on his own to the city to make a living in violation of his village's orders is an example of this process. The market order is characterized by a belief that what is currently unknown is more of a promise than a threat, and that heading off to 'make one's fortune' is likely to work to the benefit of all, even as it violates custom and tradition. When one starts from the assumption that social order emerges through conscious direction, then the individualism of the market, what Marx rightly called the 'anarchy of production', looks like chaos.

The globophobes' argument is but another version of this concern. As Hayek (1988) argues, the need to see economic processes as being the result of someone's intention is an atavistic impulse that is deep in our moral instincts. Moreover, the argument that such processes should be directed for the benefit of an identifiable group is similarly atavistic in its desire to see justice done through a conscious allocation of resources and rough equality of measured outcomes. The beliefs that: (1) the corporate world is the controlling cause of what the critics see as the negatives of globalization; and (2) a globalization process controlled by 'the people' is both possible and desirable, represent the two sides of the Hayekian 'fatal conceit'.

CONCLUSION

Aside from its emphasis on the limits to human control over social processes, there is not much that Hayekian economics can add to the standard arguments in favor of free trade and globalization. Hayek did not have much to say about these matters, and what he did say with respect to economics was largely the received wisdom of his day. What Hayekian economics can do, however, is to highlight the importance of cultural and intellectual beliefs in explaining the objections to trade-driven globalization and the important intellectual work that needs to be done to address those objections. A more sociological look at the anti-globalization arguments provides an excellent case study in the sorts of intellectual attitudes that Hayek dissects in *The Fatal Conceit*. It is a fascinating combination of hubris and atavism that explains the belief that complex economic processes can and should be consciously controlled. Add to this claim the belief that the current way in which globalization is taking place is benefitting the rich at the expense of the poor and that a more 'democratically controlled' globalization process would reverse that flow of resources, and the result is an emotionally powerful narrative.

If that narrative is that we are victims of a process that we could use to our own benefit but have allowed to be hijacked to serve the interests of a powerful few, then it has to be combated at every level. What Hayekian insights can do is to remind us that international trade and globalization are not just economic issues, and that the various facts and figures and theoretical arguments that get thrown around have to be set in a broader intellectual and ideological context. The complexities of trade test our most fundamental beliefs about the nature of society and our ability as humans to control and direct processes of social growth. Hayek's emphasis on spontaneous order and the rule of law, and his identification of the problems of seeing 'social justice' as a pattern of outcomes, all provide a larger framework for understanding both the benefits of further integration of the global economy and the arguments of those who object to it.

NOTES

1. Although this chapter does not address the movement of people across borders, I would argue that many of the same Hayekian arguments that support the case for the free movement of goods and services apply to immigration and emigration as well.
2. See Caldwell (1988, 2003), Vaughn (1994) and Boettke (1998) for more on this point. Hayek's contributions to this debate can be found in Hayek ([1935a] 1948, [1935b] 1948, [1940] 1948, [1945] 1948).
3. This process of *ex ante* coordination of production also explains how the Marxian system would eliminate alienation and exploitation. With all decisions about production being made openly and by everyone, and with exchange, and therefore the value of labor, not directing what gets produced, workers are not alienated from their work or themselves, because they are fully part of the process, and they are not exploited, as ending private property in the means of production ends the class system.
4. Engels ([1892] 1972, p.68) captured this attitude nicely: 'The difference is as that

between the destructive force of electricity in the lightning of the storm, and electricity under command in the telegraph and the voltaic arc; the difference between a conflagration, and fire working in the service of man'.
5. On the relationship between Hayekian 'organizations' and the broader social order, see Horwitz (2005a, 2005b) and Hayek (1973, especially Ch. 2).
6. This argument echoes Nozick (1974).
7. It is worth noting the underlying, and implicit, cosmopolitanism in Hayek's argument. Historically, classical liberalism's defense of free trade was premised on a belief in the irrelevance of national, ethnic, or racial identity. Trade was always among households and firms, not among members of groups or nations. One's role as a 'citizen of the world' entitled one to membership in the trading community, not one's nationality or ethnicity. This is the source of Hayek's claim that the national 'economic solidarity' created by planning is 'artificial'. The 'real' economic solidarity we should have is all of us in our role as humans wishing to improve our lives through the ability to trade freely. It is also clear how this view of trade makes the natural connection between free trade and international peace. Viewing the citizens of other countries as possible sources of benefit via trade, rather than threats to one's nation's share of world income, makes one much less likely to see war and conflict as necessary or productive.
8. After raising this point, Hayek goes on to note how it can explain the horrors of Nazism. Given their desire to plan their economy in the interests of the 'master race', they have no choice but to use brutal force. Hayek (1944, p.223) says, 'It is a mistake to regard the brutality and disregard of all the wishes and ideals of the smaller people shown by the Germans simply as a sign of their special wickedness; it is the nature of the task they have assumed which makes these things inevitable. To undertake the direction of the economic life of people with widely divergent ideals and values is to assume responsibilities which commit one to the use of force; it is to assume a position where the best intentions cannot prevent one from being forced to act in a way which to some of those affected must appear highly immoral'.
9. This, of course, is the dynamic of interventionism identified by Mises (1966, pp. 855–61; [1940] 1998) and explored in great detail by Ikeda (1997).
10. See the discussion in Hayek (1988) and Lavoie (1985, Ch. 2).

REFERENCES

Boettke, Peter J. (1998), 'Economic calculation: the Austrian contribution to political economy', *Advances in Austrian Economics*, 5, 131–58.
Caldwell, Bruce J. (1988), 'Hayek's transformation', *History of Political Economy*, 20 (4), 513–42.
Caldwell, Bruce J. (2003), *Hayek's Challenge*, Chicago, IL: University of Chicago Press.
Engels, Frederick ([1892] 1972), *Socialism: Utopian and Scientific*, New York: International Publishers.
Hayek, Friedrich A. ([1935a] 1948), 'The nature and history of the problem', *Individualism and Economic Order*, Chicago, IL: University of Chicago Press.
Hayek, Friedrich A. ([1935b] 1948), 'The state of the debate', *Individualism and Economic Order*, Chicago, IL: University of Chicago Press.
Hayek, Friedrich A. ([1937] 1999), *Monetary Nationalism and International Stability*, reprinted in Stephen Kresge (ed.), *The Collected Works of F.A. Hayek. Vol. 6, Good Money Part II: The Standard*, Chicago, IL: University of Chicago Press.
Hayek, Friedrich A. ([1940] 1948), 'The competitive solution', *Individualism and Economic Order*, Chicago, IL: University of Chicago Press.
Hayek, Friedrich A. (1944), *The Road to Serfdom*, Chicago, IL: University of Chicago Press.
Hayek, Friedrich A. ([1945] 1948), 'The use of knowledge in society', *Individualism and Economic Order*, Chicago, IL: University of Chicago Press.

Hayek, Friedrich A. (1952), *The Counter-Revolution of Science*, Indianapolis, IN: Liberty Press.
Hayek, Friedrich A. (1960), *The Constitution of Liberty*, Chicago, IL: University of Chicago Press.
Hayek, Friedrich A. (1967), 'The results of human action but not of human design', *Studies in Politics, Philosophy, and Economics*, Chicago, IL: University of Chicago Press.
Hayek, Friedrich A. (1973), *Law, Legislation, and Liberty*, vol. 1: *Rules and Order*, Chicago, IL: University of Chicago Press.
Hayek, Friedrich A. (1976), *Law, Legislation, and Liberty*, vol. 2: *The Mirage of Social Justice*, Chicago, IL: University of Chicago Press.
Hayek, Friedrich A. (1978), 'Competition as a discovery procedure', *New Studies in Politics, Philosophy, Economics and the History of Ideas*, Chicago, IL: University of Chicago Press.
Hayek, Friedrich A. (1979), *Law, Legislation, and Liberty*, vol. 3: *The Political Order of a Free People*, Chicago, IL: University of Chicago Press.
Hayek, Friedrich A. (1988) *The Fatal Conceit: The Errors of Socialism*, William W. Bartley III (ed.), Chicago, IL: University of Chicago Press.
Horwitz, Steven G. (2005a), 'Two worlds at once: Rand, Hayek, and the ethics of the micro and macro-cosmos', *Journal of Ayn Rand Studies*, 6, 375–403.
Horwitz, Steven G. (2005b), 'The functions of the family in the Great Society', *Cambridge Journal of Economics*, 29 (5), 669–84.
Ikeda, Sanford (1997), *The Dynamics of the Mixed Economy*, New York: Routledge.
Lavoie, Don (1985), *National Economic Planning: What is Left?*, Cambridge, MA: Ballinger Publishing Company.
Mises, Ludwig von ([1940] 1998), *Interventionism: An Economic Analysis*, Bettina Bien Greaves (ed.), Irvington-on-Hudson, NY: Foundation for Economic Education.
Mises, Ludwig von (1966), *Human Action: A Treatise on Economics*, 3rd edn, Chicago, IL: Henry Regnery.
Nozick, Robert (1974), *Anarchy, State and Utopia*, New York: Basic Books.
Postrel, Virginia (1998), *The Future and Its Enemies*, New York: Free Press.
Vaughn, Karen (1994), *Austrian Economics in America*, New York: Cambridge University Press.

14. Hayek on labor unions[1]
Charles W. Baird

INTRODUCTION

> It is probably... impossible in our time for a student to be a true friend of labor and to have the reputation of being one. (Hayek, [1959] 1967, p. 294)

As this epigraph implies, unions have a much better reputation than they deserve. Even today (2012) a majority of the general public thinks that labor unions are the best friend that any working man or woman could have. That is simply wrong, and in Hayek's writings on unions, from *Monetary Nationalism and International Stability* (see Hayek, [1937] 1972, pp. 21–2) wherein he first noted the inflationary dangers of collective bargaining, through *1980s Unemployment and the Unions* (Hayek, [1980] 1984), which Arthur Seldon characterized as the summation of Hayek's teaching on unions (Seldon, [1980] 1984, p. 9), Hayek explained why. He argued that while unions benefited some workers it was always at the expense of other workers and that as a whole, unions have made workers significantly worse off than they would otherwise have been.

Moreover, he saw unions as they were (and, in large measure, as they still are) in Britain and the US as major threats to the free economy as well as the free society in general. He endorsed voluntary unionism on grounds of freedom of association properly understood, but he saw actual unions in both countries as wholly involuntary organizations to which politicians had granted both immunity from the ordinary rule of law and power to wield coercive authority mainly against workers who preferred to be union free. The malign consequences of coercive unionism examined by Hayek fall into two broad categories: effects on the economy and conflicts with the rule of law. In both, Hayek saw immense problems which could only be solved by major reforms of public policy.[2]

In what follows I will first discuss what Hayek meant by 'coercive' unionism and what he saw as the sources of the unions' coercive powers in Britain and the US. Some rule-of-law issues will be addressed here. Next, in turn, I will consider his views on voluntary unions, the economic consequences of coercive unionism, and the threats of coercive unionism to the free society and the market economy. Then I will cover Hayek's views on coercive unionism and the rule of law as it relates to freedom of association, freedom of contract, and strikes and picketing. I will follow with a discussion of his views on profit sharing as an alternative to collective bargaining and on codetermination or industrial democracy. I will close by commenting on the extent to which the situation has changed since 1980.

COERCIVE UNIONISM

In *The Constitution of Liberty* (1960) Hayek outlined his views concerning the proper scope of government. He argued that the principal function of a just government is to provide the protective services of the classical night watchman state. Later, in *Law, Legislation and Liberty I* (1973) he characterized these protective services as those necessary to enforce the 'rules of just conduct' among people. I have characterized these rules of just conduct as the rules of voluntary exchange (Baird, 1995). These rules are general (applicable to all situations) and abstract (not designed to accomplish specific purposes). They set the environment within which people remain free to pursue their own purposes. To enforce such rules government must have some coercive power. According to Hayek, coercion is evil; but some coercion, exercised exclusively by government for the sole purpose of preventing people from trespassing against each other, is necessary.

In addition to limited government, Hayek's view of the rule of law requires that government apply and enforce the rules of just conduct uniformly over all people and to itself. People wielding governmental authority may grant no special privileges to, and impose no special burdens on, anyone. Equality before the law, what Hayek called '*isonomia*', is the *sine qua non* of the rule of law (1960, Part II). Moreover, the private use of coercive force, except in self-defense, is always contrary to the rule of law.

Now, unions are not governments. They are private organizations of private individuals. They should never be able to deal with any people except on the basis of voluntary exchange. Yet, in Britain and the US politicians have granted unions the unique privilege of using coercion to get what they want:

> Public policy concerning labor unions has, in little more than a century, moved from one extreme to the other. From a state in which little the unions could do was legal if they were not prohibited altogether, we now have reached a state where they have become uniquely privileged institutions to which the general rules of law do not apply. They have become the only important instance in which governments signally fail in their prime function – the prevention of coercion and violence.[3] (Hayek, 1960, p. 267)

What sort of coercion and violence did Hayek have in mind?

> The unions cannot achieve their principal aims unless they obtain complete control of the supply of the type of labor with which they are concerned; and, since it is not in the interest of all workers to submit to such control, some of them must be induced to act against their own interest ...
>
> It is the techniques of coercion that unions have developed for the purpose of making membership in effect compulsory, what they call their 'organizational activities' (or, in the United States, 'union security' – a curious euphemism) that give them the real power. (ibid., pp. 273–4)

In Britain if a union, through strikes and threats of strikes, could get employers of a particular kind of labor to agree not to hire any union-free workers, the instrument of coercion would be to present recalcitrant workers with a 'choice': join up or do not work. In the US the same sort of coercive choice was imposed through the 'union security' provisions of the National Labor Relations Act (1935). In 1947 that Act was amended, and subsequent decisions of the US Supreme Court reduced compulsory union membership to the compulsory payment of union dues. It remains true in the US that unions can coerce workers to support them as a condition of continued employment.

However, unions do not stop there. Sometimes individual workers who wish to become or remain union-free are threatened with beatings and worse. Sometimes the threats become reality. Sometimes the families of recalcitrant workers are also victims of threats and attacks.[4] And all of this has been considered proper. How could this be?

> All this has become possible because in the field of labor relations it has come to be accepted belief that the ends justify the means, and that, because of the public approval of the aims of union effort, they ought to be exempted from the ordinary rules of law. The whole modern development of unionism has been made possible mainly by the fact that public policy was guided by the belief that it was in the public interest that labor should be as comprehensively and completely organized as possible, and that in the pursuit of this aim the unions should be as little restricted as possible. (Hayek, [1959] 1967, p. 281)

Muddled thinking and widespread belief in the 'myth' that unions have benefited the working class and that those benefits would vanish in the absence of unions, leads public opinion to several false conclusions:

> [T]he fact that it is a natural aim of the unions to induce all workers to join them has been so interpreted as to mean that the unions ought to be entitled to do whatever seems necessary to achieve this aim. Similarly, the fact that it is legitimate for unions to try to secure higher wages has been interpreted to mean that they must be allowed to do whatever seems necessary to succeed in their effort. In particular, because striking has been accepted as a legitimate weapon

of unions, it has come to be believed that they must be allowed to do whatever seems necessary to make a strike successful. In general, the legalization of unions has come to mean that whatever methods they regard as indispensable for their purposes are also to be considered legal. (Hayek, 1960, p. 274)

This unthinking support of labor unions is based on confused notions of social justice:

> The struggle for the recovery of Britain may mean a struggle against those long regarded as the 'good' people, whose 'social conscience' led them to try to impose some ideal design on the distribution of incomes. These are the politicians in all parties, in the trade unions, supported by well meaning, but muddled people in high places. (Hayek, [1980] 1984, p. 47)

The principal source of the coercive powers enjoyed by British unions was the 1906 Trades Disputes Act which, unlike US legislation in the 1930s, did not actually grant any coercive powers. Instead the 1906 Act simply immunized labor unions and labor union leaders from any prosecution for acts of coercion and violence. This may sound a bit exaggerated, but it is not. Even Sidney and Beatrice Webb, staunch supporters of British unions in the late nineteenth and early twentieth centuries, regarded the Trade Disputes Act as 'nothing less than monstrous' (Hanson, 1984, p. 70). As Hayek pointed out in 1960 (p. 268) and Hanson repeated in 1984 (p. 70), A.V. Dicey, the renowned British constitutional lawyer, condemned the 1906 law for having made 'a trade union a privileged body exempted from the ordinary law of the land' (ibid., pp. 69–70). From 1906 until the Thatcher reforms of the 1980s (despite a feckless attempt by the Heath government in 1971 to make some changes) unions could, with impunity, use threats of force and violence, and actual force and violence, against employees and employers as well as customers and suppliers of strike targets to achieve whatever they wanted as long as it was in the context of a labor dispute.

Hayek cites the sources of American unions' coercive powers as the Clayton Act of 1914, and the Norris-LaGuardia Act of 1932 together with the Supreme Court decision in *Hunt v. Crumboch* (325 US 821 [1945]). Curiously he failed to cite the most important piece of legislation in this regard: the National Labor Relations Act of 1935 as amended in 1947 (Hayek, 1960, p. 268). The Clayton Act was an attempt by Congress to make unions exempt from antitrust laws. It did not work, because the 1921 Supreme Court decision in *Duplex Printing v. Deering* (254 US 443) prevented the exemption from applying to most union activities. The Norris-LaGuardia Act overrode the *Duplex* decision as far as antitrust was concerned. In addition it made it impossible for federal courts to grant injunctions against any sort of union activities in labor disputes, authorized mass picketing, even by non-employees, during strikes, and made union-free agreements between workers and employers unenforceable (Baird, 1995, section III). *Hunt v. Crumboch* was an especially egregious Supreme Court decision wherein the Court granted union leaders the privilege of driving an employer out of business simply because they did not like the employer (Baird, 2000, section III).

The National Labor Relations Act (NLRA) was and is the principal legislative source of union exemptions from the rule of law in the US. Its doctrines of exclusive representation and mandatory good-faith bargaining are the main culprits. Union security, which as we saw above was cited by Hayek, really derives from exclusive representation. Briefly, exclusive representation is the provision in the NLRA that prohibits individual workers from deciding whether they will or will not be represented by a union. Instead, the question is decided by majority vote. A union that is certified by such a vote represents all workers who were eligible to vote. Workers who voted against the union as well as workers who did not vote must accept the representation 'services' of the winning union. Individuals are forbidden to represent themselves. Moreover, once a union is certified it is presumed to have majority support indefinitely. There are no regularly scheduled future elections wherein workers can reconsider the issue. For example, the United Auto Workers union is the exclusive bargaining agent for all American General Motors assembly line workers even though all of the workers who voted for the union back in the 1930s and 1940s are now dead or retired. Current workers never got a chance to vote.

Although Hayek did not explicitly discuss exclusive representation in American unionism, he clearly condemned the principle twice in *The Constitution of Liberty*:

> Legislation has frequently gone so far as to require not only that that a contract concluded by the representatives of the majority of the workers of a plant or industry be available to any worker who wishes to take advantage of it, but that it apply to all employees, even if they should individually wish to be able to obtain a different combination of advantages. (Hayek, 1960, p. 275)

Later, while discussing how to constrain union coercion he wrote:

> It would be necessary . . . to rescind all legal provisions which make contracts concluded with the representatives of the majority of workers of a plant or industry binding on all employees and to deprive all organized groups of any right of concluding contracts binding on men who have not voluntarily [as individuals] delegated this authority to them. (ibid., p. 278)

Mandatory good-faith bargaining forces employers to bargain with certified unions on matters of wages and salaries and other terms and conditions of employment. The only sure defense an employer has against a charge of failure to bargain in good faith with a union is an unambiguous record of making compromises during the bargaining process. In Britain a union could force an employer to give in to union demands by threats and acts of violence. In America, the law itself explicitly forces employers to give in. For example, union security is a mandatory subject of bargaining. The law compels employers to bargain with certified unions on whether workers who are not union members, but who under exclusive representation are represented by those unions, shall be forced to join the union or at least pay union dues.

Hayek never discussed mandatory good-faith bargaining. Perhaps he was unaware of this feature of American law. In any case the idea is completely foreign to Hayek's conception of the rule of law. Under the common law of contracts, if any party to a contract were forced to bargain and forced to make concessions, the contract would be null and void. To be legitimate a contract must emerge from a process of voluntary exchange. This is one example of what Edwin Vieira, an American labor lawyer, calls 'the apartheid of [American] labor law' (1986, p. 35).

To perfect the exemption of American unions from the rule of law, the Supreme Court in *United States v. Enmons* (410 US 396 [1973]) exempted unions and their leaders from federal prosecution for any threats or acts of violence and coercion as long as the threats and acts were committed in the context of a labor dispute wherein unions were seeking 'legitimate union objectives' such as higher wages and collective bargaining contracts. In so doing the Court enacted its own Trades Disputes Act.

VOLUNTARY UNIONISM

Hayek begins his discussion of the legitimate functions of unions in *The Constitution of Liberty* (1960) with a rather startling statement:

> It can hardly be denied that raising wages by the use of coercion is today the main aim of unions. Even if this were their sole aim, legal prohibition of unions would however, not be justifiable. In a free society much that is undesirable has to be tolerated if it cannot be prevented without discriminatory legislation. (Hayek, 1960, p. 275)

The problem with unions, then, is not what they try to do even when those efforts are coercive. The problem, Hayek suggests, is that the unions are not subject to the rule of law. Their coercive acts go unpunished. In a free society that which is undesirable must be dealt with by a consistent application of the rules of just conduct and punishment of those who break those rules. No special, discriminatory legislation is justified.

Hayek then opines, 'as truly voluntary and non-coercive organizations, [unions] may have important services to render. It is in fact more than probable that unions will fully develop their potential usefulness only after they have been diverted from their present antisocial aims by an effective prevention of the use of coercion' (ibid., p. 276). This is in keeping with Hayek's view of the competitive market process as a 'discovery procedure' ([1968] 1978). No one can know what activities voluntary and peaceful unions might discover to be beneficial to their voluntary members and others. Unions have never had to embark on that journey of discovery.

Nevertheless, Hayek suggests some broad types of possibly useful activities for voluntary unions. Among these are a role in the discovery of preferred mixes of direct wages and fringe benefits in compensation packages, and discovery of majority opinion concerning 'the differentials between the remuneration for different jobs and the rules for promotion' (1960, p. 276). He also guesses that unions may be useful in setting up rules concerning 'self-government' among employees (ibid., p. 277).

Then he says, 'There is ... the oldest and most beneficial activity of the unions, in which as "friendly societies" they undertake to assist members in providing against the peculiar risks of their trade' (ibid.). I have doubts regarding his first three conjectures, and I join him in the fourth. But that is not the point. Anyone can make a list. Only the market can reveal outcomes. Part V of the 1984 edition of Hayek's *1980s Unemployment and the Unions* consists of an edited version of an article Hayek wrote in October 1978 for *The Times*. In that article he reiterated his 1960 conjecture that voluntary, peaceful unions would have useful things to do. Here they are limited to activities 'with respect to the internal organizations of enterprises – questions on which the arrangements of large organizations depend' ([1978] 1984, p. 61). This suggestion is no more helpful than his earlier ones.

My expectation is that whatever useful functions would be discovered for peaceful, voluntary unions they would be carried out at the level of the individual firm, not whole industries, much less for the entire economy. Hayek was not so sure. He said, 'We shall leave the question open, however, as to whether any of the above arguments justify unions of a larger scale than that of the plant or corporation' (1960, p. 277). I find this curious because, as we will see below, Hayek favored the application of antitrust laws to unions. If antitrust laws are used to prohibit two or more firms from colluding together, consistent application of the laws would also prohibit the employees of two or more firms from colluding together. My position is that antitrust law ought not to be applied to either firms or unions (Baird, 2000).

Before his discussion of the legitimate functions of voluntary unions, Hayek noted that such unions could not aspire to raise wages above market levels:

> [S]trictly voluntary unions, because their wage policy would not be in the interest of all workers, could not receive the support of all. Unions that had no power to coerce outsiders would thus not be strong enough to force up wages above the level at which all seeking work could be employed, that is, the level that would establish itself in a truly free market for labor in general. (Hayek, 1960, pp. 270–71)

The only way any union can enforce an above-market wage in any specific employment is to exclude union-free workers from being hired at the high wage. To do that, a union must have coercive power. Truly voluntary unions, working within the rule of law, would have no such power. No union-free workers would consent to be shut out of high-wage employment, and their competition with unionized workers would lower the wage to the market level.

Unless every employment is blocked by unions with coercive power, excluded union-free workers would eventually find employment elsewhere. The spillover of excluded workers into alternative employments would lower wages therein relative to what those wages would be in the absence of the coercive power of unions. In the next section it will be seen that distortions of relative wages inhibit the process of market coordination.

Hayek was even more forthright in his endorsement of voluntary unionism in his *1980s Unemployment and the Unions*:

> I do not, of course, deny the trade unions their historical merits or question their right to exist as voluntary organizations. Indeed, I believe that everybody, unless he has voluntarily renounced it, ought to have the right to join a trade union. But neither ought anyone to have the right to force others to do so. (Hayek, [1980] 1984, p. 51)

The phrase 'unless he has voluntarily renounced it' raises another question. In America prior to the Norris-LaGuardia Act (1932) it was legal for an employer to include a union-free (unionists called it 'yellow dog') provision in his offer of employment. Any worker who accepted such an offer of employment would thereby consent to abstain from any sort of union activity. As I have argued elsewhere, such agreements are perfectly consistent with the doctrine of freedom of contract (Baird, 1995). I infer from the quote above that Hayek would agree with me. However, in *The Constitution of Liberty* Hayek unequivocally condemned the 'yellow dog contracts' as agreements in restraint of trade (1960, p. 278). I will return to this issue below. Here I simply point out that Hayek must have changed his mind on this issue by 1980.

ECONOMIC CONSEQUENCES OF COERCIVE UNIONISM

The malign economic effects of coercive unionism examined by Hayek fall into four broad categories: (1) unions disrupt and impair the coordination of economic activities through the competitive market process; (2) they increase the extent and duration of unemployment; (3) they cause inflation and exacerbate the business cycle; and (4) they lower productivity, which results in lower standards of living for working people.

Discoordination of Economic Activities

Part II of Hayek's *1980s Unemployment and the Unions* is a clear and persuasive exposition of his long-held understanding of how markets achieve coordination of the diverse economic activities of all market participants without any central direction. Relative prices and relative wages, and their profit and loss implications, are central to that coordination process. In brief, within the context of voluntary exchange, all market participants attempt to do the best they can for themselves. They formulate production and exchange plans on the basis of the bid and ask prices they expect to encounter in the market. Each person formulates their own bid prices for those goods and services (including labor) they are interested in buying and their own ask prices for those goods and services (including labor) they are interested in selling. Each person also has expectations regarding the bid and ask prices of other market participants. As people attempt to carry out their plans they will discover the extent to which their expectations and planned actions are consistent with what others are willing to do. Buyers who expected to encounter lower ask prices than they do, will decide to buy less than they had planned. Buyers who expected to encounter higher ask prices than they do, will decide to try to buy more than they had planned. Sellers who expected to encounter higher bid prices than they do, will decide to sell less. Sellers who expected to encounter lower bid prices than they do, will decide to try to sell more. All the while, market participants will adjust their own bid and ask prices to make them more consistent with newly discovered production and exchange opportunities. Gradually, as expectations come to correspond to reality, more and more coordination of production and exchange activities is achieved. Since market conditions are almost always changing, coordination is a moving target. Nevertheless, freely determined prices and wages move markets toward coordination, a state where the plans and actions of all market participants are mutually consistent. Note that no one has to have knowledge of the underlying reasons other market participants do what they do. All that is necessary is that prices are free to convey the implications of those actions.

In Hayek's words:

> Each individual can rarely know the conditions which make it desirable, for him as well as for others, to do one thing rather than another, or to do it in one way or another. *It is only through the prices he finds in the market that he can learn what to do and how.* Only they, constantly and unmistakably, can inform him what goods and services he ought to produce in his own interest as well as the general interest of his community or country as a whole. The 'signal' which warns him that he must alter the direction or nature of his effort is frequently the discovery that he can no longer sell the fruits of his effort at prices which leave a surplus over costs. The signaling apparatus works as much for the employed worker as for the professional or business man....
>
> For anyone earning his living in the market, which means most of us, the most valuable contribution he can make at any time will depend on thousands of continually changing conditions of which he can have no direct knowledge. It is nevertheless possible for him to make whatever decisions are most advantageous both to himself and the community at large because the open market conveys to him, through its prices, the information he requires to make the right decisions and choices. The prices are thus the indispensable signals that communicate to him the effects of events with which he cannot himself be directly acquainted. (Hayek, [1980] 1984, pp. 28–9)

Coercive unionism cripples this coordination process. Specifically when above-market wage rates are imposed in unionized employments by the ability of unions, through coercion, to shut out competing workers, those wages will not tell the truth about the relative scarcity of workers who can do the job. Too few workers will enter those employments. Instead, many workers who should be employed therein, based on what they can do and the willingness of consumers to pay employers to hire them to do it, will be diverted to lower-valued uses of their abilities. This will depress wages in those employments again resulting in prices that do not send the right signals to market participants. Relative wages and relative prices will be distorted. They will tend to discoordinate the economy rather than coordinate it. Here is Hayek on union-caused discoordination in Britain when it was considered the 'sick man of Europe'.

> The effect of the present system of wage determination in Britain is that the country no longer has an internal price structure to guide the economic use of resources. This is almost entirely due to the rigidity of politically determined wages. If it is no longer possible to know the most efficient use of the natural talents of the British people, it is because relative wages no longer reflect the relative scarcity of skills. Even their relative scarcity is no longer determined by objective facts about the real conditions of supply and demand, but by an artificial product of the arbitrary decisions of legally tolerated [labor] monopolies. (ibid., p. 54)

Unemployment

Hayek held that unemployment is always a pricing problem. It emerges when 'there is a discrepancy between the distribution of labor (and the other factors of production) between industries (and localities) and the distribution of demand among their products' (1975, p. 19). Given the pattern of consumer demands for goods and services, suppose there is an excess demand for labor where consumer demand for goods and services is strong, and an excess supply of labor where consumer demand is not so strong. Ordinarily this would result in higher wages in the former and lower wages in the latter. This pattern of relative wages would attract additional workers into the production of goods and services for which consumer demand is strong, and induce some workers employed where consumer demand is less strong to leave those employments. The additional supply of workers seeking employment in the former will tend to lower wages there. The decreased supply of labor in the latter will tend to increase wages there. The process continues until all labor is employed in accordance with the pattern of consumer demands. Higher consumer demand becomes translated into additional production, and lower consumer demand becomes translated into less production. Any discrepancy between the allocation of labor among employments and the pattern of consumer demands is gradually remedied by changing relative prices and wages.

The only way such a discrepancy can endure is if there is a 'distortion of the system of *relative* prices and wages' (ibid.). To the extent that the markets in which there is an excess demand for labor are unionized, additional workers are prevented from seeking employment there. The high wages become permanent. Thus the high consumer demand is absorbed by the high wages rather than translated into additional production. If the markets in which there is an excess supply for labor are also unionized, the initial wage decrease will be prevented so employers have no recourse but to lay off workers. Result: durable unemployment. If the markets with excess supply of labor are not unionized, unemployment there can be avoided, but only by a substantial decline in wages. If declines of that magnitude are illegal because of minimum wage laws, or if because of the welfare state people would be paid more not to work than to work at such low wages, the result again is durable unemployment. Unions always support increases of legal minimum wages and higher unemployment benefits.

In Hayek's words:

> The normal cause of recurrent waves of widespread unemployment is ... a discrepancy between the way in which demand is distributed between products

and services, and the proportions in which resources are devoted to producing them. Unemployment is the result of divergent changes in the direction of demand and the techniques of production. If labor is not deployed according to demand for products, there is unemployment. (Hayek, [1980] 1984, p. 55)

It is the continuous change of *relative* market prices and particularly wages which can alone bring about that steady adjustment of the proportions of the different efforts to the distribution of demand, and thus a steady flow of the stream of products. It is this incessant adaptation of relative wages to the ever-changing magnitudes, at which in each sector demand will equal supply, which the trade unions have set out to inhibit. (ibid., p. 18)

The reason why I believe that the license to use coercion conceded to unions some 70 years ago [in the Trade Disputes Act] should be withdrawn is precisely that their actions have become the chief cause of unemployment. [One way they do this] is the obvious one of an increased demand for some product being absorbed by an increase of the wages of the workers already employed in it rather than by an influx of additional workers, leaving out in the cold those in the industries from which demand has turned. (Hayek, [1978] 1984, p. 62)

The chief significance of the comprehensive systems of unemployment compensation . . . is that they operate in a labor market dominated by the coercive action of unions and that they have been designed under strong union influence with the aim of assisting unions in their wage policies . . . Such a system, which relieves the unions of the responsibility for the unemployment that their policies create and which places on the state the burden not merely of maintaining but of keeping content those who are kept out of jobs by them, can in the long run only make the employment problem more acute. (Hayek, 1960, p. 302)

Hayek acknowledged another way in which union-imposed wage distortions cause unemployment. Excessive wage rates imposed by union duress will cause employers to change the capital–labor mix in ways that permit them to reduce labor costs while maintaining output. 'At wages higher than those which would prevail in a free market, employers must, in order to be able to pay them, use the limited amount of capital that is available in a manner which will require fewer workers for a given output' ([1978], 1984, p. 62).

Unions, Money, Inflation and Keynes

Hayek often cited a perverse *de facto* division of responsibility between monetary authorities and trade unions in Britain. The unions would arbitrarily set high money wage rates in key industries, and because by itself this would result in extensive unemployment, the monetary authorities would inflate the money supply enough to raise money prices which in turn would lower real wages sufficiently to avoid the extensive unemployment:

> What we have achieved is a division of responsibilities under which one group can enforce a wage level without regard to the effects on employment, and another agency is responsible for providing whatever amount of money is needed to secure full employment at that wage level. So long as this is the accepted principle, it is true that the monetary authorities have no choice but to pursue a policy resulting in continuous inflation, however little they may like it. But the fact that in the existing state of opinion [the sanctity of unions] they cannot do anything else does not alter the fact that, as always, it is monetary policy and nothing else which is the cause of inflation. (Hayek, [1959] 1967, p. 282)

The US also experienced this phenomenon on a limited scale, especially in the 1970s, but unions here were much less pervasive than in Britain so it was much less of a problem. Nevertheless we had our own discussions of the extent to which this 'cost-push' process could account for US inflation. Most US economists concurred with Hayek (and Friedman) that cost-push could not account for inflation in the absence of ratifying monetary policy.

Keynesian economics, of course, only strengthened the link between unions and the monetary authorities in causing inflation. Keynes always understood that unemployment was a result of real wages that were too high, but he simply assumed that money wages could not be reduced because of unions and other causes of wage 'rigidities'. His solution to the problem of unemployment was to increase aggregate money demand through expansionary monetary policy. Of course, this 'solution' is possible only to the extent that workers underestimate the resulting inflation.

> The essential point is that it must be once more realized that the employment problem is a wage problem and the Keynesian device of lowering real wages by reducing the value of money when wages have become too high for full employment will work only so long as the workers let themselves be deceived by it. It was an attempt to get round what is called the 'rigidity' of wages which could work for a time but which in the long run has only made this obstacle to a stable monetary system greater than it had been. What is needed is that the responsibility for a wage level which is compatible with a high and stable level of employment should again be squarely placed where it belongs: with the trade unions. (Hayek, [1958] 1967, p. 298)

The final disaster we owe mainly to Lord Keynes. His erroneous conception that employment could be directly controlled by regulating aggregate demand through monetary policy shifted responsibility for employment from the trade unions to the government. This error relieved trade unions of the responsibility to adjust their wage demands so as to sell as much work as possible, and misrepresented full employment entirely as a function of government monetary policy. For 40 years it has thus made the price mechanism ineffective in the labor market by preventing wages from acting as a signal to workers and to employers. As a result there is divided responsibility: the trade unions are allowed to enforce their wage demands without regard to the effect on employment, and government is expected to create the demand at which the available supply of work can be sold at the prevailing (or even higher) wages. Inevitably the consequence is continuous and accelerating inflation. (Hayek, [1980] 1984, p. 57)[5]

However, Hayek did not recommend that this 'disaster' be remedied by restrictive monetary policies. He thought such an effort would be far too dangerous: 'A monetary policy that would break the coercive powers of the unions by producing extensive and protracted unemployment must be excluded, for it would be politically and socially fatal' (1960, pp. 281–2). The only solution, according to Hayek, is to remove the unions' privileges, to subject them to the rule of law. This would be difficult, but the unions would come to see that it is the least bad of their alternatives:

> [I]f we do not succeed in time in curbing union power at its source, the unions will soon be faced with a demand for measures that will be much more distasteful to the individual workers, if not the union leaders, than the submission of unions to the rule of law: the clamor will soon be either for the fixing of wages by government or for the complete abolition of the unions. (ibid., p. 282)

Of course Hayek would be opposed to either government wage setting or the complete abolition of (voluntary) unions. However, I think Hayek was, at least in 1960 when he wrote these words, too optimistic about the unions' distaste for government wage fixing. American, if not British, unions supported government interference in the 1970s through 'incomes policies' and explicit wage fixing. During that period of time the unions had a lot of confidence in their ability to manipulate public policy in their interests. And the complete abolition of (coercive) unions was not then, and is not now, politically possible.

Hayek thought that Keynes's notion of 'aggregate demand' was meaningless but dangerous. Thinking in such aggregate terms diverts attention away from what, as we saw above, was in Hayek's mind really important: the distribution of individual demands relative to individual supplies and relative prices:

> If the composition (or distribution) of the demand for the various products is very different from that of their supply, no magnitude of total demand will assure that the market is cleared. The wider the difference between the composition of the demand and that of the supply, the more the achievement of a correspondence between the whole of demand and the whole of supply can be brought about *only* by a change in the relative quantities, *and* this, in turn, only by a change in the relative prices of the different products and services, including wages. ([1980] 1984, p. 16)[6]

Moreover, trade unions exacerbate the difficulty:

> Aggregate demand may well exceed the aggregate price of all goods and services offered, yet this will not create full employment if in the sectors in which demand exceeds supply the already employed obstruct the entry of additional workers by claiming all the surplus as gains for themselves. (ibid., p. 17)

Finally, Hayek joined his critique of unionism with his monetary theory of the business cycle.[7] The basis for that theory is the role of relative prices (including wages) and interest rates in the coordination of economic activities. The introduction of newly created money and bank credit distorts relative prices, sending incorrect signals to market participants who then misallocate resources. The new money does not change the underlying real supplies and demands, but makes it appear that some supplies and demands have changed. In particular, lower interest rates send the false signal that people want to consume less now and more in the future. In response, producers produce less for current consumption and instead undertake too many investments designed to yield consumer goods in the future. In the meantime real demand for consumer goods does not decrease, and the spending boom part of the cycle gets under way. Eventually, unless money inflation is accelerated to keep ahead of expectations, real supply and demand conditions will become revealed, and a correction of the misdirections of resources will get under way. This is the bust part of the cycle.

What role do unions play in this story? When discussing unions Hayek emphasized that wages are distorted by inflation and so they will misdirect labor. When monetary authorities resort to inflation in order to avoid unemployment, the new money increases particular wage rates. 'The artificial demand brought about by increasing the amount of money is simply misleading: it attracts workers into employments which cannot be maintained except by accelerating inflation' ([1980] 1984, p. 21). Moreover, after Hayek had developed his trade cycle theory and had turned his attention to the union problem, he came to see that unions were the principal influence leading monetary authorities to inflate:

> [T]he most common cause [of unemployment] is that, because of excessive credit expansion, over-investment has been encouraged and too many resources have been drawn into the production of capital goods, where they can be employed only so long as the expansion continues or even accelerates. And credit is expanded to appease trade unions that fear their members will lose their jobs, even though it is they themselves who forced wages too high to enable the workers to find jobs at those excessive rates of pay. (ibid., pp. 55–6)

Lower Productivity and Lower Standards of Living

According to Hayek, 'It is a complete inversion of the truth to represent unions as improving the prospect of employment at high wages. They have become in Britain the chief cause of unemployment and the falling standard of living of the working class' ([1978] 1984, p. 62). Misallocation of labor due to the unions' interference with the signaling functions of relative prices and wages reduces the productivity of the workforce by preventing labor from being allocated according to its most highly valued uses. Many workers are excluded from where they would be most productive and forced into employments where they are less productive; or, if there are no union-free employments, they are excluded from any employment until entrepreneurs create new, union-free alternatives:

> It is the wages maintained by the closed shops whose barriers prevented the rest from earning as much as they might have done which keeps the productivity of the majority of British workers low. Once the opportunity to earn more in a particular trade becomes the exclusive property of those already employed there, successes of individual enterprises are likely to be taken out by its present staff in the form of higher wages rather than leading to additional employment. ([1980] 1984, p. 19)

> Britain has been brought to her present [i.e., 1980] plight, not because of the lack of skill or industry of the individual worker, but because government and labor organizations, in order to appease groups of workers, have tried to relieve them of the necessity for adjustments by removing the inducements (and rewards) of changing their jobs. (ibid., p. 35)

High productivity in an economy not only requires that individual decision-makers within their respective enterprises attempt to allocate each resource to its most highly valued use, it also requires that as little as possible of each resource is used to produce any amount of any output:

> [R]educing costs means setting free resources which could produce more elsewhere. In any particular instance, the primary aim must therefore always be to use as few resources as possible for a given output... The secret of productivity which makes it possible to employ many at high wages is for each producer to do his job with the use of as few resources as possible...
> It has come to be thought in Britain [due to unions] that a prime task of economic policy was the protection of *existing* jobs. This fundamental reversal of the truth has developed into a sort of anti-economics which has misrepresented the chief social goal to be the use of as *large* a quantity of resources as possible. (ibid., pp. 34–5)

One common manifestation of this phenomenon is union-imposed workplace rules that stipulate the types and amounts of labor that must be devoted to each task. I recently gave a lecture at a convention hotel in Las Vegas. I had prepared a PowerPoint presentation, but I was tardy in requesting the organizers to provide a data projector. When I did, it was too late. I offered to bring my own projector and set it up myself. That, I was told, was impossible because in this union-impaired hotel only in-house equipment could be used and only union workers could set it up and operate it.

Hayek discussed yet another way by which unions have lowered the overall productivity of labor: through their influence on investment and the composition of the capital stock. Hayek recognized what is today called the holdup problem. Specific capital goods, those which when once acquired and set up by employers have few, if any, alternative uses, present unions with opportunities to expropriate most of the returns from the productivity of those capital goods. The cost of acquisition of capital equipment is its purchase price minus any immediate resale value it may have. If it is specific capital it has few if any other uses, and thus its resale value will be very low. This means almost all the purchase price is a sunk (unavoidable) cost. Under these circumstances it is rational for an employer to continue to operate as long as after-tax revenue is any amount over variable costs, which include labor costs. If a union drives up labor costs so that there is only a penny left over out of after-tax revenue after the other variable costs are covered, that penny would be the only return to capital. Specific capital has nowhere else to go, so the penny is better than nothing. Of course employers recognize this danger. That is why most of them try to avoid unionization. Where that is not possible, employers attempt to minimize their purchases of highly specific, relative to less specific, capital equipment, or they simply reduce their investment spending in general.

> It is true that any union effectively controlling all potential workers of a firm or industry can exercise almost unlimited pressure on the employer and that, particularly where a great amount of capital has been invested in specialized equipment, such a union can practically expropriate the owner and command the whole return of his enterprise. (1960, p. 270)[8]

> Because unions are most powerful where capital investments are heaviest, they tend to become a deterrent to investment – at present probably second only to taxation. (ibid., pp. 272–3)

> Personally, I am convinced that this power of union monopolies is, together with contemporary methods of taxation, the chief deterrent to private investment in productive equipment which we have allowed to grow up. We must not be surprised that private investment dries up as soon as uncertainty about the future increases after we have created a situation in which most of the gain of a large, risky and successful investment goes to the unions and the government, while any loss has to be borne by the investor. ([1959] 1967, p. 286)

Low productivity diminishes the flow of incomes that arise from production and exchange. It decreases the average real standard of living:

> It is more than doubtful ... whether in the long run these selfish practices [of unions] have improved the real wages of even those workers whose unions have been most successful in driving up their relative wages – compared with what they would have been in the absence of trade unions. It is certain, and could not be otherwise, that the average level of attainable real wages of British workers as a whole has thereby been substantially lowered. Such practices have substantially reduced the productivity potential of British labor generally. They have turned Britain, which at one time had the highest wages in Europe, into a relatively low-wage economy. ([1980] 1984, p. 53)[9]

The logical implication of this observation is that, at least in the long run, unions do not benefit the workers they represent. They benefit only union leaders who, in effect, are paid very handsomely to make the rest of us worse off.

The myth that unions benefit the working class dies hard. Yet the evidence is quite clear. 'Real wages have often risen much faster when unions were weak than when they were strong; furthermore, even the rise in particular trades or industries where labor was not organized has frequently been much faster than in highly organized and equally prosperous industries' (1960, p. 271–2).[10]

UNIONS THREATEN THE FREE SOCIETY AND THE MARKET ECONOMY

Apart from their malign economic effects, Hayek saw labor unions as a threat to the free society. In *Law, Legislation and Liberty*, vol. III (1979), while discussing the role of special-interest groups in unlimited majoritarian democracies, Hayek pointed out that the methods commonly employed by labor unions are especially damaging:

> It was a misfortune that these [special-interest group] problems became acute for the first time in connection with labor unions when widespread sympathy with their aims led to the toleration of methods which certainly could not be generally permitted ... One need merely ask what the results would be if the same techniques were generally used for political instead of economic purposes (as indeed they sometimes already are) in order to see that they are irreconcilable with the preservation of what we know as a free society. (1979, p. 89)

Government employee unions have indeed carried the methods of coercion into the determination of public policy in the US. The principles of exclusive representation, union security and mandatory good-faith bargaining in government employment in effect make government employee unions an unconstitutional fourth branch of government.[11]

Hayek was also concerned that the actions of labor unions were leading inexorably to the crippling of the market economy and the emergence of central economic planning:

> It is scarcely an exaggeration to say that, while we still owe our current living standards chiefly to the operation of an increasingly mutilated market system, economic policy is guided almost entirely by a combination of the two views whose object is to destroy the market: the planning ambitions of doctrinaire socialist intellectuals and the restrictionism of trade unions and trade associations. (Hayek, [1980] 1984, p. 40)

> [Unions] are using their power in a manner which tends to make the market system ineffective and which, at the same time, gives them a control of the direction of economic activity which would be dangerous in the hands of government but is intolerable if exercised by a particular group . . .

> Unionism as it is now tends to produce that very system of overall socialist planning which few unions want and which, indeed, it is their best interest to avoid. (Hayek, 1960, pp. 272–3)

FREEDOM OF ASSOCIATION

Unions claim that they are based on workers' freedom of association. The International Labor Organization (ILO) proclaims that freedom of association is the most basic right upon which union legitimacy rests. Hayek did not see it that way. The unions and the ILO have a warped understanding of freedom of association. Correctly understood, freedom of association has both a positive and a negative dimension. The former is the principle that each person is free to associate (for legal purposes) with any other person or persons who are willing to associate with him. The latter is the principle that each person has a right to refuse to associate with any person or persons who want to associate with him. If there is no effective right to abstain from unwanted association, the right to choose one's associations is meaningless. The unions and the ILO do not recognize the right of workers to abstain from association with unions. Their appeal to freedom of association as justification for coercive unionism is pure hypocrisy:

> The unions have of course now become the open enemies of the ideal of freedom of association by which they once gained the sympathy of the true liberals. Freedom of association means the freedom to decide whether one wants to join an association or not. Such freedom no longer exists for most workers.

> The present unions offer to a skilled worker only the choice between joining and starving, and it is solely by keeping non-members out of jobs that they can raise the wages of particular groups of workers above the level they would reach in a free market. ([1978] 1984, p. 61)

Hayek began Chapter 18 in *The Constitution of Liberty* with a section titled 'Freedom of association'. In it he argues that unions have transformed that principle into a right to coerce:

> Most people ... have so little realization of what has happened that they still support the aspirations of the unions in the belief that they are struggling for 'freedom of association', when this term has in fact lost its meaning and the real issue has become the freedom of the individual to join or not join a union. The existing confusion is due in part to the rapidity with which the character of the problem has changed; in many countries voluntary associations of workers had only just become legal when they began to use coercion to force unwilling workers into membership and to keep non-members out of employment. Most people probably still believe that a 'labor dispute' normally means a disagreement about remuneration and the conditions of employment, while as often as not its sole cause is an attempt on the part of the unions to force unwilling workers to join. (1960, p. 268)

In a later section of the same chapter, titled 'Constraining coercion', Hayek argued that to do so, '[t]he essential requirement is that true freedom of association be assured and that coercion be treated as equally illegitimate whether employed for or against organization, by the employer or by the employees' (ibid., p. 278).

In sum, according to Hayek, just as appeal to freedom of association was the means by which unions made their claim to legitimacy, appeal to freedom of association correctly understood is the essential means by which unions can be transformed from involuntary into voluntary (and therefore legitimate) organizations.

FREEDOM OF CONTRACT

Then, continuing in the same section, Hayek gets into what I consider to be a bit of logical trouble. He was so adamantly opposed to the closed shop as it evolved under the unions' illegitimate privileges and immunities granted by the Trades Disputes Act in Britain and the National Labor Relations Act in the US that he failed to recognize that closed-shop agreements between a truly voluntary union and a willing employer would be consistent with true freedom of association. Here is Hayek's argument:

[T]he unions should not be permitted to keep non-members out of any employment. This means that closed- and union-shop contracts . . . must be treated as contracts in restraint of trade and denied the protection of the law. They differ in no respect from the 'yellow-dog contract' which prohibits the individual worker from joining a union and which is commonly prohibited by the law. (ibid.)

He implies that 'yellow dog' contracts (which I prefer to call 'union-free' contracts) are properly prohibited by the law. I disagree. A job offer made by an employer to an employee has several components. The compensation package stipulates a direct wage or salary along with a set of other benefits of various descriptions. Hayek certainly would not argue that an employer should be prohibited from offering any compensation package he chooses. He certainly would argue that the prospective employee has the right to accept or reject the compensation package. Similarly, the job description itself (the stipulation of the time, place and manner of the employee's expected actions on the job) is another part of the job offer. Hayek certainly would not argue that an employer should not be able to make such stipulations. Again, he would argue that the prospective employee must be free to accept or reject the offer. It seems to me that if an employer wants to include a union-free agreement in the job offer, that is their right. The prospective employee would have a corresponding right to accept or reject the job offer. Any job offer will consist of some things a prospective employee likes and other things they do not like. They must settle the trade-offs in their own mind before exercising their right to accept or reject the job offer.

Now, in the absence of any special privileges or immunities for unions or employers, I think the principle of freedom of contract (which is part of the freedom of association), implies that a willing employer has a right to agree with a truly voluntary union to hire only union members as employees. I would not expect many truly free employers to do so, but I think they should be free to do so. If such agreements work in a free-market setting, they will be adopted by other employers and other unions. If they do not work, they will not be adopted. The market will sort it all out. Hayek endorsed the principle of letting the market sort things out in other settings. He was not logically consistent when he advocated government interference in market arrangements in this setting.

I will go even further. The problem with exclusive representation in American labor law is not exclusive representation itself. It is that the law compels exclusive representation. In the absence of the National Labor Relations Act, I see no reason why an employer should not be free to agree with a voluntary union that the question of union representation will be decided by majority vote among the employees. Certainly in the case of a brand new enterprise, where all prospective employees know that there will be such a vote, such an arrangement should not be prohibited. In an established enterprise the terms of each individual worker's hiring contract would determine whether they could be bound by any post-hiring vote among their colleagues on the issue of union representation. Again, I would not expect many truly free employers would choose to enter such agreements.

My position on this issue is, of course, that taken by Milton Friedman (1962, pp. 115–16). Friedman argued that American right-to-work laws (which, in the 23 states that have adopted them, prohibit a union from agreeing with an employer to require union membership or the payment of union dues as a condition of continued employment) were, by themselves, illicit interferences by government in the freedom of contract. He went on to state that the problem that should be remedied is the monopoly power that the National Labor Relations Act grants to certified unions. Friedman did not explicitly say that without such monopoly power, the right-to-work laws would be moot, but they certainly would be. If unions represented only their voluntary members, they would have no argument to justify any sort of compulsory membership or support. In any case, there is no place for right-to-work laws in a truly free labor market.

Hayek goes on, in the same section, to claim that his position on closed-shop and union-free contracts (that both should be prohibited) is consistent with the principle of freedom of contract correctly understood:

> It would not be a valid objection to maintain that any legislation making certain types of contracts invalid would be contrary to the principle of freedom of contract. We have seen before (in chap. xv) that this principle can never mean that all contracts will be legally binding and enforcible [sic]. It means merely that all contracts must be judged according to the same general rules and that no authority should be given discretionary power to allow or disallow particular contracts. Among the contracts to which the law ought to deny validity are contracts in restraint of trade. Closed- and union-shop contracts fall clearly into this category. (Hayek, 1960, pp. 278–9)

Here, again, I disagree. Closed- and union-shop contracts in the context of special privileges and immunities for unions clearly are illicit. But the best solution is to eliminate those special privileges and immunities. If that cannot be done, then as a second best, measures like American right-to-work laws could be used to protect individual worker rights.

The term 'contracts in restraint of trade' is a work of art. It means different things to different people. In particular that term has played a mischievous role in the sad history of antitrust regulations. One person's contract in restraint of trade is another's innovative arrangement to cope with market realities. As Dominick Armentano (1982) has shown, American antitrust laws have more often been used to protect particular competitors than to protect the process of competition and consumers. I infer from Hayek's condemnation of contracts in restraint of trade in the context of unions that he would support the application of antitrust laws to unions. Again, I disagree. As I have argued elsewhere (Baird, 2000) antitrust laws should be repealed. That, together with repeal of the monopoly-granting privileges of the National Labor Relations Act, would allow the market to sort out efficient from inefficient organizational architectures.

Finally, Hayek agreed with the position I have taken above concerning right-to-work laws as second-best alternatives:

> Though there ought to be no need for special 'right-to-work laws', it is difficult to deny that the situation created in the United States by legislation and by decisions of the Supreme Court may make special legislation the only practicable way of restoring the principles of freedom. (1960, p. 279)

Of course right-to-work laws do not really restore principles of freedom. They are actually an infringement on the freedom of contract made necessary to partially offset even greater infringements on freedom of association and contract. What we ought to do is abolish all such infringements.

STRIKES AND PICKETING

If a strike is defined as a collective withholding of labor services by workers who find the terms and conditions of employment offered by an employer to be unacceptable, then there is a legitimate right to strike. I call this the voluntary-exchange right to strike. In the absence of an unexpired fixed-term employment contract, any individual worker has a right to withhold their labor from an employer who does not offer satisfactory terms. If every worker has such a right they all can individually choose to exercise the right simultaneously. Even if a worker has an unexpired fixed-term contract with an employer, they cannot be forced to continue on the job. If the worker walks off the job, the employer's only recourse is to sue for breach of contract and let other employers know that the worker is an unreliable employee:

> Neither the right of voluntary agreement between workers nor even their right to withhold their services in concert is in question. (1960, p. 269)

> I am even prepared to agree that *everybody* ought to have the *right* to strike, so far as he does not thereby break a contract... But I am convinced that nobody ought to have the right to *force* others to strike. ([1980] 1984, p. 51)

When unions (and compliant politicians) claim that there is a right to strike, they mean something very different from the voluntary-exchange right to strike. They assert that union leaders, or union members by majority vote, can force workers who do not want to strike to withhold their labor. In addition, they claim the right to prevent employers from hiring replacement workers during strikes and to prevent suppliers and customers from continuing to do business with struck firms. In other words they claim the right to prevent people who do not support a strike from exercising their voluntary-exchange rights with strike targets. Unions exercise these extraordinary rights claims through picket line intimidation and violence:

> The present coercive powers of unions ... rest chiefly on the use of methods which would not be tolerated for any other purpose and which are opposed to the protection of the individual's private sphere. In the first place, the unions rely – to a much greater extent than is commonly recognized – on the use of the picket line as an instrument of intimidation. That even so-called 'peaceful' picketing in numbers is severely coercive and the condoning of it constitutes a privilege conceded because of its presumed legitimate aim is shown by the fact it can be and is used by persons who themselves are not workers to force others to form a union which they [the non-employee strangers] will control (1960, pp. 274–5)

> [A]ll picketing in numbers should be prohibited, since it is not only the chief and regular cause of violence but even in its most peaceful forms is a means of coercion. (ibid., p. 278)

The US Supreme Court addressed these picket line questions in its decision in *American Steel Foundries v. Tri-City Central Trades Council* (257 US 184 [1921]). The Court noted that even peaceful picketing can be intimidating, so it limited the number of pickets to one per entrance. Moreover, the Court ruled that only actual employees could be pickets. No strangers bussed in from union headquarters could participate. Both parts of the decision were overruled by Congress in 1932 with the enactment of the Norris-LaGuardia Act.

Hayek claimed that even the voluntary exchange right to strike, 'though a normal right, can hardly be regarded as an inalienable right' (1960, p. 269). There are certain employments (he did not give an example) where 'workers should renounce this right' by entering 'long-term obligations', and 'any concerted attempts to break such contracts should be illegal' (1960, p. 269). Twenty years later Hayek gave an example: enterprises on which the law has 'conferred a monopoly' ([1980] 1984, p. 51). He was thinking of private enterprises, but I think his point applies most obviously to the military, the police and firefighters. In the US the military cannot be unionized, but police and firefighter unions have gone on strike with impunity in several states and localities. Hayek's suggestion that strikes against private firms with government-granted monopoly power are especially harmful because consumers have no alternative sellers to whom to turn, applies to almost all strikes by government employee unions. Government employing agencies almost always have monopoly power. Private sector alternatives are often simply outlawed. Hayek had nothing explicit to say about unionism in the government sector. He probably thought his arguments against private sector unionism applied *a fortiori* to the government sector.

As an aside, most Americans accept the commonsense idea that strikes by police and firefighters ought to be prohibited. So unions representing those government employees have argued, often successfully, that strikes should be replaced by compulsory arbitration over the terms and conditions of employment. This is incompatible with a basic democratic value: there should be no taxation without representation. The terms and conditions of government employment are matters of public policy paid for by taxpayers. Unelected arbitrators should not be able unilaterally to determine the taxes that taxpayers must pay.

PROFIT SHARING AND CODETERMINATION

Hayek thought that collective bargaining, as it had evolved by 1972 in Britain, created so many problems that it simply had to be replaced by some 'alternative method of wage determination which, while offering the worker as a whole a better chance of material advance, at the same time restores the flexibility of the relative wages of particular groups' (Hayek, 1972, p. 117). He came up with a specific solution:

> The only solution of this problem I can conceive is that the workers be persuaded to accept part of their remuneration, not in the form of a fixed wage, but as a participation in the profits of the enterprise by which they are employed. Suppose that, instead of a fixed total, they could be induced to accept an assured sum equal to, say, 80 percent of their past wages *plus* a share in profits which in otherwise unchanged conditions would give them on the average, their former real income, but, in addition, a share in the growth of output of growing industries. In such a case the market mechanism would again be made to operate and at the same time one of the main obstacles to the growth of social product would be removed. (ibid.)

He recognized that such a proposal 'raises many difficult problems' (ibid.), but he did not discuss any specific examples. I think union leaders, whose incomes depend on sustaining the illusion that employers and employees are natural enemies, would fight this idea every time and in every venue in which it was proposed. Given Hayek's distaste for schemes imposed by government, I doubt that he would support any legislation aimed at forcing this outcome. It would have to be adopted, by willing employers and employees, one enterprise at a time. Still, given the success of several different sorts of profit-sharing plans in American union-free enterprises, the idea cannot be dismissed as an impossible dream.

Hayek's profit-sharing proposal must not be confused with the insidious institution, particularly popular among muddled thinkers even today, called codetermination. This idea calls for government to require that workers (and, often, other 'stakeholders') be given a role equal to the role of owners and their agents in controlling most aspects of businesses. Efficiency in the allocation of resources depends crucially on decision-makers in firms being accountable to the owners of the firms, and that the criterion for success is the maximization of long-term owner value through voluntary exchange. To maximize long-term owner value it is necessary for decision-makers to seek to serve the interests of customers, and this requires striving for cost minimization and timely adaptations to changing market conditions. If diverse groups of stakeholders, with diverse objectives, all have part control over an enterprise, decision-making therein degenerates into a political process based on a strife of interests. Even if decision-making is done democratically, as advocates of 'industrial democracy' would have it, choices among three or more alternatives could result in cyclical majorities – that is, no one alternative can beat all of the others by majority vote – and this would give rise to battles of varying degrees of civility and totally unpredictable outcomes (Barry, 2002).

Hayek was clear in his condemnation of industrial democracy and codetermination. After discussing some legitimate functions for voluntary unions he asserted that codetermination was not one of them:

> An entirely different matter ... is the claim of unions to participation in the conduct of business. Under the name of 'industrial democracy' or, more recently, under that of 'co-determination,' this has acquired considerable popularity, especially in Germany and to a lesser degree in Britain. It represents a curious recrudescence of the syndicalist branch of nineteenth-century socialism, the least-thought-out and most impractical form of that doctrine. Though these ideas have a certain superficial appeal, they reveal inherent contradictions when examined. (1960, p. 277)

IN CONCLUSION

The Thatcher reforms of British labor law by the Employment Acts of 1980 and 1982 and the Trade Union Act of 1984 went a long way toward removing the most egregious privileges and immunities British unions had enjoyed since the 1906 Trade Disputes Act, but there is still a way to go before British unions become truly voluntary. In the US, labor law has changed very little since the 1959 amendments to the National Labor Relations Act (which attempted to give rank-and-file members more control over union leaders). All the worst privileges – exclusive representation, union security and mandatory good-faith bargaining – plus the court-granted immunity to prosecution for acts of violence during labor disputes, remain. As Hayek said about the economic myths that sustain coercive unionism, '[a] departure from such a condition can come only from a truer insight into the facts, and whether this will be achieved depends on how effectively economists do their job of enlightening public opinion' (1960, p. 273). But it is not just economists who should attempt to enlighten public opinion on unionism. The rule-of-law issues raised by Hayek imply that historians, legal scholars and philosophers also have a continuing role to play. To be a true friend of labor, one cannot be a friend of coercive unionism.

NOTES

1. Although initially drafted for inclusion in this volume, this chapter was first published as two stand-alone journal articles. Subtitled 'Coercion and the rule of law' and 'Economic and social consequences', these articles appeared in 2007 and 2008 in the *Journal of Private Enterprise*.
2. Although Hayek made frequent references to labor unions in several essays, his thinking on this issue is most completely represented in just three sources: 'Unions, inflation and profits' ([1959], 1967), Chapter 18 of his *Constitution of Liberty* (1960) and the monograph he wrote for the Institute of Economic Affairs (IEA) in 1980, *1980s Unemployment and the Unions*. The IEA published a second edition of this monograph in 1984 which consisted of Hayek's original essay and a postscript by Charles G. Hanson which addressed the Thatcher union reforms of the early 1980s.
3. I do not know how unions were treated by the law in Britain in the latter part of the nineteenth century, but it is clearly not the case that in the US the legitimate functions of unions were ever proscribed or prosecuted (Baird, 1984).
4. For thorough documentation of union violence in the US see Thieblot et al. (1999).
5. See also Hayek's 'Full employment, planning and inflation' ([1950] 1967, pp. 271–2).
6. See also Hayek's *A Tiger by the Tail* (1972, p. 118).
7. What is now called the Austrian theory of the trade cycle was first explicated by Ludwig von Mises in *The Theory of Money and Credit* (1912) and developed by Hayek (1928).
8. See also Hayek's 'Unions, inflation and profits' ([1959] 1967, pp. 285–6).
9. See also *The Constitution of Liberty* (1960, p. 271).

10. The best discussion of these claims is in Reynolds (1991).
11. This argument is fully developed by Robert S. Summers (1976).

REFERENCES

Armentano, Dominick T. (1982), *Antitrust and Monopoly: Anatomy of a Policy Failure*, New York: John Wiley.
Baird, Charles W. (1984), *Opportunity or Privilege: Labor Legislation in America*, Bowling Green, OH: Social Philosophy and Policy Center.
Baird, Charles W. (1995), 'Toward equality and justice in labor markets', *Journal of Social, Political and Economic Studies*, 20 (2), 163–86.
Baird, Charles W. (2000), 'Unions and antitrust', *Journal of Labor Research*, 21 (4), 585–600.
Barry, Norman P. (2002), 'The stakeholder concept of corporate control is illogical and impractical', *Independent Review*, 6 (4), 541–54.
Friedman, Milton (1962), *Capitalism and Freedom*, Chicago, IL: University of Chicago Press.
Hanson, Charles G. (1984), 'From Taff Vale to Tebbitt: a postscript on British trade unions and the law', *1980s Unemployment and the Unions*, 2nd edn, London: Institute of Economic Affairs, pp. 65–78.
Hayek, Friedrich A. ([1928] 1966), *Monetary Theory and the Trade Cycle*, New York: Augustus M. Kelley.
Hayek, Friedrich A. (1937), 'Monetary danger of collective bargaining', reprinted 1972 in *A Tiger by the Tail*, London: Institute of Economic Affairs, pp. 21–2.
Hayek, Friedrich A. (1950), 'Full employment, planning and inflation', reprinted 1967 in *Studies in Philosophy, Politics and Economics*, Chicago, IL: University of Chicago Press, pp. 270–79.
Hayek, Friedrich A. (1958), 'Inflation resulting from the downward inflexibility of wages', reprinted 1967 in *Studies in Philosophy, Politics and Economics*, Chicago, IL: University of Chicago Press, pp. 295–9.
Hayek, Friedrich A. (1959), 'Unions, inflation and profits', reprinted 1967 in *Studies in Philosophy, Politics and Economics*, Chicago, IL: University of Chicago Press, pp. 280–94.
Hayek, Friedrich A. (1960), *The Constitution of Liberty*, Chicago, IL: University of Chicago Press.
Hayek, Friedrich A. (1968), 'Competition as a discovery procedure', reprinted 1978 in *New Studies in Philosophy, Politics, Economics and the History of Ideas*, Chicago, IL: University of Chicago Press, pp. 179–90.
Hayek, Friedrich A. (1972), *A Tiger by the Tail*, London: Institute of Economic Affairs.
Hayek, Friedrich A. (1973), *Law, Legislation and Liberty*, vol. 1, *Rules and Order*, Chicago, IL: University of Chicago Press.
Hayek, Friedrich A. (1975), *Full Employment at Any Price?* London: Institute of Economic Affairs.
Hayek, Friedrich A. (1978), 'Reform of trade union privilege the price of salvation in the 1980s', reprinted 1984 as Part V, *1980s Unemployment and the Unions*, 2nd edn, London: Institute of Economic Affairs.
Hayek, Friedrich A. (1979), *Law, Legislation and Liberty*, vol. 3, *The Political Order of a Free People*, Chicago, IL: University of Chicago Press.
Hayek, Friedrich A. (1980), *1980s Unemployment and the Unions*, 2nd edn, London: Institute of Economic Affairs, 1984.
Mises, Ludwig von ([1912] 1934), *The Theory of Money and Credit*, London: Jonathan Cape.
Reynolds, Morgan O. (1991) 'The myth of labor's inequality of bargaining power', *Journal of Labor Research*, 12 (2), 167–83.
Seldon, Arthur (1980), Preface to the 1st edition of *1980s Unemployment and the Unions*, reprinted in 2nd edn 1984, London: Institute for Economic Affairs.

Summers, Robert S. (1976), *Collective Bargaining and Public Benefit Conferral: A Jurisprudential Critique*, Ithaca, NY: Institute of Public Employment, Cornell University.

Thieblot, Armand J., Jr, Thomas R. Haggard and Herbert Roof Northrup (1999), *Union Violence: The Record and the Response by Courts, Legislatures, and the NLRB*, Fairfax, VA: John M. Olin Institute for Employment Practice and Policy, George Mason University.

Vieira, Edwin Jr. (1986), 'From the Oracles of the Temple of Janus: Chicago Teachers Union v. Hudson', *Government Union Review*, 7 (3), 1–37.

15. Hayek and economic policy (the Austrian road to the third way)[1]
Enrico Colombatto

ON HAYEK'S VIEW OF ECONOMIC POLICY

The debate on the scope and moral foundations of economic policy began as soon as economics strived to become something more than just a branch of political philosophy and attempted to acquire its own identity as a social science. By and large, its founding fathers characterized this discipline as being concerned with how individuals behave and interact in order to enhance their well-being. This justified the use of the term 'political economy' to emphasize the role of the institutional context within which human action takes place. Toward the end of the eighteenth century, prominent authors went further and suggested that political economists should not be confined to the mere description and explanation of human action. Nor should they refrain from recommending how institutions ought to be designed and modified in order to enhance welfare.[2] Adam Smith was of course a leading and effective supporter of this approach,[3] which actually owed much to Ferdinando Galiani and, to a lesser extent, Francois Quesnay.

At the beginning of the nineteenth century, Jean-Baptiste Say forcefully advocated the need for a sharper partition between the realms of political economy and of policy, the former referring to the study of human action under given institutional rules; the latter to the content of the legal rules. He did not exclude the importance of normative economics. Still, this branch was to remain an exercise in simulation, with little or no room for decision-making by the economist. Later on, the same perspective was also typical of Léon Walras and a number of more recent authors. Lionel Robbins, for instance, understood policymaking to be dependent on moral judgment; and thus unacceptable if conceived as a way of reasoning and an instrument to understand individual or group behavior. Indeed, he argued that it would make little sense to use a logical tool in order to derive normative prescriptions. In Harry Johnson's words, it would be unreasonable and probably counterproductive (see Mackintosh, 1950; Tyszynski, 1955).

Contrary to Say, Hayek chose not to consider normative economics as a mere exercise in simulation with little practical relevance. At the same time, however, he was also unwilling to accept the technocratic approach based on descriptive, atheoretical economics and scenarios. Not surprisingly, while trying to find a suitable compromise between socialist planning and radical free-market capitalism, he stumbled into a dilemma. On the one hand he could draw on the early foundations of political economy and follow the 'constitutional economics' approach. As made explicit by Buchanan (1979) and, more generally, by most of the public-choice and the ordoliberal schools, since economic action takes place within an institutional framework, the economist should analyze the features of an optimal context, so as to enhance voluntary exchange and widen the choices available to the agents. In other words, economic policy should propose constitutional solutions. When the notion of social contract is added – which implies that it exists, that its elements are well specified and that all the members of the community are required to act in accordance with them – this amoral version of policymaking develops into normative prescriptions for the production of goods and services described in the social contract.

Another possibility open to Hayek was related to the existence of social norms, informal behavioral patterns that have emerged over long time periods and are generally subject to varying degrees of enforcement. In some cases norms have become ways through which individuals identify their position in society (for example, manners). In other cases – and more important for the scope of these pages – they are a means to reduce the cost of cooperation within a community of interacting individuals. In the past, informal arrangements were characterized by repeated trial-and-error experiences within relatively close communities. Tradition and customs would thus gradually reveal the nature and stringency of social norms. Surely, little room was left for ambiguity or to the discretion of the would-be policymaker. If anything, politics was just a synonym for the procedure through which selected individuals were given the power to enforce compliance with the social norms.

Predictably, the conceptual gap separating social norms from policymaking is hard to bridge, even for Hayek. Whereas social norms do reflect an informal social contract originating from repeated voluntary interactions and trial-and-error processes, policymaking at its best would consist in anticipating the results of the social contract to which individuals would subscribe if they had enough time to appreciate its terms.[4] In other words, policymaking at its best is about guessing the terms of the social contract and – in an ideal world – conjecturing about those who would be willing to sign it.

In the end, and for reasons that remain largely unexplained,[5] Hayek opts for a view of economic policy which consists of a set of laws created by government and cleared by 'legislators'.[6] Their purpose is to replicate – or, rather, anticipate – social norms. Although he does not frequently mention it with the clarity that the subject deserves, this argument refers to the so-called 'acceleration of time'.[7] This situation materializes as informal institutions tend to emerge only gradually, so that their evaluation through a trial-and-error process becomes too slow to be of significant use, especially when the features of the problems to be solved through the individual interactions change rapidly. Under such circumstances, timely top-down rule making (policymaking) can be desirable and replaces slow bottom-up rules. In other words, the Hayekian-enriched version of constitutional economics does not preclude freedom to choose, but admits coercion when geared to reproducing a social contract that the acceleration of time makes hard to perceive.

By and large, this defines Hayek's project for a liberal society, away from laissez-faire and – in his view – strong enough to resist socialist attacks. And it also explains why from the end of the 1930s Hayek tried to find ways to replicate or anticipate a plausible social contract, and then to justify it without using constructivism. The pages that follow examine these efforts in some detail and conclude that the results attained are far from persuasive. Economic policy always requires the definition of shared goals and priorities, of the tools to be employed and of the policymaker in charge of implementation. Unfortunately, Hayek's work remains somewhat wanting on the legitimacy of both the instruments and the actors; and thus is ambiguous. As de Jasay (1996, 'p. 107) put it, 'he has no complete theory of the social order to back up his liberal recommendations', which contributes to making 'modern liberalism vulnerable to erosion and invasion by incompatible elements'.

HAYEK'S VIEWS ON POLICY ACTION

Consistent with the Austrian tradition, Hayek deals with economic policy as a social philosopher, rather than as an economic technocrat or a political theorist. In particular, he focuses on the aims of policymaking in a society in which human dignity and thus liberty are supposed to be the primary moral components and proposes to 'design the most rational permanent framework within which the various activities would be conducted by different persons according to their individual plans' (Hayek, [1944] 1979, p. 26). It is therefore manifest since the beginning of his intellectual journey that, although some elements of such a framework are the legacy of the past (customs, traditions, implicit contracts),

Hayek also considers other elements, which stem from human design and are conceived through a procedure of 'consensus behind a veil of ignorance', whereby the social designer is not allowed to act in order to benefit or damage specific individuals or groups deliberately. Compliance with this procedure provides legitimacy to policies, so as to protect and/or reproduce the results generated by the appropriate set of long-term, stable social norms that would have emerged spontaneously if agents had not been hindered by transaction costs or surprised by the acceleration of time, as mentioned earlier.

In fact, Hayek's offensive against economic policy is weaker and less comprehensive than might appear at first sight. It is a 'third way' between *dirigisme* and laissez-faire where the state plays two roles: (1) it provides a framework within which individual action develops; and (2) it meets those social needs that the market fails to satisfy because of externalities.[8] It happens to be illegitimate only when it becomes the instrument of discretionary bureaucratic interference with the social norms (loosely understood as a synonym for social contract). Interference can be direct, through rules issued by the bureaucrats themselves; and indirect, when bureaucrats arbitrarily interpret and enforce the rules conceived by the social philosophers or by the politicians.[9] Although this is surely an important limitation, it is not enough to deter Hayek from advocating state funds in favor of generalized education, sanitation, minimum-income legislation, adequate infrastructure, information, quality control, sporting and cultural activities, collective insurance vis-à-vis catastrophic, unpredictable events,[10] and also behavioral rules that do not replace individual preferences ([1973] 1983, p. 51) but nevertheless shape human action and make it more predictable. In short, the Hayekian state is 'a piece of utilitarian machinery intended to help individuals in the fullest development of their individual personality' ([1944] 1979, p. 57). Unfortunately, one does not know how to distinguish between cases in which the state helps spontaneous development and cases where it drives such development: 'Unlike classical liberalism which confines the state to the provision of a single public good, law enforcement, Hayek's social order is less, rather than more, clear-cut: it permits, if not positively mandates, the state to produce any number in any quantity' (de Jasay, 1996, p. 113).

Put differently, although Hayek emphasizes the crucial role of liberty, he reasons that nothing useful can come to birth in a vacuum (which he wrongly considers a synonym for laissez-faire). And he hastens to fill in the vacuum by appealing to common sense, search for compromise, expediency, but not rationalism.[11] By holding on to these arguments (individual liberty and *horror vacui*) and carefully avoiding the discussion of the intrinsic conflicts, Hayek's well-known condemnation of scientism actually excludes bad policymaking, rather than policymaking per se; and it leaves plenty of room for social, piecemeal engineering, to be carried out by enlightened political action applied to economic activities. He therefore succeeds in attracting consensus from the anti-socialist ranks when attacking scientism and positivism – that is, historicism, objectivism and the foundations of socialism (Saint-Simon and Comte) – and in enticing those who believe in the existence of the common interest, a notion that Hayek believes can be defined by means of an idealized version of the majoritarian democracy.[12] It is hard to say whether Hayek himself was aware of the blurred border between general rules (constitutional law-making by enlightened, possibly arrogant political philosophers)[13] and detailed rules (scientism by rational and selfish bureaucrats or shortsighted politicians). He must have had serious fears, though, since after *The Constitution of Liberty*, he repeatedly tried to keep the two categories apart and explain – without much success, in my view – why public-choice analysis applies to the latter but not to the former.

BETWEEN BAD SOCIALISM AND GOOD POLICYMAKING

As the previous pages suggest, according to the main thesis put forward in this chapter Hayek's view on economic policy depends heavily on his idea of a society of free individuals protected by super-constitutional arrangements. These arrangements should be the absolute barrier against socialism and the growing conviction that governments ought to play a major part in shaping people's daily life (Hayek, [1944] 1979).[14] This is little more than a facade, though. For in Hayek's view the real problem with socialism is not so much the violation of individual freedom, as collectivization. This approach has two consequences. It does not oblige Hayek to confront natural rights and the sacredness of private property (which he is not willing to accept, as recalled earlier on); and it leaves the door open to non-socialist coercion, to be applied whenever the results of laissez-faire are not satisfactory:

> in the ordering of our affairs we should make as much use as possible of the spontaneous forces of society, and resort as little as possible to coercion ... There is ... all the difference between deliberately creating a system within which competition will work as beneficially as possible, and passively accepting institutions as they are. Probably nothing has done so much harm to the liberal cause as the wooden insistence of some liberals on certain rough rules of thumb, above all the principle of *laissez faire*. Yet in a sense this was necessary and unavoidable ... Nothing short of some hard-and-fast rule would have been effective. And since a strong presumption in favor of industrial liberty had been

> established the temptation to present it as a rule which knew no exceptions was too strong always to be resisted. (ibid., p. 13)

and

> There were many tasks ... where there could be no doubt that the government possessed enormous powers for good and evil; and there was every reason to expect that with a better understanding of the problems we should some day be able to use these powers successfully. (ibid., p. 14)

Unfortunately, Hayek does not attempt to clarify who has to decide about the features and desirability of the exceptions, or how the decision-making process should take place. Nor does he explain when better knowledge of the problems legitimizes government to use its coercive powers.[15] For example, after having warned the reader about the dangers of government intervention, Hayek makes it explicit that 'where it is impossible to create the conditions necessary to make competition effective, we must resort to other methods of guiding economic activity' (ibid., p. 28).[16] The same applies to monopolies (ibid., pp. 29, 147) as well as to a variety of other situations.

Hayek's view about economic policy is thus characterized by two essential and persistent elements: the need to develop some kind of constitutional engineering and to adjust for externalities, which justify state coercion, as explained at length in Hayek ([1960] 1978). The former turns out to be not only desirable, but also necessary if a market economy is to generate the best possible results. The latter is always welcome, as long as intervention remains within the boundaries set by the rule of law.[17] In other words, as long as the rule of law is not violated, government intervention is admitted and leads to the production of goods and services (for example, insurance services against catastrophic events and unemployment), the redistribution of income by means of taxation (including substantial inheritance taxes) and the regulation of production ([1944] 1979, p. 60).[18]

The core question then clearly revolves around Hayek's notion of the rule of law, defined as a set of 'rules fixed and announced beforehand – rules which make it possible to foresee with fair certainty how the authority will use its coercive powers in given circumstances and to plan one's individual affairs on the basis of this knowledge' (see, e.g., [1944] 1979, p. 54; [1973] 1983, p. 108). Apparently this definition does not include freedom of contract since:

> to limit working hours or to require certain sanitary arrangements is fully compatible with the preservation of competition ... nor is the preservation of competition incompatible with an extensive system of social services – so long as the organization of these services is not designed in such a way as to make competition ineffective over wide fields. ([1944] 1979, p. 28)

Hayek will indeed modify his view later on, when the emphasis moves from certainty and predictability to the notion of just conduct 'as a means for assisting in the pursuit of a great variety of individual purposes'.[19] But his argument basically remains an attack against privileges or burdens for selected interest groups known in advance,[20] and an appeal for a political system that creates stable rules behind a veil of ignorance.[21] Sometimes the veil drops, though. For Hayek also conceives an ideal world in which a set of desirable features must be in place (including the absence of externalities). The lack of such features is characterized as market failures, and the state is called upon to fill the gap and cover the costs through taxation: 'far from advocating . . . a minimal state, we find unquestionable that in an advanced society government ought to use its power of raising funds by taxation to provide a number of services which for various reasons cannot be provided, or cannot be provided adequately, by the market' ([1979] 1981, p. 41). Furthermore, 'There are common needs that can be satisfied only by collective action and which can thus be provided for without restricting individual liberty', and '[t]here is no reason why the volume of these pure service activities should not increase with the general level of wealth' ([1960] 1978, p. 257). As a result, Hayek's spontaneous order is no longer an alternative to constructivism, but a desirable situation in which repeated interactions may have given birth to patterns of predictable behavior and in which order (that is, predictable behavior) has to be enhanced on a case-by-case basis, whenever it does not appear spontaneously.[22] As de Jasay pointed out, in Hayek's view:

> the market, law and its enforcement must first secure property and contract against violation, and then the market order will spontaneously emerge as a result of individual interactions within this framework of safety and predictability. [Put differently,] law is a product of collective choice and so is its enforcement . . . Hayek's spontaneous order, then, is not spontaneous, for it includes the government as a necessary condition, and government action is purposive. (de Jasay, 2004)

Surely, Hayek is well aware of the fact that extensive state action might distort individual behavior. But he is inclined to elude the problem by arguing that when this happens, then it means that privileges are being created and the rule of law violated. Put differently, on the one hand the reader is being told that economic policy is welcome when the market fails. On the other hand, he is warned that economic policy is not acceptable when it creates winners and losers and thus distorts incentives.

HAYEK'S NEED FOR A SOCIAL CONTRACT

As mentioned in the previous paragraphs, from the late 1930s Hayek was suggesting that market-oriented economic policy was to be preferred to central planning. But the need for economic policy, and for sensible policymaking as a whole, was not questioned.

More generally, Hayek criticized the Middle Way, but also hurried to recommend allegedly neutral, state solutions to hypothetical market failures. Unfortunately, he did not see that such failures called for (private) property-right solutions. This error prevented him from grasping the essence of the notion of externality,[23] deprived the conception of the rule of law of the only intellectual anchor it could count on – the principles of 'private property and freedom of contract' (ibid., p. 28) – and forced him to apply the rule of law according to rather questionable commonsense principles (opinion and 'universalizability', to be explained shortly). As one may have noticed, Hayek correctly refrains from referring to spontaneous order; for it would be incompatible with not-so-spontaneous rules of the game, which are however desirable according to the Hayekian vision. For example, when discussing competition he adds that 'we cannot, within the scope of this book enter into a discussion of the very necessary planning which is required to make competition as effective and beneficial as possible' (ibid., p. 31). And when arguing for redistribution and a minimum welfare state, he seems to justify them both as a way of buying consensus against special interest (ibid., p. 156),[24] and because not having them is a deficiency:

> some security is essential if freedom is to be preserved ([1944] 1979, p. 99)

> adequate security . . . will have to be one of the main goals of policy. (ibid., pp 98–9)

> [C]apitalism as it exists today has many remediable defects that an intelligent policy of freedom ought to correct. A system which relies on the spontaneous ordering of forces of the market, once it has reached a certain level of wealth, is also by no means incompatible with government providing, outside the market, some security against severe deprivation. ([1976] 1978, p. 136)

In order to overcome the logical weakness of this position, one needs to introduce new conceptual tools. Authors like Leoni ([1961] 1991) and de Jasay ([1985] 1998) clearly perceived that the only instrument that social scientists can use in order to reach a compromise is the social contract. Indeed, Buchanan's success owes a great deal to having assumed a social contract, irrespective of its moral foundations (legitimacy). Hayek never mentions it explicitly and actually denies its validity.[25] In fact, he replaced the social contract with the rule of law, the difference between the two being the same as that between a state ruled by bureaucrats with discretionary power,[26] and one composed of social philosophers (politicians) with the monopoly of violence. More subtly, by sidestepping the discussion on the social contract, Hayek could actually treat it as a fact, rather than a serious concern for the social philosopher: 'constitutions are based on, or presuppose, an underlying agreement on more fundamental principles – principles which may never have been explicitly expressed, yet which make possible and precede the consent and the written fundamental laws' ([1960] 1978, p. 181).

As a byproduct, this 'underlying agreement' explains and justifies the state monopoly of violence: 'Coercion, however, cannot be altogether avoided because the only way to prevent it is by the threat of coercion. Free society has met this problem by conferring the monopoly of coercion on the state' (ibid., p. 21).[27] And legitimacy is now maintained by reference both to the veil of neutrality, following the lines already sketched in the *Road to Serfdom*:

> Even where coercion is not avoidable, it is ... being made impersonal and dependent upon general, abstract rules, whose effects on particular individuals cannot be foreseen at the time they are laid down ... Coercion ... then becomes an instrument assisting the individuals in the pursuit of their own ends and not a means to be used for the ends of others. (ibid.)

And to a new concept – opinion – defined as:

> a common tendency to approve of some particular acts of will and to disapprove of others, according to whether they do or do not possess certain attributes which those who hold a given opinion usually will not be able to specify. So long as the legislator satisfies the expectation that what he resolves will posses those attributes, he will be free. ([1973] 1983, p. 92)[28]

A MANIFESTO AGAINST FREEDOM

When encouraging policymakers to intervene and enhance the acquisition of knowledge, improve on bad past legislation, question defective traditions and gain consensus, Hayek did perceive the problem of the abuse of power:

> restraints ... on the power of the legislator could, of course, be made more effective and more promptly operative if the criteria were explicitly stated by which it can be determined whether a particular decision can be a law. But the restraints which in fact have long operated on the legislatures have hardly ever been adequately expressed in words. ([1973] 1983, p. 93).[29]

Still, his call for explicit rules defies centuries of political history, while his proposal to submit the legitimacy of the new rules to the test of 'universalizability' remains elusive.[30] For either the policymaker is in fact just proposing social arrangements that may reduce the cost of human interaction and that individuals are free to accept or reject, possibly through a trial-and-error process characterized by competition in an evolutionary context, or the policymaker has the right to impose such social arrangements as long as they may be qualified as moral.[31]

One can of course answer by arguing that all the arrangements conceived behind a veil of ignorance or by complying with neutrality are welcome by agents. Still, this is hardly credible, even from a purely Hayekian viewpoint. It does not take much to see that the politician does not necessarily use his power of coercion to minimize transaction costs in a society, that he never operates behind a veil of ignorance, let alone his knowing how people would behave and what they would choose behind the veil. Another possibility of circumventing the individual's right to express their preferences is to claim that institutions come from the past and as a result of tradition and spontaneously developed rules. Following previous terminology, from this viewpoint the social contract has not been agreed upon but has been revealed through history ([1960] 1978, Ch. 4). Therefore, one may infer that the policymaker is not a social philosopher designing social arrangements, but one interpreting and enforcing the allegedly revealed social contract by transforming it into law. Unfortunately, it is not clear what happens if different social scientists have different perceptions with regard to revelation. And not many classical liberals would agree with Hayek's notion whereby 'liberalism regards it as desirable that only what the majority accepts should in fact be law' (ibid., p. 103).[32]

Similar remarks apply to the notion of individual freedom, often quoted as the bulwark against arbitrary policymaking. In this case, Hayek departs from the classical-liberal position based on the familiar notion of 'freedom from coercion'[33] and refers instead to the concept of responsibility: 'freedom, namely a state in which each can use his knowledge for his purposes' ([1973] 1983, pp. 55–6). In particular the 'argument for liberty . . . presupposes that a person is capable of learning from experience and of guiding his actions by knowledge thus acquired' ([1960] 1978, p. 77). Thus, liberty is no longer a (natural) right, but almost becomes part of a social contract, whereby in order to deserve it, one must show that he is able to profit from – or make good use of – it. Once again, the policymaker creeps in through the back door to assess whether individual behavior is consistent with a contract that also requires that 'in our decisions as to whether a person is to be his own master or be subject to the will of another, we must regard him as . . . either having or not having the right to act in a manner that may be unintelligible, unpredictable or unwelcome to others' (ibid., p. 78).[34]

This departure from Austrian subjectivism plays an important role, since it allows Hayek to oppose coercion and still favor constitutional constructivism. For in Hayek's world, individual A is subject to coercion not only if other individuals exercise physical or psychological violence towards him, but also if they refuse to act according to A's wishes and such a refusal can jeopardize A's existence (ibid., p. 136). The statement has important implications. First, it means that individual freedom is not valuable per se, but only if it is compatible with other agents' basic needs. How basic a basic need is remains of course a matter open to debate. For example, Hayek mentions the owner of a spring in an oasis and claims that free water should be offered to all those who cannot pay and are about to die. The owner of the spring may indeed decide to do so out of compassion. But the owner cannot be obliged to do so – as Hayek advocates – unless one violates the principle of private property. And also two other principles. One is the principle of individual responsibility, since those who adventure in the desert without enough water should take responsibility for their poor organization or sheer bad luck. The second is the principle of entrepreneurship (and the ethics of profit), which would make sure that the lack of water encourages agents to find new wells, look after the existing oases, and/or possibly establish a network of relief stations in the desert.[35]

Other examples of the effects implied by Hayek's notion of coercion apply to monopoly power and the labor market. In the former case, regulation is required whenever 'a monopolist is in a position to withhold an indispensable supply', be such an action a fact, or just a possibility (ibid., p. 136). It is easy to observe that this idea is very close to that of 'dominant position', which today pervades mainstream economics: 'whenever there is a danger of a monopolist's acquiring coercive power, the most expedient and effective method of preventing this is probably to require him to treat all customers alike, i.e. to insist that his prices be the same for all and to prohibit all discrimination on his part' (ibid., p. 136).[36] In regard to the labour market, Hayek welcomes regulation 'in periods of acute unemployment', when workers may be induced to accept unfair contracts (ibid., p. 137).

In short, individual liberty for Hayek means protection against coercion, and coercion means not only violence as commonly understood, but also resistance to the rule of law and need. And since for Hayek ([1960] 1978) taxation and compulsory military service are the outcome of – or at least compatible with – the rule of law, resistance against both turns out to be an act of coercion.[37] Put differently, the difference between the

Hayekian and the socialist versions of acceptable coercion turns out to depend on how the social welfare function is defined. In the Hayekian case, state intervention is justified when it enforces rules (of just conduct), or when dominant-position conditions are feared;[38] while in the socialist context intervention is legitimate whenever it is consistent with the social welfare function in general. But the line between the two may be faint, since one suspects that the Hayekian definitions of rules or of potential dominant position are almost as arbitrary as any other.

To conclude, Hayek's recipe to make policymaking subject to the rule of law and to rely on state violence in order to eliminate coercion is not very persuasive. In his view the rule of law is in fact equivalent to a mix between constitutional straitjackets to restrain ordinary legislation, and decision-making behind a veil of ignorance and according to general principles, with the purpose of inducing individuals to behave in a predictable way. The fragility of the veil of ignorance has already been mentioned earlier on. As regards general principles, Hayek ([1960] 1978, Ch. 10) argues that they should not be created, but just discovered, since 'they have grown through a gradual process of trial and error in which the experience of successive generations has helped to make them what they are' (ibid., p. 157).[39] Discovery is the task of the legal scholars, whereas legislators *stricto sensu* should play the role of the benevolent policeman, and 'create conditions in which an orderly arrangement can establish and ever renew itself' (ibid., p. 161). In fact, Hayek replaces collectivism with some kind of enlightened policymaking, in which neoclassical technocrats are to assist legal scholars, and legal scholars are supposed to establish what the rule of law is and make it explicit. In particular, legal scholars define when individuals are subject to state coercion, while technocrats think of effective remedies in situations in which deviations from the rule of law must be corrected.[40]

POLICYMAKING BEYOND THE RULE OF LAW

Contrary to the common belief, the role of state intervention in a Hayekian world is not confined to enforcing the rule of law and restraining the use of violence (coercion) by ordinary legislators and technocrats at large. Although one wonders whether state authorities would actually listen to legal scholars telling them what they can and what they cannot do (and hope that legal scholars all share the same opinion and resist the temptation to please state authorities), Hayek goes further and emphasizes that coercive activities 'will never be the only functions of government . . . [I]nfringements of the private sphere will be allowed . . . in instances where the public gain is clearly greater than the harm done by the disappointment of normal individual expectations' ([1960] 1978, pp. 206 and 218).[41] The implications are not really clarified or examined in any detail.

Indeed, while Hayek squeezes the debate on the aims and legitimacy of economic policy into a question of rule of law, he says almost nothing about the instruments through which policy is to be carried out.[42] He therefore reduces normative economics to a matter of personal judgment by the social philosopher, and possibly populism: rules must 'tell people which expectations they can count on and which not . . . [but] it is clearly impossible to protect all expectations . . . Which expectations ought to be protected must . . . depend on how we can maximize the fulfillment of expectations as a whole' ([1973] 1983, pp. 102–3). In Hayek's view, that seems to be enough to justify breach of contract viz-à-vis employers (pickets and strikes),[43] as well as taxation (to finance poverty-relief programs, social security, compulsory health insurance, agricultural improvements[44] and constitutional design).

Hayek does try to draw the line between the socialist welfare state and his own: the former being one where takers decide about the amount of redistribution, whereas the latter is one in which the givers have a say.[45] But of course it is not clear what happens if a giver decides to give relatively little, or nothing at all; nor is it clear whether the Hayekian system is compatible with a democratic regime.[46] In the end, Hayek seems to be less hostile to planning than is generally appreciated,[47] as long as good planning is enforced and bad planning rejected. In the case of town planning, for example,[48] good planners help the functioning of the market, operate through equitable compensation mechanisms and set reasonable standards, whereas bad planners enforce rules (without compensation) and engage in arbitrary decision-making. Yet, this position is the very core of constructivism: bad outcomes are the product of bad planners and should be discarded, whereas good planning makes human activity more effective.

CONCLUDING REMARKS

During the twentieth century, the economic profession grew more and more interested in exercises in social efficiency, following which the economic policymaker was to define sets of efficient solutions to assigned problems, and the politicians were supposed to choose the best option. The illusion of the benevolent policymaker and the true nature of the relation between redistribution, incentives and economic performance were exposed only in relatively recent times.

Still, the lesson has not been learnt, let alone applied (Nelson, 1987). This chapter has tried to argue that Hayek himself bore some responsibility in this intellectual defeat, for his recipes were based on an enlightened version of economic policy (to be driven by suitable social philosophers), more or less restrained by a new constitutional order.[49] More important, Hayek did not center his research program on a clear and well-founded justification for policymaking, but rather on the constant effort to confine policymaking within reasonable, commonsense boundaries. Such boundaries are of course Hayek's definition of the rule of law, which however proves to be unsatisfactory on two accounts. On the one hand, Hayek fails to provide a proper characterization; as a consequence, the rule of law turns out to be little more than a set of principles defined behind a veil of ignorance, possibly in accordance with a questionable version of the freedom-from-coercion principle. The word 'possibly' should remind the reader that the Hayekian rule of law is in fact compatible with some redistribution, taxation, state production of goods and services, and equitable compensation. When commenting on Hayek's view of the welfare state, de Jasay (1991, pp. 15–16) is thus justified in claiming that 'here is a clear call ... to recreate something like the "Swedish model" under the liberal banner. Horrified as Hayek would be by the imputation of such a proposal, his exposition is fully consistent with it, and must be classified as "loosely liberal" for that reason'. On the other hand, he denies the principle of spontaneous order when spontaneity is not adequate or desirable: 'there can be no justification for representing the rules of just conduct as natural in the sense they are part of an external and eternal order of things, or permanently implanted in and unalterable nature of man' (Hayek, [1976] 1978, pp. 59–60). As for assessing whether the rules of the game are appropriate or consistent with just conduct, his reference to legitimacy being based on public opinion cannot be taken seriously.[50]

Of course, by looking at today's world one can maintain that both Hayek's liberalism and the neoclassical orthodoxy describe an ideal, utopian picture. The first boils down to some kind of benevolent elite of social philosophers in charge of policymaking, while the latter is obsessed by the notion of equilibrium and overlooks transaction costs and entrepreneurship. Still, whereas the neoclassical approach is wrong, but consistent, Hayek's world of constitutional engineering is fragile from the very beginning, for it is rooted in the same rules of the game that legitimate – and therefore lead to – discretionary power. To deny this is equivalent to denying the very behavioral hypotheses of human action, which Hayek observed in Western culture and learnt from Mises ([1949] 1963). As we know, the alternative is a world featuring institutional competition, ultimately based on a notion of freedom originating from natural-rights principles. Unfortunately, this is a vision to which Hayek sometimes agrees when advocating methodological individualism and – even more – Austrian subjectivism, but which he eventually neglects in order to be able to engage in 'constitutional economics'.

In this respect, Hayek's divergence from Mises is hard to explain. Hayek's ongoing efforts not to confront Mises on major issues do not help, either.[51] Perhaps Hayek may have wanted to stop short of shocking his readers or policymakers as a whole, and thus avoid the very mistake with which he reproached the classical liberals and the laissez-faire school. This is surely a feature that runs throughout the *Road to Serfdom*, where he fails to elaborate a persuasive criterion to evaluate the legitimacy of economic policy,[52] and becomes explicit in the 1970s when he claimed that 'attempts to push a principle further than general sentiment is yet ready to support it is apt to produce a reaction which may make impossible for a considerable period even what more modest attempts might have achieved' (Hayek, [1976] 1978, p. 58). One wonders, however, whether a scholar advocating a liberal vision of society should advocate accuracy and cohesion, or rather settle for political suitability and offer some kind of a Third Way composed of a piecemeal list of government actions to meet specific goals in the economic sphere, the only perceptible policy criterion being one of consistency with the prevailing notion of just conduct. The price Hayek paid for his choice was, however, high. Not only was he forced time and again to appeal to expediency within a microeconomic context, and to go as far as denying some 50 years of Austrian business cycle economics by claiming that 'it is merely common sense that government ... will step in when private investment flags, and thereby employ resources for public investment at the least cost and with the greatest benefit to society' ([1979] 1981, p. 59). More important:

> the effect of leaving out pieces from the jigsaw puzzle of social theory is that the vacuum is only too naturally filled by a false conception of the state. This conception is hardly compatible with liberal principles. Indeed, it is hardly compatible with the very market order that Hayek wants to be spontaneous. (de Jasay, 1996, p. 118)

ACKNOWLEDGMENTS

I am grateful to Carlo Lottieri, Anthony de Jasay, Henry Manne, Alberto Mingardi and Miro Prokopijevic for many insightful comments and helpful suggestions on a previous draft of this chapter. Helpful comments were also offered by seminar participants at the Schools of Economics of the Universities of Podgorica and Lisbon (Universidade Nova), at the Schools of Law of the Universities of Paris (Panthéon-Assas) and of Reims 1.

NOTES

1. Though originally drafted for the present volume, this chapter also appeared in Alain Marciano and Jean-Michel Josselin (eds) (2007), *Democracy, Freedom and Coercion: a Law and Economics Approach*, Cheltenham, UK and Northampton, MA, USA: Edward Elgar.
2. See Fontaine (1996). As will be clarified later on, Hayek ([1960] 1978) definitely subscribed to this view. More recently, a similar approach was also advocated by James Buchanan (1979), who insisted on the notion of economics as a system of voluntary exchange generated by – and giving origin to – agreed-upon rules. These rules are called institutions and represent an essential feature of economic analysis.
3. Smith's vision is not entirely clear, though. For instance, Grampp (2000) argues that Smith supported a free-market system because he believed this to be the best way to promote the social good; in his case the accumulation of national wealth and military power. As a matter of fact, this would explain why Smith did not hesitate to claim that natural rights and individual freedom should be set aside when the public good – for example national power or even fairness – is at stake. Hayek ([1979] 1981) devotes the whole epilogue to justifying his rejection of a natural rights approach.
4. Note that this notion of the social contract is different from that advocated by Buchanan (1979). Hayekian policymaking reflects a social contract that would have emerged as a consequence of a spontaneous, time-consuming process leading to a social norm. By contrast, in Buchanan's view the social contract is what the individuals would have chosen had they been behind a veil of ignorance. This view presents two major weaknesses, though. First, policymakers cannot possibly know what individuals would choose behind the veil of ignorance. Second, people do not choose behind a veil of ignorance; indeed, the history of mankind can be described as the continuous effort to reduce the size of the veil before making a decision.
5. Even Caldwell (2004) provides very little information on this account.
6. See Hayek ([1979] 1981, Ch. 17) for his notions of 'legislative assembly' and 'constitutional court'. The former is formed by the constitutional lawmakers, the latter by their controllers. It is not clear how or by whom these should be appointed, though.
7. See Hayek ([1973] 1983, pp. 88–9; [1960] 1978, p. 286) and, more generally, Denzau and North (1994) and Fiori (2002).
8. Indeed, Hayek often failed to distinguish between an externality *siricto sensu* and a residual explanation for why allegedly desirable states of the world fail to materialize. Therefore, since he believed that direct state intervention is justified – if not required – whenever externalities are relevant and widely recognized, government intervention ends up being appropriate whenever the state of the world could be improved with no obvious costs. More on this at note 23.
9. According to Hayek ([1960] 1978, pp. 112–15) the politician does not have ideas and should merely represent conventional thought: 'His task in a democracy is to find out what the opinions held by the largest number are, not to give currency to new opinions which may become the majority view in some distant future' (ibid., p. 112). By contrast, the social philosopher is an intellectual innovator who conceives new, possibly welfare-enhancing ideas or general principles that agents may or may not accept.
10. See Hayek ([1944] 1979, pp. 89–90; [1960] 1978, pp. 141, 144, 223, 257, 258, 364, 365, 375, 383; [1979] 1981, Ch. 14). See also Hoppe (1994) for a clear account of Hayek's view on government intervention. However, for Hayek's doubts about the existence of natural state monopolies, see ([1979] 1981, p. 147).

11. See on this Hoppe (1994), who emphasizes the incongruous results generated by Hayek's rejection of rationalism, despite Mises' teachings.
12. Hayek seems to have mixed feelings about democracy: feelings that vary from unqualified praise (see *The Constitution of Liberty*) to skepticism. He deals with his doubts by distancing himself from the current version of democracy (*cum* unlimited governmental powers) and suggesting a concept closer to that predating the French Revolution: demarchy (*cum* constrained governmental powers). His ideal political construction is fully detailed in Hayek ([1979] 1981), in which democracy is somewhat naively described as 'a certain framework for arriving at political decisions, and tells us nothing about what the aims of government ought to be' (p. 98).
13. In some cases the constitution should spell out and thus impose principles that are 'too unfamiliar to expect courts to comprehend' ([1979] 1981, pp. 148–9).
14. Hayek held laissez-faire responsible for this state of affairs. He maintained that its alleged success in the nineteenth century led people to take the results of market forces for granted and concentrate on collective goals (ibid., p. 15). Curiously enough, a few years later, Hayek's interpretation of the historical causality between laissez-faire and socialism disappeared, and a large part of his Counter-Revolution of Science ([1952] 1979) was actually devoted to showing the links between rationalism, positivism and ultimately socialism. Hayek ([1960] 1978, p. 60) finally closed the circle by saving the classical-liberal school, and maintaining that laissez-faire actually originated from Rationalism 'as the very words show', rather than from the classical-liberal tradition. One wonders whether Hayek truly believed that the radical Austrian school was a by-product of the French Revolution.
15. As we know, the challenge had already been raised by the libertarian school – from Rothbard to de Jasay and Hoppe – and involved the difference between Saint-Simon's Council of Newton on the one hand, and Hayek's custodians of the rule of law on the other. Hayek's reply was elusive. In his *Road to Serfdom* ([1944] 1979, Ch. 15) he believed that an international authority should take care of drafting and enforcing proper rules at a supra-national level (constitutional engineering once again). He later addressed the question at a national scale, but the answer provided in Hayek ([1979] 1981) – elected assemblies of highly paid representatives – defined the nature of the problem once more. Surely, it did not solve it. He also favored moderate decentralization among competing local agencies in the provision of public services, subject however to centralized control as regards legitimacy. Both the central and the local agencies are also expected to compete with the private sector ([1979] 1981, pp. 47, 49), except for the fact that the latter has no right to cover costs through taxation.
16. This position is not too far from what the Saint-Simonians were advocating a little more than a century earlier. Indeed, although Hayek strongly opposed the Saint-Simonian attitude towards private property ([1952] 1979, Ch. 13), when it comes to choosing between freedom and expropriation he opts for the latter. His justification is that 'we still lack adequate theoretical principles for a satisfactory solution of some of the problems which arise in this field' ([1979] 1981, p. 63).

    More generally, Hayek sometimes seems to have doubts about the very essence of free-market principles. When it comes to inheritance taxes, for example, it is obvious that the liberal argument against taxation focuses on the fact that taxation interferes with the parents' desire to sacrifice their own consumption in order to enhance their children's welfare. Inheritance taxation is indeed a tax on altruism or family affection. Surprisingly, however, Hayek criticizes inheritance taxes by referring to their inefficiency, rather than to their immorality ([1960] 1978, Ch. 6). Other examples are provided by his view of competition, which is unfair if a successful producer 'keeps out a potential competitor by offering especially favorable terms to the customers only in the limited region in which a newcomer at first will be able to compete' ([1979] 1981, p. 84). Or by his support for progressive income taxation based on the fact that indirect taxation is necessarily regressive ([1979] 1981, p. 63).

17. See Rothbard ([1982] 1998, Ch. 28) and Hoppe (1994) for an in-depth criticism of the Hayekian notions of freedom and coercion.
18. The third part of ([1960] 1978) and ([1979] 1981], Ch. 14) offer a complete list of Hayek's public goods, which includes even entrepreneurship ('certain experimental developments', to use his own words). Hayek ([1960] 1978, Ch. 6) will subsequently change his mind about inheritance taxes. And he will also deny that being part of a national group justifies compulsory income transfers (ibid., pp. 101–2).
19. See also ([1976] 1978, pp. 5, 37): 'The chief function of the rules of just conduct is thus to tell each what he can count upon, what material objects or services he can use for his purposes, and what is the range of actions open to him'. Hayek ([1973] 1983, pp. 2, 3) was aware of the fact that the rule of law raised some problems as an operational device but attributed them to a lack of understanding rather than to the conceptual weakness of the very notion.
20. See for instance ([1976] 1978, p. 137).
21. See also ([1976] 1978, p. 132). Of course, even the abolition of a bad rule – for example trade barriers – would violate Hayek's notion of the rule of law, for it would provoke damages to selected layers of the population. Not even Hayek could deny that the victims and the beneficiaries of a transition to a free-trade regime would be clearly identified. In fact, Buchanan's position is easier to understand, in that he introduces the veil of ignorance not to justify economic policy but to justify the social contract that implies economic policy.
22. See ([1973] 1983, p. 36 and Ch. 5) and ([1973] 1983, Ch. 2). A similar logical twist also characterizes Hayek's view of the welfare state as compatible with (his vision of) the rule of law and thus with free-market principles, including subjectivism ([1944] 1979, pp. 89–91). This approach is of course rejected by the orthodox Austrians à la Mises who are critical of top-down government actions; and also by the ordoliberals, who criticize his piecemeal approach; see in particular Vanberg (1996). More generally, Hoppe (1994) has rightly pointed out that the Hayekian concept of unconscious spontaneous order is simply wrong. It is miles away from the Austrian fundamentals (Menger and Mises) and leads to a meaningless theory of social evolution.
23. In Hayek's view an externality is the effect of one's action on other individuals ([1979] 1981, pp. 43–4). Since he could not argue that all actions provoking disappointment or envy need to be regulated or require compensation, compliance with his notion of the rule of law needed to be assessed case by case, following common sense. Surprisingly, Hayek never refers to a negative externality as an encroachment of somebody else's property right.
24. Oddly enough, Hayek does not perceive the contradiction embedded in his argument. If the beneficiaries of the welfare state can be classified as 'special interest', then the Hayekian welfare state is in contrast with Hayek's fundamental rule-of-law criterion. And if the beneficiaries are not special interests, it is not clear why traditional pressure groups should be satisfied by the welfare state and feel that no more rent-seeking activities should be pursued.
25. See ([1960] 1978, Ch. 4), where Hayek states that the very notion of a social contract is the fruit of Rationalism, and thus unacceptable for any follower of the Scottish Enlightenment – including Hayek himself, of course.
26. See also Hayek ([1960] 1978, Ch. 13).
27. This view brings Hayek much closer to Hobbes and away from the classical liberals. Indeed, a classical liberal or a libertarian would never believe that a politician or a bureaucrat could pursue the private interest better than the individual involved.
28. See also ([1976] 1978, pp. 28–9), where the concept of opinion is suggested as the driving principle to evaluate the legitimacy of policy action, that is, to draw the line between arbitrary interferences and interventions within the rule of law.
29. See also ([1976] 1978, pp. 28–9).
30. The test of 'universalizability amounts to a test of compatibility with the whole system of accepted rules . . . which may either lead to a clear "yes" or "no" answer or may show

that, if the system of rules is to give definite guidance, some of the rules will have to be modified' ([1976] 1978, pp. 28–9).
31. Hayek ([1960] 1978) explains that institutions are 'convention and customs of human intercourse', which involve a moral code as well as general and 'unconscious adherence to moral rules'. Therefore, coercion is not necessary only 'when individuals can be expected as a rule to conform voluntarily to certain principles' (p. 62). At the same time, Hayek is aware that coercive rules are deplorable and are not conducive to desirable evolution. This is why they 'can be broken by individuals who feel that they have strong reasons to brave the censure of their fellows' (p. 63). Indeed, the author could not have done better to confuse his readers. See also pp. 67 and 146–7 for yet other views of the same subject.
32. The fact that he also writes that 'it is not obvious that this same majority must also be entitled to determine what it is competent to do' or that liberalism 'accepts majority rule as a method of deciding, but not as an authority for what the decision ought to be' hardly contributes to clarifying matters. See ibid. (pp. 107, 104).
33. Hayek ([1973] 1983, pp. 61–2) justifies his departure from the classical-liberal lines by claiming that they were too vague to serve any operational purpose: '*Laissez faire* ... never provided a criterion by which one could decide what were the proper functions of government'.
34. Hayek suggests infants and idiots as examples of individuals who do not deserve liberty. Nevertheless, the notion of learning from experience and guidance of actions is much wider and goes well beyond those categories.
35. Both principles occur frequently in Hayek's work. But they seem to be forgotten when it comes to their policy implications.
36. See also ([1979] 1981, pp. 84–5), where the need for government action against price discrimination is argued forcefully. It may be worth pointing out that today not even socialist policymakers would object to price discrimination.
37. See (ibid., p. 143) and also de Jasay ([1995] 2002, p. 87), who observes that 'Hayek, in making this singular distinction between coercive and non-coercive government actions, appears to be classifying taxation as non-coercive, a judgment that has an obvious bearing of his position regarding redistribution'.
38. For some unexplained reason this also applies to roads and sanitation (ibid., p. 141), information (p. 144), some kind of education and the advancement of knowledge in certain fields (p. 223), which Hayek treats as if they were public goods and thus 'a recognized field of public effort'. See also pp. 222–3 for the government production of public goods through general taxation, as long as the benefits cover the costs and 'provide a favorable framework for individual decisions'.
39. The reader may observe that Hayek also claims that at times traditional conventions and norms can be broken, for they should not be considered binding, after all. Unfortunately, Hayek provides no clear indication as for when a tradition is nonbinding and when it is rule of law. Hence, although the idea of the legislator as a finder is appealing, it still begs the question of establishing the nature of what the finder has actually ascertained.
40. Indeed, Hayek does not ignore that history has provided plenty of examples whereby constitutions have degenerated, also thanks to the introduction of the separation of powers, as he notes when discussing the French and German cases ([1960] 1978, Chs 12–13). Still, rather than drawing the obvious conclusions about the impossibility of constitutional constructivism, he simply concludes that such examples demonstrate the need for further safeguards.
41. Quite astonishingly, Hayek ([1960] 1978, p. 218) suggests that the willingness of the public administration to compensate the individual is an accepted criterion for comparing private losses and public gains. He seems to forget both that civil servants carry out compensation by using somebody else's money, and that fair compensation is actually established by the buyer (the civil service). As a matter of fact, Hayek seems to be more interested in 'fair socialism' than in individual freedom. See also de Jasay ([1995] 2002)

for a critical analysis of Hayek's position and ambiguities on redistribution and the welfare state.
42. True enough, Hayek does claim that policy action should not tamper with prices or quantities. That is hardly satisfactory, though. Income taxes do affect the relative price of human capital, while it is difficult to accept that according to a free-market approach 'subsidies are a legitimate tool of policy, not as a means of income distribution, but only as a means of using the market to provide services which cannot be confined to those who individually pay for them' ([1960] 1978, p. 264). Indeed, Hayek is advocating redistributive justice within a market system steered by allegedly wise policymakers caring for the common good and possibly constrained by general rules set by equally wise legislators.
43. See Hayek ([1960] 1978, p. 275).
44. According to Hayek ([1960] 1978, Ch. 23), farmers should be subsidized, since they lack access to good information. And 'We all have an interest in our fellow citizens' being put in a position to choose wisely . . . the question as to which of these services will be worth while and to what extent they should be carried out is one of expediency and raises no fundamental issue' (ibid., p. 366).
45. Up to a point, though, for Hayek seems to replace socialism with populist pragmatism: 'the defraying out of the common purse of the costs of services which will benefit only some of those who have contributed to it will usually be agreed upon by the rest only on the understanding that other requirements of theirs will be met in the same manner, so that a rough correspondence of burdens to benefits will result' ([1973] 1983, p. 140). The same concept is repeated in, for example ([1976] 1978, p. 7).
46. Hayek is of course for democracy, as long as people are reasonably well educated by institutions free from political interference. Still, rather than being an argument supporting democracy, it sounds more like one for compulsory education financed by taxpayers' money, or for lifetime employment for state teachers ([1960] 1978, Ch. 24). See also ([1973] 1983, p. 3) and, more generally, (1979 [1981]), where Hayek mentions the broken promises of democracy. Nevertheless, the obvious and somewhat troubling consequences are not drawn. He offers instead a 'better' political constitution.
47. Caldwell (2004, pp. 206, 289) already noted Hayek's early inclinations beyond individual planning, which make him sound 'suspiciously like what the later Hayek would consider a social constructivist or, at the very least, a constitutional political economist'.
48. See ([1960] 1978, Ch. 22).
49. As Caldwell (2004, pp. 206, 289) notes, Hayek thought this to be one of his major achievements, and the answer to Keynes's objections to his work in the area of political philosophy.
50. As an alternative to positivist legal theory, Hayek considers the possibility of 'the power of the legislator [being derived] from a state of widespread opinion concerning the kind of rules he is authorized to lay down' ([1976] 1978, p. 60).
51. See Caldwell (2004).
52. Even his rule-of-law criterion starts to shake when he recommends that most wartime restrictions be kept in place for years to come (p. 155), without even bothering to explain why.

REFERENCES

Buchanan, James M. (1979), *What Should Economists Do?*, Indianapolis, IN: Liberty Press.
Caldwell, Bruce J. (2004), *Hayek's Challenge: An Intellectual Biography of F.A. Hayek*, Chicago, IL, USA and London, UK: University of Chicago Press.
De Jasay, Anthony (1985), *The State*, Oxford: Basil Blackwell; reprinted 1998, Indianapolis, IN: Liberty Fund.

De Jasay, Anthony (1991), *Choice, Contract and Consent: A Restatement of Liberalism*, London: Institute for Economic Affairs.
De Jasay, Anthony (1995), 'On redistribution', *Advances in Austrian Economics*, 2A, 153–78, reprinted (2002) in Anthony de Jasay, *Justice and its Surroundings*, Indianapolis, IN: Liberty Fund.
De Jasay, Anthony (1996), 'Hayek: some missing pieces', *Review of Austrian Economics*, 9 (1), 107–18.
De Jasay, Anthony (2004), 'A dilemma of democracy', unpublished.
Denzau, Arthur T. and Douglass C. North (1994), 'Shared mental models: ideologies and institutions', *Kyklos*, 47 (1), 3–31.
Fiori, Stefano (2002), 'Alternative visions of change in Douglass North's new institutionalism', *Journal of Economic Issues*, 36 (4), 1025–43.
Fontaine, Philippe (1996), 'The French economists and politics, 1750–1859: the science and art of political economy', *Canadian Journal of Economics*, 29 (2), 379–93.
Grampp, William D. (2000), 'What did Smith mean by the invisible hand?', *Journal of Political Economy*, 108 (3), 441–65.
Hayek, Friedrich A. (1944), *The Road to Serfdom*, reprinted 1979, London and Henley: Routledge & Kegan Paul.
Hayek, Friedrich A. (1952), *The Counter-Revolution of Science*, Glencoe: Free Press, reprinted 1979, Indianapolis, IN: Liberty Fund.
Hayek, Friedrich A. (1960), *The Constitution of Liberty*, paperback edn 1978, Chicago, IL: University of Chicago Press.
Hayek, Friedrich A. (1973), *Law Legislation and Liberty – Rules and Order*, paperback edn 1983, Chicago, IL: University of Chicago Press.
Hayek, Friedrich A. (1976), *Law Legislation and Liberty – the Mirage of Social Justice*, paperback edn 1978, Chicago, IL: University of Chicago Press.
Hayek, Friedrich A. (1979), *Law Legislation and Liberty – The Political Order of a Free People*, paperback edn 1981, Chicago, IL: University of Chicago Press.
Hoppe, Hans-Hermann (1994), 'F.A. Hayek on government and the social evolution: a critique', *Review of Austrian Economics*, 7 (1), 67–93.
Leoni, Bruno (1961), *Freedom and the Law*, Princeton, NJ: D. Van Nostrand Co., reprinted 1991, Indianapolis, IN: Liberty Fund.
Mackintosh, William A. (1950), 'Government economic policy: scope and principles', *Canadian Journal of Economics and Political Science*, 16 (3), 314–26.
Mises, Ludwig von (1949), *Human Action*, New Haven, CT: Yale University Press, reprinted 1963 in cooperation with the Foundation for Economic Education, San Francisco, CA: Fox & Wilkes.
Nelson, Robert H. (1987), 'The economics profession and the making of public policy', *Journal of Economic Literature*, 25 (1), 49–91.
Rothbard, Murray N. (1982), *The Ethics of Liberty*, Atlantic Highlands, NJ: Humanities Press, reprinted 1998, New York: New York University Press.
Tyszynski, H. (1955), 'Economic theory as a guide to policy: some suggestions for re-appraisal', *Economic Journal*, 65 (258) 195–215.
Vanberg, Viktor J. (1996), 'Institutional evolution within constraints', *Journal of Institutional and Theoretical Economics*, 152 (4), 690–96.

16. What remains of Hayek's critique of 'social justice'? Twenty propositions
Robert Nef

It is impossible to formulate a final judgment about the success or failure of an idea or a critical position in the more or less open market of political concepts. In addition to his economic writings, Friedrich Hayek's oeuvre includes numerous publications dealing with the history of ideas and with social philosophy. One of the outstanding social philosophers of the twentieth century, his main significance today is his skeptical approach to social engineering, to collectivism and to what he called constructivism. His writings on political philosophy are conceived largely as criticisms of existing conditions and developments, always based on long-term perspectives (both retrospective and prospective), and are aimed directly at observed shortcomings. His intent was by no means merely to analyze those shortcomings; rather, his academic and personal passion was to improve political, economic and social conditions by learning from mistakes and missteps. He was especially interested in institutions of long standing, and his skepticism was directed at trends which, in his view, would not be of great duration because they lacked what today might be termed 'sustainability'.

Hayek is a versatile and well-read analyst of government, economics and society, and a penetrating observer of real, existing political structures. But anyone trying to derive from his writings a partisan program directly applicable to everyday politics is certain to be disappointed. When he makes proposals, he speaks at the constitutional level, and even there he operates in the realm of broad principle. Any attempt to construct a consistent 'Hayekism' from his writings is frustrated by the fact that his concept of 'spontaneous order' is not free of internal contradictions. It is process-oriented rather than structure-oriented.

Proposition 1: Hayek's method is not a constructivist representation of what is desirable, but rather the unmasking of illusions and phantasms.

Most critics of Hayek, who tend with remarkable frequency to adopt a thoroughly hostile tone, are familiar with only a small selection of his works and base their criticisms on distortions, prejudice and secondary sources. Thus the typical Hayek critic is generally not a Hayek reader, but rather the follower of some other school of thought in the realm of political science, the adherents of which know what is 'right' and what is 'wrong', and who therefore, not without reason, were targets of Hayek's critical analysis. On the other hand, Hayek supporters tend to contradict him on specific points, when they feel he has gone too far – or not far enough – but are grateful for and respectful of his intellectual approach, his methodology, and the sincerity of his personal engagement.

Whether directed either backwards or forwards, Hayek's critiques and proposals are long-term. His approach is based on cultural history and anthropology, and is neither ideological nor politically partisan. As his friend and adversary John Maynard Keynes once remarked, 'In the long run, we are all dead'. But the socio-cultural traditions upon which the success or failure of a social order depends do not change according to the rhythm of election cycles; at best, they shift in the rhythm of overlapping generations, or even more slowly.

Hayek's best-selling book *The Road to Serfdom* (1944), dedicated to socialists of all parties, contained a radical critique of the centrally planned economy and state interventionism. A later work, *The Constitution of Liberty* (1960), sketches the outlines of a positive system, but – as if he felt the need to apologize for the constitutional 'constructivism' into which he had fallen – near the end of the book. Hayek says that as a social philosopher he cannot translate the principles: 'I have tried to reconstruct [*sic*] by piecing together the broken fragments of a tradition into a program with mass appeal'. He leaves that task to a subspecies of humankind, the politician and statesman. Not without an element of self-doubt, he continues: 'He will do so effectively only if he is not concerned with what is now politically possible but consistently defends the great principles which are always the same' (ibid., p.411). How successfully one can pursue political goals by consistently advocating general principles is best known by those who have attempted it. But Hayek's optimism in this regard does not appear to be very firmly founded. So it is with good reason that his libertarian and anarcho-capitalist followers and critics – for example, Antony de Jasay (1994) and Hans Hoppe (1994) regard the programmatic passages in *The Constitution of Liberty* as a breach of the general skepticism vis-à-vis government, politics and democracy as expressed in classical liberalism.

Proposition 2: With his critique of rationalism, Hayek casts aside the nineteenth century's typically blind faith in science and progress without abandoning its positive achievements.

In considering such fundamental cultural achievements as verbal communication, orderly trade relations, the idea of the contract, consensual marriage, the family and private property, the pace of radical change must be measured in millennia. This realization gives rise to humility with regard to that small segment of developmental history which any individual can personally observe, and to a lessening of arrogance and impatience with regard to one's own suggestions for improvement.

A large part of Hayek's critique of the planned economy, state interventionism and so-called constructivism must be seen as an appeal for less arrogance, a warning against all forms of blind faith in the feasibility of scientific and social 'progress'. Born in the last year of the nineteenth century, with a life that spanned almost all of the twentieth, Hayek may justly be seen as a radical critic of unquestioning faith in rationalism and of the technocratic-mercantilist belief that everything is possible, a thinker who overcame naive and obsolete notions dating from the Age of Enlightenment in the eighteenth and nineteenth centuries. Those who see him only as a critic of socialism arguing from an ideological base mistake the fundamental nature of his thought. For example, the following passage is to be found in the essay 'On the "meaning" of social institutions' (1956, p. 520):

> Strangely enough, rationalism's battle against superstition gave rise to a new superstition. That struggle was of course justified, to the extent that it was directed against all those beliefs and opinions which had been proven false. But there is a great difference between the effort not to believe something demonstrably false and the effort to believe nothing which has not been proven true. The former is not only praiseworthy, but is essential to intellectual honesty, while the latter is neither desirable nor even possible.

The process of secularization in the eighteenth and nineteenth centuries attempted to substitute faith in science and statecraft for faith in God; Hayek showed this to be a new and dangerous form of superstition. In the modern system of coordinates based on prefixes, this makes him more a forebear than a disciple, more 'pre-' than 'post-'. Those who, for good reason, want to label him a conservative must follow the history of ideas backwards for at least two centuries.

Proposition 3: Hayek's notion of the development of spontaneous orders is based upon the observation of long-term normal developments. What he is concerned with is weighing up the opportunities and risks in any attempt to control this development.

In the history of economic theory, Hayek is commonly set opposite John Maynard Keynes, a positioning very timely in today's political climate. But the comparison is not between a practitioner and a theoretician; both men would doubtless have rejected such one-sided labeling. One important difference between them lies in the historical period each chose from which to derive theoretical knowledge and practical conclusions. Hayek's anthropological-historical approach, his theory of the evolution of 'spontaneous orders', cannot be verified or negated in the rhythms of pre- and post-war years or legislative periods. Many of his central statements have been proved more true than false by developments since 1989, which has resulted in his critics persistently pointing to real or alleged weak points in his thinking.

Moreover, many of Hayek's predictions about the unsustainability of policies aimed at centrally planned, interventionist redistribution have been fulfilled. Before his death, he was able to witness the collapse – which he had predicted – of the ostensibly centrally managed Soviet empire. The 'Austrian school of economics', which Hayek helped form, has a significant following, especially in the United States. A large part of today's political controversies are a 'contending with Hayek', dealing with various understandings – and misunderstandings – of his oeuvre, which, as has been mentioned, does not offer a self-contained dogma despite the consistency of its theoretical and intellectual approach.

Proposition 4: In his political writings Hayek never saw himself as a 'proclaimer' of eternal truths or discoverer of a historical universal law, but rather much more as a debunker of suspicion and counselor against the public misuse of pseudotruths and popular misconceptions.

That is emphatically the case in the second volume of *Law, Legislation and Liberty* (1976) with the title *The Mirage of Social Justice*. That is also the principal issue to which the present chapter addresses itself. For now, let me anticipate matters somewhat by formulating another proposition:

Proposition 5: In democracies, too (and especially in democracies), the promise of more 'social justice' is so popular among politicians and publicists of every stripe that few are willing to forgo its propagation. Hayek's spirited arguments against it have regrettably had little effect to date.

The reception of this critique of 'social justice' is a tale of silence, of being ignored, and of capitulation in the face of the mighty power inherent in this 'mirage'. In Chapter 9 of *Law, Legislation and Liberty*, under the title 'The conquest of public imagination by "social justice"', the following key passage is to be found:

> I believe that 'social justice' will ultimately be recognized as a will-o'-the-wisp which has lured men to abandon many of the values which in the past have inspired the development of civilization – an attempt to satisfy a carving inherited from traditions of the small group but which is meaningless in the Great Society of free men. (p. 67)

It is an open question whether that conviction will 'ultimately' become commonly accepted, doubtless dependent on the time span which one allows to 'ultimate' expectations. What seems certain is that, globally and especially in Europe, we are still far indeed from that goal, and there are few signs that Hayek's critique will ever become common coinage. He would seem to have massively underestimated the central importance of illusions in political life and of unreflected misunderstandings as the basis of political compromise. Politics lives on myths, which it must sustain and recreate, and the longing 'inherited from traditions of the small group' is so central to human coexistence that not even a highly educated and visionary Nobel Prize winner has a chance against it – at least, not within the foreseeable future. In the following paragraphs we shall offer some explanations of this phenomenon.

First, I will briefly recapitulate the basic outlines of Hayek's critique. The questions 'what is "social"', what is "justice" and what is "society"' preoccupied Hayek long before 1973, the year in which the initial volume of *Law, Legislation and Liberty* was published. In *The Road to Serfdom* (1944) we find the first statement of the impossibility of what would be termed today a 'sustainable' combination of the welfare state and the constitutional state.

Proposition 6: Hayek's skepticism of the redistributive welfare state is not hostile towards the state; it is an attempt to protect the institution of the constitutional state against the vicious circle of exploding demands for the expansion of welfare and public services.

The citizens of a constitutional state demand that their government uphold the principle of equal treatment. In reality, however, there will always be many forms of inequality suffered by many people. In a liberal constitutional state, it is the sum of anonymous and non-political decisions and developments which generates inequality. Blows of fate and disappointments which seem undeserved, and which strike innocent individuals, are not generally blamed on the government. But as soon as government begins to intervene in the name of equality, it falls into a vicious cycle of unfulfillable demands:

While people will submit to suffering which may hit anyone, they will not easily submit to suffering which is the result of the decision of authority. It may be bad to be just a cog in an impersonal machine (that is, the market economy); but it is infinitely worse if we can no longer leave it, if we are tied to our place and the superiors who have been chosen for us. Dissatisfaction of everybody with his lot will inevitably grow with the consciousness that it is the result of deliberate human decision. (Hayek, 1944, p. 80)

This key passage is cited here because it contradicts the notion that Hayek harbored a fundamental hostility towards government. Rather, his concern was to avoid a serious crisis of legitimacy by the centrally planning, redistributive state and to save the political and economic order made possible by the constitutional state from the crushing weight of escalating demands for 'justice' in the distribution and redistribution of material goods and services.

Proposition 7: Hayek wishes to protect the political system of the constitutional state from maneuvering itself, on account of its irredeemable promise to distribute and redistribute benefits justly, into a spiral of increasing dissatisfaction, which ultimately is bound to culminate in a new form of totalitarianism and leave the state in the debt trap.

So long as people can rail against fate, or can blame 'the market' or 'neoliberalism' for all inequities, the political system is relieved of an enormous pressure of expectations. Who knows what would happen if politics were suddenly to be responsible for everything and hence to blame for everything – that is, if left-wing statist coalitions no longer had a scapegoat in the opposition, or in uncooperative market forces, for which they could blame the failure of their policies?

It is no coincidence that in the former East Germany (GDR), a state with a nationalized economy and a distributive and redistributive government, nearly one-third of the populace ultimately had to be recruited, formally or informally, in the service of 'state security', which had a massive negative impact both on economic productivity and on the climate of trust in political and personal life. These old burdens have by no means been overcome today. Paradoxically, however, instead of being perceived as late consequences of a failed system, these problems are being represented as the negative consequences of East Germany's transformation in the direction of a free-market system.

Proposition 8: In the face of the world's complexities Hayek dispenses neither with attempts at explanations by way of principles and oversimplifying models, nor with the control of the environment by the exercise of conscious reason. He merely warns against the presumptuous idea that we really know what is 'social'.

Hayek's method of unmasking illusions frequently consists in confronting the unthinking use of terminology. Language is not an invention, but the result of an evolutionary process. Hayek regards it as an inexhaustible storehouse of knowledge and experience, from which a speaker can draw without being aware of what is going on. He repeatedly draws attention to the similarity between the exchange of meaning via the spontaneous use of language and the spontaneous exchange of goods and services in the marketplace. In the previously cited 1956 essay titled 'Über den "Sinn" sozialer Institutionen' ('On the "meaning" of social institutions'), Hayek reflects on the relationship of knowledge, experience, language and 'the process of civilization':

> All that we refer to as civilization and culture is clearly the result of human action. But this does not mean that those broad areas are conscious creations of the human intellect, that we understand how they function or know in what ways they help us achieve our goals. In a certain sense, of course, we are more the products of our civilization than our civilization is the product of ourselves. No human intellect initially designed this civilization; rather, our individual knowledge is a product of the process of civilization ... I would be the last person to recommend taking the desperate step towards mysticism, or to simply accept what exists as 'the best of all possible worlds'. Of course we must use our faculty of reason, even when in certain special cases the only outcome would be to show us the limits of how far we may practically exercise our domination over the environment through our conscious reason. (1956, p. 521)

Proposition 9: Hayek's 'contention with concepts' indicates that, instead of blindly adopting the knowledge stored in language, he prefers to use a creative blend of trust and mistrust vis-à-vis the contemporary use of language to encourage two processes, which he distinguishes as 'orientation' (rather than 'prediction') and 'cultivation' (rather than 'domination').

The terms 'prediction' and 'domination' may be handier and more precise than 'orientation' and 'cultivation', but in essence they contain that arrogance of knowledge against which Hayek repeatedly warned. The confrontation with the subject of 'social justice' which begins in the essay mentioned earlier is continued in another essay titled 'Was ist und was heisst "sozial"?' ['What is and what means "social"?'], which appears in the collection *Masse und Demokratie* [*Mass and Democracy*] (Albert Hunold, 1957, pp. 71–85). In the introduction, Hayek poses the question of whether it is justified to devote an entire essay to the meaning of a single word. He affirms this, pointing out that the history of that adjective's usage embraces 'an important slice of the history of ideas and the history of human error'. He is especially skeptical about the adjective in conjunction with the terms 'market economy' and 'constitutional state'.

His main objection is that the word pretends to a broad level of general agreement which in fact does not exist:

> In such a situation, in which we all make use of a word which beclouds rather than casting any light, [a word] which pretends to indicate an answer when in fact we have none, and even worse, which is used only to camouflage desires which clearly have nothing to do with the general interest, it is obviously high time for a radical operation which will free us from the confusing influence of such a magic formula and the spell it casts.

The energetic and zealous analysis of the term then leads us to the root of Hayek's unease.

But what is the original meaning of the term 'social' as used in this context? Anyone attempting to answer this question comes up against the 'sacred fury' which Hayek feels towards the contemporary use of the word. He regards the shift in its meaning as a kind of theft, or a fateful revision of an attribute which plays a central role both in Hayek's developmental theory and in classical liberalism. For when the term *sozial* took root in the German language in the middle of the last century, it was used to denote a social order which was created not by the deliberate organizational effort of the state, but rather by spontaneous development, a distinction central to classical liberalism. The line separating legislatively or governmentally ordered conditions, and that which comes about non-governmentally, through spontaneous processes, through the 'unforeseen results of the interplay of the actions of many individuals and generations', was designated by the two terms 'state' and 'social'. Hayek remarks:

> By its very nature, the social is of anonymous origin, not rational, not the result of logical thought and planning, but rather the result of a supra-individual process of development and selection, to which individuals indeed make their contributions, but the determining aspects of which are not mastered by any single intellect. It was the realization that, in this sense, there are forces for order independent of the goal-oriented desires of people, that the interplay of those forces gives rise to structures which are of use to the strivings of individuals without having been designed for that purpose, that led to the introduction of the term 'social' in contradistinction to that which is intentionally created and conducted by the state. (ibid.)

Against this background of the history of language and ideas, it becomes understandable why Hayek developed a kind of 'fury about the lost, original meaning' of a term which would have had such central importance for his theory. Imagine that the term *sozial* had retained its original meaning of 'non-governmental', 'not generated by deliberate, goal-oriented aim', 'generated in the spontaneous interplay of innovation and tradition'. In that case, anti-centralists and anti-interventionists like Hayek might well have been correctly termed 'socialists', in order to underscore their contrast to the etatists – a very fundamental and meaningful dichotomy, by the way. This might have served to obviate many misunderstandings in the realms of ideas and politics.

Proposition 10: The transformation and confusion of terms in conjunction with key political concepts is not simply a case of sloppiness in the use of language or a lack of terminological discipline on the part of politicians or media commentators and interpreters, but rather a necessary side-effect of political consensus-building in a mass democracy.

Retrospective speculation about the proper and improper use of the term 'social' is moot, for it is not just a result of blind chance that the content of political vocabularies constantly changes. It is one of the costs of democratic opinion-building in the contest for political majorities. In his visionary novel *1984* (Orwell, 1949), George Orwell pointedly underscored the links between domination, propaganda and the use of language. His observations do not apply solely to totalitarian dictatorships, but to a considerable degree also to mass democracies with competitive or consensus-based systems.

Proposition 11: Politics needs terms that can be stretched, interpreted and even turned into their opposite in order to counteract the shortage of consensus among thinking people. A lack of consensus is replaced by hidden dissent and an appeal to collectivisable emotions such as envy and xenophobia.

In political systems, Hayek's criterion of dependability can lead to the maintenance of illusions, unless one truly believes in the long-term educability of humanity; a belief which occasionally shines through in Hayek's writings and which is denigrated by his libertarian critics as demonstrating excessive faith in progress and government. But given the reality of existing political systems, his hope of being able to put an end to the illusion of 'social justice' by means of a 'radical operation' seems overly optimistic. The term 'social' (often used interchangeably with 'welfare') has become inextricably mixed with 'morally good', 'humanitarian', 'altruistic'. A 'social person' is a 'good person', and a 'good person' naturally leans towards 'social democracy', towards the left, 'where the heart is'. Social scientists whose earning power is based on the structures of the 'social' (or welfare) state naturally have a vested interest in promulgating the link between 'social' and 'government'.

Hayek prophetically anticipated this development:

> It seems to me indubitable that the entire development which has made the responsibility of the individual ever more vague, on the one hand largely relieving him of responsibility for his immediate surroundings, while on the other hand imposing on him an unclear, ill-defined responsibility for things not clearly visible, has on the whole greatly vitiated people's sense of responsibility. Without imposing clear, new obligations which the individual can fulfill through his personal efforts, it has blurred the boundaries of all responsibility and, above all, served as an invitation to voice demands or to do 'good' at the expense of others (ibid.)

At the center of the book, which is divided into five sections (comprising Sections 7–11 of the complete three-volume work *Law, Legislation and Liberty*) stands a confrontation with the term 'justice'. For Hayek, justice is an 'attribute of human conduct' and, when the term is not misused, the base of individual freedom. In two theoretical passages he criticizes utilitarianism as a 'constructivist fallacy' and legal positivism as a theory which is 'largely responsible for the progressive undermining of individual freedom' (p. 34). All of this goes to show that Hayek was not trying to replace the guideline of justice with the market, but rather that he was attempting to determine that junction at which the law serves 'an ongoing overall order of actions. If such rules are enforced because they serve an order on whose existence everybody relies, this provides of course no justification for the enforcement of other recognized rules which do not in the same manner affect the existence of this interpersonal order of actions' (Hayek, 1976, p. 58).

Proposition 12: Hayek's construct of an 'evolutionary natural law' enables him to inject content into the concept of justice. Yet it is hardly suitable for delineating what regulations legislators are actually permitted to impose on the general public in a liberal society.

Having distanced himself from utilitarianism and legal positivism with a series of complex but not always entirely convincing arguments, he states his allegiance to an 'evolutionary natural law', under which the legislator must repeatedly attempt to 'maintain a functioning spontaneous order' (ibid.). This theory is just as paradoxical as the reality it proposes to explicate; but can that be used as an accusation? The term 'spontanous order' – doubtless used by Hayek because the original, more accurate adjective 'social' can no longer be used due to its widespread misuse – already contains a dialectical tension within it. According to Hayek, a legislator, in order to maintain a functioning spontaneous order:

cannot pick up and choose any rules he likes to confer validity upon them, if he wants to achieve his aim. His power is not unlimited because it rests on the fact, that some of the rules are regarded as right by the citizens, and the acceptance by him of these rules necessarily limits his powers of making other rules enforceable. (p. 61)

Proposition 13: Hayek's notion of justice refers to formal rules and not material results.

Justice is conceived as the 'rationale of the economic game in which only the conduct of the players but not the result can be just', 'The fact is simply that we consent to retain, and agree to enforce, uniform rules for a procedure which has greatly improved the chances of all to have their wants satisfied, but at the price of all individuals and groups incurring the risk of unmerited failure' (p. 70).

This mention of the 'risk of failure' is an important springboard for a critical analysis of the chances for Hayek's critique of the welfare state to enjoy political success. Today, ever fewer individuals and ever fewer groups are willing to accept the risk of individual failure. Politics today is an 'event' in which it is maintained that risk can be almost totally eliminated. Risks these days are 'socialized', transformed into long-term collective problems. Opportunities, on the other hand, are 'privatized' and consumed as swiftly as possible as short-term benefits. But that mightily increases the larger risk of failure in large-scale systems. The only escape from it – in time – is through flight to even larger systems. In the long-term public interest, it should be the job of politics to push for the opposite trend. But in a mass democracy, politico-economic considerations compel politicians to intensify this vicious cycle.

Proposition 14: The longing for compensatory 'social justice' may often be linked with aesthetic ideals, and for many the desire for things to be simple, clean and clear is an integral part of politico-economic psychohygiene.

In conjunction with concepts of political order, there seems to be a 'natural inclination' towards equalization, harmonization, unification and clarification. But all of that is to be had only at the cost of centralization and the creation of hierarchies. Obviously, many people find it very difficult to deal with unclear, mixed and pluralistic phenomena. Their fatal premise is that the larger, the more broadly binding and more centralized the state is, the more just it will be. To someone sitting at the center of power, there is nothing more unpleasant than the idea that he can have no internal or external influence because the various threads of agreement, opposition and confusion held by competing individuals and institutions is too opaque and thus cannot be effectively influenced.

In the twenty-first century, however, it will be diversity, non-centrality, cross-pollination, competition and flexible cooperation which will characterize the adaptable and progressive structures that will determine economic and political success. Deregulation is more important than harmonization, because the former expands the field for experimentation and reduces the danger of a harmonization of unified mistakes. Small, transparent structures offer greater advantages than large, opaque structures. As long as the threat of military and economic might is not in the foreground, smallness of scale is advantageous in organizing and maintaining the necessary political order.

Proposition 15: There is no description of 'happiness' or 'unhappiness' which can be generalized, but rather a host of competing experiments to achieve one and avoid the other.

This assertion applies not only to primary social groups but to everything from the individual to a large, anonymous society. That is what offers both the risk and the opportunity of diversified, not centrally regulated, experiments, which in turn may result in more happiness or more unhappiness. If we were to have only a single model of the family and of education, standardized down to the smallest detail, all families would be the same; presumably equally unhappy. The same applies to other social groups as well as to local communities, states and nations.

This realization, based upon Hayek, may be summed up in yet another proposition:

Proposition 16: Decentralization means pluralism, diversity and choice and brings opportunities as well as risks. Those who wish to eliminate the risks also destroy the opportunities and contribute to a net worsening of the situation.

In his attack against 'social and distributive justice' (ibid., Ch. 9), Hayek explicitly refers to David Hume and Immanuel Kant, taking his superscription for the chapter from Kant's 'Die Streit um die Fakultäten' (Reiss, [1798] 1970, p. 183n):

> Welfare, however, has no principle, neither for him who receives it, nor for him who distributes it (one will place it here and another there); because it depends on the material content of the will, which is dependent upon particular facts and therefore incapable of a general rule.

But in making this connection and basing his description of 'justice' upon it, Hayek places himself far indeed from what our welfare-state-deformed contemporaries understand today by the term 'justice'. The battle against 'public opinion' must be regarded as lost. Not only the original meaning of *sozial*, but also the original meaning of 'just' in the sense of 'according to the rules', 'not arbitrary', is no longer included in the common usage of the term today.

The idea that just distribution ultimately lies 'in God's hand', and that we do not know its norms, has disappeared in the general process of secularization. The distinction between 'godly' and 'human' justice, such as was made by the Swiss Reformation leader Ulrich Zwingli (1484–1531), is hardly comprehended today. We now demand of the state what prior generations did not dare demand of God, and what Kant regarded as impossible: that is, general rules for the distribution of prosperity. Today, alas, we must assume that those who call for and promise justice generally mean the kind of 'social justice' which Hayek subjected to such a fundamental critique. As a kind of sad summation, I formulate the following proposition:

Proposition 17: Hayek's attempt to rescue the concept of 'justice' by uncoupling it from 'social justice' and reducing it to its original senses of legal justice in a society operating under private law and the non-arbitrariness of fundamentally limited government power, has foundered on the empirical reality of language usage.

Hayek graphically described the consequences. They are not so much politically dubious as morally devastating:

> But it is not only by encouraging malevolent and harmful prejudices that the cult of 'social justice' tends to destroy genuine moral feelings ... Though all these moral principles have also been seriously weakened by some pseudo-scientific fashions of our time which tend to destroy all morals – and with them the basis of individual freedom – the ubiquitous dependence on other people's power, which the enforcement of any image of 'social justice' creates inevitably destroys that freedom of personal decisions on which all morals must rest. (ibid., p. 99)

In this context, it would be an exciting challenge to undertake a politico-economic analysis of the use and misuse of language, and to pursue the question of who, in the kind of 'spontaneous order' of which language is an example, is responsible for the rules of 'proper usage'. It would probably turn out to be all the more or less rational and responsible users who participate in the construction and destruction of 'meaning'; of course not intentionally, for the most part. With good reason, Hayek feels himself to be – and behaves as – a self-appointed judge of this process. And he would doubtless also grant the office of judge to all those who can base their judgments on the authority of argumentation and on a comparable fund of traditional knowledge. Here is his stern verdict: 'It does not belong to the category of error but to that of nonsense, like the term 'a moral stone' (ibid., p. 78).

For Hayek, the concept of justice cannot be applied to the results of a spontaneous process. Those who accuse him of regarding the results of a market economy as 'automatically just' are missing the essential point. His skepticism vis-à-vis the welfare state, which is based essentially on his critique of the term 'social justice', is a consistent extension of his critique of the planned economy and government interventionism laid out in *The Road to Serfdom* The leitmotif of a criticism of 'social justice' based on linguistic analysis also appears in Hayek's late work, *The Fatal Conceit* (1988). In it, an entire chapter is devoted to this issue, under the title 'Our poisoned language'.

Proposition 18: The basic problem of the welfare state is that it is unsustainable in the long term and sooner or later will therefore bankrupt both the welfare system and the democratic state.

In Europe, the welfare state in all its various forms now finds itself facing the crisis which Hayek foresaw. But no one seems terribly upset about it. Financing is not secured for the long term. And left-wing politicians who only recently were calling for the expansion of the welfare state, or its 'completion', have switched to the idea of its 'restructuring', though no one is willing to commit themselves about what should be retained in that process of restructuring and what must be altered.

While it may be enough to use mottos such as 'Head high ... and bite the bullet', or 'Let's tighten our belts', or 'More of the same' to deal with bottlenecks, getting out of a 'dead end' demands a strategy of 'about-face', a strategy of 'orderly retreat' from a mistaken mode of behavior; or to put it even more drastically, withdrawal from addiction to the welfare state. And what is the addictive narcotic, the 'drug' of the welfare state? It can be neither welfare itself nor material prosperity:

Proposition 19: The drug destroying society is an egalitarianism driven by envy, the lack of willingness to accept the difference between the 'richer' and the 'poorer'.

Envy is of course much older than any political system or ideology. Socialism does not create envy, but it appeals to and needs envy. Some of its theoreticians are bold enough to develop programs which actually promise to ultimately eliminate all grounds for experiencing envy (by creating a 'classless society', for example). In my view that is a well-intentioned but hopeless undertaking. It is not only the propertyless, the disenfranchised and the poor who feel envy, and socialism is not the only system to politically exploit envy. Racists and nationalists of all stripes take advantage of such emotions. Socialism, however, appeals time and again to the almost unlimited resentments, open or latent, that are found in a pluralistic society, drawing a following from among those who are motivated by the promise of 'more justice through more redistribution'. That promise can never be fulfilled in a final sense, since today there is a preference for a relative definition of 'poverty' and the broad range of frustrations grows as the level of prosperity rises. The dialectic found in every society between two groups, the enviers and the envied (with frequent overlapping), is thus supplemented by a third group: the functionaries, the redistributors in the political apparatus, who exploit the envy and live very nicely off the promise (irredeemable in my view) to alleviate and even eliminate inequities through 'social justice', thereby doing away with the reasons for envy. It is indeed an alluring and quite lucrative business! But it is doubtful whether it is as 'social' or as 'just' as those who promulgate it assert.

Proposition 20: The 'modern industrial society' intensifies the vicious cycle of redistribution with the promise of more 'social justice'. Redistribution is popular, among both potential recipients and the prosperous, and can therefore often generate a political majority.

Among the prosperous, the advocacy of redistribution by the welfare state (taxing one party's wealth in order to distribute the proceeds to another) is naturally motivated by something other than active envy. Their goal is to prevent or ameliorate the envy felt by others towards them. Government-imposed redistribution is seen by many of the super-rich as insurance against social unrest, and hence is very popular among them. It need hardly be emphasized that, despite all the rhetoric to the contrary, the motivation as a rule is not especially 'social' or humanitarian. The exploitation of envy can be both lucrative and politically smart. It is quite obvious that the 'desire for ever more' can become an addiction, not only among the recipients of redistributed wealth but among all people. This applies to the acquisition of all goods, and especially to goods which the individual need not earn but which are handed to them by some apparatus or other. When there is talk of people receiving 'support' in conjunction with redistribution, this is the equivalent of the liberal concept of 'subsidiary assistance'.

I am not asserting here that everything about the redistributive welfare state was negative. Even Hayek, especially in *The Constitution of Liberty*, conceded the need for and advocated government-run redistributive institutions; which is not received at all well by his libertarian critics. In Western Europe, for a limited time, the welfare state facilitated a society in which the level of social tensions was quite low. Ultimately, however, the welfare state expanded to such a degree that social spending could be financed only through ever-increasing deficits; in effect, dumping the costs of redistribution onto the shoulders of the next generation. It is doubtful whether even those who advocate 'social justice' can tolerate that situation for very long. As to those who, based on Hayek's thinking, ceaselessly subject the term to radical critique, all of this seems lost in a fog of illusion and deception.

REFERENCES

de Jasay, Antony (1994), 'The cart before the horse: on emergent and constructed orders and their wherewithal', in Christoph Frei and Robert Nef (eds), *Contending with Hayek*, Bern: Peter Lang.
Hayek, Friedrich A. (1944), *The Road To Serfdom*, London: Routledge & Kegan Paul.
Hayek, Friedrich A. (1956), 'On the "meaning" of social institutions', *Schweizer Monatshefte*, 36 (7), 520ff.
Hayek, Friedrich A. (1960), *The Constitution of Liberty*, London: Routledge & Kegan Paul; Chicago, IL: University of Chicago Press.
Hayek, Friedrich A. (1973–79), *Law, Legislation and Liberty*, 3 vols, London: Routledge & Kegan Paul; Chicago, IL: University of Chicago Press.
Hayek, Friedrich A. (1988), *The Fatal Conceit: The Errors of Socialism*, London: Routledge.
Hoppe, Hans (1994), 'F.A. Hayek on government and social evolution: a critique', in Christoph Frei and Robert Nef (eds), *Contending with Hayek*, Bern: Peter Lang.
Hunold, Albert (ed) (1957), *Masse und Demokratie*, Erlenbach-Zürich: Eugen Rentsch Verlag.
Orwell, George (1949), *1984*, London: Secker & Warburg.
Reiss, Hans S. (ed.) ([1798] 1970), *Kant's Political Writings*, transl. H.E. Nisbett, Cambridge: Cambridge University Press.

Index

1980s Unemployment and the Unions (book) 314, 320, 321, 322
1984 (novel) 372

'acceleration of time' 345, 346
accounting prices 65, 248, 249
A Century of Bank Rate (book) 30
'adverbial rules' 210
aggregate demand 13, 96–7, 98, 106, 326, 327–8
American Steel Foundries v. Tri-City Central Trades Council (1921) 337
'Anglo-American approach' 72
anti-rationalistic approach 210–11
Aréna, Richard 28, 31
Armentano, Dominick 335–6
Arrow–Debreu model 249
Austrian Institute for Business Cycle Research 1, 47–8, 144–5
Austrian school of economics
 and capital theory 25, 26, 47–9, 57–8, 67, 73–4, 91–2, 166–7, 173–4
 and competition policy 36–7
 hostility towards 35
 intellectual paths of 11
 and Lachmann 165–6
 and macroeconomics 13–14
 and market processes 130–31
 and methodological individualism 1
 and methodological subjectivism 154
 and Mises 138–41
 and monetary policy 346, 357
 and neoclassicism 197
 and price system 60
 and socialist calculation debate 278–9, 281–2, 286, 288, 290
 and spontaneous order 226, 231, 240, 242
 and subjectivism 1

Backhouse, Roger 35, 36
bank lending 19, 21, 26, 27–8

Banking Policy and the Price Level (book) 101
Barber, Benjamin 263
Bardhan, Pranab 289, 290
Barry, Norman 7–9, 240
Bartley III, W.W. 116
Bellante, Don 23
Bentham, Jeremy 17–18
Berle, Adolf 281
Beveridge, William 110
Blaug, Mark 59–60, 62
'blind faith' 365–6
Böhm-Bawerk, Eugen von
 and Austrian school 141
 and capital theory 23, 25, 166, 168, 182–3
 influence on Hayek 12, 37, 58
 as 'master' 147
 and Mises 140
Buchanan, James 255, 344, 350
Burke, Edmund 225
business (trade) cycles
 and capital theory 25, 49, 71, 82–4, 86
 and central-bank policy 132–4
 and change in Hayek's economic theory 110
 and consumption goods 19–21, 23
 and credit expansion 133–4
 and 'cumulative process' 19
 empirical weakness of theory 30
 and enhanced factor incomes 19
 and enterprise 21
 and entrepreneurship 20
 and equilibrium analysis 196–7
 and full employment 21
 and general equilibrium theory 5
 and Hayek's relationship with Lachmann 166
 and Hayek's rivalry with Keynes 1
 and industrial fluctuations 51, 53, 57–8

381

and inflation acceleration
mechanism 26–7
and interest rates 20–21, 30, 82–3,
84, 87–8, 132–4
and intertemporal equilibrium 95–6
and investment 21, 31, 82, 83–4
and macroeconomics 21
and Mises 140
and monetary disequilibrium 83–4
and monetary expansion 19–20,
82–4, 86–7
and monetary theory 51, 53
and new classicism 30, 32
and price levels 22–3
and quantity theory 22–3
and renewed interest in Hayek 19
and Ricardo Effect 20, 21–2, 30
and static equilibrium 106–7
and technological change 132, 133
and unions 328

Cairnes, J.E. 29
Caldwell, Bruce 2, 28, 29, 173
Capital and Growth (book) 18
Capital and its Structure (book) 167
capital heterogeneity 169–73, 179–82,
183
capital theory
'Anglo-American approach' 72–3
and Austrian school 47–9, 57–8, 67,
73–4, 91–2, 166–7, 173–4
and business cycles 25, 49, 71, 82–4,
86
and capital heterogeneity 169–73,
183
and capitalism 74–5, 78, 79–80, 81,
83, 92
and complexity 173, 175–9, 182–7
and consumption goods 48–9, 72–3,
74–5, 77, 80–81, 83–4, 85–6,
88–90
and credit extension 24
critiques of 23–4, 26, 57–8
and disequilibrium 174–6, 185–6
and division of labour 48, 76, 183
and entrepreneurship 48, 74–5, 79,
81, 92
and expectations 166, 167–9, 172
and Hayek's influence on Lachmann
166, 167–9, 174–6

illustrative examples 72–3, 74, 75,
77, 84–6
and industrial fluctuations 50–51,
57–8
and institutions 185–7
and interest rates 82–3, 84, 87–8
and investment 81–2, 83–4, 85–6,
88
and Keynesian economics 71
and macroeconomics 23, 71, 92
and microeconomics 71–2, 92
and monetary expansion 82–4, 85–6
and monetary policy 67
and neoclassicism 58, 72, 79–80, 92
and 'period of production' 24–5, 48,
49, 48, 76, 103–5, 182
and price expectations 86–8
and price system 118
and *Prices and Production* 5, 17,
23–4, 48, 49
and productivity of capital 75–7
and Ricardo Effect 52–3
and river analogy 80–81
and 'roundaboutness' of production
process 48, 49, 55, 58, 72, 73–4,
75–7, 82, 84, 182–3
and stock of capital 78–9, 168–9
and 'structure of production' 48–9,
52–3, 54–5, 58, 67, 75, 78
and technological change 183–4
and 'triangles' 25–6, 48, 103–4, 118
and unemployment 105
and University of Chicago 5, 17
capitalism
and capital theory 74–5, 78, 79–80,
81, 83, 92
and commodity production 296–7
and Keynes 94, 96
and Marxian socialism 261–2
and Mises 149, 153
and price system 64–6
and socialist calculation debate
280–82, 283, 289–90, 291
Capitalism and Freedom (book) 116
'catallaxy' 66, 67, 211–12
central planning
and collapse of Soviet empire 367
and commodity production 296–7
and comparative institutional
analysis 215–16

and economic calculation 59, 248, 252
and international trade 301–4
and Mises 4, 33
and monetary policy 355
and price system 63–4, 65, 150–51
and socialism 142, 149–151
and socialist calculation debate 282–3, 287, 291
and spontaneous order 231–2, 237
and unions 332
central-bank policy 4, 132–4
ceteris paribus assumption 3
Chamberlin, Edward 281
'Choice in currency' (pamphlet) 111
'circulating capital' 49, 74
Clayton Act (1914) 317
Coase, Ronald 252
Cockett, Richard 37
Cockshot, W. Paul 290
codetermination 315, 339
'co-efficient of money transactions' 55
coercive unionism 314, 315–19, 322–31, 337
collective bargaining 314, 315, 318–19, 331–2, 338
Collectivist Economic Planning (book) 151, 247
Committee on Social Thought 2, 6, 17
communitarian socialism 262–5
comparative institutional analysis 215–18
competition policy 36–7
competitive markets
  and entrepreneurship 66, 257
  and price system 63, 66
  and socialism 62, 63, 66, 252, 257–8
  and socialist calculation debate 280, 285–6, 289
  and spontaneous order 66–7, 257–8
competitive order 66–7
complementarity 169–71, 173
complexity 173, 175–87
'compositive social theory' 235–6, 239
Comte, Auguste 258–9
constitutional economics 344, 345, 348, 356–7
constructivist rationalism 67, 229–30, 231, 232, 234, 235–7, 259
consumption goods
  and business cycles 19–21, 23
  and capital theory 48–9, 72–3, 74–5, 77, 80–81, 83–4, 85–6, 88–90
  and productivity 183
consumption spending 126–7
Cottrell, Allin 290
credit expansion 19, 24, 53, 133–4, 140, 172, 328
Critical Essays in Monetary Theory (book) 18
crystal formation 227–8, 236
cultural evolution 212–13, 233, 237–8, 239, 240–41, 257–8

Darwin, Charles 225
Darwinism 178, 225, 240, 257
Davidson, David 27
de Jasay, Anthony 345, 349, 350, 356, 365
'Denationalization of money' (pamphlet) 111
Deutscher, Patrick 34
Dicey, A.V. 317
Dickinson, H.D. 283
Director, Aaron 17
discoordination of markets 322–3
distributive principle 270–74
division of labour 48, 54, 56, 76, 149–50, 183, 198
Dostaler, Gilles 35
Duplex Printing v. Deering (1921) 317
durable capital 72–3
Durbin, Evan 17
dynamic equilibrium 5, 54

Ebenstein, Alan 5, 6, 246
Econometrica (journal) 15
economic calculation
  and general equilibrium theory 67
  and market processes 60–62
  and price system 60–61, 64–5
  and socialism 1, 4, 59, 60–62, 64–5, 149, 246, 247–9, 281–3, 284, 287–8
'Economic calculation in the socialist commonwealth' (article) 281, 282
Economic Journal 14–15, 109
Economica (journal) 108
'Economics and knowledge' (article)

and change in Hayek's economic
    theory 94
and economic calculation 247
and expectations 167
and 'human action' 152, 155
importance of 1, 2
and socialism 4
and socialist calculation debate 286
and static equilibrium 106–7
and 'transformation' of Hayek 195,
    197–8, 203
*Economics as a Coordination Problem:
The Contribution of Friedrich A.
Hayek* (book) 6
Economy and Society (book) 154
egalitarianism 267–9, 270, 271, 273,
    377–8
'elastic' currency 54
Ellis, Howard 15, 26
'emergence' 179
Employment Acts (1980, 1982) 340
Engels, Friedrich 261
enterprise/enterprises 21, 82, 95–6, 262,
    320, 329–30, 335, 337–9
entrepreneurship
    and business cycles 20
    and capital theory 48, 74–5, 79, 81,
        92
    and competitive markets 66, 257
    and expectations 187–8
    and interest rates 51
    and knowledge 204, 254
    and market processes 287
    and monetary policy 54, 56, 353
    and price expectations 56
    and price system 64–6
    and production process 50, 52–3
    and socialist calculation debate 287
    and stationary states 59
'envy' 377–8
Essays in Positive Economics (book)
    117
evolution 177–8, 225, 240–41
'evolutionary natural law' 373–4
exclusive representation 318–19, 331–2,
    334, 340
expectations
    and capital theory 166, 167–9, 172
    and entrepreneurs 187–8
    and institutions 187–8

and Keynesian economics 166–7
and market processes 188–9
experimental economics 36

falsificationism 2
fascism 108
Federal Reserve (US) 133–4
Ferguson, Adam 225, 296
'firm heterogeneity' 179–80
Fisher, Stanley 22
fixed capital 26
Fleetwood, Steve 211–12
'forced saving' 19, 20, 21, 25, 52, 84, 87,
    88, 89, 90, 101, 103, 106
'formal-similarity' argument 283
Foundation of Economic Education
    35
free trade 294–5, 303, 304–6, 309, 311
freedom of association 314–15,
    332–3
freedom of contract 315, 321, 333–6
Friedman, Milton
    commonality with Hayek 113, 116,
        117–18, 130, 135
    and Keynesianism 120, 121–2
    and 'long-run/short-run'
        relationships 128–9, 135
    and macroeconomics 113, 119–23,
        125, 130, 132
    methodology of 117, 121, 122, 132
    opposing views to Hayek 116–17,
        118–23, 124
    and quantity theory 22, 23, 120–21,
        122–3, 125
    response to *Prices and Production*
        135
    and 'simple common model' 120,
        129
    and 'transmission mechanisms'
        129–30
    and unions 335
    and University of Chicago
        economics department 5, 17
Friedrich Hayek: A Biography (book)
    246
full employment
    and business cycles 21
    and consumption goods 89
    goal of 81, 87
    and inflation 26–7, 87

and quantity theory 125
and Second World War 107
and unions 326–7, 328
Full Employment in a Free Society (book) 110

Galbraith, J.K. 264
Galiani, Ferdinando 343
game theory 36
Garrison, Roger 23, 35
GATT (General Agreement on Tariffs and Trade) 305
general equilibrium theory
  and business cycles 5
  and economic calculation 62, 67
  Hayek's commitment to 28–9
  and inflation acceleration mechanism 27
  and knowledge 199–202
  and market interdependencies 3, 5
  and market processes 185–6
  and monetary policy 53–4
  and new classicism 30–31
  and price expectations 56–7
  and socialism 197, 249, 251–2, 255, 284–6
  and statics and dynamics 5, 54, 59–60
German Historical School 148–9
'given' knowledge 249–52
globalization 294–5, 298, 300, 303–4, 305, 308–11
'globophobia' 295, 308–10
gold standard 95, 100, 109, 112, 139, 300
Great Depression 95, 107, 122–3, 145, 167, 281
'Great Society' 266, 297, 298–9
Grossman, Stanford 253, 254

Haberler, Gottfried 20, 22, 27
Habermas, Jurgen 263
Hageman, Harold 22
Hamouda, Omar 31
Hansen, Alvin 15, 110
Hanson, Charles 317
'happiness'/'unhappiness' 375
Hawtrey, Richard 14, 15, 21, 23–4, 30, 58
Hayek, Friedrich August von
  abandons equilibrium analysis 195–202, 214, 217–18, 255
  awarded Nobel Prize 18, 33–4, 99, 139
  birth of 1, 140
  broad principles of 364–5, 366–7
  career overview 32–7
  change in economic theory 94, 95–6, 99, 106–7, 110, 195–202
  citation data 33, 34
  Copenhagen lecture (1933) 4–5
  death of 2
  as debunker of popular misconceptions 367–8, 370–71
  as director of Austrian Institute for Business Cycle Research 1, 47, 144–5
  evolving perspectives of 2–5
  failure to review Keynes' *General Theory* 108, 117, 123–4
  and Friedman
    commonality with 113, 116, 117–18, 130, 135
    opposing views to 116–17, 118–23, 124
  and history of economic thought 12
  and impact of Keynes' *General Theory* 13, 32, 107, 112
  and impact of *The Road to Serfdom* 16–17
  influence on Lachmann 165, 166, 167–9, 170–71, 174–6
  influence on macroeconomic theory 113
  influences upon 11–12, 37, 47–8, 58, 138–9, 141–3, 146, 148, 157–8
  intellectual background of 11–12
  joins Committee on Social Thought 2, 6, 17
  and Keynes
    age difference 112
    commonality with 96–7, 101–2, 108–9
    'disciples' of 110
    encounters with 97–9
    'Keynesian revolution' 107–8, 112
    opposition to inflation 111–12
    as 'quantity theorist' 124–5, 126
    rivalry with 1, 3–4, 11, 14–15, 71, 97–8, 107–8, 111–14

lectures at LSE 1, 12, 66–7, 118, 145, 148
mainstream neglect of 35–6
methodology of 29–30, 110, 117, 122, 195, 218–19, 233–7, 364–5
military career of 1, 140
and Mises
  attends *Privatseminar* 1, 143
  divergence from 148–9, 151–2, 154–5
  encounters with 141, 143
  influence of 12, 37, 47–8, 138–9, 141–3, 146, 148, 157–8
as 'puzzler' 147
rejection of *a prioristic* thinking 2, 29, 155
'rejection' of macroeconomics 123–4
and religion 18
response to *Treatise on Money* 3–4, 14, 25, 101–2, 105–6, 112
scepticism of 364, 367–71, 372–3, 375–7
and Tooke Chair 1, 146
'transformation' of 195–202
turned down by University of Chicago economics department 5, 17
and verification 29–30
'watershed' in thought 2–3, 4
Hayek's Social and Economic Philosophy (book) 8–9
Heath, Edward 317
Hicks, John 12, 18, 22, 23, 27, 30, 35, 47, 58–9, 124
'hidden' market forces 120, 122, 132–4
Hirai, Toshiaki 100
'historicism' 235
hoarding 54, 121
Hobhouse, L.T. 261
Homo economicus 259
Hoover, Kevin 31
Hoppe, Hans 365
Horwitz, Steven 174, 290
human action
  and complexity 176–7
  and Mises 151–3, 154–6
  and monetary policy 343, 346, 356
  and political economy 343
  and socio-economic order 212–13, 216–17, 218

and spontaneous order 225, 226, 230, 296
Human Action: A Treatise on Economics (book) 147, 148
Hume, David 225, 279, 291, 296, 375
Hummel, Jeffrey 28
Humphrey, Tom 25
Hunt v. Crumboch (1945) 317, 318
Hutcheson, Francis 225
Hutchison, Terence 2, 6, 29
hyperinflation 26

'ideal types' 155–7
ILO (International Labor Organization) 332
index numbers 54, 65
Individualism and Economic Order (book) 247
'Individualism: true and false' (essay) 255
industrial fluctuations 50–51, 53–8
inequality 268–9, 270, 272, 368–9
inflation
  acceleration mechanism 26–7
  and full employment 26–7, 87
  Keynes' views on 111–12
  and monetary expansion 52
  and renewed interest in Hayek 18
  and unemployment 113
  and unions 325–8
Institute of Economic Affairs 18, 111
interest rates
  and business cycles 20–21, 30, 82–3, 84, 87–8, 132–4
  and capital theory 82–3, 84, 87–8
  and central-bank policy 51, 52
  and credit expansion 133–4
  and entrepreneurship 51
  and expectations 172
  and Keynesian economics 30, 87, 101
  and market processes 130–31
  and monetary policy 56
  and monetary theory 51, 133–4
  and price margins 50
  and production processes 50–51
international trade 294–5, 298, 300–305, 306–9, 311
intertemporal equilibrium 18, 23, 28, 95–6, 113, 175

investment
   and business cycles 21, 31, 82, 83–4
   and capital heterogeneity 171–3
   and capital theory 81–2, 83–4, 85–6, 88
   and consumption spending 126–7
   and Keynesian economics 88–91, 95, 100–1, 102, 105, 126–7, 172–3
   and unemployment 89–90
'Investment repercussions' (article) 171
'Investment that raises the demand for capital' (article) 171
'invisible hand' 225, 280

Jevons, William Stanley 48, 73
Johnson, Harry 343
Johnston, David 270, 273
Joseph, Emperor Franz 139

Kahn, Richard 105
Kaldor, Nicholas 15, 19–20, 21
Kant, Immanuel 375, 376
Keynes, John Maynard
   and broadness of Hayek's principles 365
   and capital theory 71
   and capitalism 94, 96
   change in economic theory 94, 95, 96, 99, 100, 106, 108
   commonality with Hayek 96–7, 101–2, 108–9
   and consumption spending 126–7
   death of 97–8
   'disciples' of 110
   encounters with Hayek 97, 99
   and expectations 166–7
   and Friedman 120, 121–2
   and impact of *General Theory* 13, 32, 107, 112
   and inflation 111–12
   influence on macroeconomic theory 113, 123–4, 125
   and interest rates 30, 87, 101
   and investment 88–91, 95, 100–1, 102, 105, 126–7, 172–3
   and 'Keynesian revolution' 107–8, 112
   and Lachmann 166–7, 172–3
   and monetary policy 94–5, 100, 103
   and partial equilibrium analysis 3
   and quantity theory 100, 124–5, 126
   response to *Prices and Production* 14–15, 102, 105–6
   rivalry with Hayek 1, 3–4, 11, 14–15, 71, 97–8, 107–8, 111–14
   and saving 100–1
   and unemployment 326–7
Kirzner, Israel 66, 254
Knight, Frank 18, 24, 79–80, 130, 283, 284
knowledge
   and comparative institutional analysis 215
   and entrepreneurs 204, 254
   and equilibrium analysis 196–202
   and globalization 295
   and language 370, 377
   and market processes 60–61, 64
   and physiological psychology 202–5, 207–8
   and price system 151–3, 156–7, 204–5, 286–7
   and private property 249, 251–2, 264
   and protectionism 307–8
   and social structures 207–10
   and socialism 249–52, 254, 259, 286–7, 297
   and socialist calculation debate 286–7
   and spontaneous order 230–31, 233, 238, 239, 241
   and technological change 184
Koppl, Roger 186

labour unions *see* unions
Lachmann, Ludwig
   and Austrian school 165–6
   and capital heterogeneity 169–73, 179–82
   and capital theory 166, 167–9, 174–6, 182–3
   and complexity 177, 179–87
   and Hayek's outsider status 12, 15
   influence of Hayek on 165, 166, 167–9, 170–71, 174–6
   and institutions 185–9
   and Keynesian economics 166–7, 172–3
   at LSE 165–7
   and subjectivism 206–7

'Lachmann problem' 186, 187
Laidler, David 14
Lange, Oscar 13, 17, 61–7, 248–9, 252, 255, 282–4, 285–6, 287–8, 291
language 234, 257, 370, 371–2, 376–7
Lausanne school of economics 3, 28
Law, Legislation, and Liberty (book)
 impact of 33
 and protectionism 307–8
 and social justice 367–8, 373
 and spontaneous order 227, 256, 257–8
 and unions 315, 331
 written 2
League of Nations 141, 143, 145
Leijonhufvud, Axel 13, 36, 96
Leoni, Bruno 350
Lerner, Abba 127, 283
liberalism
 development of 37
 Hayek/Friedman comparisons 116, 118
 and monetary policy 345, 346, 347–9, 352–3, 356–7
 and socialism 262, 264, 268
 and spontaneous order 239–40, 241, 371
Logik des Forschungs (book) 29
'long-run/short-run' relationships 128–9, 135
'loose-joint' status of money 119–20
LSE (London School of Economics) 1, 12, 66–7, 118, 145, 146, 148, 165–7
Lucas, Robert 30–31, 113
Lukes, Steven 269, 271, 273
Lutz, Friedrich 26

MacFarlane, Alan 258
Machlup, Fritz 18–19
macroeconomics
 and Austrian school 13–14
 and business cycles 21
 and capital theory 23, 71, 92
 and decline in Hayek's influence 98–9
 and disequilibrium 125–6
 Hayek/Friedman comparisons 118–23
 Hayek's 'rejection' of 123–4

 influence of Keynesian economics 113
 and Keynesian economics 87
 and new classicism 32
malinvestment 83
'Manageability of social tasks' (essay) 227
Mandeville, Bernard 224–5
Mannheim, Karl 261
Marget, Arthur 15, 23
'marginal productivity' 58
market interdependencies 3, 5
market processes
 and Austrian school 130–31
 and central-bank policy 4
 and decentralization 5
 and economic calculation 60–62
 and entrepreneurship 287
 and equilibrium analysis 197
 and expectations 188–9
 and general equilibrium theory 185–6
 and interest rates 130–31
 and monetary policy 134
 and price levels 130–31
 and price system 63–6
 and production plans 4, 185, 284
 and socialism 251–2, 253–4
'market rate of interest' 51
'market socialism' 197, 248, 253, 255, 284, 289
Marshall, Alfred 3–4, 58, 100
Marx, Karl 15, 261–2, 278, 279, 280
Marxism 13, 261–2, 278–9, 280, 296–7
'master' mind 146
Mayer, Hans 12
McCloughry, Roy 2–3, 4
Means, Gardiner 281
Meltzer, Allan 120
Menger, Carl 11–12, 37, 54, 139–41, 166, 226, 235
methodological individualism 1, 218–19, 233, 241
methodological subjectivism 154–7
microeconomics 22, 60, 71–2, 92
Mill, James 28
Mill, John Stuart 141
minimum wage 298, 304, 324
Mises, Ludwig von
 a prioristic thinking of 2, 155

and Austrian Institute for Business
    Cycle Research 144–5
and Austrian school 138–41
and business cycles 140
and capital theory 25
and central planning 4, 33
criticism of Hayek's theories 148–9
and 'cumulative process' 19
development of theories 139–40, 147
and economic calculation 60, 61,
    247–9, 281–3, 284, 287–8
encounters with Hayek 141, 143
and entrepreneurship 287
and human action 151–3, 154–6
and 'ideal types' 155–7
influence on Hayek 12, 37, 47–8,
    138–9, 141–3, 146, 148, 157–8
and knowledge 151, 153, 156–7
and Marxism 13
as 'master' 147
and monetary policy 356–7
and price levels 22
Privatseminar of 1, 143
and quantity theory 123
and socialism 4, 60, 61, 62, 142–3,
    149, 247–9, 281–3, 284, 287–8
and subjectivism 154–6
Mitchell, Wesley Clair 97, 142
Mittermaier, K.H.M. 167
modularity 181
monetary expansion
    and business cycles 19–20, 82–4,
        86–7
    and capital theory 82–4, 85–6
    and inflation 52
    and monetary theory 51–2
    and price expectations 86–7
    and quantity theory 122, 123
    and rational expectations 52
    and unemployment 113
Monetary History of the United States
    (book) 113
*Monetary Nationalism and
    International Stability* (book) 300,
    314
monetary policy
    and Austrian school 346, 357
    and capital theory 67
    and constitutional economics 344,
        345, 348, 356–7

and currency 111, 300–301
and division of labour 54, 56
and entrepreneurship 54, 56, 353
and general equilibrium theory 53–4
Hayek/Friedman comparisons 116,
    117
and human action 343, 346, 356
and industrial fluctuations 53–6
and interest rates 56
Keynes' views on 94–5, 100, 103
and liberalism 345, 346, 347–9,
    352–3, 356–7
and market processes 134
and political economy 343–4
and price expectations 56
and price levels 103
and price margins 54, 56
and private property 347, 350, 353
and rule of law 348, 350, 353–5, 356
and scientism 346–7
and social contract 344, 350–51, 352
and social norms 344–5, 346
and social philosophy 345–7,
    350–51, 352, 356
and socialism 347–9, 354, 355
and spontaneous order 349, 350
and state coercion 345, 347–8, 351,
    352–5, 356
and taxation 349, 353
and 'third way' economics 346–7,
    357
monetary theory
    and business cycles 51, 53
    and interest rates 51, 133–4
    and monetary expansion 51–2
    and price system 118–20
Monetary Theory and the Trade Cycle
    (book) 20, 22, 24, 25, 96, 116, 124,
    197
monopolies 262, 278, 280, 283, 323,
    330, 335–6, 337–8, 353
Mont Pelerin Society 18, 110
moral philosophy 224–6
multilevel interaction 177, 179, 184
mutual adjustment 227–8, 229, 230–31,
    236, 240–41, 264
Myrdal, Gunnar 57

NAFTA (the North Atlantic Free
    Trade Agreement) 305, 309

National Labor Relations Act (NLRA, 1935) 316, 317, 318, 333, 334, 335, 336, 340
'natural rate of interest' 51
Neff, John 17
neoclassicism
    and Austrian school 197
    and capital theory 58, 72, 79–80, 92
    and socialism 248, 249, 250–52, 259, 278–80, 283, 286, 287–91
    and socialist calculation debate 278–9, 283, 286, 287–91
new classicism 30–32
New York University 1
Norris-LaGuardia Act (1932) 317–18, 321, 337
North, Douglass 258

O'Brien, Denis 2
O'Driscoll Jr., Gerald P. 6, 22
Oakeshott, Michael 209
Occam's Razor 24
'On the "meaning" of social institutions' (essay) 370
Optimum Quantity of Money and Other Essays (book) 116
Orwell, George 372

Pareto optimality 217
partial equilibrium analysis 3
Patinkin, Don 14
'pattern prediction' 235–6
perfect competition 36–7, 66, 151, 248–9, 252–3, 285, 289
'period of production' 24–5, 48, 49, 58, 76, 103–5, 182
Phillips curve 113
Pigou, Arthur 17, 100, 108
plan coordination 195, 201, 205–7, 211, 214–15, 217–18
Polanyi, Karl 258
Polanyi, Michael 208, 212, 226, 227
Popper, Karl 2, 29, 236
positivism 154, 235, 347
Postan, Michael 258
Postrel, Virginia 294
Presley, John 24
price expectations
    and capital theory 86–8
    and entrepreneurship 56
    and equilibrium 56–7
    and monetary expansion 86–7
    and monetary policy 56
price levels
    and bank lending 27–8
    and business cycles 22–3
    and market processes 130–31
    and monetary policy 103
    and money supply 122–3, 128–30, 131, 135
    and quantity theory 124
price margins 50, 54, 56
price system
    and Austrian school 60
    and capital theory 118
    and capitalism 64–6
    and central planning 63–4, 65, 150–51
    characteristics of Hayek's view of 63–6
    and competitive markets 63, 66
    and coordination of markets 322–3
    and economic calculation 60–61, 64–5
    and entrepreneurship 64–6
    instability of 47
    and knowledge 151–3, 156–7, 204–5, 286–7
    and market processes 63–6
    and monetary theory 118–20
    and social structures 205–6
    and socialism 61–2, 64–5, 253–4, 264–5, 297
    and socialist calculation debate 286–7
    and unemployment 324–5
Prices and Production (book)
    and business cycles 4–5, 20, 23
    and capital theory 5, 17, 23–4, 48, 49
    change in Hayek's economic theory 107
    Friedman's response to 135
    and history of economic thought 12
    impact of 146
    and interest rates 101
    and intertemporal equilibrium 96
    Keynes' response to 14–15, 102, 105–6
    and market processes 64
    and monetary policy 54–5, 103

and price system 64
published 1
reviews of 14–15
and spontaneous order 66–7
and stationary states 58–9
Principles of Economics (book) 139
private property
  and central planning 142, 287
  and comparative institutional analysis 215, 216
  and knowledge 249, 251–2, 264
  and monetary policy 347, 350, 353
  and socialist calculation debate 248–9, 279, 282, 287, 291, 297
  and spontaneous order 238, 258
Privatseminar 1, 143
production plans 4, 82, 120, 170, 184, 185, 284
Profits, Interest and Investment (book) 20
profit-sharing 315, 338–9
Prosperity and Depression (book) 27
protectionism 294, 295, 305–8
Prychitko, David 290
'puzzler' mind 146–7

quantitative modelling 180–81
quantity theory
  and business cycles 22–3
  Friedman's approach 120–21, 122–3, 125
  and full employment 125
  Keynes' views on 100
  and microeconomics 22
  and monetary expansion 122, 123
  and price levels 124
Quesnay, Francois 343

rational expectations 31–2, 36, 52
Rawls, John 267, 270–71, 272, 274, 275
Reagan, Ronald 113
'real' factors 53, 54, 56
religion 18
Ricardo Effect 20, 21–2, 30, 52–3
Ricardo, David 15, 52–3, 73
Ricketts, Martin 8
right-to-work laws 335–6
'risk of failure' 374
river analogy 80–81
Rizzo, Mario 22

Robbins, Lionel 1, 12–13, 17–18, 24, 25, 29, 62, 112, 343
Robertson, Dennis 14, 20–21, 24–5, 100, 101
Robinson, Joan 79, 98, 281
Rockefeller Foundation 144
Roemer, John 289, 290
Roll, Erich 17
Rosenstein-Rodan, Paul 166
'roundaboutness' of production process 48, 49, 55, 58, 72, 73–4, 75–7, 82, 84, 182–3
Rowley, Robin 31
Royal Statistical Society 13–14, 30
Rühl, Christof 31
rule of law
  and monetary policy 348, 350, 353–5, 356
  and spontaneous order 238, 295, 299, 301, 305, 311
  and unions 314, 315, 318, 319, 321, 340
'rules of the game' 187, 188, 350, 356

Say, Jean-Baptiste 28, 225, 280, 343
Schumpeter, Joseph A. 11, 17, 141, 284
Schwartz, Anna 129
scientism 16, 32–3, 154, 236–7, 296, 346–7
Scottish Enlightenment 224–6, 230, 235, 240, 242, 295–6
secularization 366, 376
Seldon, Arthur 314
Shackle, George 18, 31, 47
Shearmur, Jeremy 241
Shleifer, Andrei 288
'simple common model' 120, 129
Smith, Adam 35, 48, 183, 225, 226, 279–80, 291, 343
Smithies, Arthur 28
'social' (concept of) 370–72, 376
social contract 344, 350–51, 352
social evolution 256–8, 260
socialism
  and central planning *see* central planning
  and commodity production 296–7
  communitarian 262–5
  and competitive markets 62, 63, 66, 252, 257–8

and constructivist rationalism 259
critiques of Hayek's views on 269–75
and distributive principle 270–74
and division of labour 149–50
and economic calculation 1, 4, 59, 60–62, 64–5, 149, 246, 247–9, 281–3, 284, 287–8
and egalitarianism 267–9, 270, 271, 273
and 'envy' 378
failure of 142–3, 246, 278, 288
and general equilibrium theory 197, 249, 251–2, 255, 284–6
and knowledge 249–52, 254, 259, 286–7, 297
and liberalism 262, 264, 268
and limits to reason 258–61
and 'market failures' 252–5, 278
and market processes 251–2, 253–4
'market socialism' 197, 248, 253, 255, 284, 289
Marxian 13, 261–2, 278–9, 280, 296–7
and monetary policy 347–9, 354, 355
and neoclassicism 248, 249, 250–52, 259, 278–80, 283, 286, 287–91
and price system 61–2, 64–5, 253–4, 264–5, 297
resurrection of 290
and social justice 247, 265–76, 298–300
and social sciences 258–9
and spontaneous order 149, 230–31, 232, 237, 246–7, 255–8, 259–61, 262, 263–4, 296–8
and *The Road to Serfdom* 1–2
Socialism: An Economic and Sociological Analysis (book) 4, 12–13, 142–3, 149
social justice
and centralized regulation 374–5
and 'envy' 377–8
and Hayek's scepticism 367–9, 372–3, 375–7
and redistribution 378–9
and socialism 247, 265–76, 298–300
and spontaneous order 231, 266–7, 269–70, 373–4, 376–7
and unions 317
social norms 344–5, 346

social structures 205–11, 216–17
socio-economic order 196, 201, 207, 211–13, 214–17, 218
Spadaro, Louis 35
Spencer, Herbert 225
Spengler, J.J. 17
spontaneous order
applications of 237–9
and Austrian school 226, 231, 240, 242
and broadness of Hayek's principles 366–7
and 'catallaxy' 212
and competitive markets 66–7, 257–8
and constructivist rationalism 229–30, 231, 232, 234, 235–7
and cultural evolution 233, 237–8, 239, 240–41
development of 224–6, 228–30
and freedom 239–40, 241
and globalization 295
and Hayek's methodology 233–7
and human action 225, 226, 230, 296
internal contradictions of 364, 373–4
and knowledge 230–31, 233, 238, 239, 241
and language 376
and liberalism 371
and monetary policy 349, 350
and private property 238, 258
and psychology of science 232–3
and 'Reason' 295–6
and role of government 238–9
and rule of law 238, 295, 299, 301, 305, 311
and social evolution 256–8, 260
and social justice 231, 266–7, 269–70, 373–4, 376–7
and social sciences 233–6, 239, 242, 259
and socialism 149, 230–31, 232, 237, 246–7, 255–8, 259–61, 262, 263–4, 296–8
and socio-economic order 212–13
and static equilibrium 229
terminology of 227–8
Sraffa, Piero 14–15, 16
'stages of maturity' 183
static equilibrium
and business cycles 106–7

and general equilibrium theory 5, 54, 59–60
and knowledge 196–7
and microeconomics 60
and socialism 251–2
and spontaneous order 229
and stationary states 59–60, 67
stationary states 58–60, 67
Stiglitz, Joseph 253, 254–5, 288, 289, 290
stock of capital 78–9, 168–9
Strigl, Richard 12
strikes/picketing 315, 316, 317–18, 336–8
'structure of production' 48–9, 52–3, 54–5, 58, 67, 75, 78
subjectivism 1, 12, 16, 154–5, 206–7
'subsidiary assistance' 379
substitutability 169–71, 173

'tacit knowledge' 61, 207, 208
taxation 272, 349, 353
Taylor, Charles 263
Taylor, Frederick 283
technological change 132, 133, 183–4
Thatcher, Margaret 113, 317, 340
The Affluent Society (book) 264
The Constitution of Liberty (book)
    and *Capitalism and Freedom* 116
    and Hayek's 'constructivism' 365
    impact of 33
    and monetary policy 347
    reviews of 17–18
    and social justice 379
    and spontaneous order 255–6
    and unions 315, 318, 319, 321, 333
    written 2
The Counter-Revolution of Science (book) 154–5, 261
The Economic Consequences of the Peace (book) 94, 97
The Fable of the Bees (book) 224–5
The Fatal Conceit (book) 256, 257–8, 297, 300, 308, 311, 377
The General Theory of Employment, Interest and Money (book)
    and change in Keynes' economic theory 94, 95, 106
    critique of 71

Hayek's failure to review 108, 117, 123–4
impact of 13, 32, 107, 112
and interest rates 87
and investment 89–91, 95
Lachmann's views on 166–7
reviews of 108
The Great Depression (book) 24, 107
'The meaning of competition' (essay) 247
The Pure Theory of Capital (book)
    and business cycles 20, 49
    Hayek's disillusionment with 173–4, 175
    influence on Lachmann 166, 174–6
    and Keynesian economics 71
    lack of illustrative examples 77, 80
    and monetary theory 119
    and 'period of production' 25
    practical value of 91–2
    reviews of 28
The Road to Serfdom (book)
    and change in Hayek's economic theory 110
    and Hayek's 'constructivism' 365
    and Hayek's anti-socialism 246, 269
    impact of 16–17
    and international trade 300, 301–2
    and monetary policy 351, 357
    reviews of 17
    and social justice 368, 377
    and socialism 1–2
    and Western society 33
The Sensory Order (book) 173, 202–3, 207, 216, 232
The Theory of Money and Credit (book) 123, 139–40, 147
'The use of knowledge in society' (essay) 60–61, 247, 286
The Years of High Theory (book) 18
Tout, Herbert 15
Townsend, Harry 62
Trabant car plant (East Germany) 13
Tract on Monetary Reform (book) 94, 100
trade cycles *see* business (trade) cycles
Trade Union Act (1984) 340
Trades Disputes Act (1906) 317, 325, 333, 340
'transmission mechanisms' 129–30

Treatise on Money (book) 3–4, 14, 25, 30, 100, 101–2, 105–6, 112
'trial and error' 61–2, 64, 66, 184, 344–5, 352
'triangles' 25–6, 48, 103–4, 118
Tsiang, Sho-Chieh 30
Tullock, Gordon 255
'Two types of minds' (article) 146–7

unemployment 89–90, 105, 113, 324–5, 326–7, 328
unintended consequences 32, 224–5, 226, 231, 234–5, 256, 298–9, 307, 309–10
unions
  and business cycles 328
  and codetermination 315, 339
  coercive unionism 314, 315–19, 322–31, 337
  and collective bargaining 314, 315, 318–19, 331–2, 338
  and discoordination of markets 322–3
  and freedom of association 314–15, 332–3
  and freedom of contract 315, 321, 333–6
  and inflation 325–8
  monopolies 323, 330, 335–6, 337–8
  and productivity 329–31
  and profit-sharing 315, 338–9
  and rule of law 314, 315, 318, 319, 321, 340
  and social justice 317
  and strikes/picketing 315, 316, 317–18, 336–8
  as threat to free society 314, 331–2
  and unemployment 324–5, 326–7, 328
  voluntary unionism 314, 319–21, 333, 334–5

United States v. Enmons (1973) 319
'universalizability' 352
University of Chicago 2, 5, 17
University of Freiburg 2
University of Salzburg 2
University of Vienna 1, 139, 140–41, 143

Value and Capital (book) 58
Vaughn, Karen 211–12
'velocity of circulation' 55
vice 225
Vieira, Edwin 319
Viner, Jacob 17, 18
Vishny, Robert 288
voluntary unionism 314, 319–21, 333, 334–5

'wage slavery' 280
Walras, Léon 3–4, 31, 249, 343
Waterman, Linda 7–8
Webb, Beatrice 317
Webb, Sidney 317
Weber, Max 154, 155–6, 186
'What is and what means "social"' (essay) 370–71
Whither Socialism? (book) 255, 290
Wicksell, Knut 14, 19, 48, 51, 100, 101, 102, 105, 140
Wieser, Friedrich von 3, 141, 147
Wilson, Tom 15, 20, 21
windfall profits 100–1
'work in progress' 49, 90
working capital 72–3
WTO (World Trade Organization) 305

'years of high theory' 47

Zwingli, Ulrich 376